GOLDEN DREAMS

AMERICANS AND THE CALIFORNIA DREAM

Americans and the California Dream, 1850–1915

Inventing the Dream
California Through the Progressive Era

Material Dreams
Southern California Through the 1920s

Endangered Dreams
The Great Depression in California

The Dream Endures
California Enters the 1940s

Embattled Dreams
California in War and Peace, 1940–1950

Golden Dreams
California in an Age of Abundance, 1950–1963

Coast of Dreams
California on the Edge, 1990–2003

GOLDEN DREAMS

California in an Age of Abundance, 1950–1963

KEVIN STARR

OXFORD
UNIVERSITY PRESS
2009

OXFORD
UNIVERSITY PRESS

Oxford University Press, Inc., publishes works that further
Oxford University's objective of excellence
in research, scholarship, and education.

Oxford   New York
Auckland   Cape Town   Dar es Salaam   Hong Kong   Karachi
Kuala Lumpur   Madrid   Melbourne   Mexico City   Nairobi
New Delhi   Shanghai   Taipei   Toronto

With offices in
Argentina   Austria   Brazil   Chile   Czech Republic   France   Greece
Guatemala   Hungary   Italy   Japan   Poland   Portugal   Singapore
South Korea   Switzerland   Thailand   Turkey   Ukraine   Vietnam

Published by Oxford University Press, Inc.
198 Madison Avenue, New York, NY 10016

www.oup.com

Oxford is a registered trademark of Oxford University Press

Library of Congress Cataloging-in-Publication Data
Starr, Kevin.
Golden dreams : California in an age of abundance, 1950–1963 / Kevin Starr.
p. cm. — (Americans and the California dream)
Includes bibliographical references and index.
ISBN 978-0-19-515377-4
1. California—History—1950–
2. California—Social conditions—20th century.
3. California—Economic conditions—20th century.   I. Title.
F866.2.S733 2009
979.4'053–dc22   2008050359

1 3 5 7 9 8 6 4 2

Printed in the United States of America
on acid-free paper

For Sheila Starr
—we met in this time and
began our life together.

Contents

IV ART AND LIFE

V   DISSENTING OPINIONS

Preface

A S far as the understanding of history is concerned, decades can be arbitrary. Mere numbers on the calendar do not erect impassable firewalls. Forces set in motion in one decade can often take one, two, three, or more decades, even half centuries, to work themselves through to conclusion. And yet the moment such a truism is affirmed, an equally compelling paradox surfaces. Calendar decades have a way of asserting coherence, texture, even personality, upon the years they delineate. Surveying the first half of the American twentieth century, for example, we can conveniently and with a certain sense of accuracy distinguish the expansionist first decade of the twentieth century from the Progressive decade that followed, ending in a war that no one seemed to have won. From this war emerged the creative edginess of the 1920s, followed by the grainy black-and-white decade of the Great Depression, followed by the World War II years and the transitions and opaque resentments of the late 1940s. None of these characterizations is fully true, as contemporary historical interpretation has proven; yet the texture and significance of each of these decades remain in popular memory and, paradoxically, in the research and writing of history, if only as paradigms to be challenged and rejected.

Golden Dreams, the most recent installment in the Americans and the California Dream series, is centered on a decade, the 1950s, that survives in popular American imagination as a stable landscape resting atop tectonic plates that would soon result in the earthquakes and fissures of the mid- and late 1960s. From this perspective, the 1950s can be extended through the Camelot years, 1960–63, during which the assumptions of the 1950s began to be challenged but remained by and large in force. Thus the year 1963, up until the Kennedy assassination in November, feels and looks much like the late 1950s, albeit more intensified, while the year 1964 is redolent with the emergent energies and transformations of the Age of Aquarius. In California terms, the Free Speech Movement erupting on the UC Berkeley campus in the fall of 1964 inaugurated a new era, but it must also be linked to the protests in 1960 surrounding the execution of Caryl Chessman and the hearings of the House Un-American Activities Committee in San Francisco. In many cases, to understand what occurred in the 1950s demands a return to earlier decades. Thus while *Golden Dreams* is centered on the 1950–63 period, the narrative must occasionally move backward in time.

Golden Dreams seeks at once to ascertain and evaluate what Americans in California thought they were doing in this era, even when—as history would subsequently reveal—more obscure, even contradictory, forces were at work. Too often, whether in history, cultural criticism, or political analysis, the 1950s are set up as a convenient scapegoat for one or another agenda. Fiction and motion pictures, as well as political agitprop, have depicted the 1950s as a time of hypocrisy and repression. While such elements were not absent from the decade, an even more compelling argument can be made. The interplay between surface conformity and interior rebellion—between a pervasive sense of social well-being and an angry awareness of unfinished business (in the matter of civil rights especially), between heartland repose and the growing internationalism of the American century, between a sense of fulfillment and the lonely sounds of Frank Sinatra singing in the night, with academicians C. Wright Mills and David Riesman or novelists Sloan Wilson and Grace Metalious all the while suggesting other scenarios playing out beneath the surface—confers on the 1950s, in retrospect, much of its compelling power.

Golden Dreams seeks to dramatize the achievements, ambiguities, and conflicts of this era across seventeen topical chapters that represent neither an indictment nor an unqualified celebration of this era but an effort to present aspects of these years on their own terms in a mosaic of narrative that, taken cumulatively, suggests larger processes at work. Part One examines suburban growth from the perspective of real estate development and design. Part Two addresses developments and transformations in San Diego, San Francisco, and Los Angeles. Part Three deals with politics and public construction as connected to heroic initiatives in higher education, freeways, and water. Part Four provides case studies in aesthetic, moral, and psychological responses to the transformation of California into an American epicenter. Part Five deals with dissent among the marginalized or otherwise aggrieved and the resulting culture of dissent that became a growing force in the 1960s. As in the previous volumes of the Americans and the California Dream series, the primary perspective of this book is social, psychological, and cultural, frequently realized through biography in brief. Indeed, the interaction of social and personal experience, the social psychology of the era, emerges as a frequent theme. This is not surprising, given the fact that millions of Americans migrated to California to improve their lives, and these migrations profoundly altered social expectations and structures.

It was a time of growth and abundance, and this, in turn, engendered a persistent note of optimistic boosterism in public discourse. A population of 10.5 million as of 1950 reached 15.7 million by 1960, en route to the 20 million of 1970. Southern

California and the greater Bay Area absorbed most of this growth; yet Central California—centered on Fresno County in the San Joaquin Valley in the south and Sacramento County in the Sacramento Valley to the north—also grew appreciably during these years, especially the cities of Bakersfield, Fresno, and greater Sacramento. During this time, Central California first experienced the urbanization and suburbanization that would by the end of the century transform it into a third geographical designation alongside Southern and Northern California.

Economically, this growth was at once the result and the symbol of the take-off era of what many economic historians have described as the single greatest arc of rising prosperity in American history and, quite possibly, in all of modern history as well. An unprecedented abundance connected to growth characterized California in these years and would continue to do so for the rest of the century. From this abundance arose a culture of consumerism and conformity that earned, even then, more than its fair share of critics—but also nurtured a conviction on the part of millions of Americans that this was their time and place, their reward for enduring the deprivations of a depression and a world war: a house, a car, a job, a reinforced family identity and sense of well-being served by these amenities, together with a conviction that California was the best place in the nation to seek and attain a better American life.

In these years, the national experience and the California experience became, increasingly, a converging phenomenon, building upon the national role played by California during the Second World War, which is the theme of *Embattled Dreams* (2002) in this series. Nor can the post–World War II United States—its migrations, its suburbanization, its extension of the franchise in consumerism and higher education, its diversification of cultural taste, its growing protest against racial discrimination, even its apocalyptic forebodings—be understood without reference to the California experience. From this perspective, the story of World War II and the postwar period edging into the early 1960s asserts once and for all the American dimension of California and the California dimension of America. The dreams of California, in short, were the dreams of the nation, and vice versa. And so were the tensions and ambiguities. And so remains the enduring legacy of these crowded years.

San Francisco and Los Angeles

November 2008

I

SUBURBAN ASSUMPTIONS

1

San Fernando

Homes and Happiness in Residential Subdivisions

S the single largest and most comprehensive postwar suburban development
in California, the San Fernando Valley conveniently functions as a case
study of the demographic and housing dynamics transforming California in
the 1950s. Located fifteen miles northwest of downtown Los Angeles, the 235-square-
mile San Fernando Valley—a previously agricultural region bounded by the Santa
Monica Mountains to the south, the Simi Hills to the west, the Santa Susana and
San Gabriel Mountains to the north, and the Verdugo Mountains to the east—had
by 1960 become an orchestration of tract housing, swimming pools, boulevards,
and shopping centers, serving a population of 840,500. On 5 April 1960 Governor
Edmund G. (Pat) Brown cut the ribbon on the Valley's first freeway, the Ventura
(101/134), to run across the southern edge, paralleling Ventura Boulevard. Within a
few years, the Hollywood Freeway (170) would enter the Valley from the south via
the Cahuenga Pass and link itself to the Ventura. The Golden State Freeway (5) and
the Foothill Freeway (210) would eventually serve the northeastern sector, and the
San Diego Freeway (405) would connect the Valley to Westside Los Angeles.

Since the early 1900s, developers had been dreaming of such an integration of the
San Fernando Valley into the region. In 1904 developer Leslie Brand, learning that
Henry Huntington was in the process of building an electric railway between Los
Angeles and the city of San Fernando, organized the San Fernando Mission Land
Company to develop sixteen thousand acres of the Porter Ranch. Brand and his
associates knew what a combination of interurban streetcars and water would bring
to the flatlands and gently rolling slopes of the San Fernando Valley. When water
became a certainty in 1909, with the commencement of the Los Angeles Aqueduct,
another syndicate, the Los Angeles Suburban Homes Company, was organized. In
1911 developer William Whitsett joined members of this group and began—with
a free barbecue on Washington's Birthday—sales of lots in the newly established

township of Van Nuys. With the completion of its aqueduct in 1913, the City of Los Angeles had the leverage necessary to absorb its surrounding hinterlands. In May 1915 voters on both sides of the Santa Monica Mountains voted to incorporate 170 square miles of the Valley into the City of Los Angeles. Only the City of San Fernando, incorporated in 1911, maintained its independence from the City of Angels.

Throughout the 1910s, 1920s, and 1930s, the San Fernando Valley remained a Broadacre City (to use Frank Lloyd Wright's term) of cattle ranches, agriculture, farm sites, and small towns. Established ranchers and country squires, whose names would eventually adorn the streets and boulevards of the region, occasionally built such impressive homes as Lanterman House in La Cañada, but in general the Valley remained unpretentiously agricultural into the 1930s, with San Fernando and Pacoima serving as hub barrios for 1500 Mexican American families (as of 1933) working the local ranches and farms. In 1915 movie mogul Carl Laemmle brought the film industry into the Valley, with the establishment of Universal Studios on a former chicken ranch in its southeastern corner. Warner Brothers relocated to Burbank in 1929, and Republic arrived in 1935. From the mid-1930s onward, numerous film stars and directors—Al Jolson, Clark Gable, Dennis Morgan, Bob Hope, Edward Everett Horton, Janet Gaynor, John Huston, Andy Devine—made their homes in the Valley, a tradition continued into the 1940s by Van Nuys resident Jane Russell and her husband, football star Bob Waterfield, and Betty Grable of Chatsworth. Film folk preferred the Valley for its climate, rural nature, and seclusion.

Such was a prophetic pattern, for the motion picture industry had been pacing the economy of Southern California since the 1920s. During World War II and the Cold War, aviation and other defense industries became an increasing presence. Lockheed Aircraft opened its assembly plant in Burbank in 1928 and by the 1940s was the Valley's major employer. Nine of the Valley's ten biggest employers—among them, the Rocketdyne Division of North American Aviation (Canoga Park), the Missile and Space Division of Lockheed (Van Nuys), and RCA's West Coast Missile and Surface Radar Division (Northridge)—were defense-related. The dangers of such a defense economy became painfully apparent on 31 January 1957 when an F-89 Air Force jet fighter collided with a Continental Airlines DC-7 flying over the Valley at twenty-five thousand feet. Falling onto the athletic field of the Pacoima Junior High School, an engine from the DC-7 killed three boys and injured many others. President Dwight D. Eisenhower canceled any further military flights over the Valley.

Because of Hollywood, defense and electronics industries (40 percent of all employment in the Valley by 1960), and such companies as Chevrolet and Fisher Body of General Motors (Van Nuys) and the Bendix Corporation (Burbank and North Hollywood), an array of good-paying blue- and white-collar jobs were available. Wages paid in the San Fernando Valley in 1959 came to $2.6 billion, higher than the total of eighteen states. Forty-five percent of families in the Valley had two cars. (Big Red Car streetcar service to the Valley ended in December 1952.) In 1956 alone Anthony Brothers Pools, Inc., advertising itself as the largest builder of pools in the world, built two thousand swimming pools in the Valley, selling for $1,500 to $10,000. In 1959–60, permits were issued for six thousand residential swimming pools.

And so because of jobs—240,000 of them, the California Department of Employment noted in 1960, employing 80 percent of the working population in the Valley— and the concurrent development of homes, beginning with Panorama City in late 1945, the San Fernando Valley grew, grew, and grew. By the end of 1945, the Valley had 230,000 residents. Between 1945 and 1950, the population more than doubled. It doubled again between 1950 and 1960, with 3,650 (approximately 720 families) moving into the Valley each month, until the population reached 840,500 in 1960.

It was in general an aggressively white population, with restrictive covenants in effect in most developments, and only the city of San Fernando and the Pacoima district showing any signs of racial diversity. Not until 1961 would the community of Northridge be integrated, and then only by a solitary African American schoolteacher and his family. Ironically, the best-known resident of the San Fernando Valley by 1959 was a seventeen-year-old Mexican American rock and roll singer, Ritchie Valens (changed from Ricardo Valenzuela), whose explosive singing style and driving electric guitar in such hits as "Come On, Let's Go," "Donna," and "La Bamba" placed him on the top of the national charts before his tragic death on 3 February 1959 in a plane crash en route to Fargo, North Dakota, that also claimed the lives of singers Buddy Holly and J. P. (the Big Bopper) Richardson.

In 1961 W. W. Robinson, the leading historian of land use in Southern California, toured a San Fernando Valley that had now emerged as the archetypal landscape of the newly developed post–World War II California. With the exception of the city of San Fernando, most of the Valley had been transformed into a mosaic of residential communities, joined together by great boulevards cutting through landscapes of surviving agriculture that, with the exception of the western and northern borders, would not survive the decade. Los Angeles had long since annexed these communities, but they retained their identities and postal designations. Each community, Robertson suggested, encoded a paradigmatic progression from wilderness, to Native American settlement, to Spanish exploration, to subdivision as land grant ranchos in the Mexican era, to the ensuing American ranch (cattle and sheep), wheat, and orchard era, to the foundation of townships by pioneering developers in the early 1900s, followed by the long and languorous decades that ended abruptly with post–World War II suburbanization.

As of 1950, the vast majority of the 10,586,223 people of California were living in densely settled cities and towns, as they had been doing since the nineteenth century. The planned residential subdivision—developer-driven, mass-produced and uniform in design, readily financed and affordable, marketed to millions of incoming Californians—would not destroy the urban matrix and structure of California life. It would, however, profoundly transform pre-existing communities. In the remaining four decades of the twentieth century, as California approached thirty-five million in population, such subdivisions would constitute the predominant mode of new development for a rapidly expanding state and thus alter the social and institutional structures of residential life. New communities, moreover, would come on the scene through incorporation, with the planned residential development becoming the norm after 1950 and not a postwar augmentation. For both the residentially augmented community and the newly incorporated planned urban development, values and lifestyles were changing dramatically and quite soon overwhelmed prior California identities.

As with nearly everything else in California in the 1950–63 era, changes began with the war. Altogether, the war years brought more than eight million new residents to the American West, together with three million military personnel in training or transit. The majority of newcomers, so many of them seeking defense jobs, settled in cities; and with California producing 17 percent of total defense output, no cities were more keyed to the defense industry than San Diego, Los Angeles, and San Francisco. Defense workers faced many challenges: a new city, a new job, a new skill set; discrimination based on race or gender; the anomie of being away from home; removal from the social context that had nurtured and sustained many new Californians across a lifetime. Working mothers fretted over child care, despite a number of innovative programs. Marital ties came under stress as husbands and wives spent the workweek in different locations. Neglected teenagers drifted into delinquency. Sexual disequilibrium was in the air, a sense that this was wartime and anything goes. VD rates soared. Overworked but well-paid defense workers partied hard in their off-hours: drank booze and smoked incessantly. Air pollution, recently dubbed *smog*, became a problem, especially in Los Angeles, further compounding the risks to healthy lungs that came from industrial environments and cigarettes. Crime rates soared, especially batteries and sexual assaults, sure signs of a society under stress: a society, in point of fact, that anticipated postwar California in its population surge, prosperity, mobility, and instability. The war years, in short, constituted Act One of a drama of accelerated growth and transformation that would continue for the rest of the century.

In this regard, no challenges facing defense workers were more prophetic of postwar California than housing and transportation. Where to live and how to get to and from jobs became the leading leitmotifs of life in California. Defense workers rented rooms, sometimes for a mere eight hours a day, sharing beds in shifts. They lived in barns, garages, trailers, campers, tents, chicken coops, greenhouses, and automobiles. They rented dormitory beds when available, or otherwise scrambled for shelter in single-room-occupancy hotels commandeered for the war effort. Because many workers still commuted to work by car, despite multiple efforts at mass transit and paratransit, commutes to and from defense plants could take up to four, even five, hours a day.

Wartime necessity introduced a new paradigm into housing in California: density. True, the major cities of California featured numerous apartment buildings servicing every aspect of the housing market. Southern California had already invented the bungalow court, but the commanding paradigm for housing in the first half of the twentieth century had been the detached single-family residence. The need to house defense workers and other portions of the population, however, prompted the construction of developments—Linda Vista in San Diego; Hacienda Village, Pueblo Village, Amity Compton, and Channel Heights in Los Angeles; Candlestick Cove in San Francisco; Chabot Terrace in Richmond; and Marin City near Sausalito—that with varying degrees of success presented housing density as an implied model for postwar development. While Candlestick Cove in San Francisco, housing some thirty-five thousand people at its peak population, has been described by historian Gerald Nash as an instant slum, and the three-thousand-unit Chabot Terrace in Richmond, Nash points out, had neither streets nor sewers, architect Richard Neutra's Channel Heights project in San Pedro on the edge of the Palos Verdes peninsula facing Los Angeles Harbor—with its well-designed and convenient homes, its pathways and lawns, its schools, daycare facilities, playgrounds, and shopping center—has continued to serve as a prototype of the planned urban development.

Augmenting such density prototypes were two projects of the Metropolitan Life Insurance Company, Park Merced on the southern edge of San Francisco and Park La Brea in the Fairfax district of Los Angeles. Constructed in 1943 and 1944 despite wartime constrictions, these two planned developments were designed by the firm of Leonard Schultze and Associates of New York and introduced to California a New York–style rental community of residential towers, low-rise apartment buildings, and townhouses on landscaped sites. Surprisingly, given the preference of Californians for single-family home ownership, Park Merced and Park La Brea flourished for the ensuing sixty years, serving a clientele that minded neither density nor renting.

Despite such prototypes of density, however, residential patterns of California remained fixed on the single-family house. Announced in the Los Angeles–based journal *Arts & Architecture* in January 1945, the Case Study House program sought to envision the postwar housing future in terms of homes designed by the leading architects of the region, using a host of new materials. Running for nearly twenty years and twenty-seven prototypes, the Case Study program suggested a mere two apartment buildings, in 1963–64, at the conclusion of its efforts. By that time, Bay Area developer David Bohannon had emerged as one of the few developers prepared to make a major investment in density, in his case, the Hillsdale Garden Apartments, a 750-unit rental complex on forty acres in southern San Mateo. Bohannon was joined by the Stoneson brothers, Ellis and Henry, who in 1949 began development of the even more dense Stonestown complex on the southern edge of San Francisco: four ten-story apartment houses, ninety units each, twenty-eight smaller apartment complexes, and an extensive shopping center with 780 retail outlets.

Stonestown was culturally reinforced by the densities of San Francisco, and the Hillsdale Garden Apartments, also centered on a shopping complex, kept its connection to the grid of the city of San Mateo. These developments, like Park Merced and Park La Brea, were successful but were not widely imitated in the 1950s. The housing shortage of the war and postwar period had reinforced the preference of

Americans in California to own their own single-family home. Density—whether through ownership or rental—remained a lesser option, competitive only in San Francisco, whose 46-square-mile peninsula had long since accustomed residents in its constricted older districts to apartment living.

This postwar preference for the single-family home had its psychological origins in the deepest recesses of American identity. In the 1930s, the loan programs of the federal government had given this preference a near-total advantage over those wishing to purchase apartments, co-ops, townhouses, or other forms of dense living. Holding some ten million men and women in the mass conformity of military service and millions of others in the mobilization of defense work, the war intensified the almost mytho-poetic American desire for private space in a family-owned home.

Family! It remains a mystery why an entire generation should so precipitously march en masse into marriage and childbearing in these years (after all, the children and grandchildren of this wartime generation would, beginning in the late 1960s, half-disestablish marriage as a compelling institution) beyond the notion that this was the image of the good life that had been promoted during the war: the vision of marriage, children, and a dream house cited ceaselessly in public reference, extolled in the popular media, explored at length in the pages of the Ladies' Home Journal. A tidal wave of marriage, sexuality, procreation, and family building followed the annihilations, global and personal, of the war years. Eros vanquished Thanatos. Life vanquished Death.

Marriage and children also created a self-actualizing engine of economic recovery to replace defense industries. Families were forming at the rate of 1.4 million new families a year following the war, each couple having three-plus children (peaking at an average of 3.7 children per married woman in 1957), spiking the Baby Boom generation that would dominate American life for the rest of the century. That meant houses, millions of them, equipped with appliances and, shortly after the war, television sets, together with automobiles, at least one per household. Most of this construction was government-facilitated and government-financed through construction loans authorized by the National Housing Act of 1934, mortgages administered by the United States Veterans Administration (which accounted for 28 percent of the loans to California veterans by mid-decade), and the Cal-Vet program of the California Department of Veterans Affairs, augmented in June 1959 by the sale of a $100 million bond offering. Here, indeed, was a paradox. On the one hand, government—in the form of the Los Angeles City Council, aided and abetted by the Los Angeles Chamber of Commerce, the Los Angeles Merchants and Manufacturers Association, and the Los Angeles Times—could condemn subsidized public housing as a crypto-Communist program, while at the same time lauding the federal and state programs that were fueling the boom in single-family home ownership. Thus the poor, the majority of them disadvantaged minorities, were being excluded from the same government assistance that was bringing millions of middle-class Americans, veterans especially, into home ownership.

As the housing market skyrocketed, so too did the nature of development. As late as 1938, house building across the nation remained a cottage industry, with seventy thousand to eighty thousand urban home builders constructing an average of 3.5 houses annually. From 1945 to 1960, some 1.3 million new homes would annually come on the market, with 4 percent of the home builders accounting for 45 percent of the houses. The local home builder was transformed into the mass developer, a big businessman capable of leveraging federal dollars or otherwise borrowing from banks, insurance companies, pension funds, and other sources, assembling large landhold-ings, negotiating the intricacies of zoning and land use politics, creating infrastruc-ture, assembling financial packages for buyers, marketing at an unprecedented rate.

California already enjoyed the presence of many prewar entrepreneurs, who instantly understood the possibilities of the postwar market. After all, mass develop-ment as practiced earlier in the century by such masters of the art as Harry Culver, Frank Meline, Alphonzo Bell, and Frank Havens was a time-honored California tra-dition. Their successors—among them, Henry Doelger, the Gellerts, David Bohan-non, and Fritz Burns—instinctively intuited the impending postwar housing boom; indeed, they had anticipated it prior to the war in a number of developments and had further prepared themselves for the coming boom during the war years.

In 1922 Henry Doelger opened a hot dog stand at the corner of Seventh Avenue and Lincoln Way in San Francisco, on the edge of the sand dunes of the undevel-oped Sunset district that extended west to Ocean Beach. These sand dunes, Doel-ger decided, cried out for development. Four years later, having made money from speculating in sand dune lots, Doelger bought fourteen blocks of Sunset property and began to develop housing. Finishing two houses a day at the height of his opera-tion between 1934 and 1940, Doelger developed the Sunset (Doelger City it was sometimes called) from Twenty-seventh to Thirty-ninth avenues between Kirkham and Quintara and Golden Gate Heights on Fifteenth and Sixteenth avenues. Built on narrow lots with large backyards and living quarters atop ample garages, Doelger homes adhered to a repeated five-room floor plan, with variations that included inte-rior patios, a breakfast nook, or a third bedroom. Graced with fireplaces and wood floors, and selling for $5,000 in the 1930s (by 2008 these very same homes would be selling for upwards of a million dollars), Doelger homes offered a generation of mid-dle-income San Franciscans the opportunity to live comfortably in semi-suburban circumstances within the limits of an expanding city.

Doelger was joined in the creation of the Sunset district by the brothers Carl and Fred Gellert, whose Standard Building Company (later Sunstream Homes) built twenty thousand units along similar lines. Gellert developments, such as Lakeshore Park west of Twin Peaks, were characterized by fanciful architecture that varied from Mediterranean to Tudor to Hansel and Gretel and thus staved off uniformity, despite being closely packed homes on narrow lots. The Gellerts were also adept at departing from the rigid grid of the West of Twin Peaks area when appropriate, building some of their homes on curving streets at the base of hillsides planted in eucalyptus.

David Bohannon followed an arc of development similar to his contemporary Henry Doelger's. Doelger derived his first success from hot dogs. Bohannon cornered the market on pushed sightseeing wheelchairs at the Panama-Pacific International Exposition of 1915. Starting as a real estate salesman in 1925, Bohannon founded his own brokerage company in 1928 and entered development in the 1930s, focusing his attention on the mid-peninsula south of San Francisco, where he acquired foreclosed properties. Something of a theorist as well as a practical businessman, Bohannon began to follow discussions by the Urban Land Institute, a Washington, D.C.–based real estate think tank, regarding the need for developers to think comprehensively regarding planned communities that included housing, retail centers, schools, churches, libraries, and, of equal importance, work sites, soon to be called industrial parks.

Fritz Burns, meanwhile, had been concentrating his attention on Westside Los Angeles. In contrast to Doelger and Bohannon, San Franciscans with an eighth-grade education, Burns was born and raised in a prosperous Irish-German family in Minneapolis and had been educated through the University of Minnesota and the Wharton School of Finance. Arriving in Los Angeles in 1921 as the City of Angels was entering a ten-year building boom, Burns began his West Coast career as vice president and sales manager of the real estate firm of Dickinson & Gillespie, in which he held an interest. Working with (and admiring) the legendary Harry Culver, Burns openly stated that he would be a millionaire by the time he was thirty. Investing in real estate, a pioneering professional football team (the Los Angeles Buccaneers), and directing sales for the development of the Playa Del Ray subdivision on the western Los Angeles coastline before venturing out on his own, Burns achieved his goal, becoming a millionaire by thirty and an ex-millionaire by thirty-one when another development, Palisades Del Ray, went sour in the aftermath of the collapse of the stock market. For a while, Burns was so broke he was forced to live in a tent on the ocean palisades he had hoped to develop. Recouping his losses in the 1930s through such projects as Olympic Beach (the renamed Palisades Del Ray) and Windsor Hills, a housing development capitalizing upon the newly established Federal Housing Administration (FHA) mortgage program, Burns entered the 1940s as the developer most poised to capitalize on the Westside development engendered by the aircraft industry. Burns and his partner Fred Marlow developed Manchester Village, a tract of two- and three-bedroom attached homes, centered at the intersection of La Tijera and Manchester Boulevard, two blocks east of Sepulveda—double bungalows, they were called—aimed at defense workers looking for rentals, followed toward the end of the war by the development of detached single-family homes for purchase. By 1945 Burns and Marlow had built more than a thousand homes in the former bean fields of the Westchester district.

Toward the end of the war, meanwhile, David Bohannon was accomplishing equally impressive development in the apricot orchards, and the currant and rhubarb fields outside the city of San Lorenzo in Alameda County. Like Burns, Bohannon relished the techniques of mass production in the creation of his San Lorenzo Village. Bohannon techniques included a company-owned mill yard, where a single worker could cut a hundred rafters an hour. His tractors dug 450 pier holes per shift, with a foundation ready for construction after eight hours of work. Prefabricated sections were dropped off at each site, with the construction crews moving from house to house, each worker specializing in one task. A three-bedroom home in San Lorenzo Village sold for $6,000 in 1945, a mere $300 down, or rented for $55 a month. Early homes had a separate room and entrance for rental to defense workers. There were no garages, but a cement slab was laid next to each house for the construction of a garage when the war was over.

Not only were Bohannon and Burns walking the walk, they were talking the talk as well, as chairmen of the Northern and Southern Project Committees on Postwar Home Building, established by the State Reconstruction and Reemployment Commission formed in 1944 to assess the housing needs of postwar California. The July 1945 report of the committees, *Postwar Housing in California*, which Burns and Bohannon all but wrote, called for the construction of 625,000 single-family homes by 1950, keyed to middle-income wage-earners. Already, the report stated, California enjoyed a tradition of good affordable housing for the middle class, together with a prototype, the ranch house, eminently suited for mass production.

The controlling paradigm for such postwar development is the 17,400-unit Levittown on Long Island, constructed between 1947 and 1951—and sometimes finished at the rate of thirty houses per day—by Abraham Levitt and his sons, William and Alfred. Each detail of a Levittown home—its gleaming white metal kitchen cabinets, refrigerator, and stove, its washing machine under the stairs, the built-in radio and record player (later, the eight-inch television set) in the twelve- by sixteen-foot living room with fireplace, the alcove off the living room, the two bedrooms and one bath, the reverse floor plan with the kitchen fronting the street so that an eye could be kept on the children and the living room fronting the backyard for privacy, the unfinished attic that could later be developed according to individual need and taste, all this selling for $7,990 for a Cape Cod, $9,500 for a ranch—reverberated with the hope and promise of the postwar years.

So too did the middle-class developments of Westchester and Panorama City in Los Angeles, followed by Lakewood adjacent to Long Beach, the Westlake annex to Daly City south of San Francisco, San Lorenzo Village in Alameda County, the developments created by Eichler Homes and Sunstream in the Bay Area, indeed, all the mass-produced residential housing created in this era, announce to a returning and incoming generation of Californians the brave new world they had fought for and earned, the years that would now be theirs. Like Levittown, these were mass-produced places. Panorama City in the San Fernando Valley, a joint venture between Fritz Burns and Kaiser Community Homes, equaled Levittown in mass manufacture and surpassed it in the use of prefabrication, as Henry J. Kaiser deliberately transferred to home building the production techniques his companies had mastered during wartime. Laid out on the former Panorama Ranch in San Fernando Valley, one of the largest dairy farms in Southern California, Panorama City was brought into being by two thousand workers moving in intricate synchronicity to produce homes selling from $9,195 for a two-bedroom and $10,150 to $10,850 for a three-bedroom, $500 down. The first homes were ready for sale by 1948. Salesman Herb Lightfoot sold twenty-three of them on a single Sunday.

To answer the question why millions of Americans relocated to California in the postwar period and created such an expanding market is, as USC historian Doyce B. Nunis Jr. points out, to probe the very nature of California. At the core of the California identity, Nunis argues, was a process of recruitment across a wide range of promotional literature and pamphleteering in the nineteenth century and an even more powerful presentation through motion pictures, radio, and popular music in the first half of the twentieth. The Gold Rush, the 1880s, the early 1900s, the Depression, World War II: California had developed through a series of booms in which large influxes of people in search of a better life—whether imagined as gold, land, employment, or merely a second start—had migrated en masse to the Pacific Coast. Through each of these booms, with the possible exception of the Gold Rush, the desire for an improved and more affordable domestic life—visualized as a home of one's own, a garden, family life in a sunny climate—remained consistent. Publications such as *Better Homes and Gardens* and *Changing Times*, with the up-close-and-personal details of migrating families, especially in terms of home ownership and day-to-day life in their new environment, gave new energy to this domestic quest in the postwar era. In January 1960 *Changing Times* profiled a family who had moved from metropolitan Chicago to a six-room home in Encino in the San Fernando Valley. The father, a thirty-eight-year-old industrial designer, was making $11,000 a year. His thirty-three-year-old wife did not have to work and could devote her time to home-making and child care. On most days, she could also find time to sunbathe on a chaise lounge in her backyard. For nearly half the year, the couple wore light sports clothes and dined several nights a week on their backyard patio. While they were saving for a pool, the couple next door allowed the kids to swim in their pool under supervision. Although they took occasional trips to the beach and visited Yosemite on their anniversary, their home was the center of their life. They gave at least one dinner party or backyard barbecue a month and hosted frequent afternoon gatherings for neighbors and friends on weekends. As far as *Changing Times* was concerned, this was the California way of life.

And so the people came and bought, and the developers continued to develop through the 1950s, into the 1960s, and beyond. San Diego, city and county together, doubled itself, expanding into Mission Valley and the adjacent townships of El Cajon, Santee, Fletcher Hills, Lakeside, La Mesa, Spring Valley, and Lemon Grove. Between 1950 and 1961, Orange County (population 220,000 in 1950; 704,000 by 1960) witnessed the construction of 2,500 housing tracts containing 144,000 building lots. Developers transformed Newport Beach from a yachting resort into a residential city and augmented the cities of Orange, Santa Ana, Anaheim, Fullerton, Costa Mesa, and Buena Park with housing developments. Seven new cities—Buena Park, Costa Mesa, La Palma, Cypress, Stanton, Westminster, and Fountain Valley—were incorporated in the 1950s alone. Opening in 1955 in Anaheim, Disneyland was by the early 1960s the epicenter of a residential area triangulated by Harbor Boulevard, the Santa Ana Freeway (5), and Katella Avenue. In a manner that would later be described as post-suburban, the residential developments of coastal and southern Orange County, no matter how they were affiliated in terms of local government, tended to meld their identities into a continuous suburban region.

The Inland Empire—Riverside, San Bernardino, and eastern Los Angeles County, an area larger than Rhode Island, Connecticut, and Delaware combined— was experiencing comparable growth across its dairy farms, orange groves, vineyards, walnut orchards, and bean, barley, vegetable, and flower fields. During the 1950s the population of Riverside County increased by an amazing 80 percent. In the desert the resort city of Palm Springs showed comparable growth, along with the rest of the Coachella Valley. In January 1951 the Thunderbird Country Club opened in Rancho Mirage, establishing a paradigm of golf-oriented residential development for the half century to come. By 1962 Palm Springs had a population of sixteen thousand, but more important, it had subdivided itself over forty-five square miles, comparable to the size of San Francisco. Aerial views of the Coachella Valley showed the grids of emerging communities that would eventually create a metropolitan region extending from Palm Springs to Indio. San Bernardino County grew by 66 percent, and the Pomona Valley in eastern Los Angeles County, centered on the cities of Pomona and Claremont, increased by 65 percent. The city of Ontario, the regional capital of eastern Los Angeles County, doubled itself with an impressive growth rate of 112 percent. Los Angeles County as a whole was experiencing a fury of subdivision (462,593 lots subdivided between 1945 and 1957), peaking in 1955 when 50,032 new lots were recorded.

Aerial views of Los Angeles County as of 1960 reveal cluster after cluster of housing tracts geometric in regularity. Growth came in three directions: southeast toward Orange County through Downey, Norwalk, and Whittier; eastward through the San Gabriel and Pomona valleys; and northwest into the San Fernando Valley and beyond. Developed between 1950 and 1953, the community of Lakewood in southeast Los Angeles County east of Long Beach—57,000 residents by 1954, living in 17,500 houses on 3,500 acres—equaled the scale and extent of Levittown on Long Island. Seen from the air, the streets and houses of Lakewood, gleaming in the sun, surrounded by open fields that were still agricultural, offered the quintessential example of the changes that were coming to California.

So did the community of Westlake west of Daly City immediately south of San Francisco. In 1945, anticipating postwar growth, Henry Doelger purchased from the Spring Valley Water Company six hundred acres of fog-shrouded swampy sand dunes devoted to the raising of hogs and cabbages. Doelger subdivided the property, naming it Westlake from its relationship to the nearby Lake Merced, and in 1948 he began to build. By 1950 rows of architecturally repetitive, densely packed houses were sweeping across the former sand dunes. Doelger continued construction until 1962, then moved southwest down the coast to develop a similar tract on four hundred acres in the city of Pacifica.

South of San Francisco, meanwhile, the city of San Jose was experiencing a 69 percent growth rate. The majority of newcomers were settling into a myriad of middle-class housing tracts springing up to meet the market. By 1960 San Jose, a predominately agricultural marketing town through the 1930s, had a population of 161,000 and was decidedly urban/suburban in character. Through annexation of lands to its south, San Jose would eventually encompass nearly a hundred square miles, although most of that land remained agricultural. In income and housing, San Jose, outside of a few districts, was blue collar and middle class. The towns of the southern peninsula, by contrast—Palo Alto, Mountain View, Sunnyvale, Cupertino, Santa Clara, Los Altos—were already showing the demographic and cultural effects of the electronics industry (IBM, Ampex, Hewlett-Packard, Litton, Varian, Fairchild, the missiles and space division of Lockheed, the research division of United Aircraft) developing in this region, centered on Stanford University and bringing into Santa Clara County thousands of highly qualified professionals. One builder, Eichler Homes, made a specialty of meeting the tastes of this clientele with houses that blended the wood traditions of the Bay Region style with modernist simplicities of roof, pillar, beam, glass wall, and patio.

What was life like in this new California, this suburbia? Is it enough to say that it was white, native born, young, married, child-rearing, middle class, and conformist? Or are there more subtle meanings and textures to be explored? Highbrow commentary has in general not been kind to life in these residential developments nor to the decade, the 1950s, in which they expanded so rapidly in California and elsewhere. Ironically, most of the criticism, whether in print or in films, has come from Baby Boomers who were raised in such places. But so has the defense of these communities.

Urban historian Greg Hise, for example, has argued that the taken-for-granted distinction between city and suburb is a false dichotomy, especially if the suburbs are perceived as monochromatic dormitories. Historians and sociologists, Hise argues, tend to assume that the characteristics and amenities of urbanism—jobs, parks, schools, churches, synagogues, retail and public spaces—were ignored in the new developments. Not so, he contends. From Panorama City onward, the major residential developments in California had their intellectual origins in the Garden City ideal first advanced by Ebenezer Howard at the turn of the century that envisioned new developments as complete communities—housing, jobs, schools, parks, retail—separated from each other by open space. Developers such as Levitt and Sons on the East Coast, David Bohannon in San Lorenzo Village, and Fritz Burns in Westchester and Panorama City, Hise points out, were the self-aware heirs to more than four decades of research and theorizing spearheaded by, among others, the Regional Planning Association of New York City, the Urban Land Institute of Washington, D.C., and various planning commissions in California, each of them calling for the development of the new residential districts as comprehensive and full-service as possible within their boundaries.

The very notion of suburb versus city, Hise argues, represents a red herring when applied to the major postwar developments of Southern California, which were conceptualized as decentralized regional cities, sustaining as fully as possible a rich and varied life. Panorama City, for example, had a business and retail district from the beginning, which it later developed into a regional shopping center, as did Lakewood with its Lakewood Center organized around a flagship May Company department store. The problem was, the engineers of Kaiser Community Homes and the planners and developers involved in a number of the other developments neglected to designate a permanently protected greenbelt surrounding Panorama City. Hence, Panorama City and other newly developed decentralized regional cities tended to sprawl and, eventually, to blend into each other, which weakened their autonomous identities. The freeway systems constructed in the late 1950s and 1960s further linked these new developments into a contiguous mass.

But even then, can it be argued that these new places were devoid of psychological, imaginative, even moral meaning? Not so, argues University of Washington urban historian John Findlay. These new cities fully met the needs and assumptions of the postwar generation. First of all, westerners liked their new cities the way they were: on accessible grids lined by single-family houses, crisscrossed by boulevards and freeway systems, served by shopping centers and strategically sited community institutions. When critics of such developments claimed that they did not resemble the cities of the East Coast, much less Europe, they were exactly on point. Western cities deliberately rejected congestion, zoning, and land use. They were consciously kept low density and multi-centered. They were, in point of fact, collections of urban villages centered on shopping centers and industrial parks, not on downtowns. A resident of a western city had a clear picture of what aspects of the city—which freeway, which boulevard, which street, which house, which shopping center, which church, synagogue, or school—was applicable to his or her life; and this mental map was internalized with all the detail and affection of the familiar. The rest of the city was either ignored or kept on the periphery of awareness.

By the 1950s seasoned observers as intellectually astute as architect Richard Neutra, housing and urban planner Catherine Bauer Wurster, cultural critic Bruce Bliven, sociologist Nathan Glazer, and urban theorist Reyner Banham were each recognizing the voluntary and crypto-utopian nature of the newly developing western city, together with its deliberate rejection of Atlantic seaboard or European models. Far from being accidents or impositions by greedy developers, Findlay argues, these new places were magic kingdoms, theme parks for a better life on the part of an equally new class of people: the family-centered middle class, defining itself as a consumer. This new population, the wealthiest third, felt true affection for their places of residence; indeed, they regarded them as small towns within a larger mosaic, animated by an *Our Town* feel.

Opening in 1955 in Anaheim, Disneyland perfectly expressed this sustaining mythology of small-town life and identity via the schematized intensity of a theme park that was a metaphorical landscape for the new cities that were being developed across the American West. Walt Disney intended Disneyland to be, literally, the happiest place on earth. Like the new communities it prefigured, Disneyland was family-oriented and child-centered, definitely not Coney Island, which is to say, raucous, demotic, spontaneous, alive with the fleshy exuberance of a Reginald Marsh painting and taking its vitality from the big city, like Playland-at-the-Beach in San Francisco. Disneyland was, rather, a controlled development, orderly and restrictive, staffed by well-trained and polite middle-class employees, attuned to an equally middle-class and well-behaved clientele.

At the entrance to Disneyland was Main Street USA: that mythologized small town fixed forever in the American imagination, whether positively or negatively, now being transferred west and reimposed onto the new suburban developments. Like these new developments, Disneyland was based on a mythologized reverence for the past as expressed by Main Street USA and the adjacent Frontierland, which anchored Disneyland in the larger myth of the West. Like the new communities, Disneyland could be fun. Adventureland proved that. And it could also nurture the imagination, as Fantasyland indicated. But it was faith in the future, centered on Tomorrowland, that projected Frontierland and Main Street USA forward into a gloriously unfolding history of technology, prosperity, and social order. As science fiction writer and urbanologist Ray Bradbury was quick to recognize, Disneyland constituted a probe into the urban future, most notably in its monorail but also in its conception of the city as planned and controlled environment, as opposed to the spontaneous product of site and historical circumstances.

Thus Disneyland, like the successful expositions of the nineteenth and early twentieth centuries, was structured by present value and utopian statement. The themes and values of Disneyland mirrored the themes and values that an entire generation was bringing to California and the West. These values, argues urban theorist Constance Perin, were fundamental to American social practice as expressed in home ownership and the spatial organization of American cities. By the twentieth century, certainly by the post–World War I era, home ownership, Perin asserted, had come to represent the deepest possible participation by the individual citizen in American history itself. Home ownership constituted the most powerful agency for the pursuit of life, liberty, and happiness on the part of the individual citizen. It also embodied what Americans considered the correct and acceptable sequence of life: birth, education, maturity, family formation, and maximized personal sovereignty through wealth and property. In an increasingly complex and corporative world, one still could be the master of one's home, a sovereign and prelapsarian Adam or Eve in one's own house and garden. Renters, alas, whom Americans tended to regard as an historically unfulfilled, hence unstable, sector of society, failed to attain such sovereignty and permanency. Renting was by definition a transitional stage, even if this transitional stage lasted a lifetime. Even owners of condominiums and attached townhouses, in point of fact, fell short of this moral/mythic formulation. Thus the single-family home took on a near-sacred character, while the apartment building remained mundane. Government policy, as expressed by FHA loan practices and the tax policies of the Internal Revenue Service, clearly reflected this bias, as did most zoning regulations, which tended to classify apartment buildings as businesses rather than residential enclaves.

Americans believed, moreover—so Perin reports—that home ownership provided the middle class a means of deliberately separating itself from people who were racially or ethnically different, disruptive for one reason or another, or merely lower down the social ladder. Life in the big cities, by contrast, was based upon elaborate and complex rituals of avoidance through which the middle and upper classes avoided threatening elements. Middle-class Americans preferred to live among their own kind of people: people, that is, who looked like they looked, earned what they earned, had been raised the same way they had been raised, and generally shared the same philosophy of life. Home ownership—especially on the mass scale practiced in the new California developments—ensured such a willful segregation. Families voluntarily came to these places to be with their own kind.

Home ownership, Perin argues, was also believed to protect sexual stability and propriety. In the mid-nineteenth century, housing historian Gwendolyn Wright tells us, New Yorkers were scandalized that newly constructed Paris-style apartment buildings allowed unrelated men and women to live along the same corridor. Into the twentieth century, urban apartment buildings continued to sustain hints of that larger promiscuity that was an ongoing component of urban life. The single-family home in the new developments of the post–World War II era, by contrast, provided shrines and cordons sanitaires to marriage and the family as sacramental and social subsumptions of sexuality. Encoded in each home—or at least in the myth of each home—was a crypto-theological, even overtly theological, concept of marriage as a most sacred and most necessary institution, based on committed sexuality, procreation, the nurture and education of children. So, at least, went the most accepted story line of the postwar era.

And so a generation, in California and elsewhere, took to the new developments that, despite the later arguments of urban theorists, were then and now considered the suburbs. "Suburbia, of thee I sing!" rhapsodized light verse writer Phyllis McGinley in the December 1949 issue of Harper's. In full detail, McGinley described life in a suburb north of New York City: the commuting husband, chauffeured to the station each morning by a dutiful spouse, met each evening at the train station in a daily ritual of renewed family life, the children running to greet their father as if he had been gone for months; the housewife with a few hours to herself each day while the children were in school, time for gardening, reading, or other hobbies, or the sheer pleasure of getting together with the other educated and aspiring women of the neighborhood; the way the children played together in the outdoors without parental fear for their safety; the nightly dinners around the family table; the get-togethers on weekends over a highball or two. Just about the same time McGinley was rhapsodizing, short story writer John Cheever was removing himself to a similar New York City suburb, Westchester, finding there both a life and the theme for his art, albeit from a slightly more noir perspective. Although McGinley and Cheever were describing life in suburbs north of New York City, their commentary was applicable to California as well. Despite the fact that most of the new developments required an automobile for the daily commute, the suburbs south of San Francisco enjoyed a train service as far south as San Jose. A New York style of suburban commuting grew up along the peninsula townships of Burlingame, San Mateo, Belmont, San Carlos, Menlo-Atherton, Palo Alto, and Santa Clara. In the evenings the commuter train, run by the Southern Pacific, featured bar service in its lounge car.

Prosperous by definition, suburban homes were filled with freezers, refrigerators, the latest models of stove, washer, and dryer (gas or electric), chrome and Formica kitchen tables and chairs, double beds for adults, twin or bunk beds for the children, modern furniture in living rooms dominated by a television set and, for those with more advanced tastes, a high-fidelity phonograph (1958) and long-playing records (1948). Housewives had at their disposal an increasing array of convenient food products: Reddi-Whip (1947) to spray on cakes from pre-packaged mixes (1949), Sugar Pops (1951) or Sugar-Frosted Flakes (1952) for the children's breakfast, Oreo cookies (1949) and later (1960) Hawaiian Punch to pack into their Davy Crockett lunch boxes (1955), Minute Rice (1950) for the starch of the evening meal, Tupperware (1951) to store leftovers in the refrigerator. In 1954 Gerald Thomas, an executive with C. A. Swanson and Sons, a poultry wholesaler, found himself in the aftermath of Thanksgiving with ten refrigerated railroad cars of unsold turkeys. Thinking of the meals served on trays in airlines, Thomas commissioned five thousand frozen turkey dinners: turkey, cornbread dressing, gravy, buttered peas, sweet potatoes, placed on a tripartite aluminum tray, packaged in a box printed to resemble a television set, and selling for ninety-eight cents. Swanson sold ten million of these TV dinners, as they were called, in 1954 alone and soon expanded its line to include meatloaf, Salisbury steak, and fried chicken.

Families were being encouraged to eat pre-prepared meals in front of the television set, which would seem contrary to the family-centered ethos of the suburban lifestyle. But at least they were eating together in their homes. In San Bernardino, fifty miles east of Los Angeles, at the corner of Fourteenth and E Street, the McDonald brothers, Richard and Maurice, more familiarly known as Dick and Mack, were revolutionizing the drive-in restaurant business through the rapid production and serving of hamburgers, fries, and milkshakes. Henry Ford himself would have appreciated the efficiencies and assembly-line techniques introduced by the McDonalds, which enabled relatively unskilled workers to become, quite rapidly, the equals of the most skilled of short-order cooks. In 1952 the McDonald brothers began to franchise their Speedy Service System, but on a limited basis. In many instances, competing vendors merely observed, then plagiarized, the system. In the summer of 1954, however, Ray Kroc, an ambitious food-service equipment salesman, saw the expansionist possibilities of the McDonalds' San Bernardino operation. Kroc persuaded the McDonalds to appoint him their sole franchiser. In 1961 Kroc bought the brothers out for $2.7 million in cash. In time, thanks to McDonald's and other fast-food enterprises, millions of Americans would be eating outside the home, and the Swanson TV dinner would seem, in retrospect, a bulwark of domesticity and family values.

Suburban culture was child-oriented, and this orientation was strengthened by developments great and small. In 1947 two new television programs—*Howdy Doody* and *Kukla, Fran, and Ollie*—ushered in a half century of children's entertainment. Two years later, Hopalong Cassidy, as played by William Boyd, showed the potential for a young-audience-oriented television program to stimulate millions of dollars of sales in related consumer products. On an infinitely more profound level, the polio vaccine developed by Jonas Salk was introduced in 1955, and a major scourge of modern American childhood was thereby curtailed. The Salk vaccine coincided with the Davy Crockett craze that saw millions of children sporting frontier-style coonskin caps in imitation of the frontiersman played by Fess Parker on TV. Beginning in 1955 as well, smaller children could enjoy Play-Doh. Two years later, older children could enjoy the Frisbee and the Hula Hoop, each of which sold into the millions. Barbie—the doll, the drama, the fantasy—made her appearance in 1959. Her friend Ken debuted two years later, and the couple went steady for the rest of the century. Mothers, meanwhile, had the convenience of Pampers disposable diapers, beginning in 1956. When things got too hectic around the house, there was always the Miltown tranquilizer, introduced the previous year.

Based in the consumerist haven of the single-family home, the newly established family in its newly constructed house—centered in the home, entertained in the home, with the home serving as a compelling symbol of personal and social arrival—nevertheless sought community, finding it in equally newly established schools, churches, synagogues, shopping centers, parks, and playgrounds. Once again, there emerged a dichotomy between the suburbanized middle class and its critics. In 1962, for example, University of Chicago ethicist Gibson Winter castigated its religious life in *The Suburban Captivity of the Churches*, which accused the suburban Protestant church of reinforcing a lifestyle based upon a deliberate withdrawal into an isolated, racially restrictive enclave, contrary to the spirit of the Gospel. In *The Noise of Solemn Assemblies* (1961), Hartford Seminary professor Peter Berger castigated mainline Protestantism for its wholesale embrace of secular suburbanism.

Yet local histories covering this period, by contrast, chronicle an exfoliation of newly constructed Protestant, Catholic, and Jewish places of worship in developing communities. In the case of Catholics, the newly constructed parish church usually supported a parochial grade school or, in fewer cases, a regional high school, which could either be attached to a parish or freestanding. Churches and synagogues offered residents of the new communities a way of regrouping and reaffiliating themselves in their new environment. For Jews, Catholics, and Protestants alike, the synagogue or the church, after the home, provided the primary modality of social organization and identity. A new generation of rabbis and ministers, graduates of distinguished theological schools, came west to assume pulpits in the new developments. The expansion coincided with a golden age of vocations to the

Roman Catholic priesthood. Seminaries teemed with candidates, and in the field
a generation of parish priests were experiencing the pleasures of construction and
development. Youth groups and ministries aimed at teenagers proliferated in an
era that was especially sensitive to problems of alienation and delinquency among
the young. Churches and synagogues also helped integrate prior residents with the
newly arrived, which could be a problem, especially in such places as Newport
Beach in Orange County, possessed of strong prior identities; indeed, the term "new
people" was in common usage in Newport throughout the decade as older residents,
who had long enjoyed life in the neo-Mediterranean seaside community, enclavish
and arty, saw their privileged city surrounded by residential tracts and the streets
of Newport, especially on weekends, crowded with suburban types. Friday night
or Sunday morning, however, brought segments of these two populations together
for worship.

Within a few short years, longtime residents would be a distinct minority throughout the state as the population pushed past twenty million in 1970. The marvel of
it all was that the institutional life of California was sustained through this growth.
The new communities were quickly integrated into a composite and somewhat pre-
existing California life not only through worship in the private sector but through
an epic of construction of schools, high schools, and colleges. Keyed to this was the
emerging two-year community college movement, emphasizing lower-division and
vocational education, and the newly established (1960) California State University
system, which had as its goal the establishment of colleges granting bachelor's and
master's degrees and credentials to the students of the surrounding communities. By
the early 1960s, millions of young Californians were in school; and in this alembic
of public education was being forged a new California for whom the postwar boom,
including life in the suburbs, was the norm.

Within this suburban idyll, there were problems. First of all, there could be problems with the house itself. Prior to the war, most contractors took a craftsman-like
approach to construction. Homes built in the 1920s and 1930s remained notable for
fine materials and finish. While the mass production of homes in the postwar period
produced a surprisingly acceptable product, the very nature of the house—its rapid
construction, its prefabricated materials, its assembly-line plumbing and wiring, its
rapidly installed Sheetrock interiors, and in some cases its unstable sites—could
make for a host of problems, as portrayed in John Keats's *The Crack in the Picture
Window* (1956), a novelized version of everything that could go wrong with a newly
built suburban house. An admixture of fiction, social science (including footnote
citations), and docudrama intended as satire, *The Crack in the Picture Window* represents one of the most lambasting attacks against the suburban lifestyle to appear
in the 1950s. As Keats tells his story, shoddy workmanship was a problem in and of
itself as well as a metaphor for the difficulties, disappointments, and banalities of
life in the suburbs. In the course of the novel, Keats's protagonists, John and Mary
Drone and their two small children, experience just about everything that can go

wrong with suburban life: a cramped and poorly designed home; careless construction; deceptive regulations and inadequate government services; conformity and enforced association with neighbors; the isolation and marginalization of women and the overworking of men; financial anxiety arising from mortgages; an obsession with children, together with alienation and juvenile delinquency among teenagers; the loneliness that comes from deracination and the absence of an extended family; and a kind of sexual instability, however obliquely expressed or acted out, arising from the miscellaneous mixing in close residential proximity of men and women in the prime of life in post-Kinsey America.

Published in 1948, the 804-page *Sexual Behavior in the Human Male* by Alfred Kinsey, Wardell Pomeroy, and Clyde Martin, more commonly known as the Kinsey Report, was perhaps the most notorious, even influential, book of the 1950s, especially as augmented in 1953 by the publication of *Sexual Behavior in the Human Female* by the same team. As cultural critic Lionel Trilling suggested in a long essay published in *The Liberal Imagination* (1950), the Kinsey Report, for all its deficiencies—and there were many—had to be reckoned with because of its sheer ambition to document the sexual behavior of ordinary Americans. To everyone's surprise, that behavior, or so the Kinsey Report claimed, encompassed considerable amounts of sexual activity—including homosexual activity and masturbation, generally considered deviant. According to the Kinsey Report, the average American male had a statistical tendency to begin his sex life early, to indulge in experimental homosexual contacts when young, to resort to prostitutes later in life, and, after marriage, to sustain surprisingly high levels of masturbation and infidelity.

Critics from the medical, psychological, and psychoanalytic establishment had a field day attacking Kinsey's research methodology. Still, whatever its deficiencies, the Kinsey Report, a runaway best-seller, had an electrifying effect on the nation at large. The report was purporting to map a vast and largely ignored submerged continent of sexual behavior among middle-class Americans, defying ancient taboos and reticences in the process. So too must the Kinsey Report be placed in the context of the Second World War, during which it was largely researched and written on a grant from the Rockefeller Foundation. As psychiatrist Howard Kitching reported in *Sex Problems of the Returned Veteran* (1946), the war years had been fraught with sexual problems and frustrations born of danger, death, the fear of death, separation, and sexual temptations abroad and on the home front. Millions of returning veterans, together with the women in their lives, Kitching opined, would have to enter a process of readjustment in which they could re-stabilize themselves sexually.

Most gratifying, the Kinsey Report spoke to and facilitated such a process of sexual adjustment by scientifically (or so it was alleged) validating the widest possible bandwidth of sexual behavior as statistically normal. Americans who were unfaithful during the war or indulged in homosexual activity, or who were evaluating their renewed sexuality in terms of numerical orgasms, now had plenty of company. Thus the Kinsey Report, as Lionel Trilling noted, was energized by elements of manifesto:

a declaration, that is, on the part of the American people that sexuality, including its borderlands, was now open for continuing discussion.

Not surprisingly, given the popularity of the Kinsey Report and all that it stood for, commentary on the postwar suburban lifestyle frequently included an assessment of its sexuality. The soaring birth rate of the suburbs testified eloquently to the intensities of heterosexual activity within the bonds of marriage that could logically be expected from a young population that included millions of men and women whose normal arc of sexual activity had been interrupted by the war. Yet there was also a suspicion on the part of commentators that the suburbs offered new forms of sexual tempta- tion through the promiscuous amalgamation of sexually active younger adults, living in totally new circumstances, beyond the mediating influence of the extended family and religious and/or cultural institutions. Sometimes, this suspicion could be good- humored, as in the film *Good Neighbor Sam* (1964), starring Jack Lemmon, with Robert Q. Lewis as a particularly lascivious neighbor. It constitutes a more pressing threat, however, in *The Crack in the Picture Window*, in which Mary Drone is the recipient of a neighbor's hand on her thigh while her husband is suspiciously linger- ing with the neighbor's wife behind closed doors in the kitchen or when, in another scene, the neighbors play a parlor game with sexual overtones.

In John McPartland's *No Down Payment*—the novel and the film, both released in 1957—the sexual tensions of four couples, living in the same California suburb (Northern California in the novel, Southern California in the film) constitute the chief risk and almost miasmic atmosphere of suburban life. McPartland, a Northern Californian, was the author of *Sex in Our Changing World* (1947), an early version of the Kinsey Report that sold three million copies and was translated into eight lan- guages. Like *The Crack in the Picture Window*, *No Down Payment* offers readers a guided tour through suburban consumerism, with nearly forty machines and appli- ances making their appearance. Aberrant sexual attractions and conflicts, however, constitute the heart of McPartland's story, which includes an adulterous date-rape and the revenge for that offense, a savage beating, by the offended husband.

Still, for all their problems, the characters of *No Down Payment*—in their con- sumerism, their detachment from established institutions, their lifestyles, even their anomie—resemble each other more significantly than they differ. Conformity, in suburbia and elsewhere, was very much on the minds of commentators in this era, beginning with University of Chicago social scientist David Riesman, whose *The Lonely Crowd* (1950) set the leitmotif for a decade aware of a growing conformity and, paradoxically, a growing sense of isolation. In 1955 two best-sellers, a social- scientific investigation and a novel, continued the critique. In *The Organization Man*, sociologist William Whyte depicted the corporatization of the American economy, with its attendant creation of a highly conformist white-collar and profes- sional class. In *The Man in the Gray Flannel Suit* (1955), novelist Sloan Wilson told the story of advertising executive and suburbanite Tom Rath, who turns his back on a high-powered position in order to spend more time with his family. Yet *The Man in the Gray Flannel Suit* does not indict suburbia. A former paratrooper who survived fierce combat in Italy during the war, Rath finds in his suburban life, at the end of the novel, a comforting setting in which to be with his wife and children, after the trauma of being forced to kill seventeen enemy soldiers in order to survive on the battlefield. And besides: Rath's family is not that typical, for at the conclusion of the novel it includes his young son by an Italian woman, who has died and whose child the Rath family will now raise.

In a world that had so recently been life-threatening for so many thirty-something veterans, family life was everything that had been dreamed of during the war years. Which is perhaps one of the reasons why *The Adventures of Ozzie and Harriet* played so successfully on radio from 1949 to 1952 and on television from 1952 to 1966: because it so easily celebrated in such an informal way the healing presence of family. The Nelsons played themselves: Hollywood bandleader Ozzie, his stay-at-home wife Harriet, and teenagers David and Ricky, with Don DeFore playing the fictional neighbor Thorny Thornberry. The fact that they were playing themselves, albeit in highly scripted circumstances, added to the convincing nature of the show, as did the fact that in time David's friends from USC and Ricky's friends from Hollywood High School played versions of themselves on various programs. A near decade and a half of suburbanites could, with some wishful thinking—no family, after all, could be that ideal—mark their own family's progress through life as the Nelson boys went through their teenage years, played sports (football for David, tennis for Ricky), matured into adulthood, found their careers, dated, and married, and as, time and again, Harriet saw the family through challenges facing her husband and sons with wifely and motherly good humor. In December 1959 the *Los Angeles Times* selected Harriet Nelson as one of its Women of the Year. For the time being, at least, the Nelson family remained conformist, with David—and here the script departed from reality—becoming a lawyer and Ricky edging into a singing career, which actually happened.

Cultural critics, meanwhile—Lewis Mumford, Jane Jacobs, and Paul and Percival Goodman among them—were launching a counterattack in favor of the density, variety, culture, and community of cities: arguments that would give rise to the New Urbanism of a later era. These writers, it must be said, did not violently castigate the suburbs, although they did tend to dismiss them as cultural wastelands, if they noticed them at all. Not, however, Berkeley-based folksinger Malvina Reynolds, whose song "Little Boxes" (1962)—prompted by the uniform houses of the Westlake suburb south of San Francisco—represented an attitude toward suburbia shared by most intellectuals, including Reynolds, a UC Berkeley Ph.D. in English, raised in a Jewish socialist household in inner-city San Francisco. For Reynolds, the homes of Westlake were

> Little boxes on the hillside,
> Little boxes made of ticky tacky,
> Little boxes on the hillside,
> Little boxes all the same

that appropriately housed a conformist generation that went to the same colleges and universities, played on the same golf course, drank the same dry martinis, and sent their similarly pretty children to the same schools and summer camps, where they learned to be just like their parents.

Westlake residents Jack and Sally Klein might very well have agreed with Reynolds's assessment. The Kleins found themselves locked in a ferocious legal battle with the Westlake Subdivisions Improvement Association for replacing their lawn with ivy, contrary to association regulations, when their lawn succumbed to a local fungus. Jack Klein was a Lutheran and Sally a Presbyterian; but they received anonymous calls ("Kike bitch!" "Communist!") with decidedly anti-Semitic overtones. Vandals poured gasoline on their ivy, and Sally was hostilely pointed out to a group of children as the Ivy Woman at a local supermarket.

The same 25 September 1962 issue of *Look* magazine that chronicled the Kleins' plight also carried a blatantly hostile photo-essay entitled "The Tract Way of Life," describing the life of defense engineer Johnnie Irwin and his wife Joanie, who lived in an $18,800 home in a tract development in Orange County twenty-five miles southeast of Los Angeles. "In the Land of the Vanishing Orange Grove," *Look* noted, "bulldozers clear about 375 acres of farmland every day for newly arrived Californians who need backyards and bedrooms badly and find them in huge tracts full of interchangeable houses." Describing the Irwins' suburban life—"two daughters, two cars, three bedrooms, one cat, a few books, a few records... beer in the refrigerator... waxed fruit on the end tables... a swing in the backyard, a laurel tree in front of the picture window," friendly neighbors, bowling one morning a week for Joanie, coffee klatches, during which the housewives on the block did one another's hair and nails, afternoon card or Tupperware parties, in which the housewives played parlor games and had humorous names for themselves (Amiable Amy, Ticklish Trudy, Marvelous Mary), shopping at the local supermarket, building an artificial waterfall in the backyard—the unsigned *Look* article dripped with condescension and contempt, text and photographs alike. Neighbors on the 2400 block of Jackson in the tract outside Orange, *Look* reported, rode men in front, wives in back when they went out together. Husbands played nickel-limit poker. Couples had few books in the house, voted for Richard Nixon in the 1960 election, rarely went to church, and had few convictions regarding war, peace, bomb testing, or nuclear disarmament. "It's really limited when you think about it, isn't it?" one housewife remarked of life in Orange. "It was like this in Tipp City, Ohio, where I lived. I suppose it will be about the same with my kids."[1]

Were it not for Herbert Gans's *The Levittowners* (1967) and D. J. Waldie's *Holy Land: A Suburban Memoir* (1996), one might search high and low for coherent defenses of the suburban way of life against attacks from highbrow and mass media critics. Mixing personal observation and social science after a two-year residence in Levittown, Gans made a spirited defense of the individuality of Levittowners and the way that home ownership had intensified their sense of self. Through personal memory, suburban history, and confessional aphorism, Waldie countered critics with an evocation of Lakewood as hopeful paradigm for a better life.

Developed in the early 1950s by the Lakewood Park Company—an entity controlled by developers Ben Weingart, Louis Boyar, and Mark Taper—Lakewood was the Levittown of California: 17,500 homes on 3,500 acres (ten square miles) adjacent to Long Beach, a recent sugar beet field transformed within three years at the rate of fifty houses a day into a model planned community. With seventy thousand residents by 1954, Lakewood faced a decision: to be annexed by Long Beach, to remain unincorporated, dependent upon county services, or to incorporate as a city. In 1954 residents voted to split the difference: to incorporate as a city but contract for municipal services from Los Angeles County.

In almost every detail, Lakewood paralleled Levittown on the opposite coast, beginning with the assembly-line construction of houses on their one-foot-deep concrete foundations, taking less than fifteen minutes to dig by machine and only slightly longer to fill with concrete. At one point, at the height of construction, 2,113 foundations were poured within one hundred days. A specialized angle iron called a scafflejack made it possible to frame a Lakewood home in rapid time by providing carpenters a ready-made scaffold. Telephone and other wires were buried underground. Houses were lightly but durably constructed: wood framing covered by stucco, walls hollow within, roofs sturdy against fall and spring rains.

The very financing of Lakewood was symptomatic of postwar conditions. The federal government provided 100 percent financing ($100 million in construction loans and mortgage guarantees) for construction under Section 213 of the National Housing Act, an obscure provision that allowed the federal government directly to subsidize cooperative housing ventures. Once the homes were sold, however, the cooperatives dissolved, and the banks owned the property. A Senate subcommittee investigating the matter in 1954 did not like such a wholesale leveraging of federal financing by a private developer, but it was perfectly legal. The syndicate headed by Weingart, Boyar, and Taper derived the bulk of its profits from land sales to the cooperatives and from subsequent retail development. Even here, development costs were leveraged. The Lakewood Park Company got the Prudential Insurance Company to invest $8 million in 1951, after signing up the May Company department store as anchor tenant. Opening in February 1952, filled with the consumer goods of the era, the three-story, 357,000-square foot May Company department store, surrounded by a hundred-acre parking lot, constituted the true center of the new community.

By 1953 families were moving into Lakewood at the rate of thirty-five a day. On 13 July 1953 *Life* ran a photo by J. R. Eyerman that has now become a classic. Entitled "Moving Day," the photo depicted a phalanx of moving vans parked at uniform angles on Lakewood Street, each of them surrounded by families and the uniformed movers who were delivering their furniture. The Waldie family was proud to be among such people, moving into this new suburbia, so fraught with hopeful reverberations of the future. From 1942 to 1945, Waldie's father had served as a gunnery officer aboard the destroyer USS *Bradford* in the Pacific. Now he had a job designing pipelines for the Southern California Gas Company, where he would work for thirty years. The Waldies paid $6,700 for a two-bedroom home.

The Waldies were proud of their home: proud of the house, the pyracantha bushes in the backyard, the jacaranda tree in front, the streets named after entertainers and other Hollywood folk, Vice President Richard Nixon and First Lady Mamie Eisenhower, the Lakewood float in the 1985 Rose Parade that featured Timmy and Lassie from the popular television show, the consumer paradise at the shopping center. Later, D. J. Waldie would remember growing up in Lakewood during these years: the long Monopoly games with his brother, the excitement of a new electric train on Christmas morning, the way it rained for an entire week in 1953 and the streets flooded, the shock when nine-year-old Emmett Gossett suffocated to death after a mound of sand collapsed on him at a construction site. Twenty-five percent of the population of Lakewood was under ten years of age as of 1953. Already, parents were expressing anxiety about juvenile delinquency when these children would reach their teenage years. They called for the construction of more parks. In 1955 the city council of Lakewood outlawed crime and horror comic books.

Waldie's parents were grateful to be among people who had arrived: people averaging $5,100 a year in income, $2,000 above the national average. They shared this sense of well-being with the noticeable number of Lakewood residents from border states who had come to California during the 1930s to work in the fields or the early 1940s to work in the aviation industry—Aviation Okies, journalist Ernie Pyle had dubbed them—and they remained sensitive about their accents and about the word *Okie*, which they never allowed to be used in their presence. Occasionally, having had a drink or two in the course of a backyard barbecue, former Oklahomans would allow their twanging accents free rein, and they would talk of the tarpaper shacks they had once lived in. No wonder they could not believe their luck: to have come into such a place and to live in such homes, to enjoy the sunshine, and to have bearing fruit trees in their backyards.

The Waldies were of different stock, Catholics from Manhattan and Long Island, where his mother grew up. Something about these new developments seemed to attract Catholics of the newly arrived middle class. Half of Levittown was Catholic, and Lakewood supported a lesser but impressive Catholic population. Immigrant Catholic people had been city dwellers since the migrations of the mid-nineteenth century and were now taking the next step up the ladder as members of a first-generation of Americans of Roman Catholic immigrant stock to attain middle-class status and hence become eligible for the suburbs. Three of D. J. Waldie's uncles had become priests, and his father had spent a few years in a religious order and functioned as a kind of unofficial sacristan in the shiny new church built by the two young Irish-born priests assigned to Lakewood. The Waldie brothers wore their parochial school uniforms proudly each schoolday morning, and D. J. served as an altar boy, remembering especially Good Friday afternoons when the line of Lakewood residents waiting to venerate the crucifix extended outside the church and around the block. Suburbia, Waldie tells us, promised a bright new beginning in the 1950s, and in some sense it delivered on its promise, but that promise involved no exemption from the ordinary disappointments of life. Still, once that is recognized and acknowledged, another level of meaning reveals itself. Waldie calls his memoir *Holy Land* because Lakewood is in some sense exactly that: an intersection of time and eternity, a place where middle-class Americans might love, reproduce, succeed, fail, live, and die in American circumstances enlivened by day-to-day hope and the immemorial pleasures, struggles, questions, and rhythms of daily life.

2

Designs for the Good Life

Modernism, Tiki, Ranch

SEARCHING for the postwar American lifestyle, *Life* found it in Southern California. Climate, the automobile, a rising affluence, *Life* reported on 22 October 1945, had created a Southern California way of life suggestive of the future, which the magazine proceeded to illustrate through profiles of three families, living on $3,000, $10,000, and $50,000 a year respectively. Not surprisingly, the $50,000 a year family—that of MGM film composer Herbert Stothart—was living luxuriantly in Santa Monica, enjoying a two-story house, a swimming pool, a patio and garden, a live-in cook, two Studebakers, a Ford, and a Chevrolet. Given the value of money in 1945, the $10,000 Arthur Campbell family (he worked as a sales manager for Pacific Coast Borax) lived comfortably as well in an $18,000 rambling ranch-style home on three-quarters of an acre in the foothills of western Los Angeles County. The Campbells had no help, and only one car, but they enjoyed a patio and a swimming pool nevertheless, together with a portable barbecue, a Bendix electric washing machine for Betty Campbell, and a horse named Keeno for sixteen-year-old Nancy. What was surprising, however, was how well fire department engineer Leroy Loeffler, his wife Joyce, and their two small daughters lived on $3,000 a year in Glendale. The Loefflers lived in a fully equipped two-bedroom, two-fireplace bungalow, purchased at $7,800 on an FHA loan, with payments of $37.50 per month; they had a refrigerator and an electric range in the kitchen, an electric washing machine on the service porch, a backyard patio, and orange and lemon trees on the property. There was no swimming pool, alas, but they made frequent visits on weekends to the beach in the family car.

The women and girls of all three families were photographed at least once in shorts, slacks, or sundresses, and nearly everyone made at least one appearance in a bathing suit, especially the Stotharts and their friends. Southern Californians, *Life* tells us, lived casually, as often as possible in the outdoors. They loved to swim, to lunch alfresco on the patio, to hang out at golf and tennis clubs (the more affluent), and to drive their cars to nearby beaches, which were publicly owned, hence available to all, and where Southern Californians spent innumerable hours lazing on the sand, basking in the sunshine, cooling off in the surf. To support such a lifestyle, Californians had their own way of dressing, with sportswear, such as that designed and marketed by Koret of California—shorts, slacks, colorful open-necked shirts, sandals or canvas shoes—the norm after business hours and on weekends.

Whether in the north or the south, the California way of life was taking the home into the outdoors. The deck, noted landscape architect Thomas Church, could give even the most sloping of sites the leveled convenience of an outdoor room. The deck, Church suggested, continued the American tradition of the southern veranda and the Victorian front porch. The deck offered a place to sit and escape time. It mediated between house and garden and supplemented any deficiencies of topography. The deck was part of the outdoors, yet open a sliding door and it became a room of the house. Throughout the day, the deck changed its atmospherics: quiet and contemplative by morning, sunny at luncheon, mysterious in the purple twilight of the cocktail hour. The deck was as venerable as the Minoan civilization of ancient Crete—in which the Cretans constructed summer pavilions at high places so as better to enjoy the mountain coolness—and as contemporary as the Sunset edition of *How to Build Decks for Outdoor Living*, which appeared in 1963.

Deck, patio, barbecue, swimming pool: here was being articulated the vocabulary of the good life, California style. The editors of *Sunset* magazine and Sunset Books interpreted and showcased this ideal into a residential text for western living. *The Sunset Patio Book* (1952), for example, set forth an array of patio designs, each of them suggestive of privacy, leisure, and the enjoyment of sunshine and garden through sequences of day and night. Like the deck, the patio went back to ancient times, to Rome especially, and was further enhanced by Moorish Spain before being brought to Mexico and Alta California. As in the case of the deck—or the barbecue, for that matter—the classical Islamic, Iberian, Mexican, and Old Californian origins of the patio gave its proponents, such as the editors of *Sunset*, a sense that in California they were working within an immemorial tradition of domestic living.

Likewise did *The Sunset Barbecue Cookbook* (1957) and *Ideas for Building Barbecues* (1961) also revel in the historicity of the indoor/outdoor vocabulary for domestic living that was being annotated and enhanced. Suggestions for barbecues ranged from simple brick-lined fire pits to moveable metal structures to unpretentious backyard installations to elaborate affairs—whether in the backyard or integrated into the kitchen—capable of barbecuing whole lambs, suckling pigs, turkeys, or sides of beef. The connection of the barbecue pit to Homeric Greece, classical and medieval times, colonial Latin America, and Alta California under Spain and Mexico transformed the grilling meat in the outdoors into a cultural statement. The grand barbecue master of the late 1940s and 1950s, William Patrick (Bill) Magee, seemed a living encyclopedia of California history. Formerly manager of the Rancho Santa Margarita straddling Orange and San Diego counties, Magee was a direct descendant of Lieutenant Henry Magee of the First New York Regiment of Volunteers, arriving in California in 1847, and Victoria de Pedroreña of San Diego, daughter of a transplanted Spaniard from Peru. What Bill Magee did not know about barbecuing, it was argued—whether beef, pork, venison, fish, fowl, or rabbit, and the exquisite variety of spices and sauces accompanying them—was most likely not worth knowing. Magee's *Western Barbecue Cookbook* (1949) was the most ambitious guide of its sort prior to Sunset's. Like the deck and the patio, the barbecue could be intimate; but it was also available for super-sized entertaining, as evident in the annual barbecue for thousands given by Sheriff Eugene W. (Gene) Biscailuz of Los Angeles County on behalf of the Sheriffs' Relief Association.

The swimming pool—as outlined by the editors of *Sunset* in *Swimming Pools* (1959)—boasted as well of classical origins, most particularly among upper-class Romans. The swimming culture of San Francisco in the 1860s and 1870s—as nurtured by the Olympic Club, the Dolphin Club, the South End Rowing Club, and other local swimming and boating associations—introduced the idea of recreational swimming to the Pacific Coast. In 1896 philanthropist Adolph Sutro, mayor of the city, donated to the people of San Francisco a three-pool steel-and-glass structured natatorium that remained in use until 1952. In Southern California, recreational swimming in the ocean surf was a common activity by the 1890s, even by young women; indeed, families would spend the entire month of August encamped on the beach to enjoy swimming in the surf. Greater Los Angeles also supported a number of indoor plunges, privately sponsored, available to the public. During the 1920s and 1930s, California began to democratize through municipal and county subsidy a number of recreational pursuits—golf, tennis, swimming—previously restricted to the upper classes. Dedicated in 1925, the Fleishhacker Pool in San Francisco, fed by saltwater from the nearby ocean, advertised itself as the largest outdoor swimming pool in the world. By the 1950s the backyard swimming pool had become an emblem of the good life for middle-class Californians. Hollywood was perhaps the first community to envision the pool as the perfect symbol of serenity and escape from care. From the 1930s onward, innumerable photographs of movie stars at poolside helped popularize the postwar boom in swimming pools.

In *The Simple Home* (1904), Berkeley poet and aesthetician Charles Augustus Keeler argued that the true California style in domestic design was the effort to keep things as simple as possible. In his novels, Jack London frequently depicted and praised this simple style, with its emphasis upon Craftsman furniture, locally known as Mission, hardwood floors, and Native American or Oriental throw rugs, with objets d'art or bric-a-brac kept to a minimum. While the Keeler look, as one might call it, remained popular in Northern California into the 1920s, it was by no means exclusive, even in the Bay Area. In San Francisco, for example, Asian furniture and objets d'art were employed dramatically alongside period revival European furniture so as to suggest the East-West formula that was at the aesthetic core of the Bay Area.

By the 1950s interior design in California was displaying an inclusive eclecticism. Santa Barbara was especially abundant in Spanish-style furniture, whether antiques or revivals. Modernism, however, grew as a preference south of the Tehachapi Mountains, most notably as practiced by Charles and Ray Eames in their Venice studio by the sea, where since the mid-1940s the husband-and-wife team had been producing modernist furniture built with industrial materials. A graduate of the Cranbrook Academy of Art in Michigan, which his lifelong friend Eero Saarinen also attended, Charles Eames and his wife, the former Ray Kaiser, had been enamored since the late 1930s with such products as stainless steel, plywood, and other factory-produced materials. The Eameses designed leg splints for the military and movie sets for MGM during the way, their own home in Santa Monica, built entirely of prefabricated parts, and in 1956 the molded plywood, leather-upholstered Eames Lounge Chair 670, mounted on the slenderest of pedestals, along with an attendant ottoman, that remains one of the best-known icons of modernism. As practiced by the Eameses and a slew of West Coast–based and national furniture designers, modernism fit in perfectly with the minimalism of avant-garde architecture in Southern California during the 1950s. At the core of this design tradition was an effort to reconcile the industrial with the organic; hence the almost biological kidneys, hearts, and amoebic forms of every sort mounted on slender legs that fill so many of the photographs of interiors in this period. Here was furniture suggesting the brave new world of California, in which nature and technology were reconciled, it was hoped, at the macro and micro levels.

Such an effort to reconcile nature and the machine had been a persistent quest—a tension even—since the Gold Rush. American California had begun with the techno-industrial assault of the Gold Rush based in the movement of land and water; and this technology of land and water, in turn, served the agriculturalization of the state through irrigation in the late nineteenth century and was available, in turn, when damns, reservoirs, and aqueducts metropolitanized California through such water projects as the Los Angeles Aqueduct, the Hetch Hetchy system, the Hoover Dam, and the Metropolitan Water Department projects delivering Hoover Dam water to Southern California, together with multiple federal Bureau of Reclamation projects and, eventually, the comprehensive State Water Project. From this perspective California was an artificial—indeed, industrial—creation based on technology, in which the majority of the population lived in densely settled enclaves supported by aquatic and hydroelectrical lifelines.

At the same time, however, this very same society—so heroically engineered through public works—had a tendency to take nature as its primary symbol of social and cultural identity, beginning with the successful effort in 1860 to set aside the Yosemite as a wilderness preserve. Virtually the entire cultural history of American California revolved around this nature-technology dialectic: this tension of opposites, so tenuously reconciled. Surveying the society they had wrought by the 1950s, Californians could legitimately take the machine as the primary icon of their culture, for rarely had nature been so thoroughly reorganized through public works. Since the early 1900s, moreover, another technology, aviation, had also been insinuating itself and its key by-product, electronics, into a California economy now on the verge of the transistor revolution. From one perspective, California—so concentrated in its population, so dependent upon technology, so creatively responsive to technological development—had become by the 1950s a multi-faceted techno-metropolis, which was one reason why the most creative architects of the 1950s were so enamored of industrial materials.

On the other hand, California remained a garden, albeit a highly engineered garden in its semi-arid regions, meaning most of the Central Valley and the desert resorts. This California garden possessed multiple dimensions: wilderness, managed wilderness, agriculture, urban and suburban landscapes of various kinds (frequently dominated by stands of eucalyptus trees, imported from Australia), and gardens of every sort, public or private. Strictly speaking, there was no pure wilderness left by the 1950s, since the entire state had by then been surveyed and apportioned to public (federal, state, local) or private management. Despite this technicality, a significant portion of California—the mountain ranges of the far north, the Sierra Nevada, the great southeastern desert—remained, for all practical purposes, as pristine as they had been in the era of Native American stewardship. Although the scars of the Gold Rush still remained and were especially discernible to the trained eye, the mountain regions of the Mother Lode had made a remarkable recovery. Yosemite had long since become a federal preserve, along with the nearby Sequoia National Park; and the California Department of Parks and Recreation was administering a growing network of state parks, many of them wilderness preserves of one sort or another.

In addition, the federal and state government each maintained extensive forest preserves that were, in effect, preserved wildernesses, although generally not accessible to the public. Much of the California coastline remained a type of wilderness, especially in the Big Sur region and the coastline north of San Francisco, while the beaches of Southern California, from Santa Barbara southward, had been transformed over time into recreational parks for adjacent cities and suburbs. A century of agriculture, meanwhile, had created a preserved garden throughout the state: a landscape of vineyards, orchards, and fields such as Thomas Jefferson—steeped as he was in Hesiod, Virgil, and the Physiocrats of France—had dreamt would one day extend across the nation.

So too did the artificially created urban and suburban landscapes of California constitute a series of macro-garden environments. In the late nineteenth and early twentieth centuries, the eucalyptus had been particularly employed to create such scenic effects in the central and south coastal regions. The campuses of Stanford, UC Berkeley, and UCLA, for example, enjoyed glorious eucalyptus gardens by deliberate design. So too was the palm tree—not a true native to the region (with the exception of Palm Springs)—effectively employed in innumerable urban and suburban landscapes. The cities and towns of California, meanwhile, by and large each maintained one or more public parks, including such impressive achievements as Balboa Park in San Diego, Griffith Park in Los Angeles, Golden Gate Park in San Francisco, Tilden Regional Park in the East Bay, Land Park in Sacramento, and Bidwell Park in Chico, winding for ten miles along Big Chico Creek. The park movement had come early to California, in the 1850s, and the growing urbanism of California had sustained this parkland orientation. Thus the entire landscape of California—wilderness, agriculture, urban and suburban land-scapes, parks and public gardens of every sort—nurtured an expectation for the private domestic garden as well. The history of the private garden in nineteenth and early twentieth century California remains to be written. When it appears, it will chronicle the efforts of thousands of Californians—amateur and professional alike, drawing upon the seed stocks of four continents—to bring into being the fabled Garden of the West, one garden at a time. The suburban novels of Wallace Stegner—*A Shooting Star* (1961), *All the Little Live Things* (1967), *Angle of Repose* (1971), and *The Spectator Bird* (1976)—celebrate, in part, the continuing nature of this quest, made even more urgent by the fragmentations and ambiguities of mod-ern life. Stegner himself found such a domestic and professional garden in 1945 when he accepted a professorship of creative writing at Stanford University. With his wife Mary and son Page, he settled into a hilltop home, complete with deck, in the Los Altos foothills, awash in oak and madrone, the epicenter of a new fictive Stegner Country: the upper-middle-class townships clustered around Stanford.

Private value was in the ascendancy in the 1950s; and the private garden was receiving increasing attention from such master landscape designers as Thomas Church, Garrett Eckbo, and Lawrence Halprin, whose lives intersected at various times at UC Berkeley, Harvard, and San Francisco. Born in Boston in 1902 and raised in the Ojai Valley of Southern California and Berkeley, Thomas Dolliver Church, the senior figure among the three, matriculated at Berkeley in 1918 with the intention of going on to law school. A purportedly snap course in garden design offered by the College of Agriculture changed Church's life. He dropped law and took up landscape architecture. Graduating in 1922, Church went on to the Harvard Graduate School of Design. Born in Cooperstown, New York, in 1910 but raised in California from the age of four, Garrett Eckbo took his degree in landscape archi-tecture at UC Berkeley in 1935, then, like Church, went on to the Harvard Graduate School of Design, where he received his master's degree in landscape architecture in 1938. Born in Brooklyn in 1916, Lawrence Halprin as a teenager spent two years on a kibbutz in Palestine, to which he traced his lifelong obsession with the interac-tion of human beings and the environment. Graduating from Cornell with a degree in plant sciences in 1935 and from the University of Wisconsin in 1941 with a master's degree in horticulture, Halprin likewise enrolled in the Harvard Graduate School of Design, where he took a bachelor's degree in landscape architecture in 1944.

The UC Berkeley experienced by Thomas Church in the early 1920s and Garrett Eckbo in the mid-1930s adhered to a traditional approach, historical and formal, to landscape design. One of Eckbo's qualifying projects at Berkeley was the design of an estate in the style of Louis XIV. The Harvard of the early and mid-1920s was also historical and formalist in its traditions: a legacy built upon by Church when he toured Europe in the mid-1920s on a Sheldon Traveling Fellowship, observing the landscapes and gardens of the Old World. The Harvard that Eckbo and Halprin shared, by contrast, was electric with the modernist influences—Cubism, Constructivism, the Bauhaus—brought there by such figures as Fletcher Steele, Christopher Tunnard, and Walter Gropius. Tunnard's *Gardens in the Modern Landscape* (1938) provided Eckbo and Halprin with ideas that would reverberate through their work for the next half century. Both in terms of its practitioners (Steele himself would design more than seven hundred gardens) and its theories, Harvard was by the mid-1930s advancing a philosophy that garden design was a high art form fully compatible with—indeed, brought to new levels of intensity and significance by—the modernist impulse.

Connections among Church, Eckbo, and Halperin continued back in California. Following his return from Europe, Church opened an office in San Francisco. Eckbo joined Church's practice in 1938 but lasted a mere two weeks before taking on the job he truly wanted (Eckbo had a strong social imagination and reformist streak), the design of migrant camps and recreational facilities for the Farm Security Administration. Halprin spent two years as a naval officer on a destroyer in the Pacific. Released from service, Halprin joined Church's practice, remaining there through the design and construction of El Novillero in Sonoma County, a garden almost immediately recognized as a modernist classic and considered one of the great gardens of American history. Halprin opened his own office in San Francisco in 1949.

In one sense, these were three very different men. A dapper WASP called by his middle name, Dolliver, when he was growing up—tall, spare, exquisitely mannered, given to Madras jackets, button-down shirts, and wide-brimmed straw hats—Tommy Church, as his clients called him, was the perfect Tommy: the essence of the Californian as transplanted Yankee, the kind of jaunty Anglo-American gentleman one could expect to run into at an Ivy League reunion. In his combination of a Cal degree and a Harvard and European finish, in his amiable blend of tradition and modernity, Church was also the quintessential elite San Franciscan of his era. Eckbo, by contrast, a Norwegian American of middle-class origins, was intense, focused, and reformist, much more the pure intellectual than either Church or Halprin, typically Scandinavian in the complexities of his inner life. Following the war, during which he worked on housing projects, Eckbo relocated to Los Angeles, where he joined the USC School of Architecture, then entering a golden age, and formed a highly successful partnership with Robert Royston and Edward Williams. However brief their first association, Eckbo and Church would be reunited as members of the Berkeley faculty in 1965. Of Eastern European Jewish ancestry, Halprin maintained an office in San Francisco, but his true home, intellectually and imaginatively, was Marin County, with its outdoor lifestyle and environmental mysticism: its amalgamation of Mount Tamalpais and Shangri-la. A devoted outdoorsman, backpacking each year into the high country of the Sierra Nevada, Halprin epitomized the

Californian as outdoor trekker (a trait he shared with another contemporary, poet Gary Snyder) although, paradoxically, he would eventually become the master of large-scale urban projects.

As would Tommy Church, despite his mastery of the private garden. In 1935 Church designed the courtyard connecting the San Francisco Opera House and the War Memorial Building. In 1940 he designed the gardens for the Golden Gate International Exposition on Treasure Island. Paradoxically, for a designer devoted to the private gardens of an upscale clientele, Church first burst onto the national scene in the early 1940s with his designs for the Valencia Public Housing project in San Francisco (1939–43), which the Museum of Modern Art in New York voted the most outstanding project of its kind in the country. Architect William Wurster, Church's dean at UC Berkeley, helped Tommy secure a number of large-scale projects. These included the Stanford Medical Center, the *Sunset* headquarters in Menlo Park, Hewlett-Packard headquarters in Palo Alto, and portions of the campuses of UC Berkeley and UC Santa Cruz. Garrett Eckbo's larger projects included the Plaza in Old Monterey, the Ladera residential community on the Stanford campus, and the Berkeley waterfront. Halprin's large-scale projects included Sproul Plaza at UC Berkeley and in San Francisco Justin Herman Plaza and Ghirardelli Square, one of the first adaptive reuse projects of its type. Halprin became involved in larger and larger and more urban projects—college campuses, shopping centers, urban design and redevelopment, hospitals, the siting and landscaping of freeways—as his practice became national, then international. The large-scale projects of Church, Eckbo, and Halprin asserted their individual mastery of their profession on its most grand and public scale; and it was projects such as these that won them an array of awards from the American Institute of Architects, the American Society of Landscape Architects, the American Academy of Arts and Sciences, and other organizations. Halprin, in fact, can be considered almost entirely in terms of such ambitious efforts.

In the case of Church and Eckbo, however, it was the more intimate and private garden—photographed and promulgated by such mass media publications as *House Beautiful, House and Garden,* and *Sunset*—that provided them with the most gratifying of ongoing livelihoods and artistic fulfillment. Because he was there first and designed so many gardens (2000 in all), Tommy Church must be considered the lead personality for an entire generation of landscape architects—Eckbo, Halprin, Robert Royston, Theodore Osmundson, and Douglas Baylis among the most notable—responsible for what was variously called the California style or the Quality California look. Garrett Eckbo, however, was the better designer and theoretician, as evident in the gardens he was designing in Southern California in the late 1940s and his book *Landscape for Living* (1950), the manifesto of modernism as it related to the private California garden.

There was a minimalist force to *Landscape for Living*: its conception of space as the fundamental building block. "Gardens are fragments of space," Eckbo states, "set aside by the planes of terraces and walls and disciplined foliage."[1] The primary plane of reference in a garden, Eckbo believed, was approximately five feet above the surface, at the level of the human eye. The elements of a garden each stood in relationship to this plane, whether the overall design be free-form or geometrically structural. (The most successful gardens, Eckbo argued, combined both approaches.) Space was organized by materials; and each material element of a garden—earth, rock, water, wood, brick, stone, fence, structure, flora, fauna, art, plants and planting—conditioned the space around it in a distinctive manner and, assembled by the human eye at the five-foot plane, created the perception of space that was the first premise of the garden experience.

The garden, in short, was not a painted canvas or a three-dimensional tableau. It was, rather, a deliberate reconstruction of space itself, a renegotiated universe. Not surprisingly, Eckbo considered the Japanese Zen tradition one of the most compelling of garden designs, referring to it frequently and providing illustrations of Zen gardens in his various writings. Nature did not create gardens, Eckbo emphasized. People did. But people created gardens in the way that nature wanted them to. A garden was meaningless without people. The garden space, moreover, came into its highest existence as an art form when it was nurturing daily life, whether the leisure of adults or the play of children. Both Eckbo and Church were especially sensitive to the children who would be using the gardens they were designing. Pervading *Landscape for Living* and all the books by Eckbo that followed was a humanistic concern for family life on the part of a designer who had begun his career creating better spaces for migrant agricultural workers. The photographs illustrating Eckbo's books, many of them taken by Julius Shulman, constitute a portfolio of the ideal garden, California style, from the late 1940s through the 1960s. In these gardens one can glimpse an entire nexus of hope for domestic life: the desire of Californians, that is, to live in privacy, to live in the family, to live at well-wrought intersection points of architecture and designed landscape.

In comparison to Eckbo's analytically rigorous writings, Thomas Church's *Gardens Are for People* (1955) reads like a chat between Church and his clients. Church himself describes the book as a garden tour with commentary and photographs. This was his essential style as practitioner and theorist, to make things seem easy, to conceal effort and smooth out angularities. Coming of age professionally before the ascendancy of modernism, Church transformed himself into the first great modernist landscape architect in California, but he was also the last of the state's great garden design traditionalists, as evidenced by the erudite range of historical examples and quotes from garden literature with which Church embellished his arguments. Like so many designers of the period, Church went out of his way to underscore the Mediterranean, especially the Spanish, antecedents of the California gardens he was discussing.

On the other hand, Church believed—and conducted his practice accordingly—in the assumption that the American garden, including the California garden, had to break off its haphazard, even slavish, thralldom to Europe and refound itself as reconstructed modernist space. This is what Church had done so deliberately in his design of El Novillero, the garden he completed for Dewey Donnell in Sonoma County between 1947 and 1949. El Novillero brought to the California garden the full power of abstract modernism, especially Cubism and the Bauhaus. Writing in *The Oxford Companion to Gardens* (2006), Michael Lancaster describes El Novillero as a Cubist construction presenting a garden that can be seen from any number of viewpoints: a garden without a beginning or an end. Still, there was a residual formalism to Church's designs, evident, among other traits, in the way that his gardens could absorb statuary, be it classical or modernist in inspiration. This residual formalism, however, was deconstructed (Church favored the asymmetrical) and kept informal: a Californianizing, if you will, of European traditions.

At its most basic level, the Church garden consisted of a surface supporting other raised surfaces. A Church garden ascended into as well as across space. Church preferred to free the garden from the tyranny of the uninterrupted lawn. Lawns were allowed at intervals, but they were offset by pathways and surfaces of brick or flagstone. Steps were frequent in his designs, as well as raised flower beds. Church would even surround a tree with a raised bed to appear as if the tree itself had been deliberately planted there. At various levels, there were benches at differing heights. Church was a master of the deck; but the deck belonged to the house as well as to the garden. Within the garden itself, Church favored the raised terrace, which unlike the deck, was its own autonomous place, rising from one level to another, perfect for family meals or entertaining. For beachfront houses, Church used the wood deck as a way of moving out over the sand in stable defiance of its shifting surfaces. Church embraced the swimming pool, considering it a center for outdoor living, not just a place for exercise. He insisted that whenever possible some form of pool house or shelter be adjacent so as to enhance its usability. From the same reasons, he welcomed the barbecue and incorporated its raised surfaces into his designs. He also openly accepted the automobile and made provisions for double garages. This serviceable side to a Church design made it amenable to tract housing, especially the Eichler homes springing up on the San Francisco peninsula, Tommy Church country because of the hundreds of gardens he had designed there.

Similarly, Marin County was Lawrence Halprin country. For Halprin, the process of design was itself an art form and a philosophy of total engagement. During his years at sea as a naval officer, Halprin began a lifelong habit of keeping extensive sketchbooks of concepts and images he saw at work in specific situations, which could, in turn, lead to general design patterns. These sketchbooks eventually totaled five thousand pages. A sensual empiricist, Halprin sought to align his designs with the very processes of nature, especially as observed in, on, or around Mount Tamalpais in Marin County, the north coast, where he maintained a cabin, or the High Sierra, where he trekked each summer.

Halprin's early notebooks emphasized gardens, but as time went on, he became increasingly concerned with larger environments. Thus Halprin's very methods of observation and theorizing were moving him by the 1960s beyond the private garden. (Garrett Eckbo himself was making a similar—but less total!—transition.) For

Halprin, the garden of California was becoming, increasingly, the landscape of the
city, the region, even the freeway. While his sketchbooks might show him capable
of observations appropriate to the private garden, the very integrated movement he
sought as the basis for his designs was demanding a larger and larger canvas: such
as Sea Ranch (1962) on the Mendocino Coast north of San Francisco, a second
home development for which Halprin designed plans for eighteen hundred acres of
homes and gardens intimately connected to the larger natural processes of the north
coast. Through Sea Ranch, Lawrence Halprin regionalized the garden in a comprehensive and circular scheme that suggested, most compellingly, that if the California garden was to attain its highest effectiveness and identity, it could not remain
a private affair. Landscape design, rather, would have to embrace the public sector
as well. That meant landscaped campuses and other public institutions, correctly
sited and landscaped freeways and highways, ribbons and wedges of agriculture
adjacent to human settlement, protected and accessible coastlines, neighborhood
playgrounds for underprivileged children.

New Dealer Garrett Eckbo understood this as well as did Tommy Church,
gardenmeister for the privileged. If California should neglect or trash its public
landscapes, the private garden would become a flight from reality, a retreat into
unearned privilege, a mode of self-deception. Within each private California garden
could be found California itself; hence the visual well-being of that larger California
was crucial to the success of those arrangements of earth, rock, water, stone, trees,
shrubbery, and flowers that mysteriously reordered the world for purposes of private
recreation and renewal.

All this, by and large—the enjoyment of California as designed and private garden—
remained the prerogative of the affluent. This did not particularly bother Thomas
Church, who once stated offhandedly that his favorite minority group was the rich
because, if their tastes were correctly formed, the rest of the population would follow. Garrett Eckbo, by contrast, devoted the last decades of his career to the social
aspects of landscape design. Architecturally, California was facing a major challenge
in the postwar period: the design of appropriate, affordable, and aesthetic housing
on a mass scale. Could this be done? From one perspective, the housing created
in Panorama City and Lakewood, like the housing of Levittown on Long Island,
proved that a serviceable product could be delivered through the techniques of mass
construction. Highbrow critics, however, would not describe them as architecturally
distinguished. Defenders of such homes, on the other hand, might very well say
that in proving so serviceable across more than half a century, such mass-produced
homes were fulfilling the first requirement of architecture, usefulness and sustain-
ability, which more than compensated for their lack of distinguished design.

The challenge to fuse industrial materials, mass production, and distinguished
architecture was a continuing concern of modernism, foreign and domestic. In
California terms, it went back to the work of modernist *Urmeister* Irving Gill of
San Diego in the first two decades of the twentieth century. Almost spontaneously,

Gill devised an architecture that was breathtakingly modernist for its era, begging comparison to Secessionist Vienna: oriented to industrial materials, concrete most notably; adaptable to tilt-up construction; and—in its clean lines, simple windows, uncluttered interior surfaces, innovative heating, ventilating, and cleaning systems— thoroughly reformist in intent. Gill was also involved in the development and design of the city of Torrance in southern Los Angeles County as a model community show- casing the appropriateness of modernism to a blue-collar industrial town in terms of its housing, churches, schools, libraries, streetcar stations, roads and bridges, hotels, retail stores, banks, electricity plants, and industrial sites, many of which were built. Torrance, in short, as Gill and others envisioned it, would assert the ability of mod- ernism to serve everyday life.

Frank Lloyd Wright, by contrast, the next notable modernist on the Southern California scene, designed homes—the Storer House (1923) in Hollywood, for example, or La Miniatura (1923) in Pasadena—that, like all of Wright's Southern California oeuvre, provide interesting examples of Wright's idiosyncratic talent but point nowhere as far as the ability of modernism to create prototypes for mass housing. Architect-driven and client-customized, obsessed with privacy (the Storer House did not even have a front door) and impractical (located at the bottom of an arroyo, La Miniatura was frequently flooded), a Wright house offered an anti-social statement in its inefficiencies and idiosyncratic design, as far as Southern California was concerned.

Viennese émigrés Rudolf Schindler and Richard Neutra, by contrast, were each interested in the social dimension of modernist architecture and successfully cre- ated across their long careers (Schindler died in 1953, Neutra in 1970) numerous homes that pioneered designs, materials, and construction techniques that could, if anyone were so inclined, be applied to the creation of mass housing. Schindler, for example, was a pioneer in the use of plywood and other industrial materials. Neutra described his brand of modernism as Biological Realism, which is to say, an architecture keyed to the socio-biological realities of a healthy everyday life. The problem was, however, virtually all of Schindler's and Neutra's clients in the 1920s and 1930s were exactly that—clients, capable of affording an architect, willing to venture themselves into the avant-garde realms of the International Style. So too did contractors and bureaucrats rebel at the designs and materials of Schindler's and Neutra's work. Only individuals of means and highly developed tastes, in short, could face the cost and, frequently, the bureaucratic ordeal before, during, and after construction to acquire a home that was, ultimately, more a work of art, transcen- dent and autonomous, than an instance of social statement.

A paradox was involved. As in the case of Europe and the eastern United States, the modernists of Southern California—whether their modernism be reflected in architecture, painting, photography, or printing as a fine art—were by and large progressive, which is to say, liberal in their political orientation, hence, it could be presumed, interested in the social question of creating an architecture for the mid- dle and working classes. For the time being, however, they were finding themselves confined to personal architectural statements, although just before the war Neutra was designing tract housing in Burbank that represented an exhilarating effort to bring modernism to working- and lower-middle-class Californians.

Streamline Moderne, by contrast, was proving itself thoroughly agreeable to the affordable, if not mass, market. True modernists viewed this style with distaste. Its ostensibly up-to-date designs, they claimed, were little more than decorative rhetoric, masquerading behind an industrial metaphor. This argument would be hard to make, however, regarding Gardner Dailey's Coral Casino (1937) beach club in Montecito, in which Streamline Moderne was fused with Regency Revival, or the small weekend home (1936) he designed for William Lowe Jr. in Woodside south of San Francisco, which in its simplicity, affordability, and grace might very well have served as a prototype for postwar tract housing in California. Developers of apartment buildings up and down the state, however—whether atop Telegraph or Russian Hill in San Francisco or in Westside Los Angeles, oceanside Santa Monica, Long Beach, or San Diego—together with contractor-developers reentering the housing market in the late 1930s when the economy was recovering, found Streamline Moderne, along with the Art Deco style that had preceded it, easy to sell to middle-class clients who, in turn, considered themselves thoroughly up-to-date, thoroughly modern, for living in such structures.

America's entry into the war liberated modernism into social extension. Neutra's wartime Channel Heights Housing Project in San Pedro, together with a number of other similar developments, represented a prophetic paradigm of socially attuned housing and community facilities, designed and constructed at minimum expense, intended for working people. With its convenient floor plans, its appropriate and serviceable furniture, its efficient kitchens, its outdoor play spaces and pathways, its retail center, and its accessibility to jobsites, Channel Heights prophesied, through modernism, the Southern California lifestyle to come. After the war, Neutra entered a partnership with Robert Alexander, and their work from the 1950s and early 1960s, while lacking the pure and austere modernism of Neutra's prewar work, shows a serviceable and direct response to creating the schools, motels, banks, public and private office buildings, and in one instance—the Miramar Naval Base Chapel in La Jolla (1957)—the worship spaces of the postwar Southland.

The architects who came of age in the 1930s as apprentices to Neutra, Schindler, or various combinations thereof were by and large obsessed with the effort to render modernism relevant to mass housing. Raphael Soriano, for example, pioneered the use of prefabricated steel framing (he later turned to aluminum) as a superior and cost-competitive substitute for wood. Julius Ralph Davidson demanded that architects pay attention to how people actually live within their homes. Good design, Davidson argued, began and ended with a floor plan that served the needs of everyday life. A house, in fact, was basically a floor plan protected from the elements. So focused was Gregory Ain on the social dimensions of modernist design, his architecture stood in danger of becoming so self-effacing as to be near-invisible, absorbed almost entirely by social statement. Raised for a time by his Russian Jewish socialist parents in the cooperative colony of Llano del Rio in the Antelope Valley in eastern Los Angeles County, Ain came of age formed by the closest thing one could have to a kibbutz experience in Southern California. Inspired by the communitarian traditions of his family and the austere modernism of Schindler and Neutra, Ain graduated from the USC School of Architecture in 1927 and by 1935, after a stint with Neutra, began to devote himself to the conceptualization and design of housing for middle- and low-income clients. As a modernist, Ain most obviously rejected historicism. He went, however, even beyond the bounds of modernism in his conceptualization and practice of architecture as an unpretentious, near-anonymous social art. The attached four-unit Dunsmuir Flats south of Wilshire near Fairfax in Los Angeles that Ain designed in 1937 epitomized his conjoined ideals of dense housing, up-to-date materials, and an architecture of austere and ego-less purity.

In 1940 Ain received a Guggenheim Fellowship to research low-cost housing; while his researches were rewarding enough, Ain never connected in the postwar period with a mass-housing developer willing to implement his ideas. There were, however, more modest successes, such as the Avenel Terrace complex off Rowena Avenue in the Silver Lake district of Los Angeles, commissioned in 1946 by ten couples of moderate income. Completed in 1948, the ten units of attached housing, slightly more than nine hundred square feet per unit, cost their owners $11,000 (they were selling for $350,000 in 2004) and established a paradigm of modernist urbanism that went largely unrecognized by all but Ain's satisfied clients. In the postwar period Ain and various partners devoted themselves to such communal housing and/or socially integrated projects as the Park Plan Homes in Altadena (twenty-eight houses on two rows facing each other across one long block, for which Garrett Eckbo did the landscaping) and the Mar Vista housing complex in Venice, an integrated cluster of fifty-two small homes. Ain also continued a practice that included single-family residences, apartment buildings, and schools. From 1953 to 1963, Ain taught at the USC School of Architecture, where—arriving on campus in either a Pierce-Arrow, a Cadillac, or a 1938 Packard, depending upon his mood that day—he devoted himself to his teaching and expanding his theories of architecture as a social art.

Ain's lifetime obsession, architecture as an ego-deflated social process aimed at the enhancement of everyday life, was also shared in Northern California by William Wurster, dean of the School of Architecture at UC Berkeley from 1950 to 1959. Born in Stockton in 1895 and graduating from Berkeley in 1918, Wurster became in rapid order a lifelong member of the Northern California architectural establishment. A summer residence he designed for Mrs. Warren Gregory in the Santa Cruz Mountains, completed in the spring of 1928, established him as a master of an easygoing Bay Region style of modernism, favoring wood over the hard-edged industrialized International Style of Southern California. Like Gregory Ain, his social and cultural opposite, Wurster eschewed show-off architecture in favor of a restrained and modest modernism. Such modesty, however, infuriated the most egomaniacal show-off in the profession, Frank Lloyd Wright, who in the mid-1950s—at a

UC Berkeley meeting of architects, with Wurster present—described Wurster as a shack architect who had exercised a chilling effect on Bay Area design. The Bay Area establishment, however, disagreed with Wright's rude dismissal, and throughout the postwar period the firm of Wurster, Bernardi and Emmons, formed in 1944, remained the firm of choice for the Bay Area elite.

Wurster's upscale practice had its ironies. Since the late 1930s Wurster had become increasingly preoccupied with social-architectural and housing questions, under the influence of his wife Catherine Bauer. A Vassar graduate who had tasted the bohemianism of Paris and Greenwich Village in the 1920s, Bauer turned her formidable intellect to housing questions in dialogue with her mentor and lover Lewis Mumford, over whose thought she was equally influential. In 1934 Bauer published *Modern Housing*, describing and analyzing the social housing programs of Europe: not for imitation, Bauer insisted, but to stimulate Americans to pay attention to public policy issues regarding housing development. A year earlier, Bauer had broken off her romantic relationship with Mumford, although the two of them remained friends, and she would eventually transfer her affections to Wurster, whose developing social theories she helped to explicate and expand. In the late 1930s, Wurster competed for and won the commission for the design of Valencia Gardens, a municipal housing project in San Francisco, evidence of his developing interest in social questions. Just before the war, he designed a highly experimental defense workers housing project on Carquinez Heights in Vallejo. In 1945 Wurster and his partner Theodore Bernardi collaborated with Ernest Kump on a Pre-Bilt house prototype that was assembled in San Anselmo. The Museum of Modern Art in New York included a display of that Pre-Bilt house in its "Tomorrow's Small House" exhibition. Returning to UC Berkeley from MIT in 1950, where Catherine Bauer was also appointed to the faculty, Wurster continued to promote the conceptualization of modern architecture keyed to social need.

A case would seem to be building in the architectural community, among modernists especially, for an innovative approach to postwar housing, in terms of cost, suitability, and design. Here was an opportunity for modernism to seize the moment: to align itself with postwar growth so as to create a mass housing in California of distinction and durability. Certainly that was the intent in January 1945 when John Entenza of Los Angeles, editor of the Los Angeles–based *Arts & Architecture* magazine, announced the Case Study House project. The idea was simple: commission the best modernist architects of the region to create houses that would serve as prototypes for postwar development. The homes would be financed by clients who agreed to participate in the program. The Case Study House (CSH) project extended across two decades and involved the talents of the best modernists in the Southern California region. CSH #1, designed by Julius Ralph Davidson for a West Los Angeles lot in 1946 and actually built in 1948 in North Hollywood, was conditioned almost entirely by wartime scarcities and restrictions. Nevertheless, Davidson, employing the simplest of materials—Douglas fir siding, glass walls, birch plywood, plaster boards—achieved what architectural critic Esther McCoy has aptly described as a brave little house full of fruitful suggestions for the postwar era.

The argument can be made, in fact, that Davidson's CSH #1 was the most realistic of all the twenty-seven CSH projects in its inexpensiveness, its spatial arrangements, its dependence upon modest materials, and its orientation to indoor/outdoor living. Among other amenities, CSH #1 featured radiant heating built into its concrete slab foundation, bright colors and varied textures within and without, rubber tile floor covering, an efficient kitchen, built-in storage spaces, a screened service yard in front of the house, parents' and children's bedrooms as far away from each other as possible, a bath for each bedroom, glass walls looking out on the garden, the opening of each bedroom onto a garden space, a walled-in terrace off the living room, built-in provisions for a home entertainment center, and, finally, a guest bedroom. CSH #1 asserted that even an inexpensive 1,800-square-foot house on a 100' × 70' lot, with a fifteen-foot setback from the street, could achieve a level of housing—inexpensive, easy to build, thoroughly humane in its arrangements—that might have that provided the prototype for postwar tract housing in the region.

From one perspective, Case Study House #1 was emerging from the defense housing projects of the wartime era, in and through which modernism had gotten off its high horse, rolled up its sleeves, and produced mass housing for ordinary people. From another perspective, CSH #1 looked to a future in which ordinary people might be challenged to buy and live in a home representing an improved level of taste. If the Case Study House program had stopped then and there with CSH #1, and an effort had been made to interest lenders, FHA officials, local planners, and, most important, tract developers in Davidson's prototype as being easy to build, hence affordable, and appealing to ordinary taste, modernism might very well have gained a market share of the mass housing created in the postwar era.

The Mutual Housing Tract project on eight hundred acres of undeveloped land in the Santa Monica Mountains of West Los Angeles, extending from Bel Air to the bay, was even then, beginning in 1947, in the process of financing and building 150 architect-designed homes (the initial proposal was for 500), together with a community center, a co-op store, a medical office, a nursery school, and a gas station. It was also a communal enterprise in which those seeking housing organized and directed the Mutual Housing Association, which in turn supervised development. The homes designed by A. Quincy Jones (another USC architect) for this project incorporated the best aspects of the Case Study House prototypes, which is to say, a skilled use of modernist design and industrial materials. The cooperative nature of the Mutual Housing Association project provided a model whereby like-minded clients might band together to form their own development companies. As in many such communitarian enterprises, however, the cooperative impulse eventually flagged, and few communal facilities were built. Tragically, the great Bel Air fire of 1961 destroyed many of the original Mutual Housing Association homes. Scorched from the landscape, they were not even available as challenging prototypes.

The Case Study House project, meanwhile, was veering in the direction of name-brand modernists (among them, William Wurster, Theodore Bernardi, Charles and Ray Eames, Eero Saarinen, Richard Neutra, Raphael Soriano) designing signature statements for discriminating clients. Among such work, Soriano's and Ellwood's steel-framed pavilions (Soriano's 1950 published study and Ellwood's CSH #16, #17, and #18) most closely approached Davidson's CSH #1 as mass-marketable prototypes.

The orientation of the Case Study House project toward signature buildings was accelerated as steel framing became available after the Korean War, and architects such as Soriano, Craig Ellwood, and Pierre Koenig turned to it in their designs. Only one Case Study House project completed in the 1950s—Don Knorr's CSH #19 (1957)—was wood-framed, but this project was built in Atherton on the San Francisco peninsula and hence participated in the Northern California wood-building tradition. For more than three decades, modernist architects—Mies van der Rohe and Le Corbusier most notably—had been in love with steel, seeing in it a fusion of industrialism and art, especially in the ability of steel to sustain new and dramatic configurations and spaces. Steel enabled modernist architects to soar across sites, to create expansive and uninterrupted spaces, to achieve hitherto impossible masses and volumes. Richard Neutra had used steel framing for the Lovell House (1929) in the Hollywood Hills, the acknowledged masterpiece of the prewar International Style in Southern California. Because of steel, the Lovell House ascended its hillside site as a series of soaring, fenestrated, and interconnected pavilions, worthy of comparison to the montane monasteries of Mount Athos or the precariously sited lamaseries of Tibet.

The best-known house of the Case Study House program—Pierre Koenig's home for Carlotta and C. H. (Buck) Stahl (1960), CSH #22—vividly demonstrated the ability of steel to enable an architect to work on a difficult site and to create spaces that were almost aerodynamic in their ability to soar. Born in San Francisco in 1925, Koenig studied engineering at the University of Utah before earning three battle stars as an artillery observer in Europe. Initially rejected by the USC School of Architecture, Koenig pursued the subject at Pasadena City College before literally—after being rebuffed by USC the second time—camping outside Dean Arthur Gallion's office for a week until he was admitted. There, from such faculty members as Gregory Ain, Richard Neutra, Harwell Hamilton Harris, William Pereira, and Garrett Eckbo, Koenig absorbed the pure and vibrant modernism that was making USC such an epicenter of contemporary design.

Following graduation in 1952, Koenig went briefly to work for the master of steel, Raphael Soriano, before establishing his own practice. Three steel-framed houses—the Lamel House in Glendale, the Squire House in La Cañada, and the Scott House in Tujunga—were designed and built within the first two years of his practice. Envisioning each home as a steel pavilion, Koenig used steel in the framing, the roof, the walls, even the floors. He also advocated the use of the swimming pool as an essential part of the design and favored an overall ambience of Spartan simplicity.

From this perspective, there was an almost Japanese quality to Koenig's work: an orchestration of a pavilion, its roof seeming to float atop glass walls, with the still water of the pool adding to the Zen-like effect. The steel and glass pavilion that Koenig designed for a canyon site in the Hollywood Hills, the Bailey House (CSH #21, 1958), was almost completely surrounded by water. Many critics believed that this simple pavilion represented the most significant steel and glass breakthrough of the Case Study House program in the 1950s and might therefore have served as a useful prototype for mass construction, which was Koenig's intent.

It never happened, yet Koenig's next Case Study House project, thanks to a single architectural photograph, was destined to become one of the most celebrated icons of postwar Los Angeles. For the Stahl family of Hollywood, Koenig designed an L-shaped structure that soared off its hillside site atop a ten-foot steel cantilever that supported the living room. The house afforded a 270-degree view of Los Angeles, and at night the living room seemed to hover over the lights of the city like a mirage of light in flight. On one such evening, architectural photographer Julius Shulman, standing near the edge of the swimming pool framed by the L-shaped house, photographed the glass-walled living room as two women sat talking against an expanse of nighttime light flowing in three directions from Sunset Boulevard.

Born in Brooklyn in 1910 and arriving in Los Angeles at the age of fifteen, Shulman had in the late 1930s mastered his craft—architectural photography, concerned almost exclusively with modernist buildings in Southern California—under the encouragement of Richard Neutra. Almost immediately, photographs by Shulman became the means through which the works of Neutra, Schindler, Ain, Soriano, and other modernists became appreciated and accepted. A master of light, Shulman instinctively understood that modernist architecture needed to be enlivened by light if it were to be liberated from its severity. The photograph Shulman took of two young women in cocktail dresses visiting together in the Stahl House by night orchestrated the nighttime lights of the city and Sunset Boulevard, the global fixtures in the living room, and an indirect light from outside the house. The result: a liberation of the metaphor for a better life contained within Koenig's house; an evocation of modernism as urban, urbane, and humane; a fleeting Southern California moment that seemed to say everything this region had to offer American life.

But could such a home attract developers on the plain below? Could the steel-framed pavilions of Soriano, Ellwood, and Koenig compete with the ranch, the Cape Cod, the ever-morphing Streamline Moderne, or the boxy utilitarianism so close to non-architecture, the tracts of ticky tacky earning the contempt of Malvina Reynolds? To answer this question in the negative—modernism did not make such a crossover—requires us to summon a number of causal factors: the scarcity of steel during the Korean War, the highly efficient wood-frame construction techniques being employed by tract developers, the resistance of the housing bureaucracy to the avant-garde nature of what the Case Study House program was suggesting. Then there were the limits of ordinary American taste, both in terms of design and materials. First-time home buyers of the era, millions of them, were by and large working-class and/or blue-collar people who had absorbed either from their own experience or from Hollywood a non-modernist conception of what a house and its furnishings should be. Millions of American men had recently spent time in barracks and Quonset huts and hence evaluated the concept home not in terms of the austerities of modernism, but in terms of the frilly historicism of the wood-frame home Cary Grant was building for his family in the movie *Mr. Blandings Builds His Dream House* (1948), which made their tastes congruent with the prevailing feminine preferences of the era, if one is to judge from women's magazines.

The clients willing to finance and live in the Case Study houses were educated, affluent, upper-middle-class, and, as Esther McCoy describes them, energized by Rooseveltian progressivism. Modernism might triumph in Palm Springs, thanks to the designs of émigré Albert Frey, but Palm Springs, a resort for the affluent, constituted a clustering of like-minded clients. So too did the unpretentious modernism of Wurster, Bernardi, and Emmons flourish in the upscale suburbs of the San Francisco peninsula. Harwell Hamilton Harris, another distinguished Southern California modernist of the prewar and postwar era, together with Gardner Dailey and Joseph Esherick in Northern California, practiced an engaging, easygoing modernism, sensitive to historical reference, that might also have passed over into a broader production, had it ever been taken up by developers of tract housing.

Lewis Mumford praised this Bay Region style, as he first termed it, in his "Skyline" column in the *New Yorker* in October 1947. Beginning with such architects as Bernard Maybeck, Willis Polk, Bruce Porter, and Louis Christian Mullgardt in the fin de siècle and early 1900s, Mumford argued, and continuing through the next generation, so strongly influenced by John Galen Howard of UC Berkeley, the notable architects of the San Francisco Bay Area had absorbed the best of modernism—clean lines, concern for a view, simple surfaces, an integration of outdoors and indoors, a free flow of space—without succumbing to a worship of the machine or practicing architecture as a form of hard-edged industrialism. This tradition, Mumford conjectured could be traced, in part, to the apprenticeship served by many of the first generation of Bay Area architects in the offices of that great proto-modernist Louis Sullivan in Chicago, where they absorbed a taste for the organic as well as the functional, for the texture of materials—wood and stone especially—as well as their efficiencies. They translated these lessons, in turn, to the Bay Area, where they were most compatible. The Bay Area, after all, was about wooded hillsides and water, redwood groves and abundant stone. There was no rigid ideology in the Bay Region architecture of the past half century, Mumford argued, but rather a like-minded response on the part of various architects, each with his or her (Julia Morgan) own orientation, to the ideals of simplicity, naturalism, unpretentious efficiency, and appropriateness.

It was perhaps this Bay Region tradition that underlay the success of the Eichler Homes building program—ten thousand homes over eighteen years—one of the few tract developments, if not the only one, to practice modernism at its highest levels of appropriateness and taste. The founder of Eichler Homes, Inc., San Francisco business investor Joseph Eichler—self-educated, hard-driving, short-fused—was in one sense a highly improbable developer of such architecturally distinguished tracts. He was neither a college graduate nor even much of an intellectual, in the formal sense of that term, although he did adhere to an ahead-of-its-time sympathy for minorities and loathed discrimination of any sort. Joseph Eichler, in short, had the temperament of a pragmatic reformer, and this oriented him, however obliquely, to the culture of modernism.

In 1943 Eichler and his family moved into the Bazett House (1939) in Hillsborough, designed by Frank Lloyd Wright. The house stimulated in Eichler an interest in modern architecture. During the war, Eichler was also intrigued by the rapid construction techniques of defense housing projects in the Bay Area. In 1947, while thinking about getting into the development business, Eichler studied the construction techniques of builder Earl Smith, especially the poured concrete floors and flat roofs Smith had used in constructing defense workers' housing in Richmond. In 1949 Eichler formed his own company and hired the architectural firm of Anshen and Allen (Robert Anshen was a disciple of Frank Lloyd Wright) to design a prototype in Sunnyvale, a T-shaped two-bedroom home that went on the market in 1950. Over the next decade, Eichler refined this prototype with the assistance of such architects as Anshen and his partner Steven Allen, A. Quincy Jones and partner Frederick Emmons, and Claude Oakland and Associates, all of them adaptable modernists.

Joseph Eichler wanted none of the usual—the ranch or Cape Cod style, or the boxy faux Moderne, itself a faux style, of Stonestown, Lakeside, Park Merced, and Daly City on the north peninsula. He wanted modernism: an architecture of glass walls, low-pitched roofs, concrete floors, and steel framing, based on floor plans serving family life across the decades. Eichler homes positioned the children's room off the atrium, so that the children would have an element of independence as they grew older, and directly adjacent to the enclosed garden, where they could play safely. Eichler had learned about the atrium—a light-flooded foyer at the entrance to the house, forming a transition from outdoors to indoors—from Robert Anshen. The Romans used atriums, architect Anshen informed Eichler. Give me some atriums! Eichler replied with the speedy forthrightness of a businessman who knew when to take advice.

As tract homes went in this period, an Eichler home was a little pricey: $18,000 to $25,000 (as of 1957) for four bedrooms, two bathrooms, and a family room. Even so, the homes were a bargain. Eichler kept expenses down by employing speedy and standardized construction techniques on some five hundred homes per year during the 1950s. His construction superintendent, John Hooten, was a no-nonsense former Navy Seabee chief petty officer with extensive experience building military installations. The foundation of an Eichler home was a concrete slab on grade, embedded with radiant heat piping. The house was steel-framed. Utilities were gathered in a centralized core; hence few interior partitions were needed. All lumber was precut, including post-and-beam framing and Philippine mahogany plywood for interior wall finishes. (No plasterboard for an Eichler home!) Eichler kitchens were glorious, with Zolatone-treated kitchen cabinetry, sliding rather than opening doors, and a dramatic use of color. To this day, many Eichler kitchens remain functional after more than a half century of use. The house was oriented toward indoor/outdoor living; but beyond that, Eichler also provided, when he could, flowing curved streetscapes, cul-de-sac streets, and mini-greenbelts throughout the development.

Eichler country was the San Francisco Bay Area: the peninsula between Burlingame and San Jose, centered on Palo Alto (2,700 houses) and Sunnyvale (1,100 houses); the East Bay between Concord and Castro Valley; and southern Marin County, where Eichler built some two thousand homes. Architectural critics have suggested an affinity between the climate of the San Francisco Bay Area and an Eichler home. Yet the company also built six hundred homes in Southern California—in Thousand Oaks, Granada Hills, and Orange; sixty homes in Sacramento; and three in Chestnut Ridge, New York.

Joseph Eichler had a strong progressive streak, anchored perhaps in his Jewish identity. Eichler homes were sold to minority clients who could afford them, and a number of them could, in contrast to most tract developments, which used covenants to exclude potential minority buyers. Marketing director James San Jule recalls how Eichler threw a prospective buyer out of the office when the man complained about minorities being able to buy an Eichler home, telling the guy he was unworthy to be his client. Eichler also hired ex-convicts as construction workers, willing to give them a second chance. With only the slightest stretch of imagination, an element of social democracy can also be discerned in the fact that Eichler did not build individual swimming pools. He constructed, rather, communal swimming pools as well as communal nurseries and meeting halls.

In contrast to the photography of Julius Shulman, so deliberately focused upon the daydream of pure abstract modernism, with people rarely present, Joseph Eichler hired photographer Ernie Braun to do his publicity. Braun featured an array of actors and models living the California Dream in their new Eichler home: reading to their children, gardening, sunbathing, preparing meals in a state-of-the-art kitchen, lazing with the newspaper on a sunny Sunday morning in the garden, sitting at the end of a weekday in a living room fitted with modernist designer furniture (by Eames, Nelson, Saarinen, or Bertoia), entertaining over cocktails on a Saturday night, the men in the short hair, black horn-rimmed glasses, skinny ties, and narrow lapels of the era, the women in high heels and billowing skirts. In retrospect, the Braun photos constitute a montage of 1950s middle- and upper-middle-class aspiration: the *Sunset* syndrome, it can be called (the magazine's Menlo Park headquarters stood at the epicenter of Eichler country); indeed, in the Braun photographs one can almost catch a glimpse of the latest *Sunset* on the coffee table.

Purchase of an Eichler home signified at least a mid-level of affluence, a mid-level of liberalism, and more than a mid-level of taste. Ten thousand of them were constructed and sold. Ten times that number would have had to have been brought online for modernism to make credible presence in the mass market. Were there millions of Californians, it could be legitimately asked, who would be comfortable in a modernist house, even in such a elegant and non-threatening modernism as Joseph Eichler and his architects were providing? The argument could be made that Tiki—which is to say, Polynesian Revival, ranging from pop to kitsch, in bars and restaurants, apartment buildings, motels, backyards, a portion of Disneyland—provided middle-class Californians a more welcomed ambience for those times when they were experiencing the joy of life and wanted to celebrate.

Polynesian primitivism, paradoxically, had highbrow roots (as did modernism) in such figures as Paul Gauguin, who had fled the bourgeois constraints of his banker's life in Paris for the primitivism of Tahiti, and Pablo Picasso, who had a transforming aesthetic experience upon viewing the exhibits at the Musée d'ethnographie du Trocadéro in Paris. Igor Stravinsky's *The Rite of Spring* (1913) provided the overture and grand march of the primitivist parade that reached Southern California in the late nineteenth century in similarly highbrow terms. The San Francisco–based writer Charles Warren Stoddard traveled extensively in the South Pacific and wrote of his observations in *South Sea Idylls* (1873). A few years later, Stoddard introduced his friend Robert Louis Stevenson to the region. Another San Franciscan of the era, the French-born artist Jules Tavernier, spent the last years of his life in Hawaii, painting volcanoes. By the time of Tavernier's death in 1889, a strong San Francisco–Honolulu connection had already been established, with the Polynesian royalty and the New England elite of Hawaii visiting the city, staying at the Palace Hotel. In 1898 Hawaii was annexed to the United States, and the Hawaii-California connection became even stronger. Jack London discovered the islands in the early 1900s and, as in the case of anything he encountered and liked, wrote extensively on the subject. Then Tin Pan Alley discovered the ukulele, and a cycle of Hawaiian-themed ukulele songs continued through the 1920s.

San Francisco architects, meanwhile, were receiving a growing number of commissions from the Islands, resulting in a Hawaiian–Beaux-Arts style only now beginning to be documented and appreciated. In the early and mid-twentieth century, the San Francisco–based Matson Lines served the islands on a regular basis, with connecting voyages to the South Pacific. The Bay Area elite, in short, had Hawaiian business connections and Hawaiian tastes: a connection that was expanded and democratized with the establishment of a California-based Pacific Fleet and the development of a major naval installation at Pearl Harbor. Even the Folks of Los Angeles, the pensioners and midwestern émigrés, had their own South Seas place: Clifton's Pacific Seas Cafeteria on South Olive Street in Los Angeles, with an entire wall built three-dimensionally as a lava mountain and waterfall.

As a style, Polynesianism tended to be confined to recreational furniture, especially for gardens and bars, public or private, and could be found in the most tasteful of homes. On a more popular basis, it had also begun to make inroads as a restaurant design. In 1934, in the aftermath of Prohibition, Ernest Beaumont-Gantt, a restaurateur from New Orleans, opened a Polynesian-themed bar in Hollywood called Don the Beachcomber, specializing in rum drinks. At this point, the Zombie (a blend of Jamaican, Barbadian, and Puerto Rican rums, apricot brandy, papaya nectar, and pineapple juice) was invented, given that name because it transformed its first consumer into something resembling that creature, or so he told Don the Beachcomber the following morning. The restaurant was so successful that Beaumont-Gantt legally changed his name to Don Beach and in 1937 opened an even larger establishment, lavishly decorated in Oceanian motifs. Artificial rain flooded the roof at intervals, and even more elaborate rum drinks were served in hollowed pineapples and coconuts.

In Northern California, meanwhile, another restaurateur, Victor Bergeron, owner of Hinky Dink's, a small but successful establishment on San Pablo in Oakland, upgraded Beaumont-Gantt's beachcomber persona to that of a roguish and informed island trader. In the South Sea novels and short stories of W. Somerset Maugham and the prewar films they inspired, a trader was higher on the social scale than a beachcomber. A trader was a good businessman, spoke a number of languages, and, as Bergeron put it, knew his chow and grog. Having a wooden leg, the result of a childhood bout of tuberculosis, Bergeron, now Trader Vic, could easily play the part, which he did across the next half century in and through a network of Trader Vic restaurants, anchored in the Bay Area, that further elaborated Don the Beachcomber's array of rum drinks and expanded Don the Beachcomber's sweetened faux Chinese cuisine through the addition of authentic Indonesian, Malaysian, Vietnamese, and Southeast Asian cookery.

World War II nationalized this largely California-based preference for Polynesian décor and cuisine. Millions of Americans had experienced the region at the most impressionable time of their lives. Writer James Michener upgraded and romanticized their memories through such fictional accounts as *Tales of the South Pacific* (1948), which won the Pulitzer Prize and formed the basis for one of the most successful Broadway musicals of all time, followed by a highly successful CinemaScope movie. Ever since the publication of Herman Melville's fictionalized South Sea memoirs *Typee: A Peep at Polynesian Life* (1846) and *Omoo: A Narrative of Adventures in the South Seas* (1847), the South Seas had been for Americans, to one degree or another, a place for sexual liberation or sexual license, depending upon one's point of view. In the twentieth century, the newly influential science of anthropology expanded and rationalized the sexualization of the South Pacific through such works as Margaret Mead's *Coming of Age in Samoa* (1928) and Bronislaw Malinowski's *The Sexual Life of Savages in North-Western Melanesia* (1929), which postulated a more flexible, even easygoing, attitude toward sexuality in the South Pacific than one encountered in the developed world. Michener's *Tales of the South Pacific* was, in part, an erotic-escapist idyll, whose protagonist, Lieutenant Cable, finds himself on Bali Ha'i, where the girls of the surrounding islands have been gathered for safety during the war. The outcome is inevitable. Buoyed by the success of his novel and the Broadway show and film that followed, Michener continued his South Seas saga through *Return to Paradise* (1951), *Rascals in Paradise* (1957), and the blockbuster *Hawaii* (1959), keyed to the admittance of Hawaii as a state that same year.

The admission of Hawaii to the Union in 1959 capped a decade in which tourist travel to Hawaii increased dramatically, democratized by low-priced charter airplane flights and hotel tourist packages. Across the 1950s millions of Americans enjoyed vacations in the islands that gave psychological and imaginative depth to an identity based in postwar affluence. Returning to the mainland, they remembered Hawaii as an enchanted place, now become a permanent part of their lives. Tiki helped them re-create the experience. In the early part of the decade, Waltah Clarke (yes, that is how he spelled his first name!), a clothier who had moved to Honolulu from Los Angeles in 1938 to manage a Trader Vic's restaurant, began to popularize recreational Hawaiian attire—shirts, swimwear, and muumuus—on the mainland. In 1950 Thor Heyerdahl's *Kon-Tiki*, an account of a three-month voyage by raft from Peru to Polynesia, intended to prove that the settlement of the South Seas had come from South America, hit the best-seller list. The following year, the film documentary version of the voyage won the Academy Award. Hollywood remade *Bird of Paradise* in 1951, starring Debra Paget, and *Rain* in 1953, starring Rita Hayworth. In 1952 Les Baxter released the best-selling album *Le Sacre du Sauvage*, which introduced South Sea sounds into mainstream music, a trend followed up later in the decade by Martin Denny, whose 1959 hit "Quiet Village" seemed a soundtrack for a decade of Tiki development. A popular television series, *Hawaiian Eye*, aired from 1959 to 1963; and in 1961 Elvis Presley went Tiki with *Blue Hawaii*, followed by *Paradise Hawaiian Style* (1966). In 1963 Walt Disney opened an Enchanted Tiki Room at Disneyland, featuring technically advanced audio-visual entertainment: singing birds, drumbeats in the distance, the chanting of warriors, the rain forest, the roll of surf.

Tiki was helping to create a myth and identity for ordinary Americans: a design and style that contained within itself a strong note—at least on the level of fantasy— of sexual liberation, of escaping the Puritan restraints of American life. The icon of the style, the Tiki figure, frequently resembling the statues of Easter Island but appearing in other variations as well, was in its multiple meanings either the first man, who made the first woman and procreated the human race, a phallic symbol, or the god of art. Tiki was, in any event, a good-time guy, and his image could be found nationwide, in California especially: in bars, restaurants, motels, coffee shops, bowling alleys. In restaurants such as Don the Beachcomber, Trader Vic's and its franchises, the Luau in Beverly Hills, Christian's Hut in Newport Beach, the Zombie Village in Oakland, the Outrigger in Monterey, where the connection between alcohol and sexuality was made explicit on menu cartoons and other illustrations depicting bare-breasted *wahines* associated in one way or another with elaborately concocted and named (Navy Grog, Cobra's Fang, Vicious Virgin, Islander's Pearl, Scorpion) rum drinks. A number of Tiki restaurants featured Las Vegas–style floor shows celebrating faux primitivism and exotic dancing.

It would be a mistake, however, to exaggerate the erotic-escapist or demimondaine dimensions of the Tiki craze, which was not revolutionary in intent. Tiki, rather, allowed suburban Americans to have a night out in acceptably exotic circumstances. The gang from the office could go to a local Tiki place for a celebratory luau. The Tiki luau migrated to the suburban backyard through the installation of Polynesian torch lights and the use of sauces and condiments franchised from Trader Vic's and other establishments. Teenagers going to the Tonga Room in the Fairmont Hotel in San Francisco for dinner before their senior prom, posing for pictures before one or another of the Tiki idols, were hardly attempting to throw off three centuries of Puritan restraint. Like modernism at the opposite end of the cultural spectrum, Tiki—all of it, including the most kitschy of kitsch curios, the bamboo, the rattan furniture, the tropical plants, the paintings, the Tiki motel or hotel architecture, and above all else the emblem of Tiki himself, grinning his enigmatic grin—constituted a way for ordinary Americans to escape, momentarily, into a fantasy world that helped mitigate, if only for an evening, the hard-charging, relentless pace of modern life. Tiki defied the modern, like a Maori warrior wagging his tongue at an adversary. Tiki suggested that cops and firemen could be beachcombers for a night, stockbrokers could be South Seas traders, suburban housewives in leis, muumuus, or sarongs could imagine themselves elsewhere, in a place transformed and magical. Modernism—as high art, as architecture—extolled the intelligence, precision, and machinery of contemporary life. Modernism demanded an elite level of cultivation and taste. Tiki said to hell with it. If only for tonight, let's party!

Tiki or no Tiki, ordinary Californians were getting more than their fair share of modernist buildings during the 1950s: schools and colleges, hospitals, banks, office buildings in the public and private sector, shopping centers, theaters, parking structures, synagogues and churches. Indeed, by the early 1960s the public face of Southern California and the newer regions of Northern California as well were decidedly modernistic, with ordinary people using modernist structures virtually every day. Did the overwhelming (and, if the truth be told, frequently undistinguished, sometimes even brutalist) modernism of public California encourage not only a taste for Tiki but a desire, even among discriminating clients, that home architecture be as comforting and familiar as possible?

Hence, it can be speculated, arose the persistence and ultimate triumph of Ranch. For the editors of *Sunset* magazine, arbiter of western value and taste, the ranch house represented the quintessential California style, and its prime proponent and practitioner was Cliff May. In 1946 *Sunset* and May joined forces to publish *Sunset Western Ranch Houses*. Revised and expanded in 1958, this extensively illustrated study served as the predominnt guide to the ranch house for the rest of the century. Cliff May was a designer-contractor, not a professional architect, and he had but one genre in his oeuvre, the ranch house, which he had been designing and building since the early 1930s, starting out in San Diego and Los Angeles. *Sunset* covered May's work extensively and in 1951 commissioned him to design its headquarters in Menlo Park, one of the few institutional buildings May ever attempted. (Thomas Church did the landscaping.) Comprised of linked ranch-style segments around a patio garden, the headquarters was soon attracting fifty thousand visitors a year to a place that was in effect ground zero of western living.

Cliff May revered the ranch house format, including the home he designed for himself in West Los Angeles in 1939, for a number of reasons. The ranch house represented a residential language stable across 150 years of usage. As a building type, the ranch house had its origin in Spain (with some Moorish influences evident in the interior patio) and from there was brought to Mexico. Here was the type of house in which the *rancheros* of Old California conducted their later mythologized existence through the first half of the nineteenth century. The contemporary ranch house, May believed, had sprung almost organically from the topography and historical memory of California; indeed the very earth of California, as adobe, was still being used in contemporary structures as it had been used in the first half of the nineteenth century. There was something appropriate, May suggested, in the very silhouette of the California ranch house: its low and leisurely lines; its gently sloping roofs, conveying at once a sense of authority and shelter; its ability to ramble comfortably across a site; its lofty and unencumbered interior spaces; its sustained vocabulary of wall, window, *corredor* (a covered walkway), patio, and garden; its indoor/outdoor rhythms. In its simplicity and flexibility, its closeness to the earth, its adaptability to topography and trees, its nurturing of domestic life in protected interiors, the sunshine of its gardens and patios, its naturally cool interiors on hot days, its great central fireplace so congenial on chilly nights, and, of great importance, its adaptability to the new postwar materials, the ranch house was virtually a symbol of California itself, past, present, and future.

So useful a prototype could not be confined to California. For the editors of *House Beautiful*, the ranch style Cliff May was describing had become the quintessentially American look for domestic housing. "Here is the new norm," *House Beautiful* editorialized in 1957, "the new standard for our homes. It is clearly the American tradition of today, our typical way to build for our fuller ways of life."[2] Whether built from wood or adobe (in the sun-scorched Central Valley city of Fresno especially), whether upscale and architect-designed or in a middle-priced tract, Ranch was holding its own by 1963. The style had, in fact, reached out—like California itself—to the rest of America.

II

URBAN PERSPECTIVES

3

Urban Expectations

San Diego Leverages Itself into Big-City Status

ARLY in 1944, with the end of the war only vaguely on the horizon, the post-war planning committee of the San Diego Chamber of Commerce commissioned the urban research firm of Day & Zimmermann of Philadelphia to prepare a report on the impending prospects of greater San Diego. Field investigations began in April, and it took six months to collect and analyze the relevant data and almost another six months to write the report. Finally, on 31 March 1945, the report was issued: more than a thousand pages of double-spaced typescript in eleven volumes, replete with plates, maps, plans, tables, and diagrams, gathered into one hefty black box with gold lettering. The Zimmermann Report, as the survey was called, represented a formidable inventory of San Diego, city and county, as place, society, infrastructure, and economy, past and present, and predicted an optimistic future for city and region. Greater San Diego, the report argued, had all the makings of a metropolis. It enjoyed an impressive and beautiful topography and one of the finest climates in the country. It was strategically located at the intersection of Latin America, the American Southwest, California, and the Pacific Basin. Thanks to the United States Navy, it possessed one of the finest harbor and port infrastructures in the world. It also enjoyed a direct railroad connection to the East, and its geography allowed for highway expansion. The war had brought its manufacturing capacity to high efficiency. Within that context, aviation had secured for San Diego a highly skilled and motivated workforce.

Most important, greater San Diego contained within itself every element of the built and natural environment—urbanism, suburbanism, adjacent agricultural hinterlands, and a desert border to the east—conferring coherence upon the entire region. Indeed, no one aspect of California, whether natural or man-made, was absent. San Diego could therefore develop simultaneously along urban, suburban, agricultural, and resort/tourist lines. It was at once international in its port and

autonomous in its geographical and sub/urban completeness. In order to flourish in
the postwar era, San Diego did not have to change itself or to add any urban sector
then lacking. It only had to know itself for what it was—a coherent sub/region of
Southern California—and build upon that identity.

Thus the Zimmermann Report, in its presentation of facts, statistics, and recommendations, re-confirmed an existing San Diego identity that the war had intensified and—in the case of housing, most conspicuously—had put under severe stress,
but had not altered substantially. As dramatic as the developments of World War
II in terms of intensity and growth might be, the San Diego formula that had been
established earlier in the century had held and would continue to hold for the fore-
seeable future. Metropolitan San Diego knew itself as the Gibraltar of the Pacific: a
Navy and aviation town, a port, a resort, an enclave, complete unto itself and happy
with its lot, a society given to the sun, the sea, sport, and an easygoing lifestyle. Like
most other American cities, San Diego was governed by an oligarchy—only more
so. It was an oligarchy at once conservative and business-oriented but also touched
by Progressivism; hence the parks and impressive public amenities of the region. It
was an oligarchy that favored growth as long as growth proved profitable and could
be kept under control. For various reasons, especially the dock strike and free speech
demonstrations of 1912 in which the Industrial Workers of the World (IWW) had
threatened to take over the town, it was an oligarchy, finally, that harbored a special
fear of radicalism, which dovetailed with a certain caution and restraint in civic temperament: a concern for privacy, stability, and moderation in life, art, and politics.

In order to achieve, simultaneously, stability and growth, the San Diego oligarchy had joined the Navy in the first three decades of the twentieth century. Spearheaded by William Kettner, at once a congressman and a continuing director of the
chamber of commerce, the San Diego establishment had persistently and painstakingly wooed the Department of the Navy to locate its primary presence on the
Pacific Coast in San Diego. No San Diegan was more eager to see the development
of San Diego as a naval center than Marine Colonel Joseph Pendleton, commander
of the Fourth Marine Regiment, who joined with Congressman Kettner to convince
the Department of the Navy to establish a Marine training center on Dutch Flats,
to which the city of San Diego donated five hundred acres of adjacent tidelands.
The fused Navy, Marine, and San Diego urbanism of Pendleton's and Kettner's
venture was evident in the selection of the famed New York architect Bertram Gros-
venor Goodhue, creator of signature buildings at West Point, to plan and design the
Marine base as well as the naval air station on North Island. Goodhue had been
responsible for the majestic Spanish Colonial complex of the 1915 Exposition in Balboa Park. For the Marines, he designed a similarly impressive ensemble of Spanish
Colonial buildings that constituted an urban military campus thoroughly Southern
California in its ambience that was soon acknowledged as one of the most beautiful
examples of military architecture in the nation. In time, San Diego would support
a number of naval and Marine establishments reflective of San Diego as Navy and
the Navy as reflective of San Diego. (By 1930, a third of the workforce would be in

one way or another on the Navy payroll.) When Pendleton retired in 1924 as a major general, he settled in the adjacent community of Coronado, where he served fourteen years on the school board and two terms as mayor.

Naval and Marine officers were especially prized in social circles; their wives (many of them from San Diego) were invited onto local boards and offered membership in local clubs and had their names mentioned in local newspapers. In time, the national naval establishment itself, an interlocked elite in the most conservative and rank-conscious of the services, became strongly San Diego–oriented as a matter of sentiment and policy. Most of the leading Navy and Marine commanders of World War II shared a San Diego experience from some earlier point in their careers. Officers and senior NCOs alike returned to San Diego in retirement because it was so congenially a Navy town, with a full array of support facilities, and because they had had good experiences there; 20 percent of all retired Navy personnel by the 1950s were living in Southern California, the majority of them in metropolitan San Diego. As senior Navy and Marine officers approached retirement, they frequently angled for assignment in San Diego, where they became active in charities and on civic boards in an effort, in part, to facilitate their transition into the private sector. The corporations, government agencies, educational institutions, and non-profit sector of greater San Diego were honeycombed with retired brass serving on boards or in administrative positions, where their prestige and expertise could be fully exploited. World War II hero and retired Rear Admiral Leslie Gehres, for example, served as coordinator for the various enterprises of downtown oligarch C. Arnholt Smith.

The vivid social stratification of the Navy and Marine Corps dovetailed with oligarchic preference. Flag officers were especially prized, followed by Navy captains and Marine colonels, followed by retired commanders and lieutenant colonels. Skilled and experienced in hands-on management, former warrant officers, senior petty officers, and sergeants were also absorbable upon retirement into foreman-level supervisory positions. A tension existed, however, as historian Mike Davis has pointed out, between San Diego and lower-ranking enlisted men, whom Davis describes as the proletariat in the San Diego formula. They were young, first of all, and tended to come from the less privileged sectors of the nation, and there were thousands of them at any one time in the vicinity, most with very little money. Young and single, sailors and Marines liked to raise cain in their off-hours, which led, Davis points out, to the creation of honky-tonk zones in San Diego and elsewhere abounding in bars, bordellos, and tattoo parlors, toward which local police cast a lenient eye, provided that things did not get out of hand.

The Second World War intensified this Navy and Marine relationship and further expanded an equally strong culture of aviation. An enlarged Naval Training Center transformed hundreds of thousands of recruits into sailors. In 1942 the Marine Corps acquired through federal court order (and later payment) the sprawling 122,798-acre Rancho Santa Margarita y los Flores forty-five miles north of the city, which it quickly developed into Camp Pendleton, where three Marine divisions and numerous replacements were trained for combat service in the Pacific. Throughout the war years, the streets of San Diego teemed with sailors and Marines in various stages of training or deployment. Seventy-five thousand civilians, meanwhile, were employed in the construction of Navy and Army Air Forces aircraft. Since the mid-1930s Consolidated Aircraft had been building flying boats for the Navy—the famed PBY Catalina, most notably, designed by Mac Laddon, a plane that constituted a masterpiece of Art Deco design fusing sailing on the sea and flight. During the war, Consolidated turned its attention to an even more impressive version of this aircraft—the 200 PB2Y Coronado Patrol Bomber, which soon became the work-horse plane for bombing runs, submarine surveillance, high-priority freight, and VIP transportation. In 1943 Consolidated merged with Vultee Aircraft of Downey in Los Angeles County to form the even more impressive Convair, which produced B-24 Liberator bombers for the Army Air Forces—nearly seven thousand of them built in San Diego in Convair's harbor-side plant—along with a continuing stream of PBYs.

All this created a boom of unprecedented proportions as the San Diego city pop-ulation of 203,321 in 1940 jumped to 390,000 in 1943, not including military person-nel, leveling off to 334,387 by 1950. San Diego County, meanwhile, mushroomed from 289,348 in 1940 to 556,808 by 1950. It was a boom toward which the perma-nent prewar population sustained a high level of ambivalence. Who, after all, was going to pay for it all: the housing, the water, the sewage, the schools, hospitals, and social services, especially since so much city property was federally owned, hence tax exempt? It was one thing to be a Navy town in peacetime, with an economy sustained by federal dollars. It was quite another matter entirely to be responsible for the creation of a civic infrastructure supporting a military mega-center. Signifi-cantly, given the San Diego–Navy symbiosis, the Navy itself got into the housing business, creating thousands of units, and in 1944 the Navy financed the construc-tion of an emergency aqueduct from the Colorado River. The San Diego Aqueduct was completed in 1947, and a second pipeline—financed this time by San Diego—was added in 1952.

The stress of the wartime boom, moreover, had to be perceived from the perspec-tive of San Diego's love-hate relationship with a big-city identity. For three decades, beginning with the smokestacks-versus-geranium debate of the mayoral elections of 1913 and 1917, San Diegans had been struggling with the problem of wanting it both ways: wanting San Diego to remain an unchanging enclave resort while enjoying the prosperity that comes only from growth. The entire history of San Diego since the 1870s, in fact, could be written from this perspective. Oligarchic San Diego was energized by the Progressive impulse that wanted things orderly, efficient, and kept to scale. San Diego featured one of the most ambitious park systems in the nation because in significant measure the city envisioned itself as a park, aesthetic and rationalized. If growth meant industrialism, then industrialism meant disorder, as in the case of the violent strike led by the IWW in 1912. Not only did San Diego join the Navy to deal with this dilemma—and thereby create a safe and stable economy—it developed itself as well as a retirement center, with retirees bringing income into the region, although by the early 1930s, as Edmund Wilson pointed out, San Diego had also briefly become the suicide capital of the nation when retirees lost their assets and in unprecedented numbers decided to end it all. In the decade to come, the 1950s, San Diego would replay this ambivalent drama of growth versus stasis, smokestacks versus geraniums. It would do this, however, not through a program of unified urbanism but through a confederated model that the very landscape of the region, with its succession of mutually exclusive canyons, facilitated.

The oligarchy that facilitated this development was a mixture of new and old players. Not until 1946 did George White Marston, the predominate oligarch from the Progressive Era and the second founder of San Diego after Alonzo Horton, pass from the scene at the age of ninety-five. A few San Diegans whose fortunes dated from the late nineteenth or early twentieth century were still around or were represented by second or third generations. Their identifications were centered, among other places, on the downtown Cuyamaca Club, founded in 1888, and the Corte Madera Ranch, a 3,400-acre retreat near Pine Valley fifty miles east of the city, which a dozen or so families had developed in the 1920s as an upper-register resort, complete with its own lake and polo field. Still on hand as well were two towering figures from the earlier aviation elite. T. Claude Ryan, who built Charles Lindbergh's *Spirit of St. Louis* in 1927, prospered during the war as an aircraft (including the jet-assisted Fireball fighter of 1944) and aviation components manufacturer and in the postwar era was heading Ryan Aeronautical, which was developing cutting-edge aircraft, missiles, and radar technology. Likewise still in the game was Reuben Fleet, who had moved Consolidated Aircraft from Buffalo to San Diego in 1935. Presumed retired, Fleet remained at the epicenter of San Diego's military-industrial complex. His home on Point Loma was considered ground zero of political and industrial influence in a city in which the oligarchy exercised the decisive power, with city government following its direction.

To no one's surprise, it was a conservative, Republican-oriented culture, sustained on the journalistic front by James Copley, owner and publisher of the two dominant newspapers, the morning *Union* and the *Evening Tribune*. During the war, Clinton McKinnon, a Democrat, had secured permission (authorizations for newsprint and machinery) from the Roosevelt administration to establish a competing newspaper, the *San Diego Daily Journal*, which McKinnon ran as an alternate voice until selling it in 1948. By 1950 the *Journal* had been absorbed by the *Union-Tribune* publishing company and merged into the *Evening Tribune*. The fact that San Diego had only one television station until 1953, KFMB-TV, Channel 8, which carried programs from all three networks, further underscored the information monopoly characterizing the city.

Oligarchies of American cities tended to run to type and genre, and San Diego was no exception. While Ryan and Fleet were near-heroic figures from an earlier era, the 1950s oligarchy also included, aside from publisher Copley, the usual assortment of developers, property owners, corporate bigwigs, lawyers, city officials, and religious leaders, most conspicuously the Roman Catholic Bishop Charles Buddy, who would spend the late 1940s and the 1950s building an architecturally recherché university campus on a mesa overlooking the city. A graduate of the North American College in Rome, the West Point of American Catholic seminaries, Buddy, a native Missourian, had absorbed a strong preference for Mediterranean culture during his student days: a preference that dovetailed with the European orientation of many of the Roman Catholic hierarchy, especially those educated in Rome or elsewhere on the Continent. Arriving in San Diego in January 1937 as the first bishop of the newly established Diocese of San Diego, Buddy—learned, hard-working, a skilled administrator—soon earned for himself a respected place in the San Diego oligarchy.

Buddy was especially taken with the European origins of San Diego, settled by the viceroyalty of New Spain in 1769, formally dedicated on 3 June 1770, and symbolized in the surviving Mission San Diego del Alcalá, named in honor of a Spanish Franciscan brother canonized in 1588. By 1945 Buddy was making plans to memorialize this historical connection architecturally and, simultaneously, to express the presence of San Diego as a continuing Roman Catholic town through the construction of Alcalá Park, a multi-functional academic campus and chancery atop Kearny Mesa overlooking the city. To this project he recruited the equally European-oriented Religious of the Sacred Heart, more commonly known as the Madames of the Sacred Heart, a religious order founded in Paris in 1800 in the aftermath of the French Revolution to educate the daughters of the displaced nobility and upper classes. Construction at Alcalá Park began in September 1950 with the pouring of concrete foundations for the San Diego College for Women, to be staffed by the Madames as the first component of a larger University of San Diego campus that would include by the end of the decade a men's college directed and staffed by diocesan clergy, a law school, a theological college for the training of priests, a basilica chapel, and chancery offices for the diocese.

To the consternation of some architectural critics, such as James Britton of *San Diego* magazine, who would have preferred modernism, Buddy insisted that the entire complex be designed in the style of the Spanish Renaissance. Buddy considered such an ensemble reflective of the Spanish Catholic origins of San Diego, the golden age of Spain, with specific reference to the great universities of that era, and the Spanish Colonial city created by Bertram Goodhue in Balboa Park for the Exposition of 1915. By May 1959, his campus nearing completion, Buddy was featured on the cover of *San Diego* magazine as founder and president of an institution that embodied San Diego as a city alive with Mediterranean associations, while at the same time between 1936 and 1966 establishing 150 new parishes, thirty mission chapels, seventy-five elementary schools, and a diocesan newspaper. Many parish priests, however, the majority of them from Ireland, resented Buddy's assessments for the university and were complaining, so it was later revealed, to the apostolic delegate in Washington.

With the exception of Buddy's clerical attire, photographs of the San Diego establishment from the period reveal a uniform procession of late-middle-aged white men in dark suits. Two oligarchs from the era, however—C. (for Conrad) Arnholt Smith and Roger Revelle—emanated something more distinctive and complex: the suggestion, that is, that they were not exclusively members of the corporate and professional crowd but something else as well, something more elusive, more autonomous even. Smith and Revelle were each at the top of their respective games, business and academic leadership, but they had got there by significantly different means. Their life stories constituted, in fact, a diptych of San Diego as upward mobility versus patrician privilege, with Smith being played by Fred McMurray and Revelle by his friend and fellow La Jollan Gregory Peck in the movie that was never made. Yet, despite surface similarities and their mutual membership in the San Diego oligarchy, no two figures could have been more unlike each other while playing parallel roles in the same establishment. Each possessed a certain prepossessing power that emanated from his physical presence, especially Revelle, who stood six foot four. Each embodied various aspects of San Diego value. Each accomplished much in his respective realm. One, however, the more privileged in his origins and connections, would help bring San Diego to a whole new level of civic maturity; and the other, the self-made one, would fall like Icarus into the San Diego sea.

Each of them was born in Washington state, Smith in Walla Walla in 1899, Revelle in Seattle in 1909. Smith was the son of a small-town businessman, active in politics, who by 1907 was facing prison as a felon convicted for perjury in a political case. Hence the Smith family's abrupt removal to San Diego. Revelle's parents, by contrast, were graduates of the University of Washington, his father a lawyer, his mother a teacher in local schools. The family moved to Pasadena in 1917 when Revelle's mother was diagnosed with tuberculosis. His father reestablished his law practice there, as well as gaining a position in the local junior high school. Smith was raised in blue-collar and lower-middle-class neighborhoods in San Diego, a smart but indifferent student, more interested in athletics and dramatics than scholarship. He quit high school at the age of fifteen to go to work in Heller's Grocery and Bakery. Revelle, equally athletic, did well in high school and went on to Pomona College, where he majored in geology. While Revelle was absorbing the educational values and genteel ambience of Pasadena and Pomona, Smith was unloading groceries, making chocolate éclairs and cream puffs, handling the cash at the counter, and keeping the books. He showed a distinct talent for bookkeeping and, despite his lack of a high school diploma, was hired as a teller at the Merchants National Bank. Thus Smith was formed by a rather free-and-easy, unsupervised boyhood and early employment and, in some ways, by the compromised past of his father. Revelle, meanwhile, who had excelled at Pomona, entered UC Berkeley in 1930 as a graduate student in geology.

C. Arnholt Smith had ambition to rise in the world and to improve his social standing. To compensate for not going to college, he took up the most collegiate of sports, crew, at the San Diego Rowing Club, earning distinction in four-man and single shells. Placing in regattas up and down the Pacific Coast, Smith was considered a candidate for the 1920 Olympics but could not afford the year away from employment necessary for training. Crew nevertheless made a gentleman of C. Arnholt Smith: tall and tan and handsome in his early twenties, his hair slicked back and parted in the center. In 1922 he married a fellow bank employee. Shortly thereafter, A. P. Giannini's Bank of Italy bought the Merchants National and three other San Diego banks, and the young Smith proved his mettle by helping Giannini consolidate the Bank of Italy branch system throughout the region. Giannini wanted Smith to take a higher position in Ventura County, but Smith's wife refused to move. Instead, Smith took over the commercial banking department as a regional vice president of the Bank of Italy, responsible for Southern California, Nevada, and the Southwest. He lived at the Jonathan Club in Los Angeles, commuting to San Diego on weekends for a year before his wife, with reluctance, joined him in L.A. All in all, it had been a remarkable rise, earning Smith the admiration of, among others, the Nixon family of Whittier, whom the Smith family had befriended in the 1920s.

In June 1931 Roger Revelle married Ellen Virginia Clark, whom he had met when she was at Scripps College adjacent to Pomona. Clark was the grand-niece of the English-born Ellen Browning Scripps, half-sister and business partner to newspaper mogul Edward Wyllis Scripps, founder of a chain of dailies and of the United Press. Attracted to San Diego for his health, E. W. Scripps had moved there in 1891 with his half-sister, where he built an estate called Miramar atop a dry mesa overlooking the Pacific, and the two of them proceeded to develop a second successful newspaper chain on the Pacific Coast. Five years later, Ellen Browning Scripps, who never married, settled permanently in the northern San Diego suburb of La Jolla.

The Scrippses, brother and sister, were fascinating figures: wealthy beyond belief, but it was self-made wealth from a newspaper business they had personally managed. There remained in each of them, moreover, an intellectualism—an interest in science, education, Progressive social theory, philanthropy and social improvement, the rights of labor and public ownership—that linked them, if only by sympathy, to the Fabian Socialists of England and, more locally, to Fabian Pasadena. Brother and sister enjoyed their money, but they also—and this in an era before the graduated income tax and tax deductions—were willing to give some of it away to make the world a better place. In doing this, they fit into the larger pattern of philanthropy in the early twentieth century, when private money was migrating into universities, colleges, hospitals, foundations, and philanthropic enterprises of every sort.

In the case of the Scrippses, this generosity resulted in the endowment of the San Diego Marine Biological Institution established at La Jolla in 1903, which became affiliated with the University of California in 1912 as the Scripps Institution of Oceanography. In 1927 Ellen Browning Scripps, who in California had made a further fortune on her own in real estate, endowed a women's college in Claremont, adjacent to Pomona, its campus designed in exquisite Spanish Revival by architect Gordon Kaufmann. Roger Revelle was thus married into the family that had endowed the Scripps Institution, which he joined in August 1931 as a research assistant, settling with his wife in a seaside cottage on campus in La Jolla. Five years later, the Scripps family trust was dissolved (E. W. Scripps died in 1926, his sister in 1932), and a bequest from the dissolved trust made Roger and Ellen Revelle financially independent for life. Financial security, however, did not slacken Roger Revelle's ambition. Over the next quarter century, he became one of the most respected oceanographers in the world. In 1936 he earned his doctorate and was appointed instructor at the Scripps Institution. Returning to California in 1937 after a year of post-doctoral study at the Geophysical Institute in Norway, Revelle taught at Scripps and UCLA and conducted seagoing research expeditions, which led to a reserve commission in the Navy, with a specialty in oceanographic research. In July 1941 he was called to active duty and assigned to the Navy Radio and Sound Laboratory in San Diego, the first step in a distinguished six-year career in naval research.

C. Arnholt Smith, meanwhile, tired of working for others, was busy assembling financing for the purchase of the United States National Bank in San Diego. It was a small bank, with approximately $1 million in deposits as of 1933, but the Depression was on, and banking had become a risky business, which to Smith, age thirty-four, meant that it was a good time to buy. Assembling his savings and money raised by his older brother, and securing the vote of the bank's Massachusetts-based majority stockholder, Smith gained control of the United States National Bank through astute maneuvering, only to have it closed during the Bank Holiday of March 1933 and be forced to raise an additional $50,000 in new capital before being allowed to reopen for business in 1934. Smith's brother John, an oil promoter and original investor, helped raise the necessary second round of cash from a number of Southern Californian oilmen.

Across the next sixteen years, Smith leveraged his control of the United States National Bank into a series of complex real estate deals that included investments south of the border in the Agua Caliente Casino and Racetrack developed in the late 1920s by Los Angeles and San Diego investors as an accessible and legal escape from the constraints of Prohibition. During these years—as Roger Revelle was making his reputation as an oceanographer, Navy officer, and government consultant—Smith was assembling a diverse portfolio, frequently in partnership with his longtime friend John Alessio, a onetime shoeshine stand operator whom Smith had brought into the banking business. During this time as well, Smith was rising steadily as a fundraiser and influence wielder in Republican Party circles. From 1943 to 1949, he served as a commissioner on the all-important state highway commission during the first phases of its heroic construction program. A Mr. San Diego in the making, Smith also threw himself into a number of local enterprises—tuna, baseball, resorts, and the stewardship of the Cuyamaca Club—as well as continuing his labyrinthine investments in real estate and allied interests through his Westgate-California Corporation.

In entering the tuna business, Smith was gaining a stake in the third lead element in the San Diego economy after the Navy and aviation, averaging $30 million a year by the late 1940s. By 1951 the San Diego tuna fleet stood at more than seven hundred vessels, manned by some twenty-seven hundred fishermen. Five canneries employed more than three thousand workers, trying to keep up with the nation's insatiable taste for tuna, which could be traced to meat rationing during the war. Following the war, Americans were eating more tuna than ever. As of 1950 there were more than two hundred white-hulled clippers in the San Diego tuna fleet—diesel-driven, in the main, capable of remaining at sea for up to five months or fifteen thousand miles, whichever came first—and choice albacore was selling for as high as $500 a ton. It would take a train of fifteen hundred box cars, it was estimated, twelve miles long, to transport the tuna that was canned in San Diego in that year alone.

The trouble was, the Japanese were getting into the tuna business as well and undercutting San Diego tuna by $20 a ton. Smith's response—and he was not alone in this effort—was to industrialize and de-unionize the fleet, most of whose workers belonged to the Cannery Workers and Fishermen's Union, AFL. In acquiring the United States National Bank, Smith had also acquired control over one of the six shipbuilding operations in the city, National Ironworks (later National Steel and Shipbuilding Corporation). At this facility, Smith began to build highly industrial-ized tuna clippers, which he sailed under the Peruvian flag with non-union crews. He replaced individual fisherman and their bamboo poles with nylon nets that could haul from the water tons of tuna at a time (unfortunately destroying dolphins in the process). He also set up two freezing plants in Peru, shipping the frozen tuna back to the Westgate San Diego Marine Terminal in two refrigerated freighters for canning in a Westgate cannery for distribution under the Breast-O'-Chicken and Carnation labels.

In 1955 Westgate California acquired the San Diego Padres of the Pacific Coast League for $300,000. To own the Padres, as Smith now did, was to own a significant portion of the San Diego soul; for since 1936 the Padres, playing in Balboa Stadium, had been providing San Diego with its only big-ticket connection to professional sports, hence civic identity. The 1937 championship team had featured the talents of San Diego native Ted Williams. After two seasons Williams had gone on to the Boston Red Sox and during the war, a true San Diegan, enlisted in the Marine Corps and distinguished himself as a combat aviator. In 1948, a year after Jackie Rob-inson joined the Dodgers, the Padres broke the racial barrier on the Pacific Coast when the front office brought aboard San Diego native Johnny Ritchey, an African American, who had made All-City three times consecutively in the late 1930s when playing for San Diego High School before going on to star in football and baseball at San Diego State, followed by decorated service in the combat engineers in Europe during World War II. For the Padres, Smith built a new stadium, Westgate Park, which opened in 1955 in Mission Valley, and in 1968 he won a National League franchise that officially made San Diego a big-league city.

Tuna and baseball; now Smith got into another iconic endeavor, tourism. Smith was a member of the San Diego Yacht Club, but he found the facilities shabby and run-down. He envisioned something much more lavish, something more expres-sive of the conspicuous prosperity of the 1950s: a Hawaiian-style yacht club and luxury resort catering to the motor yacht crowd who were willing to spend money, as opposed to the more penurious blue bloods at the San Diego Yacht Club, obsessed with the rituals and protocols of sailing competition. Characteristically, Smith acted on his vision. In the early 1950s, Westgate California embarked upon the development of the Kona Kai Yacht Club and Inn on a filled-in sandbar in San Diego Bay, designated Shelter Island. A successful private club by the mid-1950s, with motorized yachts packing the quays and the Lawrence Welk Orchestra playing for weekend dances at the side of an oversized outdoor swimming pool, Kona Kai welcomed an influx of new San Diegans who were making money and seeking ways to enjoy the good life.

Nor did Smith ignore upper-register clubdom. When the Cuyamaca Club ran into financial difficulties in 1960, due to the movement of professional and business elites to the suburbs, Smith took control of this club as well, intending to install it in the twenty-story office building he was planning for the downtown. By 1963 the Cuyamaca Club was comfortably ensconced on the twenty-third and twenty-fourth floors of the United States National Bank Building, with C. Arnholt Smith dropping in for lunch three or four days a week: majestically tanned, wearing his characteristic beige suit and Buster Brown shoes, enjoying a scotch before lunch, followed by a chicken salad sandwich. Such regularity befit Mr. San Diego, as Smith was officially named in 1961 by the Grant Club: banker, real estate power, tuna mogul, baseball team owner, resort developer, director of the convention and visitors bureau, key player in Republican politics (a delegate to several national GOP conventions), chairman of the Arthritis and Rheumatism Foundation, director of the San Diego Symphony; married now to a second wife who loved art and antiques. Aside from a major league baseball franchise, Smith was also in the process of gaining control of the Yellow Cab franchises in San Diego and half a dozen other western cities, a bus company, and the statewide commuter airline Air Cal. Roger Revelle, meanwhile, was also advancing up the ladder of San Diego importance. During the war, Revelle rose to the rank of commander and was decorated by the Secretary of the Navy for research he had conducted and directed on behalf of the Navy and the Division of War Research in San Diego and Washington and, at sea in the Pacific, dealing with the oceanographic aspects of the planned invasion of Japan. At the request of the Navy, Revelle remained on active duty following the war, assigned to Operation Crossroads, planning the first postwar atomic tests on Bikini Atoll, which took him once again to sea. In 1946 Revelle was named commanding officer of the hydrographic office in the Office of Naval Research in Washington. As such, he brought the Navy and the Scripps Institution into close cooperation.

When Revelle returned to Scripps in 1948, he returned as a paragon of San Diego value: a decorated naval officer who had held a series of top-level assignments that had put him at ground zero of the military-academic establishment. Add this to Revelle's marriage to a beautiful local blue blood, the couple's wealth, his commanding personal presence (well over six feet, in superb shape from tennis), and his appointment in 1947 as professor of oceanography and associate director of the Scripps Institution, and a portrait emerges of a figure who could inspire but who was also coming dangerously close to arousing envy among his colleagues. In January 1947, for example, a coterie of senior faculty at Scripps vociferously opposed—to the point of writing directly to UC president Robert Gordon Sproul—the appointment of Revelle to the directorship of the institution when it was first proposed by the then director, the eminent Norwegian oceanographer Harald Sverdrup, when announcing his retirement. Faculty opposition to Revelle succeeded in derailing his appointment as director until 1950.

Despite the presence there of the Scripps Institution, La Jolla was hardly an average academic community. It was, rather, a highly social upper-class enclave on a point north of downtown San Diego that, while technically part of the city, was its own highly self-regarding township with its own postal designation: to be compared to Santa Barbara, Carmel, Palo Alto, and Berkeley in the same time period in its self-contained Tory bohemian aestheticism. If C. Arnholt Smith is to be understood within the context of downtown San Diego, with its self-made men and aspirations toward plutocracy, then Roger Revelle has comparably to be considered within the context of La Jolla.

Anglo-American Protestants, many of them from New England, came into La Jolla at the turn of the century; and from the beginning they envisioned their community as an enclave of cultural value and taste, enlivened by the outdoor life. At the core of the La Jolla identity was the resort metaphor. It was a place for people who had already made or inherited their money and for those who served them. In the first decades of the twentieth century, La Jolla developed as a combination of Carmel and a New England township. It was artsy and bohemian, given to reading circles and the outdoor presentations of Greek and Shakespearean plays in full costume, as well as paying attention to its schools, playgrounds, library, clubs, Presbyterian, Episcopal, and Congregational churches, the landscaping of its near-bare peninsula with a multitude of hedges and trees, the construction of snug cottages, a community bathhouse on the beach, and, at Scripps, a center for oceanographic research.

Gregory Peck was born in La Jolla in April 1916. His father ran the local pharmacy. Peck retained a lifelong interest in his home community. And this suggested the next phase of La Jolla's development, starting sometime in the 1930s and gathering momentum after the Second World War: the evolution of La Jolla, building on its New England base, into a celebrity-oriented enclave, the Hamptons of San Diego if you will, affluent (two blocks of the quaint downtown, called the Village, were devoted to branch brokerage offices) and oriented toward an increasingly glamorous version of the good life. In 1947 Gregory Peck, Mel Ferrer, and Dorothy McGuire established the La Jolla Playhouse, which each summer brought to La Jolla top-ranked Hollywood stars (David Niven, Olivia de Havilland, Jennifer Jones, Ginger Rogers, Tallulah Bankhead, Jose Ferrer, James Mason) eager to keep alive their stage talents and Actors' Equity memberships through little theater. The presence of such stars in La Jolla each summer created a Hollywood–La Jolla connection, impressive to such young La Jollans as Cliff Robertson and Raquel Welch, already attracted to the Business. Dancer Ann Miller and her fiancé, Texas oilman Bill Moss, were married in La Jolla in the mid-summer of 1958, and the resulting mix of show business, Texas money, Hollywood stars, and syndicated journalists (Walter Winchell among them) enlarged the La Jollan formula, with La Jolla becoming a favorite destination for big-ticket Texans.

La Jolla also featured two other little theater groups, the Drury Lane Players and the La Jolla Community Players, together with an art gallery. The La Jolla Beach and Tennis Club grew in glamour and intensity, its combed sands teeming with well-tanned men and women basking in the sunshine. The Beach Club, the La Jolla Country Club, the restaurants and cocktail lounges of the town (Morrie's Grill, La Plaza, the Marine Room), and a growing number of private residences with some of the most elaborate landscaping in California sustained a year-round pageant of golf, tennis, cocktail and dinner parties, benefits, and charity balls. The annual Jewel Ball at the La Jolla Beach and Tennis Club began in the late afternoon with an outdoor cocktail party, at which the formally dressed crowd wore sunglasses, and moved on to dinner and dancing, then fireworks, followed by an early morning swim. The magazine *San Diego*, owned by John Vietor, heir to the Jell-O fortune, covered these events extensively as well as running a regular column devoted to La Jollan comings, goings, and gossip. In early December, Christmas decorations came out in force. According to local agreement, Americans of Jewish background were discouraged, indeed actively prevented, from buying homes in the community.

In this swirl of high life, old and new money, Anglo-American ascendancy, and, at Scripps, internationally respected academic endeavor, Roger and Ellen Revelle were at the top of the A list as embodiments of the best possibilities of life in La Jolla. The 1950s proved a golden age for Revelle as oceanographic investigator and statesman. Thanks to his Navy connections, the Scripps Institution's seagoing fleet was augmented by three new research vessels. Revelle spent a lot of time at sea in the 1950s, supported by grants from the federal government and the Rockefeller Foundation. In the relatively new field of oceanography, each voyage yielded impressive results. It was proven, for example, that the ocean beds were not, as previously thought, as old as the planet itself but were, in many places, formed as recently as one hundred million years ago. An expedition to the central Pacific resulted in the discovery of the previously unknown Mid-Pacific Mountain Range. In 1955 Revelle represented the United States on the International Advisory Committee on Marine Sciences established by UNESCO. Revelle's published research in ocean geology and currents, carbon dioxide and global warming, fisheries, and the disposal of atomic waste—a gamut of topics in a field that was by its very definition interdisciplinary—won him election to the National Academy of Sciences in 1957. Increasingly respected as an expert in scientific policy, he served on a number of important national and international panels and boards concerned with the ocean, the atmosphere, and the environment. He also maintained Washington connections as a consultant to a number of House and Senate committees and the Department of Defense.

Navy officer, scientist, power player, social lion: Roger Revelle emerged in the 1950s as the embodiment of San Diego value, La Jolla style, just as C. Arnholt Smith epitomized the downtown establishment. San Diego was expressed in each of these men, the upper class and the newly arrived, the international scientist and the wheeler-dealer. Each of them, in turn, was furthering the San Diego formula: Smith in the direction of growth, Revelle in the direction of science. It is testimony to the representative nature of each of these men to say that in the 1950s, their respective passions—growth and science—were converging.

San Diego had always been planning for the growth that it knew would eventually come and toward which it remained ambivalent. It took the Navy and the emergency conditions of a world war to secure for San Diego the first phase of a water supply that would allow for the metropolitanization of the region. An aqueduct bringing Colorado River water to the city from Hoover Dam was dedicated in December 1947. Eventually the San Diego County Water Authority, part of the Metropolitan Water District (MWD) since November 1946, reimbursed the Navy and constructed a second pipeline, financed by a bond issue passed in the same election approving the MWD merger and completed in 1954. A third pipeline was completed in 1960, and a fourth put into construction. Thus San Diego, somewhat belatedly in comparison to the rest of Southern California, availed itself of the water resources of the Colorado River made possible by the Hoover Dam and the MWD distribution system.

Other efforts at urbanization, however, did not fare as well, due, in part, to the ambivalence toward urbanism—Los Angelesization it was called—that had been part of the San Diego formula since the early 1900s. In June 1945, thanks in significant measure to the urgings of San Diego planning director Glenn Rick, voters approved a $2 million bond issue to develop the tidelands, marshes, mudflats, and open water of the Mission Bay to the north of the city—2,600 acres in all, with eleven miles of shoreline—as a municipal recreation, hotel, and resort area, a Miami Beach for San Diego, as the *San Diego Union* described it when an additional (and successful) $5 million bond issue for Mission Bay was placed on the ballot in June 1956. But this was for recreation and sports-related tourism, an essential and unambiguous component of the San Diego formula. In April 1947 voters rejected plans for an ambitious city-county administration center on Cedar Street near the harbor; and when it came time to approve a sewer bond issue for $16 million in 1954 to curb pollution of the bay, the voters again said no, despite the fact that swimming in the bay waters was now considered a health hazard. When it came time in 1956 to approve an $8.5 million bond issue to build a downtown civic auditorium and convention hall, designed to attract national conventions, the voters said no in two separate elections. Nor could San Diego bring itself to find a new or supplemental site for its already inadequate Lindbergh Field at harborside. Following the war and prior to the Korean conflict, San Diego had neglected opportunities to expand its airport onto Kearny Mesa in cooperation with the Navy. When the city council looked to North Island in 1956, the Navy refused, recommending instead that Lindbergh Field be expanded onto the southern marshlands of Mission Bay. In 1957 the Civil Aeronautics Administration rejected plans to expand the existing airport to accommodate jet traffic within its present boundaries, a restriction that was eventually lifted. In March 1959, however, Lindbergh Field had its first commercial jet landing. It was unplanned: Fog had prevented a jet passenger plane from landing in Los Angeles.

As San Diegans suburbanized themselves, the interest of voters was turning elsewhere. For three-quarters of a century, San Diego had been centered on its harborside grid. Now, thanks to the automobile, it was expanding in every direction. Like everyone else in Southern California, San Diegans had embraced the automobile with a vengeance, as testified to by the proliferation of roads, highways, freeways, and drive-in movie theaters and restaurants throughout the region. Oscar's Drive-In restaurant on University Avenue was by the 1950s a cherished local landmark, as was the first Jack-in-the-Box, opening in 1951 on El Cajon Boulevard, the main thoroughfare leading into the city. The neon sign announcing the Campus Drive-In near San Diego State—a gigantic drum majorette bedecked as an Aztec—was featured in *Life* as a model of its type. San Diegans did not want their city to be like Los Angeles, but between 1950 and 1970 the metropolitan region grew from 99 to 307 square miles, as a virtually uninterrupted urban area extended from the Mexican border to Camp Pendleton and from the coast as far inland as Escondido. The automobile and the freeway system made this possible. During the war, the streetcar system had carried up to 375,000 passengers a day. By 1949 it was no longer in business. In 1948 the Cabrillo Freeway (State 163) had been punched through Balboa Park, intersecting with Interstate 8 and connecting downtown with the previously undeveloped Mission Valley. Crossing Balboa Park with a freeway had been a controversial decision, given the reverence San Diegans had for this vast tract on what was once the edge of the city, so the state Department of Highways was forced to landscape the Cabrillo Freeway with more than a half million plants and trees to create a scenic parkway; but the park had stood as a barrier to the suburbanization of the city hinterlands, which a rising population was now demanding. By August 1959 visiting social critic Nathan Glazer, writing in *Commentary*, was stating that the extensive road, highway, and freeway system of San Diego, as well as the Navy, provided the key clues to local identity.

However ambivalently, San Diego was in the process of changing its most fundamental image of itself. Ever since the 1870s, San Diego had been a harbor-side city centered on a grid-determined downtown. Such a unity, however, based as it was on the topographical coherence of a harbor-side shore, could by definition not survive metropolitan growth; for as MIT city planners Kevin Lynch and Donald Appleyard would soon be pointing out, the topography of metropolitan San Diego—in contrast to the seashore, plain, mountain, and valley of Los Angeles and the circumscribed peninsula of San Francisco—was a complex confluence of seaside plain, broad valley, mountains, high mesas, and deep canyons that by its very nature fragmented development into distinct, even autonomous, districts. Spread San Diego outward, however, as it was being spread in the 1950s, and it fragmented itself into a myriad of self-reflecting neighborhoods and villages. When in 1941 the United States Housing Authority created the Linda Vista housing project—two thousand permanent homes, one thousand units of temporary housing, 750 dormitories—on four square miles atop Kearny Mesa, some sixteen thousand defense workers and their families found themselves by April 1943 in an isolated development connected to the city water system by one ten-inch pipe and served by one over-clogged road, together with an excruciating scarcity of grocery stores and retail outlets. Not until the late 1940s, after the Linda Vista community had been privatized, was it integrated into the city, although even then it continued to maintain a quasi-autonomy suggestive of future metropolitan development. Similarly, the 3,500-home Clairemont subdivision of 1951 atop Morena Mesa overlooking Mission Bay remained a semi-isolated mesa-top village within the city into the early 1960s.

For the first half of the twentieth century, Mission Valley had remained a river-watered agricultural and dairy region, and certain forces wanted to keep Mission Valley that way, as an agricultural preserve and adjacent greenbelt, with the possibility of some recreational and/or park development. Mission Valley, after all, was a riverbed, hence liable to periodic flooding, as had happened most recently in 1952. Still, C. Arnholt Smith received a zoning variance from the city council to build a baseball stadium there, and, starting in 1953, hotel mogul Charles Brown, who had also secured zoning variances, was developing hotels and motels alongside Interstate 8 (the Town and Country, the Hanalei) in an area later designated Hotel Circle. As San Diego expanded, US 80 (Interstate 8 after 1958) and the intersecting US 395 (later State 163) provided the key freeway links between downtown San Diego and the new communities developing to the north and northeast. In 1957 the strategic location of Mission Valley between old and new San Diego caught the attention of the May Company of Los Angeles as an ideal site for a shopping center. Earlier, in 1952, the May Company had been the anchor tenant in Lakewood Center in Lakewood north of Long Beach, one of the largest shopping malls in Southern California, with, eventually, a hundred stores and a 154-acre parking lot, capable of handling twelve thousand cars. The May Company had similar plans for Mission Valley. Based on preservationist considerations as well as the danger of flooding, city planning director Harry Haeslig and the planning commission rejected the May Company proposal, as did an association of downtown merchants, who argued that the proliferation of shopping centers would change the very nature of San Diego. Residents of the new developments, however, wanted big shopping centers or at least were not radically opposed to them. Ignoring the downtown merchants, the city council unanimously approved an ordinance authorizing the May Company to build its shopping center. By 1961 the May Company had completed in Mission Valley the mother of all shopping centers, surrounded by the mother of all parking lots, and throughout the 1960s Mission Valley, only recently a sylvan enclave, was sub/urbanized into a hotel, retail, stadium, and high-density residential corridor. Four other major shopping centers—College Grove and El Cajon Parkway Plaza to the east, Chula Vista to the south, and Grossmont on Interstate 8—soon made their appearance.

Once an intimate harbor-side city, San Diego had moved outward from its grid-core commercial downtown (Central Business District, Harbor View, Old Town) and its older grid-core residential districts (North Park, South Park, Logan Heights) and coastal communities (La Jolla, Pacific Beach, Mission Beach, Point Loma) to a complexity of mesa-top residential communities (Middletown, Mission Hills, College) and rolling hillside tract developments (Clairemont, University City, Linda Vista, Serra Mesa). Metropolitan San Diego also included once rural settlements overwhelmed by the spreading city (La Mesa, Spring Valley, Lemon Grove, Casa de Oro, El Cajon), industrial and residential satellite cities (Coronado, National City, Chula Vista), corridor ranch residential developments, and rural inland and mountain towns. All things considered, it was an extraordinarily complex in-gathering of communities old and new. Although San Diegans would be loath to have it put that way, San Diego had been recast into the Sunbelt prototype first established by the City of Angels.

Downtown San Diego, meanwhile, was struggling to reinvent itself as a high-rise corporate center. In 1958 San Diego stood fifth in the nation behind New York, Los Angeles, Chicago, and Houston in total volume of downtown construction. In the early 1960s, Home Federal Savings & Loan and C. Arnholt Smith's United States National Bank each built high-rises. In the mid-1960s as well, San Diego at long last got its planned civic center, financed in part by funds borrowed from the city's employee retirement fund, a complex that included an impressive three-thousand-seat civic theater, opening in January 1965. By then, metropolitan San Diego also had a state-authorized (1962) five-city Unified Port District, responsible for the port, the airport, and most harbor activities. This led San Diegans to embark upon a project that had been on their minds for decades now: a bridge from San Diego to Coronado–North Island, which formed the western edge of San Diego Bay. Opening in August 1969, the San Diego–Coronado Bridge—a masterpiece of bridge design: 2.12 miles long, turning ninety degrees in mid-span, at two hundred feet high enough to allow the clearance of an empty aircraft carrier—that gave a Golden Gate Bridge-like finish to the San Diego cityscape.

How to interpret this city, en route through the 1950s to its new identity: a sleepy enclave, a quiet Navy town, now an emergent Sunbelt corporate headquarters, tourist center, and core of what would become by the end of the century the sixth-largest city in the United States? It could be said, through the 1950s, that San Diego was a privileged provincial place: a city, enjoying the cultural amenities of urbanism—an impressive central park with a restored Spanish Revival complex of museums at its center, a world-class zoo, an internationally ranked oceanographic research center, a state college, a private Catholic university, an orchestra, a civic light opera company, visiting performances by the San Francisco Opera and other troupes, a flourishing tradition of little theater—while at the same time remaining (so it told itself frequently) a laid-back kind of a place, blessed with the best climate in the nation.

Perhaps San Diego came closest to its best definition of itself in its collective love of athletics, amateur and professional. San Diegans swam, rode, golfed, and played tennis in impressive numbers. Its roll call of Olympic and other title champions in these fields dated from the early 1900s, men and women who began their careers at Hoover or San Diego High School or otherwise locally, went on to play at San Diego State, then proceeded to win national titles, amateur and professional. The list included Ted Williams, of course, a graduate of Hoover High School, playing for the Padres in 1936 and 1937 before going on to Boston and baseball immortality; rough-water swimmer Florence Chadwick, who thrice prevailed over the English Channel, and tennis star Maureen Connolly, who prevailed at Wimbledon, equally well known; but also Olympian divers Clarence Pinkston and Dutch Smith; basketball champion Milton Phelps, killed when his Navy torpedo bomber went down in World War II; 1948 Olympic broad-jump champion Willie Steele; pole vaulter Bob Gutowski, who broke the world record in April 1957, but also died too young while on active duty with the Marines at Camp Pendleton; boxers Lee Ramage, a heavyweight contender, and Archie Moore, light heavyweight champion of the world; Wimbledon champion Karen Hantze; golfers Gene Littler, who won the U.S. Amateur in 1953 and the U.S. Open in 1961, and Billy Casper, who won the Open in 1959 and 1966; and San Diego Yacht Club Star-boat champions Milt Wegeforth (1938), Gerald Driscoll (1944), Malin Burnham (1945), and Lowell North (1957, 1959, 1960). San Diego fostered athletes because it had the climate for sport twelve months a year and because prowess in sport was a fixed mode of civic distinction and recognition.

As much as they said about San Diego life, however, athletics remained—and properly so—ends in themselves and hence could not bear the burden of interpreting San Diego. While also ends in themselves, art and literature—literature especially—were capable of more directly interpreting the city. The 1930s, continuing into the 1940s, witnessed some first-rate murals work being produced in and for the city by Maynard Dixon and Belle Baranceanu. Sculptor Donal Hord carried the mood of the 1930s and early 1940s into the 1950s through ambitious sculptures representing a fusion of modernism and pre-Columbian art. Hord's continuing viability testified to the fact that an older San Diego identity—that of being the capital of the Spanish Southwest—remained in force: was on the verge, in fact, of a dramatic re-intensification as the cities of the American Sunbelt developed into a new and populous urban tier, and Mexican immigration emerged as a transforming dynamic in Southern California.

Through the 1950s the Mexican American and Mexican immigrant population of San Diego was growing and developing, moving toward that majority it would become by the end of the century. Mexican American San Diego was a self-contained society, centered on the older portion of the city. While not oppressed, it was not favored either. The Mexican American community still retained vivid memories of earlier discrimination, segregation, and the forced repatriations of immigrants and Mexican Americans alike during the early 1930s. In early 1931 the Mexican

American community of Lemon Grove had successfully sued, with the help of the Mexican consulate, when the school board, urged by the chamber of commerce, had tried to segregate Mexican American and Mexican immigrant students into separate school buildings. Some seventy-five Mexican American and Mexican students went on strike until the conflict was favorably resolved by the superior court. Eight years later the Mexican community, largely Roman Catholic, took on Bishop Buddy himself when Buddy replaced Spanish-born, Spanish-speaking priests of the Augustinian Recollect order with Irish-born, non-Spanish-speaking diocesan clergy in a number of Mexican parishes. It was a full-scale revolt, with the Mexican community appealing directly to the Pope via the apostolic delegate in Washington. Buddy enlisted the district attorney and the Immigration and Naturalization Service to put pressure on the dissidents. The bishop won the battle but lost the war when many Mexican American and Mexican immigrant Catholics began to cross the border to Tijuana for marriages, baptisms, and confirmations. Nor did the quarrel, or Buddy's heavy-handed response to it, do him much good in Vatican circles.

Crossing the border for religious services emphasized another still veiled reality in the postwar era: the growing interconnectivity between Southern and Baja California, between San Diego and Tijuana. No border—on an abstract level—was more problematic, even illusory, than the border between Mexico and the United States, between brown and white, Spanish- and English-speaking, affluent and poor. To the Spanish Colonial way of thinking, Baja and Alta California had been a continuity, two phases of the same geographical entity. New Spain and, subsequently, the Republic of Mexico saw San Diego as, potentially, the mid-section capital of the Californias as well as a port city linked overland to Arizona and Mexico via the Old Spanish Trail. Following the settlement of Alta California, El Camino Real began at Veracruz on the Gulf of Mexico, crossed Mexico to Mexico City, proceeded to the west coast of Mexico at San Blas, was linked by ship across the Gulf of California to Baja, proceeded up Baja to San Diego, then continued north to Monterey. In and of itself, then, El Camino Real expressed the interconnectivity of Mexico, Baja, and Alta California. As recently as the 1870s, the United States could have purchased Baja California for a modest price.

Not until the mid-twentieth century, however, would Mexico be able to populate its northern regions, Baja California included. In the meantime, Baja California remained for Southern California an arena for land investment, aqueduct construction, scientific exploration, and recreation. Tijuana began its existence as a scruffy outpost, a town on the frontier of northward migration. In the winter and spring of 1911, during the Mexican Revolution, when Tijuana had between seven thousand and eight thousand people, it captured San Diego's attention rather dramatically. Mexican revolutionaries under the ideological sway of anarchist Ricardo Flores Magón, augmented by IWW Wobblies, a handful of American military deserters, and assorted soldiers of fortune, seized Tijuana from federal defenders by force of arms on 10 May 1911 and raised the red flag of rebellion emblazoned with *Tierra y Libertad*, Land and Liberty. It took a pitched battle on 22 June 1911, bringing the total dead in two battles to more than seventy, including the lieutenant governor of Baja California, for Mexican federal forces to dislodge the rebels.

As Tijuana grew in the years before and after the Second World War, its relationship to San Diego became increasingly complex. Pristine and primal, desert and shoreline, the Pacific on one side, the Gulf of California on the other, Baja California became the unexplored—yet persistently historical—wilderness annex to American Alta: the place to which one sailed to observe the mating of the great gray whales, to explore the marine riches of the Gulf, the Sea of Cortez, as amateur marine biologist John Steinbeck called it, or to excavate Jesuit missions from the seventeenth century. It was also a place to acquire land, cheap and on a vast scale. (The Otis-Chandler dynasty at the *Los Angeles Times* held 832,000 acres in Baja California, extending from Mexicali to the Gulf.) Tijuana became San Diego's playground, whether in the upscale elegance of the Agua Caliente Casino and Racetrack or the bars and bordellos of downtown. The use of Tijuana as sexual playground was especially degrading to the larger question of Mexican identity—but revelatory nevertheless of the unequal relationship between the two communities.

As Tijuana matured as a city, however, it began to assert itself simultaneously as Mexican in sovereignty and Mexican-Californian in culture. By the 1950s the beginnings of a Twin Cities relationship had begun to assert itself, forecasting that time in the mid-twenty-first century when metro San Diego/Tijuana would be a bi-sovereign metropolis, the second most populous urban region on the coast after metropolitan Los Angeles. Anticipating this unity, this Spanish-speaking future, was San Diego's second television station, Spanish-language XETV, Channel 6, from Tijuana, which began broadcasting in January 1953. Channel 6 carried English programs as well, at least for a few years, until another station, XEWT, Channel 12, began broadcasting exclusively in Spanish and XETV followed suit.

One looks in vain, however, for Mexican-related interpretations of San Diego in this era, although San Diego revered its Spanish past and restored its surviving Spanish and Mexican buildings. San Diego also enjoyed Mexican food and in August 1955 the city council set in motion plans for a large-scale *Fiesta del Pacifico* to run the following summer. Produced under the direction of Vladimir Rosing of the New York City Center Opera, its symphony orchestra and hundred-voice choir under the direction of composer (*The Music Man*) Meredith Willson, *Fiesta del Pacifico* filled Balboa Stadium with men and women in Spanish, Mexican, and mid-nineteenth-century American costumes, as it told the story of California from the arrival of Juan Cabrillo in 1540 to the early twentieth century. *Fiesta del Pacifico* was a throwback to a more naïve pre-television time, when such pageants and festivals had proven staples of local civic celebration. Not surprisingly, it failed to yield the income that was promised. Neither San Diegans nor tourists were in the mood to buy Spanish or Mexican costumes. Nor were residents of San Diego all that interested in Spanish and Mexican history, most of them having come to the city in recent times. The pageant stumbled along for three summers before it was scrapped.

Of the ninety-plus Hollywood films to be set in San Diego during the 1940–65 period, one looks in vain for Mexican- or Mexican American–related scenes, actors, or actresses (despite the fact that Raquel Tejada Welch graduated from La Jolla High School in 1958 and that year won the Fairest of the Fair beauty contest in Del Mar). With the exception of a few noir films after the war—*Nightmare Alley* (1947), for example, or the low-budget *Tuna Clipper* (1949) from Monogram—most San Diego–based films ignored civilian San Diego in favor of the Navy, the Marine Corps, even the *Fighting Coast Guard* (1951). That is what made Billy Wilder's *Some Like It Hot* (1959) so welcomed. Its scenes set in or around the Hotel del Coronado suggested San Diego as something other than a military garrison: the kind of place that *San Diego*—the first city magazine in the nation—had been saying San Diego was since October 1948. Put together by ex–New Yorkers Frank Sherwood and the husband-and-wife team of Ed and Gloria Self, and headquartered in its early existence in surplus offices at Convair, *San Diego* saw itself as a talk-of-the-town monthly that would cover San Diego as a sophisticated grown-up city. When Jell-O heir and La Jollan John Vietor became an investor and merged his La Jolla–oriented *Point Magazine* with *San Diego* in September 1955, the monthly began to take on an even brighter sheen, as it expanded its coverage with articles by art and planning critic James Britton, cultural historian James Mills, and *Collier's* and *Saturday Evening Post* veteran Mary Harrington Hall, with Gloria Self covering fashions and an unknown correspondent writing the "La Jolla Is Talking About" column. The magazine also increased its circulation to 14,500 by 1960 and its paid advertising to 865 pages. *San Diego* made contact with a newly arrived and upwardly mobile San Diego readership: college graduates (68 percent), with 30 percent of them holding graduate degrees, 39 percent of them serving on various boards of directors, and all of them bringing home incomes well beyond the national average. *San Diego* established an entirely new magazine genre: a city-based magazine, keyed to an upscale market within the context of the news, interests, gossip, and developing identity of a metropolitan region. By September 1962 there were thirty such magazines operating in the United States, with a centralized advertising office in New York, most of them following the *San Diego* formula.

As of the 1950s, San Diego, city or county, had not inspired much successful locally oriented fiction. The best book, in the literary sense of that term, to come out of San Diego in the prewar period—reporter Max Miller's classic *I Cover the Waterfront* (1932)—was a non-fiction memoir, anchored in reportage. The most distinguished San Diego-area novelist of the 1930s and 1940s, Judy Van der Veer, set her minimalist fictions in the rural backcountry. Erle Stanley Gardner, working in his three-thousand-acre hilltop Rancho del Paisano south of Temecula—dictating up to twenty thousand words a day to three secretaries, four novels under way at any one time, soon to be added to the 107 million Perry Mason volumes already in print in English and sixteen other languages—was socially connected to the San Diego literary community.

Hence the great hope in the first half of the 1950s when San Diego–born and –bred (Hoover High, San Diego State) Oakley Hall produced three novels—*So Many Doors* (1950), *Corpus of Joe Bailey* (1953), and *Mardios Beach* (1955)—asserting San Diego as dense enough sociologically to support fiction in the realist manner of John O'Hara and J. P. Marquand. In October 1956 *San Diego* magazine ran a portfolio of buildings and places mentioned in Hall's fiction, captioned with excerpts from the novels. Two years later, however, Oakley Hall, turning in another direction, produced *Warlock* (1958), an existentialist western set in Arizona. *Warlock* represented a departure toward a larger and more mythic West that would end Hall's career as a San Diego writer. Lawrence Madalena's *Confetti for Gino* (1959)—set in the Italian-American fishing community centered on Our Lady of the Rosary parish, where young men were dealing with the complexities of liberated young women from non-Italian San Diego—carried on the San Diego novel for one more title, before the genre faded from view. While there was nothing so coherent as a La Jolla school of writers, H. H. Lynde, Max Miller, Ted Geisel, Raymond Chandler, and Neil Morgan were living and active as writers in La Jolla through the 1950s, knew each other, and, through Neil Morgan especially, were linked to each other in supportive friendships. The author of a series of nationally focused novels—*Remember Matt Boyer* (1944), the story of an isolationist United States senator; *The Slender Reed* (1949), published in England under the title *No Safe Harbor*; *Which Grain Will Grow* (1952); *The Adversary* (1957)—Helen Huntington (Mrs. Reuben Morgan), who wrote under the name H. H. Lynde, was living quietly in La Jolla through the 1950s. A reserved and well-bred widow, writing each morning by longhand and typewriter, Morgan had honed her craft, in part, as a member of the MacDowell Colony in New Hampshire. She described herself as a realist committed to chronicling the contemporary American scene, and not a regional writer, although *The Adversary* did have a California setting.

So too would it be hard to link Theodore Geisel—Dr. Seuss—to any regional consideration, aside from his residency in La Jolla. The Geisels had moved there from Hollywood in September of 1948, building a home atop Mount Soledad with a view that swept past downtown San Diego to the hills of Baja California and on clear days included the snowy peak of Mount San Jacinto in Palm Springs. Geisel maintained his studio in a tower already on the property, built there in the 1920s to dramatize La Jolla views to prospective real estate clients. He worked there seven days a week, if not on vacation or on the road, across the next four-plus decades of his life, producing his whimsical classics. Helen and Ted Geisel joined the magic circle of La Jolla life centered on Roger and Ellen Revelle, other scientists from the Scripps Institution, the Max Millers, the Neil Morgans, and other jolly assorted haute bourgeoisie of La Jolla. As non-localized as might be his work, Ted Geisel was interested in California. He was particularly worried about its rapid growth, as evidenced in his semi-satirical fable *Whither California?* and his campaign before the La Jolla town council to ban billboards from highways and scenic places.

In *It Must Be the Climate* (1941), Max Miller made an intriguing analysis of San Diego as a place to write. Interestingly enough, it dovetailed with observations that Edmund Wilson had concurrently made in *The Boys in the Back Room* (1940). For some time in the 1930s, Miller wrote, he had been gathering notes for a big book—an epic narrative, perhaps even an historical pageant that could be produced—on California, starting from the Spanish period. "Before the droning of this shoreline, year after year," Miller admitted, "finally knocked ambition out of me, just as it has knocked ambition out of others, I would have liked to put a book on California into story form." The Pacific, Miller suggested (something that Edmund Wilson was suggesting as well), especially the vast Pacific as he had been living by it, day by day in La Jolla, "forever upon an ocean-cliff overlooking timelessness," tended to burn away human considerations.[1] The longer he lived on the lazy shoreline of an ancient coast, Miller admitted, the more difficult it became to sustain an interest in human character as opposed to the timeless drama of nature, the endless repetitive nature of time as expressed in the rolling of the surf onto shore.

Raymond Chandler would agree. La Jolla, Chandler said repeatedly, especially when in his cups, which was frequently, numbed the brain. Yet he himself had been living there since 1946. Chandler and his wife Cissy had discovered La Jolla in the Christmas season of 1939, finding there "that intangible air of good breeding, which one imagines may still exist in New England, but which certainly does not exist any-more in or around Los Angeles."[2] Tiring of Hollywood, Chandler and Cissy, eigh-teen years older than her husband and suffering from fibrosis of the lungs, moved to La Jolla in the late summer of 1946, paying $40,000 for a newly built white stucco corner home at 6005 Camino de la Costa with a view of the Pacific, Point Loma, and the lights of San Diego after sunset. Among other comforts, they furnished it with an oversized Dumont television and a Steinway piano. Across the next decade and more, working each morning for four hours, Chandler would continue his writing career—*The Little Sister* (1949), *The Long Goodbye* (1953), *Playback* (1958)—based in an upscale San Diego community which he basically found congenial yet sati-rized in that affected English Public School style of his that allowed him to reject the country in which he was born and the scenes in which he set his fiction. Chan-dler was on the wagon during these early La Jolla years and making excellent money from the Hollywood he despised: $140,000 from Universal for the unproduced script that would eventually become the novel *Playback*; $750 a week for a wildly success-ful (10.3 million listeners by 1949) radio program, with Philip Marlowe being played by Van Heflin on NBC and Gerald Mohr when the program moved to CBS.

The English novelist Somerset Maugham and director George Cukor visited the Chandlers shortly after they moved to La Jolla. Like other visitors, Maugham and Cukor found them, Cissy especially, quaintly Edwardian in their lifestyle: a domes-tic staff, a personal secretary for Chandler, a formal tea—sandwiches and cake each afternoon at four, served off a silver tray in the living room. Ill and fragile—a kind of Miss Havisham, Maugham noted—Cissy spent most of the time in the rear of the house in quasi-seclusion, waited on by Chandler, but could be coaxed to come to the living room, an ethereal figure emanating the mood of 1910, to play Chopin on the Steinway. The couple was childless but doted on their large black Persian cat named Taki, which they had owned since 1931 and treated as almost human. Like the country squire he had always wanted to be, Chandler relished his afternoon trips in his Oldsmobile to the local shops, where he delighted in kibitzing with the locals—grocers, butchers, garage men, postal clerks, booksellers—from whom he garnered the gossip of the town: material he would employ, obliquely, when he used La Jolla (Esmeralda) as the setting for *Playback*. Being on the wagon made it extremely difficult for Chandler—who suffered from a mixture of shyness and arrogant superiority—to relate socially, and he relished these casual contacts, as he relished his extensive correspondence, which also kept him company.

When he went off the wagon—which was inevitable perhaps, given his lifelong history of heavy drinking—Chandler became much more sociable. Reporter Neil Morgan interviewed Chandler for the *Daily Journal* shortly after Chandler's move to La Jolla, and the two of them became good friends. By the early 1950s, Chandler was a regular in an Inklings-like circle meeting for drinks and conversation at the El Toro Bar adjacent to the La Plaza Restaurant that included Morgan, Miller, Geisel, and crime novelist and screenwriter John Latimer. Chandler also made the acquaintance of Erle Stanley Gardner and was fascinated by Gardner's ability to dictate a novel within a week or ten days. Chandler's drink of choice was the gimlet—two jiggers of gin, one of lime juice, shaken with ice. He held his gin gimlets, drink of the Raj, in a hand covered by a white glove worn to protect his allergy-ravaged skin. If Cissy was feeling up to it, he would take her to La Plaza for dinner. (Chandler refused to join the La Jolla Beach and Tennis Club because it discriminated against Jews.) One evening, so local legend has it, FBI director J. Edgar Hoover was dining at La Plaza with his great and good friend Clyde Tolson and other company, and sent word by a waiter that he would like Chandler to come over to his table and say hello. Chandler sent word back that Hoover was welcome to come over to his table and say hello. A furious Hoover sputtered that he would have Chandler investigated.

Raymond Chandler's La Jolla life can be divided into two phases, pre- and post-Cissy. As long as Cissy was alive, Chandler could control his drinking. Cissy's death in 1954, however, plunged Chandler back into that bleakness, that abyss, that, among other causes, was in some measure a form of post-traumatic stress due to his being the only member of his immediate unit in the Canadian Gordon Highlanders to survive an artillery barrage on the front during the First World War. That bleakness, that abyss, could serve productively as an imaginative matrix for fiction; but in life it could get the best of him—which is to say, drive Chandler to heroic levels of drink—after he lost the stabilizing influence of his wife. The last years of Raymond Chandler's life constituted a downward spiral of gin gimlets (for which he had Rose's lime juice delivered to his house by the case), a bottle of scotch a day, and wine with meals. Not surprisingly, he began to experience blackouts on a regular basis and showed signs of alcoholic dementia. Neil Morgan did the best he could to watch over Chandler in these years, getting him into rehab after one particularly ferocious bender. On his last of a number of trips to the hospital—this on 23 March 1959, to the Scripps Clinic in La Jolla—Chandler contracted pneumonia and died three days later at the age of seventy.

Chandler's La Jolla friend Neil Morgan stood at the center of the literary circle meeting at the El Toro Bar in the early 1950s. Morgan was Raymond Chandler's friend, Max Miller's friend, Theodore Geisel's friend and co-biographer (along with Morgan's wife Judith), and the friend and co-biographer (again with Judith Morgan) of Roger Revelle, La Jollans all and figures expressive of San Diego's aspirations and prospects in the postwar era. Morgan was also highly connected to the downtown establishment, including a friendly acquaintance with C. Arnholt Smith and the other oligarchs and politicians of the period. Like his counterpart Herb Caen in San Francisco, Neil Morgan—as reporter, columnist, social commentator in a number of well-received books, newspaper editor, and celebrity figure in his own right—was in these years in the early stages of a six-decade career as the prime interpreter of the San Diego experience. Appropriately, for someone so important to the interpretation of San Diego, as it developed, Neil Morgan was a newcomer, brought to San Diego as a young officer by the United States Navy during the war, after graduating from Wake Forest College in North Carolina, and serving a stint as assistant state editor for the *Raleigh News and Observer*. Released from the service, Morgan returned to Raleigh for a total of two days before deciding that he preferred to take his chances in San Diego. Hitching a ride back to the coast on a military flight, he took his discharge and went to work for Clinton McKinnon's *Daily Journal*, a Democratic paper with a lively interest in arts, culture, and the local scene. Admittedly, Morgan later remembered, he at first found San Diego a small city and more than a little on the quiet side. It was, he believed, basically a city of migrants from Midwestern and Southern small towns who wanted to keep it that way. Over time, Morgan had the opportunity to chronicle in the "Crosstown" columns he filed in the *Daily Journal* and, after 1950, in the *Evening Tribune* the evolution of San Diego into something else: not yet a big city, he admitted, but the Lisbon of the Pacific Coast: a smaller city, that is, slightly out of the way, modest in its expectations, protective of its privacy, but complete in its urban amenities and spectacularly situated. Morgan was a journalist, working on deadline, but he frequently caught the poetry of San Diego—its relationship to the sea, the sapphirine hue of the city at sunset, its winter rain squalls—along with the honky-tonk of the sailor- and Marine-oriented parts of the downtown. Like Herb Caen in San Francisco, Morgan became himself part of the establishment—a long-term Mr. San Diego—and a tireless socializer on the La Jollan scene.

The San Diego Neil Morgan was covering was by the mid-1950s staking its economy on aviation and the Cold War. Such an orientation intensified San Diego's existing relationship to science and technology. This intensification, in turn, prompted Roger Revelle and others to push for an expanded Scripps Institution, which led to the establishment of a comprehensive University of California campus at La Jolla and stimulated the ancillary founding of a number of other science and technology enterprises, beginning with the Salk Institute. As Roger Revelle phrased it, San Diego was en route to becoming the Boston of the Pacific Coast, a city keyed to science, technology, and biotech; this, in turn, as Neil Morgan would later point out, changed the nature of the city.

In November 1941 Consolidated Aircraft of San Diego—responding to fears that England would fall and that the United States would hence need to be able to bomb Germany from the American mainland—had developed plans for a gigantic bomber prototype, the XB-36, designed to carry its ten-thousand-pound payload up to twelve thousand miles at a top speed of 450 miles per hour. When England did not fall, and Consolidated ran into design problems, the project was put on hold. After Vultee and Consolidated merged into Convair in 1943, the project was eventually revived, and a prototype was first flown on 8 August 1946, the largest aircraft ever to fly. Designated the B-36, its six Pratt and Whitney piston engines augmented by four jet engines mounted under its wings, the lumbering B-36 served as the workhorse of the Strategic Air Command throughout the 1950s.

Designing, manufacturing, and testing the B-36 got Convair executives to start thinking about commercial jet transportation. For short hauls, Convair—functioning as an autonomous unit of General Dynamics since April 1954—had already produced the extraordinarily successful two-propeller-engine Convair 240, which it sold to airlines throughout the world. Even more ambitiously, Convair began to develop a medium-range, four-jet passenger plane, the Convair 880, scheduled to be put into service in the early 1960s. It was intended to be the largest, fastest, and safest passenger jet in existence, and, Convair executives hoped, it would out-compete Boeing's proposed 707 and Douglas's proposed DC-8 in a growing worldwide commercial market. Convair even had a client for the 880, Howard Hughes of Trans World Airlines, who in June of 1956 ordered thirty 880s for TWA. Hughes constantly interfered with design and development and was short of cash. It took him until December 1960 to obtain financing, which meant that Convair had to bear the burden of three and a half years of development costs with no money up front. Equally bad, American Airlines reneged on its order for the 990, a more advanced version of the 880, although it eventually ordered fifteen planes. All this—combined with technical difficulties, problems at the executive level, and tough competition from Boeing and Douglas—resulted in the failure of Convair to capture the jet passenger market, which led, in turn, to a $425 million loss by Convair in the early 1960s, surpassing the hit Ford Motor Company had taken on the Edsel. In May 1965 a reorganized General Dynamics transferred its airplane manufacturing elements to Fort Worth, Texas, and focused Convair–San Diego on space and missile development. In 1957 Convair–San Diego had employed 32,400 people. By 1965 it was employing 3,300.

In aerospace, by contrast, General Dynamics/Convair was achieving success. In 1956 Convair scored big: a multi-million-dollar Air Force contract, kept secret until the following year, to design, build, test, and deliver the Atlas, an intercontinental ballistic missile, capable of carrying an atomic warhead across either ocean in slightly more than thirty minutes. To serve this contract, Convair built a state-of-the-art plant on Kearny Mesa east of Highway 395: modern in its steel-and-glass buildings, resembling a university campus more than a warfare center. In contrast to the 880 project on the shoreline below, the Atlas missile project atop Kearny Mesa was a go, with the first Atlas rocket being tested on 11 June 1957. When the USSR launched *Sputnik* into space on 4 October 1957, the space race was on, which meant the further development of the Atlas rocket for space flight. A San Diego–built Atlas rocket took Alan Shepard into sub-orbital flight in May 1961. The following year, on 20 February 1962, John Glenn rode an Atlas rocket into space, circling the earth three times.

Roger Revelle of the Scripps Institution, meanwhile, had been arguing that the University of California should expand the Scripps Institution into a full-fledged campus. Revelle had Caltech in mind as a model: a cluster of science- and technology-oriented research schools and institutes, keyed primarily to the interests of faculty and graduate students. Such a campus, he believed, could be easily grafted onto the Scripps Institution of Oceanography. Revelle prepared a memorandum to this effect for distribution to the Scripps faculty in March 1954, which he broadened at the request of the UC regents into a larger report. Revelle did not envision the UC expansion in San Diego as a comprehensive campus, committed to the teaching of undergraduates and to the social sciences and humanities as well as science, engineering, and technology. He was advocating, rather, a focused, top-down model. Critical masses of research-oriented scientists, he stated in a speech at Princeton in December 1958, were transforming science, hence the world. An expanded San Diego campus should stay focused on research.

Across town, at their Spanish Revival campus atop Montezuma Mesa, the faculty and staff of San Diego State College breathed a sigh of relief. They did not need the competition from a UC campus. Founded in 1897 as a state normal school and brought to its present campus site on a promontory overlooking Alvarado Canyon in 1931, San Diego State was the school of necessity for the upwardly mobile and/or academically challenged of the region: the place for blue-collar kids or those whose grades were not competitive enough for Stanford, Berkeley, or UCLA. Given these restrictions, it was remarkable how vibrant an institution San Diego State managed to become: how urban in its feel, in fact, and staffed by such scholars as California historian Abraham Nasatir and physicist Louis Smith, who managed to remain productive as researchers despite their heavy teaching schedules. As in the case of low-cost urban colleges across the nation, most of the area's politicians and judges had gone to San Diego State, as well as such notables as Admiral Eugene Wilkinson, the first skipper of the *Nautilus*, celebrity broadcaster Art Linkletter, and Raquel Welch.

In 1952 another undergraduate institution, Balboa College, was reorganized as the Methodist-affiliated California Western University and relocated to a newly constructed campus atop the Point Loma peninsula. Noting these developments—the success of San Diego State, the founding of California Western—the regents of the

University of California, considering the population growth in the region, began to envision for San Diego a full-fledged, comprehensive university campus departing from Revelle's Caltech model. When such a proposal surfaced in the late 1950s, San Diego State, California Western, and even UCLA dropped their support.

Revelle persisted, advancing his cause on a number of top-down corporate, political, and academic fronts. Thanks in significant measure to Revelle's lobbying of the San Diego Chamber of Commerce, John J. Hopkins, chairman of Convair and General Dynamics, pledged $1 million to the proposed institution. More, he announced plans to build his own $10 million atomic research center atop Torrey Pines Mesa. (Dedicated in July 1956, the laboratory would eventually spin off some fifty companies.) Revelle's friend Fleet Admiral Chester Nimitz, a longtime UC regent, announced that he was solidly behind the project, citing the importance of keeping the United States competitive in science and technology with the Soviet Union. The San Diego City Council chimed in. On 20 August 1958 city council members—thoroughly lobbied by the oligarchy, including Roger Revelle—voted to put a proposition on the ballot offering 450 acres of pueblo lands to the University of California for the development of the new campus. That same month, Revelle was named director of the newly announced Institute of Technology and Engineering at Scripps. In November, the proposition passed. The proposed institute, en route to becoming a comprehensive university, now had its campus. Nobel Prize–winning chemist Harold Urey, discoverer of heavy hydrogen, arrived in September 1958, recruited by Revelle from the University of Chicago as part of his of top-down strategy. By the end of 1960, were anyone outside academic or political circles asked who would be the first chancellor of the University of California at San Diego, the obvious answer would have been Roger Revelle. Those in the know, however, would not be so sure. In 1950 Revelle had openly lobbied against the loyalty oath being demanded of the UC faculty. This had especially offended conservative San Diego oligarch James Archer. Revelle and Archer had quarreled over the oath through a boozy all-night encounter at Archer's home in La Jolla, and Archer had a long memory, a decade-long memory, in fact, declaring himself opposed to Revelle's appointment as chancellor: an opposition that reverberated in Sacramento circles. Other La Jollans were opposed to Revelle because of a number of speculative land deals he had personally made in the area, anticipating, they suggested, rising land prices once a full-fledged university was established.

Revelle had an even more formidable opponent in regent Edwin Pauley, an independent oilman and real estate developer who chaired the regents in the late 1950s. Pauley was a Democrat, with excellent connections to Governor Edmund G. (Pat) Brown. The exact cause of his opposition to Revelle never fully surfaced. Initially Pauley had been friendly to Revelle, but the friendship had cooled, Revelle later remembered, when Revelle had refused to accompany Pauley on a polar-bear-hunting expedition to Alaska. Whatever the cause—simple envy, perhaps; Revelle's patrician style, galling to a self-made Indiana-born oilman; the declined invitation to hunt polar bears—Pauley was implacably opposed by the late 1950s not only to Revelle but to the expanded campus that represented Revelle's most cherished ambition. Among other things, Pauley claimed that noise from jets landing at nearby Miramar Naval Air Station made the La Jolla site unsuitable for a university campus. Pauley retained Los Angeles architect Charles Luckman to argue such a case before the regents. Revelle, however, had in hand a report Luckman had written some years earlier stating that noise from Miramar would prove no threat to an expanded Scripps Hospital. Believing that he had checkmated Revelle, Pauley called on Luckman to give his report. Luckman went on at length, citing evidence that flight paths to Miramar would destroy the peace and quiet of the proposed campus. When Luckman sat down, it seemed that the La Jolla site was a goner. UC president Clark Kerr, however, tipped off by Revelle, read aloud from the Scripps Hospital report, arguing against debilitating noise over the site from Miramar. "Who wrote this report?" Pauley asked. "Charles Luckman," Kerr replied. An awkward silence gripped the room. The La Jolla location was never re-questioned.[3] Humiliated, Pauley took his case against Revelle and the UC San Diego campus to Sacramento, in particular to his good friend Governor Brown.

The bad vibes created by Pauley against Revelle were having their effect, and so was opposition from a number of Revelle's colleagues at Scripps. In 1948 faculty opposition had delayed Revelle's appointment as director. Now, with the prospect of an expanded campus in view, the anti-Revelle coalition within Scripps re-formed and began to broadcast its message. Revelle was a haphazard administrator, the group claimed. He made decisions unilaterally, without consulting. He was more interested in his national and international commitments than his local position, as evident from his flying into San Diego from some distant place at midnight, dictating correspondence and memoranda all day, flying out that night. And, although this was never openly stated, he was too rich, too social, too privileged in his style and demeanor. He could have appointed Revelle, UC president Kerr admitted three decades later, but he would have had to put his own job on the line to do so, and, given the strength of the opposition, the situation would not have stabilized. The regents would continue to be bombarded by back-channeling Revelle dissidents. Telling Roger Revelle that he would not be the first chancellor of UCSD, Kerr later recalled, was one of the most difficult things he had ever had to do as president of UC. "Roger," Kerr admitted, "deserved it."[4]

In February 1961 Kerr and the regents turned instead to thirty-nine-year-old Herbert York, a Manhattan Project *Wunderkind* who directed the Lawrence Livermore Laboratories, followed by a stint as chief scientist of the Advanced Research Projects Agency of the office of the Secretary of Defense, followed by an appointment from President Eisenhower as director of research and engineering for the Department of Defense. York was a classic Cold War academic warrior. Revelle knew and respected him—and flew to Washington to offer his support. For some time, Revelle had had inklings that his cause was waning. On 7 June 1960, in a memo redolent of the classic kiss-off, Kerr notified Revelle that he was appointing a UC vice president to take charge of all plans for expanding the La Jolla campus. "The University long will be indebted to you," Kerr wrote Revelle, "for your great contribution in leading the initial stages of its growth at La Jolla. Please accept our grateful thanks." Following York's appointment, Revelle wrote a letter to Kerr in which he praised York as a bright man and an administrator of wide experience, but unproven as a leader. "For the past eleven years," Revelle noted, "I have been leader of one of the University's campuses, and, for many people in the San Diego area, the personal symbol of the University's presence.... To be superseded now, and to lose that independence, may affect me personally in such a way that I cannot continue to serve the University effectively at La Jolla."[5]

Revelle agreed to stay on as director of Scripps. But the hurt persisted. In September 1961, he took a leave of absence to serve in Washington as science adviser to the Secretary of the Interior. As might be expected, Revelle rose rapidly in the Kennedy administration and served on a number of national and international projects. Upon his return to Scripps in July 1963, Kerr created for Revelle the previously non-existent position of university-wide dean for research, with an office in University Hall in Berkeley. After three years as chancellor, York resigned for reasons of health. Clark Kerr had a number of names on his desk to replace York, who wished to return to the faculty. Among them was Secretary of State Dean Rusk, presidential adviser and former Harvard dean McGeorge Bundy, and Roger Revelle. At a dinner in San Diego in honor of James Archer, a group of San Diego businessmen cornered Kerr and argued against Revelle's appointment. In recent testimony on Capitol Hill, they complained, Revelle had described San Diego as "as far from being an intellectual center as one could get."[6] Rejected for the second time, Revelle accepted the Richard Saltonstall Professorship of Population Policy at Harvard, where he served for the next twelve years as director of the Center for Population Studies. Roger and Ellen Revelle fit quite easily into Harvard, Cambridge, and Boston social circles. His friend Neil Morgan continued to cover and interpret the city that Roger Revelle had left behind.

As envisioned by Revelle in his Boston of the Pacific Coast comparison, the multiplying effects of the new UCSD campus on San Diego were soon evident. By 1964 UCSD had two Nobel laureates and thirteen Academy of Science members on its faculty. Soon the Salk Institute for Biological Studies, established alongside the university by polio vaccine perfector Jonas Salk, would be ensconced on North Port Torrey Pines Road in La Jolla in an architecturally stunning complex designed by Louis Kahn. In time, stimulated by UCSD and the Salk Institute, San Diego exfoliated in research institutes and corporate laboratories devoted to biotechnology. Faced with an influx of Jewish faculty and constrained, eventually, by state law, La Jolla dropped its anti-Jewish real estate covenants and club restrictions. Bagels, Neil Morgan could report by the end of the 1960s, were now on sale in the bakery department at Jurgensen's, the upscale La Jolla market. A new kind of newcomer, moreover, was arriving in the city: not the small-town midwesterners and southerners of a previous generation but urban academics with advanced degrees, liberal political opinions, and upscale tastes.

By this time, Bishop Charles Buddy was long gone, having in July 1963 been abruptly removed from authority by Vatican officials concerned with reports from certain San Diego clergy that the Fortress on the Hill, as Buddy called his university on Alcalá Park, was soaking up too much revenue. Buddy denounced the Irish-born priests who had denounced him to the Vatican as "the illegitimate descendants of Judas Iscariot." Still, it was a very rare thing for an American bishop to be thus removed from office, and it humiliated Buddy, who had presided for so long as Catholic bishop of the city.[7]

C. Arnholt Smith, Mr. San Diego, managed to hang on a lot longer: co-owner of a major league baseball team, schmoozing with President Eisenhower and, a decade later, spending election evening in November 1968 in the company of his longtime friend soon-to-be president-elect Richard Nixon, who considered San Diego his lucky city, watching the returns on television. It was Smith's last hurrah. On Wednesday, 16 April 1969, the *Wall Street Journal* published an article disclosing a host of irregularities in the relationship between the United States National Bank and Westgate-California. Smith, it was alleged, was using the bank as a secret source of cash for his many ventures and buying off bank investigators by offering them cushy jobs. On 18 October 1973, the United States National Bank went into receivership, the biggest bank collapse since the Great Depression. By July 1974 Smith was facing a federal grand jury indictment on twenty-five felony criminal counts, alleging the manipulation of $27.5 million in loans through the now-defunct bank. At age seventy-five, Mr. San Diego was facing up to 125 years in prison. Smith was later sentenced to three years for income tax evasion and grand theft, a sentence that was reduced to a year in deference to his age and ill health. After nearly a decade of appeal, C. Arnholt Smith served seven months at the San Diego County honor camp, where he occupied his days tending roses.

4

Baghdad by the Bay

Herb Caen's San Francisco

B Y 1950 a new identity, Baghdad by the Bay, being advanced by newspaper columnist Herb Caen, was gaining strength in San Francisco. The composite identities of the past did not disappear. The myths and realities they expressed remained. Yet newly arriving San Franciscans wanted a new narrative, a postwar story to tell about themselves, which Herb Caen and other writers were happy to provide. By 1960 San Francisco stood secure in this new formulation. A Republican city had become Democratic. Bohemia had yielded to café society. The Second World War had replaced the Earthquake and Fire of 1906 as defining event. Charm and enchantment had taken an equal place alongside a sense of the past. The Queen of the Golden West, the Paris of the Pacific, had become Baghdad by the Bay.

The Baghdad metaphor had as its first premise a sense of enchantment, of San Francisco being an alternative to something else, to some other place, to another way of living American life. The first premise of this identity was beauty in terms of site, weather, and urban fabric. San Francisco was—so stated the Baghdad by the Bay formulation—a city so beautiful, so favored by nature and history, that it was not quite real and hence offered newcomers a setting in which to remake themselves anew: to leave Cleveland (it was always Cleveland, poor Cleveland, that served as the place left behind) and start a new and better life.

Few would quarrel with the notion that San Francisco was beautiful. That was, perhaps, the most important thing one could say about it. As a totality, as a marriage of site and urban fabric, the city was the best symbol of itself: a hilly peninsula (forty-two hills in all, ten of them dominant) encompassing 46.38 square miles, with the Pacific on its western edge and on its northern and eastern edges one of the great bays of the planet. Two earthquake faults swept laterally from Fort Point to Hunters Point on the north, from Land's End past City College Mound in the southeast.

The peninsula itself was hilly in its central and northeastern quadrants. It rested on great deposits of serpentine rock and volcanic greenstone. Rolling savannahs dominated its northwestern edge. Sand dunes characterized its Pacific quadrant, culminating in Golden Gate Heights, a soaring sandstone and chert redoubt. Lagoons and marshes watered its northern edge, and a lake rested on its southern border. Every kind of imported tree grew in such an environment, the Australian eucalyptus especially; but two native trees, the Monterey pine and the Monterey cypress, their Dantesque grandeur silhouetted against the sky, provided the city with its most signature statement. On the western edge there was always the roaring of the surf breaking relentlessly onshore, treacherous in its undertows and currents. The Bay, by contrast, seemed calmer although its currents, equally powerful, could run with even greater force.

Fog provided San Francisco with its most signature statement as far as weather was concerned: fog that muffled the night in stillness, save for the steady lament of foghorns or the cries of foraging seagulls in the early morning. Fog could be light and wispy, speckling the sunlight like a white gauze, or so heavy that it registered as rain. Prevailing westerlies, moving across ocean currents, pushed the fog across the peninsula on rivers of wind through coastal gaps at Muir Woods, Tennessee Valley, the Golden Gate, and San Bruno. Beginning in late spring and continuing through the summer, layers of warm air from the interior created an overhead barrier of heat that stabilized the fog over large portions of the city. The coldest winter he ever spent, Mark Twain is reported to have said, was the summer he spent in San Francisco.

Over time, Americans had on this site constructed—then re-constructed after April 1906—a white, pastel, and Camembert city (so Edmund Wilson described it in December 1946), rising like Atlantis from the sea, linked to its hinterlands by two great bridges (one of them, the Golden Gate, among the engineering and artistic marvels of all time) and graced by some of the most expressive architecture in the nation. In 1847 surveyor Jasper O'Farrell imposed a grid directly upon the hilly topography; hence the streets of San Francisco at once defied topography and enhanced it by rising dramatically to the horizon until the Bay came in view. In the reconstruction of the city following the Earthquake and Fire of April 1906, O'Farrell's grid held, and was augmented by a grand city hall and civic center inspired by a City Beautiful plan presented to the city just days before the earthquake by Daniel Hudson Burnham. In time, a number of public squares and plazas—Union Square at the core of the city, most dramatically, but Washington Square as well in the North Beach, together with Alamo Square in the Hayes Valley, Lafayette Park in Pacific Heights, and Buena Vista Park in the Haight-Ashbury—would open up the crowded streetscapes in which house stood adjacent to house on the narrow fifty-vara lots inherited from the Mexican era.

From an aesthetic perspective, the Baghdad by the Bay, Arabian Nights comparison—first introduced almost casually by Herb Caen in a *Chronicle* column on 1 October 1940, following a catalog of atmospheric San Francisco places—was not that far-fetched. Of Alsatian Jewish ancestry, born (1916) and raised in Sacramento, Caen had moved to San Francisco in 1936, an internal émigré with a taste for newspapering. From 1936 to 1938, Caen wrote a radio column for the *Chronicle*. In July 1938 he began "It's News to Me," a talk-of-the-town column for the same paper. With the exception of the years he served in England and France as an Army Air Forces public relations officer during the war, Caen's column—inspired by Walter Winchell, with a rat-a-tat-tat plethora of items—would run in the *Chronicle* (Caen moved it to the *Examiner* for most of the 1950s) until his death in 1997. When Caen was awarded a specially designated Pulitzer Prize for his fifty-eight years of columnizing, he was described as the voice and conscience of San Francisco. Already, by 1941—to judge from the collection of his columns issued that year by the *Chronicle* under the title *This Is San Francisco*—Caen commanded the town: was indeed depicted on the cover of this publication as an oversized figure bestriding the city. At age twenty-five, the outsider—the junior college dropout, by his own description, from Sacramento—had become the ultimate insider, the preeminent citizen of the city.

How did this happen? Caen was, first of all, an assiduous newspaperman. For each day's column (he wrote six a week for most of his career), Caen assembled dozens of items with the assistance of his longtime aide and researcher Jerry Bundsen, which either he or Bundsen scrupulously fact-checked before using. Second, Caen was a first-rate writer—capacious, inventive, clever, clear and frequently brilliant of phrase—who had gotten his start in an era when American journalists often edged into literature. Caen was also a drummer, with an encyclopedic appreciation of big band music, Benny Goodman especially, and a high regard for virtuoso performances on the skins. With *Front Page* panache—in shirtsleeves, his tie loosened, a cigarette at the ready—Caen pounded out his daily columns on an upright Royal typewriter; and something of the music of that machine—crisp, staccato, rhythmic, like a drummer backing a smoothly playing jazz combo—seeped into his prose.

Caen knew intuitively, almost from the time he arrived in San Francisco and certainly by the postwar era, that the city would require a new identity, a new myth. Had Caen surrendered himself totally to high provincial San Francisco, he might have become a talented antiquarian. His formidable intelligence, however, was free of all such mindsets, thanks in part to his truncated education. Nostalgia and, to a lesser extent, history were some of the tools he used, but he could never be seduced by them as ends in themselves. It was the present that Herb Caen wanted—the ever-present, ever-changing, ever-engaging, ever-fascinating present—and the present was telling him by the late 1940s that the war had unsettled the provincial certainties of San Francisco and the nation, and that the generation that had won the war now wanted the good life, now wanted its time in the sun, and that hundreds, then thousands of them were choosing San Francisco or its immediate environs as the place to find it. Providing them with a myth, an identity, a story line, was a sure ticket to journalistic success. Columnizing was a form of entertainment, true; but properly employed—had not Walter Winchell showed this so clearly?—it was also a slipstream to influence for the Sackamenna Kid, as Caen described himself.

First, Caen had to colonize high provincial San Francisco by assimilating, as much as possible, its themes and identities. *The San Francisco Book* (1948), Caen's first collection of postwar columns, presents San Francisco with an exactitude equal to the accompanying black-and-white photographs of Max Yavno. Although Caen employs the Baghdad by the Bay metaphor in his preface, he rarely, if ever, returns to it. This is a no-nonsense guide to a high provincial city, not a rhapsodic love song to Baghdad by the Bay. Caen ends the book, in fact, with a quote from George Sterling, the poet laureate of pre-Baghdad high provincial San Francisco. The very next year, however, the Baghdad by the Bay comparison emerges in full force in a collection of postwar columns bearing that name and representing a transformation of high provincial materials and themes: a restructuring by a onetime outsider who was now the quintessential Mr. Insider at the top of his game. *Baghdad by the Bay* (1949) was succeeded by *Baghdad, 1951* (1950) and *Don't Call It Frisco* (1953), anthologizing a stream of columns in which Caen has successfully fused old and new identities.

In the opening and closing essays of *Baghdad by the Bay*, Caen attempts to do for San Francisco what on a more ambitious level the English writer Lawrence Durrell would soon be doing for Alexandria: fuse the city, that is—people, places, sunlight, fog, seabirds, and bridges—into an alembic of magic memory: make of San Francisco a unified symbol, an image in the mind, a work of art. "That is some of San Francisco," writes Caen at the conclusion of one of his poetic catalogs. "That, plus a thousand other things, blended in with the mixed-up moods of the city—the old landmarks and the brave new plans, the battered traditions and the newcomers that never heard of them, the familiar hills and the unfamiliar problems that dwarfed them. And always the Bay, always the restless fog, always the people running round as though they knew what they were doing—but always glad they're doing it in San Francisco."[1]

The business of such a busy city was exactly that, business. Throughout the 1950s, the economy of San Francisco remained anchored on such traditional high provincial pylons as manufacturing; banking, law, and insurance; shipping, receiving, and freight forwarding; corporate and governmental administration; and food processing, retail, and hotels, with only the last, hotels, suggesting the tourism that would become the lead element in the economy by 1962. In times past, San Francisco had functioned as the dominant manufacturing center for California and the Far West. Between 1939 and 1947, however, San Francisco lost 182 manufacturing companies. Planning economist Mel Scott described this process—Alameda County gaining two hundred manufacturing entities in the same period, Santa Clara County gaining more than one hundred—as industrial dispersion. Census 1950 revealed that only 16.9 percent of the San Francisco workforce was in manufacturing. Still, a significant number of San Franciscans were earning a good living making things with their hands: jeans for Levi Strauss in the Mission district, heavy machinery for the Pelton Water Wheel Company south of Market, mattresses for Simmons at the base of Potrero Hill, and locks for Schlage in Visitacion Valley. Related to this manufacturing sector were thousands of jobs in canning (S&W Fine Foods, Del Monte), brewing (Pabst's, Burgermeister, Lucky Lager, Hamm's, Acme, Anchor Steam), spices (A. J. Schilling, Armanino Farms), coffee (MJB, Folgers, Hills Brothers), candy (Ghirardelli, Blum's). These were steady and reasonably good-paying jobs for ordinary workers, most of them unionized, in companies of local ownership.

The Port of San Francisco, together with the affiliated piers along the Carquinez Strait and Oakland waterfront, remained in flourishing condition. Steamship companies such as American President, Matson, and Dollar ran extensive operations, with Matson serving the profitable Hawaiian tourist market with its *Matson* and *Lurline* liners, and Crowley Maritime dominating the tugboat business for the entire Pacific Coast. During the Korean War and its aftermath, the military maintained extensive shipping services out of the sheds and piers at Fort Mason fronting San Francisco Bay. To the southeast, Hunters Point remained a busy shipping, receiving, and repair facility for the Navy. Longshoreman Eric Hoffer, already a published author of national reputation, had been working the docks of San Francisco since 1943. Hoffer's diaries reveal a steady succession of assignments on the Embarcadero: the *Lurline*, Grace Line ships, freighters from the U.K., Denmark, the Netherlands, Norway, West Germany, Chile, New Zealand, South Korea. The entire Embarcadero was served by freight trains that entered the city from the south and skirted the shoreline, loading and unloading freight. The very passage of these trains in full view of Telegraph Hill and the downtown suggested the continuing industrial vitality of the port, although since 1950 shipping tonnage had been slipping behind the Port of Los Angeles. While a profitable tourist attraction since the 1930s, graced with some of the best restaurants in the city (Scoma's, Alioto's, DiMaggio's, Sabella's, Tarantino's, the Franciscan), Fisherman's Wharf remained a collection of working piers for the still vital Wharf-based San Francisco fishing fleet (sole, salmon, sea bass, the indigenous sand dab, Dungeness crab) and the shoreside fish-icing and -packing sheds where families such as the Lazios and Aliotos were in the second, even third, generation of the fish business. Throughout the 1940s and 1950s, blue-collar San Franciscans could afford a life. They could buy an automobile and a home in the Richmond, Sunset, Mission, Eureka Valley, Noe Valley, Excelsior, or Visitacion Valley districts. As of 1949 San Francisco ranked fourth among the twenty largest cities in the nation for family income. Blue-collar culture was showing early signs of an eventual decline, but it was still part of the social, cultural, and political structure of the city.

So were the thousands of white-collar jobs connected to governmental and corporate administration. San Francisco sustained an imposing federal presence—courts, administrative agencies, the Federal Reserve Bank, Headquarters Sixth Army in the Presidio, district headquarters for the Army Corps of Engineers on New Montgomery Street, numerous naval and Coast Guard installations, Headquarters Twelfth Marine District on Treasure Island—each of these agencies generating white-collar employment. State government was also noticeably present, despite the fact that the capital was officially in Sacramento. The state supreme court and the state public utilities commission sat in San Francisco. And since San Francisco was both a city and a county, local government sustained a near-complete array of city and county services, employing thousands.

The world's largest bank, the Bank of America, was headquartered in San Francisco, as were Wells Fargo, the Bank of California, founded in 1864 (and still the favored bank of old families), the Hibernia Bank (1859), the bank of choice of the Irish Catholic community, and the Crocker-Anglo bank formed in February 1956 by the consolidation of two earlier institutions. In addition to a Federal Reserve Bank, San Francisco had its own United States Mint, ensconced atop a rocky promontory in the center of the city. The roll call of corporations maintaining their headquarters in the city—Standard Oil of California, the Southern Pacific, Transamerica, Crown Zellerbach, Levi Strauss, Fireman's Fund, Bechtel, Stauffer Chemical—together with the headquarters of two giant regulated public utilities, Pacific Gas & Electric and Pacific Telephone & Telegraph, further testified to the continuing vitality of San Francisco as the corporate power center of the Far West and a white-collar job machine. These were venerable companies, many of them founded in the Gold Rush and its immediate aftermath, companies with national and international reach and reputations. The Bank of America, for example, had long been globalizing itself across Asia and Europe. Founded in 1863, Fireman's Fund Insurance in 1957—a year after it had settled numerous claims related to the sinking of the *Andrea Doria* off Nantucket, drowning fifty-one passengers—opened a ten-acre campus headquarters on California Street atop Laurel Hill. There executives would soon be processing claims relating to the death from heart attack in November 1958 of actor Tyrone Power on the set of *Solomon and Sheba* in Madrid, which threatened to sink Twentieth Century–Fox, and the fire at Our Lady of Angels School in Chicago in December, in which ninety-five children and nuns lost their lives.

Like so many of these companies and corporations, the retail sector serving high provincial San Francisco was dominated by companies with comparable nineteenth- or early twentieth-century origins. Urban geographer Michael Johns has chronicled how the 1950s represented the last incandescence of downtown America. Nowhere was this more true than in San Francisco, where the downtown—centered on Market Street from the Ferry Building to Civic Center—abounded in department stores, hotels, restaurants, theaters, and a cluster of high-rise buildings from the prewar period. Market Street provided a sixteen- to twenty-hour pageant of urban life. Women considered it de rigueur to wear hats and gloves when shopping or socializing in the downtown. Most San Franciscans had at least one photograph of themselves strolling downtown, dressed to the nines, taken by an equally ubiquitous street photographer.

Aside from the thousands of white-collar jobs located in the downtown, retail was driving much of this pedestrian traffic. Throughout the 1950s upscale San Franciscans continued to buy their furniture at W. & J. Sloane (1875), their jewelry from Shreve & Company (1852), their pianos, musical instruments, sheet music, and records from Sherman Clay and Company (1876), their stationery at Schwabacher-Frey (1906), their flowers and floral arrangements from Podesta and Baldocchi on Grant or the many sidewalk flower stands in the area. Gentlemen might shop for clothes at Roos Brothers (1865) or the more recently founded Atkins, Bullock & Jones, Pauson's, Cable Car Clothiers, and J. Press. Brooks Brothers of New York opened a San Francisco store in May 1957. For women, such venerable stores as I. Magnin (1876) and Ransohoff's (1902) remained perennial favorites. Under the guidance of the socially prominent Hector Escobosa, I. Magnin constituted the epicenter of haute couture for the city. The department stores of San Francisco—the City of Paris (1851), the White House (1854), and the Emporium (1872) —were equally thriving. Following the war, Macy's of New York purchased the venerable O'Connor Moffat (1866) near Union Square, and Macy's became a leading department store of the city.

Like all great urban department stores, these San Francisco establishments were at once private and public places: crossroads, caravansaries, bazaars, points of psychological reference and demarcations of season. Bruce Porter's great stained-glass dome at the City of Paris, for example, depicting a galleon returning to port with its cargo of luxury goods, was one of the most revered creations of its type in a city rich in stained glass. Each Christmas season, a decorated forty-foot tree was placed beneath its opalescent light. The grandson of Hugenot Felix Verdier, who had founded the Ville de Paris in 1851 to cater to the French community, Paul Verdier had taken over management of the City of Paris from his father in 1904 as a twenty-three-year-old. A graduate of the University of Paris, Verdier was eminently suited to the management of a department store designed just after the Earthquake by Arthur Brown, John Bakewell and the French architect Louis Bourgeois, each of them an alumnus of the École des Beaux-Arts, intended to reflect Paris as much as possible. When war broke out in August 1914, Verdier returned to France and enlisted, surviving the war and winning the Croix de Guerre and a chevalier's ribbon from the Foreign Legion. Throughout his career, Verdier was very deliberate about having the City of Paris continue to make a statement to the effect that San Francisco enjoyed a direct connection to the culture and taste of France. As soon as Prohibition ended, he opened the Verdier Cellars and imported the finest French vintages to the city. Located behind the Cellars was Verdier's private dining room, dominated by a large circular table where chef Victor Faure-Brac prepared sumptuous lunches (conversations tended to be in French) for local notables. Symphony maestro Pierre Monteux was a frequent guest, as was Jeanne Salinger, whose son Pierre would soon be JFK's press secretary, together with such visiting French firemen as playwright Louis Verneuil, novelist and playwright Georges Duhamel, a member of the French Academy, and assorted consuls general, visiting diplomats, musicians, or opera singers. In a tour de force of retailing, Verdier re-created a provincial French street, Normandy Lane, running through the City of Paris basement, featuring a variety of food and wine stations, a restaurant, an offering of French books and newspapers, and other imported products.

The Emporium on Market Street, a stately building first designed in 1896 by the Beaux-Arts–trained Albert Pissis, was surmounted by an equally ambitious dome that had been incorporated in the rebuilt structure following the Earthquake. Escalators were added in 1936, the first in the city. The Emporium provided San Francisco with one of its most popular public spaces: a café beneath the dome, where there would be a great tree, children's rides, and a Santa Claus at Christmas; and adjacent to this the most comprehensive bookstore in the city. By profession, department store executives were alert to tradition and to shifts of fashion and were hence sensitive to the emergence of Baghdad by the Bay amidst the continuing splendors of high provincial San Francisco. Cyril Magnin, for example, was keying Joseph Magnin's department store to the newcomer, the upwardly mobile younger woman: the secretary with an English accent (such secretaries were all the rage in the important front offices throughout the 1950s); the San Francisco–based stewardess, living in a rented apartment in a better district, shared with two or three other flight attendants, each on the look-out for an eligible male; the young marrieds with college backgrounds, having recently moved to the city or to one of its suburbs. Here were women of the middle class, but eager for something more, something glamorous, eager to upgrade their taste, and find their place in Baghdad.

Equally distinguished were the great hotels of the city and equally crucial to the local economy. It had long been the custom for high provincial San Franciscans to live in apartment suites in such venerable institutions as the Fairmont (1906) atop Nob Hill, where poet-heiress Agnes Tobin kept a suite into the 1930s; or the Palace Hotel (1873, reconstructed in 1909) on Market, where crusading newspaper editor Fremont Older and his wife maintained their apartment; or the Whitcomb on Market, where as of January 1957 Elizabeth Bender, eight-six, had been living forty years and retired superior court judge Isidore Harris, eight-five, would live on until his death in December 1958. Young professionals coming to work in the city had the option of living in any one of nearly forty well-appointed residence clubs in the downtown or the southern side of Nob Hill, where for reasonable rates they could enjoy a well-furnished room, breakfast and dinner on weekdays, and, within the rules of house, agreeable socializing. Hotels such as the Clift (1915) on Geary, the Sir Francis Drake (1928) on Powell, the Mark Hopkins (1926) atop Nob Hill, and, most conspicuously, the St. Francis (1904) on Union Square were, like the department stores, overtly public places, whose restaurants (the Garden Court at the Palace, the Mural Room and English Grill at the St. Francis), bars (the Top of the Mark, the Redwood Room at the Clift, the Pied Piper at the Palace), and lobbies sustained much of the coming and going, meeting and greeting, and high-end socializing of the city. To meet someone under the clock in the lobby of the St. Francis was a local ritual.

The executives heading up these enterprises, many of them owners as well, constituted the oligarchic elite of the city. In the early decades of the twentieth century, Raphael Weill, manager of the White House, was so popular a figure that he was urged to run for mayor and lead the effort to rebuild San Francisco following the

Earthquake. A French Jew, Weill had immigrated from France to San Francisco in 1855 at the age of eighteen. Upon his death in 1920, a public school and the Rodin sculpture *The Thinker* at the California Palace of the Legion of Honor in Lincoln Park were dedicated in his honor. Elected to the board of supervisors in 1921, florist Angelo J. Rossi became mayor in 1930 when Mayor James (Sunny Jim) Rolph Jr. was elected governor. Roger Lapham, president of the American-Hawaiian Steamship Company, succeeded Rossi as mayor in 1944. In the late 1920s and early 1930s, Charles Kendrick of Schlage Lock led the bond campaign that financed an opera house and a museum of modern art as part of a War Memorial complex.

San Francisco businesses tended to be multi-generational. In 1953 Kendrick stepped down as president of Schlage to become chairman of the board, and his son Marron stepped in. By 1950 the Folgers of Folgers Coffee, founded in 1850 by direct descendants of Peter Folger of Nantucket, an ancestor of Benjamin Franklin, were in the third generation of executive ownership, the helm now being held by James A. Folger III, a Phi Beta Kappa from Yale, under whose leadership Folgers Coffee would soon command a quarter of the far western market. Founded in 1881, MJB Coffee was in the third generation of leadership as well, with the brothers Robert and John Bransten, Dartmouth graduates, succeeding their father, Joseph, who had succeeded the brothers Max and Manfred, the founders. In 1962 MJB introduced instant coffee to the nation. So too was the all-powerful San Francisco–based Bechtel Company, now a global enterprise (the Trans-Arabian pipeline in Saudi Arabia and Kuwait, nuclear power plants in North and South America and elsewhere throughout the world), entering its third generation of owner-management as Stephen Bechtel Jr. succeeded his father, Stephen Bechtel Sr., in 1960, who had succeeded his father, founder W. A. Bechtel, in the 1930s. The Zellerbach brothers, James David and Harold, were likewise the third generation of owner management at Crown Zellerbach, eighty-plus years since those days when their grandfather Anthony Zellerbach, who had arrived in San Francisco in 1868 and gone into the paper jobbing business, was pushing a handcart through the downtown streets to deliver his product to stationers.

Some oligarchs of the high provincial city succeeded to their positions. Others— such as real estate moguls Lou Lurie and Ben Swig—brought their assets with them. Born in Chicago in 1888 into a poor family, Lurie had begun his career Horatio Alger style as a newsboy before going into real estate at the precocious age of sixteen. By the 1920s he was investing not only in Chicago but in Vancouver and Seattle as well, and in San Francisco, where he purchased a number of theaters preparatory to going into the motion picture business with Sol Lesser in the 1930s. In 1923 Lurie began investing in a chain of Pickwick Stage Line hotel-bus terminals up and down the coast. Increasingly his attention was turning to San Francisco. By the early 1950s, Lurie had built and/or owned some 258 buildings in the city. All in all, some nine hundred buildings throughout the country had passed through his hands in the course of his career. A well-known figure in the downtown—a diminutive, dapper, genial septuagenarian, featuring the pince-nez of an earlier era—Lurie lunched each weekday at a reserved table at Jack's (1864), a high provincial eatery on Sacramento Street (men only at lunch), where he was joined by such regulars as banker Parker Maddux, president of the San Francisco Bank, founded as the German Savings and Loan Society in 1868, defense attorney Jake Ehrlich, *Examiner* editor Bill Wren, press agent Bernie Averbuch, and a moveable feast of local notables, including the sitting mayor and assorted supervisors, and visiting firemen. (George Jessel was a regular when in town. Even Herbert Hoover would drop by.) Lurie would do the ordering from Jack's menu, which he proudly stated had not changed for nearly a hundred years.

By the time Ben Swig arrived in San Francisco in his early fifties following the war, he was already one of the most successful solo real estate entrepreneurs in the country. The son of a Lithuanian Jewish immigrant living in Taunton, Massachusetts, and like Lurie a newspaper boy in his youth, Swig had regained his momentum after his bank had been destroyed in the stock market crash of 1929, specializing in assembling real estate sites for department store chains. By the time he reached San Francisco, Swig owned more than twenty highrise office buildings throughout the country and three premier hotels, including the Fairmont, where he ensconced himself in its twelve-room penthouse. By the 1950s Swig had become an important *macher* in city politics, legendary for the fundraisers he held in his penthouse suite on behalf of this or that candidate or philanthropic cause.

Entrepreneurs such as Richard Gump, Howard Gossage, Walter Landor, and Chuck Williams, meanwhile, were bringing the innovative spirit of Baghdad by the Bay to San Francisco business as they democratized good taste and projected the dream of a better life to postwar consumers. Founded in 1865, Gump's on Post Street played an important role across the decades in informing the taste of the high provincial city and evolving its signature style. Toward the end of the nineteenth century, Gump's began to specialize in Asian furniture, jewelry, and object d'art. By the 1920s a distinctive style of blended European and Asian furniture and art characterized upscale interior design in San Francisco. Even Edmund Wilson, who in general refused to be taken in by San Francisco during his 1947 visit, found in the Gump's store a wonderland of exquisite objects. When Abraham Livingston Gump—who along with actor-retailer Ching Wah Lee of Chinatown was the most learned connoisseur of things Asian among his generation in San Francisco— passed on, the store came under the ownership and management of his son Richard Gump, forty-two, who soon revealed himself as an enthusiastic Baghdadian. An accomplished Orientalist like his father, Richard Gump's monograph *Jade—Stone of Heaven* (1962) earned him the respect of experts in his field. Like his father, Richard Gump kept his store as a museum of Asian art and a destination-clearinghouse for people throughout the world interested in the field as either collectors or academics. Whereas Abraham Livingston Gump was cautious and conservative, and oriented toward the sale of individual objects at impressive prices, Richard Gump was convinced—and this made him a leading citizen of Baghdad—as he wrote in *Good Taste Costs No More* (1951), that an entire generation of postwar Americans was eager to improve its taste and lifestyle and that Gump's could play a role in this evolution through catalog sales as well as San Francisco–based retail. Commissioning agents to fan throughout Asia in search of art and furniture, Gump projected through his books, store, and catalogs an image of Baghdad San Francisco as a city of taste, catering to a worldwide clientele.

Advertising guru Howard Gossage was a leading Baghdader, a good friend of Herb Caen's, the two of them batching it together at one point when Caen was between marriages in a restored firehouse on Pacific that Gossage had developed as a work/living space years ahead of the time when such recycled live/work developments became commonplace. A Chicago-born graduate of the universities of Kansas City, Paris, and Geneva, Gossage had served as a naval aviator during the war, then chose San Francisco in the postwar era as a place where an outsider could be at home in an atmosphere open to new ideas. Gossage's big idea, inspired in part by his good friend Marshall McLuhan, was that advertising was a medium, a communications system related only tangentially to the sale of goods and services. Its primary purpose was, rather, beyond mere salesmanship. Advertisement was comparable to literature and the arts. It was thus an end in itself, or, as McLuhan might put it, the medium was the message. Once advertising was seen as an autonomous mode of communication, Gossage argued, its power for the good, for the communication of beneficial value, could be appreciated, and likewise its current abuse, its being used merely to sell products, could be understood and corrected.

Graphic designer Walter Landor was also intensely aware of the fact that imagination — in his case, the visual imagination — branded and transformed experience. For Landor, the logo was, like advertising, a communications medium existing for itself and on its own terms. Born in Munich in 1913, Landor grew up under the influence of the Bauhaus and Werkbund design movements, with their emphasis on the power of design to shape social and economic experience. Moving to England in 1931 to complete his education at the Goldsmith College School of Art at London University, Landor, twenty-two, commenced his career as an industrial design consultant. Work on the British Pavilion at the World's Fair in New York in 1939 brought him to the United States and to San Francisco, where he decided to settle. In 1941 Landor established Walter Landor & Associates in his Russian Hill flat. By 1964 the firm was operating out of the ferry boat *Klamath* anchored at Pier 5. What Landor understood and what he created for Coca-Cola, Levi's, Kellogg's, General Electric, Dole, Del Monte, Wells Fargo, Bank of America, and his many other clients was the power of branding through design: of speaking directly to millions of clients by establishing a vivid and immediate subliminal connection through a logo. The logo was intended to sell, true, but it was also making a statement on its own terms and could be thus appreciated as art.

Hardware retailer Chuck Williams, meanwhile, brought his French cookware store down from Sonoma to Sutter Street in San Francisco in 1958. Williams comparably understood that cooking, cookware, tableware, and the other accoutrements of food preparation and dining were not only tools; they were, rather, if properly understood, sophisticated statements of cultural value and identity. Upgraded from a hardware store, the cooking emporium of Williams-Sonoma was more than a retail outlet. Williams-Sonoma, the store and the catalog alike (like Richard Gump, Williams pioneered the use of the catalog for direct sale), was an artful statement, a museum even, of aspiration and taste, in this case materialized through aesthetic arrangements of French or French-inspired cookware that added its strength to San Francisco's already flourishing wine and food culture. What Gossage, Landor, and Williams understood—and what made them such exemplary entrepreneurs of Baghdad by the Bay—was the notion that imagination transformed experience, just as Herb Caen was transforming San Francisco through his columns. Through slogans, logos, cookware, catalogs, and advertising campaigns, these salesmen were communicating a message not just about the products they were selling but about the place, San Francisco, where new levels of taste and cleverness were being imagined and projected. From this perspective, Baghdad by the Bay was speaking directly to the same rising tide of postwar aspiration and taste, tied to lifestyle and consumer products, that was re-formulating America itself.

From the 1850s onward, San Francisco had orchestrated most of the business of the Far West and had hence been a lawyering town. The city even had its own freestanding Hastings College of the Law, founded in 1878 and part of the UC system, where Dean David Snodgrass was busy assembling an outstanding faculty by recruiting, all in all, seventy-six retired legal eminences from the great law schools of the nation for second careers at Hastings. But the lawyers of blue-chip downtown firms as Pillsbury, Madison & Sutro or Chickering & Gregory or Brobeck Phleger and Harrison were by culture, necessity, and preference buttoned-down, three-piece-suit kinds of guys, graduates of name-brand schools, living in the better districts, rarely if ever seeing their names in the newspapers. This was the world of corporate law, so characteristic of the mid-twentieth-century economy. It was also high provincial—dominated by men whose fathers and grandfathers had founded the firm.

Yet the brilliant solo practitioner, especially in the field of criminal defense, was also a high provincial tradition that Baghdad by the Bay found highly adaptable to its own sense of the city. Attorneys such as Jake Ehrlich, Melvin Belli, Vincent Hallinan, James Martin MacInnis, George Davis, and Nate Cohn were by definition colorful, as were the private investigators who helped them research their cases: shamuses such as Hal Lipset, a close associate of MacInnis, each of them appearing regularly in the Herb Caen column. Lipset was, in fact, the preferred private eye from Baghdad in that he eschewed tough-guy tactics in favor of research, interviews, and a pioneering use of electronic surveillance. With the advance of miniaturization, Lipset once recorded a conversation by concealing a listening device in the olive of his martini!

The leading solo practitioners of San Francisco tended to have a taste for well-known clients and were themselves highly expressive personalities. MacInnis loved to quote Shakespeare in his opening and closing statements and achieved national prominence when he defended Edmund Wilson against charges that Wilson's novel *Memoirs of Hecate County* (1946) was obscene. MacInnis also defended singer Billie Holiday on drug charges. Nate Cohn earned the sobriquet "Attorney to the Stars" for his defense, among other cases, of Duke Ellington, Josephine Baker, Gisele MacKenzie, Billie Holiday, and Anna Maria Alberghetti. George Davis made a specialty of defending clients facing the death penalty, including Burton Abbott and Caryl Chessman in two of the most notorious cases of the era.

The three best-known criminal defense attorneys of high provincial San Francisco—Vincent Hallinan, Jake Ehrlich, and Mel Belli—were easily assimilable to Baghdad by the Bay, as signified by frequent mentions in the Herb Caen column because they were such good copy: criminal defense attorneys, solo practitioners, in the robust style of Old San Francisco. Despite his sobriquet, Jake "Never Plead Guilty" Ehrlich nevertheless pleaded drummer Gene Krupa guilty to a lesser charge in a marijuana case, earning Krupa ninety days in the county jail, to avoid felony charges that could have sent him to San Quentin. In early 1949 Ehrlich won acquittal for Billie Holiday, charged with possession of opium. By the mid-1950s Ehrlich had handled fifty-six homicide cases with not one first-degree murder conviction. When Howard Hughes retained Ehrlich to defend *The Outlaw* (1943) on obscenity charges based in large part upon a discussion of Jane Russell's cleavage, Ehrlich brought into court an oversized blow-up of the painting *Madonna and Child* by Leonardo da Vinci and asked an embarrassed prosecutor if the same portion of the female anatomy depicted in the Vatican-approved painting as was depicted in the film excited in him feelings of lust. Not only did Ehrlich win the case, the presiding judge urged the public to see the film. Not surprisingly, Ehrlich developed a sizeable Hollywood clientele, especially after he got Hollywood director Walter Wagner off on reduced charges when Wagner tried to pump his wife Joan Bennett's agent full of lead in a Hollywood parking lot. Hollywood friends who were not in trouble—Zsa Zsa Gabor, Humphrey Bogart, Jean Hersholt, Martha Raye—were wont to look up Jake when they were passing through San Francisco, just in case things ever took a turn for the worse. When Jimmy Roosevelt, son of the late President, was faced with a messy divorce, he knew where to turn.

Famous for his tailored suits, luxuriant neckties, and prominent cuff links—he shot his cuffs with mesmerizing panache when addressing a jury—Ehrlich was instantly recognizable to those greeting him frequently as he moved through the downtown, en route, perhaps, to Jack's, where he was a regular at the Lou Lurie roundtable. On Thursdays, Ehrlich also joined Lurie at the weekly luncheon of the Saints and Sinners, another Lurie-inspired group, organized around fundraising efforts to provide free milk for impoverished schoolchildren. At the lunches, Lurie would raise money for the milk fund by leveling fines against members and guests: $100 against Chief Justice Earl Warren for being too popular, $1,000 against lobbyist Artie Samish for refusing to take his seat when Lurie told him to do so. Saints and Sinners regular Tommy Harris (real name, Milton Colberg), a longtime radio singer now the owner of Tommy's Joynt on Van Ness, would regale such visitors

as Irish prime minister Eamon de Valera and San Quentin warden Clinton Duffy
with his songs and rapier wit. Thanks to Lurie's fundraising efforts, which included
a citywide raffle and a benefit at Bimbo's 365 Club in North Beach, the Saints and
Sinners milk fund had by 1954 reached a million dollars, which Lurie put into a
trust. Attorney General Edmund G. (Pat) Brown was not amused. It was one thing to
raise and spend money for charitable purposes within a fixed period of time, Brown
argued. It was another thing to create a trust fund via raffle tickets that would have to
purchase millions of bottles of milk ever to be expended for its stated purpose. The
Saints and Sinners, Brown charged, were in effect running an illegal lottery. Jake
Ehrlich leapt to the organization's defense, and a compromise was reached involving the expenditure over time of the trust fund on milk for needy children, with a
cap on further fundraising efforts.

One of Ehrlich's arguments was that Brown was setting a precedent that would
end fundraising bingo games by the Roman Catholic Church. This would have
been perfectly fine with Vincent Hallinan, whom a lengthy Jesuit education at
St. Ignatius High School, the University of San Francisco, and the USF Law School
had turned into a militant atheist and frequent opponent of the Catholic Church,
starting from the time that Hallinan's divorced and remarried brother, having died
from alcoholism at age forty-four, was denied a Catholic funeral. Coming from an
Irish Catholic family of ten, Hallinan was the epitome of Irish San Francisco in
everything save religious belief: a dedicated amateur boxer in his youth; a devoted
husband and father to his four sons (to whom he gave pugnacious nicknames); a
noted criminal defense attorney since the 1920s, with a reputation for wrangling
with the bar association and with judges in court (a tendency that occasionally
landed him behind bars for contempt); and the lawyer of choice for the left, including such celebrity clients as singer Paul Robeson and longshoreman leader Harry
Bridges, whom Hallinan was defending between 1950 and 1955 against the United
States Immigration Service, which was trying to deport Bridges as a Communist. In
1952 Hallinan ran for President on the ticket of the Independent Progressive Party, a
Communist Party affiliate.

MacInnis, Ehrlich, and Hallinan were high provincials with deep roots in one
or another aspect of the prewar San Francisco identity. Melvin Belli, by contrast—
the flamboyant King of Torts, as *Life* magazine dubbed him in October 1954—was
pure Baghdad by the Bay. Of Italian-Swiss descent, born in the Gold Rush town of
Sonora and raised on a ranch near Stockton, Belli arrived with no connection in
San Francisco in 1933 after graduating from Boalt Hall in Berkeley. Like Balzac's
Rastignac shaking his fist at nighttime Paris from his roof-level garret, Belli vowed
one day to have San Francisco at his feet. Belli's first two clients, assigned him by
the public defender, met their doom at the end of a rope in San Quentin; but very
soon Belli earned a reputation for winning in court, especially when it came to his
specialty, personal injury. For all his flamboyance—his Rolls-Royce; his tailored
suits; his five wives; the human skeleton dubbed Elmer used to great advantage
in court to describe various injuries; his hoisting of a black and white Jolly Roger

atop his office on Montgomery Street when he won a case (flying the skull and bones at half mast when he lost)—Melvin Belli was not only a brilliant court-room performer, he was also a formidable legal scholar. Not only did Belli argue cases with erudition and verbal skill, he also wrote them up, and others as well, with credible scholarship, including extensive library research, beginning with the series *Modern Trials*, which Belli, fueled on Holland gin and Dexedrine, began to dictate into a Dictaphone in the summer of 1953. Within the year, Belli had com-pleted three thousand pages and secured a contract with Bobbs-Merrill for an edi-tion in three volumes. *Modern Trials* (1954) eventually ran to six volumes. Belli's *Trial and Tort Trends* (1955) ran to fifteen. Other Belli books, researched in the libraries of Japan, Russia, the British Museum, and Boalt Hall and in the Library of Congress and dictated in the midst of a busy practice, included *Ready for the Plaintiff* (1956), *Life and Law in Japan* (1960), *Life and Law in Russia* (1963), and *The Law Revolt* (1968) in two volumes, *Civil* and *Criminal*. Roscoe Pound, dean of the Harvard Law School, so admired Belli's *Modern Trials* he became a personal friend, staying at Belli's home when visiting San Francisco. In 1962 Belli, who could manage Italian, was invited to give a seminar on forensic medicine at Rome University. Like many Baghdad San Franciscans, Belli delighted in the Victorian era. In January 1960 he moved his offices to historic quarters at 722 Montgomery Street (1851), which he decorated in a style he described as Mother Lode Whore-house Victorian. An actor attired as Emperor Norton was on hand to dedicate the building and dub Belli knight. With the red velvet draperies of his windows drawn, Belli worked in full view of the public, sitting in front of a roll-top desk. His clut-tered and distinctively decorated office soon became a must-see stop on the Gray Line Bus tour.

By the mid-1950s Caen's column in the *Examiner* had become a daily requirement for the newspaper readers of San Francisco and environs, providing them with the local color, gossip, and inside scoop they increasingly needed not only to be enter-tained but to anchor themselves in time and place: to become convinced, paragraph by paragraph, that they were living in, as one sobriquet had it, Everyone's Favorite City. A dedicated luncher (rumor, which he angrily denied, had it that he rarely picked up a tab), Caen mastered the restaurants and restaurant culture of the city, whether in terms of commenting on the food (he was reputed to be able to make or break a new restaurant with one mention), picking up the gossip, or covering the action: the pols and celebrities, the quips, the laughter, the crash of liar's dice on the bar, the rhythmic marimba of ice in a cocktail shaker, the reporters, racetrack touts, and professional drinkers, the cops lunching in the kitchen, the notable trying to be invisible as he hunched into a back banquette with a young lady not his wife, the whole Walter Winchell three-dot scene of it all. Caen's coverage of restaurants and nightclubs in his column and in books such as *Herb Caen's New Guide to San Francisco* (1958) constituted a vivid and useful inventory of this essential aspect of the San Francisco economy and lifestyle.

Like so much else in San Francisco in the 1950s, the restaurant and nightclub scene consisted of high provincial and Baghdad places and, of equal importance, high provincial places taken up by Baghdad. From the Gold Rush, a city of solitary strangers had been a restaurant town. A number of restaurants surviving into the 1950s, in fact—the Tadich Grill (1849), the Poodle Dog (1849), Jack's (1864), Sam's (1867), Maye's Oyster House (1867)—could trace their origins to the open-air downtown California Market at the corner of California and Kearny, to which each morning the fishermen, farmers, butchers, and bakers of the city would sell their products. These surviving Gold Rush places were still featuring in the 1950s a century-old cuisine based upon salads, seafood, grilled fish and meats, freshly baked thick-crusted sourdough French bread, potatoes and vegetables awash in creamy, buttery sauces, and desserts of custard, bread pudding, or rice pudding. The waiters at such establishments were male, middle-aged or older, and professional: never deliberately rude, but possessed of a high self-regard that precluded any unnecessary intimacy.

Another category of San Francisco restaurant was already en route to Baghdad before Herb Caen's arrival: places like Julius Castle and Shadows on the Bay side of Telegraph Hill, the Blue Fox on Merchant, Ernie's and Paoli's on Montgomery, Omar Khayyam's on O'Farrell at Powell, and, above all others, Trader Vic's on Cosmo Place. All of these restaurants were from the beginning highly themed places, self-consciously aware that they were offering a stylized and theatrical performance along with food and drink: San Francisco as Europe in the case of the Blue Fox, as Baghdad in the case of Omar Khayyam's, as Italy in the case of Paoli's, as Belle Époque San Francisco in the case of Ernie's, as South Pacific crossroads in the case of Trader Vic's. When Alfred Hitchcock filmed *Vertigo* in San Francisco, he located a key scene in Ernie's, already a well-known tourist attraction, and heightened business as diners came to sit amidst the grand Victorian décor, expecting to see, at any moment, Kim Novak and Jimmy Stewart being seated at the next table. Each of these establishments had celebrity owners: George Mardikian, an Armenian immigrant, also known as a writer, at Omar Khayyam's, and at Trader Vic's, Victor Bergeron, with his wooden leg and South Seas trader manner, who was also distinguished in another art form, sculpture.

By 1953 San Francisco could boast some 3,000 restaurants, 1,330 bars and nightclubs, and 438 churches. In contrast to the restaurants of the city, the bars and nightclubs were of more recent vintage; indeed, many of them, such as Barnaby Conrad's El Matador on Broadway, were strictly the creation of Baghdad. The Fairmont Hotel atop Nob Hill dominated the mainstream nightclub market with its Venetian Room featuring name entertainers, its Papagayo Room and Le Cirque Room catering to the late-night crowd, the mid-America-oriented Tonga Room, with its Tiki motif, Hawaiian music, and a regularly scheduled rainstorm, and frequent appearances in the Grand Ballroom by Ray Hackett, the Lester Lanin of San Francisco, and his Society Orchestra. The other hotels of the city—in such places as the Top of the Mark and the Lochinvar Room at the Mark Hopkins, the Starlight Roof at the Sir Francis Drake, the Mural Room and

Patent Leather Lounge at the St. Francis, the Redwood Room at the Clift, and the Happy Valley and Pied Pipers rooms at the Palace—were also committed to upscale entertainment, aimed primarily at tourists and affluent high provincials. Other night-clubs flourishing in the 1950s included Coffee Dan's on Mason near Geary, an after-hours establishment (bring your own bottle, and breakfast was served); the Black Hawk at Turk and Hyde streets, featuring such jazz players as Cal Tjader, Dave Brubeck, and Paul Desmond in the early years of the decade; Charlie Low's Forbidden City in Chinatown, with its all-Chinese chorus line; Club Hangover on Bush, a jazz joint; the supper club Station J, a reconverted PG&E substation in the downtown; Gorman's Gay Nineties on Pacific in the International Settlement; the nearby Gold Street, where New Year's Eve was celebrated every night; Bimbo's 365 Club at Columbus and Chest-nut in North Beach, showcasing a nude chorine in a fishbowl (achieved by projecting a number of diminishing images through a series of mirrors); the Jazz Cellar on Green, a favorite with jazz-and-poetry Beats; Finnochio's on Broadway, with its female imper-sonators; and the Old Spaghetti Factory on Green, a former pasta factory with skylights and clerestory windows decorated by owner Freddie Kuh, who described himself as a bohemian businessman and whom Herb Caen proclaimed the Father of Funk.

The spirit and style of Baghdad was most evident in two North Beach clubs, the Purple Onion at 140 Columbus and the hungry i farther north on Columbus at Jackson. The Purple Onion was owned and managed by Bud Steinhoff. The hungry i, like Enrico's on Broadway, was the brainchild of club owner-impresario Harry Charles Banducci, who rechristened himself Enrico, the son of a Bakersfield bootlegger who ran away from home to San Francisco in 1936 at the age of thirteen. No matter: The bars and restaurants of Chinatown and North Beach offered Ban-ducci employment and a home of sorts, and Harry Charles had by the 1950s devel-oped into the renamed Enrico, bar and nightclub owner and North Beach celebrity extraordinary. At Enrico's on Broadway, Banducci created the essence of the Medi-terranean-style sidewalk café, fronting a more ambitious restaurant and club within. At the Purple Onion and the hungry i, despite their limitations of space, Steinhoff and Banducci, drawing upon an overlapping pool of emergent performers, mounted a cavalcade of entertainment throughout the 1950s that helped define Baghdad by the Bay to itself as the essence of the hip, the sardonic, the anti-establishment, the subversive, that was itself a counter-establishment. Like all good nightclubs, the Purple Onion and the hungry i featured music and singers—Miriam Makeba, Maya Angelou, Barbra Streisand, Vicki Carr, the Limelighters, the Kingston Trio, Peter, Paul, and Mary—each of them in the early stages of their career. But it was another specialty, stand-up comedy, that most displayed their Baghdad orientation—in such comics, also at the beginning of their careers, as Irwin Corey, Tom Lehrer, the Smothers Brothers, Pat Paulsen, Jim Nabors, Bob Newhart, Mort Sahl, Shelley Berman, Dick Gregory, Woody Allen, Mike Nichols and Elaine May, Bill Cosby, Jackie Mason, Jonathan Winters, Phyllis Diller, Richard Pryor, and Lenny Bruce: comics—Sahl, Gregory, and Bruce especially—who were launching a critique, sar-donic to the point of bitterness, against what they considered the hypocritical values and postures of the Eisenhower era that would explode into a full-scale critique, with accompanying street theater, in the decade to follow. KSFO radio personality Don Sherwood, a shock-jock ahead of his time as well, was also pushing the envelope through acerbic comedy appealing to Baghdad. Sherwood was not an outsider, as were the majority of Baghdaders, but a native son, born in the Sunset district in 1925. San Francisco had always been an important radio town. KCBS claimed to be the oldest commercial radio station in the country, tracing its origins to 1909. In the late 1930s San Francisco had emerged as a center of national broadcasting from the coast second only to Hollywood, with such figures as Art Linkletter, Merv Griffin, and, later, Johnny Mathis getting their start on local stations. Singers such as Tommy Harris, before he went into the restaurant business, and Stan Noonan, a stalwart performer at the Bohemian Club, continued to make a steady income on local stations. Nor was more ambitious music neglected, with Albert White and the Morris Plan Masters of Melody broadcasting on Friday evening on KCBS, Doug Pledger playing opera and serious music some twenty-five hours a week on KNBC, and native son Dave McElhatton (a 1951 graduate of San Francisco State, where another native son, Johnny Mathis, was excelling on the track team) providing the same fare on his all-night program *Music Until Dawn* on KCBS. In a high provincial town such as San Francisco, local radio personalities such as news analyst William Winter, talk show hosts Dean Maddox and Ira Blue, and bandleader Del Courtney made a good living and wielded enormous influence. With erudite commentary on foreign affairs, Winter, a combat correspondent in the Pacific during the war and a law school graduate, flattered high provincial San Francisco's sense of itself as a world city. Dean Maddox, the best-known voice in local radio, had spent time in China in the early 1930s as a correspondent. For more than twenty years, Maddox presided over a Sunday morning live interview program from the Cliff House, in addition to daily live interviews of visiting celebrities and other notables from a booth near the cable car roundabout at Powell and Market, with the clang-clang of the cable car bell serving as the signature sound of the program. Maddox called himself the Buddha, as if to suggest the becalming influence of his sonorous and modulated baritone.

Maddox's station, KFRC, part of the Mutual–Don Lee Broadcast Network, was until the rise of KSFO the most listened-to station in the region, with such programs on its docket as *Red Ryder, Captain Midnight, The Cisco Kid, The Shadow,* and *Superman* for the younger crowd; *Queen for a Day, Nick Carter, The Roy Rogers Show,* and *Life Begins at Eighty* for the older set. By the 1950s KFRC alumni who had made the big time included singer Merv Griffin, television emcee Ralph Edwards, and composer Meredith Willson. The times, however, were a-changing, decided the executives at independent radio station KSFO (560 on the AM dial), located atop Nob Hill near the Mark Hopkins Hotel. Most local radio personalities were venerable figures, high provincial in style and attitude. Looking in another direction, KSFO decided to reach out to the Baghdad market of hip newcomers, the kinds of people who took their identity from Herb Caen and jammed the shows at the Purple Onion and the hungry i. To do this, KSFO, paradoxically, employed as its lead personality local boy Don Sherwood.

A high school dropout who had served briefly in the merchant marine in the Pacific as a radio operator during the last months of the war, Sherwood had read widely when at sea. His autodidacticism, resembling Herb Caen's, fit congruently into the mood of the city in which Baghdaders were frequently redefining themselves outside the traditional matrix of lineage or college degrees. A now-and-then big band singer, Sherwood had a mellifluous voice as well as a quick wit. In a buttoned-down era, his only homage to conventional dress was the dark horn-rim glasses he wore in tribute to his hero Dave Garroway. Otherwise, Sherwood anticipated the 1960s in his proclivity to dress down in jeans and T-shirts, rarely if ever wearing a tie, even when hosting his own television show on KPIX. In March 1953, KSFO gave Sherwood his own early-morning program, from six to nine. Sherwood was supposed to be a disc jockey, and he did occasionally play a record or two, especially Latin music, but if he did not like a song, he would bring the record to a grinding halt in mid-play. An excellent mimic, like his friend Jonathan Winters, Sherwood would occasionally sing in the voice of one or another well-known singer as part of his routine.

What soon gained Sherwood an audience of a million listeners, however, was not his music but his humorous and unpredictable patter. In true Baghdad by the Bay style, Sherwood, the Peck's Bad Boy of local radio—a heavy drinker and smoker, bouncing from marriage to marriage—himself became the medium and the message and the primary entertainment of his program. Sherwood was frequently too hungover to show up for work, and his very absenteeism became part of the program, which KSFO announcers frequently dubbed "The Will Don Sherwood Show?" Far from being grateful to the KSFO management for not canning him, Sherwood was constantly berating the front office on the air and off for a myriad of real and imagined offenses. Edgy, ever in therapy and talking about it, Sherwood was a frequenter of the hungry i and the Purple Onion, where he especially appreciated Lenny Bruce and Mort Sahl and sometimes himself did impromptu stand-up comedy. Like the humor of Bruce and Sahl, Sherwood's humor was ahead of its time in its acerbic and semi-subversive satire. Also avant-garde were Sherwood's interest in Zen Buddhism and his advocacy of Native American political rights.

An ardent 49ers fan, Sherwood helped transform the popular perception of the 49ers—and hence the eventual reality of that team during the Bill Walsh era—from a local team of likeable players to a team with an urban sophisticate touch, playing thinking man's football. Like Herb Caen, who ragged the Northern California city of Chico as a place where Velveeta was found in the gourmet food section, Sherwood played to his audience as people belonging to a sophisticated and an enchanted circle, far from such squaresville places as Chico or Stockton, against which Sherwood organized a mock invasion. Much of Sherwood's patter—his edgy menu of sports, commentary, humor, and traffic reporting from a helicopter, which KSFO pioneered—was oriented toward commuting listeners. At one point, hearing of a traffic jam on the Golden Gate Bridge, Sherwood played a police siren loudly over the air and encouraged his listeners to open their windows, turn up their radios, and move through traffic like a police car in hot pursuit. Needless to say, Don Sherwood was at times a daily item in the Herb Caen column. Sherwood, Caen, and writer Barnaby Conrad would frequently lunch together, and Sherwood did a lot of his late-night drinking at Conrad's El Matador.

Sherwood's advocacy of the 49ers offered a case study in the Baghdadization of sport, as did the arrival of the New York Giants in April 1958. Whereas the Giants were in-migrants to San Francisco, hence bona fide citizens of Baghdad, the 49ers were transformed into a Baghdad team. Founded by two quintessential locals— the brothers Tony and Vic Morabito, Italian Americans, graduates of St. Ignatius High School and Santa Clara University, lumbermen until 1949, when Tony, who owned 75 percent of the team, sold his business to go full-time into football—the 49ers were high provincial. Coached by local coaches, manned by graduates of Cal, Stanford, Santa Clara, and the University of San Francisco, the 49ers played home games in Golden Gate Park at Kezar, a municipally owned stadium, where high school games were played as well, before a loyal local audience. By the late 1950s, in yet another instance of Baghdadization, the 49ers had become a cerebral, quarterback-dominated team in which the brainy coaching of Frankie Albert, him-self a former quarterback with Stanford and the 49ers, and after 1959 the coaching of Howard Hickey melded with the equally cerebral style of quarterback Y. A. (Yelberton Abraham) Tittle. Also relevant to this new style of play were the glide-run style of fullback Joe Perry, a pioneering African American pro footballer, the canny maneuvers of "Alley Oop" receiver R. C. Owens, another African American early in the pro game, and the anticipatory downfield maneuvering of receiving end Gordy Soltau, all of it backed up by the scientific defenses and offenses of linesmen Leo Nomellini and Bob St. Clair, each of them bringing discernible intelligence to his gladiatorial calling.

The championship football and basketball teams being fielded in this era by the University of San Francisco, a one-hundred-year-old Jesuit institution on Ignatian Heights overlooking the western edge of the city, were likewise contributing to the emergence of San Francisco as a sports town. Coached by former Notre Dame great Joe Kuharich, the USF Dons played an undefeated season in 1951 but were not invited to any bowl games. The excuse given: USF had not played an impressive array of teams. It was suspected, however, that USF was not invited to any of the southern bowls because of the prominence of African Americans Ollie Matson and Burl Toler on the team. Football played at such a high level was an anomaly for such a small institution. Even in that championship season, football was costing USF a $70,000 deficit; and so, that very same year, Jesuit president William J. Dunne ended the program. Tackle Bob St. Clair transferred his two years of remaining eligibility to the University of Tulsa before turning pro with the 49ers. In the fall of 1954, USF was back in the headlines when coach Phil Wolpert fielded one of the best college basketball teams of all times, sparked by such players as Bill Russell, K. C. Jones, and Hal Perry. Winning the National Collegiate Athletic Association tournament in Kansas City in March 1955, the Dons were greeted back in San Francisco with a ticker-tape parade down Market Street led off by Mayor Elmer Robinson and USF president John Connolly, followed by a victory luncheon at the Fairmont Hotel. In 1956 USF repeated its NCAA championship performance. Once again there was a ticker-tape parade, followed by a banquet at the Palace Hotel to raise money for a new gymnasium.

It was all very high provincial, a local Catholic school thrusting itself unexpectedly into the big time and winning local support. For years, San Francisco had been happy with local teams such as this: the St. Mary's Gaels football team from across the Bay, coached by Slip Madigan to national prominence; the USF Dons on both the grid-iron and the hardwood, asserting themselves into national prominence; and the San Francisco Seals of the Pacific Coast League, playing since March 1931 in a munici-pally owned stadium at Sixteenth and Bryant, considered one of the finest inner-city ballparks in the nation, whose urbanism and intimacy reflected the rapport the Seals enjoyed with their home city and the excellence that over the years had produced a number of major league players of note, including the ultra-great Joe DiMaggio. By 1953, however, as high provincial San Francisco was being colonized by Baghdad by the Bay, the city was growing tired of being a minor league town. And besides: the Seals were in the cellar that year.

By the following fall, the new mayor of San Francisco, George Christopher, had persuaded voters to pass a $5 million bond issue to build a major league stadium to attract a major league team. When owner Walter O'Malley moved the Brooklyn Dodgers to Los Angeles in 1957, Christopher saw his opening and began success-ful negotiations with owner Horace Stoneham to move the New York Giants to San Francisco. On 14 April 1958, more than a hundred thousand San Franciscans turned out to greet the Giants, returning from spring training in Phoenix, with a ticker-tape parade down Market Street, followed on the fifteenth by a winning game, 8–0, over the Los Angeles Dodgers in a renovated and expanded Seals Stadium, where the Giants played their first season. During negotiations, Christopher prom-ised Stoneham a state-of-the-art stadium, with parking for ten thousand. Contractor Charles Harney donated land at Candlestick Point on the southeastern edge of the city, provided that he get the construction contract, which occurred, although a grand jury later took a long and searching look at both the land deal and the park-ing leases. The Teamsters also struck during construction, and the fire department came up with a whole list of correctives. The Giants themselves rejected Harney's first version of the playing field, and it had to be reconfigured. On 12 April 1960 a sellout crowd of 42,269 flocked for the first time into a twin-deck reinforced concrete stadium surrounded by seven thousand of the ten thousand parking spaces Stone-ham had demanded.

Candlestick Park soon revealed itself to be challenged by fog and by the wind gusts created by surrounding mountains: gusts strong enough during the All-Star game of 1961 to blow relief pitcher Stu Miller off the mound. Outfielders learned to judge the winds at Candlestick when pursuing fly balls. But no matter: Baghdad by the Bay had its big league stadium and its big league team that went to the World Series in 1962 and missed winning it by one run in the seventh game. Soon such New Yorkers–turned–San Franciscans as Willie Mays, Orlando Cepeda, and Willie McCovey, manager Bill Rigney, and the Voice of the Giants, Russ Hodges, had become celebrity Baghdaders, and the Giants had become the best possible way of redefining San Francisco as a major league town. High provincial San Francisco, by contrast, discredited itself when certain homeowners resisted the efforts of center fielder Willie Mays to buy a home in a posh all-white neighborhood. An enraged Mayor Christopher offered the Mays family the use of his own home while they continued house-hunting.

Along with its love of sports, San Francisco was a hard-drinking town and had the bars to prove it. A city of tightly defined neighborhoods, each of them character-ized by distinctive topographies, climates, architecture, and ethnic demographies, San Francisco abounded in hundreds of neighborhood bars, many of them dating back to the nineteenth century, which constituted local clubs of an informal nature: bars such as McCarthy's in the Mission, the Lucky Club in the Haight-Ashbury, the Philosophers Club in West Portal, the Miraloma in Miraloma Park, the Laurel Lodge in Presidio Heights, the Final Final facing the eastern entrance to the Presidio, Club Alabam in the Western Addition, Harrington's, Breen's, Hanno's in the Alley, the House of Shields downtown, Cookie Picietti's Blue Star Buffet on Kearny near the Hall of Justice, Red's in Chinatown, Gino & Carlo's in North Beach. Each had its steady clientele, its *Cheers* ambience of locals and off-duty newsmen in the case of the House of Shields, Breen's, and Hanno's in the Alley, or off-duty cops and lawyers at Cookie Picetti's, off-duty scavengers at Gino & Carlo's, or off-duty firemen at the Miraloma. San Francisco had more than its fair share of bars because, for all its surviving family life, it was increasingly becoming, as Census 1950 showed, a city of singles, of newcomers or older longtime residents whose families had melted away. The good news was that bars and taverns offered a haven, a way of belonging, for the lonely or those merely seeking camaraderie and a measure of magic in the night. The bad news was that San Francisco had one of the highest rates of alcoholism in the nation, with an average of 360 people a year dying of cirrhosis of the liver. Sui-cide, much of it alcohol-related, ran at three times the national rate.

Still, for all the sadness of such statistics, for all of San Francisco's underside as an alcoholic Lonely Town, it was still a fun place to live for the coping middle and working classes. San Francisco brewed its own beer (Acme, Hamm's, Anchor Steam, Lucky Lager); baked its own bread (Laraboux, Boudin, Colombo); prepared its own salami (Gallo, Molinari's); and even had its own ice cream treat, the It's It sandwich, two oatmeal cookies on either side of a slab of vanilla ice cream, the whole drenched in frozen chocolate and covered with nuts. The It's It had origi-nated at Playland-at-the-Beach, a Coney Island–like amusement park at Ocean Beach under development since the 1920s by George and Leo Whitney, conces-sionaires who had learned their calling at the Alaska-Yukon Exposition of 1909 in

Seattle and Luna Park in Melbourne, before returning to San Francisco at the outbreak of World War I. Although Playland-at-the-Beach was a private concession, it
was also an extremely successful civic space, a strong point of reference, in fact, for
the overall San Francisco identity. Its roller coaster, merry-go-round, and fun house,
presided over by Laughing Sal, an oversized mechanical marionette laughing away
at the entrance, its Parachute Drop and Diving Bell, its House of Horrors, its myriad
of carnival concessions, attracted thousands of San Franciscans each weekend and
holiday, creating a pageant of popular fun that Reginald Marsh would have loved to
paint, had he ever visited San Francisco.

Ocean Beach had been a popular resort since the nineteenth century. Adolph Sutro
had built his estate on its bluffs, and until it closed in 1952 San Franciscans could still
swim at the great steel and glass natatorium Sutro had donated to the city in 1896,
situated on the rocks just north of the Cliff House, where one might rent the scratchy
wool one-piece swimsuits from the 1890s and swim in one or another of the three saltwater pools, sliding down a steep water slide, and, before or after the swim, ice-skate
in the rink that was also on the premises or visit Sutro's privately sponsored museum
of Egyptian and classical antiquities, all this for the admission price of forty cents for
adults. The Cliff House of the 1950s was a modest successor to the great Victorian
pile that had burned to the ground in 1907, but it was still serving meals and offering binocular views of Seal Rocks four hundred feet offshore, crowded with raucous
Stellar sea lions at various times of the year. Farther south down the Great Highway,
fronting the rolling surf, was Roberts at the Beach, a vast public dance hall favored for
high school proms and college dances and the nearby Fat Boy sandwich concession,
surmounted by a gigantic figure of a fat boy eating a sandwich, that replenished the
strength of hungry dancers or other assorted late-night revelers with barbecued beef
sandwiches dripping in sauce. South of that, where Sloat Boulevard flowed into the
Great Highway, was the municipally sponsored Fleishhacker Zoo and the seawater-fed
Fleishhacker Swimming Pool, the largest outdoor swimming pool in the world, where
lifeguards patrolled in rowboats and where one might dive or jump from a horrifically
high platform offering three levels of challenge. Running for more than fifty blocks,
Golden Gate Park ended at Ocean Beach and continued eastward into the Haight-
Ashbury in the interior of the city. It took book-length guides to enumerate the attractions of the park, which had been patiently under development for more than eighty
years. Successive waves of philanthropy and bond issues had developed the park into a
triumph of horticulture, landscape design, and recreational and cultural architecture,
all of it keyed to a popular usage. In its statues and monuments—Prayer Book Cross,
commemorating the first Book of Common Prayer service in North America, during
the Drake Expedition of 1579; Junípero Serra, suggesting the Mission era; the Pioneer
Mother; the Portals of the Past, a legacy of the 1906 Earthquake—the park, like a medieval cathedral, suggested the history of the city.

The de Young Museum (1917) in Golden Gate Park, the Palace of the Legion of
Honor (1924) in Lincoln Park at Land's End, and the Museum of Modern Art in

the War Memorial complex (1932) on Van Ness Avenue near Civic Center were not, as museums go, notable institutions: as Edmund Wilson, among other visitors, noted in his journal for December 1946 and another visitor, Alice McIntyre, writing in *Esquire*, was still noting, even more emphatically, as late as May 1963. When it came to art, the elite of high provincial San Francisco had not shown itself to be overly ambitious, or even venturesome. The most popular exhibit at the de Young seemed to be the armor, swords, pikes, World War I tanks, rifles, and other associated weaponry on the first floor. The one notable collection of Old Masters at the de Young had come from the estate of Samuel H. Kress, a Pennsylvanian. Thomas Carr Howe, the director of the Palace of the Legion of Honor, privately described his institution as Aida's Tomb, an empty palace on the Pacific. Dr. Grace Morley, director of the Museum of Modern Art, had improved her institution across her long career; yet no one would list it on any national register. Still, these provincial institutions—not even high provincial institutions by museum standards—did sustain a strong sense of intimacy and appreciation with the non-elite majority of the city, who continued to support them from the public treasury and to visit them with gratifying frequency.

What was truly vital in Bay Area art in this period—the abstract expressionism of such figures as Clyfford Still, Elmer Bischoff, Mark Rothko, Richard Diebenkorn, and Sam Francis, followed by the figurativism of David Park, Manuel Neri, Joan Brown, and others—was far beyond the reach of popular taste. While an avant-garde elite comprised of Baghdaders whose tastes had been formed elsewhere, together with assorted high provincials, most of them from the Jewish community, might appreciate abstract expressionism, the majority of San Franciscans of all classes preferred to see what they could easily understand. Take public sculpture as an example. Haig Patigian, the leading artist in this genre, had been active since the mid-1930s in an organization calling itself the Society for Sanity in Art. From August to October 1940, the society sponsored a highly successful exhibit of approved painting and sculpture at the Palace of the Legion of Honor. By the time of his death in September 1950, sculptures by Patigian—among them a Lincoln in front of City Hall, the Volunteer Fireman's Memorial in Washington Square, Friendship at the entrance of the Olympic Club at Lakeside, a bust of tennis star Helen Wills, a statue of Thomas Starr King in the Statuary Hall of the United States Capitol—had helped define and strengthen the conventional tastes of high provincial San Francisco in matters of public art. Even the most ambitious public statuary in the city, an original cast of Rodin's *The Thinker* at the entrance to the Palace of the Legion of Honor and the collection of Rodins within, presented art that was understandable to majority tastes, as did *El Cid* and *Jeanne d' Arc* by Anna Hyatt Huntington flanking the entrance.

Even the most bohemian and avant-garde of San Francisco sculptors, Beniamino Bufano—a true radical, who had cut off a finger to protest the draft of World War I—created sculptures (rabbits, owls, seals, sea birds, nursing bears, multiple St. Francis of Assisis) that, while stylized, were comprehensible to public taste;

indeed, Bufano's work was emplaced in housing projects, union halls, the airport, and the Steinhart Aquarium in Golden Gate Park; and Bufano became a revered public figure, supported free of charge by the Press Club on Post Street, where he lived and took his meals. So too were the two most popular artists of the city—the Bolivian-born Antonio Sotomayor and the Hong Kong– and Paris-trained Dong Kingman—committed to representational art, however variegated. Arriving in San Francisco in 1923 and going to work as a dishwasher at the Palace Hotel, Sotomayor—a magical realist in the fairy-tale style of Marc Chagall—emerged by the late 1930s as the muralist of choice for establishment San Francisco, as symbolized by his murals for the Cirque Room at the Fairmont and, eventually, a panel of historic murals in Grace Cathedral atop Nob Hill. By the 1950s watercolorist Dong Kingman—a Chinese American whose style melded classical Chinese painting, French Impressionism, and touches of Walt Disney—was dividing his time between New York, where he taught at Columbia, and Hollywood, where he was producing award-winning opening screen credits, and San Francisco, where he did the murals for the Bank of California, pursued a freelance magazine cover practice, sold his work in local galleries, and co-produced a book on San Francisco with Herb Caen.

Ballet, orchestra, opera, and theater had an easier time making the transition to Baghdad, for these art forms, with the possible exception of theater, were being advanced by high provincial San Francisco at such a level of ambition, taste, and performance that even newcomers confessed themselves impressed. Tracing itself to the opera ballet established in 1933, the San Francisco Ballet had been developed since 1952 by Lew Christensen, a former associate of George Balanchine at the New York City Ballet, into an impressive regional company, worthy of three State Department tours of Europe and Asia in the late 1950s. A talented dancer and choreographer, Christensen seemed to understand instinctively that if he were to succeed, he would have to satisfy high provincial and Baghdad tastes simultaneously: hence the value of his full-length signature *Nutcracker*, repeated each holiday season, balanced off against *Filling Station*, a paradigm of ambitious avant-garde dance.

Likewise impressive—on a regional basis—was the Actors' Workshop located in the Marines' Memorial Theatre on Sutter. In times past, high provincial San Francisco had been an important touring vaudeville and theater town, both before and after the Earthquake, in such venues as the Alcazar, the Orpheum, the Columbia, the Valencia, and the Savoy. By the 1950s only two theaters, the Curran and the Geary, were hosting touring or pre-Broadway try-outs. In 1952, however, two veterans of New York theater, Herbert Blau and Jules Irving, founded a repertory company, Actors' Workshop, specializing in the experimental and avant-garde. It was pure Baghdad by the Bay: Baghdad and high provincial audiences, eager to escape their provinciality by sitting through frequently incomprehensible plays such as Samuel Beckett's *Waiting for Godot* (1952). But even Baghdad could not endure a steady diet of Beckett, Brecht, and Genet, especially when a recent Broadway comedy or musical was in town. By 1965 Actors' Workshop had folded for lack of local support, and Blau and Irving decamped for New York. Two years later, a new company, the

American Conservatory Theater (ACT), moved into Marines' Memorial with more lasting results.

No figure better embodied the desire of high provincial San Francisco to take itself seriously as a center for performing arts than Pierre Monteux, maestro of the San Francisco Symphony. High provincial San Franciscans were grateful to Monteux, a classically trained Parisian conductor, because he rescued and reinvigorated a failing orchestra upon his arrival in 1935. Herb Caen featured Monteux constantly in his column: a portly and genial maestro, high in color, eyes alight, smiling behind a luxuriant fin-de-siècle mustache, walking his poodle Fifi in the company of his wife Doris atop Nob Hill in his leisure hours, receiving the clang-clang salute of a passing cable car, sweeping onstage at a near-trot before each performance, then bounding to the podium in defiance of his portliness and conducting from memory, rarely using a score, dining after major performances at the Captain's Table in Trader Vic's, exchanging one or another bon mot with locals and visiting celebrities. For Caen and for Baghdad by the Bay, in general, Monteux offered an unambiguous embodiment of San Francisco as a reprise of Europe, an *outre-mer*, a daydream of Parisian chic. When Monteux returned to the city in 1952 for his final season, a fire department tug escorted his ferry boat across the bay with a running cannonade of seawater, the maritime equivalent of a ticker-tape parade down Market Street.

Following Monteux's return to France, San Francisco nevertheless soon had another equally expressive European maestro on hand, the Vienna-born Kurt Herbert Adler, artistic director of the San Francisco Opera since November 1953, artistic and musical director since 1956, general director since 1957. As a young man, following his graduation from the University of Vienna and the Vienna State Academy of Music, Adler had worked as an accompanist and conductor for Max Reinhardt at the Volksopera before accepting in 1938 a position as choral director at the Lyric Opera of Chicago. From his apprenticeship with the great showman-impresario Reinhardt, the Flo Ziegfeld of European opera, Adler had learned a very important lesson. Opera had to be entertaining. There was, in fact, no contradiction between artistic excellence and the effort to reach as broad an audience as possible by emphasizing costume, scenery, lighting, staging, and acting as well as singing and music. Adler hence entered upon his duties simultaneously able to meet the tastes of high provincial San Francisco for lavish performances of the standard repertoire and the tastes of Baghdad for the new, the challenging, the avant-garde. In his debut season—which he inherited from his predecessor Gaetano Merola, when Merola suffered a fatal heart attack at the podium, but which Adler had also helped to select—Adler catered directly to established tastes; indeed, he persuaded the beloved Monteux to conduct the season, which was dominated by such war horses as *Rigoletto*, *La Forza del Destino*, *Manon*, and *Tosca*. At the same time, Adler salted this standard stew with the recherché (Cherubini's *The Portuguese Inn*) and the avant-garde (Honegger's *Joan of Arc at the Stake*).

Throughout the rest of the decade—in pioneering productions of Sir William Walton's *Troilus and Cressida* in 1955, Zandonai's *Francesca da Rimini* in 1956,

Richard Strauss's *Ariadne auf Naxos* and the American premiere of Poulenc's *Dialogue of the Carmelites* in 1957, Carl Orff's *Die Kluge* in 1958 (on a double bill with the first operatic performance of Orff's *Carmina Burana*), Richard Strauss's *Die Frau Ohne Schatten* in 1959 (an opera Adler had loved as a young man but one that was generally considered un-assimilatable to American audiences), the American premiere of Berg's *Wozzeck* in 1960—Adler, who had himself fled Hitler, showed that a new sensibility, an émigré Baghdad sensibility blending scholarship and showmanship, connoisseurship and a regard for popular support, was defining the program at the War Memorial Opera House. Seasons were fully subscribed, and in such figures as soprano Leontyne Price, singing in *Dialogues of the Carmelites*, up-and-coming singers were making their mark in San Francisco. Only Maria Callas refused to come, canceling in September 1957 a scheduled performance of *Lucia di Lammermoor*, which Callas demanded be rescheduled; Adler refused, launching instead a formal complaint against the diva with the American Guild of Musical Artists. Callas never performed in San Francisco, but the very fact that Adler had the confidence to refuse a last-minute and very expensive rescheduling underscored the confidence felt by the entire company in the validity of what *Chronicle* cultural critic Allan Temko was announcing in *Horizon* magazine for January 1959: namely, that San Francisco now ranked with New York and Chicago as one of the three best permanent opera companies in the nation.

In April 1958 Billy Graham came to San Francisco to conduct a two-month Crusade for Christ at the Cow Palace exposition hall. It was a great success, with Graham taking his Bay Cities Crusade to the naval station on Treasure Island, to the Greek Theater at the University of California, to the campus of San Francisco State, to the Commonwealth Club, and to San Quentin, where 623 convicts decided for Christ. At the final rally at the Cow Palace, a choir of two thousand voices sang under the direction of musical director Cliff Barrows. Billy Graham was taking on Sin City, local newspapers had announced upon his arrival. The success of Graham's crusade suggested that San Francisco was not as sinful as it would like to be. All things considered, San Francisco remained a religiously oriented city. Atop Nob Hill, the Very Reverend C. Julian Bartlett, dean of Grace Cathedral—a Tulane-trained chemical engineer and a descendant of Washington Bartlett, the first alcalde of San Francisco during the period of military government in the 1840s—was spearheading the completion of Grace Cathedral, under construction since 1910. Bartlett's bishop, the Right Reverend James Albert Pike, was Baghdad personified, which is to say, an improbable admixture of substance and self-invention. A former Roman Catholic who had left that church while an undergraduate at Santa Clara University because he could not accept the doctrine of papal infallibility, Pike had gone on to the Yale School of Law, practiced with the Securities and Exchange Commission, taught law at George Washington University, converted with his second wife from agnosticism, joined the Episcopal Church, studied divinity at the Virginia Theological Seminary and the Union Theological Seminary in New York, was ordained an Episcopal priest, then began a rapid climb up the ecclesiastical ladder: rector of a big parish in Poughkeepsie, chaplain at Vassar, chaplain and chairman of the department of religion at Columbia, dean of the Cathedral of St. John the Divine, coadjutor bishop of the Diocese of California. At his consecration ceremony, held at Grace Cathedral on 15 May 1958, the preacher, the Very Reverend John Bowen Coburn, had urged the new bishop to avoid controversy in his ministry. Ignoring this advice, Pike was quite soon questioning such basic Christian doctrines as the Trinity and the Virgin Birth, positions that would help him to lose his job by 1966. In the meantime, Pike played Bishop of Baghdad, questioning the very institution he served—or at the least, probing its ambiguities—in the same way that Howard Gossage was challenging advertising.

As far as Pike's affronts to orthodoxy were concerned, Roman Catholic San Francisco—or mainstream Protestant San Francisco, for that matter—was not amused. Certainly, one could not imagine such heterodox musings emanating from the Most Reverend John J. Mitty, Archbishop of San Francisco since 1935. Mitty was, in point of fact, a leading member of the last generation of American Roman Catholic bishops to experience the near-monarchical power granted them by an immigrant community grateful for such leadership, especially if carried on with a certain in-your-face assertion of Roman Catholic muscle on behalf of the working classes. Seated at his desk in chancery headquarters adjacent to Mission Dolores, Mitty ruled over an archdiocese that extended from San Jose to the Oregon border, encompassing everything except the separately established Diocese of Sacramento. The most salient thing one could say about Mitty was that he was a New Yorker, a powerful and vibrant New Yorker, as was his Los Angeles counterpart and former student at Dunwoodie Seminary when Mitty was teaching there, James Francis Cardinal McIntyre—and his presence as archbishop brought to San Francisco some of the standards and certainties of New York Catholicism. On Good Friday, between the hours of twelve and three, so many downtown workers would crowd Old St. Mary's (1854) on California at the entrance to Chinatown, the proto-cathedral of the city, loudspeakers had to be installed in the park across the street to handle the overflow. The Paulist Fathers had assumed responsibility for St. Mary's in 1894 and were conducting a dual ministry: one aimed at downtown workers (a library, inquiry classes, a variety of social programs serving more than six hundred singles), the other toward the nearby Chinese community, where the Paulists had established a Chinese mission in 1903 on Stockton and where now the Old St. Mary's Chinese Center (1921) teemed each day with meetings of Boy Scouts, Cub Scouts, Campfire Girls, the Holy Name Society, a boys' club, a girls' club, and rehearsal sessions of a drum and bugle corps featured in every major parade, marching in full uniform behind dragon dancers.

Frontier San Francisco—indeed, frontier America—had proven an especially congenial setting for German-Jewish immigrants of the Reform persuasion. Among the founders of San Francisco, their names adorned its most conspicuous monuments and philanthropies, and one could not even consider the economic, cultural, or political vitality of San Francisco in the 1950s without reference to the participation of San Francisco Jews in every aspect of civic life. Here was the community that had opened the first stores of the city, invented the first copper-riveted denim jeans, imported the coffee, tea, and spices, pioneered in the Alaskan and Asian trade, brought hydroelectricity down from the mountains, opened the most venturesome banks and insurance companies, served on cultural boards and commissions, produced two violin prodigies (Yehudi Menuhin and Isaac Stern, both instructed by local teacher Louis Persinger), served as reforming mayor and patron to the city (Adolph Sutro), represented the city in Congress (Julius Kahn, succeeded by his wife Florence following his death), produced the first female to win tenure at UC Berkeley (Jessica Peixotto, economics), patronized the arts and scholarship (Sydney Ehrman, Albert Bender), gave depth to local law and medicine, imported psychiatry and psychoanalysis, raised its public schools to the first rank. In 1956 Lowell, the high school of preference for the Jewish community, was celebrating its centennial. A consolidation in 1894 of a number of previously established institutions, including the pioneering Boys' High School and Girls' High School, Lowell had developed over the years into a rigorous and academically comprehensive academy—the Boston Latin, the Horace Mann, the Stuyvesant of San Francisco—feeding its graduates almost automatically into Cal or Stanford.

Rabbi Alvin Fine of Temple Emanu-El, a former Army chaplain with World War II experience in the China theater, was called to San Francisco in 1948 at the age of thirty-one from his post as assistant to the president of the Hebrew Union College in Cincinnati by a search committee headed by Harold Zellerbach, president of the congregation. The liberal politics of Alvin Fine, a Baghdad rabbi brought into town by a high provincial congregation, underscored the political transformation of San Francisco—from right to left—that while not a fait accompli was nevertheless discernible throughout the 1950s. For all its flamboyant politics on the left, the predominant political cast of high provincial San Francisco was either Republican or union-oriented, meat-and-potatoes New Deal Democrat. Adopted in 1932, the charter of San Francisco, a product of Progressive reform, envisioned and implemented a city that was as insulated as possible from the vagaries of politics. Nine major departments, for example, were run by an appointed chief administrative officer (CAO) holding lifetime tenure. Nearly all departments, whether reporting to the CAO or to the mayor, were governed by citizen commissions. By the postwar era, San Francisco resembled a fully serviced, semi-autonomous city-state, characterized by efficient departments (the fire department was one of the best in the nation), a civil service appointed by examination and supervised by a quasi-autonomous civil service commission, elegant public buildings, most of them Beaux-Arts classical revival or Mediterranean in style, a nationally ranked public school system, graced by some of the finest school architecture in the nation, and such amenities as a distinguished park and library system, neighborhood playgrounds and recreation centers with professional staff on hand, public swimming pools and playing fields, two municipally supported golf courses, a number of publicly supported tennis courts, publicly subsidized opera, symphony, museums, and a municipal zoo.

The fundamental conservatism of San Francisco was based, in part, on its monolithic culture. For all its diversity of ethnic and linguistic groups—the Italians of North Beach and the Excelsior, the Greeks south of Market, the Irish and Hispanics of the Mission, the Russians and Germans in the Western Addition and Inner Richmond, the Jewish community in the northwest quadrant, the Maltese of Butchertown—Census 1950 revealed San Francisco (population 775,357) to be a city that was 89.5 percent white: 74 percent of them native-born, 15.5 percent foreign-born immigrants. (Hispanics, not yet a separate category, were classified as whites.) San Francisco, in short, was an overwhelmingly white city, with its African American population standing at 5.6 percent, its Chinese population 3.2 percent, its Japanese-population at 0.8 percent, and all other non-whites comprising a mere 1.0 percent of the total population. While its single population was showing signs of growth, the city remained a family-oriented community, with the majority of the population living in single-family or extended-family households. All this made for a cautious high provincial practice of politics among Republicans and Democrats alike, inspired by the Republican-Democrat détente that had shaped the charter. San Francisco was governed by negotiated arrangements among the corporate sector, small businesses, centrist unions, the civil service, and white homeowners living in family arrangements. All this made for a fundamentally conservative political culture.

Since 1912 all mayors of San Francisco had been Republicans: shipping executive James (Sunny Jim) Rolph Jr. from 1912 to 1930, florist Angelo Rossi from 1931 to 1944, another shipping magnate, Roger Lapham, from 1944 to 1948, former superior court judge Elmer Robinson from 1948 to 1956, dairy owner George Christopher from 1956 to 1964. Whatever their differences—Rolph the flamboyant Tory bohemian, Rossi the conservative businessman, Lapham the large-living clubman and bon vivant, Robinson the Masonic jurist and book collector, Christopher the up-from-the-streets autodidact and hands-on manager—these mayors had in common a consistently cautious Republican philosophy of government that when it got off course usually veered to the right.

By the mid-1950s a Harvard man and a Yalie, thirty-something Republicans, were representing San Francisco in the state assembly. San Francisco–born Caspar Weinberger held undergraduate and law degrees from Harvard, had served on General Douglas MacArthur's staff during the war, and clerked for a federal judge before winning election to the assembly in 1952. John Busterud, a University of Oregon graduate, had distinguished himself as an Army infantry lieutenant in Europe during the war, gone on to Yale Law School upon his release from the service, where he served as an editor of the Yale Law Journal, returned to San Francisco to practice, rising through Young Republican ranks before winning election to the assembly in 1956 in a preponderantly Democratic district centered on the Haight-Ashbury. Republican Congressman Bill Mailliard was representing San Francisco in Washington. Rising through the ranks of city and state government, meanwhile, en route to becoming chief administrative officer in 1964, was electrical company executive Thomas Mellon, a San Francisco native with undergraduate and law degrees from USF.

Mellon was an Irish Catholic Republican, a category that was somewhat ahead of its time in this era, but not unknown to San Francisco. The Jewish community was predominately Republican as well, as evident in such past figures as Congressman Julius Kahn and his wife Florence, who succeeded him following his death; city and county supervisor Jesse Coleman; Assemblyman B. J. Feigenbaum; city supervisor and Assemblyman Jefferson Peyser; Assemblyman Albert Wollenberg; and the presently sitting Assemblyman Milton Marks and city supervisor Harold Dobbs. None of these Republicans, however, with the possible exception of Dobbs, was hard right, although this being the 1950s they were all aggressively anti-Communist. While tending to be fiscal conservatives, however, San Francisco Republicans were at home in the public sector; indeed, they administered it well and cut sustaining deals with public sector constituencies. The Republican presence of San Francisco was so strong that it won two national conventions, the convention of 1956 that renominated Dwight Eisenhower and Richard Nixon, and that of 1964, nominating Senator Barry Goldwater.

If the Republicans of San Francisco in that era could get along with Democrats, it was in part because the Democrats showed the same signs of centrist moderation. Congressman John Shelley was an old-time pro-union Democrat who avoided any ideological edge. Lawyer William Malone, the longtime (1938–61) chair of the Democratic county central committee and the closest thing the city had to a Democratic political boss, was a centrist Truman Democrat (Truman was, in fact, a longtime personal friend), another practicing Catholic and USF graduate, culturally cautious in the midst of his commitment to the New Deal. George Reilly, a longtime (forty-four years) member of the State Board of Equalization for San Francisco, responsible for establishing taxes on retail sales, cigarettes, liquor, timber, and gasoline, was the epitome of the old-time Irish politician: local (born in the Mission district), Catholic (a graduate of Sacred Heart High School), a genial toastmaster (serving as chairman of the annual St. Patrick's Day parade for twenty-seven years, a Supreme Governor of the World of the Loyal Order of Moose, a founder of the Irish-Israeli-Italian Society), and two-time candidate for mayor. While never elected to office, barkeep John Monaghan, a veteran of fierce fighting in the South Pacific with the Marine Corps, wielded considerable political influence from behind the brass rail and polished mahogany at his Log Cabin watering hole on Upper Market Street and, by the 1950s, at his Ten Club at Sanchez and Duboce. Speaking in the rapidly vanishing South of Market accent of the early twentieth century in a voice that *Chronicle* writer Carl Nolte compared to crushed gravel, Monaghan practiced the ward-heeling politics of Irish America (one of his brothers was a fireman, the other a priest), delivering precincts (Eureka Valley, the Castro, Upper Market) and doing favors. A Democrat such as Monaghan, and the cops, firemen, teamsters, retirees, and other ordinary folk he served as barkeep and ward-heeler were by definition committed to a politics of give-and-get as opposed to ideological, much less dialectical, conflict based on class warfare.

The détente between Republicans and Democrats structured and nurtured the political career of Edmund G. (Pat) Brown, a Republican turned Democrat who served as San Francisco district attorney from 1944 to 1950 and was from 1950 to 1959 serving in Sacramento as attorney general of the state. A graduate of Lowell and evening law school, Brown had switched from Republican to Democrat in 1934 without much alteration to his basically centrist point of view. In November 1958 he was elected governor, taking two San Franciscans to Sacramento with him. *San Francisco Chronicle* reporter Hale Champion, Brown's press secretary, later became director of finance for the state, and attorney William Coblentz, Brown's research secretary, eventually returned to San Francisco to become the most influential political lawyer in the city and a longtime regent of the University of California.

The unions of San Francisco, openly Democratic in their preference, were, like Malone, Reilly, and Monaghan, cautious and pragmatic. Joe Mazzola, for example, business manager for Local 38 of the Plumbers and Pipefitters Union, was busy negotiating some of the most remarkable collective bargaining agreements in the history of labor, bringing to the West Coast for the first time such benefits as paid vacations, health and welfare coverage, and pension plans. Harry Lundeberg, president of the Sailors' Union of the Pacific, was a leading anti-Communist. Even Harry Bridges, the notorious leader of the Great Strike of 1934, a man whom the federal government spent the first half of the 1950s trying to deport back to Australia as a Communist, registered himself—perhaps tongue in cheek—as a Republican. At the center of the decade, mayor from 1956 to 1964, was the greatest high provincial Republican of them all, George Christopher. Born in Greece and brought to San Francisco at the age of two, Christopher had grown up in the Greek community South of Market, his father running a diner at Third and Minna, working from four in the morning to seven at night. A man of formidable intelligence and sensitivity, learning to play the violin as a boy, Christopher was forced to leave Galileo High School in the early 1920s without graduating to go to work in the advertising department of the *San Francisco Examiner*. Leaving Galileo, Christopher, an ardent reader, continued his education through the American Hellenic Education and Progress Association, a group that met for discussion of great books and the practice of public speaking. Going into the milk distribution business, Christopher became a millionaire by age thirty-eight, married to a strikingly beautiful wife, Tula, also of Greek descent, from whom he was inseparable. In 1945 he won election to the board of supervisors. Defeated for mayor by Elmer Robinson in 1951, Christopher won election on his second try in 1955, taking office in 1956.

The *Holiday* April 1961 special edition covering San Francisco featured a two-page photograph of Christopher standing before a cable car stopped in the intersection of Powell and California, at the cusp of Nob Hill, on which were sitting restaurateur Joe Paoli, restaurateur and former Seals manager Frank (Lefty) O'Doul, nightclub owner and writer Barnaby Conrad, model Lily Valentine, Charlie Low, noted polo player and owner of Forbidden City, advertising executive Howard Gossage, and Herb Caen. The picture said it all: George Christopher was the all-commanding, totally in charge mayor of the town, its number one citizen and spokesman, the man who more than anyone else had brought the Giants to San Francisco. A Republican, Christopher nevertheless had the near-total support of Democratic voters and wielders of influence. In his early years of self-education, he had learned to respect the Irish for their love of learning and their virtuosity as public speakers. As mayor Christopher sustained the Irish hegemony at the fire department, appointing veteran William Murray chief, and, to the surprise of many, he promoted homicide inspector Frank Ahern up through the ranks to be chief of police. When Ahern succumbed to a heart attack at a Giants game in September 1958, Christopher turned to another Irish Catholic, Thomas Cahill, then serving as deputy chief, and placed yet another Irish Catholic, Al Nelder, in the deputy chief's slot.

Christopher had been impressed, initially, with the way that Frank Ahern had taken on the abortion racket in San Francisco and had led the raid on 1275 Bay Street that brought down the infamous madam Mabel Malotte, who had eluded the authorities for nearly a quarter of a century. For all his South of Market gutsyiness, there was in George Christopher a strain of the puritanical, motivated in part by the fact that he had in 1940 been arrested for violating milk pricing laws: a conviction that had been almost totally forgotten but that prompted, perhaps, Christopher's decision to reverse the somewhat laissez-faire attitudes of the Elmer Robinson administration and turn up the heat on prostitution, gambling, abortion, and homosexual activity, which gave great irony, incidentally, to charges by city assessor Russell Wolden Jr. seeking to unseat Christopher in 1959, that the Christopher administration was soft on homosexuals. High provincial San Francisco had always been liberal in matters of private life. Mayor Rolph had once opened a municipal ball with one of the leading madams of the town on his arm. Mayor Robinson—in his personal life an upright married man—believed that if San Francisco were to maintain its reputation as the Paris of the West, it would have to take a Parisian attitude toward certain matters, within limits. Christopher's anti-vice initiatives hence represented the beginnings of a break with the old high provincial attitudes.

The politics of Baghdad were, in general, liberal to left, as symbolized most conspicuously in the left-liberal point of view of Herb Caen, the social activism of Rabbi Alvin Fine, and the liberal Democratic politics of two newcomers to the Jewish community, hotelman Ben Swig and real estate investor Walter Shorenstein. The rising star of a new Democratic politics, moreover, Assemblyman Phillip Burton, defeated Republican incumbent Tommy Maloney in November 1956 without the support—indeed, in the face of the active hostility—of the centrist-oriented William Malone machine. Raised by his physician father in the comfort of St. Francis Wood, Burton, of Irish Catholic origins, could have been expected to become a high provincial centrist. He became, instead, a hard-edged left-liberal infighter, in the first phases of building an equally left-liberal machine that would dominate San Francisco for the rest of the century, thanks, in part, to the continuing support of African Americans and Baghdaders. In June 1958 John Bussey was sworn in as the first black judge in San Francisco history. That December Governor-elect Pat Brown named Cecil Poole of San Francisco, a graduate of Harvard Law, his clemency secretary, making Poole the first African American to serve in the cabinet of a California governor. Things were changing, as a politically ambitious young African American lawyer by the name of Willie Brown knew full well. High provincial San Francisco had long been a closed town as far as black political participation was concerned, but those days would soon be over.

Even George Christopher was showing himself capable of the unexpected, as in the case of the visit in September 1959 by Soviet premier Nikita Khrushchev. On a tour of the United States at the height of the Cold War, Khrushchev had been treated rudely, or so he alleged, by Los Angeles mayor Norris Poulson and was in a foul mood by the time he reached San Francisco. Christopher welcomed Khrushchev to the city enthusiastically, personally showing him around town. Khrushchev in turn proclaimed San Francisco the best city in the United States and invited Christopher to tour the Soviet Union, which the mayor did in March 1960. It was a public relations coup worthy of Baghdad by the Bay: a conservative high provincial anti-Communist Republican soothing a Soviet premier on behalf of world peace.

Other native sons were joining Baghdad as well. Journalist Warren Hinckle, for example, an Irish-German Catholic from USF, founded *Ramparts*, a left-liberal journal originally concerned with the reform of the Roman Catholic Church that would soon be playing an important role in the far left politics of the 1960s. Governor Pat Brown's son Jerry was studying for the priesthood in the Jesuit order in Los Gatos, where he was absorbing a comparable radicalism nurtured on Thomas Merton, Dorothy Day, Ivan Illich, and others, together with Catholic social democratic teaching, that would also shape his distinctive brand of radical politics as governor of the state in the 1970s. On 4 October 1950, the feast of St. Francis of Assisi, Franciscan Father Alfred Boeddeker, pastor of St. Boniface Church in the inner-city Tenderloin district, opened St. Anthony's Dining Room at 45 Jones. Within a few months, the Dining Room was daily feeding some 350 hungry transients, unemployed, or otherwise impoverished. Within six months, some 1,200 to 1,500 people per day were showing up for meals, and Father Alfred bought the first of two farms to grow produce for his operation and offer some of his clients an opportunity to get their lives together through outdoor work. Soon the nearby Glide Memorial Methodist Church would begin to offer a similar program of free food service. Glide's pastor, the Reverend Cecil Williams, an African American, was especially skillful in securing federal funds to support his program and making Glide an epicenter for left-liberal Democratic Party activity. In September 1963, as conservative Republican Harold Dobbs was running for mayor against Democratic Congressman Jack Shelley, African American activists conducted a sit-in at Mel's Drive-in on Geary, owned by Dobbs, protesting its hiring practices. In November Jack Shelley won the mayoralty, and the Jewish vote, despite the strong Republican registration of the Jewish community and the fact that Dobbs was Jewish. A high provincial centrist with Baghdad support, Shelley was the first Democratic mayor of San Francisco in fifty-five years.

When it came to a most crucial element of municipal governance, planning and development, the high provincial/Baghdad dichotomy asserted itself with surprising results. Far from being nostalgically antiquarian or preservationist, high provincial San Francisco wanted to remake and modernize the city. Baghdad San Franciscans, by contrast, who had chosen the city in part because of its urban and architectural charm, grew strongly preservationist in their orientation as high provincials sought to tear down and revamp the city.

Pushing the permanent and transient population of the city well past the million mark each working day, the war had put an enormous strain on the urban fabric of San Francisco. Already in 1942, the San Francisco Planning Commission was talking about the need to revamp the city. The Western Addition, J. C. Geiger, M.D., director of the Department of Public Health, warned a congressional committee, was a blighted area of decaying and unhealthy Victorians, in the process of becoming a ghetto for the African Americans flooding into the city. That same year, the planning commission began to turn its attention to the produce market near the Embarcadero, claiming that it, too, required redevelopment. In July 1944 the planning commission issued *Postwar Improvements: A Handbook*, calling for the postwar development of San Francisco as a business and manufacturing center. In early 1945 Mayor Lapham appointed a Citizens Postwar Planning Commission to consider the whole question of postwar infrastructure development and redevelopment where necessary. The chamber of commerce, meanwhile, was calling for the creation of a comprehensive Bay Area–wide plan. In 1945 Governor Earl Warren signed the Community Redevelopment Act, allowing cities to create governmental entities empowered to acquire and redevelop urban areas. Almost immediately, San Francisco formed its redevelopment agency and turned its attention to the Western Addition and the produce market.

By 1947 San Francisco had a total black population of fifty-one thousand, ten times its prewar number. Some thirty-five thousand of them lived in the Fillmore district of the Western Addition. In May of that year, District Attorney Pat Brown documented the decrepit conditions of housing in the older parts of San Francisco, including the Western Addition, Chinatown, and the South of Market. The respected city planner Mel Scott, meanwhile, was calling for the redevelopment of the entire Western Addition, which he described as blighted. There was much anxiety in the city regarding the fact that 30 percent of the unemployed in San Francisco were blacks, and that the Fillmore district had more tuberculars than any other area except the Skid Row south of Market. While the Western Addition comprised only 8 percent of the total population of the city, it was accounting for 16 percent of its crime. In 1948 the board of supervisors designated the 280 blocks of the Western Addition as a blighted area to be redeveloped. Thus was unleashed, with some delays, a twenty-year war on the aging Victorians of the district, which were demolished by the hundreds, eventually the thousands. Whatever its motivations—and the question of redevelopment as black removal has to be raised—high provincial San Francisco was certainly not showing much sentiment in the matter of preserving the historic housing stock of the city.

In 1951 the Redevelopment Agency turned its attention to Diamond Heights, 325 hilly and rocky acres south of Twin Peaks, which Redevelopment envisioned as an enclave of townhouses and apartment buildings for more than two thousand families, served by shopping centers, schools, parks, and playgrounds. Planned in part by architect Vernon DeMars, Diamond Heights eschewed the quaint and the picturesque in favor of an aggressively modern idiom. When litigation slowed down both the Western Addition and the Diamond Heights projects, Redevelopment turned its attention to the razing of the forty-four acre produce market on the northern edge of the downtown, whose buildings and protocols went back to the mid-nineteenth century, to be replaced by the Golden Gateway, an equally modernist enclave designed by Skidmore, Owings & Merrill, of apartment and office buildings and a 1,300-car garage topped by a pedestrian mall. Like the Western Addition and Diamond Heights projects, the Golden Gateway project also became stalled in litigation. Yet, however delayed these projects might be, a pattern had asserted itself. High provincial San Francisco was interested in modernizing itself, with little regard for antiquarian and/or preservationist values.

At this point, in 1955, the business community threw its influence solidly behind redevelopment in the form of a Committee of Eleven—more popularly known as the Blyth-Zellerbach Committee, after its two leaders: J.D. Zellerbach, president of Crown Zellerbach, and investment banker Charles Blyth—which breathed new life into the Western Addition, Diamond Heights, and Golden Gateway projects. San Francisco, the Blyth-Zellerbach Committee decided, needed a redevelopment czar, a Robert Moses figure. In May 1959 Mayor George Christopher and the Redevelopment Agency found such a director, Justin Herman, fifty, a Phi Beta Kappa graduate of the University of Rochester and the Harvard Business School, a career federal civil servant then heading the United States Housing and Home Finance Agency in the western states. Feisty, imperious, driving himself and others, Herman over the course of the next decade pushed these and other redevelopment projects to conclusion and, in so doing, significantly remade the city.

One of the key proposals of the Blyth-Zellerbach Committee was that the Embarcadero Freeway, first proposed in 1947, be built underground. This did not happen. In an astonishing display of pragmatic, even brutalist, modernism, the state—without aggressive resistance from the city—spent the year 1957 and the first half of 1958 constructing a two-decker freeway along the Embarcadero that sealed off from view, even from pedestrian access, major portions of the waterfront. It was the triumph, or the nadir, of modernist transportation planning—high provincial planning, if you will—with next to no Baghdad concerns for aesthetics, access, or view. True, another program was under way: a Bay Area Rapid Transit (BART) interurban system first proposed in 1947 but not funded until November 1962. BART was for the future. For the time being, the automobile remained triumphant in San Francisco despite its crowded streetscape and—the two great bridges notwithstanding—the narrowness of its accessibility to its hinterlands.

As early as 1945, the state was planning a series of freeways to link the Bay Area before veering south to Los Angeles. The plan was augmented and further refined in 1953. In 1957 the state opened a new bridge across the Bay, linking Richmond and San Rafael. The following year, the state completed a bridge across the Carquinez Straits, facilitating automobile traffic between San Francisco, Sacramento, and the northern interior. In 1958 a freeway running down the East Bay, linking San Jose, Oakland, and San Francisco—the Nimitz Freeway, named in honor of Fleet Admiral Chester M. Nimitz, a San Francisco resident on Yerba Buena Island—was ready for service. High provincial San Francisco not only approved of these developments, but played a considerable role in implementing them.

Nor did high provincial San Francisco mourn the past. In 1947 Mayor Roger Lapham had come close to closing down the city's cable car system until thwarted by an early Baghdad by the Bay campaign led by activist Frieda Klussmann. In September 1956, however, the Washington-Jackson cable car line was closed down with minimal resistance. Throughout the 1950s many of the streetcar lines of the city were replaced with buses; and in May 1958 the remaining boxy two-man streetcars on Market Street were replaced with new one-man models, streamlined and efficient. Ferry boat service on the Bay, meanwhile, went into steady decline, and in October 1961 the ferries, removed from service, were auctioned off. High provincial San Francisco had other modes of transportation on its mind. In November 1956 voters approved a $25 million bond issue to build a second terminal at the San Francisco International Airport and to lengthen its runways to accommodate jetliners. On 18 November 1958, the first DC-8 jetliner, from United Airlines, made a demonstration landing at San Francisco Airport. On 20 March 1959 TWA inaugurated jet service between San Francisco and New York.

The city, meanwhile, seemed in a frenzy of demolition as historic structure after historic structure fell to the wrecking ball. Down in May 1958 came the Crystal Plunge Salt Water Baths on Lombard Street between Taylor and Columbus, closed since 1956. Down in 1959 came the Montgomery Block, a landmark since 1853. Down in late 1959 came the Crystal Palace on Market Street at Eighth, a cavernous food court constructed in the aftermath of the Earthquake. Down in February 1961 came the nearby Fox Theater, one of the great movie palaces of the era, opened in June 1929; and down in February 1962 came the State Theater at Fourth and Market, built in 1917 as the California Theater. Down in June 1961 came the ornately Italianate Hall of Justice on Kearny Street. Closed in September 1952, the historic Sutro Baths at Land's End were incinerated within the decade by an arsonist's torch. Any one of these structures, had they survived into the Baghdad era, would most likely have been redeveloped as themed properties: the Fox Theater as the new symphony hall for the city; the Crystal Palace as the epicenter for an emergent food and wine culture; the Sutro Baths as a Chelsea Piers–like indoor recreation center; the Hall of Justice as mixed-use office/retail complex. But high provincial San Francisco was not interested in such things because, it claimed, preservation did not pencil out, although the Maiden Lane Promenade dedicated in August 1957 did transform a disreputable alley into a profitably chic shopping street, but more because the very idea, the Baghdad by the Bay idea, of preserving these structures was not part of its modernist mindset.

What high provincial San Francisco had in mind for its future, by contrast, was the ultra-modern Crown Zellerbach Building at Bush and Market dedicated in January 1960, a steel and glass structure by Hertzka & Knowles and Skidmore, Owings & Merrill, instantly compared to Lever House in New York City, also by SOM, and cited by San Franciscans as the signature building for the downtown future. The existing skyline of San Francisco, it was argued, was cluttered with too many pseudo-historical references—Doric, Gothic, Florentine, even Mayan—what Le Corbusier once described as an architectural zoo. Forget such fussy antiquarianism, high provincial San Francisco argued. What was needed was buildings like the Crown Zellerbach headquarters, the adjacent circular branch of the American Trust Company, also by SOM, and the nearby John Hancock Western Home Office Building, another SOM design, and such other modernist buildings as the Equitable Life Building on Market, the Masonic Temple and Auditorium atop Nob Hill, the Jack Tar Hotel and Office Building at Van Ness and Geary: buildings that suggested the impending San Francisco as a triumph of integrated modernism.

Herb Caen loathed the Jack Tar, sitting atop its six-hundred-car garage, in all its modernist splendor, and had equally hostile things to say about the brutalist arrogance of the new Federal Building on Golden Gate and the new Hall of Justice on Bryant. Caen loved, however, the crumbling Palace of Fine Arts, a Piranesian dome and colonnade designed by Bernard Maybeck for the Panama Pacific International Exposition of 1915, during the visiting of which from Sacramento, Caen claimed, his parents had conceived him. As early as 1952 a Citizens Committee for the Preservation of the Palace of Fine Arts had argued that it would be barbaric for San Francisco to allow the Palace of Fine Arts to fall into ruin, much less demolish it. Maybeck himself, shortly before his death in Berkeley at the age of ninety-five in October 1957, told Caen that he thought the Palace should be allowed to decay like the ruin it was intended to suggest. Surround the Palace with redwoods, Maybeck urged Caen. They will grow as the Palace falls into ruin and provide a tableau vivant of nature replacing art. As the spokesman for Baghdad value, however, Caen continued to call for the restoration of the crumbling icon.

High provincial San Francisco remained unmoved, and in November 1958 voters rejected a municipal bond issue, Proposition B, that would have allotted $3.6 million toward the restoration of the Palace, despite the fact that Assemblyman Caspar Weinberger had already secured a $2 million grant from the state. Then a Baghdader, lumberman Walter S. Johnson, president of the Palace of Fine Arts League, announced in May 1959 a $2 million gift to the city to restore the Palace in conjunction with the state funds. Shamed by such generosity, the voters of San Francisco that November approved a $1.8 million bond issue to be added to the state funds and to Johnson's gift. Not only was the saving of the Palace of Fine Arts a Baghdad gesture against the demolition going on elsewhere in the city, it provided a metaphor for the reconstruction of the San Francisco identity. The Palace of Fine Arts was not only saved. It was taken down, rotunda and columns, and rebuilt in steel and concrete through the mid-1960s, its ornamentation recast from molds made from the originals. In its efforts to save the signature expression of San Francisco, Baghdad was actually creating a new structure, just as Baghdaders would soon be stripping Victorians down to the studs and building new identities within.

Baghdad, meanwhile, was likewise reconstructing what was to become by 1963 the city's leading newspaper, the *Chronicle*. Like nearly all American cities in this era, San Francisco defined itself through its newspapers. An earlier frontier era witnessed the founding of three of the four San Francisco newspapers—the *Call-Bulletin* (1855), the *Chronicle* (1865), the *Examiner* (1887)—that survived into the 1950s. The fourth, the *News*, a Scripps-Howard paper, was founded in 1903. The postwar period was for San Francisco a *Front Page* time, with four newspapers—the *Chronicle* and the *Examiner* in the morning, the *Call-Bulletin* and *News* in the afternoon—battling each other for circulation. With 212,000 subscribers, the *Examiner* led the field. The flagship of the Hearst empire, the *Examiner* was, as might be expected, a conservative, straightforward, no-nonsense kind of a newspaper, although such *Examiner* writers as Alexander Fried on music and the arts, Luther Nicholas on books, Robert Patterson (writing as Freddie Francisco) on talk-of-the-town, and Prescott Sullivan on sports were lively and accomplished writers. The afternoon *Call-Bulletin*, another Hearst-owned paper, emphasized fast-breaking news, crime, local politics, and sports. Although not a writers' paper per se, which went against the curent Hearst policy favoring strong editorial control, the *Call-Bulletin* (a merger in 1925 of two frontier-era papers, the *Call* and the *Bulletin*) possessed a certain breezy attitude. Sections of the paper were published on either pink or green newsprint. Mark Twain had once written for the *Call*, and turn-of-the-century editor Fremont Older had put the *Bulletin* on the forefront of crusading reform. The *Call-Bulletin* also had on its staff as a talk-of-the-town columnist Paul Speegle, a Stanford graduate with a Hastings College law degree, a former Hollywood actor, toastmaster-in-chief to the city, and future president of the Press and Bohemian clubs. Despite the fact that it was intended for the working people of the city, the *News*, as of the early 1950s, supported an impressive array of columnists and feature writers: Arthur Caylor on politics, Jack Rosenbaum on talk-of-the-town, and the syndicated column of Robert Ruark. The *News* also maintained the most extensive program of home delivery, with three thousand carriers distributing it daily from its six-story plant at 812 Mission Street. The *Recorder*, the legal newspaper, was also a respected publication, edited by Edward Francis O'Day, a reporter with a lineage extending to the pre-Earthquake era. So too was the African American paper, the *Sun-Reporter*—published by Carlton Goodlett, a Ph.D. in child psychology from UC Berkeley, and edited by longtime reporter Thomas Fleming—gaining momentum throughout the decade. The

Press and Union League Club on Post Street offered hotel rooms, food service, a library, a bar pouring generous drinks, slot machines (dubious in their legality), and a swimming pool in the basement. Practically every week, celebrities of every sort made their pilgrimage to the Press Club to speak off the record at lunches or dinners before a statue of the Club trademark, a sleek and self-satisfied black cat.

The fourth leading newspaper of the city, the *Chronicle*, entered the 1950s with an identity crisis. Its longtime editor Paul Smith, who had risen from private to lieutenant colonel in the Marine Corps during the war, envisioned the *Chronicle* as a West Coast version of the *New York Times*—a news-oriented, editorially conservative paper, that is, owned by and speaking for the establishment—and ran it accordingly. By the early 1950s, however, both Paul Smith and the *Chronicle* were losing their edge. Seeing himself as a mover and shaker on the national and international scene, Smith was traveling a lot, neglecting his day job. The paper was flat, despite the presence on its staff of such talented writers as music and arts critic Alfred Frankenstein and the San Francisco–born investigative reporter Pierre Salinger. In 1950 Herb Caen transferred his flag to the *Examiner* after a quarrel with Smith, taking more than twenty-five thousand subscribers with him. By 1952 the *Chronicle* circulation stood at a mere 145,000, and the paper was losing a million dollars a year.

With the resignation of Paul Smith, *Chronicle* publisher George Cameron turned to Sunday editor Scott Newhall, who had joined the paper in 1935 at the age of twenty-one as a photographer, and appointed him executive editor. It was a brilliant decision. In his lineage and attitudes Scott Newhall was high provincial enough to satisfy the high provincials: the San Francisco–born grandson of frontier land baron Henry Mayo Newhall, a graduate of the Webb School for Boys, with three years at UC Berkeley. At the same time, Newhall was flamboyant enough, ironic enough, even zany enough at times, to earn his Baghdad credentials. He also had a Bay Area–wide perspective. While born in San Francisco, Newhall had not been raised in the city but in Marin and Southern California. Even at the height of his tenure at the *Chronicle*, he lived in Berkeley. Having lost part of one leg as the result of an accident on an exploring expedition in Baja California, hence draft exempt, Newhall had distinguished himself as a correspondent in London during the Battle of Britain and had put himself in harm's way covering high-speed gunboats engaged in combat off the coasts of Holland and Germany.

Thus Newhall was Baghdad in his non–San Francisco upbringing, his wartime experiences, his savoir faire and ironic approach to life, his preppie background, his love of vintage cars, which he personally restored (in 1961 winning the Concours d'Elegance at Pebble Beach with a 1930 Packard rumble-seat roadster), his Tory bohemianism (he was at once a member of the old family establishment and the longtime drinking buddy of Herb Caen and other newsmen), his conviction that the San Francisco Bay Area was the most favored place on earth, the just reward for the war generation lucky enough to live there. What the Bay Area needed, Newhall decided, was a newspaper that would further define and intensify this sense of San Francisco and its hinterlands as chosen place, as Baghdad by the Bay. While

Newhall realized the importance of news, he saw the key to this new identity for the *Chronicle* in columns and feature writing by talented writers, with even straight news stories being given a literary edge. In the back of Newhall's mind was something like the *New Yorker*—knowledgeable, sophisticated, assured, ironic, amused by it all—within the context of a daily newspaper staffed by Ivy League Baghdaders or Baghdaders with comparable degrees who wore tweed jackets, button-down shirts, rep ties, slacks, and loafers to work, (for ladies, Seven Sisters attire) and considered themselves the professional equivalent of Berkeley or Stanford faculty.

From the start, Newhall knew he had a problem. Herb Caen was working for the *Examiner*. In the meantime, Newhall recruited and/or promoted from within a slew of Baghdad-oriented writers and editors with the requisite panache: staff such as city editor Abe Mellinkoff, a Stanford graduate, who dressed like an English squire and wore a monocle. To cover architecture and planning, he promoted the byline of the University of Paris–educated Allan Temko, who in 1955 published a highly respected book on Notre Dame Cathedral. From the *New Yorker* Newhall recruited Kevin Wallace. Harvard graduate Art Hoppe, promoted from copy boy to reporter, was given key assignments. (Other Harvard graduates included reporter Maitland Zane and music critic Robert Commandy.) Newhall eventually gave Hoppe his own column dealing with political satire. Hoppe was a local boy, a graduate of the Presidio Hill School and of Lowell High School, with Baghdad attitudes, as were such other favored reporters as Pierre Salinger of the French community, Carolyn Anspacher of the Jewish establishment, James Benét, nephew of the poet Stephen Vincent Benét, reporter George Draper, and Peck's Bad Boy Warren Hinckle, who as editor of the USF student newspaper, the *Foghorn*, had taken it daily into competition with the other four newspapers. Having lost an eye in a childhood accident, Hinckle wore a piratical black eye patch, the moral equivalent of Mellinkoff's monocle, dressed in Brooks Brothers, and, ever the dandy, was invariably shod in black patent leather dancing pumps with grosgrain ribbon bows. Newhall increased attention paid to books (Joseph Henry Jackson, followed by William Hogan after Jackson's death in 1955), jazz (Ralph Gleason, one of the founders of jazz criticism as a genre), the environment (Harold Gilliam), modern art (Thomas Albright), radio and television (Terrence O'Flaherty), travel (Stanton Delaplane), society (Frances Moffat), and editorials (Templeton Peck), and Margot Patterson Doss wrote of her rambles about the city by foot, something that few high provincials would even think of doing.

When it came to the news stories in the front of the newspaper, Newhall encouraged unusual angles of approach. Art Hoppe, for example, covered the execution of Burton Abbott in 1957 at San Quentin strictly in terms of the reactions of the fifty-three witnesses. At the height of the space race, Newhall dispatched Hoppe to Zambia when that tiny African nation declared its intentions to enter the competition. In 1960 Hoppe covered a debate between Kennedy and Nixon strictly in terms of their small talk before the main event. When reports surfaced of a continuing slave trade in the Middle East, Newhall dispatched reporter George Draper (a Baghdad émigré from New York, once married to a Guggenheim) to go to the Arabian peninsula and try to buy a slave. In response to fears regarding thermonuclear war, Newhall assigned reporter Bud Boyd to live in the wilderness as the Last Man on Earth. (Boyd is said to have filed the story from the comfort of a well-stocked cabin.) Newhall also sicced his reporters on mock-investigative stories or encouraged them to crusade against one or another deficiency in the community. Some of them (the lack of good coffee in San Francisco) were amusing; others (a campaign to clothe naked animals) utterly bizarre. An Emperor Norton Treasure Hunt, Newhall's first promotion, named in honor of the mid-nineteenth-century San Francisco eccentric, was highly successful as hundreds of readers, following a series of clues, took to the outdoors, picks and shovels in hand.

But it was columns and columnists that Newhall most had on his mind. He wanted Herb Caen back from the *Examiner*, of course, but until he could pull that off, Newhall wanted to develop as many home-grown columnists as possible. When he could—in the case of Art Hoppe, Allan Temko, and Stanton Delaplane— Newhall encouraged his writers to become columnists. In 1959 he persuaded rewrite man Charles McCabe to start a sports column, "The Fearless Spectator," despite— or was it because of?—the fact that McCabe believed that sports were largely a waste of time. The talents of McCabe, a native of New York City and an erudite and epigrammatic disciple of Montaigne, had come to Newhall's attention when Newhall had sent him to Virginia City to cover a dispute between a bordello and the pastor of the local Catholic church, who wanted the bordello moved from the vicinity of his school. McCabe's brought to Newhall's attention Lucius Beebe, a flamboyant émigré from New York, formerly with the *Herald Tribune*. Newhall persuaded Beebe, a Boston heir of independent means, once profiled in the *New Yorker* as the leading dandy of his era, to join the *Chronicle* as a weekly columnist, covering wine, food, manners, and the good life.

Ever on the lookout for talent, Newhall was introduced to a well-mannered sometime hairdresser, former actor, drama critic, soap opera writer, beauty parlor owner, and wounded veteran of the Tarawa invasion by the name of Marc Spinelli, now working as a producer at the *Chronicle* affiliate KRON-TV. Spinelli wanted to write a column for women. After listening to Spinelli's persuasive spiel, Newhall gave him a column Newhall designated "Beauty and the Beast." Ever inventive, Newhall recast Spinelli as Count Marco, complete with a coat of arms that Newhall himself designed. The count's assignment: to write a glamour column aimed at women, but with the proper amount of Baghdad tongue-in-cheek and playful salaciousness. Newhall provided the newly ennobled count with a Rolls-Royce to drive about town, which the Count did, attending various events, usually in black tie. Perhaps the count's most famous column, published on 4 August 1959, was his advice to wives to bathe jointly with their husbands, being careful to enter the bathtub decorously. In typical *Chronicle* fashion, the count also ran campaigns, such as his Fat Venus series, which conducted a search for an overweight woman whom the Count promised to turn from an ugly duckling into a swan. Chauffeured to Los Angeles in his Rolls-Royce to cover the murder trial of Dr. Bernard Finch alongside such press luminaries as Dorothy Kilgallen, the count covered the trial strictly in terms of whether or not the doctor's girlfriend was truly a blonde. Although at least one of Count Marco's columns earned him a slap in the face from an outraged reader, toward thirty newspapers were soon negotiating to run his material.

Critics derided the *Chronicle* as an unserious and frivolous newspaper, a critique gaining in crescendo after October 1962 when the *New York Times* established a West Coast edition. Newhall got so tired of being criticized at Berkeley parties, he cut back on his socializing in that town, although he was gratified to hear that no less a luminary than Lewis Mumford, then a visiting professor at UC Berkeley, had defended the news section of his paper: perhaps with tongue in cheek, however, in that Mumford said that everything he read on the front page of the *Chronicle* could also be found on the front page of the *New York Times*. And yet the Berkeley criticism was ambivalent, for while the ownership of the *Chronicle* kept it conservative on its editorial pages, most of the writers recruited by Newhall—with the conspicuous exception of the ultramontane Lucius Beebe—were Baghdad liberals, as was the general tone of the newspaper. Even its critics from the School of Journalism at UC Berkeley, grimacing as they dismissed the *Chronicle* as fluff, were reading it on a daily basis, as were so many others in the Bay Area, finding in the newspaper, day by day, corroboration for their choice to live in the San Francisco Bay Area.

Still, Newhall wanted Herb Caen back, and by late 1957 Caen, too, was growing homesick for the *Chronicle*, which had now become such a decidedly Baghdad publication. After almost eight years at the *Examiner*, Caen met with Newhall over a Friday lunch at Bernstein's Fish Grotto on Powell. Send me your new *Examiner* contract, Newhall told Caen. Just cross out *Examiner* and substitute *Chronicle* when appropriate. The *Chronicle* will match the *Examiner*'s offer for you and your assistant Jerry Bundsen. The following Monday, Newhall found the revised and signed contract in his Berkeley mailbox. Caen's return to the *Chronicle* in January 1958 represented, Newhall estimated, a net gain of thirty-five thousand to forty-five thousand subscribers. In desperation, the *Examiner* hired a forty-eight-year-old ex-screenwriter, Art Cohn, to take over the Herb Caen slot. In short order, Cohn bombed. In 1963 the *Chronicle* passed the *Examiner* in circulation. In January 1964 the *New York Times* folded its western edition. Baghdad was trumping the high provincial and, for the time being at least, was holding its own against the eastern establishment.

5

The Cardinal, the Chief, Walter O'Malley, and Buff Chandler

Redefining the City of Angels

FOUR ongoing pieces of civic business—the rapid rise of the Roman Catholic Archdiocese of Los Angeles, the modernization of the Los Angeles Police Department, the building of a stadium for the Dodgers baseball team, and the construction of a Music Center atop Bunker Hill—offer case studies in the transition Los Angeles was making in this era from regional capital to supercity. The individuals directing these developments—James Francis Cardinal McIntyre, Archbishop of Los Angeles; William Henry Parker, chief of police; Walter Francis O'Malley, baseball entrepreneur; and Dorothy Buffum Chandler, philanthropist and arts activist—were each in his or her way pursuing a vision of modernity for the city, county, and region. However differently each of these civic leaders envisioned a new definition for the region—an expanded and efficiently run Roman Catholic archdiocese, the most professional and up-to-date police department in the nation, a major league stadium for a newly arrived major league baseball team, or a world-class venue for music and the performing arts—each enterprise was also resulting from an imposition of will by a single individual on the titanic forces of an emergent metropolitan region. Each protagonist, each enterprise, succeeded; yet each success had its downsides as well.

James Francis McIntyre brought to Los Angeles the big-city attitudes and efficiencies of clerical Catholic New York. As the Auxiliary Archbishop of New York and the longtime chancellor (chief operating officer) of the New York Archdiocese, McIntyre's installation in March 1948 as the second Archbishop of Los Angeles in elaborate ceremonies held in St. Vibiana's Cathedral—an appointment engineered by his boss Francis Cardinal Spellman, Archbishop of New York, from whom McIntyre received the crozier staff of office during the ceremony—can be seen as the ecclesiastical equivalent to the arrival of the Dodgers a decade later. Although Baltimore was the founding diocese of the Roman Catholic Church in the United States and remained the primary see, the Archdiocese of New York—established by Rome in 1808, raised to the dignity of a metropolitan (archepiscopal) see in 1850—emerged in the mid-nineteenth century, in terms of population and political clout, as the epicenter of Roman Catholicism in the United States, as symbolized by St. Patrick's Cathedral on Fifth Avenue, its cornerstone laid in 1858, the most architecturally ambitious Catholic church in the nation. In the decades to follow, the Archdiocese of New York flourished as the American center of Catholic life and culture. Its seminary, St. Joseph's in the Dunwoodie section of Yonkers, rivaled the Catholic University of America in Washington, D.C., as an intellectual center of Catholic thought, as evidenced in its faculty-sponsored *New York Review*, the leading American Catholic theological journal of its day.

It was to Dunwoodie that James Francis Aloysius McIntyre came as a mature man of thirty in October 1916, donning the black cassock of an aspirant to the priesthood. McIntyre was some fifteen years older than the average member of his entering class, having pursued a career on Wall Street since his teenage years, working his way up from messenger boy to stockbroker in the investment firm of H. L. Horton and Company. Following his mother's death, McIntyre had postponed plans for the priesthood in order to support his brother and invalid father, a New York City mounted policeman who had been seriously injured on duty. While taking night classes at Columbia and City College, McIntyre rose steadily on Wall Street, and by age twenty-nine, he was offered a partnership at Horton.

The death of his father that year, however, together with the self-supporting success of his brother, freed McIntyre to reconsider thoughts of the priesthood. Initially, he was attracted to a missionary career with the recently founded Catholic Foreign Missionary Society of America, Maryknoll, headquartered in Ossining, New York, but on the advice from his spiritual director he chose the diocesan priesthood instead. Devoid of Latin and even a regular high school education, McIntyre spent a year in the minor seminary, sitting in classrooms with high school students half his age, preparing for admittance to Dunwoodie. After considering his age and experience, seminary officials at Dunwoodie reduced for McIntyre the usual six-year course to five; and in May 1921, in St. Patrick's Cathedral, the thirty-five-year-old McIntyre, along with forty-one younger men, was ordained to the priesthood by Archbishop Patrick Hayes. Two weeks later, McIntyre was assigned to St. Gabriel's Church on East Thirty-seventh, a low-income, predominantly Irish parish, where he spent two years as a curate.

Not for McIntyre, however, would there be the career that he truly wanted—and that he practiced part-time throughout his life, even as he rose in rank, and full-time following his retirement in 1970—that of a parish priest: saying mass each morning, hearing confessions, visiting the sick, conducting baptisms, marriages, and funerals. McIntyre already stood out from his peers: marked for his financial and stenographic skills and Wall Street credentials. Within weeks of his first assignment, McIntyre was invited on a part-time basis into the chancery to use his skills at shorthand to transcribe testimony in marriage cases. After two years in parish work, Father McIntyre was transferred to the archepiscopal residence at 452 Madison Avenue; and there he remained for the next twenty-five years, living in a small suite on the third floor, traveling each day across a few yards from the residence to the Chancery at 477 Madison Avenue, saying mass each morning at St. Patrick's Cathedral at the side altar of St. Thérèse of Liseux, hearing confessions when possible, offering instruction when he could find the time (a young woman by the name of Dorothy Day sought his counsel) and rising from assistant to Archbishop Hayes, created cardinal in March 1924, to vice chancellor to chancellor with the rank of monsignor to auxiliary bishop and finally to auxiliary archbishop reporting to Cardinal Spellman.

These were for Francis McIntyre glorious New York years: friendships with renowned preacher Monsignor Fulton J. Sheen and former governor Al Smith, the only Catholic thus far to be nominated for the presidency; the other great and near-great who returned his telephone calls; the respect accorded the Church and its representatives by politicians marching past the cathedral on St. Patrick's Day; the near daily dealings with bankers, contractors, and other chancery officials; the splendid ceremonies of the cathedral or his quiet morning mass at a side altar; the hours he stole to sit in the confessional, one of the ways he most preferred to exercise his priesthood; the close association with Cardinal Spellman, who discussed with his auxiliary archbishop in October 1947 the possibilities of either Washington, D.C., or Los Angeles. McIntyre was unwilling to express a preference, perhaps out of reluctance to leave New York, which had been his whole life. At McIntyre's farewell mass, 14 March 1948, St. Patrick's Cathedral was packed, three thousand strong. Monsignor Sheen preached, praising McIntyre as the epitome of the dedicated New York diocesan priest.

When McIntyre arrived by train in Los Angeles, he had never seen the City of Angels, or California for that matter. McIntyre's archepiscopal colleague John J. Mitty of San Francisco, a New York priest who had taught him at Dunwoodie, had at least spent some seasoning time in the West as bishop of Salt Lake City before being transferred to San Francisco. In McIntyre's case, by contrast, the style and values of New York were being directly translated to the woefully inadequate Archdiocese of Los Angeles. The second-in-command of the most developed archdiocese in the United States was now at the helm of one of the least developed. Despite his success in the church, however, McIntyre was not pampered or, for that matter, even very worldly. He was personally austere, rarely if ever took alcohol, and was considered a kind confessor and a compassionate disciplinarian when discipline was required. There was, in fact, a certain austerity to McIntyre, an impression, compounded by his angular leanness, of a certain asceticism, perhaps related to the deprivations of his early life. Yet McIntyre was also a ranking ecclesiastic produced by an intricate culture, a dedicated anti-Communist, a churchman accustomed to authority, efficiency, and the urban milieu. The New York priests under his supervision dubbed the Union-Pacific train taking McIntyre to Los Angeles "the Freedom Train," meaning their freedom from his demanding jurisdiction.

The first four bishops to hold jurisdiction over Los Angeles were Mexican- or Spanish-born. The fifth, George Montgomery, came from old Anglo-American Catholic stock in Kentucky. The last two bishops were Irish-born, including John J. Cantwell, the first archbishop, a gentle and somewhat remote prelate, plagued by ill health in his later years, his household managed by his sister. Father John Dunne, another Irishman, who edited the *Tidings* archdiocesan newspaper for Cantwell, described Cantwell as lacking the commoner's touch but "the right man for this rinky-dink diocese at the time."[1] The very fact that the Reverend Dunne could use such a deprecating term regarding his own diocese underscored the contrast McIntyre was experiencing in the months following his arrival. Governor Earl Warren, Supervisor Raymond Darby of the county, and Mayor Fletcher Bowron of the city were on hand to welcome McIntyre at the official civic reception for the new archbishop that took place on 20 March 1948 at the Philharmonic Auditorium. Still, here was a churchman who had spent the majority of his working life in midtown Manhattan, now governing a rinky-dink archdiocese centered in a city uncertain of its center. Here was a prelate from an archdiocese nearly 150 years in the making, now at the helm of an archdiocese whose fundamental identity, despite its ability to trace its origins back to the Franciscan missionaries of the late eighteenth century, was the futurity—the uncertain and sometimes raw futurity—that lay ahead.

In order to anchor this Archdiocese of Los Angeles onto a more certain identity, Archbishop Cantwell, McIntyre's immediate predecessor, had in the last years of his life raised over a million dollars for a new cathedral to replace the aging St. Vibiana's (1876), now enveloped by Skid Row across from the Union Station and near the Plaza where Los Angeles had been founded in September 1781. Cantwell planned to build the $1.5 million Cathedral of Our Lady of the Angels, a Gothic structure seating twenty-five hundred, on the more fashionable Wilshire Boulevard. Within months of his arrival, however, McIntyre wrote donors to the cathedral asking that they allow him to use the funds for the construction of schools and saying that if such permission were not granted, he would return the disapproving donor's funds. McIntyre's immediate commitment to school and church construction—sixty-four new parochial schools by September 1953, together with eighteen high schools, a minor seminary, and twenty-six new parish churches—represented his response to futurity, which is to say, to growth. Enrollment in the parochial schools of the archdiocese increased from fifty-two thousand to ninety thousand between 1948 and 1953, which still left half of the Catholic children in public schools: which was exactly McIntyre's point. While Archbishop John Ireland of Minneapolis–St. Paul and other midwestern prelates of the liberal wing favored sending Catholic children to public schools with released time for religious instruction, Michael Corrigan, Archbishop of New York from 1885 to 1902, was the leader of those who held the opposite point of view: namely, that Catholics, while proud of their Americanism, required their own institutions to preserve their Catholic identity. The New Yorker in McIntyre, in short, wanted to tone up, toughen up, and consolidate the Catholic presence, New York style, in Los Angeles by making sure that there were enough grammar schools, high schools, parish churches, hospitals and other institutions to serve the burgeoning Catholic community. Between 1948 and 1963 he would build 206 schools, an average of one a month.

McIntyre took the same New York approach to the ecclesiastical administration and culture of the Los Angeles Archdiocese. He made of it, in fact, a Catholic New York on the Pacific, which included the exercise of political muscle. In May 1951 Governor Warren signed a bill ending the taxing of Catholic school buildings, in effect since 1879. When a taxpayers' group sought, via Proposition 3, to reverse this legislation, McIntyre spearheaded a campaign that defeated the referendum at the ballot box. Rather soon, McIntyre brought onto his staff as executive secretary Father Benjamin Hawkes, a financial wizard like his boss. Like McIntyre, Hawkes had delayed his entry into the seminary, in his case to study business administration at Loyola University and to work as an accountant at Lockheed during the war. Ordained by McIntyre in April 1950, Hawkes served—again like McIntyre—a mere two years in parish ministry before being taken into the chancery, where he was made monsignor a mere five years after his ordination. Hawkes spent the next thirty-three years (eight more than McIntyre) as chancellor and second in command. Novelist John Gregory Dunne would later study Hawkes carefully as the model for the Hawkes-like chancellor in his *True Confessions* (1978), a novel set in the Archdiocese of Los Angeles at the time of the Black Dahlia murder.

As of September 1953 McIntyre, Hawkes, the Irish-born auxiliary bishop Timothy Manning, and Inky, a Kerry blue terrier, were in residence at the archbishop's mansion on Fremont Place in the exclusive Hancock Park district, served by an Irish housekeeper, a Chinese cook, and a Filipino gardener-chauffeur. Having lived at Madison Avenue headquarters for nearly all of his priestly career, McIntyre enjoyed the community of Fremont Place, using its spacious rooms for meetings of his council of priest consultors and giving receptions there for various Catholic groups. By this time the cassock buttons, cincture, cape, and skullcap McIntyre wore on such occasions had changed from purple to scarlet. On 29 November 1952 McIntyre had been awakened by an early morning telephone call from a *Los Angeles Examiner* reporter informing him that Pope Pius XII had named him to the College of Cardinals in recognition of the rising importance of Los Angeles and McIntyre's own long and distinguished service. It was the first red hat to come to an American Catholic prelate west of the Mississippi, and it galvanized Los Angeles, Catholic and non-Catholic alike, as yet another proof of the emergent status of the city. Traveling to Rome in mid-January with his entourage on a TWA Constellation hastily named *Prince of the Church*, McIntyre received the red biretta from Pius XII in ceremonies at the Apostolic Palace. The next day, in ceremonies in St. Peter's Basilica, he received the red galero, the thirty-tasseled wide-brimmed hat bespeaking his rank, along with the other new cardinals, this being followed on Sunday by the final ceremony in which McIntyre took possession of his titular church, Santa Anastasia atop the Palatine Hill near the Roman Forum. When the newly invested cardinal returned to Los Angeles, two thousand people jammed St. Vibiana's Cathedral and another thousand stood outside at the installation mass, followed by a luncheon for clergy at the Biltmore Hotel and, a few days later, a civic reception at the Shrine Auditorium, where an audience of sixty-five hundred heard Governor Warren, John Anson Ford, chairman of the Los Angeles County Board of Supervisors, and Mayor Fletcher Bowron thank McIntyre for bringing the honor of the red hat to the City of the Angels.

Meanwhile, another executive of Irish Catholic origins, William Henry Parker, chief of police since 1950, was doing his best to transform the Los Angeles Police Department into a similar paradigm of modernist efficiency. Just as the cardinal had been attracted to his calling since early youth, William Henry Parker, born in Lead, South Dakota, in 1902, the grandson of a United States attorney, the son of a geologist for the Homestake Mining Company, had always wanted to be a policeman— so he would tell his audience in the course of one of the innumerable speeches he made as chief—ever since he had been presented at the age of eight with a small silver badge making him an official deputy of the Deadwood, South Dakota, police department. As a high school student, Parker had served as a bellhop and sometime house detective at the Franklin Hotel in Deadwood, three miles from Lead, where his grandmother ran a boarding house. Parker was especially adept at preventing local daughters of joy from marketing their services in the lobby or upstairs corridors of the hotel, marking the beginning, perhaps, of his lifetime crusade against prostitution. Parker's family moved to Los Angeles in 1923, part of the mass migration of midwestern Folks into the Southland. Parker got a job driving a cab and started to work for a law degree at night at the Los Angeles College of Law. He joined the Los Angeles Police Department in August 1927, working the graveyard shift and finishing his law degree by day. In 1930 he graduated and passed the bar. Like the cardinal, then, Parker was a night school graduate who had achieved professional status the hard way. Like McIntyre as well, Parker had risen steadily in his profession, assisted by a well-deserved reputation for personal rectitude and a near-genius for taking civil service exams.

The LAPD in which Parker served had its own form of covenant with the people and, more important, with the establishment of the city. As far as policing was concerned, Los Angeles offered a unique challenge. It was a city filling up with hundreds of thousands of strangers, people from elsewhere, many of them of dubious stability and inclinations, as testified to by a series of bizarre murders and other forms of exotic misbehavior during this period. Los Angeles was also a city in the process of spreading itself across hundreds of square miles through in-migration and the absorption of adjacent suburbs. The oligarchy wanted Los Angeles policed. The Los Angeles Police Department was willing to do this, on the condition that it be granted—in both the charter of 1925 and the ongoing politics of the city—a high degree of autonomy. The chief of police, for one thing, held office as a civil servant, promoted through examination and appointed by a near-autonomous police commission, as opposed to the straight political appointment of most eastern cities. The force the chief commanded rarely walked a beat as in the East but patrolled vast areas through a pioneering use of radio-equipped police cars. Thus in prewar Los Angeles a garrison or constabulary relationship developed among the police, the city, and the people they served and protected, as the LAPD motto claimed.

To a high degree, the LAPD, especially its uniformed branch, had a tendency to define itself against Los Angeles as much as by or through the city. Chief James Edgar Davis, for example, who served from 1933 to 1938, prided himself on the paramilitary culture of his department. Just as McIntyre was ever at the side of Cardinal Hayes in these prologue years, Lieutenant William Henry Parker was ever at the side of Chief Davis, from whom he absorbed a model of the LAPD as a paramilitary organization. Davis, in fact, had helped to persuade voters to pass Charter Section 202, which authorized the LAPD to review all charges of misconduct internally and for the police commission, as opposed to the district attorney, to recommend any appropriate charges. Thus the LAPD became a self-policing police department, with its chief holding civil service tenure, following a civil service exam.

Praetorian guards, however—for as such the LAPD could now be described— have a tendency to become political and corrupt, or at the least laws unto themselves. The buying and selling of LAPD examinations and promotions by the brother of Mayor Frank L. Shaw led to Shaw's recall in 1938. Interestingly enough, in comparison to the East, the upper power structure of the LAPD was Anglo-Protestant and Masonic, a direct reflection of the Folks who had flooded the city from the Midwest in the 1920s. Herein resulted a tension, an institutional paradox. On the one hand, the LAPD, the creation of the Folks, had within itself a strong evangelical impulse, especially when it came to policing vice, with the leading ministers of the city forming a kind of shadow commission in this particular regard. On the other hand, individual members of the LAPD, being human, could and frequently did succumb to payoffs from the vice culture they were expected to suppress. Working his way up the ranks, Parker encountered this corruption most painfully when he placed first in the lieutenant's examination but, having paid no one off, was placed number ten on the promotion list. By World War II, Parker held the rank of captain despite the fact that, once again, he had placed first in examinations for inspector (commander) and deputy chief. No matter: He was soon in uniform as an Army captain of military police and in 1944, as a major, he was placed in charge of all police and prison operations for the Normandy invasion. Strafed by a German plane, Parker was awarded the Purple Heart along with the Croix de Guerre. Further assignments took him to Sardinia, where he helped reestablish civil government, and to postwar Germany, where as a lieutenant colonel he supervised the reorganization of the police departments of Frankfurt and Munich.

Returning home, Parker once again found himself odd man out in an LAPD where the fix was in at a number of levels. Homicide, for instance, was a semi-autonomous enclave within the nearly autonomous LAPD, its detectives solving a crowded calendar of cases but doing it on their own terms as far as legal procedures and the use of force were concerned. This was the LAPD of the late 1930s and 1940s, whose detectives—with their overcoats and fedoras, their expensive watches and wrist bracelets, their tough talk and even tougher actions—are mirrored in the fiction and films noir of the era. Here were detectives who might or might not pursue a case, depending. Sixty years after the fact, credible evidence would surface that certain detectives had a rather strong idea of who had perpetrated the Black Dahlia murder but let the alleged perpetrator, a physician who had functioned briefly as a consultant to the LAPD during the war, skip town with no charges filed rather than have its bungled investigation—three hundred suspects interviewed, no results— come to light. In any event, a 1949 grand jury noted the evasive answers made by certain detectives when questioned regarding the Black Dahlia case, but the matter was never pursued.

Mickey Cohen succeeded Benjamin (Bugsy) Siegel, the New York gangster sent to Los Angeles before the war by the Mafia to establish a beachhead on the coast, after Siegel was assassinated in June 1947. Born in New York of Russian-Jewish parentage, Cohen moved with his family to Los Angeles as a boy in the 1920s and grew up in Boyle Heights, the largest Jewish community west of Chicago. The diminutive (five feet, five inches) Cohen had been a lifelong racketeer since the time he began to run dice games as a teenager, but he was also colorful and quotable, a flashy dresser, and in his own way a likeable personality appreciated by hordes of newspapermen in search of copy. His rivals, East Coast mobsters such as Jack Dragna, were not members of the Mickey Cohen fan club. Reporters had a field day covering the gunning down of Mickey's personal bodyguard Neddie Herbert in front of a crowded Sunset Strip restaurant. Cohen and three of his associates, including his bodyguard Johnny Stompanato, were wounded in the hail of gunfire but survived. This drive-by at Sherry's was followed by the mysterious disappearance of two of Cohen's business partners, Frank Niccoli and Dave Ogul, all this covered by a gleeful press. Then it turned out that detectives assigned to monitor Cohen were being wined and dined at expensive restaurants by the ever-generous Mickey, whom they were supposed to be shadowing.

Then there was the Brenda Allen case. Brought before the grand jury, Marie Mitchell, a.k.a Brenda Allen, a drop-dead-gorgeous redhead with a taste for tailored suits, the leading madam of the city—114 girls at the height of her operation, generating $9,000 a day—revealed that her lover and business partner was LAPD Sergeant Elmer V. Jackson of the Hollywood vice squad, whom Allen paid a hefty $50 weekly kickback for each girl in her employ. Jackson was in turn responsible for paying off other vice squad members. These and other scandals led to the forced resignation of LAPD Chief C. B. Horrall in the summer of 1949. The reform-oriented Mayor Fletcher Bowron replaced Horrall with William Arthur Worton, a retired Marine major general, with explicit instructions to clean up the department. Worton did what he could, but since he had not come off the civil service list he could only serve for a year and stepped down in March 1950. Once again, William Henry Parker, then serving as deputy chief and head of Internal Affairs, stood at the top of the examination list for chief but was overshadowed by insider

Thaddeus Brown, chief of detectives. Loyal, genial, respected by reporters, Brown stood in dramatic contrast to the cantankerous Parker, outspoken in his calls for reform. For weeks, it seemed a slam-dunk for Brown. Only the death of one police commissioner and a change of vote by another gave Parker, then forty-seven, the job of chief in August 1950.

Parker's reputation as a hard-ass reformer, blunt and contentious, had almost cost him the top slot at the LAPD. From one perspective, this was perhaps a good thing, given the challenges Parker faced. First of all, Parker had a crime-plagued city to police, its population swollen to two million across the 1940s by the in-migration of a half-million new residents, bringing along what often seemed more than their fair share of the criminally inclined. For all the colorfulness of Brenda Allen and Mickey Cohen, the real crime story in the Los Angeles of 1950 was a more anonymous epidemic of murders (especially of women), rapes, abductions for robbery or sexual violence, burglaries, and sex crimes against children, the latter prompting Governor Warren to call a special session of the legislature. Given the one-story construction of most Los Angeles homes, hot prowls—entrance by burglars while residents were in their homes—was a local specialty, and burglaries of homes with residents absent a near-commonplace.

In his brief tenure as chief, General Worton had done a credible job correcting abuses and upgrading the department. Testing and training standards had been improved in what was the youngest police department of a major city in the nation, average age thirty-two. Some 3,500 officers (out of an authorized strength of 4,493) were veterans, hence graduates of military basic training and qualified in one or another military specialty, thereby fitting into the already established paramilitary nature of the LAPD. Some fifteen hundred officers were pursuing advanced educations on a part-time basis, five hundred of them at a special program in police science and management offered by USC. Thus Parker inherited a police department already in the process of reforming itself. Still, old habits die hard, especially among plainclothes detectives so used to running their own show.

On Christmas Eve 1951, a group of hard-partying police at Central Station in Lincoln Heights severely beat (using wet towels and gloved fists so as to leave minimal identification) seven Mexican American young men in the mistaken notion that one of the policemen who had arrested them at a free-for-all at a bar in the San Fernando Valley was in danger of losing an eye. The two officers initially trying to make the arrest were themselves badly beaten and had to call for backup. Bloody Christmas, as it came to be known, provoked a grand jury investigation that was extremely critical of internal discipline in the LAPD. Parker himself took charge of the investigation. Four hundred and fifty officers were interviewed. When it was over, eight officers were indicted. Four eventually went to jail, and two were dropped from the force. Another thirty-six had official reprimands placed in their files. Bloody Christmas and its aftermath confirmed to the rank and file and upper echelons of the LAPD what they already knew: namely, that Parker was not running a popularity contest.

Nor was Bill Parker easy on himself. Nor was he particularly likeable, or did he even care to be. Parker was a driven man, and his driving force was the crusade to transform the LAPD into the most modern and efficient police department in the nation. As in the case of J. Edgar Hoover and the FBI, Parker lived in and through and only for the department he headed. Being chief was more than a job. It was a calling, a vocation, a crusade. Parker and his wife, a former policewoman, were childless but doted on their Weimaraner Lex (Latin for *law*), lived simply in their Silver Lake home, rarely if ever entertaining. Rising early, Parker devoured the morning newspapers and was at his desk by seven. Cardinal McIntyre, a virtual teetotaler, would retire each evening at Fremont Place with a glass of milk. Parker preferred bourbon; he was a heavy drinker with a taste for double shots of Bourbon deLuxe (Parker Specials he called them). Booze was about the only thing that could help Parker unwind. Behind his back he was known as Whiskey Bill as a result of a number of public indiscretions he had committed when loaded. The officer assigned to drive the chief in the early 1950s, Daryl Gates, frequently had to help his boss into his home after a night of heavy imbibing. In 1957, however, faced with a serious heart problem, Parker gave up both booze and his two packs of unfiltered cigarettes a day. He then became, noted Gates, a really, really mean son of a bitch.

Parker controlled the LAPD through personal supervision of the divisions of Intelligence, Internal Affairs, Planning and Research, and Administrative Vice, a unit charged with overseeing all vice operations in the city. He monitored and orchestrated all information, all internal investigations of corruption or malfeasance, and the policing of vice, which was especially vulnerable to infiltration and payoffs. In February 1964, thanks to a young officer willing to whistle-blow, the Bureau of Internal Affairs cracked a scheme by bookmakers with a sub rosa connection to an officer in Central Vice that threatened to reestablish the prior practice of payoffs, indeed, to infiltrate Central Vice with up to five officers on the take.

Through the Intelligence Division—headed in the mid-1960s by Inspector (Commander) Daryl Gates, who like his boss had worked his way steadily up the ladder through examination—Parker waged a proactive and relentless war on the Mafia. The Mafia, Parker believed, could only re-establish itself in Los Angeles if it infiltrated Intelligence and Internal Affairs, but the mob showed no signs of being able to do that. Yet the mob could also try to establish a field presence in Los Angeles, now that it had established itself in Las Vegas. At Intelligence, Mafia movements and relationships were tracked on a national basis. Should Mafiosi arrive in Los Angeles on business, they were met at the airport by LAPD plainclothesmen, who put them back on the next plane, or they were invited downtown for an interview during which it was explained to them the world of hurt that would be their lot, should they decide to remain in the city. LAPD officer Roger Otis was a specialist in personally delivering messages of warning at one or another Mafia hangout: Tracton's steakhouse on the Westside, Sneaky Pete's, Sherry's on the Strip, the Losers, the Laurel Inn, the Scene, the Four Trees, or the Red Velvet Supper Club, frequently crowded with pimps and prostitutes.

By July 1965 a mere thirty Mafiosi, it was estimated, were living in greater Los Angeles, many of whom had come to California to retire. A few operatives remained: Frank Desimone, for example, an attorney who had done time in the aftermath of the Grand Council Meeting at Apalachin, New York, in 1957; Nick Licata, seventy by 1965, deriving his income from apartment houses he owned, together with a few other legitimate businesses, spending his days at the racetrack; or Louis Dragna, the nephew of the late longtime Mafia boss Jack Dragna. Nephew Louis served as arbiter of Mafia matters in the region, such as they were, spending his days on the golf course, his nights wining and dining at Perino's on Wilshire. But these Mafiosi represented a holding action at best, Parker claimed, in contrast to the cities of the Midwest and East. Mickey Cohen, meanwhile, was spending the years 1961–72 (as he had 1952–55) in federal prison for income tax evasion.

To maximize such anti-Mafia operations by Intelligence, together with the ongoing investigations of Internal Affairs and other divisions, Parker fought a decade-long battle on behalf of wiretapping, which the legislature had made a felony unless approved by the courts. Session in and session out, before legislative committees in Sacramento, Parker tried for such a court-approved blanket permission for wire-tapping by the LAPD, especially after the California Supreme Court in 1955 declared that bugging constituted illegal search and seizure and that evidence obtained from it could not be used in court. Parker failed to obtain the wiretapping permission he sought and was not foolish enough to commit the LAPD to a program of felony wiretapping unuseable in court. Non-felony bugging, however, while not providing court evidence, nevertheless helped the LAPD track suspicious characters. It was also rumored, but never conclusively proven, that Parker, like J. Edgar Hoover, maintained a private file on politicians' peccadilloes, just in case.

As far as day-to-day crime was concerned, Parker also practiced proactive policing, which is why he so prized Intelligence. It was not enough for police to respond to crimes, Parker argued; they had to anticipate what crimes would be committed, and where, and prevent them from happening. Thus Parker replaced as many uniformed police who were in clerical positions with civilians as possible and put as many police as he could (1,925 officers on patrol duty by 1951) in the nearly 1,300 cars cruising the 453 square miles of the city, responding to 434,000 radio calls in 1951 alone. He also created an LAPD Air Force: seventeen Bell Jet Ranger 206-B helicopters and one fixed-wing patrol plane, supported by the seventy-five officers of the Air Support Division, in the air eighteen hours a day, seven days a week, hovering over the city like gigantic dragonflies, their searchlights by night tracking fleeing suspects through the vacant lots and backyards of the city.

A graduate of one of the best Roman Catholic seminaries in the United States, Cardinal McIntyre believed in professional training; indeed, three of his seminarians from the 1950s would themselves become cardinals and nearly a dozen others become bishops, all of them, taken together, constituting an ecclesiastical Los Angeles–based political machine for the rest of the century. For his part, Parker focused in on the Police Academy with similar intensity, expanding its program from three weeks to thirteen and adding instruction in law, sociology, psychology, public policy, and public relations, as well as intensifying its Officer Candidate School–like program of boot camp formation, although Parker would allow no swearing or untoward harassment. Still, it was a military model of police formation, favoring veterans of the military who were at least five foot nine and (although this was never formally stated) Caucasian, and it had a tendency not only to militarize further the LAPD but to militarize as well most major police departments in Southern California.

Thanks to the *Dragnet* television series starring Jack Webb—the production of which Parker, with the help of Stanley Sheldon, captain in charge of public information, meticulously monitored, as technical consultant—the LAPD became the best-known police department in the nation. Parker was thanked by name at the conclusion of each broadcast. This, as well as the Mafia campaign, stuck in J. Edgar Hoover's craw. In times past, Hoover and his longtime companion Clyde Tolson loved to vacation in Hollywood and Palm Springs, hobnobbing with the stars. Following the success of *Dragnet*, however, Hoover was rarely seen in the Southland. Parker, by contrast, became an accepted Hollywood figure, paid court to by the industry. Parker strained the relationship, however, when he lambasted Twentieth Century–Fox for its biopic *I Want to Live* (1958). Susan Hayward's portrayal of convicted murderer Barbara Graham's execution at San Quentin won her an Oscar for Best Actress, and the scene of her execution at San Quentin remains one of the most harrowing depictions of its kind in American film. *I Want to Live*, however, suggested that Graham had been framed by the LAPD. Nonsense, Parker fumed. Graham, a convicted prostitute and perjurer, had cold-bloodedly assisted in the beating and strangling of Mabel Monahan, an elderly, crippled widow, in a botched robbery. Parker felt doubly aggrieved given the fact, he alleged, that the LAPD had once saved Hayward's life following a suicide attempt. He also resented the anti-death-penalty message of *I Want to Live*, with its depiction of a sobbing Graham being taken by force into the gas chamber. In reality, Graham had met her fate with considerable sangfroid. Advised by a San Quentin guard to take a deep breath as soon as the gas pellet was dropped, so as to make her death easier, Graham wisecracked in reply: "How the hell would you know?"[2]

Each week *Dragnet* announced itself with an unforgettable opening theme and a shot of Los Angeles City Hall, where the LAPD was headquartered until 1955, when it moved into an eight-story ultra-modern steel-and-glass administration building on Los Angeles Street. Restrained, skeptical, fact-oriented, beyond bribery or corruption—almost ascetic in the same tweed sport jacket, black-knit tie, and snap-brim fedora he wore in episode after episode—Jack Webb's Sergeant Joe Friday epitomized the laconic professionalism prized by Parker. Sergeant Friday also bespoke another LAPD value that was part of the 1920s covenant. Friday was in the city but not quite of it. Friday considered Los Angeles a moral battleground in which criminals and con men would be winning, were it not for the LAPD. And such were the themes that Parker took to the people in speech after speech, sometimes three a day. Human nature, Parker argued, was fallen, hence prone to crime. To be a policeman was to be called to a vocation as old as civilization itself. Like the clergy, police were a breed apart, kept at a distance by the society in which they exercised such decisive authority on behalf of the greater good. Faced with the moral crisis of contemporary society, a favorite Parker theme, a police department had a responsibility to be as modern as the society it policed and as efficient as it was beyond corruption. Both the moral battleground that was Los Angeles and the efficiency of the LAPD might find corroboration, Chief Parker suggested, in the fact that in 1956 alone the LAPD arrested some 220,000 suspects, which is to say, 10 percent of the population of the city or, as Chief Parker phrased it, "over twice the number it would take to fill the Memorial Coliseum."[3]

Despite such dire arrest statistics, Los Angeles remained a pleasant place to live. Whatever its problems, a successful city must provide multiple sources of pleasure for its residents. From this perspective, the arrival of the Dodgers in April 1958 built upon and brought to a new level a recreational capacity developing in the pre- and postwar eras.

The park movement had been strengthening these bonds since the mid-nineteenth century. And while Los Angeles, city and county, lagged somewhat behind in this regard, having gotten a late start, the county Department of Parks and Recreation was supporting by 1959 some 140 parks comprising 11,393 acres along with 10.5 miles of beaches, and its City of Los Angeles counterpart was administering some 350 parks totaling 15,098 acres, dominated by Griffith Park, the largest city park in the nation: 4,226 acres of hills, valleys, and flatlands in the very heart of the city. In so many other places, public access to the beach remained an intermittent and highly regulated privilege, as it was in stretches of the Malibu coast above Santa Monica. In Los Angeles County, by contrast, the beach was the most important public park in the metropolitan area, and the people used it enthusiastically. Photographs from the 1930s, 1940s, and 1950s depict an increasingly utilized countywide beach parkland running from Santa Monica to Long Beach, with the bulky swimwear of the 1930s morphing over time into the trunks and one-piece bathing suits of the 1950s and the bikini making its appearance in the 1960s. Organized in association with the county fire department and staffed by professional lifeguards—a number of whom served as frogmen during the war—the Los Angeles County Lifeguard Service constituted one of the finest services of its kind in the world.

Urban parks, by contrast, expressed the reverse but complementary identity of Los Angeles as urban place. Exposition Park near USC was almost as old as the American city itself. Set squarely in the center of the city on the Santa Monica mountain range dividing the Los Angeles plain from the San Fernando Valley, Griffith Park subsumed unto itself, nearly, the entire storyline of the city in geological and human terms. In ages past, the Tongva people wandered the mountains and ravines of the area. In 1796 the tract became part of the Rancho Los Feliz granted to Corporal José Vicente Feliz, who had helped establish the pueblo in September 1781. The land then passed into the ownership of Antonio Coronel, one of the leaders of the Mexican era, then to Leon Baldwin, who sold it to Griffith J. Griffith in 1884. In 1896 Griffith donated the property to the city. Following his release from prison for the attempted murder of his wife, Griffith donated $700,000 for the construction of the Griffith Observatory (1935), although the city council was initially reluctant to accept further money from a convicted felon. By the 1950s Griffith Park had in one sense been developed, with picnic areas, a golf course, an archery range, a merry-go-round, a nature museum, a zoo, and even a cricket field, named in honor of the English actor Sir C. Aubrey Smith, captain of the Hollywood Cricket Club. The Chavez Ravine section of the Park remained the site of an informally organized Mexican American settlement, connecting Griffith Park to its Hispanic past.

And this threw into bold relief, as parks are expected to do, the traditionally urban aspects of the City of Angels encircling Griffith Park, as expressed by the region's restaurants. One cannot make a special case for Los Angeles in this regard. Any flourishing American city was by the mid-twentieth century offering its citizens places to eat, drink, congregate, and recreate. In terms of haute cuisine, not overly abundant in the Los Angeles of that era, Perino's, on Wilshire adjacent to Hancock Park, presided over by debonair Alexander Perino, an immigrant from Northern Italy, held the lead. In 1932, at the depth of the Depression, hocking his Packard and signing a slew of promissory notes, Perino had opened the restaurant with the assistance of chef Attilio Balzano, still with the establishment twenty-plus years later. In 1950 Perino relocated Perino's—by now the restaurant of choice for the beau monde—to newly constructed quarters designed by Paul Williams, architect to the stars. "Early Thirties Grand Hotel," one restaurant critic would later describe the décor at Perino's: an interplay of luxurious banquettes, noiselessly efficient waiters and Perino himself, the ever-present maitre d' as tasteful in his fine tailoring as any Hancock Park patron, as attention-getting as any of the Hollywood stars in attendance. Nancy and Ronald Reagan were regulars.

Los Angeles abounded in nightclubs: the Biltmore Bowl in the Biltmore Hotel on Pershing Square, or the Cocoanut Grove in the Ambassador on Wilshire; the Trocadero, Ciro's, the Mocambo, Earl Carroll's on Sunset Boulevard; Romanoff's on North Rodeo Drive in Beverly Hills, each combining ambitious dining with dancing and live entertainment. Arrayed around these expensive venues, known internationally because of their Hollywood clienteles, was an extraordinary network of more affordable clubs featuring a similar program of dinner, dancing, and a show; indeed, for what it was worth, Los Angeles remained the nightlife capital of the United States west of Chicago and held that honor against a rising Las Vegas through the 1950s, thanks to a complexity of Latin-, African American–, Polynesian-, and jazz-oriented establishments, a number of them aligned along a portion of Sunset Boulevard better known as the Strip.

The sporting set, meanwhile, was enjoying, according to its various sub-sets and inclinations, a culture that had been in place since the 1920s. Golf—an upper-class game that became middle-class in the 1920s—could be enjoyed at minimal cost at more than a dozen publicly supported courses in the city and the county. The

Wilson Municipal Golf Course in Griffith Park had the reputation of being one of the most challenging and scenic public golf courses in the state. The more affluent had access to an almost equal number of private country clubs, such as the Los Angeles, the Wilshire, the Bel-Air, Lakeside, Hillcrest, and Annandale, where the approach to the fourteenth hole was (so Bob Hope, among others, observed) one of the most difficult of all approaches to a green of any private club in Southern California. Like golf, tennis was another once-aristocratic sport that Southern California had quasi-democratized through the creation of high-quality public courts. Although the public could not walk into such establishments as the Los Angeles or Beverly Hills Tennis Club, there were some seven constellations of public courts available throughout the city, and it had to be remembered that the first generation of Southern California tennis champions had by and large come from such public places.

Los Angeles abounded in bowling alleys, which ran the gamut from small neighborhood places to multi-lane complexes combining bowling, cocktailing, dining, retail shopping, nurseries, daycare, and live entertainment. In the 1950s Southern California emerged as an epicenter of bowling in the United States (five thousand lanes by 1962), as bowling alleys provided points of social consolidation for newly emergent suburban neighborhoods. The bowling set, augmented by a phalanx of swells in the front row, could also enjoy an ambitious schedule of boxing and wrestling at the Olympic Auditorium on South Grand or the American Legion Stadium in Hollywood. Boxing was in the second-to-last decade of its golden age; and as far as wrestling, which appealed to a slightly less discriminating clientele, figures such as the perfumed, peroxided, permed, gender-bending Gorgeous George, otherwise known as the Human Orchid, entering the ring attired in a silk kimono and carrying a floral bouquet, were inaugurating a golden age of television wrestling.

For those addicted to the sport of kings, Los Angeles represented a veritable paradise, with Hollywood Park in Inglewood near the airport and Santa Anita Park in Arcadia in the San Gabriel Valley, two of the most noted racetracks in the nation, offering more than one hundred days of racing each year. The more democratic of these two tracks in terms of its diverse clientele—although for years its prize money was among the highest in the nation—Hollywood Park opened its gates at 7:30 A.M. and allowed the public to watch early morning workouts free of charge. Santa Anita, by contrast, was more upper-crust, with its opening day an Ascot-like event in the annual social calendar, covered in the society columns. Santa Anita and Hollywood Park each featured sulky racing in mid-March or harness racing in the fall following the regular season.

When it came to the more conventional sports—basketball, football, and baseball—Los Angeles was similarly blessed. USC and UCLA supported nationally ranked basketball teams, and the professional Lakers moved to the city from Minneapolis in 1960. USC and UCLA satisfied the football needs of the region, along with the Rams, a National League team that moved from Cleveland in 1946 and across the next thirteen years proceeded to win one NFL and four divisional titles, and to finish second three times in its division and in third place twice, thanks to such crowd-pleasing players as Bob Waterfield (married to actress Jane Russell), Elroy (Crazy Legs) Hirsch, and Ollie Matson. Playing in the Coliseum, coached by Sid Gillman, managed by Pete Rozelle, the Rams enjoyed an excellent rapport with their fan base. Tickets were reasonably priced, and more than 125 restaurants throughout the region sponsored pre-game brunches as well as chartered buses to and from the Coliseum. In the pre-season, fans were invited out to Redlands in southwest San Bernardino County to watch practice. Coach Gillman was a regular speaker on a fan-driven luncheon and dinner circuit. Each Sunday before a home game, radio station KMPC broadcast a morning show keyed to the impending contest. Rams souvenirs and memorabilia—jackets, cigarette lighters, ash trays, hi-ball glasses—moved so quickly at the Coliseum and Los Angeles–area department stores, the club opened its own retail outlet.

Thanks to the Rams and to the Los Angeles Angels and Hollywood Stars, baseball teams of the Pacific Coast League, Los Angeles was more than showing its potential as a venue for professional sports, with the Angels and the Stars attracting enthusiastic crowds to the Spanish Revival Wrigley Field (1925) in south Los Angeles and Gilmore Field (1934) just west of the Pan Pacific Auditorium in the Fairfax district. The Hollywood Stars, as might be expected, were owned in part by a number of Hollywood personalities and attracted a host of celebrity fans throughout the season.

"When I became Mayor in 1953," Norris Poulson later reminisced, "Los Angeles was 'big league' in everything but baseball: big league track, big league freeways, big league entertainment, big league business. But in baseball, it was strictly minor league."[4] The arrival of the Dodgers in April 1958 and the dedication of Dodger Stadium in Chavez Ravine four years later formalized this big league status. Even as Mayor Poulson began his administration, Walter O'Malley, owner and president of the Brooklyn Dodgers, on the lookout for a new venue, was surveying the Los Angeles scene, especially its baseball culture, media environment, and transportation networks. Like Cardinal McIntyre and Chief Parker, O'Malley was yet another Irish Catholic who had risen to prominence through hard work and night school and had been helped along by powerful mentors in earlier years. Like McIntyre, O'Malley was also a consummate New Yorker. Born in the Bronx in 1903, O'Malley was reared as the only child of upwardly mobile parents. A dry goods merchant, O'Malley's father rose to commissioner of public markets, making the transition from immigrant to lace-curtain status. A comfortable home on Long Island, the Boy Scouts, the Culver Military Academy in Indiana, the University of Pennsylvania, where he majored in engineering, followed by the Columbia Law School: O'Malley received a solid upper-middle-class upbringing until his father went broke during the Depression and O'Malley was forced to withdraw from Columbia. Yet he finished his law degree by night at Fordham while working days as an engineer and surveyor for the City of New York and developed a private company that published information on the New York City building code. Tragedy struck when O'Malley's childhood sweetheart and fiancée Kay Hanson contracted cancer of the larynx, underwent experimental surgery, and was for the rest of her life unable to speak above a whisper. Nevertheless, the couple was joyously married in a quintessentially Irish Catholic New York wedding at the historic actors' church of St. Malachy's off Times Square. Passing the bar in 1933, O'Malley made the transition from engineering to law, commuting to the Lincoln Building in Manhattan from an apartment on St. Mark's Avenue in Brooklyn, where he became a Dodgers fan.

In his rise in the church, McIntyre was mentored by Cardinal Hayes. Chief Davis saw the value of Lieutenant Parker and helped advance his career. In O'Malley's case, Brooklyn banker George V. McLaughlin—former New York City police commissioner, president of the Brooklyn Trust, a powerful civic leader known as George the Fifth, and a friend of O'Malley's father—mentored O'Malley beginning in his college days. As bank president, McLaughlin asked O'Malley, then in law practice, to monitor the financial affairs of the ailing Brooklyn Dodgers. In time, O'Malley mastered the intricacies of corporate baseball. When the former presidential candidate Wendell Willkie, then serving as vice president and general counsel of the Dodgers, left the team to promote his book *One World* (1943), O'Malley left his law firm and took Willkie's place. The next year, O'Malley joined Dodgers president Branch Rickey and Brooklyn insurance executive Andrew Schmitz to purchase 25 percent of the team's stock from the estate of a deceased part-owner. In August 1945 Rickey, O'Malley, and chemical baron John Smith purchased another 50 percent from the estate of Charles Ebbets. Thus by 1945, after further sales and adjustments, O'Malley belonged to a triumvirate owning 75 percent of the team.

Such a rapid rise to ownership suggests Walter O'Malley's business acumen, although it might not seem so at first glance, given the declining fortunes of the Dodgers. Built in 1913, Ebbets Field was in poor condition and had parking for only seven hundred cars, a growing disability given the fact that a generation of Dodgers fans was along with the rest of urban America, in the process of suburbanizing and would increasingly prefer to commute by car back to Brooklyn for games. O'Malley and his colleagues had three choices: either improve Ebbets Field, or find a more convenient location for a stadium in the vicinity, or—and this idea was only dimly on the horizon—move the Dodgers elsewhere. As early as 1946, O'Malley was in dialogue with retired Navy design engineer Captain Emil Praeger for suggestions regarding the upgrading of Ebbets Field, on the theory that a stadium resembled a landlocked ship. O'Malley also conferred with visionary designers Norman Bel Geddes and R. Buckminster Fuller regarding, in Bel Geddes's case, the renovation of Ebbets Field as a domed stadium, and, in Fuller's case, the design of a brand-new fifty-thousand-seat geodesic clear-span dome with a retractable roof for another Brooklyn site.

O'Malley wanted that site to be at the intersection of Atlantic and Flatbush, adjacent to the Long Island Rail Road terminal and a variety of New York subway connections. He also wanted the Dodgers to pay for the stadium out of their own pocket, provided that the proper deal could be structured under Title I of the Housing Act of

1949, which would apply if the proposed ballpark could also double as a community parking garage. Robert Moses, however, parks commissioner and planning czar for New York, was in the process of orienting metropolitan New York to automobile traffic and nixed O'Malley's public-transportation-oriented proposal. Moses wanted the Dodgers to build a car-oriented stadium at Flushing Meadows in Queens, a semi-suburban venue that later hosted a world's fair.

Despite their difficulties with Ebbets Field, the Dodgers were doing better and better as a team. In 1952 and 1953 they won National League pennants but lost to the Yankees in the World Series. O'Malley thereupon replaced manager Charlie Dressen with Walter Alston, an up-from-the-minors manager, content to work on an annual contract, as opposed to Dressen, who was demanding a long-term commitment. The Dodgers won their first world championship in 1955, defeating the Yankees, their archrivals, in seven games. Attendance, however, continued to decline, which led O'Malley to consider the example set by the Milwaukee Braves, who had left Boston two years earlier for a new municipally built ballpark and were now drawing more than two million admissions a year, twice the draw of the Dodgers.

Something had to give. The Dodgers were at the top of their game. They had integrated major league baseball in 1947 by calling Jackie Robinson up from the Montreal Royals, one of the many minor league teams affiliated with the Dodgers, based on Branch Rickey's belief that the best way for the Dodgers to develop talent was to promote it from within. Each year since 1948, the Dodgers had brought some six hundred young ballplayers from twenty-six minor league teams for spring training at a leased former naval air station in Vero Beach, Florida, renamed Dodgertown. Players lived in barracks, ate together in mess halls, trained in large groups, and showed their stuff in the five-thousand-seat Holman Stadium designed and engineered by Captain Praeger. Inspired by the mobilizations of World War II, Dodgertown also expressed modernist values of large-scale corporate training and strong corporate identity.

In 1953 *Los Angeles Examiner* sports columnist Vincent Flaherty wrote O'Malley regarding moving the Dodgers to Los Angeles. O'Malley replied that he preferred to stay in Brooklyn and had high hopes of building a domed stadium. In September 1954 the Los Angeles City Council sent a circular letter to all major league team owners expressing the desire of Los Angeles to begin negotiations to acquire a major league team. The following year Los Angeles City Councilwoman Rosalind Wyman, a dynamic young newcomer to city politics, wrote O'Malley to express her interest in having the Dodgers move to Los Angeles. The new mayor of the city, former congressman Norris Poulson—a Mason, a Republican, an accountant by profession, the chosen candidate of the *Los Angeles Times*—together with county supervisor Kenneth Hahn, another young politician, joined Wyman in openly supporting an effort to lure the Dodgers to the Coast. Dodger advocates experienced a setback when voters in June 1955 turned down a measure to finance a baseball stadium with public funds at an undisclosed location in an effort to attract a major league team. This turndown, however, was not a deal-breaker as far as O'Malley was concerned; for O'Malley favored private construction and ownership, provided there be adequate incentives from the public sector.

At some point in the mid-1950s—as early as 1955 perhaps—O'Malley began to listen more closely, albeit discreetly, to his Los Angeles supporters as he wrangled with Robert Moses over a stadium site, while publicly remaining an advocate of keeping the Dodgers in Brooklyn. By 1956 O'Malley was having private conversations with Horace Stoneham, owner of the New York Giants. Stoneham admitted to O'Malley privately that he, too, was fed up with sagging attendance, in his case at the dilapidated Polo Grounds (1911) in Harlem, and was planning a move to St. Paul, where he owned a Triple-A minor league team. O'Malley suggested to Stoneham that he consider moving the Giants to San Francisco and O'Malley arranged for San Francisco mayor George Christopher to fly to New York and begin discussions with Stoneham.

Nineteen fifty-seven turned into an annus mirabilis for the Dodgers. In February O'Malley made a trade with Philip Wrigley, owner of the Chicago Cubs. O'Malley would give Wrigley ownership of the Fort Worth Panthers of the Texas League in exchange for Wrigley Field and the Los Angeles Angels. O'Malley was now the owner of a Los Angeles ballpark and a Los Angeles team. O'Malley also paid $450,000 personally, along with another $450,000 from the Dodgers as a corporation, for league territorial rights to move the Dodgers to Los Angeles if and when such a move was in the best interests of the team. In March Mayor Poulson, city council president John Gibson, city administrator Samuel Leask, and county supervisor Kenneth Hahn led a delegation to Dodgertown in Vero Beach to discuss with O'Malley the possibility of the Brooklyn Dodgers moving west. In the course of discussions, Poulson later remembered, O'Malley expressed his interest in Chavez Ravine. (Almost on the sly, O'Malley had hired a team of engineers the previous year to reconnoiter the ravine as a possible stadium site.) Among other things, O'Malley—whom Moses was trying to force out to semi-suburban Flushing Meadows—liked the ravine's downtown location. "The meeting was primarily a sparring match," Mayor Poulson later remembered. "One of our officials promised O'Malley the moon, and Walter asked for more. You couldn't blame him. He had a valuable package in the Dodgers, and he knew it. I assured him we wanted desperately to get the team, but made it clear we would have to come up with a plan that wouldn't get all of us run out of the city."[5] These Vero Beach negotiations resulted in what subsequently became known as the Tablets—as in the stone tablets brought down by Moses from Mount Sinai—listing O'Malley's irrevocable conditions and commandments.

Matters were coming to a head. In April O'Malley flew out to Los Angeles to inspect his new acquisition, Wrigley Field, and his new team, the Angels, and to meet and greet the city's pro-Dodgers political and business establishment. On 2 May 1957, O'Malley surveyed Chavez Ravine by helicopter, courtesy of the county sheriff. He loved the terrain, although he estimated (correctly, as it turned out) that some eight million cubic yards of earth would have to be moved to create a stadium site and surrounding parking lots. O'Malley also loved the way that the site was directly served by the Pasadena and Hollywood freeways. On 28 May, meeting in Chicago, the National League granted permission to the Giants and the Dodgers to move to San Francisco and Los Angeles, provided that the clubs move together by 1 October. Harold McClellan, former undersecretary of Congress for international affairs in the Eisenhower administration, was appointed to continue negotiations.

Two days after McClellan and O'Malley met in Brooklyn, the Giants announced on 21 August 1957 that they were moving to San Francisco, which further strengthened the possibility of O'Malley moving as well, despite last-minute efforts by New York mayor Robert Wagner and banker Nelson Rockefeller to assemble a competitive counter-offer. In October, the Los Angeles City Council voted ten to four officially to invite the Dodgers to move to Los Angeles. More dramatically—and controversially, as it turned out—the council also approved a deal, hammered out across the summer and early fall, to trade the Chavez Ravine site for Wrigley Field and to require O'Malley to fund privately and build a fifty-thousand-seat stadium and to put Chavez Ravine back on the tax rolls as private property. The very next day, 8 October 1957, O'Malley announced that the Brooklyn Dodgers were moving to the City of Angels.

The move of the Giants to San Francisco was relatively painless. The move of the Dodgers to Los Angeles, however, was fraught with controversy and might never have been finalized, given the fact that O'Malley had the right (thus sayeth the Tablets!) to return to Brooklyn within two years if a suitable stadium site did not become available. From the point of view of Brooklyn, the removal of the Dodgers represented a cultural and psychological affront to an embattled borough whose glory days now seemed long gone. For the pro-Dodgers faction in Los Angeles, city and county, the arrival of the Dodgers finalized with a flourish the emergence of the region into big league status. Yet there were many in the city and county who resented the way that O'Malley held all the winning cards from the beginning. Many bitterly resented the way that Chavez Ravine, so recently intended for high public purposes of redevelopment and affordable housing, should now be turned over to a profit-making baseball team. Mexican Americans especially resented the fact that a flourishing Mexican American community had been removed from the ravine on the promise of public housing: a promise now voided by the Dodger contract.

It was a tangle of motivations, this Battle of Chavez Ravine as it came to be called, dating back to the National Housing Act of 1949. Among other provisions, the act allowed the federal government to form and operate redevelopment agencies to acquire slum, marginal or otherwise under-utilized properties and redevelop them as public housing. In the case of Los Angeles, the provisions of the act resulted, among other projects, in an agreement between the city council and the housing authority, signed in October 1950, to acquire and redevelop Elysian Park Heights, which included Chavez Ravine, and to create there with federal funds a master-planned community to be designed by the noted architects Richard Neutra and Robert Alexander. It was a bold and visionary proposal, solidly backed by Mayor

Fletcher Bowron and the majority of the council: the creation of a Corbusian community of twenty-four thirteen-story apartment towers and 163 garden apartments of two stories served by an infrastructure of nurseries, schools, churches, retail zones, landscaped parks, and gathering places.

Despite the endorsement of the mayor and the city council, however, the Elysian Park Heights project faced a number of obstacles. First of all, Chavez Ravine supported what was in effect a Mexican American village, complete with church, school, chickens and goats, religious processions, festivals, and dances: a Mexican Brigadoon, as UCLA historian Tom Hines described it, in the heart of the city, symbolically presided over by the noted Mexican actor Crispin Martin (the Cisco Kid), who lived on a peak of the ravine in a Spanish Revival villa and walked its streets, greeting "my people," like a Mexican *patrón*.[6] Some might consider Chavez Ravine as a slum, a haphazard collection of shanties. Hundreds of Mexican American Los Angelenos, however, called it home.

Which was why the City Housing Authority (CHA), as it began to acquire properties, either purchased homes from Chavez Ravine residents or, if they were renters, paid their relocation costs and guaranteed to owners and renters alike first rights of return to the Elysian Park Heights community, once it was constructed. Opponents of the project argued that Mexican Americans were essentially villagers and would never adjust to ultra-modern high-rise or garden apartment life. In any event, the clearing of the Chavez Ravine barrio proceeded on course through 1951. A second source of objections coming from the private sector proved more troublesome. Developer Fritz Burns—who had created thousands of homes in Westchester, North Hollywood, and Panorama City—led the charge, joined by such groups as the National Apartment Owners Association, the local chapter of the Home Builders Association, the Small Property Owners League, the Los Angeles Chamber of Commerce, and the *Los Angeles Times*. Yes, there was a housing shortage in postwar Los Angeles, Burns argued, but the private sector—empowered by veterans' loans at the state and federal level and by liberal housing loans from private banks and other sources—was more than capable of meeting this need and was, indeed, in the very process of doing so.

Quite soon, however, the anti-Communist crusade spearheaded by the junior senator from Wisconsin fused with the anti-public housing movement, and kerosene was poured on the flames. The argument against Elysian Park Heights and the other public housing developments proposed by the CHA now became—under the furious and effective leadership of Frederick Dockweiler, chairman of the Citizens Against Socialist Housing, and all four Los Angeles newspapers, especially the *Los Angeles Times*—the notion that these projects represented a form of creeping socialism. Mayor Fletcher Bowron, the unions, the NAACP, the League of Women Voters, and a variety of church and veterans groups continued to advocate for the projects, but the tide was soon turning. Matters went from bad to worse when State Senator John B. Tenney, chair of the California Senate Committee on Un-American Activities and the leading Red-hunter in the state, launched an investigation of alleged Communist infiltration into the CHA. Three officials of the authority, being asked "Are you now or have you ever been a member of the Communist Party?" took the Fifth. The city council immediately began to backtrack on its support. On 26 December 1951, in an eight-to-seven vote, the council canceled its contract with the CHA, and the CHA in turn filed suit to have this cancellation declared null and void, a position upheld unanimously by the State Supreme Court in April 1952 and reaffirmed by the United States Supreme Court in October.

The city council trumped each of these court decisions by placing a referendum, Proposition B, on the June 1952 ballot upholding its decision to cancel the CHA contract. Proposition B prevailed, 378,000 to 258,000. Not satisfied with the trashing of the Elysian Park Heights project, the city council, now thoroughly on the anti-Communist bandwagon, voted ten to one to request an investigation by the federal House Un-American Activities Committee into Communist infiltration into the CHA. Mayor Bowron, meanwhile, running for reelection, found himself increasingly vilified as a soft-on-Communism mayor. The portly and bespectacled Bowron got into a fistfight when a demonstrator outside the city council chambers accused him of being "a representative of Stalin."[7] Even more devastating to Bowron's hopes for re-election, State Attorney General Edmund G. (Pat) Brown came personally to Los Angeles to investigate Communist influence in the CHA. It was no surprise, then, when in the fall 1953 election Bowron lost to Poulson, the anti-public-housing candidate backed by the *Los Angeles Times*. By 1953, then, Chavez Ravine, still owned by the federal government, stood vacated, although there were some significant holdouts, especially among the Arechiga family.

The Dodgers arrived in Los Angeles on 18 April 1958 and were greeted with a parade down Broadway. Later that day, a record crowd of 78,672 packed Memorial Coliseum, reconfigured for baseball, to watch the Dodgers prevail 6–5 over the Giants on the opening day of big league baseball in Los Angeles. (After considering the Rose Bowl in Pasadena and the team-owned Wrigley Field, O'Malley opted for a two-year lease on the Coliseum.) Booster rhetoric went into overdrive, but support for the deal cut between O'Malley and the city was not universal. A strong opposition had already surfaced: a cobbled alliance of embittered public housing advocates, smarting over the Elysian Park Heights defeat; developers who owned property in and around Elysian Park Heights and believed that the private development of housing there was a better option; owners of the San Diego Padres, concerned that minor league baseball would soon be a thing of the past; and a vaguely defined group resenting the way O'Malley had presented the Tablets to Los Angeles, and the elected officials of the city, led by the mayor, had thereupon fallen on their knees in worship. Despite the glories of opening day, the Dodgers had arrived in a city where anti-Dodger forces had already placed on the June 1958 ballot a referendum, Proposition B, asking the voters to approve or disapprove the Dodger deal. According to the Tablets and the consent of the city council, Dodger Stadium would sit atop a reconfigured Elysian Park Heights. Without this agreement, O'Malley would not have come west. Now this agreement stood in jeopardy.

Proposition B constituted a referendum on Los Angeles itself. What did the City of Angels wish itself to be? Did Los Angeles wish to hand over a portion of its identity, hence a portion of its sovereignty, to one man, Walter O'Malley, and his baseball team? In the case of working- and middle-class Brooklyn, now abandoned, the Dodgers had embodied and expressed the civic meaning of the borough. Did Los Angeles now wish to make the same transference, especially to a man and a team it had wooed, indeed seduced, from an earlier and long-standing relationship? Cardinal McIntyre was embodying the notion that metropolitan Los Angeles, for Catholics at least, was represented in its comprehensive and well-run archdiocese. Chief Parker was saying that Los Angeles was the LAPD. And now Los Angeles was being asked to affirm yet another covenant, among the city and a team and the jowly New York businessman who was demanding not only a prime piece of public property but a portion of the Los Angeles identity as well. Baseball had a way of helping people believe that they belonged to a place. That is why, significantly, Dodgers games were from the beginning broadcast in Spanish by Rene Cardenas, a Nicaraguan-born journalist living in Los Angeles, and in English by Vin Scully, a New Yorker and Fordham graduate already on board with the team, and his partner Jerry Doggett. The voices and personalities of these men became, almost immediately, iconic, suggesting a bilingual, bicultural identity for Los Angeles that had been whitewashed in the Anglo-American ascendancy but would in time be reemerging in full force. As arrangements to bring the Dodgers to Los Angeles were being finalized, a native Angeleno, Francis Marien, a Jesuit teaching in Spokane, speculated in *America*, the Jesuit weekly, that the City of Angels was in the process of discovering, even earning, its soul and that the coming of the Dodgers was part of that process. "May their coming mean that we will soon speak a common language with something like a Brooklyn accent and be capable of expressing something like a Bronx cheer. Something like it—but distinctively Angeleno," Marien urged.[8]

But first Proposition B had to be passed. In an early instance of celebrity politics, stars such as Joe E. Brown, Dean Martin, George Burns, Jerry Lewis, Debbie Reynolds, and Ronald Reagan flocked to a live five-hour Dodgerthon on 1 June 1958 held over KTTV, the *Los Angeles Times* station, centered on live coverage of the Dodgers arriving at the Los Angeles International Airport for a new round of games. Sixty-two percent of the 1.1 million voters in the city cast their ballots in the largest turnout outside of a presidential election in Los Angeles history. The Dodgers barely won—by a mere 25,785 votes out of nearly 700,000 votes cast. Los Angeles had made up its mind. There were a few more obstacles ahead, including a legal challenge to the United States Supreme Court, which was not heard. But even before the court took a pass, the result was all but certain. The Dodgers would stay in Los Angeles and build at Chavez Ravine.

Like the reorganization of the archdiocese and the LAPD and the coming of the Dodgers to the city, the creation of a Music Center was, essentially, a top-down enterprise on the part of a social elite, led by Dorothy Buffum Chandler, determined to put Los Angeles on the map as a center of serious music and the performing arts. For all the talk of its Johnny-come-lately identity, Los Angeles, like every other American city, had its founding families, its self-recruiting oligarchy, its downtown establishment. The grand mansions of West Adams, Chester Place, Fremont Place, Windsor Square, and Hancock Park bespoke the wealth of the Edwardian era moving into the mid-twentieth century; indeed, each of these developments—strictly from the roll call of families who built these mansions, the lives they led, and the city they were building through business enterprise—suggested an unwritten novel of the city, had there been a Balzac or an Edith Wharton or a Thomas Mann on hand to write such a narrative. Corporate culture came to Los Angeles in full force in the 1920s, as it had come to other American cities; and an oligarchy of corporate leaders had been guiding the city since that time, as also was the case with most other American cities, and was guiding Los Angeles through the 1950s as well: corporate oligarchs such as insurance executive Asa Call, Edward Carter of the Broadway-Hale department store chain, and banker Howard Ahmanson, each of these present and powerful at the opening of the 1950s, and others—Charles (Tex) Thornton of Litton Industries, Norton Simon of Hunt Foods—moving into prominence as the decade unfolded; and still others—financier Mark Taper, Lew Wasserman of MCA, Rabbi Edgar Magnin of Wilshire Temple—becoming more prominent following the détente between downtown and the Westside, Christians and Jews, that was a direct dividend of the Music Center campaign. Insurance executive Asa Call headed an informal but influential Committee of Twenty-Five that met regularly for lunch at Perino's on Wilshire to discuss the issues of the day and, if necessary, to take action. While loosely organized—in one sense, it was little more than a luncheon club—the committee, when it chose to do so, could call upon an extensive arsenal of private resources and political contacts among its membership to exercise influence.

Like all oligarchies, the Los Angeles establishment sought to preserve and develop the city as a place to do business, but also as a source and matrix for social recognition: which is why Society with a capital S had asserted itself in Los Angeles as it had in every other American city. The Los Angeles region enjoyed a social register beginning in 1903, the *Southwest Blue Book*, with seven hundred listings, which continued to publish for the next sixty years. There was also the *Los Angeles Blue Book*, begun in 1917, and the more recently established *California Register* (1954), listing socially prominent families throughout the state. Venues such as the California Club (1887), the Jonathan (1895), the Los Angeles Country Club (1898), and the Valley Hunt Club (1888) in Pasadena served, expressed, and reinforced social status, as did a variety of private schools (Cate, Flintridge, Harvard, Thacher, Webb, Marlborough, Westlake) and debutante balls for which local orchestras did their best to replicate the East Coast Society Sound of Meyer Davis and Lester Lanin. that sound of snobbery, as columnist George Frazier described it in *Esquire*, "of money and breeding and social position."[9] Governed by a discreet committee centered on Hancock Park, the annual Las Madrinas benefiting Children's Hospital was the oldest and most prestigious of these debutante balls. Roman Catholics could and did participate in Las Madrinas, but they also had their own Presentation Ball, benefiting the Sisters of Social Service, in which the debutantes, wearing white, made a deep curtsey before the cardinal. Las Damas, benefiting the Holy Family Adoption Service, was also Catholic and had strong connections to the founding families of Old California, as symbolized by the debutantes' wearing of white lace mantillas. The Coronet debutante ball was Westside and New Money in orientation; the Valley Hunt Club annual event was restricted to young women whose parents or grandparents had been members of the club. Various other groups supported comparable annual balls: the Rose of Castile (Latin American), the Sakura (Japanese), the Paradise Ball, the Links' Cotillion, the Questionettes' Courante Ball (African American), the St. Nicholas (Greek), and the Blue Danube (Hungarian). There were also exclusions: no movie people, for example—with Walt Disney's daughter (Las Madrinas) the first and sole exception—and no Jewish girls, especially at the more upper-crust events, until this exclusion was lifted by Las Madrinas in 1967, yet another by-product of the thawing of Christian-Jewish relations brought about by the Music Center.

Children's Hospital was the charity of choice for the ascendant oligarchy, along with Good Samaritan (Episcopal), Queen of Angels and St. Vincent's (Roman Catholic), and Cedars of Lebanon (Jewish), which merged with Mount Sinai in 1961. For socially ambitious younger (under forty) married women, Los Angeles supported a flourishing chapter of the Junior League, whose annual Moulin Rouge Review not only raised money for charity but allowed otherwise proper matrons to dance onstage in the skimpiest of showgirl costumes. In mid-winter, the oligarchy repaired to the desert, with the family-oriented Smoke Tree Ranch in Palm Springs remaining the dude ranch of choice. Summertime witnessed a southerly migration down the coast to Balboa, a group of islands, a slice of bay, and nineteen miles of scenic shoreline near Newport Beach forty-two miles southeast of the city, the Hamptons of Los Angeles, where the summertime population increased (as of 1957) by more than two hundred thousand vacationers, and sun-drenched weeks were spent in sailing, swimming, sunning, and socializing.

Oligarchs collect art, at once for the pleasure of collecting and connoisseurship and as a reinforcing sign of financial and social achievement. Few oligarchs in the nation, however, were collecting with the energy and resources of Norton Simon. Following his arrival in Los Angeles from San Francisco in 1927, Simon had made a fortune in sheet metal, real estate, steel, orange juice, canned fish, pet food, tomato sauce and tomato paste, matches, railroads, and publishing. Just as he acquired Hunt Foods, the Ohio Match Company, McGraw-Hill, Condé Nast, and McCall's, the one leading to another, Simon began acquiring art in much the same manner, beginning with *Andrea en Bleu* (1918), an oil portrait by Renoir of his daughter-in-law, for which Simon paid $16,000 in December 1954. Within two decades, through a series of rapid purchases (corporate takeovers, one is tempted to call them) of important paintings from all eras, medieval to modern, Simon—guided by the great art dealers of his era and his own unerring instincts—assembled the last comprehensive collection of its kind to be acquired by a single individual (or a single institution, for that matter): a museum of masterpieces from medieval to post-Impressionist, with a gallery of Old Masters at its core, together with an ancillary collection of Asian art of comparable caliber. By its very presence in the city, moreover, Simon's collection was by the early 1960s helping to reinforce the drive for the long-delayed creation of a first-rate art museum.

As her field of interest, her way of leveraging Los Angeles into an improved civic identity, Dorothy Buffum Chandler chose music and the performing arts, which was not surprising, given the fact that Los Angeles already had significant strength in this area. Music, in fact, was the most compelling art form when it came to getting Los Angelenos to leave their homes and commute considerable distances to attend performances. Hence the nationally ranked Los Angeles Philharmonic and the continuing success of the annual concert series at the Hollywood Bowl. Still, when it came to evaluating Los Angeles as a serious center for the performing arts, especially if such assessments were being offered by non-Angelenos, two factors—distances and Hollywood—were frequently offered as trump cards to any effort by the City of Angels to claim for itself status as a cultural center. As far as legitimate theater was concerned, New York drama critic Maurice Zolotow was opining in April 1956, Los Angeles was a wasteland. Even the most notable plays on tour, staged in such well-known venues as the Biltmore Hotel Theatre in the downtown, played for a half or a third the time they had played in other cities. A recent production of *The Caine Mutiny Court-Martial* with Lloyd Nolan, Barry Sullivan, and John Hodiak had closed in a mere six weeks. Some argued that the dispersion of Los Angeles made legitimate theater difficult. Zolotow believed, however, "that the real explanation for the cultural barbarism of Los Angeles is not to be found in geographical diffusion or outdoor mores. It lies in human deficiencies. The average Angeleno is spiritually apathetic, intellectually enervated, and emotionally dehydrated. He resides in a huge vacuum. He is a walking dead man." Zolotow blamed this apathy on the dominance of Hollywood culture and mores on the city. "The principal goal in Hollywood," he argued, "is the avoidance, at all costs, of thinking, of feeling, of being aroused, of, in short, living on any human plane of intensity. Since the theatre seeks to arouse emotions and to propound ideas, to challenge the spectator with the issues of life and death, the theatre is one of those experiences that must be shunned."[10]

This was a devastating critique, and unfair in many ways, but it was also an assessment frequently made of Los Angeles when it came to serious culture as represented by the performing arts. In cultural terms, went this critique, Los Angeles was dominated by the worst banalities and superficialities of Hollywood. Dorothy Buffum Chandler and her fellow oligarchs had long lived with such criticism. Indeed, dating back to the 1920s, this harsh assessment had created a nearly impassable gulf (Walt Disney and Fred Astaire were exceptions) between the film colony and the downtown establishment that was in part motivated by anti-Semitism and in part propelled by the oligarchy's desire to differentiate itself from Hollywood. Which is perhaps why serious music meant so much to the elite of Los Angeles and why serious music, in contrast to the other performing arts, flourished on such a high level. At the core of Anglo-American Protestant Los Angeles culture, for one thing, was a tradition of choral music in hundreds of churches throughout the region that had supported ambitious performances of ambitious music on a weekly basis for the past sixty years. Churchgoing Protestants knew, revered, and practiced serious music. This appreciation, among other causes, led to the establishment of the Los Angeles Philharmonic Orchestra in 1919. This taste for serious music also led to the near-simultaneous creation in the mid-1920s of the Hollywood Bowl in an outdoor amphitheater in Cahuenga Pass previously used for church-related performances of choral music.

The arts and the prestige they brought to a city were very much on the mind of the Los Angeles oligarchy of the 1950s and very much on the mind of Dorothy Buffum Chandler, wife of *Los Angeles Times* publisher Norman Chandler and a driving force at the *Times* in her own right, responsible, among other things, for the *Mirror*, a city-centered tabloid published by the *Times* since 1948. Although Buff Chandler, as she was known to her close friends—or Mrs. C to a wider network of acquaintances—stood at the apex of the oligarchic pecking order, she was also in her own way one of the Folks, born (1901) in La Fayette, Illinois, raised in Long Beach, with her father serving as mayor of the city from 1921 to 1924 and the Buffum family flourishing from the proceeds of a chain of sixteen retail stores founded by her father and uncle. Dorothy Buffum attended Stanford but did not graduate, having met Norman Chandler at a college dance. In marrying Norman as she did in 1922, the eldest son of Harry Chandler, publisher of the *Los Angeles Times*, she moved from Long Beach to a larger metropolitan influence centered on the Chandler newspaper and real estate holdings. Dorothy Buffum had a strong identity before becoming a Chandler and resisted having that identity dissolved in Chandler status and self-regard. She was, in one way or another, a flapper, a 1920s girl, loving parties and dancing and participating in theatrical productions. By temperament, she was not cut out to be a staid society matron, sealed off into an oligarchic enclave that was in so many ways a kingdom unto itself. In that Chandler kingdom, she was expected to be grateful just for being there: this girl from Long Beach, up from the middle-class minor leagues as far as her oligarchic status was concerned; and Norman's siblings had a way of subtly keeping her aware of her social origins lower down the pecking order.

Ten years and two children into her marriage, Buff Chandler fell into a depression regarding her inability to fit into the Chandler clan, and it took six months in a private psychiatric clinic in Pasadena to return her—fully cured, according to psychiatrist Josephine Jackson—to her life as a Chandler. All such breakdowns have complex origins. One of them for Buff Chandler was her visceral reluctance to remain ornamentally on the sidelines. She wanted work, action, involvement; and she sought it, initially, in a classic oligarchic venue, volunteer work for the Children's Hospital of Los Angeles. Once there, she did not remain mere window dressing but in short order tackled the dysfunctional personnel culture at the hospital, which she helped adjudicate with proposals for better wages, more days off, and longer vacations.

In the last year of World War II, when Norman, now *Times* publisher, was frequently away on government service, Buff Chandler became, in effect, his administrative deputy and was given direct oversight of the *Mirror*. She took a crash course in journalism at USC. As in the case of her involvement in Children's Hospital, Mrs. C was once again hands-on in her approach, meeting with top staff over beer for nightly critiques of that day's edition and, among other things, reorganizing the so-called women's pages into a more ambitious arts and cultural review as well as a more comprehensive chronicle of women in all phases of Los Angeles life. In 1950 she established a Woman of the Year award that quickly gained strong regional support. Like so many Los Angeles women who went to work as Red Cross volunteers during the war or joined the assembly line in aircraft factories or otherwise involved themselves in the war effort, Buff Chandler was a woman for whom the challenges of the Second World War and the postwar era brought to fruition latent possibilities for a more active engagement in the world around her.

In 1950 actor Jean Hersholt, president of the Hollywood Bowl, impressed by Buff Chandler's leadership on the board of the Southern California Symphony Association, asked her to join the board of the Bowl, then on the verge of financial collapse. Once again, Chandler's approach was direct. She spearheaded an abrupt suspension of the season's program, followed by a hastily organized series of fundraising concerts, in which musicians played for free. Within two weeks, enough money was raised to resume the season. The rescue of the Hollywood Bowl led Dorothy Chandler fully to experience the power of music as a unifying social force and her own powers as a community leader.

Los Angeles had been on the lookout for a new music center since the late 1930s. However distinguished the Los Angeles Philharmonic had become, it was still performing on a long-term lease from the Temple Baptist Church for an auditorium in a 1906 mixed-use structure facing Pershing Square. Since the Los Angeles Philharmonic was the best thing about Los Angeles in terms of the performing arts, the upgrading of the Los Angeles identity in the postwar period included the financing and construction of a more suitable music center, especially now that the city also had its own Civic Light Opera Association (1952) and Los Angeles Opera Company (1955), along with annual visits by the San Francisco Opera Company and the Metropolitan Opera of New York. (Los Angeles even had a pioneering classical radio station, KUSC-FM of the University of Southern California.) The proposal for a new music center, first made in the late 1930s—to be financed by a county bond issue—called for a mixed-use complex combining a music auditorium with a trade or exhibition hall in an effort to please as many voters as possible. Three times, however—in 1951, 1953, and 1954—voters failed to give the project the necessary two-thirds majority. Falling short by less than 1 percent, the failure of a 1954 bond issue was especially galling to serious music backers since the proposal also included a fifteen-thousand-seat auditorium for sporting events as well as an exhibition hall for trade and industrial shows and only a smaller auditorium for symphony, opera, chamber music, or other classical music recitals.

The Los Angeles County Board of Supervisors favored the project but knew that it could not go to the voters for the fourth time with yet another proposal to finance a music center with public money. What was needed was a public-private partnership in which the private sector would raise the majority of funds and the board of supervisors would assist the project through grants, a favorable land deal, and other subventions that did not require voter approval. In the winter of 1956, while vacationing in the Bahamas, Buff Chandler received a telegram from the board of supervisors asking her to join a 125-person county-wide Citizen Advisory Committee to raise private funds for the music center project. The twelve-person executive committee to which Chandler was appointed commissioned the consulting firm of Arthur D. Little to make a feasibility study. Released the following year, the Little report called for yet another mixed-use trade-fair and performance-space building, this time in a high-rise in the downtown. After some deliberation, the executive committee, dissatisfied with this recommendation, decided to call a time-out on the project. Twelve years of planning screeched to a halt.

This was not an acceptable solution to Buff Chandler, executive vice president of the Southern California Symphony Association. Already, she and Grace (Mrs. Henry) Salvatori had in March 1955 raised an impressive $400,000 reserve fund for the project at a star-studded fundraising gala at the Ambassador Hotel, raffling off an El Dorado Cadillac as first prize. Chandler had also interested herself in the selection of a better site, finding one on a county-owned promontory on the western edge of Civic Center on seven acres atop Bunker Hill bounded by Grand, First, Hope and Temple. Becoming president of the Los Angeles Symphony in late 1958, Mrs. Chandler organized a new music center building fund committee of seventy-six members, with herself as chair. It included an A-list of corporate movers and shakers (Henry Salvatori, Leonard Firestone, Justin Dart, and Howard Ahmanson, among them) as well as Cardinal McIntyre, Sam Goldwyn, and Dolores (Mrs. Bob) Hope. Within three months, the committee had raised $4 million toward the purchase of the Grand Avenue site atop Bunker Hill and the construction of what now had morphed into a three-building complex encompassing a music pavilion seating 3,200, with underground parking for 3,000 cars, an 1,800-seat performing-arts-oriented theater; and an 800-seat forum for other kinds of plays and performances. All in all, the committee raised more than $19 million toward the $33.5 million complex, with the remaining funds coming from revenue bonds and public subventions that did not have to go before Los Angeles County voters, thanks to changes in the law passed by the legislature and signed by Governor Pat Brown. The money came from large donations ($1 million from financier and philanthropist S. Mark Taper alone) and 12 percent of it from small cash donations by individual citizens, money gathered in large blue canvas Buck Bags designed by the Walt Disney Studios.

It was, all things considered, an extraordinary tour de force of fundraising, legislative maneuvering, and negotiation with the county on the part of the oligarchy as led by Buff Chandler, whose prowess as a fundraiser was in and of itself a form of performance art. True, she was the wife and, after 1960, the mother of the publisher of the *Los Angeles Times*, a director of the Times Mirror Corporation, a regent of the University of California, and a trustee of Occidental College; but that alone could not explain her commitment and her success. There was something almost obsessive about the way that Mrs. C had labored on behalf of the music center project across a decade: something that blended her own private needs for useful action with her vision for an upgraded identity for Los Angeles. At times, Buff Chandler seemed to be almost stalking the oligarchy: challenging it, in effect, to back its boosterish claims with cash. Seated weekdays for lunch at her favorite table at Perino's—to the left of the entrance, commanding the room—she would interrupt conversations with prospective donors to pounce upon other prospective donors at other tables, then return to leverage her first prospect with the news of how much so-and-so at another table had just pledged. From this perspective, her quest paralleled that of Cardinal McIntyre, Chief Parker, and Walter O'Malley as a fusion of personal and civic actualization. The full implication of what Mrs. C was accomplishing, however, was not immediately apparent, although when ground was broken on the Bunker Hill site in March 1962 it was already apparent that Los Angeles was moving in a new direction.

After two and a half years of construction, the privately financed fifty-six-thousand-seat Dodger Stadium was ready for baseball by April 1962. The site and structure had been meticulously planned by Walter O'Malley and a team of Dodger administrators and consultants. O'Malley moved into the Statler Hotel on Wilshire Boulevard to be near the project. What O'Malley wanted was the ultra-modern stadium he had been dreaming of for more than a decade; and his architect, retired Navy Captain Emil Praeger, did not disappoint him. In every instance—its freeway-served site, its column-free construction, its clear sightlines, an unobstructed view of home plate from every seat, its escalators serving four levels, its exclusive private box seating, the comfortable seats for fans, the availability of restrooms—the $23 million stadium was state-of-the-art. Eight million cubic yards of earth had been moved to create the plateau on which the stadium sat, surrounded by the mother of all parking lots, with space for sixteen thousand automobiles. Architectural critics chided O'Malley for a shortage of drinking fountains (there were only two in the entire stadium!), an error soon rectified; yet by and large they recognized Dodger Stadium almost immediately as not only a place to play baseball but a paradigm of futurist Los Angeles. Indeed, as if to suggest even further this prophetic paradigm, the site itself—with its views of the downtown and the San Gabriel Mountains—was lavishly planted, at the cost of $1.5 million, in acacia, pepper, olive, palm, pine, elm, ash, and other trees, together with more than three hundred rosebushes.

During the planning and design process, O'Malley and his team closely studied Disneyland from the perspective of access, egress, convenience, and crowd control. As in Disneyland, access and egress was by car along convenient feeder roads from the freeway leading to ample parking. Uniformed attendants were likewise on hand to guide visitors to their section of the stadium. Disneyland-like as well was the care paid to food services, including a milk bar for children. Most important, Dodger Stadium, like Disneyland, constituted an idealization of what was being presented, in this case, baseball: not as enjoyed by the boisterous fans of Ebbets Field, yelling and screaming for their beloved Bums from seats with obstructed sightlines, but an entertainment being appreciated by well-behaved middle-class Los Angelenos, decorously enjoying the game or listening by radio to the skilled play-by-play narrative of Vin Scully and Jerry Doggett. If all this were not enough—this ultra-modern stadium, the most impressive in the nation at the time, in an Acropolis-like setting—the Los Angeles Dodgers were already a world champion team, having won the pennant in their second season at the Coliseum and going on to defeat the Chicago White Sox in the World Series. Los Angeles was now not only a major league city; it had become a World Series city as well.

All this came at a cost. First of all, there were those still smarting over the passage of Proposition B in June 1958, giving O'Malley the store, they believed, bowing down before the Tablets, together with the subsequent defeat of their legal appeals. Then there had been the evictions by sheriff's deputies of the Arechiga family and two other households from their Chavez Ravine homes on 8 May 1959. The Arechigas—four adults and three children—had barricaded themselves in their home. Three sheriff's deputies kicked in the door, and one of the Arechiga daughters, Aurora Arechiga Vargas, a war widow, went limp and was forcibly carried down the stairs, as nearby bulldozers, almost immediately, moved in against the houses. Other Arechigas and neighbors scuffled with deputies. One of them, a woman, was handcuffed and taken to a squad car. The Arechigas children, meanwhile, were crying hysterically. The Arechigas set up a tent in a nearby vacant lot and refused to leave the property. All this was replayed on television that evening in Los Angeles and across the country, inflaming not only opponents to Dodger Stadium but countless others who believed that the Arechigas were being evicted so that the stadium could be built.

In reality, the Arechigas had been evicted early in the decade by the California Housing Authority so that the Elysian Park Heights Housing Project could go forward. The family had been offered $10,050 for its property, which the court had upheld as fair compensation, but the Arechigas had demanded $17,500. The Arechigas had also refused an offer of three apartments in Ramona Gardens because there would have been no place to coop their flock of 150 chickens. Then there was the fact, as was soon disclosed, that the Arechiga family owned and rented out seven homes throughout the region. This last news tended to blunt the moral intensity of their case, but not before the spectacle of their removal had resulted in a local and national uproar. Even with the news that the Arechigas were prosperous property owners, the anti-O'Malley faction could legitimately ask the question: Why were the Arechigas denied a mere $7,500 when O'Malley was given millions in public subsidies? Counseled by Mexican American city councilman Edward Roybal, the Arechigas abandoned their tent and moved to a house owned by their daughter in

Santa Fe Springs, vowing to carry their case forward (futilely, as it turned out) in the courts.

Still, the spectacle of upright Mexican Americans, including a war widow, being forcibly evicted from their property on behalf of what many considered a sweetheart deal with a white multi-millionaire from New York, reverberated throughout the city and in time would prove an inflammatory icon to the Chicano activists of a later generation. Whether intentionally or not, such activists frequently gave the impression that the Arechigas were made homeless by their eviction and that, subsequently, there was a cleavage between Mexican Americans and the Dodgers that reflected the chasm between brown and white in metropolitan Los Angeles. Such an argument, however, overlooks the popularity of the Dodgers among Latinos, whether in the stadium or listening for forty-five seasons to Spanish-language radio broadcasts by Jaime Jarrin.

In the case of the Music Center, there was nothing comparable to the Battle of Chavez Ravine. There was, in fact, the very opposite effect: a reconciling of tensions among various groups. Not only had Buff Chandler raised money from the usual suspects among the Anglo-American establishment centered on Hancock Park, Palos Verdes, the downtown, Pasadena, and San Marino, she had also involved the significantly Jewish Westside of the city in the fundraising effort. This work of cross-town reconciliation, of introducing the Hillcrest Country Club to the California Club, the movie industry to the downtown establishment, Joan Didion would later claim, ranked Dorothy Buffum Chandler alongside Phoebe Apperson Hearst, Jane Lathrop Stanford, and Eleanor McClatchy as a powerful woman who upgraded her community to the point of re-foundation.

The dedication of the Music Center in early December 1964 landed Dorothy Chandler on the cover of *Time*, with a favorable profile of Mrs. C and the center, although the 2,100-seat Ahmanson Theater and 750-seat Mark Taper Forum would not be paid for, named, built, and opened for another two years. Designed by the local firm of Welton Becket and Associates, the 3,250-seat Music Center Pavilion, a restrained blend of classicism and modernity, with sub-structure parking for two thousand cars (guaranteeing an exit time of no more than fifteen minutes), soared atop its freeway-girded Bunker Hill site at the western edge of the Civic Center as a compelling icon of the Los Angeles, city and county, that had now arrived. The entire structure was surrounded by a continuous colonnade of columns rising against walls fenestrated in honey-colored onyx. Thus the Pavilion presented itself as a totality to every part of the city. Within, a grand hall and foyer encircled the auditorium. Orchestra seats arced in uninterrupted rows in the European manner, with access only from side aisles; yet these rows were separated enough so that no one had to stand for anyone making a late entrance. The stage was high and deep (you could do *Aida* here with live elephants, noted one wag) and was designed to handle symphony, opera, ballet, and musical theater with equal ease. Composer Richard Rodgers, whose *The King and I* was scheduled for an early performance, predicted that the Pavilion, together with the John F. Kennedy Center in Washington, would

breathe new energy into American musical theater by allowing Broadway productions to play more conveniently while on the road and for Broadway-bound tryouts
to show themselves to full advantage.

On opening night, 6 December 1964, a packed house in formal attire sat expec-
tantly as Zubin Mehta—the twenty-four-year-old conductor of the Los Angeles
Philharmonic whom Dorothy Chandler had personally selected three years earlier—strode to the podium. Raising his baton, Mehta led the orchestra in the *Fan-
fare* by Richard Strauss, followed by Beethoven's *Violin Concerto in D Major*, with
Jascha Heifetz as soloist. "We have given it bricks and mortar," remarked Mrs. Chandler in the course of the festivities. "Now we must give it a soul."[11] Five nights later,
Nat King Cole performed to an equally enthusiastic, if more casually dressed, audience. Two years after opening night, the Pavilion was named in honor of Dorothy
Chandler.

6

Downsides and Dividends

Los Angeles as Supercity

HE Music Center catalyzed the performance culture of metropolitan Los Angeles. It had also run parallel to a number of other related developments. Four months after the dedication of the Pavilion, an equally impressive Los Angeles County Museum of Art (LACMA) opened its doors in Hancock Park on Wilshire adjacent to the La Brea Tar Pits. Like the Music Center, the three-building LACMA complex fulfilled more than a half century of hopes. Founded in 1910, LACMA began its existence as part of the county Museum of History, Science, and Art in Exposition Park and limped along for the next four decades as a promise of things to come. In 1958 oligarch Edward William Carter, president of the Broadway-Hale retail chain in Southern California, joined the museum's board of governors and became chair of its fundraising committee. The time had arrived, Carter announced, for the county art museum to detach itself from the museum of science and industry, build its own complex, and fashion itself into an institution worthy of the metropolis that was forming around it. Carter was backed in this campaign by Richard Fargo Brown, the great-grandson of the founder of Wells Fargo serving as chief curator of art at LACMA since 1954. A Ph.D. from Harvard, Fargo also had the ear of Norton Simon, whom he advised on acquisitions, and a number of other oligarchs already involved in the Music Center campaign.

Learning from the thrice rejected Music Center campaign, the museum backers avoided the ballot box in favor of private fundraising, combined with an advantageous purchase of county property and a mixed public-private operating budget when the institution went into operation. Once county supervisor Kenneth Hahn set aside certain objections, the support of the county board of supervisors was almost immediate. Banker Howard Ahmanson, meanwhile, pledged two million dollars to get the fundraising campaign rolling. Norton Simon came through with a promise of one million and the even more compelling promise that the art collection administered by the Norton Simon Foundation would be loaned to LACMA on a long-term basis.

While the LACMA campaign was open and straightforward regarding its public-private pact between supervisors and oligarchy, it was in psychological terms a clash of egos and wills of titanic proportions. Furious that Carter had secretly agreed that the museum would be named in honor of Ahmanson in exchange for Ahmanson's $2 million gift, Norton Simon withdrew his offer of $1 million. Even the National Gallery of Art in Washington, Simon argued, had not been named after its donor, Paul Mellon. After some struggle, it was agreed that the museum would be divided into three buildings, with only one of them named after Ahmanson. That necessitated more money, and so in the late fall of 1961 Carter brought aboard UCLA chancellor Franklin Murphy to head the fundraising campaign.

Bart Lytton, meanwhile, chairman of the Lytton Financial Corporation and Lytton Savings and Loan Association, came through with a $500,000 gift, and Simon, mollified by the three-building solution, pledged $250,000 for a sculpture plaza bearing his name. Then Anna Bing Arnold, a Broadway actress in her youth and the widow of real estate magnate and art collector Leo S. Bing, agreed to pay for a building named in honor of her late husband. LACMA thus consisted of the Ahmanson Gallery for its permanent collection, the Lytton Center for traveling exhibitions, and the Leo S. Bing Center, housing an auditorium, restaurant, classroom, and seminar facilities.

Still, there was still not yet peace in the valley. Curator Brown wanted either the internationally renowned Mies van der Rohe or, as a second choice, the equally famous Eero Saarinen to be brought to Los Angeles to create an iconic complex. Ahmanson, meanwhile, wanted the more conservative Edward Durrell Stone, who had done for him a number of buildings; and Ahmanson, being the major donor, had the ability to bring things to a standstill, which he did. As a compromise the trustees gave the commission to the local firm of William Pereira and Associates. The resulting complex, while impressive, was not iconic as far as international architecture was concerned. In the year following its opening, nonetheless, more than 2.5 million visitors flocked to the new museum to enjoy an impressive collection centered on the gifts of the William Randolph Hearst Foundation and the collection on loan from the Norton Simon Foundation.

The role played by Franklin Murphy in the LACMA fundraising effort underscored another coming of age, that of UCLA and its chancellor. Among his many accomplishments, Chancellor Murphy forged an emotional and imaginative connection between UCLA and Los Angeles, arguing that UCLA, like the Music Center and LACMA, underscored the rise of the metropolitan region. Dramatically expressive of this relationship was UCLA's highly successful adult education program, presided over by Paul Sheats, a Harvard-trained literary scholar. By 1964 nearly sixty-eight thousand participants in the UCLA Lifelong Learning program were commuting to the UCLA campus or to homes throughout the region for a wide range of courses taught by regular and adjunct faculty. While Harvard had long since entered the continuing education field with its Lowell Institute, few if any nationally ranked universities were supporting a program of adult learning on such a scale. The Lifelong Learning program at UCLA was making of the entire region a UCLA campus and thereby bonding to UCLA a supportive cadre of thousands of adult learners. Within eight years of his arrival in the City of Angels, Franklin Murphy had become chairman and CEO of the Times Mirror Company, parent company of the *Los Angeles Times*, and a member of countless boards, including LACMA and the Getty Trust. More, he had become Doge of the City as far as culture and philanthropy were concerned, a metropolitan icon.

Norman Topping, meanwhile, another physician turned academic executive, was pursuing a parallel, if less flamboyant, program of development at the University of Southern California. Appointed president of USC in May 1958 from the deanship of the medical school at the University of Pennsylvania, Topping assumed control of a confederation of professional schools and an undergraduate college known primarily for its football team. Topping's predecessor Fred Fagg Jr., a legal scholar, had been hampered in his efforts to improve USC by the continuing presence on campus of Rufus Bernard von KleinSmid, president of USC from 1921 to 1946 and chancellor since 1947. Ensconced in a wood-paneled office adjacent to the rare book collection in the library, von KleinSmid continued to second-guess Fagg and semi-direct the institution, using his influence with alumni as leverage.

Topping, however, refused to be intimidated by von KleinSmid or anyone else. Rather quickly, he came to certain conclusions. Founded in 1880, USC had for more than a half century functioned as a de facto land grant university, training the professionals of the region. During the 1920s, like the rest of Los Angeles, USC had experienced significant growth, as evidenced in the architecturally impressive buildings from that era dominating the campus. During the Depression, however, growth had come to a standstill; and during the Second World War USC had become almost exclusively a facility for military training. The university, moreover, missed out on the first phase of post–World War II growth, which went to UCLA, a state-supported institution. Now was the time, Topping decided, for USC to recover its momentum.

Between 1958 and 1961, Topping threw himself into a self-described Thousand Days devoted to planning the turnaround of USC: an improved and expanded campus, the upgrading of faculty and faculty salaries, the creation of endowed chairs, and, above all else, a new identity and mission: to become a nationally ranked research university. Empowered by a board of trustees growing in strength across the decade (it included, among others, Howard Ahmanson, Asa Call, Justin Dart, Leonard Firestone, and Seeley Mudd), Topping improved the law, business, and medical schools and all but re-founded the schools of music and cinema-television. Almost for the first time in its history, USC began to attract and reward research scholars to its college of arts and sciences. Topping brought in nationally ranked architects to design campus buildings: Edward Durrell Stone, for example, for the social sciences and education buildings, I. M. Pei and Associates for the business school. Dwight Eisenhower, John F. Kennedy, Richard Nixon, and Robert Kennedy came to campus, and in 1961 USC awarded an honorary degree to alumna Patricia Ryan Nixon. Even more deliberately than Dorothy Chandler, perhaps, Topping worked at scrubbing away traces of anti-Semitism remaining from the prewar era; and from the ties Topping formed with Jewish students and supporters USC—an institution founded by a Protestant, a Catholic, and a Jew—achieved a renewed relationship with the Jewish community that would in time yield impressive results in terms of students, faculty, trustees, fundraising, and national ranking.

In December 1962 the Ford Foundation awarded a breakthrough $6.5 million grant to the USC endowment, which stood at a meager $7.7 million at Topping's arrival. In December 1964 the Ford Foundation made a second grant, for $7.5 million, the first time in its history that it had made a double grant to a single university. By the end of the 1960s, a revitalized USC was admitted to the American Association of Universities, the Washington-based organization representing the leading research universities in the country. The entrance of USC into the athletic Association of Western Universities, furthermore, aligned the Trojans with the major universities on the Pacific Coast.

Like Murphy at UCLA, McIntrye at the archdiocese, Parker at LAPD, O'Malley at the Dodgers, Chandler at the Music Center, and Carter at LACMA, Norman Topping at USC was doing his part to upgrade and intensify the institutional culture of greater Los Angeles, now approaching the status of a supercity. The Los Angeles County colleges founded in the 1880s, meanwhile—Occidental (1887), Whittier (1891), and Pomona (1888)—were experiencing equal periods of upgrading and growth. In 1960 President Arthur Coons of Occidental chaired the crash effort to formulate the Master Plan for Higher Education for the entire state of California. Whittier College, the Quaker institution that Richard Nixon had attended, enjoyed its first Rhodes Scholarship, conferred in 1963 on Stan Sanders, an African American born and raised in Watts. In eastern Los Angeles County, Pomona and Scripps (1926), the nucleus of the Associated Colleges of Claremont, were joined by the newly formed Claremont Men's College in 1946, which by the late 1950s had become the West Coast epicenter of the conservative revival being spearheaded by William F. Buckley Jr. and the *National Review*. In 1955, thanks to a gift from Los Angeles philanthropist Harvey Mudd, an engineering school was added to the Claremont complex, followed in 1963 by Pitzer College, emphasizing social science and the liberal arts. By then, the Claremont complex—the five undergraduate colleges, the Graduate School, and the School of Religion—had emerged as a cooperative cluster on the Oxbridge model, edging into national reputation.

The Henry E. Huntington Library and Art Gallery in San Marino, meanwhile, was bringing to Southern California a host of accomplished English and American scholars responsible for some of the most notable historical and humanities writing of the postwar era. To experience the Huntington in the 1950s was to rub shoulders with such Oxford luminaries as Shakespearean scholar A. L. Rowse of All Souls, Sir George Clark, president of Oriel and historian of seventeenth-century England,

and medievalist Vivian Galbraith, Regius Professor of Modern History. Also in residence, together or singly, were such respected figures as James Wardrop, curator of early English manuscripts at the Victoria and Albert Museum; historian Marcus Cunliffe of Manchester; scholars Merrill Jensen of Wisconsin, Edmund Morgan, Wilmarth Lewis, and Howard Lamar of Yale; Ezra Styles, David Donald, Marjorie Nicolson, and Allan Nevins of Columbia; James Silver of the University of Mississippi; Louis B. Wright of the Folger Library; and such eminent Californianists as Robert Glass Clelland of Occidental, Robert Hine of Riverside, Franklin Walker of Mills, and John Caughey of UCLA. To converse with such scholars over luncheon or play bowls with them on the great lawn during the second half of the luncheon hour was to experience to an impressive degree the fulfillment of founder Henry Huntington's vision, augmented by that of the institution's first director, Professor Max Farrand of Yale, of metropolitan Los Angeles as a congenial crossroads of historical and humanistic research. From this perspective, the Huntington, opening itself to scholars in 1928, constituted a prewar prototype of what USC, UCLA, the Claremont Colleges, the Music Center, and the Los Angeles County Museum of Art would bring to fruition in the postwar period: high culture in Southern California, centered on, sustained, and nurtured by metropolitan Los Angeles.

Equally expressive of greater Los Angeles—perhaps even closer to the true identity of the city as a place for demotic self-invention—were its best-selling writers. Living in Hollywood since 1943, Ariel and Will Durant were writing up a storm. A Massachusetts native of French-Canadian extraction, Durant had studied for the priesthood with the Jesuits before leaving the order (and Catholicism) for philosophy studies at Columbia and a peripatetic teaching career. At twenty-eight, he married his brightest pupil, Ariel—appropriately named, for she was to become his lifelong muse and partner. At first glance, the Durants would seem headed for a lifetime of poverty; indeed, they lived on $300 the first year of their marriage. Pushing their infant daughter Ethel along the sidewalks of New York, however, Durant, ever the contemplative, happened upon a notion that would determine his entire life. "The meaning of life," he mused, "is losing yourself in a larger life."[1] That larger life, that larger enterprise, Durant soon decided, was the writing of large-scale works for a general audience. (At the time, Durant was directing the Labor Temple School in New York, lecturing to working men and women on historical subjects and contemporary social and industrial problems.) As the first product of this new vocation, Durant wrote a general history of philosophy. Its publisher, Simon & Schuster, expected *The Story of Philosophy* (1926) to sell sixteen hundred copies. It sold more than a million and continued to sell for the rest of the century.

Will and Ariel Durant were now financially independent. What to do? The answer: *The Story of Civilization* (1935–63), tracing the history of the Western world across a cavalcade of volumes aimed at a general audience. While working on the first three volumes at their home in Great Neck, Long Island, the Durants spent 1938 in Los Angeles, where Will taught a course at UCLA. The two of them came to love the city and the climate and moved to Hollywood in 1943, following the completion of volume three. In the two decades and more to come, working steadily together and eventually listed as co-authors, the Durants produced the next eight volumes of *The Story of Civilization*, which sold steadily in English and numerous translations.

There was something very typical of Los Angeles in the cottage industry established by the Durants in their Hollywood home where the two of them—working together, side by side, consulting innumerable books at UCLA and the Hollywood Public Library, gathering more than a thousand pages of notes per published chapter—produced year after year, volume after volume, thick and compendious studies centered on major epochs. Did Los Angeles offer the Durants more than a good climate? Did Los Angeles offer them a certain freedom from the dense but intimidating academic culture of the East Coast in exchange for the non-intimidation, indeed the encouragement, of a neo-Mediterranean city aside an azure sea, as Will Durant put it, where one might think and write independently for a general audience of intelligent readers? Whatever the answer to this question, the Durants did become iconic figures suggestive of Los Angeles and Southern California as a popular, democratic, and intelligent place.

It would be a mistake to evaluate Los Angeles strictly in terms of its importation of culture—texts, performances, art and artifacts—from older and elsewhere places. Los Angeles was its own complex place, capable of sustaining high culture when necessary—as in the 1940s when it emerged as the capital of German literature—but also of nurturing various forms of popular culture in writing, music, movies, radio, and television that were distinctive to the region. Highbrow, middlebrow, and popular culture frequently blended in Los Angeles as in the case of detective stories and film noir, and as a result the creative output of Los Angeles would help force a later generation of critics to ask themselves whether the distinctions between high and popular culture could be either made or sustained in the first place, at least as far as Los Angeles was concerned. Popular writers felt at home in Los Angeles, ground zero of the Hollywood dream factory: a metropolitan region in which so many residents were up-from-nowhere, up-from-elsewhere people, looking for a second or third chance, figments frequently of their own imaginations, anxious for instructive entertainment or entertaining instruction that would shore up spotty educations and identities.

Best-selling historical novelists Irving Stone, Harold Lamb, and Paul I. Wellman knew this, each of them coming from elsewhere and settling in the metropolis to spin out their fictions. Stone, for example, a San Francisco native, moving to Los Angeles from New York, interspersed life and writing in his hillside home in Beverly Hills with sojourns abroad to research his best-selling novels in partnership with his wife Jean, a parallel couple in historical fiction to Will and Ariel Durant in history. Even more easily than the Durant histories, which required close reading, the historical novels of Irving Stone educated readers through solidly researched entertainment, almost painlessly, in a way that ran parallel to the extension courses at UCLA. Thanks to Stone, mass audiences were being introduced to Vincent van Gogh, Camillo Pissarro, and Michelangelo in a non-intimidating manner, hence to art history and an appreciation of painting. The major Irving Stone novels became motion pictures, which cinched the popular connection. It was not Harvard, true; but it was en route to Merchant-Ivory and *Masterpiece Theatre*.

Defending champion of the popular novel in the region was the best-selling Brentwood-based popmeister Irving Wallace, whose ever so soft soft-porn *The Chapman Report* (1960), inspired by the Kinsey Report and set in Los Angeles, suggested an underground epidemic of nymphomania in middle-class L.A. and resulted in an early film for an aspiring actress named Jane Fonda. Wallace's *The Prize* (1962) ran to more than three hundred thousand words and dealt with the race for the Nobel. The mid-1960s saw Wallace break his previous hardcover record with *The Man* (1964), the story of an African American who becomes President, selling 105,000 in hardback. Then came *The Seven Minutes* (1969), dealing with efforts to suppress a pornographic classic, with a barely disguised Catholic prelate modeled on Cardinal McIntyre getting the novel in question placed on the Vatican's Index of Forbidden Books. By the end of the decade, when Wallace was working on *The Word* (1972), dealing with biblical paleography and exegesis, his combined sales were approaching $30 million, and his movie contracts had become legendary.

Highbrow critics could easily dismiss Irving Wallace as a schlockmeister or first-draft movie writer—*movelist* in Richard Schickel's terminology. But what was one to say about the equally prolific Ray Bradbury, whose novels and short stories, while not as outrageously best-selling as Wallace's, nevertheless earned Bradbury a steady income, a home in Cheviot Hills in West Los Angeles, a comfortable life for himself and his wife and four daughters, and, in literary terms, the approval of highbrow critics such as Christopher Isherwood and art scholar Bernard Berenson, who became a personal friend? From one perspective, Bradbury was a pulp fiction writer, in his case of science fiction (or science fantasy, as Bradbury preferred to describe his work), initially published in pulp science fiction magazines before Bradbury broke into the big time. Bradbury's *The Martian Chronicles* (1950) earned high praise as ambitious literature, a success followed in 1953 by the equally compelling collection of linked short stories, *The Golden Apples of the Sun*, dealing with the harnessing of the sun's energy via rocket-mining, and the full-length novel *Fahrenheit 451*, an indictment of McCarthyism in the guise of a futurist society that burned all books.

If any one writer best epitomized the fusion of cultural levels so characteristic of Los Angeles, it would be Bradbury: a midwesterner, born in Waukegan, Illinois, brought to Los Angeles as an adolescent at the age of thirteen after a precocious, hard-reading childhood soaked in L. Frank Baum, the John Carter of Mars series by Edgar Rice Burroughs, Jules Verne, the Lon Chaney silent films *The Hunchback of Notre Dame* (1923) and *The Phantom of the Opera* (1926), the pulp science fiction magazine *Amazing Stories*, Buck Rogers and Flash Gordon comics, and live performances by Blackstone the Magician, who when Bradbury was eleven presented him with the live rabbit extracted from his hat, which led

Bradbury himself to devote a number of years to the study and practice of magic. The primary influences on Ray Bradbury, then, with the notable exception of Edgar Allan Poe, were those of popular culture, and Poe himself wrote for a popular audience.

Arrived in Los Angeles, a movie- and radio-obsessed Bradbury haunted the entrance to Paramount Studios in hopes of catching a glimpse of a star or two or rummaged in garbage cans outside radio studios in search of discarded scripts. As a student at Los Angeles High School from 1935 to 1939, Bradbury fell in love with Thomas Wolfe, began to write poetry, received his only instruction in writing from two dedicated teachers, saved his lunch money to buy a typewriter, and wrote for the school paper, to which he submitted byline reports on live radio performances by Jack Benny and Fred Allen. Following graduation from Los Angeles High, Bradbury forwent college in favor of peddling the *Los Angeles Daily News* at the corner of Olympic and Norton, reading omnivorously in the Los Angeles Public Library, taking acting lessons from Laraine Day at the Wilshire Players Guild, watching repeated performances of Walt Disney's *Fantasia* (1940), the most influential film in his life, and, returning to his room in a tenement at Figueroa and Temple in off time from selling newspapers, writing, writing, writing, fifty-two short stories in 1941 alone. Sundays he spent at Muscle Beach, where Hollywood writer Leigh Brackett would review Bradbury's drafts between workouts. By 1943, kept out of the military because of poor eyesight, Bradbury was supporting himself selling science fantasy stories to *Weird Tales* and *Famous Fantastic Mysteries*. The next year, turning to detective fiction, he sold stories to *New Detective, Detective Tales, Dime Mystery,* and *Flynn's Detective Fiction.* In 1945 his story "The Big Black and White Game" sold to the more upscale *American Mercury.* It was selected for *Best American Short Stories.* By 1947, the year he married Marguerite McClure, a UCLA grad working as a clerk in Fowler's Bookstore downtown, Bradbury was selling scripts to the CBS radio program *Suspense.* The day before his marriage at the Church of the Good Shepherd, Episcopal, on 27 September 1947, Bradbury burned a million manuscript words of his apprentice writing. Later that week, he sold a short story, "I See You Never," to the *New Yorker,* and at the end of the year it was selected for the O. Henry Awards *Prize Stories of 1947.* By then, Bradley was making $250 a month and selling to better and better magazines.

Then came the astonishing productivity of the early 1950s and the critical praise of Isherwood, Berenson, J. B. Priestley, Angus Wilson, and Arthur C. Clarke, and the gold medal from the Commonwealth Club of California in 1954 for *Fahrenheit 451,* followed by a sojourn in London and Ireland working with John Huston on the script for *Moby Dick* (1956), followed by the writing of *Dandelion Wine* (1957), in which Bradbury returned nostalgically to the world of his Illinois childhood. The decade to come would see Bradbury continue to produce short stories on a steady basis, write travel literature, work intermittently with the movie studios, lecture alongside Aldous Huxley at UCLA, and turn his attention to city planning (Bradbury favored monorails) and a variety of other topics.

It is nearly impossible to categorize the prodigious output of a writer who later claimed to have written every day of his life or to fix Bradbury into any one or another literary category or level of literary importance. He was, in short, like Los Angeles itself, eclectic and unintimidated, an entertainer whom highbrow critics took seriously, a self-instructed urban planner respected by professionals, and a jack-of-all-writing-trades: scriptwriter for movies, radio, and television (*The Alfred Hitchcock Hour, The Twilight Zone*), a produced dramatist, a writer for national magazines. Bradbury was, in short, a latter-day Jack London for Los Angeles: and doing all this without benefit of a driver's license (or even learning to drive, for that matter!) and staying away from air travel except when absolutely necessary.

Were literary historians to have only Bradbury to consider, they would be able to disentangle the quirks, oddities, byways, and multiple levels of pop, schlock, mass media, and flashes of highbrow in the literary Los Angeles of those years. Indeed, with the testimony of literature alone—fiction, poetry, memoir, highbrow, middle-brow, or pulp—the entire city could be excavated and recovered. Here was a paradox: the one American city that was supposed by its critics to have been so lowbrow, so hostile to literature and related arts, had, in fact, been receiving since the 1930s the testimony of notable writers from the United States, Europe, and Latin America to a degree unequaled by any other city in the United States. Whether they loved or hated Los Angeles or were unable to make up their minds, writers wrote about the City of Angels; and, taken cumulatively, such testimony by the mid-1960s had created a formidable density of literary reference and commentary. Like the city itself, this literature was a mixture of indigenous and imported energies. A later generation of critics would find in it a meta-narrative based on utopian expectations frequently gone awry, together with a cumulative sense of the City of Angels as a physical place that was, in effect, an urban jigsaw puzzle that had to be disassembled and reassembled as part of the plot. Here was a city of neon-lit boulevards, of roads winding up and down dark canyons, of bungalows with their shades pulled against the sunshine, of the blue Pacific and shoreline, the palm trees, the jumbled architecture of every era, Santa Ana winds, brilliant sunsets, and by night a sea of light sweeping across the plain. Themes in this meta-narrative included sex, violence, racism, the Big Fix—whether among cops, politicians, or oligarchs—the terrifying loneliness endemic to a city of strangers, and the consequent longing for home and homeland left behind, as testified to by the coffins shipped from the city each day, returning recent Angelenos to the places from whence they came.

The success of Ray Bradbury in the 1950s signaled the emergence of a thoroughly indigenous point of view. Other writers—Norman Mailer, for example—were passing through with mixed results. Others still were deciding to stay. Accepting a professorship at UCLA, the Italian novelist P. M. Pasinetti, among the most noted writers of his era, settled in, dividing his time between Venice and Beverly Hills, writing in Italian. Aspiring novelist Alison Lurie sojourned in Los Angeles from 1957 until 1961. During that time, she gathered the impressions that would help make her novel *The Nowhere City* (1965)—a chronicle of adjustment, East to West, in a

Beverly Hills and Westside setting—the best fictive portrait to capture Los Angeles as it made the transition to supercity.

While novels can cover their times, they frequently do so in a spotty way. For day-to-day coverage of a community, as far as the written word is concerned, one turns to newspapers; and as far as the *Los Angeles Times* is concerned, this newspaper, along with so much else in the city, was making a transition in this era: from a discredited right-wing provincial bully sheet, second only to the *Chicago Tribune* as the least-respected newspaper in the nation, to a contender for top honors against the best newspapers of the East Coast and, in terms of revenues, the most profitable news-paper in the nation. Once again, Buff Chandler stood at the center of a transition, one that would be comprehensively chronicled by David Halberstam in *The Powers That Be* (1979).

It was a story in which psychological motivation—rejection and resistance, one woman's willpower, a husband and son's response—drove a complex process of cor-porate and journalistic upgrade. It was the Chandlers, after all, who had driven Buff Chandler into psychiatric care and against whose rejection she had redefined herself as a willful activist on a number of fronts. Becoming publisher, Buff's hus-band Norman, a talented if conservative businessman, recognized that the *Times* was on shaky ground. What bothered him most was the long-term financials and the competition offered by the Hearst *Examiner*, which bested the *Times* in circulation. Thanks in great measure to counsels being offered by his wife, Norman Chandler recognized as well that the *Los Angeles Times*, as far as metropolitan Los Angeles was concerned, was caught in a time warp. It was a narrowly sectarian newspaper, for one thing, edited and staffed by too many hacks transparently pushing a Chan-dler family agenda based on a prewar hegemony in a much more provincial and tractable city. As the 1950s approached, the region was growing at a near-geometric rate, attracting all kinds of new people, including hundreds of thousands of newspa-per readers accustomed to better newspapers in their city of origin or at the least to newspapers that did not so transparently slant news and editorials to fit a Republican and real estate investment agenda.

One of Norman Chandler's early responses to changing times was to establish in 1948 a tabloid, the *Mirror*, which he all but gave to his wife to operate. At the *Mir-ror*, Buff Chandler put into operation many reforms and innovations: the expanded coverage of women, including women in the workplace, and the journalistic recog-nition of social groups outside the establishment. Running the *Mirror*, as much as saving the Hollywood Bowl, put Buff Chandler into direct connection and exercise of her formidable powers. She loved the power of running a newspaper, for one thing, and the fulcrum it offered her with which to leverage herself against all those other Chandlers who had once pushed her into such a crippling personal crisis. *Mirror* veterans would later recall how Mrs. C would wear assertive hats to the office and place her desk so that the sun shone through the window behind her, shading her face and giving the impression—the hat, the blinding sunlight precluding eye contact, the directives coming from a shadowy and mysterious source—to staffers called in for a conference that they were being interviewed by a reincarnated Queen Victoria herself, as Buff Chandler was also known, behind her back.

If so, Mrs. C was a Queen sensitive to the future of the realm and the question of succession. Buff Chandler knew that the innovations of the *Mirror* would soon have to be taken up by the parent newspaper if the *Times* were to remain competitive. That meant new leadership on both the editorial and the publishing sides of the aisle. At her urging, Norman Chandler in 1958 replaced editor L. D. Hotchkiss, a take-no-prisoners Chandler family retainer, gruff, imperious, blindly Republican, with Nick Williams, a courtly southerner with a taste for Greek classics and diverse points of view, who provided a more nuanced editorial direction. Williams, in turn, hired as managing editor Frank McCulloch, the West Coast bureau chief for *Time*, who would in turn help recruit national talent and further open up the editorial philosophy of the paper.

Buff and Norman's son Otis, meanwhile, spent the mid- to late 1950s working at various positions throughout the newspaper in preparation for taking over as publisher. Some scions of lineage and wealth remain exactly that throughout a lifetime, tucked away, if they are working at all, in the family enterprise. Others make a reasonable transition into productive careers. A smaller number, such as Otis Chandler—driven by superego and a desire to prove themselves on their own terms—outperform themselves in the businesses that brought wealth to the family in the first place. Born in 1927, educated at the Cate School, Phillips Academy, Andover, and Stanford, Otis Chandler was a prince of the realm enamored of democratic competition and engagement. At Stanford, where he served as president of Delta Kappa Epsilon, he was captain of the track team and came within a foot of setting a new world record in shot put. Only a sprained wrist kept him from making the 1952 Olympics. Joining the *Times* following a three-year tour in the Air Force, Chandler kept himself fit working out with weights in an improvised gym in the ventilation room. He served his apprenticeship until April 1960 when, according to his mother's plan, Norman Chandler became the full-time CEO of the Times Mirror Corporation, and thirty-three-year-old Otis became publisher of the newspaper.

It would be a mistake to consider Otis Chandler merely a product of his mother's will. Yet it would be a mistake as well not to see Otis Chandler as the fulfillment of the Buffum quotient in the Chandler formula. Not only had Dorothy Chandler brought Otis into the world, she had literally brought him back into the world when at the age of eight he fell from a horse and was driven by his mother to a nearby hospital, where he was pronounced dead. "My son is not dead!" Buff Chandler cried out, driving him to the Huntington Hospital in Pasadena, shouting as she drove, David Halberstam tells us, that her son was alive! alive!—and having that life confirmed when a shot of adrenaline to Otis's heart brought back his pulse beat and vital signs.[2] And now Otis was embarking upon what would be a twenty-year stint as publisher that would see the *Times* fulfill Buff Chandler's second but equal obsession alongside the Music Center: namely, that the *Times* become a paper worthy of mention in the company of the *New York Times* and the *Washington Post*.

Many of the Chandlers had no such ambition to be ranked alongside the Sulzbergers and the Grahams. They liked things as they were, and when the *Los Angeles Times*, under its new regime, in March 1961 ran a series critical of the John Birch Society and fifteen thousand readers canceled their subscriptions, the family went into an uproar. Still, while the Birch brouhaha slowed the transition being made by the newspaper, a combination of business astuteness and new recruits—Bob Donovan, Washington bureau chief of the *New York Herald Tribune*; Jim Bellows, Sunday editor of that newspaper; cartoonist Paul Conrad of the *Denver Post*; Pulitzer Prize winner Ed Guthman, formerly of the *Seattle Times*, and others—launched the *Los Angeles Times* into two decades of outstanding performance. The two-year presence of the *New York Times* in California from 1962 to 1964 stimulated Otis Chandler's determination to improve the family newspaper with better writers, better stories, national and international coverage, and more advertising. Los Angeles and its newspaper were mano a mano with New York and its newspaper, the leading newspaper in the nation. The *Los Angeles Times* prevailed, on its own territory at least, earning national rank. By the end of the 1960s, a supercity had the supernewspaper Otis Chandler and his mother felt it deserved.

Since the nineteenth century, the tendency of Los Angeles to expand outward into the great plain in which it was centered had been the driving dynamic of the city. Movement was twofold: from the center south prior to World War I, westward to the sea from the 1920s onward. The north-south axis followed, in one way or another, the course of the Los Angeles River. Westward expansion followed an axis that dated back to Native American times, proceeding along trails developed in the Spanish, Mexican, and frontier American eras. Since the early twentieth century, westward expansion had been paced by Wilshire Boulevard. The Big Red Cars of the Pacific Electric Railway pushed settlement south to Long Beach, west to Santa Monica, northward along the Arroyo Seco to Pasadena, and eastward toward Riverside along axes that had made the transition from Native American pathways to Spanish and Mexican trails, to American trails and roadways, to railroad and electric rail routes, and, finally, to automotive boulevards. Here, then, was the fixed nature of the urban form of Los Angeles since the Pueblo era: a center moving south, west, east, and north horizontally across the plain, ceasing only at mountains and sea.

By the 1950s a network of automotive boulevards—Central, Figueroa, Vermont, Western, Crenshaw, La Cienega, Sepulveda in one direction, crossed by Pico, Olympic, Wilshire, Hollywood, Sunset, to name but a few—defined the form of the city. Los Angeles had its neighborhoods—the Downtown, West Adams, Hancock Park, Silver Lake, Los Feliz, for example—but unlike San Francisco, Los Angeles was not a neighborhood-defined city. The boulevards, rather, defined the dominant spatial aggregates and determined place. The African American community, for example, defined itself via Central Avenue; the Mexican American community defined itself through Boyle Avenue on the eastern side of the Los Angeles River. As far as the entertainment industry was concerned, the axis of place had for some time been shifting from Hollywood to Sunset Boulevard slightly to the north and west.

Twenty years earlier, the Garden of Allah at Sunset and Havenhurst, a Spanish Revival hostelry opened in 1921 by actress Alla Nazimova, had served as a hangout for the film industry. Here the Hollywood writers of the 1930s—Robert Benchley, F. Scott Fitzgerald, Dorothy Parker, Somerset Maugham, George S. Kaufman, Alexander Woollcott, among others—had worked and partied in the company of the stars, creating an Algonquin West legend. Yet the Garden of Allah bade farewell to its last tenants in August 1959 and would soon be torn down and replaced by a bank. As far as film folk were concerned, the action had been shifting by the late 1950s further west along the Sunset Strip—as Sunset Boulevard between Sweetzer and Doheny on the boundary of Beverly Hills was called—and by August 1961 writer Bernard Wolfe was covering Sunset Strip for *Esquire* as the new place for the film industry to see and be seen. "You can get pretty much anything you want, or think you want, on the Strip these days," Wolfe observed. "This is where you go to rent a car, buy an Alfa Romeo or a Ferrari, hear Mort Sahl (at Gene Norman's Crescendo) or Ray Charles (at the Cloister), drink a cappuccino (at the Largo, Le Crazy Horse, the Body Shop), get custom-made holsters for your six-shooters, acquire an Italian suit (at the Leading Man), enjoy foreign cooking (at Scandia, La Rue's, the Cock 'n Bull, the Har-Omar, Frascati's, Imperial Garden, Villa Nova, Dino's, the Golden Violin, Le Petit Trianon) or perhaps an organic meal (at the Aware Inn, where the liver comes from 'non-diethyl stilbestrol cows'), discuss career problems with a writers' or actors' agent, receive hypnotherapy (at the American Institute of Hypnosis), linger over a marshmallow parfait (at Wil Wright's), hire a press agent or a public-relations man, record a mambo band (at the 'Gene Norman Presents' recording studio), consult an interior decorator, listen to Miles Davis' cool jazz (at the Renaissance) or Afro-Cuban bongos (at Pandora's Box) or fold-singing guitarists (at the Unicorn), make a deal with an independent movie-producing organization...."[3] What Wolfe was observing was not an ill-defined suburb but a dense, intensely atmospheric urban place arranged along and intersecting a busy automotive boulevard. Los Angeles, as Wolfe encountered it on the Strip, was growing up as a city. It now had its own Greenwich Village, its Soho, North Beach, Chelsea, and Left Bank, with the nearby UCLA filling in for Columbia, the New School, and New York University. Sunset Strip was Bohemia, keyed to films over the other arts: vain, brittle, superficial, hollow even; but urban, nevertheless, and resonating with the magic of place.

Dating back to Native American times, Wilshire Boulevard was in and of itself a sixteen-mile spatial repository of Los Angeles history and aspiration, a chromosomatic strip of the past, the present, and the unfolding future of the city. Wilshire began at Grand Avenue in the downtown and crossed 206 streets en route to Santa Monica. Along the way one encountered architectural remnants of every phase of Los Angeles development, more or less in sequence: from 1890s MacArthur Park, to

1920s Bullocks Wilshire, past the Brown Derby and the Miracle Mile of the 1930s, to the emerging quadrangle and campus of UCLA. In doing so, Wilshire passed two instances of classic urbanism amidst the more suburbanized Los Angeles landscape: Park La Brea and the Farmers Market. Begun by the Metropolitan Life Insurance Company during the war, Park La Brea eventually encompassed 4,213 rental apartments in a complex of twelve-story towers and two-story garden apartments spread across 176 acres. As such, Park La Brea represented an island of New York City on the Plains of Id, to use Reyner Banham's phrase: density (toward seven thousand residents), a rental culture, pedestrian values. Likewise did the Farmers Market, opened in July 1934, offer an even more venerable instance of urbanism: a European-style town square of shops and food stalls that demanded that Los Angelenos leave their cars and walk around. Ahead of its time as well as historic, the Farmers Market anticipated the manner in which eating and retail complexes of independent vendors would at the end of the century be brought back to abandoned or unimproved districts.

That Los Angeles was destined to expand across its plain between mountain range and sea, from Ventura County to Orange, had been a fixed point of reference for booster rhetoric since the early 1900s. Between 1906 and 1935 there appeared more than a dozen studies with recommendations as to how exactly Los Angeles, city and county, should handle the metropolitan region that was being created. Should the city and county consolidate into one government, as was the case in San Francisco? Or should the city of Los Angeles secede from the county and form its own city/county entity? Or should Los Angeles remain a city within a county structure but implement a borough system within the city so as to federate and localize growth alongside the other local entities of the county? Or should the county absorb all cities into one unified countywide metropolis that could, in turn, be subdivided into smaller administrative units?

So the debate continued, from the report of the Los Angeles Consolidation Commission of 1906 to the reports of the City Bureau of Budget and Efficiency and the Committee on Governmental Simplification of 1935. In the first half of the 1950s, the debate was renewed with fervor via the sixteen-volume *Metropolitan Los Angeles: A Study in Integration* issued between 1952 and 1955 by the John Randolph Haynes and Dora Haynes Foundation, which took up once again the question of how exactly to govern the developing mega-metropolis. In September 1955, just as the final volume of the Hayes study was released, *U.S. News & World Report* devoted a special issue to chronicling what it described as the emergence within twenty years of a two-hundred-mile-long metropolis stretching from Santa Barbara to San Diego, centered on Los Angeles, city and county. Already, the magazine reported, the Los Angeles metropolitan area, taken at its greatest extent, contained 42 percent of the population of California.

Year by year, the 1960s witnessed the continuing chronicling by major magazines—*Life* in June 1960, *National Geographic* in October 1962, *Fortune* in March 1965, the *New Yorker* across a series of articles in 1966, along with a number of articles in *Los Angeles* magazine throughout the same period—of the emergence, if not the two-hundred-mile-long city predicted by *U.S. News & World Report*, then certainly a metropolitan leviathan heading in that direction. For Richard Austin Smith, writing in *Fortune*, metropolitan Los Angeles was the American prototype of the supercity, a "speeded-up version of the process of urbanization that is even now engulfing the fewer and fewer islands of darkness in the vast sea of light that stretches from Philadelphia to Boston."[4] For Christopher Rand, writing in the *New Yorker*, Los Angeles was a developing paradigm of the Ultimate City, meaning the form mega-urbanism would eventually take across the United States. The majority of these articles were illustrated with maps of the metropolitan region prominently depicting its integration through freeways and suggesting through recent ultra-modernist architecture its futurist dimension.

Here, then, by the late 1960s could be experienced a Los Angeles that had exfoliated into a metropolitan region offering a model for the urban future. English residents and visitors alike seemed to understand and empathize with this new and surprising city with the most enthusiasm. Aldous Huxley might satirize Los Angeles, but he was happy to be living there, as was Christopher Isherwood. And so it was perhaps not so unexpected that the most enduring tribute to the emergence of Los Angeles as super city should come from Reyner Banham, an English expatriate. An erudite urbanologist and historian of design, Banham was, among other freelance occupations, a BBC correspondent based in Southern California. Throughout the 1960s, in various venues, including a series of BBC broadcasts, Banham drew parallels between metropolitan Los Angeles and metropolitan London—two concatenations of suburbs fused into a city—while at the same time extolling what was distinct to the urban form of this improbable Southern California metropolis shaped by the automobile. Banham eventually distilled his ruminations into *Los Angeles: The Architecture of Four Ecologies* (1971), a study that provided Los Angeles with its Magna Carta as innovative metropolis and supercity.

Dividing metropolitan Los Angeles into four dominant environments—seashore, plain, foothills, and freeway—Banham launched a contrarian defense of everything that was lacking in Los Angeles as far as classic urban forms were concerned. Los Angeles was different, radically different, Banham argued; but the city made sense once you started to consider it on its own terms as a new kind of urban entity. Anchoring the horizontality of this supercity—its tendency to spread outward from its center—to transportation routes that remained consistent from the Native American era to the present, Banham defended the uniqueness of Los Angeles by basing it in an historical process. Metropolitan Los Angeles, Banham argued, was in its basic form, its core identity, a transportation grid, and had always been such, engendering suburbs along the way.

But what about the downtown? Was it the center from which, in classic urban terms, movement outward originated and back toward which movement tended? Or was the downtown merely another suburb left behind along the way? It was a combination of both, Banham argued. Even in the Spanish and Mexican eras, the

center of Los Angeles had a tendency to shift. In the first American decades, dispersion throughout the region, as opposed to concentration around the downtown, had
been the rule. True, the downtown supported classic urban structures—a cathedral,
a city hall, a train station, courts of law, clubs, hotels, office and business districts—
but these did not over the long run constitute a center that would hold. They were,
rather, archipelagos of traditional urban forms asserting themselves against a tide
flowing in an outward direction.

But what about the Music Center? When the Dorothy Chandler Pavilion was
dedicated, hopes had been expressed that the finished Music Center would revi-
talize the downtown, by then in deep trouble along with the downtowns of many
American cities. "Detractors of downtown Los Angeles love to list its deficiencies,"
noted urban critic Ray Duncan in November 1963. "By day they see a snaggle-tooth
city lacking in unity, shoving mismatched buildings together without unity or style,
putting skyscrapers next to shack stores among too many ugly rugs of asphalt parking lots. They see a dispirited, carelessly-dressed populace, indifferent to their city,
with a high percentage of obvious transients and semi-detached persons who carry
mysterious belongings about in wrinkled shopping bags. They see streets without
excitement where even the pigeons seem poor in spirit. They see third-rate stores
or empty shops lined up against a scarred and naked hillside, chopped out like a
vacant lot standing on edge. And by night, they see worse—almost deserted streets
dominated by derelicts or aimless lonely strollers in front of blank dark buildings—a
scene from which the daytime population has fled in horror into a giant traffic jam
escaping the city."[5]

The very fact, however, the Pavilion had parking for two thousand automobiles
and that the nearby Civic Center Mall provided an additional thirteen hundred
spaces reinforced an irony. Booster rhetoric might describe the Music Center as the
renewed heart of the city, but it served people arriving and departing by automobile;
indeed, the fifteen-minute egress of two thousand cars following a performance—
the roar of engines, the screeching of tires, the jockeying for position—constituted
a Grand Prix of suburbanites desperate to return home as quickly as possible. The
famed urbanist UC Berkeley professor Catherine Bauer fully accepted this parking
paradox. Yet the Music Center, she hoped, would stimulate a new kind of cultural
centrality in the downtown: one based upon an emergent Civic Center that was the
largest public space of its kind outside of Washington, D.C. Extending between City
Hall and the Music Center, bordered on each side by government buildings, Civic
Center, Bauer argued, might very well offer a new means for localizing the region.

The problem was, people were living elsewhere and building their homes elsewhere, and new business districts were emerging elsewhere. UCLA, meanwhile,
the social and psychological epicenter of the western part of the city, was offering an increasingly attractive program of educational programs and cultural performances. A counter-argument could be made, indeed, that Los Angeles had been
moving westward along the Wilshire corridor since the 1930s: a momentum that
had resulted in the location of the UCLA campus on the Westside as the new goal

for urban expansion just as USC had beckoned the city south in the 1880s. The 1950s witnessed the acceleration of this westward movement, culminating in the 1963 opening of the Santa Monica Freeway. In January 1958 Twentieth Century–Fox announced that in partnership with the Alcoa Corporation it intended to transform the majority of its 284-acre property on the Westside into an entirely new master-planned business and residential community called Century City. It took more than a decade for Century City to come completely on-line, but its implications were clear from the beginning. The City of Los Angeles was in the process not only of spreading its suburban-style housing tracts across the plain but of polynucleating itself into dense master-planned centers (fourteen by the early 1990s in one count) competing with the downtown.

Even earlier, in 1946, the city council had approved rezoning on the western portion of Wilshire, allowing for the construction of high-rise apartments. Development of such buildings was initially cautious, but by the late 1950s it was evident that a phalanx of Park Avenue–like luxury apartment buildings was creating a new residential density on western Wilshire. Westwood itself near UCLA, meanwhile, together with the nearby Barrington Plaza, was showing the first signs of becoming a new high-rise district, and the UCLA Medical Center was en route to becoming an urban behemoth. In Santa Monica, on the very western edge of it all, the Ocean Park Redevelopment project was by the early 1960s gearing up to line the Santa Monica beachfront with high-rise, low-rise, and garden apartments, together with an attendant hotel, retail, and restaurant infrastructure.

Under the auspices of the Bunker Hill Redevelopment Project and other programs of the Community Redevelopment Agency of Los Angeles, a similar process of densification was under way by the mid-1960s in the downtown, now renamed the Central City: office towers, high-rise apartment buildings, hotels, a museum, assorted plazas, all this in an ultra-modernist mode of urban planning and architecture that would ultimately confer on downtown Los Angeles what it had always lacked, a skyline, rising in huddled height from its freeway grid.

The Music Center, in short, could not create for the city of Los Angeles a dominant center, even in cultural terms. Nor could the developing Civic Center fulfill Catherine Bauer's hopes for a new kind of centralism. Dodger Stadium could develop a crowd on the edge of the downtown, and the Music Center could draw impressive audiences; but for the time being, the revitalization of the downtown remained an open question. It became a point of snobbery, in fact, for Westsiders to suggest that they never went downtown, ever. One Hollywood starlet told *Los Angeles Times* columnist Jack Smith that no one in her set ever went downtown except to get a divorce.

This localizing of identity and sentiment—my house, my block, my shopping center—argued UC Riverside political scientist Francis Carney, was the fundamental fact of Los Angeles politics. For all the talk of the downtown establishment, for all the maneuverings of the oligarchic Committee of Twenty-Five, Carney argued, the City of Los Angeles had by and large failed to come under the control of either a political machine or a ruling elite. Politics in Los Angeles was the very opposite of the boss system in Eastern cities or the ward system of Chicago. Los Angelenos tended to see politics almost exclusively in terms of local issues and, now and then, in terms of a standout galvanizing issue or a slogan with high entertainment content.

Thus Mayor Norris Poulson, put into office with the backing of the oligarchy and the *Los Angeles Times*, was finding himself in deep trouble as far as a third term was concerned when in January 1961 a suburbanite from Studio City in the San Fernando Valley, Nebraska-born Sam Yorty, one of the Folks, went downtown to City Hall with his wife Betty and filed papers to run for mayor in the forthcoming election. Yorty was everything that Poulson was not. An accountant by profession, Poulson was a genial corporate type, a generic Republican in gray flannel suit and black-rimmed glasses who could have come from any number of American cities. Sam Yorty, by contrast, was an edgy hardscrabble lawyer and frequent officeholder (the state assembly and Congress) who had been out of office for the past six years, practicing law in the San Fernando Valley, and living there as well in Studio City with his wife "Betts," a pert blonde homemaker, their son Bill, and a Dalmatian dog named Jett. Poulson was a Dave Garroway look-alike, smiling and assured, a Chamber of Commerce regular. Yorty was insecure, uncertain, a thin-skinned populist with buried resentments, featuring a slickster's pencil-line mustache (which he shaved off for the campaign) and a mean streak that now and then surfaced. In 1936, when he first went to the assembly, Yorty had been a left-leaning Democrat, advocating public ownership of utilities and supporting the Republic in the Spanish Civil War. In 1938, however, Yorty's name had surfaced before the California Un-American Activities Committee as a Communist sympathizer, and the committee cautioned the ambitious young politician to distance himself from the Far Left. Returning from military service in the Pacific, Yorty regained his assembly seat, then went on to the House of Representatives in 1950, was reelected in 1952, but lost a second race for senator in 1954. The shock of being branded a Communist in 1938, however briefly and erroneously, had been the tipping point for Yorty's turn to the right, which accelerated during the Cold War. Although he remained a registered Democrat, Yorty was in the vanguard of the populist conservatism that would soon revolutionize Sunbelt politics, fueled by a suspicion that the privileged classes, especially privileged liberal Democrats, had in one way or another betrayed the nation.

Edgy, high-strung, quick to talk, and when talking, speaking in a discernibly midwestern accent (pronouncing Los Angeles as "Los Ang-gah-leez"), Sam Yorty was definitely not Norman and Buff Chandler's kind of mayor, although Yorty did endorse Nixon in the presidential election of 1960, thereby earning the enmity of the national Democratic Party. Symptomatic of this cultural divide between the Chandlers and the Folks, the key issue in the 1961 campaign—the issue that did the most to get Yorty elected—was not the impending destiny and greatness of Los Angeles, or even the Music Center, but garbage! Specifically, the right of Los Angelenos to submit their wet, paper, and metal garbage in one bin rather than be forced to sort it, as was then the case. The Folks were not in a mood to sort and recycle, and so Yorty came in second in the primary and first in the general election, weathering charges that he had underworld connections because of legal work he had done for Las Vegas interests. Throughout the campaign, Yorty presented himself as just another San Fernando Valley resident, who wanted to keep Los Angeles an accommodating and livable place. Greatness could come later.

In the midst of delicate negotiations with the city and county regarding the Music Center site, Buff Chandler had to make nice with the new mayor, although it must have galled her. Yorty was, after all, from the Chandler perspective, a culturally chthonic figure from the Plains of Id, San Fernando Valley section, living in a Studio City home once owned by Mickey Rooney. Lobbied by the Chandlers, Yorty, who had run against the downtown establishment, did play a crucial role in finalizing negotiations for the Music Center site. This détente lasted, however tenuously, through the December 1964 dedication of the Pavilion. By mid-decade, however, the *Los Angeles Times* was hammering away at Sam Yorty on an almost daily basis. Yorty took his case directly to the people via appearances on *The Tonight Show*, hosted by his fellow Nebraskan Johnny Carson, projecting a down-to-earth image, resistant of high-falutin talk, slyly playing a cat-and-mouse game with the establishment.

So too was there resistance gathering in the ecclesiastical engine created by Cardinal McIntyre: this transformation of the sleepy Archdiocese of Los Angeles into the Archdiocese of New York of the Pacific. Across the 1960s McIntyre would be transformed by dissenting Catholics into a poster boy for everything they rejected in what they believed to be the outdated system. Convened by Pope John XXIII, an engaging career diplomat with reformist tendencies, the Second Vatican Council, meeting in Rome between 1962 and 1965, was in the process of undertaking an historic reorientation of the Roman Catholic Church. *Aggornimento* was the term Pope John XXIII used, an updating to the modern era. What was also being launched by Vatican II was a forty-year crisis in the American church, pitting liberals against conservatives. In this conflict, McIntyre emerged in the minds of the liberal wing as the embodiment of an oppressive ecclesiastical system that had to be overthrown.

Vilification began on 10 June 1964 when a twenty-nine-year-old priest of the archdiocese, William DuBay, announced at a press conference that he had sent a fourteen-page telegram to Pope Paul VI calling for the removal of McIntyre for "gross malfeasance in office." The cardinal, DuBay charged, had "perpetuated inexcusable abuses" by refusing to combat racial discrimination and by a "vicious program of intimidation and repression against priests, seminarians and laity who have tried to reach the consciousness of white Catholics in his archdiocese."[6] Ordained four years earlier, DuBay—a slender, boyish figure, wearing a black cassock and Roman collar in his public appearances—was devoted to racial justice and the civil rights movement and had already been removed from a parish in Northridge in the San Fernando Valley for writing in the parish bulletin against segregation. Chided for his behavior, DuBay requested a missionary assignment in Kenya but was sent instead to a black parish in Compton, where he became active on behalf of the implementation of the Fair Housing Act authored by Assemblyman W. Byron Rumford, an African American from Berkeley. Enacted in 1963, the Rumford Act called for an end to all housing segregation based on race. The very next year, an amendment went before the voters, put there by initiative, to recall the measure. McIntyre had refused to comment publicly on the controversy, saying that it was a matter of politics. DuBay, by contrast, said that it was a matter of Catholic teaching; hence his telegram to the Pope.

What followed, as far as Father DuBay was concerned, was an effort by the chancery, meaning the cardinal, to handle the matter as canonically and as quietly as possible. DuBay was asked to sign a statement of loyalty to the church and the archdiocese, which he did, twice, once in the sanctuary of Immaculate Conception Church and again in the presence of the Cardinal and 231 priests on retreat at St. John's Seminary in Camarillo. The rebellious cleric was thereupon reassigned to a parish in Anaheim, and the controversy seemed to have passed, at least as far as the cardinal and his chancellor Monsignor Hawkes were concerned. DuBay, however, was only temporarily silenced. Within a short time, he had resumed his campaign, offending yet another all-white parish with his political activism and was again transferred, this time to a hospital chaplaincy, where he was once again at odds with his constituency and removed. Within the year, DuBay was calling for the unionization of the fifty-eight thousand Catholic priests in the United States, and in 1966 he published *The Human Church*, calling for a liberalization of church structures and procedures. Suspended from the practice of the priesthood by the archdiocese, DuBay appealed his case to the Vatican and continued his campaign for the unionization of the clergy.

The DuBay case eventually fizzled. Toward the end of the decade, DuBay left the priesthood, married, and became an environmental activist. The media firestorm that surrounded the DuBay case in its first years, however, had uncovered vulnerabilities and fault lines. For many non-Catholics, DuBay seemed another Martin Luther nailing his ninety-five theses to the door of the castle church at Wittenberg. For liberal Catholic dissenters, DuBay stood as a hero, defending African Americans, complaining against repression in the church. In July 1964 *Commonweal*, the liberal Catholic weekly, devoted an entire issue to Catholicism in Los Angeles, with essays overwhelmingly favorable to DuBay. A month later, Robert Blair Kaiser, a former Jesuit covering the Second Vatican Council for *Time*, wrote an article for *Los Angeles* in which he extolled DuBay as the essence of the New Breed of younger, radicalized clergy, active in the civil rights movement and deeply opposed to the by-the-book regimes of prelates such as McIntyre, whom Kaiser singled out as especially insensitive on racial issues.

None of this was completely fair, of course; and McIntyre had more than his share of defenders. But the DuBay case and the subsequent media blitz from the left chipped away at the cardinal's image. And now, as the decade progressed, came something even worse: a stand-off between the cardinal and a group of nuns eager for *aggornimento*. Founded in Catalonia in 1848, the Sisters of the Most Holy and Immaculate Heart of the Blessed Virgin Mary had been brought to the Diocese of Monterey–Los Angeles in 1871 by Spanish-born Bishop Thaddeus Amat. Across the decades, Immaculate Heart Sisters became a mainstay of the educational system of the archdiocese. In 1924 the Vatican approved the separation of the Los Angeles–based sisters into their own canonically independent institute. By the 1950s Immaculate Heart Sisters, headquartered in Hollywood, were active as faculty and teachers at Immaculate Heart College, Immaculate Heart High School, and twenty-eight elementary and eight secondary schools throughout the four counties of the archdiocese as well as other schools throughout California.

Immaculate Heart Sisters had panache, no two ways about it. Their aristocratic Spanish origins suggested a connection with an upscale Iberian heritage that was most prized in Southern California. Their blue, black, and white habits emanated a certain ecclesiastical chic. Drawing upon a Southern Californian recruitment base, the order took in more than its fair share of attractive, physically fit young women and encouraged them to stay in shape as novices, postulants, and professed sisters. At their novitiate and motherhouse located in a posh estate in Montecito, the sisters enjoyed swimming, tennis, and other outdoor pursuits in their leisure hours. Opportunities for higher studies were made available. The majority of sisters teaching at Immaculate Heart College held doctorates. Sister Mary Corita Kent of the art department was en route to becoming a superstar in the Pop Art movement. It was a young order. More than half the sisters were under thirty-five as of the early 1960s; and this pervasive youthfulness engendered a more than average intensity when it came to responding to the calls for updating and reform coming from the Second Vatican Council, from the liberal Belgian Cardinal Leon-Joseph Suenens in his influential *The Nun in the World* (1963), and from Pope Paul VI himself in a *motu proprio* declaration urging religious orders to examine and renew their way of life and, if necessary, to experiment with new modes of service.

As if all this were not enough, the Immaculate Heart Sisters also embarked upon a program of non-directive psychotherapy under the supervision of psychologist Carl Rogers in preparation for a general chapter, a meeting on behalf of the whole, in which they would reevaluate their entire situation. Under Rogers's guidance, groups of sisters, meeting together, were encouraged to explore their lives and values with as little agenda or control as possible. The archivist and historian of the Archdiocese of Los Angeles, Monsignor Francis Weber, would later speculate that these group-therapy sessions drove many sisters, indeed a majority of the order, into a condition of meltdown, or at the least into a condition of extreme restlessness regarding their current situation. Already, Cardinal McIntyre was concerned about the number of Immaculate Heart Sisters requesting dispensations from their vows, as well as complaints, coming from parents, regarding what their children were being taught by the sisters in parochial school religion classes.

Forty-three elected representatives of the Order convened at the Montecito novitiate in July 1967 and across the summer hammered out what was by traditional

Catholic standards a revolutionary manifesto. First of all, the sisters demanded that all their teachers hold State of California credentials, classrooms be limited to thirty-five students, and principals not have to teach. These were by and large overdue reforms, addressing the tendency of American Catholic school systems to put nuns into the classroom with a minimum of training, even in many cases without degrees. More innovatively, the sisters called for the right to dress as they wanted, whether in modified habits or lay clothes, to resume their family names, to pursue careers outside the church if they preferred, and, most innovatively, to abandon their semi-monastic convent-based lifestyle for a re-clustering in small democratically governed communities.

What followed across the next four years was a struggle between the cardinal and the sisters that like the contretemps with Father DuBay left the cardinal savaged by the liberal Catholic and secular press and, in the opinion of one observer, Monsignor George A. Kelly, writing in 1995, signaled the end of the American Catholic parochial school system—staffed by nuns, hence affordable and promotive of a Catholic identity—as it had developed and functioned over the previous seventy-five years across the nation. What an irony for an archbishop who had built more schools than any prelate in American Catholic history: to be drawn into such a no-win imbroglio! In his biography of Cardinal McIntyre, Monsignor Weber emphasizes repeatedly that Cardinal McIntyre did not fire the Immaculate Heart Sisters from the archdiocese, nor was the cardinal overly concerned, Weber argues, with the modernization of their habit. But when it came to their abandonment of traditional convent life, McIntyre was adamant. Either the sisters continued to live in convents in recognizable communities, or he would not renew their contracts.

The sisters refused to budge on this issue, and because they were canonically independent of the Archdiocese of Los Angeles, they appealed their case to Rome. When the sisters lost their case at the Vatican, they appealed personally to the Pope, while continuing their innovations. An increasing number of sisters returned to lay life. In the end, the sisters disestablished their order as a canonical entity and reorganized it into a non-canonical secular association independent of Church supervision. Thirty-plus sisters elected to remain under traditional conditions in a newly organized archdiocesan order. The Immaculate Heart Sisters, in any event, were no longer in the classrooms of the Archdiocese of Los Angeles in full force, and Cardinal McIntyre had become the poster boy, the fall guy, for a crisis in Catholic culture that was taking place across the nation.

As stressful as all this might be it paled in comparison to the Watts Riots of August 1965, which involved an even greater irony than an education-oriented cardinal at odds with his teachers. Parker believed that by building up the Los Angeles Police Department as an ultra-modernist constabulary, he was ensuring the peace of the city. Yet here was erupting across six days of August something that was more than a riot. It was, rather, a civil insurrection of historic magnitude—a rebellion even, some would insist—with thousands of Los Angelenos taking to the streets (estimates vary between ten thousand and fifty thousand) and several thousand police, sheriff's deputies, and California Highway Patrolmen and fourteen thousand National Guardsmen brought in before the violence could be quelled. And when it was over—the looting, the burning, the murders, the assaults, the burglaries, the countless crimes of violence—thirty-four Los Angelenos, most of them African Americans, were dead and a thousand injured. More than 3,400 were under arrest, and property damage totaling $40 million extended over eleven square miles of the city. It was the worst riot of its kind in the United States to that point in the twentieth century.

The emergent supercity had, in short, experienced a super riot that had underscored the limits of modernist reform. Chief Parker had based his modernization of the LAPD upon the longstanding covenant between the police and the white people of Los Angeles. As far as police-community relations were concerned, Mexican American Los Angeles had borne the negative brunt of this covenant in the 1930s and 1940s. Now another minority group was to become the object of LAPD disdain. During the war, more than a hundred thousand African Americans had poured into the city from Texas, Louisiana, Mississippi, Alabama, and Georgia. Black Americans continued to arrive at the rate of two thousand a month in the postwar period, leveling off to one thousand a month by the 1960s. As of 1965 African Americans comprised 16 percent—about 425,000—of the total population of the city. Los Angeles had been boomed into one of the centers of African American urbanism in the nation. While there was stability (coming from the churches especially) and prosperity along Adams and Western boulevards and in Baldwin Hills, there was also a 30 percent unemployment rate as of 1965, as well as high levels of welfare.

It was an ambiguous and unstable situation. On the one hand, Sam Yorty had in 1961 demonstrated the power of the black vote and might even have suggested a political détente between the San Fernando Valley and South Central. In 1963 three African Americans—Tom Bradley, Billy Mills, and Gilbert Lindsay—were elected to the city council, providing African American Los Angeles with its first official taste of political clout. On the other hand, police-community relations in much of South Central were catastrophic. Between 1963 and 1965, sixty black Los Angelenos were killed by police officers. Even more disturbing: Twenty-seven of them had been shot in the back. There were no statistics on how many young black men had been harassed or beaten, since such malfeasance was obviously not reported; nor how many middle-class African Americans—men in suits and ties, women tastefully dressed—had been gratuitously stopped and questioned. Councilman Tom Bradley—a UCLA graduate and a career LAPD officer who had gone to night law school and qualified for the bar before taking retirement and running for office—was especially concerned over the deteriorating situation, particularly when in the summer of 1964 African American communities in Harlem, Rochester, Jersey City, Paterson, Elizabeth, Chicago, and Philadelphia erupted into riot.

In an interview in *U.S. News & World Report*, Chief Parker, responding to these East Coast and midwestern uprisings, downplayed police brutality as a legitimate explanation for such disturbances. "I think that actually the charge of police brutality," Parker told his interviewer, "is used to more or less cover over the real and basic problems that have led to violence. Furthermore, the police officer, wherever he may be, is the visible symbol of *status quo*—the 'power structure,' the 'establishment,' the authority of government by whatever name you wish to brand it. In other words, the policeman is a physical object against which persons believing themselves to be oppressed can vent their frustrations."

Why, then, were so many in the black community so frustrated, Parker was asked? His answer: The federal Civil Rights Act of 1964 had promised blacks too much. "So, when the next day dawned, and the sun came up in the same portion of the eastern sky and illuminated the same squalor that existed the day before, I'm inclined to believe that this increased frustrations. And eventually, the safety valve to frustration is physical violence." Another Parker bête noir revealed in the interview was the American Civil Liberties Union and the very idea of an independent review board to handle charges of police brutality. "If they get one in Los Angeles," he said of such a board, "then I will walk out. I would not share my administration of this department with a group of persons who are selected primarily from minority elements— many of them demagogues with axes to grind." Parker also revealed that should a riot break out in Los Angeles as those breaking out that summer of 1964 in the East, he would have to call in the National Guard, given the fact that he had only 4,900 policemen to police 450 square miles with a population of 2.7 million.[7]

It was as if, a year before the actual event, Parker was having premonitions that a riot was on the verge of erupting. In *To Protect and to Serve* (1994), police reporter and historian Joe Domanick offers a detail-by-detail description of how the Watts Riot erupted. On the sweltering summer evening of 11 August 1965, Domanick relates, in the predominately African American community of Watts in South Central Los Angeles, California Highway Patrol motorcycle officer Lee Minikus pulled over a 1955 Buick Special being driven by a twenty-one-year-old African American by the name of Marquette Frye. The young man was good-humored about the pullover, and cooperative, and, no doubt about it, he was under the influence of alcohol. It seemed a routine event.

But then Frye's mother Rena, who lived nearby, arrived on the scene with her other son Ronald and began to bawl out not Officer Minikus but her son Marquette, for driving while drunk. A crowd had gathered, meanwhile, and witnessed Rena's chewing out of her son: a ripping that, understandably, put Marquette Frye in a surly mood. When Officer Minikus tried to arrest him, Frye evaded his hold and began to harangue Minikus, a white highway patrolman in a sea of black faces. Minikus radioed for backup, and by the time other patrol cars arrived, the crowd had grown to four hundred and become increasingly menacing. When Marquette Frye tried to leave the scene, a backup officer cracked him across the forehead with a baton: the very weapon Parker had defended in his *U.S. News & World Report* interview as an effective means of riot control.

The baton attack infuriated Marquette Frye's mother and brother, who had initially been neutral toward Officer Minikus. Mother and son attacked the highway patrolman, and the crowd, now approaching a thousand, cheered them on. After more scuffling and verbal resistance, all three Frye family members were jammed into a patrol car, which managed to leave the scene. When police arrested another woman for allegedly spitting on an officer, the crowd surrounded the second patrol car. More patrol cars arrived, broke through to the surrounded patrol car with its arrested suspect, formed an escort, and inched their way through the noisy protesters, who were by then showering the departing cars with rocks and bottles.[8]

Domanick argues that Officer Minikus, seeing the crowd gather, should have let Marquette Frye go. Arresting him in the face of a hostile crowd was only making a bad situation worse. Domanick also argues that the LAPD fought the riot ineffectively because, in part, Chief Parker, age sixty-three, was weakened by an aneurysm in his aorta. In modernizing the LAPD, Domanick argues, Parker had emphasized intelligence and communication; and now each of these functions was proving inadequate. The Intelligence Division had failed to predict that such a full-scale riot could ever break out; and when it did, communications to the command center were chaotic. The initial tactic of the LAPD, moreover—to withdraw from Watts in the hopes that the riot would wind down—was equally flawed. "The LAPD," writes Domanick, "had either allowed itself to be run out of Watts or decided it was not worth defending. Then it stood by and watched as it—along with vast sections of black LA—were consumed in flames."[9] A massive show of force, Domanick argues, was required to break the riot, but it took until the third night of the disorders for the National Guard to arrive.

By the time the riot was over, it had been literally burned into public awareness that Los Angeles—supercity, ultimate city, metro-city of the future—sustained in the south central regions of its interior an angry population that had been left behind. It was not the fault of the LAPD, Parker argued on *Meet the Press*. The California Highway Patrol had provoked the incident through its inept arresting techniques. Nor was Watts a race riot, insisted the chief, meaning one race against another, "since the rioters were all Negroes." Yet even as he said this, Parker invoked the specter of a race-based *Götterdammerung*. "It is estimated that by 1970," Parker stated on a Los Angeles television program, "forty-five percent of the metropolitan area of Los Angeles will be Negro. If you want any protection for your home...you're going to have to get in and support a strong police department. If you don't, come 1970, God help you."[10])

Mayor Sam Yorty, meanwhile, began to distance himself from the black community that had helped put him into office. Following the Watts Riot, Chief Parker went in for surgery on his aorta at the Mayo Clinic and returned to work in fragile condition. In June Parker was honored as Headliner of the Year at a banquet at the Biltmore Hotel hosted by the Greater Los Angeles Press Club. Jack Webb served as master of ceremonies. On the night of Saturday, 16 July 1966, Parker was honored at yet another banquet, this time by the Second Marine Division Association in the Pacific Ballroom of the Statler Hilton. Actress Betty Hutton and comedian Joe E. Lewis were also being honored. A thousand Marine veterans were applauding the chief when he slumped into his chair and expired.

III

POLITICS AND PUBLIC WORKS

7

Warren, Nixon, Knight, Knowland

The Demise of Republican Centrism

A S of early 1956, it remained an open question whether President Dwight David Eisenhower would seek a second term. In September of the previous year, while vacationing in Denver, the President had experienced a left anterior myocardial infarction and had been hospitalized. Nine months later, he was operated on for a bowel obstruction. While his physicians assured the President that he was fit for a second term, Eisenhower himself had his doubts, and these doubts opened floodgates of speculation. In February 1956 the seasoned political reporter Theodore H. White, writing in *Collier's* magazine, speculated that should Eisenhower not run, the Republican nominee and, presumably, the next President of the United States would most likely be a Californian: either Vice President Richard Nixon, Senator Joseph Knowland, or California governor Goodwin J. Knight. Even Chief Justice Earl Warren, White speculated, the longtime governor of California, could conceivably be tempted to lay aside the majesty of his current office in pursuit of the presidency that had eluded him.

These were new men, White continued, from a new state as far as national political influence was concerned. In times past, California had represented "a faraway scouting ground for Eastern leaders seeking collateral strength beyond the Rockies."[1] But now, with its 13.25 million citizens—a population destined to make it the largest state in the nation by the early 1960s—California was no longer a sideshow. By 1965, given the present rate of growth, one-tenth the membership of the House of Representatives would be Californians, which suggested great implications for the way that national policy would be determined. And as far as the future of the Republican Party was concerned, the Republicans of California had for decades mastered the art of winning elections despite being outnumbered by Democrats by three-quarters of a million voters. White's argument that the politics and politicians of California were now of national importance dovetails with so many other aspects of the rise of

California in the postwar period. The entrance of California into the political big leagues, moreover, would erode the Republican center represented nationally by Eisenhower and the patrician northeastern political establishment that had ushered Ike into office. In its place would develop a more democratized and radicalized Republican Party on the right and an equally democratized and radicalized tilting of the Democratic Party to the left. A paradigm shift in American politics was about to occur, and it would be most clearly on display in California.

The ability of California to register and pace such shifts of political sentiment was anchored, paradoxically, in the very Progressivism, centrist and non-partisan, that would soon be a thing of the past. A newcomer to politics with no previous experience of elective office, Progressive reformer Hiram Johnson became governor, in significant measure, because in 1909 the state legislature passed a Direct Primary Law that replaced state party conventions with direct primaries as the means of nominating candidates. Immediately upon Johnson's taking office in 1911, Progressives sought and won voter approval for a few simple but powerful protocols. Through the initiative, referendum, and recall approved by the voters in January 1911, a partial direct democracy was put in place. The voters of California could now use the election process to pass legislation, judge public policy, or recall elected officials. In 1913 the Progressive-dominated legislature added cross-filing to the Direct Primary Law, allowing candidates of one party to enter the primary of other parties without the necessity of declaring their own party affiliation. In 1915 yet another Progressive measure, the State Non-Partisan bill, removed party designations on the ballot for all elections in California, local and statewide, with the exception of federal elections for the Senate or House of Representatives.

In 1917 Assemblyman Henry Hawson, a Fresno Democrat, successfully sponsored an amendment to the Direct Primary Law stating that any candidate who cross-filed would have to win the nomination of his or her own party in order to be placed on the ballot in the general election. Thus in 1918 Mayor James Rolph Jr. of San Francisco, a Republican, cross-filed as a Democrat in the gubernatorial primary and won the Democratic nomination. Rolph lost the Republican nomination, however, to incumbent governor William Stephens. Democrats took Rolph's case to the California Supreme Court, which upheld the validity of the Hanson Amendment. Hence in the general election of 1918 the Democrats had no candidate for governor, although Democrat Theodore Bell, running as an Independent, tried to fill that role. In 1919 the Direct Primary Law was yet again modified by the legislature to allow party state central committees to fill any vacancies resulting from the Hanson Amendment.

In California, then, as a result of the Progressive suspicion of party organizations dominated by political cliques that were in turn dominated by special interests, the two-party system was seriously weakened through the 1940s. Initially, Progressives profited most conspicuously through cross-filing. During the suburbanizing pro-business 1920s, Republicans emerged into ascendancy; but as the Democratic Party began to regain its strength during the Depression, Republican candidates effectively used the cross-filing system to remain in office. Throughout his long career in the Senate, until his death in 1945, Hiram Johnson enjoyed strong Progressive, Republican, and Democratic support. In 1940 Johnson won both the Republican and the Democratic nominations to the Senate. In June 1946 incumbent governor Earl Warren did the same thing, winning both the Republican and Democratic nominations for reelection. Also winning the nomination of both parties that year were the secretary of state, the controller, the treasurer, four members of the Board of Equalization, fifteen out of twenty state senators, and sixty out of eighty assemblymen up for election, together with twelve of the state's twenty-three representatives in Congress.

As of June 1946, then, partisan politics and a strong two-party system seemed thoroughly on the ropes in the great state of California. No one had profited more conspicuously from this situation than Governor Earl Warren. In later years, after Eisenhower had appointed Warren Chief Justice in 1953, and Warren was leading the Court in reformist directions, commentators frequently cited Warren's allegedly miraculous transformation from a hard-charging law-and-order attorney general and a moderate-centrist governor to a liberal reformer Chief Justice. Such commentators, however, fail to take into consideration Warren's success as a cross-filing Republican with strong Democratic support at the polls, together with the influential Democrats on his staff: most conspicuously, Warren's chief of staff William Sweigert, a brilliant Catholic attorney from San Francisco, strongly influenced by the liberal social teachings of the papal encyclicals of Leo XIII and Pius XI. Warren, a dedicated Mason, had a continuing interest in Catholic social thought. Under Sweigert's influence, Warren supported such liberal programs as workers' compensation, health care, and equal opportunity in employment. Then again, the Warren-Sweigert relationship could have been even more subtle, as some suspected, with Warren deliberately choosing Sweigert as his alter ego so that the two of them, forming a Masonic-Catholic odd couple, could pursue programs that Warren believed in but had to be cautious about, given his Republican base of support. From this perspective, when Warren became Chief Justice of the United States, he at long last had the opportunity to allow his liberal beliefs to surface on their own terms.

Earl Warren, in any event, was an enigma flourishing within California's cross-filing system. He was a crime-fighting attorney general who took no prisoners, and to his later sorrow (but not repudiation) he had in early 1942 supported the internment of Japanese Americans. He was a Republican, but not too much of a Republican to be unable to win Democratic support. He rarely supported other Republicans in major elections, in any event, and by the time of his second term seemed to have emerged for all practical purposes as a Party of One, which Warren would consider the Party of California, anchored in a strong and continuing Progressive foundation of bipartisanship.

Designed to weaken control from the top, cross-filing had also made of each elected official in California a Party of One, loyal not so much to the Republican or Democratic Party but to his or her own autonomy as an elected official. That autonomy meant that elected officials could be wooed, one by one, outside a frame-work of party discipline by lobbyists representing special interests. In 1946, the very year he won the nomination of each major party, Warren openly stated that in terms of influence in the legislature Ur-lobbyist Artie Samish was in many respects as powerful as the governor himself. In 1956 UC Berkeley political scientist Eugene Burdick published a best-selling novel, *The Ninth Wave*, chronicling the rise of a real estate developer as a behind-the-scenes political power in Southern California. The rapid growth of California, Burdick suggested, had outstripped traditional poli-tics, already weak in the state. In a California that was developing exponentially, developers held, clandestinely, the determinant political power.

Party identification—indeed, politics itself—was further weakened by the ascen-dant culture of the state, especially in the developing suburbs. The average Califor-nian was neither a joiner nor a political activist. He or she was, rather, someone from elsewhere who had come to California to avoid problems, not to engage them. In the suburbs, a mere 30 percent of male householders, if that, belonged to organiza-tions of any sort. Even unions, in areas where union membership was high, limped by with a ten percent participation rate. The sheer size of California discouraged participation. People spent long hours commuting and were home-oriented when it came to leisure and entertainment, especially in the suburbs. Even barbershops lacked the kibitzing culture of their counterparts in other regions, with the men of California sitting silent, and certainly not talking politics, as they awaited their turn in the barber's chair. The average Californian, then, participated in politics only intermittently, and when he or she did participate, it was not through traditional party organizations but through media-driven campaigns. "What they've got," a dis-gruntled Democratic operative said of Republicans to Theodore H. White in 1956, "isn't a party. It's a star system, it's a studio lot. They don't run candidates—they produce them like movie heroes, everyone cast in just the right part."[2]

No one understood this better than the husband-and-wife team of Clem Whita-ker and Leone Baxter; indeed, the duo had for all practical purposes invented the system. The son of a Baptist preacher, Clem Whitaker was as of the early 1930s an aspiring public relations consultant. In the 1920s Whitaker had made the transition from employment—the *Sacramento Union*, where he became city editor at nineteen, followed by an editorship at the *San Francisco Examiner*—to owning his own Capitol News Bureau that distributed state government stories to smaller newspapers. By 1929 Whitaker had recruited eighty subscribers and was netting $25,000 a year but was experiencing health problems, compounded by overwork. Seeking a more congenial way of life, Whitaker in 1929 sold the Capitol News Bureau to the United Press and launched himself into the as yet vaguely defined profession of public relations con-sulting. Leone Baxter, meanwhile, was as of 1933 a self-supporting widow of twenty-six, managing the chamber of commerce in Redding, Shasta County, and doing a bit of freelance writing. That year, the state legislature passed a bill authorizing an ambitious Central Valley Project (CVP) designed to provide irrigation and flood and salinity control for central California. Naturally, the privately owned Pacific Gas

& Electric Company resented the intrusion of such a massive public project onto its turf and sponsored a statewide referendum to scuttle the proposal. Retained by sponsors of the CVP, Whitaker and Baxter teamed up to defeat the PG&E referendum by 33,603 votes by providing small-town newspapers with pro-CVP editorial material and making a pioneering use of radio advertising—all this on a spartan budget of $40,000. Defeated, PG&E was so impressed it put Whitaker and Baxter on retainer, where the couple stayed for the next quarter of a century.

As conservative Republicans, Whitaker and Baxter no doubt felt more at home on the PG&E side of the spectrum. In any event, they had discovered a thing or two about California politics. Voters, for one thing, were apathetic regarding most issues but could be engaged if a campaign involved a contest and provided entertainment. Second, voters could be reached directly, with no mediating agencies involved, and certainly not political parties, which were negligible in their influence. Instead, voters could be reached by well-crafted radio spots, and smaller newspapers could be wooed through a campaign of equally lively news stories and editorials. Then there was the newly proven efficiency of direct mail, whether letters, which could be expensive, or an equally effective and much more thrifty use of postcards and flyers.

In 1933, in their first campaign, Whitaker and Baxter had formed Campaigns, Inc. They had also established the Clem Whitaker Advertising Agency to handle all advertisements for future campaigns and in 1936 had organized the California Feature Service to keep in contact with newspapers on behalf of their clients. In 1938 the partners married and moved to a rambling home with a kidney-shaped swimming pool on the slopes of Mount Tamalpais in Marin County. Meanwhile, as business increased through the 1930s and 1940s, they continued to refine their campaign strategies.

First of all, Whitaker and Baxter prized exhaustive research into issues and the backgrounds of candidates. That done, they came up with a plan of attack, always on the offensive. They also created with equal care an opposition plan outlining the best possible attack that could be launched by their opponents. As far as their own strategy was concerned, it had to be based upon a message, pithily and pungently expressed and kept as simple as possible. No one would ever accuse Whitaker or Baxter of over-estimating the intelligence of the average California voter, who, as they put it, preferred corn to caviar. Nor did Whitaker and Baxter over-estimate the attention span of its audience. Election strategies, they believed, should be planned well in advance but should only be fully implemented in the last month of any campaign. Seventy-five percent of all resources should be reserved for the final month, the final week, the final days of the contest.

By the mid-1950s Whitaker and Baxter were claiming victory in seventy of the seventy-five campaigns they had run since 1933. In 1942 they ran Earl Warren's first campaign for governor. In 1944 they successfully secured a raise for teachers, the first of three successful campaigns for the California Teachers Association. In 1946 they ran the successful campaign of Goodwin Knight for lieutenant governor and in that same year defeated an effort to recall San Francisco mayor Roger Lapham. In 1947 they secured the election of Lapham's successor, Elmer Robinson. In 1948 they conducted and won a statewide initiative to end mandatory staffing in the railroad industry. In 1949, going national for the first time, they spearheaded a successful campaign by the American Medical Association to defeat the mandatory health insurance program being advocated by President Harry Truman. In 1950 they defeated yet another old-age pension plan, this time to be financed by a state lottery. In 1954 they managed the successful effort of Goodwin Knight, who as lieutenant governor had succeeded Earl Warren when Warren went to the Supreme Court, to win a full term in his own right.

Each of these campaigns had been characterized by the typical Whitaker and Baxter media blitz, by the late 1940s on television as well as radio, and by the constant pounding away at a simple and sustained message. In the case of Earl Warren, Whitaker and Baxter persuaded the stolid-faced attorney general to smile now and then and to be photographed in the company of his large and attractive family. For the California teachers, they pointed out that teachers were on the average earning a third the salary of a well-placed receptionist. In defense of Mayor Roger Lapham, they covered San Francisco with billboards depicting the Faceless Man (first sketched by Leone Baxter on a cocktail napkin) who was trying to remove Lapham from office and went so far as to have the embattled mayor—in a gesture of "bring it on!" bravado—personally sign the recall petition being circulated against him so as to get the matter over with once and for all. In 1948, taking on the unions on behalf of the railroads, Whitaker and Baxter campaigned against the full-crew law on trains by playing on innumerable radio stations across the state the song "I've Been Loafing on the Railroad" and distributing for wide dissemination a cartoon depicting a railroad employee lolling on a bed atop a freight car. Their message on behalf of the American Medical Association was simple but effective: Mandatory health insurance would lead to socialized medicine; and as far as the old-age pension plan proposal of 1950 was concerned, was not the lottery that would finance it akin to gambling, and did Californians wish to introduce gambling into their state? In the case of Goodwin Knight, Whitaker and Baxter toned down Knight's garrulousness and taught him to get quickly to the point.

Themselves conservative Republicans, Whitaker and Baxter took special pleasure in helping to ensure the continuing Republican ascendancy by providing California Republicans with effective campaign strategies. Indeed, they can be seen to have created a new profession, campaign management, blending the skills of public relations, advertising, direct mail, radio and television, opposition research, and related techniques keyed to the distinctive political climate of California. In the opinion of Carey McWilliams on the left, Whitaker and Baxter were political hucksters, yet McWilliams was forced, however reluctantly, to admit the success of their techniques. For Irwin Ross, writing in *Harper's* in July 1959, Whitaker and Baxter represented a phenomenon that could never be exported to the rest of the country, although Ross was forced to admit that in the 1952 presidential campaign

Eisenhower and Stevenson had been media-merchandized in a way that could point to the future of presidential campaigns. Back in California, meanwhile, such figures as Murray Chotiner, Herbert Baus, William Ross, and the husband-and-wife team of Hazel Junkins and Robert Voigt in Los Angeles, and Harry Lerner, Len Gross, and Curtis Roberts in San Francisco, following in the footsteps of Whitaker and Baxter, were running increasingly effective and expensive media-savvy campaigns, mostly on behalf of Republicans.

Forces were coalescing, meanwhile, that would over time redefine and reenergize party affiliation in California and would by 1959 end the cross-filing system. Amateur activism, for one thing, began to assert itself on both the right and the left. More and more Californians were becoming engaged in politics on the basis of ideological orientation. While such activity initially remained on the margins, it had the effect in liberal and conservative circles alike of eroding the non-partisan and frequently indifferent center that by default dominated California politics.

When it came to politics, the suburbs of California were overwhelmingly moderate to conservative, hence tending to vote Republican. Already, by the 1920s—the first golden age of suburban development in the United States—this pattern had asserted itself. Suburban California, for example, solidly supported Herbert Hoover. Even the city of San Francisco, for all its radicalism and labor heritage, was by the 1920s putting Republicans into local office; and Los Angeles—which some defined as a series of suburbs in search of a city—after a strong flirtation with the Left that in 1911 had almost put socialist Job Harriman in the mayor's office, proceeded through the 1920s in a moderate to conservative fashion. Cities embodied, in one way or another, immigration, ethnicity, working people and their unions, machine politics in the manner of the East Coast. The newly emerging suburbs of California, north and south, by contrast, bespoke traditional middle-class Anglo-American values, significantly Protestant and supporting an orderly way of life centered on family and religion.

In October 1949, writing in *Harper's*, veteran California commentator Carey McWilliams pointed out that between 1940 and 1947 some three million new residents had relocated to the Golden State: a rate of growth that would continue through the 1950s. McWilliams was interested in the practical challenges faced by such migration—jobs, housing, schools, transportation infrastructure, and the like—but, being Carey McWilliams, he also explored the social, cultural, and political dimensions of this burgeoning new society. As a dedicated left-liberal, McWilliams was fully aware that migration into Los Angeles County from Dust Bowl states during the Great Depression had revitalized the Democratic Party in that region. What, then, did the future of the rapidly growing, rapidly suburbanizing postwar era hold for California, once its overnight growth had settled into patterned communities? Would the suburbs cohere into stable communities with defined social, political, and governance structures? Or would they emerge as disorganized dormitories for the disconnected and indifferent, devoid of meaningful public life?

Fourteen years later, in their pioneering study *Southern California Metropolis* (1963), political scientists Winston Crouch and Beatrice Dinerman argued that the social and political chaos that McWilliams feared might happen had not occurred. Far from it: Los Angeles County had localized itself into seventy-two independent municipalities, while the City of Los Angeles had localized itself into some fifty place-named communities within the municipal structure; indeed, many of these communities, especially in the San Fernando Valley, were cited as psychologically distinct places, many with their own post office designations, as if they were not part of the City of Los Angeles at all. The same patterns were true of adjacent Orange County, northern San Diego County, the San Francisco peninsula, and the East Bay. Almost overnight, then, suburbs—recently laid out on agricultural land as dormitory grids—had achieved a measure of community coherence. In Los Angeles terms, Crouch and Dinerman discussed this localization and emergence of community in terms of retail patterns centered on shopping centers, branch banking and other forms of business diversification, public utilities offices, local newspapers, grammar and high schools, churches and synagogues, social organizations, and— more elusive, but present nevertheless—local loyalties motivating, among other things, volunteerism and political activity. The assertion, then, being advanced by social critics, nightclub comics, song writers, novelists, and screenwriters that every California suburb was a wasteland of anonymity and alienation represented an overstatement. True, those suburban communities centered on pre-existing cities and townships—whether San Mateo or San Carlos on the San Francisco peninsula, Walnut Creek or Concord in the East Bay, Pasadena, Burbank, or Palos Verdes in the Los Angeles basin, the La Jolla district of San Diego—had experienced a head start in the matter of community development; but even the brand new communities, so recently dormitory suburbs, were showing signs of social development.

Not unrelated to such localized community development was the assertion in 1954 by Stanford political scientist Dean Cresap that California was in need of a revived two-party system. Supported by the John Randolph Haynes and Dora Haynes Foundation of Los Angeles, Cresap probed the central paradox of contemporary California politics. Thirty plus years ago, Cresap argued, the Progressives had virtually disestablished political parties in California as a means of ending domination by special interests, but special interests had become more powerful than ever in the ensuing political vacuum. With no strong party allegiance or discipline to guide them, legislators were being lobbied on a one-by-one basis. Voters, moreover, never knew exactly who they were voting for in terms of political orientation. Bernadette Doyle, for example, supported by the Communist Party of California, had in 1950 received more than six hundred thousand votes for superintendent of public instruction from voters, Cresap suggested, who most likely thought that Doyle was a moderate Irish Catholic, whether Democrat or Republican. Civil service reform, moreover, had mitigated against the Progressive notion that strong parties equaled strong, if not outrightly corrupt, patronage. And then there was the absurdity of the fact that the speaker of the assembly and the president pro tem of the state senate were elected at large by legislators of both parties, which boiled down to having influential lobbyists make the decision. The reforms of the Progressive Era, Cresap concluded, had been enacted at a time when California had slightly more than three million people. As of the early 1950s, a complex and growing urban industrial/agricultural state with triple the population was being ill served by the blurring of party lines. Contemporary California required the discipline, competition, and programmatic alternatives of honest, well-managed political parties.

The question was, how to get there? Such a reform of previous reforms could not be expected to come from elected officials, since cross-filing favored incumbents. Party rejuvenation might come from the parties themselves, however, which is what was beginning to occur following the revivification of party identity offered by Adlai Stevenson and Dwight Eisenhower in the 1952 presidential campaign, resulting in legislation that cross-filing candidates would henceforth be required to state their party affiliation. By law each party already had central committees on the county and state levels. Since 1935, moreover, Republicans had a statewide California Republican Assembly, open to all, which took policy positions at its annual convention. By the 1950s as well, California Democrats were sponsoring a growing number of local Democratic clubs that were taking an increasing role in the political process. Then there was the rise of political activity on the margins, left and right, which was having the effect of squeezing the center into party alignment. As far as Republicans were concerned, this activism, marginal but edging toward the center, was coming from an increasingly defined and militant Right, most of it originating and flourishing in the suburbs.

Between 1948 and 1951, for example, Pasadena—established in the nineteenth century but experiencing explosive suburban growth—found itself nearly in a condition of civil war regarding its public school system. On the one side of the conflict stood school superintendent Willard Goslin, a committed disciple of educational theorist John Dewey of Columbia, author of *The School and Society* (1899), which progressive educators—progressive with a small *p*, meaning, in postwar terms, on the liberal left—regarded as possessing near-scriptural authority. The goal of the school, Dewey argued, was not to drill or to motivate through competition but to set in motion a process of social actualization through cooperative programs. Taking the helm at Pasadena, Goslin pursued a Dewey-oriented program with a vengeance. Competitive performance and grades were de-emphasized in favor of joint teacher-student reviews. The transmission of fixed values was set aside in favor of an open-ended inquiry into systems and procedures that could never be finally fixed in their meaning. Teachers were required to discuss their own personal progress toward progressive goals at mandatory retreats, and summer camps were established for students to encourage similar self-scrutiny.

Naturally, there was resistance from conservatives not buying into the Dewey program. Where was the American value, they asked? Why was there so much discussion in class as opposed to old-fashioned teaching? Did not a lot of this progressive palaver, with its emphasis upon equal results, sound socialistic, or even worse?

And what was all this disturbing talk of racial justice? And sex education, even in the lower grades? Did this belong in the classroom? Growing increasingly bitter, the debate and the divisiveness in the Pasadena school district attracted national attention, appearing to be, as it was, not only an educational debate but a rehashing in classroom terms of Henry Wallace's 1948 run for President on a left-of-center progressive ticket.

After three years of ferocious controversy, Goslin lost the support of the Pasadena Board of Education and in February 1951 was asked to resign. Conflict, meanwhile, had moved to nearby Los Angeles, where UNESCO, the United Nations Educational, Scientific, and Cultural Organization, became a matter of growing debate. UNESCO advocated a species of one-world socialism or worse, anti-UNESCO activists argued. Why should students be encouraged to write essays on UNESCO, given its fundamentally socialist orientation? The *Herald-Express*, a Hearst newspaper, a women's Republican group calling itself Pro-America, the American Legion, a network of Freedom Clubs associated with the Congregational Church, and the *Tidings*, the newspaper of the Roman Catholic Archdiocese of Los Angeles, backed the anti-UNESCO campaign, which had resulted by 1953 in a scuttling of all pro-UNESCO programs in the Los Angeles Unified School District and the election of anti-UNESCO candidates to the school board.

A tempest in a teapot, some might say; but as House Speaker Thomas (Tip) O'Neill would later remark, all politics are local. From one perspective, the UNESCO controversy underscored the dramatic shift in Los Angeles politics in the early 1950s from left-liberal to an anti-Communist, isolationist right, as symbolized by the abandonment of the Elysian Park Heights public housing plan, the defeat of the liberally-oriented Fletcher Bowron by conservative Republican Norris Poulson in the mayoral election of 1952, and the histrionic anti-Communist posturing of Los Angeles city councilman Edward Davenport. Before succumbing to alcoholism in June 1953, Davenport functioned as a local stand-in for Senator Joe McCarthy, as evident in Davenport's reckless demagoguery, opposition to rent control (there was strong posthumous evidence that Davenport was on the take from apartment owners), and race-baiting (Davenport once accused Councilman Ed Roybal, a Mexican American, of hiding a knife on his person during council meetings).

The climax of more than a decade of school-related controversy came in November 1962 when the fiercely anti-progressive Max Rafferty was elected state superintendent of public instruction. A graduate of the academically rigorous Beverly Hills High School, Rafferty obtained his degree from UCLA in 1938, followed by a teaching credential. While an undergraduate, majoring in history, Rafferty managed the football and rugby teams, served as president of his fraternity, and was active in the UCLA Americans, an anti-Communist athletic group opposed to the larger left-liberal culture of the campus. At the UCLA School of Education, Rafferty later claimed, he had only studied John Dewey and given nominal assent to Dewey's theories because he was forced to. From 1940 to 1948, Rafferty taught English and history and coached football at Trona High School in rural San Bernardino County, exempted from the draft because of flat feet, although his critics later claimed that Coach Rafferty discarded his cane shortly after V-J Day. Obtaining a doctorate in education from USC, Rafferty rose steadily up the ranks of various Southern California school districts. Academic year 1961–62 found him superintendent of the prosperous northeastern Los Angeles suburb of La Cañada. By then, Rafferty had gained a reputation as an outspoken critic of John Dewey and the New Deal. As state superintendent, Rafferty hammered away at his anti-Dewey message, linking progressive education to a larger drift toward collectivism. An almost stereotypical scrappy Irish politician—outspoken, pugnacious, with a message similar to Ronald Reagan's but without Reagan's amiability—Rafferty served as an advance guard for the Reagan Revolution soon to come.

Max Rafferty found a degree of political support from a national organization, the John Birch Society, that was establishing itself in Southern California, in San Marino and Orange County especially. Founded in February 1959 by Robert W. Welch Jr., a wealthy retired candy manufacturer from Boston, the John Birch Society was named after an American Baptist missionary in China, who, while serving as an intelligence captain in the flying forces commanded by General Claire Chennault in support of Chiang Kai-shek, was assassinated by Chinese Communist soldiers. Well financed and skillfully employed as a lobbying force, the John Birch Society never attained the status of a mass movement in Republican circles, although it did exercise notable influence in the nomination of Barry Goldwater in 1964. The society, however, stayed on message: The United States was a republic, not a democracy; the United Nations was pushing the world toward collectivism; a mega-conspiracy favoring a one-world solution was at work in international corporate and banking circles as well as in the Kremlin. This message struck a chord with a certain kind of suburban Republican activist. When it came to Republican party politics, John Birch Society activists played an impressive game of hardball. In California that meant getting members of the society elected to the state central committee, the California Young Republicans, the California Republican Assembly, and the California delegation to the 1964 Republican National Convention. By 1964 some six thousand John Birchers were exercising considerable influence in California Republican circles, achieving, eventually, the election of two congressmen: John Rousselot from San Marino and John Schmitz from Orange County.

Another campaign of the emergent Right, opposing the fluoridation of drinking water, surfaced and prevailed in San Luis Obispo in 1953 and Palo Alto in 1954, as well as in the rural township of Los Banos in 1957. Even when failing at the polls, however, anti-fluoridation efforts in Glendale (1953), Long Beach (1957), Pomona (1957), and Manhattan Beach (1960) managed to garner 28, 41, 36, and 44 percent of the vote respectively: respectable showings, given the overall impression of nuttiness attached to the anti-fluoridation movement. As eccentric, even paranoid, as some of its manifestations might be, a New Right was emerging in the suburbs of California, Orange County in particular.

Standard-bearer for this emergent suburban Right was the senior United States senator from California, William Knowland. Virtually forgotten after the crash of his political hopes in 1958, followed by a long descent into gambling indebtedness, marital strife, and suicide, the William Knowland of the 1950s was the quintessential Mr. Republican from the great state of California, a commanding paradigm of the Anglo-American Masonic Republican establishment dominating Northern California for most of the twentieth century. The senator's grandfather Joseph Knowland had migrated to California from New York in 1857 and after a rocky start acquired a fortune in lumber and mining, based out of the East Bay community of Alameda. Joseph Knowland Jr., the senator's father, earned election to the state assembly at the age of twenty-five, followed by election to the state senate, followed by an appointment to the House of Representatives to fill a vacancy, followed by re-election to four ensuing congresses. In 1914 Joe Knowland was defeated in a three-way race for the United States Senate in the first popular election to be held for that office in California. But no matter; the very next year Joe Knowland acquired control of the *Oakland Tribune* and for the next half century, ensconced in an architecturally elegant Tribune Tower dominating the Oakland skyline, exercised decisive influence in East Bay and statewide Republican politics. Son William, meanwhile, born in 1908, was launched into an even more rapid rise following his graduation from UC Berkeley: appointment to the California Republican Central Committee in 1930, election to the state assembly in 1932, the youngest person thus far to be elected, election to the state senate in 1934, appointment to the Republican National Committee in 1938. By age thirty, family influence and his own driving ambition had made William Knowland a force in California politics: the heir apparent, it seemed obvious, to either the governorship or a Senate seat and—in distant view, but glimpsed nevertheless—the presidency.

In June 1942—despite his age, thirty-four, and his three children—William Knowland was drafted into the United States Army. Knowland had the connections, to say the least, to arrange for a direct commission or to secure a deferment. He could have secured an exemption as a state senator. To be drafted to serve in the ranks, however, had its own political appeal for someone interested in national office. Knowland did well as an enlisted man, rising to first sergeant in an anti-aircraft unit. Pushing the envelope, he applied to Infantry Officer Candidate School at Fort Benning and earned a commission the hard way. Although he was never assigned to combat, Knowland served in the European theater of operations as a staff officer, winning promotion to major, and was wearing his uniform when he showed up at the United States Senate in late August 1945, appointed senator at the age of thirty-seven by Governor Earl Warren, whose political career had been solidly backed over the years by the *Oakland Tribune*, when the incumbent senator, Hiram Johnson, died in office. As in the case of the other senator from California after 1950, Richard Nixon, the preponderance of journalistic, even historical, critiques of William Knowland seemed concerned only with the noir aspects of his personality and the right-wing nature of his politics. It was easy to stereotype Bill Knowland. He was a large beefy-faced white man in a double-breasted suit, rhinocerine in person and style, who walked and talked in a hurry and never blunted his opinions. His defense of Chiang Kai-shek earned him the sobriquet "the senator from Formosa." His vehement opposition to organized labor made him the man-you-love-to-hate in national union circles. President Eisenhower would eventually castigate him as impossibly stupid. Yet the senior senator from California remained a force to be reckoned with in Republican circles.

If William Knowland can be typecast as an Old Blue fraternity scion of third-generation privilege anxious for so much more, Richard Milhous Nixon can be characterized as a self-made Southern California suburbanite with a composite of personal traits Shakespearean in complexity. Elected to Congress in 1946, the United States Senate in 1950, and the vice presidency in 1952, defeated for the presidency in 1960 and for the governorship of California in 1962, then coming back to win the presidency in 1969—Nixon's story belongs, primarily, to national history and must be considered in this context. Even he, running desperately for the governorship in an effort to restore his flagging career, once referred to California as the boondocks, and noted on another occasion that he was running for the presidency of California. No matter how much he attained, how high he had risen in the world, how many times he had come back from defeat, it never seemed enough to assure him that he was once and for all removed from the boondocks of his hardscrabble youth in Yorba Linda, Orange County, Southern California, with all the hurts and snubs and disappointments such a rise, such an escape, entailed.

As of the spring of 1945, Richard Nixon was a somewhat rumpled Navy lieutenant commander, returned from duty in the South Pacific, reviewing defense contracts in Baltimore when a fateful letter from Herman Perry, branch manager of the Bank of America in Whittier, arrived at Nixon's apartment in Middle River, Maryland, inquiring whether he would be interested in running for congressman from the Twelfth Congressional District in the forthcoming election against the liberal Democratic incumbent Jerry Voorhis. Here, coming from nowhere, or so it initially seemed, was the breakthrough Nixon had been dreaming about since graduating from Whittier College in 1934 and from Duke Law School in 1937. Turned down by a New York law firm, his application to the FBI deep-sixed, Nixon had joined the small-time Whittier law firm of Wingert & Bewley in early 1938, where he became a partner within the year. This would have been it, most likely: local practice, membership in the Kiwanis Club of La Habra, service as a trustee to his alma mater, Whittier College, marriage to the strikingly attractive Thelma Catherine Ryan, more commonly known as Pat, a USC graduate teaching commercial subjects at Whittier High School, possibly election to the city council or the county board of supervisors, or even to the state assembly. Not a bad life by most standards, but certainly not the life he had hungered for, read about, dreamed of, across those years of lonely ambition when he had helped his parents run their grocery store in Yorba Linda, witnessed two brothers succumb to tuberculosis, and felt that persistent gnawing within for something more and that equally knowing fear that it might never happen.

Something more, something big, did happen, of course, the Second World War, although this had its ironies for a Quaker, an identity Nixon had vaguely inherited from his mother Hannah. Like William Knowland, Nixon did not get into frontline fighting during his time in the South Pacific, although he tried on a number of occasions to do so, spending his time instead first in Noumea, New Caledonia, then later in Bougainville, the largest of the Solomon Islands, as a ground operations officer for air transport, gaining a reputation as an astute poker player and the operator of a hamburger stand providing free burgers and beers to fatigued flight crews. Nixon finished his South Pacific tour as an air operations officer with New Zealand troops on Green Island in the Northern Solomons and returned to San Diego in August 1944 before being assigned to Baltimore where he handled contract terminal negotiations; Pat was expecting her first child by early 1946. Within six years, the reserve lieutenant commander huddling over contracts was Vice President of the United States.

The wave Nixon rode to the vice presidency was anti-Communism, as employed by his campaign manager Murray Chotiner in campaigns against Jerry Voorhis in 1946 for the House and Helen Gahagan Douglas in 1950 for the Senate. Neither Voorhis nor Douglas knew what hit them when they found themselves attacked from every possible direction in a variety of media for their alleged soft-on-communism voting record. Also propelling Nixon into the national spotlight was his standout role on the House Un-American Activities Committee; Nixon doggedly pursued patrician Communist Alger Hiss across two years and two trials for perjury. If nothing else, Nixon's role in helping to bring down such an establishment figure for lying under oath regarding his membership in the Communist Party earned him the lifetime enmity of the liberal wing of the eastern establishment, embarrassed by Hiss's conviction but equally affronted by the unintimidated doggedness of the suburban Southern Californian congressman and his key witness Whitaker Chambers, homosexual, fat, sweating profusely under the lights. In these years of HUAC activity, compounded by his Red-baiting, take-no-prisoners campaigns against Voorhis and Douglas, was born an enmity between Nixon and the liberal establishment that would play a determining role in the low points of Nixon's up-and-down career that might have ended abruptly in September 1952, had it not been for his Checkers Speech, a tour de force of spontaneous self-defense by an embattled candidate seemingly beyond hope.

Named in honor of the Nixon family pet, a black-and-white cocker spaniel sent to the Nixons by a Texas admirer, the Checkers Speech remains a classic of spontaneous oratory. When supporters of the Democratic nominees for President and Vice President, Governor Adlai Stevenson of Illinois and Senator John Sparkman of Alabama, revealed that supporters of Nixon had created an $18,000 fund for his use while in the Senate, it looked for a while as if Nixon's meteoric career would be just that, a meteor, flaring forth, then disappearing from view. Almost immediately, calls came forth—and not just from Democrats—for Nixon to be dropped from the ticket. Eisenhower withdrew and stood by, offering neither condemnation nor support, as Nixon leapt to his own defense in a nationally televised speech broadcast from Hollywood.

Speaking spontaneously, with only the barest of notes, Nixon not only saved himself but in the finale of the speech played shepherd boy David to Eisenhower's King Saul, becoming the young and strong right arm of the aging warrior and, even more brazenly, the spokesman-in-chief for the campaign.

Such a speech, so spontaneously delivered under such enormous pressure, must by definition depend upon a pre-existing rhetorical persona. Nixon had such a persona at the ready. He presented himself as the suburban man, a veteran, a junior executive from humble circumstances, released into upward mobility by the Second World War, married and starting a family, buying a house, experiencing the suburban dream, getting by on a tight budget. Nixon introduced himself to the American public as if applying for a home loan. First of all, as a United States senator, he pointed out, he earned $15,000 a year; and that only went so far. The $18,000 fund established by his supporters was in no way used for personal gain, and he had an audit from Price Waterhouse and a legal opinion from the Los Angeles firm of Gibson, Dunn & Crutcher to prove it. The fund was used to support legitimate political activity—travel, speeches, mailings—that could never be paid for with tax monies. Unlike Senator Sparkman (even in his opening and very defensive salvo, Nixon took to the offense), he did not have his wife Pat on a public payroll. Pat, of course, was a skilled stenographer who had taught commercial subjects in high school. On many a weekend, Nixon pointed out as the television camera panned in on Pat sitting in a suburban-like setting listening to her husband's speech, Pat volunteered her skills and time, and no bills were ever sent to the taxpayer.

At this point, Nixon embarked upon an itemized listing of his assets that in their simplicity and stark realism must have struck a chord with millions of suburban viewers. He owned a home in Whittier, Nixon itemized, and rented when he first came to Washington, $80 a month. He now owned a house in Washington costing $41,000, on which he owned $20,000. He had $4,000 in life insurance and a GI policy that would run out in two years. The family drove a 1950 Oldsmobile. The Nixons owned their furniture but had no stocks or bonds of any type, no interests of any kind, direct or indirect, in any business. In addition to his mortgages, he owed his parents $3,500 for a personal loan and was paying them 4 percent interest. Pat Nixon did not own a mink but did have "a respectable Republican cloth coat." ("And I always tell her that she'd look good in anything.") And then, following Pat and her cloth coat, came Checkers, the cocker spaniel sent to them by train by a Texas admirer. "And our little girl—Trisha, the 6-year-old—named it Checkers. And you know the kids love the dog and I just want to say this right now, that regardless of what they say about it, we're going to keep it."[3] With Pat's cloth coat and Checkers, Nixon had reached a turning point in the debate, as evident from his personal recovery in the remainder of this spontaneous speech from the embattled accused to a righteous prophet launching his own *j'accuse* in every direction: toward Stevenson, Sparkman, Truman, Dean Acheson, and all those others who, soft on

Communism, he charged, were betraying the American Dream. Following this indictment, in his most daring move of all, Nixon launched into a paean of praise of the five-star general who was allowing him to hang by his fingernails: praise that must have galled Eisenhower as, along with everyone else, Ike sat before the television set and beheld this dark-haired, five o'clock-shadowed young man from nowhere, this veteran of the family grocery store, this small-town lawyer rejected by New York, his cunning partially concealed (but only partially!) behind his suburban persona, end his speech, which saved his career, with the suggestion that Dwight David Eisenhower was a good man because Richard Milhous Nixon believed him to be so.

The rise of the fiercely partisan Richard Nixon proceeded in tandem with the decline of Earl Warren as a Republican candidate for national office. As of the early 1950s, Nixon knew instinctively that Warren offered the greatest barrier in California to his own continuing political future and must in some way be checkmated. For all practical purposes, Warren belonged to an earlier era of Progressive bipartisanship, while Nixon was an early and preeminent protagonist of partisanship. Within two years of becoming governor, Warren was being lambasted by conservative Republicans as a Trojan Horse for the New Deal. By November 1948, shortly after he lost the vice presidency as Thomas Dewey's running mate, a strong coterie of Southern California Republicans were attributing Warren's loss to his "non-partisanship" and "New Dealism," which stood in contrast to "the principles of real Republicanism."[4] As governor, Warren appointed Democrats to directorships of the Department of Social Welfare, the California Youth Authority, the Department of Agriculture, the Department of Public Works, the Bureau of Motor Vehicles, and the commissioner-ship of corporations. Warren went against his friends in the Masonic fraternity when in 1951 he refused to veto on constitutional grounds a bill sponsored by Cardinal McIntyre of Los Angeles exempting Roman Catholic colleges from state taxation.

Even more controversial was Warren's earlier sponsorship in 1947 of a hike in gasoline taxes to create a highway fund for freeway construction, which the oil companies opposed and many Republicans considered socialistic. In 1953 Warren successfully advocated a ten-year program of freeway construction. Between 1945 and 1950, under the guidance of his chief of staff William Sweigert and other Democrats, Warren launched four unsuccessful efforts to establish a visionary publicly administered statewide prepaid health care insurance program. Elements of Warren's proposal, dovetailing with a health insurance plan being advocated by President Truman, which Warren also supported, eventually found their way into Medicare. Warren also fought unsuccessfully for the passage of a fair employment act ending discrimination in the workplace. Other bipartisan proposals backed by Warren that in one way or another went against the conservative Republican grain included workmen's compensation and expansions of unemployment insurance and social welfare. Warren was in the habit, moreover, of sponsoring and presiding over town hall meetings throughout the state dealing with a host of social problems and proposed solutions.

No wonder, then, that under cross-filing Warren captured both party primaries in 1946 and did well among Democrats against FDR's son James Roosevelt in Warren's successful run for a third term in 1950.

Appreciative of what government could accomplish in its proper sphere, Warren was devoid of personal wealth and lacked any experience whatsoever in the private sector, having spent a lifetime raising a family of six children on the middle-range salary of a public official. All this stood in contrast to the tide of wealth and the pro-corporate point of view asserting itself in the Republican Party, in Southern California especially. Still, Warren managed to emerge as a national figure in Republican circles, serving as a national committeeman from 1936 to 1938, a favorite son candidate for President in the 1936, 1944, and 1948 primaries, the Republican nominee for the vice presidency in 1948, and a candidate for President in 1952. By this time, however, Warren's philosophy and practice of bipartisanship, his bland personal style, and his lack of corporate connections were making him seem, increasingly, a figure from an earlier era, lacking the bite necessary for survival in an age of partisanship. No one held this view more intensely than the very partisan Richard Nixon, who believed that he had a chance at the second spot on an Eisenhower ticket and no chance whatsoever if Warren were the nominee.

As the Warren Special train headed east to the Chicago convention in early July 1952, there ensued the Great Betrayal, as history and legend would later remember it. When the Warren Special stopped briefly in Denver, it took on the one California delegate not yet on the train, Congressman Richard Nixon, who by definition was pledged to Warren's favorite son candidacy, which Warren hoped could be parlayed into something more, should Senator Robert Taft and Eisenhower pummel each other into a stalemate. Moving from car to car, delegate to delegate (the Warren family oblivious to what was going on, the Warren girls happily dancing with delegates to piano music in the club car) Nixon lobbied nonstop against a Warren candidacy and left the Warren Special at a suburban station just before the delegates detrained in Chicago. Adding insult to injury, a gigantic I LIKE IKE banner was affixed to the bus taking the California delegation to its hotel.

Eisenhower's victory in Chicago and his selection of Nixon as his running mate should have spelled the end of Warren's political career, since, following the convention, a bitterly disappointed Warren announced that he would not seek a fourth term as governor. The election of Eisenhower as President, however, and the death of Chief Justice Fred Vincent precluded retirement when on 30 September 1953 Eisenhower appointed Warren the fourteenth Chief Justice of the United States.

The man to whom Warren turned over the reins as governor of California, former lieutenant governor Goodwin J. Knight, while not as openly non-partisan as Warren, was, all things considered, a moderate Republican with centrist tendencies. Born in 1896 in Provo, Utah, Knight came from prosperous, well-connected Mormon stock. (His English-born maternal grandfather had served as secretary to Brigham Young.) Knight's father, a lawyer and mining engineer, made the transition from

Mormonism to Episcopalianism following a move to Los Angeles in 1904. Personally and politically, young Goodwin Jesse Knight was early in life exposed to the
Progressive mindset that would keep Republicanism a power in California into the
1950s, despite the fact that by the mid-1950s Democrats outnumbered Republicans
by a million. As a student at the Manual Arts High School in Los Angeles (fellow
members of the class of 1914 included aviation great James Doolittle, opera star
Lawrence Tibbett, and film director Frank Capra), Knight worked as a volunteer on
the first Hiram Johnson campaign and came under the influence of campaign manager Meyer Lissner, a lawyer who was one of the founders of the Lincoln-Roosevelt
League that had inaugurated the Progressive movement in California. One should
not underestimate the formative influence of such an early experience of statewide
politics, as evident as well in Knight's almost obsessive determination as a youngster
to get as physically close as possible to William Jennings Bryan, William Howard
Taft, and Woodrow Wilson when these luminaries were passing through Los Angeles or his lifelong devotion to Theodore Roosevelt, America's über-icon of Republican Progressivism. Young Knight wanted to make his way in life, like the heroes of
the Horatio Alger novels he devoured or, indeed, the Horatio Alger–inspired *Good's
Budget* (1910), a novel that took its sixteen-year-old hero from Idaho to Seattle to
China in an effort to reestablish family fortunes, which Knight wrote at the age of
thirteen and his father had printed, along with two short stories, in an edition of five
hundred copies. There was something prophetic in all this, whether consciously or
subconsciously on young Knight's part. Initially, Knight's father had prospered as a
street and grading contractor in Los Angeles County. During the First World War,
however, he lost both his business and $250,000 in cash-on-hand in a disastrous
municipal bond investment. When Knight junior graduated from high school, his
father told him there was no money for Stanford, which Knight had hoped to attend.
At this point, young Knight, pursuing his own Horatio Alger scenario, drove a bus,
did reporting for the *Los Angeles News*, and, most dramatic, worked in the lead and
zinc mines of southern Nevada to accumulate funds for Stanford, which he entered
in 1915, majoring in law (then an undergraduate program).

At Stanford there surfaced the outgoing, genial, sunny side of Goodwin Knight,
the fraternity boy, at ease with himself and the world, that in later years would
obscure his success as a self-made millionaire, jurist, and politician. Working as a
hasher in the women's dining hall, shoveling coke for the Santa Fe Railroad, driving
a delivery truck or returning to the southern Nevada mines during vacations, Knight
refused to become a grind. On the contrary, he distinguished himself as a debater,
an actor in student productions, a rugby player (breaking his nose in the process,
which only served to masculinize even further his rugged good looks), a writer for
the *Stanford Illustrated Review*, the manager of the campus yearbook the *Quad*, and
a leading light, along with David Packard, in Alpha Delta Phi. Knight even managed to master the art of tap dancing, and for the rest of his life, given the opportunity, he would put aside his judicial or gubernatorial dignity, don his dancing shoes,
and tap a riff or two, just to show that he could do it. Thus Knight was combining

in his emerging persona the twin identities of privileged Stanford undergrad and self-supporting man of the people, an identity he further intensified by enlisting as an apprentice seaman in the United States Navy in World War I, serving aboard a sub chaser in the Atlantic and the Pacific before returning to Stanford to graduate in June 1919 as class orator.

At Cornell, where Knight matriculated on scholarship, intending to pursue joint degrees in history and law, his academic side—reinforced by shipboard reading while in the Navy—came to the fore. Knight wrote an M.A. history thesis on the American presidency and solidified a taste for serious reading that became part of his complex nature, running parallel to his hale-fellow-well-met Rotary persona that so charmed Republicans and irritated Democrats. "Whenever two Californians get together," Democratic National Committeeman Paul Ziffren would later remark, "up pops Goodie Knight." Democratic Attorney General Robert W. Kenny, in a not unfriendly way, characterized Knight's corny jokes, his steady eye contact, strong handshakes, and remembered names: "He has such a wholesome insincerity."[5]

Forced out of Cornell when money ran out, Knight managed to pass the California bar in March 1921, based on his Stanford and Cornell studies, and within the decade, in partnership with Stanford classmate Thomas Reynolds, was running one of the top-grossing law firms in Los Angeles and driving a Stutz Bearcat. An experienced miner, Knight invested part of his earnings in the Elephant-Eagle Gold Mines in the Mojave Desert, in which his father had once had an interest, managing the investment while practicing law and eventually selling it for $425,000, which, together with his law earnings, made him financially independent by his mid-thirties.

Knight thereupon entered politics, more or less on a full-time basis, later stating that the first thing a politically ambitious young man should do, before entering politics, is to secure his financial future. Active in the Young Republicans, Knight distinguished himself as a supporter of Frank Merriam in Merriam's race for governor against Upton Sinclair in 1934 and was awarded with an appointment to the Los Angeles Superior Court. Knowledgeable in the law, Knight proved a first-rate judge (a mere fourteen reversals in seven thousand decisions); yet he regarded his judgeship as a springboard to higher office, accepting as many Republican-oriented speaking engagements as possible and hosting weekly radio programs in Los Angeles and San Francisco, commuting each weekend on the overnight train. Knight's Los Angeles program—the Sunday evening *Open Forum* on KMPC—earned him an audience of three hundred thousand. By 1946, when he declared for lieutenant governor in his first bid for statewide office, Knight had attained wide popularity. He won the lieutenant governorship with a majority of 333,000 votes, the largest majority thus far in the political history of California for an opposed candidate.

Richard Nixon won election to Congress that same year, and between these two Republicans soon ensued a ferocious rivalry: the awkward, introverted Nixon, so scarred by poverty and past slights; the sunny, outgoing Knight, so delighted with his own Horatio Alger rise to financial independence. What both men had in common was a successful marriage to a formidable and attractive woman: in Knight's case, the socially well positioned Arvilla Cooley, a chic blonde whom he met at a dinner dance in Santa Monica and married in 1925; in Nixon's case, the angularly good-looking and intelligent redhead Pat Ryan, who had flirted briefly with Hollywood before settling into teaching, whom Nixon had married in 1940 at the Mission Inn in Riverside, the two of them bonded by shared memories of hardscrabble earlier years and a fierce determination to do better. Knight and Nixon would also eventually have in common the fatherhood of two attractive and brainy daughters. Goodwin J. Knight, however, was a tap dancer, possessed of the flamboyance and panache skirting self-parody tap dancing requires. Nixon played the piano on occasion, but one could never imagine him tap dancing.

The Knight/Nixon antagonism began, so it was later reported, when in July 1952 Lieutenant Governor Goodwin J. Knight stood on the tarmac of the Los Angeles International Airport as part of a party welcoming back to California the newly nominated candidate for Vice President. Suddenly, Nixon backers—or were they staffers, as Knight later suspected?—yanked Lieutenant Governor Knight out of the front-ranked welcoming party and relegated him to the sidelines. Here, then, was Goodwin J. Knight—Stanford man, self-made millionaire, distinguished jurist, winner in 1950 of both the Republican and Democratic nominations for lieutenant governor, receiving more votes than any candidate for statewide office had ever received in the entire history of the state—extracted from the VIP section and pushed into the rear ranks of those welcoming a candidate for Vice President of the United States who six years earlier had been a broke Navy lawyer in search of employment.

The pushing of Knight out of the lead party only emphasized certain transitions and appropriations of political turf that each man was making. Nixon was the candidate of choice for the emergent Southern California Republican right, oligarchic and ferociously anti-Communist. Knight himself had flirted with the Right in the late 1940s, going so far as to consider a run against Earl Warren in 1950 on the grounds that Warren was not proving Republican enough. It was a temptation Knight prudently resisted. He was anti-Communist, of course. Everyone was. But he was not a McCarthyite. And when it came to labor, Knight's own experiences as a hard-rock miner warred against the anti-labor policies of the Southern California Republican establishment; indeed, in the elections of 1946 and 1950, Knight had garnered solid support from labor, based in part on his hard-rock mining past.

Thrust into the governorship when Warren left for the Supreme Court, Knight—one of the few California governors fluent in Spanish—wrapped himself in the bipartisan mantle of his predecessor. Playing the governorship like opening night, Knight flew about the state in his official DC-3, *The Grizzly*, speechifying constantly, eighty-four speeches in his first fifty-nine days in office. In one sense, Knight was faking it. In October 1952, in his last year as lieutenant governor, his wife Arvilla had succumbed unexpectedly to a coronary thrombosis. Devastated, Knight went into isolation, spending his evenings in his Sacramento hotel room brooding over his loss. When Knight became governor, his vivacious elder daughter Marilyn acted as his hostess. While serving out Earl Warren's third term, Knight began to keep company with a longtime family friend, Virginia Carlson, an attractive widow who had lost her husband, an Army Air Forces bombardier, during the war. In August 1954, in the midst of his campaign for election as governor in his own right, Knight and Virginia Carlson were married at the Episcopal Church of Our Savior in Los Angeles and honeymooned off Catalina Island on a borrowed yacht. An Associated Press photographer photographed Knight as he carried his new bride across the threshold of the governor's mansion in Sacramento. Suggesting as it did middle-aged marital bliss in the handsome and virile governor and his attractive bride, the AP photograph ran in hundreds of newspapers and in November helped Knight cruise to victory over the Democratic nominee, Richard Graves. As first lady, the fashionably dressed Virginia Knight accompanied her husband on his frequent trips throughout the state. Once a year, the couple held an open house at the governor's mansion, personally greeting hundreds of drop-in visitors. As in the case of Earl Warren, whose photogenic family constituted a major political asset, Warren and his new bride, together with Knight's two attractive daughters and, in time, their husbands and children, projected an equally compelling image of California well-being.

Knight, meanwhile, continued his Warren-inspired agenda. Five of his top staffers were Democrats. Endorsed by the AFL in his reelection campaign, Knight kept a union-busting right-to-work bill stalled in committee for the duration of his governorship. Espousing the Progressive program of public works begun by Warren, he reorganized the twenty state agencies with jurisdiction over water into a single Department of Water Resources under the leadership of the respected water engineer Harvey Banks and jump-started the Feather River project, the first installment of a comprehensive State Water Project organizing California's water resources. Knight raised unemployment and senior citizen benefits, appointed the first women to serve as regents of the University of California, increased the state education budget, fought air pollution in Los Angeles, tightened state control of alcohol and boxing, and successfully negotiated with the Hearst family for the donation of Hearst Castle at San Simeon to the state. Knight also downplayed the Red Scare, openly declaring at one point that he was no Joe McCarthy.

Still, there was looming amidst all this bipartisan fulfillment the specter of Vice President Nixon vying for control of the Republican Party in California. When Knight proposed that Los Angeles Savings and Loan executive Howard Ahmanson be named chairman of the state Republican Party for 1956, a routine prerogative of the governor, Nixon, a federal official with no standing in the matter, entered his own candidate, wealthy cattleman Ray Arbuthnot, and an internecine struggle broke out among Nixon and Knight Republicans. Knight was badly bruised in the battle, for it took the intervention of Senator William Knowland, another rival of Knight's, to win the chairmanship for Ahmanson, and even with this victory, Ahmanson suffered a heart attack and was unable to take office. On Knight's side of the rivalry, he was no doubt listening to suggestions—coming most strongly from Harry Finks, vice president of the AFL-CIO—that President Eisenhower was not particularly happy with Nixon's outspoken anti-unionism and would dump him from the ticket lest labor be lost in the 1956 election. Who better to replace Nixon than Knight, Finks and other labor leaders suggested? An even more compelling possibility: Eisenhower, beset by ill health, might not run in 1956 at all, leaving Knight to enter the Republican Convention to be held at the Cow Palace in San Francisco that summer as a favorite son. This depiction of Knight as possible presidential contender was made even more credible in May 1955 when *Time* ran a cover story advancing such a scenario. Then came a laudatory article by Theodore H. White in the February 1956 *Collier's* positioning Knight, Nixon, Knowland, and Warren as possible successors to Eisenhower, should Ike decide not to run. By this time, Knight was openly opposing the renomination of Nixon as Vice President. When the convention convened, Senator Knowland, now solidly behind Nixon, hijacked the California delegation from Knight in favor of a total support for Nixon's renomination. Even before Eisenhower declared that Nixon was his choice for a second term, Knight had been bested, even humiliated, by his archrival.

All this would pale in comparison to the humiliations in store for Knight in the gubernatorial election of November 1958, which would bring an end to the non-partisan political culture of California, put the Democratic Party in charge of the state, and end the political careers of Knowland and Knight. The ambitions of limited men can frequently be dangerous; and, as far as California politics were concerned, there was no more ambitious—or more limited—a politician on the national scene than Senator William F. Knowland, who wanted to be elected President of the United States in 1960. Already, Knowland had come tantalizingly close to the presidency when Senator Robert Taft had seriously considered him as his vice presidential running mate. Had Taft been nominated and elected in 1952, Knowland told himself, and succumbed to cancer as he did in 1953, Vice President Knowland would have moved into the Oval Office. To win election as President in 1960, Knowland strategized, he would need executive experience. And what better executive experience could there be than a term as governor of California? And so, in early 1957, at the height of his authority as Senate minority whip, Knowland announced that he would not seek reelection in 1958 but would return to California to spend more time with his family.

As rumors of Knowland's impending run gained strength, Goodwin J. Knight on 19 August 1957 made a preemptive strike, declaring his intention to run for reelection in 1958 and warning Knowland not to seek the governorship as a stepping-stone to the presidency. Two months later, Knowland declared his candidacy at a press conference in the Hotel Senator in Sacramento. Thus Goodwin J. Knight, who might otherwise have expected to breeze into a second full term, found himself fighting for his political life.

Quite clearly, Knight embodied a moderate-to-liberal Republicanism, inherited from Earl Warren. Although he came from Northern California, Knowland was the candidate of the Southern California anti-labor conservative Republican insurgency centered on the *Los Angeles Times*. In the months that followed the announcement of the competitive Republican candidacies, *Times* publisher Norman Chandler privately communicated to Knight on two occasions that he should step aside from the governor's race and declare for Knowland's vacant Senate seat. On the third occasion, Chandler sent his wife to deliver the message personally to an increasingly beleaguered governor. With the cooperation of Rexall Drug executive Justin Dart, chairman of the Republican State Finance Committee, and Charles Sparks Thomas, chairman of the Republican National Committee, Chandler also began to cut Knight off from Republican fundraising. Southern California aircraft industry executives were especially anxious to replace Knight with the outspoken Cold Warrior Knowland. Even Bay Area Republican fundraising began to dry up for Knight. In November 1957 Los Angeles industrialist John A. McCone took the pro-Knowland argument to the White House; and Ike (who had once entered into his diary regarding Knowland, "In his case, there seems to be no final answer to the question, 'How stupid can you get?'")—went along with the scenario being advanced by the *Los Angeles Times* and the aircraft and oil industries.[6] Nixon, meanwhile, was openly stating that there should be only one Republican candidate for governor in the primary if the Republicans were to have a chance of keeping control of Sacramento.

Not surprisingly, Goodwin J. Knight came down with a serious case of flu and had to go to Arizona to recuperate, promising as he left to stay in the race "come hell, high water, pressure from friends, or threats of withholding of campaign funds."[7] A few days later, however, speaking from his desert retreat, Knight announced that he would withdraw from the governor's race and seek Knowland's vacant Senate seat. The problem was, George Christopher, the respected Republican mayor of San Francisco, had already declared for the Senate seat. Vacationing in Greece at the time of Knight's announcement, Christopher accused Knight of a double-cross and vowed to stay in the race. Knight, meanwhile, recovered from the flu, flew to Washington, where he secured the blessings of President Eisenhower and—bitter wormwood and gall!—the endorsement of Vice President Nixon.

In less than a year, Goodwin J. Knight had been reduced from a successful and popular governor of California, a possible candidate for President of the United States, and a shoo-in for reelection as governor in 1958 to a humiliated reject of his own party. The Republican Party was officially backing Knight for the Senate; but at the California Republican Assembly convention meeting in San Jose in mid-March 1958, Christopher put up a fierce resistance. Although he won the assembly's endorsement over Christopher, 109 to 44, Knight suffered grave damage from the San Francisco mayor's outspoken charges of ethnic bias and double-cross.

The Democratic Party, meanwhile—long dormant and disorganized despite its million-voter majority—was regaining momentum. In 1950 Earl Warren had trounced Jimmy Roosevelt in the race for the governorship, with Attorney General Edmund G. (Pat) Brown of San Francisco being the only Democrat to win statewide office. Although he failed to win California in 1952, the Democratic candidate, Los Angeles–born Adlai Stevenson, galvanized liberal Democrats into new optimism. All across the nation there was emerging, political scientist James Q. Wilson would later document, a new kind of Democrat: urban, college educated, middle to upper middle class, persistently liberal, and committed to Democratic Party activism. These were not, in short, politicians in search of office or up-from-the-ranks union leaders or party hacks on the payroll involved in gatekeeping and related bread-and-butter issues. These were, as Wilson described them, educated, prosperous, ideologically oriented amateurs, willing to form clubs and serve as a reforming elite.

In November 1953 this new breed of Democratic activist met in convention in Fresno and formed the California Democratic Council, introducing an element of statewide party discipline into a network that would eventually encompass more than 450 local clubs. A year earlier, cross-filing had been amended by the legislature to include the designation of a candidate's political party. Thus Democrats could now run openly as Democrats, capitalizing on their majority in statewide elections. Cross-filing Republicans, moreover, could no longer conceal their party affiliation. By the mid-1950s, then, the stage was set for what would soon be occurring in the gubernatorial election of 1958: hardball partisan politics, open and unashamed.

Initially, Attorney General Brown had not planned to seek the Democratic nomination to oppose Knight's bid for a second full term. Brown and Knight were friends, two of a kind, twins separated at birth, with Brown replicating in an Irish Catholic San Francisco Democratic idiom Knight's genial centrism and bipartisan spirit. Like Knight, Brown had an Horatio Alger–style boyhood. Brown's father was a small-time owner/operator of, at various times and in various combinations, souvenir shops, cigar stores where bets were taken and poker played in a back room, a movie theater, and other local enterprises. Born in Colusa County of German descent, Brown's mother was outspokenly anti-Catholic, although in 1904, having moved to San Francisco, she married the Irish Catholic Edmund Gerald Brown, destined to live his life as one of those men who are promising in their youth but never fully connect. The couple had four children, including their oldest, Edmund Gerald, born in April 1905, but would eventually separate over religious and other differences.

Edmund Gerald Brown Jr. acquired the nickname Pat, which remained with him for a lifetime, in the course of quoting Patrick Henry's "Give me liberty or give me death" in a speech he made in the seventh grade, urging the purchase of Liberty Bonds. Like Knight at Manual Arts in Los Angeles, Pat Brown was a big man on campus at Lowell, San Francisco's most prestigious public high school: president of the camera club, the debating society, the rowing club, and president as well of a fraternity, the Nocturnes, which he founded when his previous fraternity would not admit a Jewish friend. As head yell leader, the widely popular Brown brought to a fine point his socializing skills. His girlfriend at Lowell, Bernice Layne, a Protestant, was the daughter of a prominent San Francisco police captain. Following graduation from Lowell, Bernice earned a teaching degree at UC Berkeley, while Brown, too much in a hurry to spend four years in college, enrolled in night law school and passed the bar in 1927. In October 1930 he and Bernice eloped to Reno, where they were married in the Episcopal cathedral.

From the beginning, Pat Brown wanted a career in elective office. At age twenty-three, he ran unsuccessfully for the assembly as a Republican. He then organized a young (under forty) political club, aimed at getting candidates elected to local office. San Francisco at the time was a Republican town, but in 1934, under the influence of the Depression and the New Deal, Brown became a Democrat and began a mildly successful rise as a party apparatchik while pursuing a moderately successful legal practice. Brown's breakthrough would not come for another ten years, when he won election as district attorney. In 1950 he was elected attorney general, the lone Democrat in statewide office. Like his good friend Earl Warren, with whom he would commute to the Bay Area on weekends, Pat Brown would spend the bulk of his career on a middle-income public salary.

Fourteen years after winning his first election, Attorney General Pat Brown, watching the Republican meltdown, declared for governor. Going on the attack, Brown denounced Knight—who as yet had not abandoned the governor's race—as a "confused and wavering incumbent deserted by his own party" and Knowland as a "reactionary who views the state's highest office only as a pawn in presidential power politics."[8] In the primary campaign, Knowland linked his candidacy to Proposition 18, a right-to-work initiative banning closed union shops and any form of enforced union membership, put on the ballot in January by an employers' group calling itself the Citizens Committee for Democracy in Labor Unions. Galvanized into action, the unions countered with an anti–Proposition 18 campaign that would eventually cost more than $2.5 million. Thus Knowland made of himself a one-issue candidate facing a unified and powerful opposition. Nor was the gruff and combative Knowland, painfully awkward when he tried to be nice, a particularly skilled campaigner compared to the instinctively amicable Brown. In the June primary, with cross-filing still in effect, Brown not only won the Democratic nomination but acquired an aggregate margin over Knowland of combined Democratic and Republican votes totaling 662,000. In effect, Brown had won the election at the primary, and Senator William F. Knowland was facing the end of his political career.

As a senatorial candidate, Goodwin J. Knight was hanging on, just barely, winning 49.2 percent of the primary vote to Christopher's 34.7 percent, with the cross-filing Democrat Clair Engle, a congressman from Red Bluff in Tehema County, taking a respectable 10.8 percent of the Republican vote. On the Democratic ticket, a cross-filing Knight managed to win 17.8 percent of the vote, yet Engle had taken 72 percent, testifying to his strong support within his own party. All things considered, the stunning victories of Brown and Engle—which included strong cross-filing showings in the Republican primary—forecast a Democratic landslide in November 1958. Which is exactly what happened. Brown won the governorship by more than one million votes, winning 60 percent of total votes cast. Engle went to the United States Senate in a much closer race, and Democrats were elected lieutenant governor, attorney general, controller, and treasurer. The right-to-work initiative lost by a million votes. Even more important, Democrats won their first numerical majority in the state senate since 1890 and their first majority in the assembly since

1942. The election also erased the seventeen-to-thirteen Republican advantage in the House of Representatives in favor of a small but comforting sixteen-to-fourteen Democratic majority.

Goodwin J. Knight and William F. Knowland, each so powerful a year ago, were finished politically. Knowland took up the editorship of the *Oakland Tribune*. Knight returned to Los Angeles and went into the insurance business. While the newly elected Pat Brown was promising that he would govern in the spirit of Earl Warren and Hiram Johnson—and would by and large do so in the years that followed—a culture of partisanship had reasserted itself in state government. The newly elected lieutenant governor, Glenn Anderson, attorney general, Stanley Mosk, and controller, Alan Cranston, were highly credentialed liberals, with Cranston serving as one of the founders of the California Democratic Council. In the years to come, a spirit of partisanship, a left/right dialectic, would become increasingly characteristic of California politics.

This was the buzz saw into which Richard Nixon blundered when, defeated for President in 1960 and wanting to stay alive politically, he declared for governor against Pat Brown in 1962. Pat Nixon had warned her husband against it, and Nixon himself, who had barely taken California in 1960 thanks to absentee votes, had serious doubts about his ability to win a job about which he was highly ambivalent. On Election Day in November 1962, Richard Nixon, for the time being at least, found himself once again falling into political oblivion. A decade earlier, Nixon had saved himself with his largely impromptu Checkers speech. Now, having lost the presidency and, even more humiliating, being beaten by Brown for the lesser office of governor, Nixon faced the press in the Beverly Hilton Hotel and, in an equally impromptu performance (his last press conference, he described it) unleashed on reporters a monologue of paranoia, bitterness, and self-pity, exacerbated by fatigue and disappointment—and some truth as well. The press had not been favorable to Nixon during the campaign, or even fair, reporting with glee his verbal gaffes about running for governor of the United States and, on another occasion, suggesting that he was running for President in 1964 rather than for governor in 1962. The very modesty of Brown's victory, however, some three hundred thousand votes, testified to the underlying liberal-conservative face-off now at the core of the political culture of California, as Governor Pat Brown, seeking a third term, would find to his dismay when in 1966 he lost to Ronald Reagan.

8

Cold War Campus

The University of California and Other Secret Places

ON 26 April 1960, Governor Edmund G. (Pat) Brown signed into law Senate Bill 33, otherwise known as the Donohoe Higher Education Act in honor of the recently deceased assemblywoman from Bakersfield, Dorothy Donohoe, chair of the assembly's Education Committee, who had shepherded the bill through its early stages. Governor Brown described the Donohoe Act as "the most significant step California has ever taken in planning for the education of our youth."[1] The governor was not exaggerating. The Donohoe Act called for the implementation of the Master Plan for Higher Education in California. Negotiated by a blue-ribbon team headed by Arthur Coons, president of Occidental College, the plan organized California into an higher educational utopia, a *multiversity* as President Clark Kerr of the University of California would soon be defining it, serving the economic, social, health, and cultural needs of the state, as well as its defense against foreign foes. The prosperity that was bringing California to such a lofty place was based upon a defense-related Cold War economy that had as its primary goal the arts and sciences of nuclear warfare. As of 1960 the competitive edge of the overall California economy was coming from an ongoing ingestion of Defense Department steroids. The strength of California was that of a garrison state. Hence ambiguities hovered in and around the announcement of the Master Plan for Higher Education. Was it Dr. Coons of Occidental and Dr. Clark Kerr of the University of California leading the charge? Or Dr. Strangelove?

In the nineteenth century, mining and agriculture drove the development of the University of California, as evident in the immediate creation of programs in these subjects. Such an orientation remained the case for the rest of the nineteenth century as mining and agriculture continued to dominate the economy. Agriculture remained the leading element of the California economy through the 1950s. An entire UC campus at Davis in the Sacramento Valley was devoted to agricultural research. While mining receded as a force in the Northern California economy, it was replaced by the oil industry of Southern California, which lent its strength to university-based programs in engineering and the geological sciences. The World War II era saw petroleum production in California jump from 250 million barrels in 1938 to 350 million barrels per year by the end of the war. By 1956 California was still producing an impressive 350 million barrels annually.

Thanks to World War II, California tripled its manufacturing capacity between 1930 and 1956. As of 1957 Los Angeles—second only to Akron, Ohio, as a center for tire manufacture—was second only to Detroit as a national center of automobile assembly, with an annual capacity of 650,000 cars. Aside from the standard Detroit brands being assembled in the state (by 1949 Ford was producing 14 percent of its cars in California), there was even a regional offering: the Kaiser-Frazer auto plant in Long Beach, established by Henry J. Kaiser in the late 1940s, producing a line of compact automobiles far ahead of its time. Manufacturing, however, never achieved the kinetic connection with the University of California achieved by agriculture and mining. As defense-related industries grew in importance in the Cold War era, moreover, a question lingered. Did Californians truly desire an industrial and manufacturing economy separate from but equal to defense spending, or had the state's economy by the 1950s passed a point of no return? Had the Cold War fixed California forever as garrison state?

Since free-market economies rarely articulate formal industrial policies, it is difficult to locate this question explicitly in California in the immediate postwar period; but it was there—in boardrooms and union halls, among investors and consumers, in government and university circles—as the state emerged from the wartime boom that had tripled its manufacturing economy through defense. There was much talk of beating swords into ploughshares following the end of the war, which translated, among other proposals, to turning airplane factories into places where buses, refrigerators, kitchen appliances, motor scooters, even aluminum recreational canoes, were made; but at the same time, in the midst of such proposals, between 1945 and 1950, as the manufacturing capacity of the state, deprived of defense dollars, plummeted, there was also a pervasive fear of a future primarily based on private-sector industrialism. The state, after all, had only one integrated steel mill, at Fontana in San Bernardino County, and that had only come about during the war when Henry J. Kaiser got tired of scrounging for steel on the East Coast. The Kaiser steel mill, moreover, was keyed to defense production and would have to be retooled for peacetime use.

California had a good supply of labor and was its own best market for manufactured goods, yet it remained expensive to ship manufactured products to the population centers of the East. And could California compete with the established industrial capacity of the Northeast and Midwest, even if it wanted to? The state was without coal, its hydroelectrical generating capacity appeared to be maxed, and the burning of fossil fuels had created a smog crisis in the Los Angeles Basin and would have to come under some form of curtailment by government. This meant an increased reliance on natural gas, which as of the late 1940s was not yet served by interstate transmission lines of the magnitude that would be necessary.

Thus Californians found themselves, collectively, in whatever mysterious way a free-market society thinks through its economic alternatives, remembering with longing and regret the prosperity of wartime; and by 1948, with the Berlin Airlift and the outbreak of the Cold War, defense spending loomed once again on the horizon as the newly independent Air Force began to lobby for the return of an international capacity for air power, including the design, manufacture, and servicing of global strategic bombers capable of delivering the awesome atomic bomb anywhere on the planet. A sigh of relief could be heard among the industrialists of California with the outbreak of the Korean War: They could now get back to what they really liked doing—fulfilling defense-related government contracts.

As in the case of the Second World War, aviation led the way. Altogether, California experienced a 140 percent increase in employment in the aircraft industry during the Korean War as the 88,400 jobs of 1950 became the 213,000 jobs of 1953. In 1948 the Department of Defense spent $100 million on aircraft. By 1953 national military spending for aircraft had reached $7 billion—for 10,000 jets for the Air Force and 3,500 for the Navy, sophisticated aircraft, labor intensive, requiring big budgets— with an additional $300 million being spent on the next phase of air defense, the guided missile. The statewide unemployment rate of 9.2 percent in 1949 dropped to 3.4 percent as of 1953. When the Korean War was over, Secretary of State John Foster Dulles announced that massive retaliation was replacing containment as the nation's lead element in defense and that the Strategic Air Command was replacing conventional ground forces; and the spending continued. Throughout the 1950s— as aviation led to missiles, and missiles led to aerospace—national defense spending increased by 246 percent, reaching the staggering sum of $228 billion in 1959. The Department of Defense awarded one-quarter of all its contracts to California in the 1950s. Between 1952 and 1962, the Department of Defense funneled more than $50 billion into California, twice the amount received by any other state.

By its very definition—involving as it did the futurist intricacies of jet flight, missile technology, aerospace, and finally, fully surfacing at the beginning of the 1960s, space travel itself—the defense sector in California was research-oriented; and this underscored its ongoing connection to the universities of the state. As applied engineering, aviation was by definition a research activity. The electronics aspects of aviation, for example, increased with the complexity of aircraft. A B-17 or B-29 of World War II had several thousand electrical components. Jet bombers had many more. The B-47 had twenty thousand electrical components; the B-52, fifty thousand; the B-58, ninety-five thousand. Thus the electronic aspect of aviation began to intensify even before the introduction of complex missiles. As early as October 1942 the Army Air Corps established a secret facility in the Edwards Air Force Base in Kern County for the testing of a jet aircraft produced in less than 150 days of all-out effort by Lockheed at a secret unit called the Skunk Works because of its remote location in a skunk-infested field. From Edwards, on 14 October 1947, Chuck Yeager, a P-51 ace from World War II, flying the experimental X-1, dropped from the belly of a B-29 Superfortress, broke the sound barrier: which was a form of research, as was all test-piloting, proving not only that Yeager had the Right Stuff but that the sound barrier could be broken in the first place, without the plane falling apart.

The Air Force at this time, however, had been reduced to one combat-ready squadron, and so the research emphasis shifted to passenger flight. During the war, the Air Transport Command of the Army Air Forces and the Naval Air Transport Service, operating a fleet of four thousand aviation transports on a worldwide basis, prophesied an era of large-scale national and international global air travel. With its DC-4 and DC-6, Douglas Aircraft of Santa Monica led in the research, development, manufacturing, and marketing of passenger aircraft. By the late 1950s, Douglas was testing its DC-8 jetliner.

By this time, a new entity, the rocket-propelled guided missile, and a new concept, aerospace, had entered the picture. Missiles began to replace aircraft in defense arsenals by the mid-1950s. The manufacturing of missiles included the production of missile frames, propulsion units, ground support equipment, warheads (which were not produced in California), and intricate electronic guidance, control, and telemetering systems. Between 40 to 50 percent of the cost of each missile was in its electronic guidance system. Between 1953 and 1957, employment in missile electronics, much of it based in California, more than doubled, as expenditures rose from $300 million in 1953 to $2 billion as of 1957. To test missile engines, Rocketdyne, a division of North American Aviation—which had gotten its start rebuilding German V-2s following the war—in April 1956 opened a Field Propulsion Laboratory in the Santa Susana Mountains thirty-five miles northeast of downtown Los Angeles. There, the propulsion systems of such missiles under development as the Navajo, Redstone, Atlas, Thor, Saturn, Jupiter, Skybolt, Polaris, Titan, and Minuteman were anchored onto gigantic concrete and steel stands, fired, and tested. Any one of these missiles was the product of horizontally and vertically integrated cooperation. The Polaris, for example, first fired in 1960, had been produced by the Lockheed Missiles and Space Division, with General Electric (electronic guidance) and Aerojet-General (propulsion) acting as subcontractors. Aerojet-General, in turn, held subcontracts on the projects with another 211 companies (Northrop, for example, supplied the electronic subsystems), and these subcontractors in turn were sub-subcontracting with another 464 smaller concerns. Forty percent of all work on the Polaris had been done in Southern California.

For testing of the completed missile, the Air Force in 1956 staked out 64,700 acres near Lompoc in Santa Barbara County, which it named in honor of United States Senator Arthur Vandenberg. There it built a brand-new military installation—maintenance sheds and other industrial buildings, laboratories, launch sites (those for the Titan in 146-foot-deep underground silos), barracks, and fourteen hundred housing units for missile men and their families—constituting an entirely new Santa Barbara County community, albeit a secret place.

The largest producer of rocket engines was Aerojet-General, headquartered in the unlikely suburban community of Azusa, nestled alongside the rocky San Gabriel River as it emerged from the San Gabriel Mountains: 142 acres of nondescript warehouses, steel-and-glass laboratories, trailers, sheds, Quonset huts left over from World War II. An estimated six hundred thousand rocket engines had already been produced there since Army Air Corps chief Henry H. (Hap) Arnold had commissioned a team of Caltech-associated scientists and engineers to work on a booster rocket to assist heavily loaded bombers to take off from short runways. Such jet assisted take-off (JATO) technologies propelled thousands of Allied bombers into the air throughout the war. Running such a company was beyond the mission and ability of Caltech, and so in March 1942 Caltech scientist Theodore von Kármán and four associates established the Aerojet Engineering Corporation, which in 1944 was refinanced by the General Tire and Rubber Company as Aerojet-General. With its impeccable Caltech lineage, its sterling record during World War II, and its commanding position as the largest producer of rocket engines in the nation, Aerojet-General—33,500 employees working across Southern California; Sacramento; Frederick, Maryland; and Miami, Florida—epitomized the evolution of the defense companies of Southern California.

By the time the Soviets put *Sputnik* into orbit in October 1957, the transition to aerospace had already begun, given the ballistic capabilities of the advanced missile systems. By 1956 nearly one-third of federal purchases from California companies, sustaining more than four hundred thousand jobs, was connected to the aerospace industry, which was accounting for more than 5.7 percent of all manufacturing jobs in the United States. *Sputnik* created a boom within a boom. In 1959 Congress created the National Aeronautics and Space Administration (NASA), which became a prime player in defense contracting after President Kennedy stood before Congress on 25 May 1961 and promised to put a man on the moon within the decade.

As of July 1962, the Aerospace Corporation—a public/private entity first conceptualized in 1954 and incorporated under California law in June 1960—was operating on a $50 million annual budget at Cape Canaveral, Florida, and Vandenberg Air Force Base in California. Funded largely by the Air Force to accelerate the advancement of space science and technology, the Aerospace Corporation was headquartered in the semi-suburban community of El Segundo just south of the Los Angeles International Airport. Its trustees and past trustees—among them Roswell Gilpatric, the first chairman of the board and later Deputy Secretary of Defense; William Foster, the second board chairman and later director of the United States Arms Control and Disarmament Agency; Jerome Wiesner of MIT, special assistant to the President for science and technology; Harold Brown, director of defense and research engineering at the Pentagon, later president of Caltech and, after that, Secretary of Defense; and Najeeb Halaby, secretary-treasurer and general counsel, later the administrator of the Federal Aviation Agency—testified to the integration of the military-industrial complex that was playing such a conspicuous role in the

California economy. Nearly a third of Aerospace's 3,600 employees were professionally qualified. Twenty percent held doctorates.

Academic as well in staffing, mood, tone, and physical place were the research and development divisions of these aerospace companies. Rocketry had initially been developed by academic engineers but also by such a talented amateur as John (Jack) Whiteside Parsons, an eccentric, even bizarre, USC dropout nurtured on daydreams from Jules Verne, who joined the staff of Theodore von Kármán at the Guggenheim Aeronautical Laboratory at Caltech in the mid-1930s to begin experiments that would lead to the further establishment of the Jet Propulsion Laboratory (JPL) during World War II. The Second World War had gotten the federal government into defense-oriented research and development on an expanded basis. By 1945 the Office of Scientific Research and Development was spending $114.5 million a year. Stimulated by the outbreak of the Cold War, federal security research and development had risen to $871 million by 1950. By 1956 $3 billion was being spent. By 1963 research and development had risen to an astronomical $8.5 billion. California was receiving approximately 40 percent of all such contracts.

To the genre of archetypal Californians—the Forty-niner, the rancher, the Hollywood producer, the real estate developer—was now added, especially in Southern California, but in Sacramento and Palo Alto as well, a new figure, the defense research scientist and/or engineer: seventy thousand of them in Southern California alone by 1963, technically trained, proficient, a cadre comparable to the civil engineers creating the freeway system and the water engineers creating the State Water Project. Moving from their suburban homes and families each morning by automobile and freeway to the Cold War campuses where they worked, look-alikes in their short haircuts, white shirts, narrow ties, and dark Robert Q. Lewis–style horn-rimmed glasses, they spent the work day bent over their desks or drawing boards or gathered around seminar tables discussing one or another cutting-edge problem of missile engineering and/or deployment.

Here was a new California place, the Cold War campus: installations such as that maintained by the Hughes Aircraft Company on a ridge in Malibu in a Y-shaped air-conditioned campus: a mid-twentieth-century Tibetan monastery of stone, steel, and glass suspended between the green-to-brown hills of the Santa Monica Mountains and the endless blue of the Pacific. There some 145 scientists, 49 of them with Ph.D.'s, guided by top consultants from Caltech, UCLA, Stanford, and UC Berkeley addressed a range of defense-related issues, involving pure and applied theory in chemistry, physics, nuclear radiation, and electronics, aided by state-of-the-art laboratories, a full-service library, and a support staff of 255. On staff at Hughes since 1946, Simon Ramo, a double Ph.D. from Caltech, had led the invention of the electron microscope while at General Electric. At Hughes, Ramo concentrated on the integration of radar with wing-gun controls and air-to-air missiles. Tiring of Howard Hughes's eccentricity, Ramo and a number of other engineers left Hughes in 1953 to form their own firm: a move that led the Defense Department to force Hughes out of any management responsibility in matters of research. In 1958 Ramo's firm was reorganized as TRW; and in rapid order, yet another Cold War campus came into being, this time on a hundred-acre site in Redondo Beach.

At the RAND Corporation in Santa Monica, researchers were proving equally ambitious as they entertained and answered questions that would be some of the defining issues of the twentieth century. Established in December 1945 as a cooperative effort between the Army Air Forces and the Douglas Aircraft Company of Santa Monica, Project RAND (an acronym for "research and development") originated from a memo by General Arnold to the Secretary of War stating that the Pentagon would need in some way to institutionalize and project forward its wartime research and development activities, with an emphasis upon ensuring teamwork among the military, government agencies, industries, and the academic establishment. By May 1948—when it was separated from Douglas Aircraft into a freestanding non-profit institution—Project RAND, now the RAND Corporation, had a staff of some two hundred organized in a Cold War campus in sight of the sea in downtown Santa Monica into academic-like departments of mathematicians, engineers, aerodynamicists, physicists, chemists, economists, and psychologists, all of them tackling an array of separate but interrelated problems and programs intended, as the founding statement of the new non-profit asserted, "to further and promote scientific, educational, and charitable purposes all for the public welfare and security of the United States of America."[2]

As early as May 1946, Project RAND produced for the Air Force the seminal report *Preliminary Design of an Experimental World-Circling Spaceship*, setting forth the rocket and satellite technology necessary for American entry into space. In its boldness and sweep as well as its details—its discussion of fuels, its advocacy of multiple-stage rockets, its communication and telemetric proposals—this RAND report can be said to have jump-started the space program, or at the least to have announced the notion that it was now time to begin seriously to think about space technology as part of an overall defense strategy.

RAND did social science and systems analysis (a term it first coined) as well as science and engineering technology. Based upon an advanced practice of mathematical logic and game theory, systems analysis at RAND took on such questions as: Where should the Air Force base its nuclear bombers? (The answer: In the continental United States, not abroad.) In 1954 RAND performed the preliminary calculations regarding the technology and yield for the delivery of nuclear warheads by rocketry that the very next year jump-started the Air Force's missile program. RAND pioneered the use of computer technology for advanced analysis, developing its own Johnniac computer, named in honor of mathematician and game theory pioneer John von Neumann. Among other defense-related projects in the 1950s, RAND performed pioneering studies in infrared detection that would result, ultimately, in a space-based early warning system against Soviet attack. Its Project Feedback report (1954) commited the Air Force even further to the creation of a space-based defense shield.

Photographs of RAND from this period depict lean and lanky scientists and engineers confabulating around Danish Modern furniture in their Cold War campus just yards from the Santa Monica beach, with the men keeping their jackets on, perhaps in deference to the uniformed Air Force officers also present. As in the case of the Hughes campus atop its hill in Malibu, the ocean-side campus at RAND suggested that a new kind of institution, the defense-related think tank (a term coined by the British during the war), had arrived in the United States, academic in ethos and organization, but without formal teaching duties, although RAND, the first such think tank in the United States, would eventually be authorized to grant the Ph.D.

The fusion between academia and the federal government, meaning the Department of Defense, was marked by the rise of academic-like research institutes such as Hughes, RAND, and the Stanford Research Institute both inside and outside of the academy or—in the case of such research-oriented enterprises as Lockheed, Aerojet-General, Douglas, and Northrop—within the corporation itself. So extensive was this network of research efforts, and so multiple were its organizational forms, the question could very well be asked by the mid-1950s: How did the university as an academic institution fit into this new and pervasive mobilization of research for defense purposes?

The University of California, dominated by the Berkeley campus, and Caltech in Pasadena each played crucial roles in the creation and rise of the academic wing of the military-industrial complex. The relationship of the University of California to the wartime and postwar military-industrial complex represented one of the most powerful and pervasive connections of its kind in the history of American academia. The University of California was itself a branch of government, established by the second state constitution in 1879 as a permanent public entity, supported by public revenues and governed by regents appointed by the governor and confirmed by the state senate. Mining and engineering had early on oriented UC toward science and technology as a cutting edge of its institutional identity. By the 1930s, with the development by UC physics professor Ernest O. Lawrence of a cyclotron for research in nuclear physics, UC was edging into the atomic era. By 1940, a year after Lawrence was awarded the Nobel Prize for developing the first atom-smasher, the university was constructing on the steep and thickly wooded hills above its Berkeley campus the second version of the cyclotron, twenty-two times larger than the first 225-ton machine, thanks to a $1.1 million grant from the Rockefeller Foundation. The very next year, in the spring of 1941, Glenn Seaborg and other UC scientists, using the new cyclotron, discovered a second fissionable isotope, plutonium, that like uranium-235 could be used as fuel for an atomic weapon. The day before Pearl Harbor, Lawrence took this news to Washington, D.C., where he met with Harvard president James Conant, chairman of the National Defense Research Committee, and other academics and government officials. In the course of the meeting, they were given the news that Roosevelt had given the go-ahead for the development of an atomic bomb, lest the Germans or the Japanese get there first.

The creation of the atomic bomb, hence the inauguration of the nuclear era for either war or peace, is not an exclusively University of California story; but it did depend upon Lawrence's early research, and it was directed at Los Alamos, New Mexico, by UC physicist J. Robert Oppenheimer, and it did involve the efforts of hundreds of UC scientists and technicians. The Korean War stimulated the development of the even more terrible hydrogen bomb. The hot war in Korea (officially not a war at all but a police action) was part of a larger Cold War pattern that would keep the University of California in the defense business well into the next century. In 1952 Edward Teller, father of the hydrogen bomb, joined Lawrence to found the Radiation Laboratory at Berkeley, renamed in 1958 in honor of Lawrence, who had died that year at the too-early age of fifty-seven. Attached to the existing cyclotrons was a new generation of accelerators—the proton linear accelerator (1948), the bevatron (1954), the heavy ion linear accelerator (1957), and the eighty-eight-inch spiral ridge cyclotron (1962)—for which the Atomic Energy Commission was paying the bills. In 1953 Teller, Dr. Strangelove himself, joined the Berkeley physics department, and in 1958, following Lawrence's death, he became the second director of the Lawrence Livermore Laboratory. By then more than a hundred faculty members were affiliated with the laboratory, now located in an architecturally impressive Cold War campus in the Berkeley hills, assisted by nearly three hundred graduate-student research assistants. A steady succession of Nobel laureates, meanwhile—six in chemistry and five in physics between 1946 and 1968—testified to the continuing preeminence of UC Berkeley in pure science.

Advancing the far frontiers of knowledge, such science represented the highest possible formulations of the academic calling. Yet it would be disingenuous to separate such science from the more generalized and practical upgrading of such academic institutions as UC Berkeley, Caltech, and Stanford brought about by the Cold War. Caltech had been a founding member of the military-industrial complex. Two Caltech pursuits in the 1930s—aeronautics at its Guggenheim Aeronautical Laboratory under the direction of German émigré Theodore von Kármán and the more informal experimentations in rocketry at the nearby Arroyo Seco—were intrinsically defense-oriented. During the Second World War, Caltech designed, tested, and produced hundreds of thousands of military rockets in an affiliated operation formalized as the Jet Propulsion Laboratory in 1944. Following the war, JPL continued its research in jet propulsion and rocketry on behalf of the military in a Cold War campus adjacent to Caltech. In 1958 JPL became the research and development arm of NASA, which put it on the cutting edge of space research for military and peacetime purposes. Thus World War I, World War II, the Korean War, and the Cold War had transformed Caltech into what many considered the finest center of scientific and technological research in the nation.

Up north in Palo Alto, the power elite at Stanford—trustees, deans, superstar faculty—were doing their best to have their university make the same transition. As far as science and technology were concerned, Stanford represented a paradox. On the one hand, it had helped bring about the modern era of electronic technology through its sponsorship of such inventions as the Audion vacuum tube converting alternating current to direct current and functioning as an amplifier (Lee de Forest, 1912), the electronic scanning and transmission of images leading to television (Philo T. Farnsworth, 1927), the klystron vacuum tube amplifying microwave signals into an ultra-high-frequency current (the Varian brothers, Russell and Sigurd, 1937), and the audio oscillator leading to high fidelity (David Packard and William Hewlett, 1938). On the other hand, Stanford had missed out on the big defense research contracts during the Second World War and had to content itself with the less prestigious role of turning its campus into a training center for officer candidates and various military specialists.

A partial cause of this second-tier status was ambivalence on the part of many administrators, faculty, and alumni who, while restive with the lack of defense-oriented dollars pouring into their school, were nevertheless determined to keep Stanford autonomous, or at least to prevent it from turning itself wholesale over to the military-industrial complex. Even before the war was over, however, sentiment was building in the opposite direction, thanks to the newly chosen (1943) Stanford president Donald Tresidder, a non-academic executive from the private sector, chosen from the board of trustees. The selection of Tresidder led to a more competitive pursuit of federal dollars by Stanford, a policy that electrical engineering professor Frederick Emmons Terman—now on loan to Harvard, working on the top-secret radar project—had long been advocating. Returning to Stanford as dean of engineering in 1946, becoming provost in 1955 and senior vice president in 1958, Terman was put in charge of plans to make Stanford and Palo Alto an epicenter of scientific and engineering research and development. That meant securing federal dollars and the recovered overhead from such grants that could go into the general fund for the further improvement of the university; and that meant an increasing involvement by Stanford in defense research as a stated policy—indeed, the primary means of institutional improvement—for what had been until recently an elegant, if cash-strapped, school for the upper middle class. A sizeable commitment to defense research, some faculty argued, would in effect federalize Stanford and downgrade its moral and intellectual relationship to undergraduates. As a way of dealing with this objection, Tresidder in 1946 established a quasi-autonomous entity, the Stanford Research Institute, to contract for and conduct defense research outside the ongoing obligations of undergraduate and graduate instruction. Like other Cold War campuses, the institute would be a place apart, a classified place, devoted to defense research and the recovery of federal dollars through overhead that was in the process of transforming Stanford into something more than a socially privileged regional institution.

Tresidder died unexpectedly of a heart attack in January 1948 while in New York on business, but Frederick Terman remained a commanding figure at the helm of the transformation of Stanford into a Cold War campus. Terman believed that Stanford should be entrepreneurial in the fullest sense of that term, which is to say, the university and individual faculty members should participate in the financial rewards of applied research, another point of contention with faculty who saw the university as obliged to pursue knowledge for its own sake. In 1951, at Terman's urging, Stanford established the Stanford Industrial Park, with the Varian brothers as its first tenant. All told, Stanford University would recover $2.56 million in licensing fees before patents expired in the early 1970s for the $100 in seed money it had provided the Varians in 1937. When profit margins such as this became known, investors such as Arthur Rock of San Francisco took notice and began to pioneer a new form of business financing—venture capital Rock called it—in which investors, including Stanford, took risks alongside company officials and had a say in the development and management of the enterprise and shared in profits.

Three factors, Roger Lotchin points out in *Fortress California* (1992)—defense spending, population growth, and defense-related suburban development—recast California in this period into one vast Cold War campus, with the newly developing suburbs serving as campus dormitories. To bolster his argument, Lotchin presents maps of what he calls the metropolitan-military complexes of San Diego, Los Angeles, and San Francisco, together with the military hinterlands of these regions scattered throughout the rest of the state. By 1961 each of these regions constituted an intricate and interactive network of military installations, defense-oriented industrial sites, associated military housing, and sub/urban development, together with the infrastructure of freeways, water, and public agencies necessary to support each metropolitan-military complex.

The engine driving this development was defense spending and the jobs it created. In 1953 California passed New York as the leading state for defense spending. By 1959—a year in which defense contracts with California industry and academia amounted to $2.1 billion, or 40 percent of all defense contracts for manufacturing and research nationwide—California had a labor force of six million. Four hundred thousand of this workforce were employed in defense industries, which is to say, approximately one out of every fifteen working Californians was being supported by the Cold War. By 1962 California had more military personnel stationed within its borders than any other state, and they too, spending their money locally, supercharged an economy already in overdrive.

This meant growth, and plenty of it. Between July 1947 and July 1959 the total population of California grew from 9.8 to 15.3 million. More than 5 million of these Californians arrived during the 1950s, a decade in which $50 billion of defense spending was funneled into the state. Not surprisingly, the regions that received the most money experienced the most growth. By 1958 three counties—San Diego, Los Angeles, and Santa Clara—were doing 90 percent of California's defense business. Metropolitan San Diego thus continued its development as the Gibraltar of the Pacific, under way since the First World War. By the late 1950s, more than three-fourths of the seventy-five thousand San Diegans employed in manufacturing were working in defense industries, two of the largest employers being Ryan and Consolidated Vultee, later Convair, owned by General Dynamics, where such Cold War necessities as the eighty-foot Atlas intercontinental ballistic missile and, later, the all-purpose Tomahawk were being assembled.

Within the defense economy of California, aviation and aerospace were the driving forces; hence the extraordinary development experienced by the Los Angeles metropolitan-military complex and its adjacent hinterland in Orange County. The Korean War had led to a 75 percent increase in the aircraft industry of this region, centered in such companies as Douglas, Lockheed, North American, and Northrop. As aviation made the transition to aerospace in the mid-1950s, this 75 percent figure held. As early as 1954, the Los Angeles Chamber of Commerce issued a report showing Los Angeles County to be the premier electronic manufacturing center of the nation. Some 413 defense-related electronics companies were inventoried, ranging from the giants—Aerojet-General in Azusa, Lockheed in Burbank and Van Nuys, Northrop in Hawthorne, Hughes in Glendale—to a sheltered workshop in Santa Monica where handicapped employees were producing cable assemblies. All this defense spending—all these jobs created, all these people pouring in to take these jobs—was materializing a megalopolis twice the length of New Jersey, extending from Vandenberg Air Force Base in Santa Barbara County to the Mexican border. In the San Fernando Valley alone, the population tripled between 1950 and 1960, and the once remote Antelope Valley straddling Los Angeles and Kern counties grew by 800 percent during the same period. Semi-suburban and exurban enclaves, meanwhile, such as Alhambra, Azusa, Downey, Culver City, El Segundo, Glendale, Hawthorne, and Palmdale were transformed into commercial and residential centers. In Orange County, the city of Anaheim grew by sixfold through the decade; the city of Fullerton tripled. If San Diego were the Gibraltar of the Pacific, Los Angeles and Orange counties comprised an aerospace neo-Sparta, a metropolitan-military complex in which by 1963 toward 30 percent of its economy was dependent upon defense spending.

In the Santa Clara Valley south of San Francisco, the Cold War was similarly functioning as a catalyst for urbanization. Santa Clara County ranked third after the counties of Los Angeles and San Diego in defense spending across the decade and fourth in population growth, which translated to a growth rate of 348 percent, much of it spurred by Department of Defense spending such as that in the Lockheed Aircraft Missile System division in Sunnyvale. San Jose, Mountain View, Sunnyvale, and Palo Alto were already showing signs of creating the multi-centered metropolis known as Silicon Valley. One company alone, Aerojet-General, was stimulating the urbanization of Sacramento County, transforming a quiet agricultural town and decorous state capital into a booming suburban region.

Still, a number of observers were arguing that California was being transformed into a welfare state dependent upon Cold War spending. As early as April 1942, Robert Pettengill, an associate professor of economics at the University of Southern California, was pointing to a specific problem that the defense industry in California would face following the conclusion of the war. Eastern industries, Pettengill pointed out, had existed, with focused tooling and markets, prior to being converted to wartime production. After the war, eastern industries could revert to normal functioning. Southern California, by contrast, had no stable industrialized economy, no prior tooling, no prior markets. Could the wartime industries of Southern California find a peacetime role? This was an extraordinary if prescient question to ask a few months into the war, but very much the question to ask as the war approached its conclusion, and an even more pertinent question when the economy of Southern California went into a slump in the immediate postwar era. Although not asked specifically by Pettengill, the question also had its social democratic implications. Wartime mobilization had brought to the industrial culture of California and to the other states where defense industries were located a range of social democratic benefits for workers such as health care, child care, transportation pools, a growing equality for women in the workforce, and the beginnings, slender but discernible, of better (if not yet fair) treatment for minorities. Could these benefits be maintained outside the mobilizations of wartime?

In the immediate aftermath of the war, discussion of such diversification and maintenance of industrial culture ran ahead of performance. Very few companies learned how to beat their swords into ploughshares. The Berlin Crisis and the Korean War, then, came as a mitzvah to the faltering California economy. In any event, it was as if California were proving itself—outside of its agricultural, tourist, and entertainment economies—to be incapable of an industrial culture not dependent upon defense spending, and even these sectors of the economy had their connections to defense. An entire generation of California businessmen, economic analyst Joel Kotkin has observed, thought they were big-time entrepreneurs, true creators of jobs and wealth, because they were fulfilling defense contracts, rubbing shoulders with high-ranking military officers, exercising a growing influence in the Republican Party, getting rich beyond belief.

Still, there could be glitches, especially for the little guy. When the Air Force canceled work on the Navajo missile in July 1957, North American laid off 15,600 workers, and the Los Angeles suburb of Downey, where many of them lived, went into shock. The nearby Rocketdyne division of North American picked up a contract to build the air-to-surface Hound Dog missile, the B-70 bomber, and the F-108 fighter, and all seemed well for a while—until the Department of Defense canceled the B-70 and F-108 projects a year later. No wonder that James Gillies, a professor of business administration at UCLA, was warning that the economy of Southern California was too dependent on defense. A "peace scare," in Gillies's phrase, such as might come about following the forthcoming visit of Nikita Khrushchev to the United States, would throw the region into an economic panic.[3]

Already the aviation companies of the region were talking about diversification, not into refrigerators and high-fidelity sets, however, but into missiles, guidance systems, and other aspects of avionics. Yet such internal diversification would not be enough, the Stanford Research Institute was warning by 1960, predicting a steady decline in the aircraft industry. Lockheed claimed that it was already making the transition, sobered as it was by its flawed and failing Electra passenger plane program;

yet its day job was still the Polaris, supplemented by the building of four Navy ships on Puget Sound, a step away from aerospace, true, but still a diversification dependent upon the military. Douglas, whose mainstay was the Thor missile, was venturing into microfilm miniaturization; and North American, whose B-70 supersonic bomber had been canceled, was keeping afloat by making rocket engines for satellites.

By 1963 anxieties over a downtrend in defense spending were resulting in two isotonic arguments. The space race announced by President Kennedy would keep the good times rolling, yet all the same it was time to get truly serious about diversification. Governor Pat Brown came as close as anyone to making these arguments converge by saying in his down-to-earth-way that it was time to use the Space Brains of California to make the world, and hence the California economy, a better place. Brown was especially intrigued with the notion of using aerospace expertise to create a statewide transportation system incorporating planes, trains, and ships, to include ferries, to integrate California as a transit system just as it was being integrated through the State Water Plan.

As usual, Governor Brown was thinking big-picture: the integration of the entire state into one high-speed air, land, and sea commuter system, based on the technology and expertise of aerospace. The Vietnam War, however, refocused California on defense. For another quarter century, the hot war in Vietnam and the Cold War, climaxing in the spending fury of the 1980s, followed by the breakup of the Soviet Union, would continue as an engine driving the California economy. Was it worth it, some were asking, this Faustian pact with defense: all this growth, this fixation with sheer bigness and numbers? Had California exchanged its regional identity for a mess of defense pottage, thereby inviting its re-colonization by the East? And if so, had something very valuable been lost, a previous California identity, with its emphasis on agriculture, small-town life, and moderate-size cities? Had the state lost its culture and autonomy, turning its agricultural fields into sprawling suburbs that were in so many cases defense-related dormitories, whoring its universities into defense-related think tanks, narrowing its industrial culture?

Being a Quaker and hence sensitive to anti-war sentiment, Clark Kerr, chancellor of the Berkeley campus since 1952 and president of the university since 1958, had little trouble grasping these tensions and ambiguities. Nor was Kerr without personal experience of how such hostilities could flare forth into social conflict, having begun his career as a labor economist covering the great agricultural strike of 1933. The defense function of UC was obvious to no one more than to Kerr, who was administratively responsible for it all under the supervision of the board of regents. But Kerr also recognized that a broader base of justification was necessary—an ideological diversification, if you will—if UC was to avoid either internal or external disturbances if and when its defense identity became too strong for those, within the university and without, who increasingly resented the political and economic control of the defense establishment over UC.

The so-called Silent Generation of students currently on campus had generally proven itself to be apolitical. By the late 1950s and early 1960s, however, Berkeley was supporting a growing free-floating community of non-registered non-students, bohemian in lifestyle, radical in politics, who sat in on classes, used library facilities, and in other ways formed a shadow student body that could very well erupt into dissent. Even the registered mainstream student body was showing signs of rebellion. On 20 October 1959, eighteen year-old freshman Fred Moore, the son of an Air Force colonel, went on a hunger strike for seven days in front of Sproul Hall, protesting compulsory ROTC: and this at the very epicenter of the Cold War campus. Worse, undergraduate David Armor won election as student body president on an anti-compulsory-ROTC platform. In December 1960 student demonstrations erupted against compulsory ROTC, and tensions heightened when an ROTC student, wearing his uniform in a picket line, was given an automatic F in his military science course. By June 1962 ROTC was no longer compulsory at Berkeley.

If the defense economy should ever fail in California, the mainstream Center, as well as the Left, might very well express resentment against UC. For the university to steer a safe and sure course into the future, Kerr decided—not all at once, but in increments of analysis and decision—it would be necessary to reconnect higher education in general and UC in particular to the people of California and the legislators they elected, who paid the bills. With this in mind, Kerr began to formulate an advanced paradigm for the university: the multiversity, he called it, formally dedicated to the betterment of society across a wide range of fronts. Thus, forces began to coalesce that would result in a Master Plan for Higher Education for the entire state.

By 1960 it seemed that everyone was going to college, or at least 39 percent of college-age Americans were. With the Baby Boomer generation born after 1946 only four years away from entering college, the statistics promised to become even more impressive. What a high school diploma had meant in the nineteenth century was now represented by the college degree. Virtually every profession was being trained and credentialed through graduate programs, and the Ph.D. had become a near-universal requirement for a research career, whether in the university or in industry. How did Clark Kerr—a bald, bespectacled, mild-mannered Quaker in a white shirt, dark tie, and blue suit—embody, for the time being at least, this victory of institutionalized higher education throughout the United States? Those who knew him well might have some suggestion of an answer in Kerr's distinctive blend of Quaker rectitude, self-assurance, and—although Quakers had no formal clergy—near-ministerial presence. Intellect and will emanated from the dark blue eyes peering steadily through the rimless glasses.

Kerr came from a background redolent of Anglo-American probity and high-mindedness. His father Samuel was an apple farmer near Jacksonwald, Pennsylvania, who turned to farming and high school teaching after mastering four languages—Latin, Greek, German, and French—and taking a master's degree at the University of Berlin. Kerr's mother Caroline, a milliner with a sixth-grade education, revered higher learning and would not accept Samuel's offer of marriage until she had personally accumulated a fund for her future children's college education. Clark Kerr was raised in an environment of reading, discussion, and outdoor work. At Swarthmore, where he majored in economics, Kerr became captain of the debating team and student body president and converted to Quakerism, which he would consider a source of strength throughout his life. Following graduation, he spent the summer of 1932 in California, touring with a Peace Caravan sponsored by the American Friends, intended to raise public consciousness via street-corner presentations on issues relating to world peace and the need for the United States to join the League of Nations. Visiting Stanford that fall, Kerr—who planned to attend Columbia Law School—encountered a registration line. What's going on? he asked the last person in line, Dean McHenry. The line was for graduate school registration, McHenry replied. Having his Swarthmore transcripts on hand, Kerr stayed in the line and was summarily admitted to the graduate school, so casual was the admission process at Stanford in that student-short Depression year of 1932. Kerr and McHenry became lifelong friends and colleagues. After taking a master's degree in economics from Stanford, Kerr, on the advice of his economics professor at Swarthmore, transferred to Berkeley for the Ph.D., which he took in 1939 under the direction of labor economist Paul Taylor, writing his thesis on self-help cooperatives among the unemployed.

Thus Clark Kerr came to Berkeley at the very center of the decade, the 1930s, that John Kenneth Galbraith would later regard as a golden age; and like so many alumni of that period, Kerr the Quaker convert found himself equally converted to the University of California at Berkeley—Cal, California, UC, the University—as something more than a merely secular ideal, a university that was a kind of faith as well, an ethos and a way of life. He also met and married in 1934 an attractive UCLA co-ed, Catherine Spaulding (Dean McHenry married Catherine's roommate), whose UCLA connection helped broaden the range of Kerr's UC identification. UCLA chancellor Franklin Murphy would later claim that despite everything—despite being president of a multi-campus system—Kerr would always see things from the perspective of Cal, meaning the Berkeley campus. Even if this were not true, or as completely true as Murphy would have it, it testified to the Cal faith once delivered to the saints that had so transformed Kerr in the 1930s and had presented him with his life's work.

It took Kerr six years to find his way back to Berkeley after taking his Ph.D. But they were not wasted years—teaching at Antioch College in Ohio, the London School of Economics, Stanford, and the University of Washington—for it was during this time that Kerr not only prepared *Industrialism and Industrial Man: The Problems of Labor and Management in Economic Growth* (1960), published by the Harvard University Press, but also acquired his chops as the most respected labor negotiator on the Pacific Coast, which was one of the reasons why UC president Robert Sproul called Kerr back in 1945 to serve as professor of labor economics and director of UC's newly established Institute of Industrial Relations. During the Loyalty Oath controversy of 1950, Kerr—although he himself signed the required oath only reluctantly—showed courage aplenty, albeit in his non-flamboyant way, in opposing Sproul and the regents in open meetings in the matter of firing those faculty members who refused to sign and successfully lobbied for their back pay once the courts returned them to work. When it came time for Sproul and the regents to appoint Berkeley's first chancellor in 1952, Kerr—who had never served as a department chair, dean, or higher administrator of any sort—was enthusiastically recommended by the Academic Senate, meaning Kerr's fellow faculty members, and was given the job. Thus a Quaker, religiously committed to peace, was now chancellor of a campus fueled by defense spending and the recovered overhead from such spending, and proud of the military men, politicians, and industrialists who had gone forth from its hallowed halls. Speaking at Charter Day ceremonies at the Greek Theatre in March 1962, President John F. Kennedy would remark: "When I observe the men who surround me in Washington, I am forced to confront an uncomfortable truth— the New Frontier may well owe more to Berkeley than to Harvard."[4]

While Kerr might joke that his job as chancellor was to provide "parking for faculty, sex for the students, and athletics for the alumni," he quickly showed himself to be a talented campus planner and faculty leader. By the time his name was being circulated in 1958 to replace Robert Gordon Sproul (also under consideration: Chancellor Franklin Murphy of the University of Kansas; Dean Rusk, president of the Rockefeller Foundation; John Gardner of the Carnegie Foundation; McGeorge Bundy, dean of the Faculty of Arts and Sciences at Harvard), Kerr had established the chancellorship as a viable office, turned Berkeley in the direction of creating student housing on an ambitious scale, brought to the campus eminent and rising academicians in the humanities and social sciences, and kept Berkeley on the cutting edge of federal spending from defense or other sources.[5]

This involved keeping UC, dominated by Berkeley, as the sole and exclusive proprietor in the public sector of advanced research and doctoral programs. Which was more complicated than it might seem at first glance, given the higher education boom in California. In times past, the constitutionally established University of California had felt no threat whatsoever from the state colleges. Many of these institutions began as normal schools and remained committed to teacher training. In the postwar boom, however, many of the state colleges had expanded their ambitions and programs. Some were en route to becoming impressive institutions, especially the polytechnics at San Luis Obispo (1903) and Pomona (1938). State colleges, moreover, had strong local attachments. Every community wanted one, and by the late 1950s there were more than twenty proposals before the legislature to expand the fifteen-college system, which had tripled in enrollment (from thirty thousand to ninety-five thousand) in the 1950s. These colleges, moreover, were under the general supervision of the state board of education and the state superintendent of public instruction, which in reality meant that they were functioning as semi-autonomous fiefdoms under the control of campus presidents. California had in effect created a multi-centered second higher educational tier, and it was growing and gaining strength.

How did this fit into the constitutionally established role of the University of California to teach and conduct advanced research? Sproul favored the option of bringing individual state colleges into the UC system once they had reached a certain point of maturity, as had been done in 1944 when UC acquired the freestanding state college at Santa Barbara. But this acquisition was due to political pressure, others argued, not academic merit, and as of the late 1950s the Santa Barbara campus remained a state college in all but name. The postwar boom in higher education, meanwhile, was producing more and more Ph.D.'s, many of whom were taking jobs in the state colleges and were increasingly resentful of the fact that they were teaching twice as many courses as their UC counterparts (four courses per semester as opposed to two) and were discouraged from doing advanced research.

In 1959 matters reached a crisis. There were too many bills to build state colleges before the legislature. The administration of those that existed was uncertain, and there were signs aplenty that, if matters were allowed to drift along on their present course, a rival public institution, a California State University equivalent in prerogatives to UC, or worse, a number of freestanding state-supported research universities growing out of the more advanced state colleges, would develop. A Liaison Committee had been in existence since 1945 to coordinate between the regents and the state board of education on matters of higher education; and it was here and before the assembly and state senate committees on education that the debate became most focused. Clark Kerr was very much part of these public debates and very much part of the behind-the-scenes conversations that were beginning to coalesce around the notion of a comprehensive master plan for higher education in California. Finally, Assemblywoman Dorothy M. Donohoe, a Democrat from Kern County and a former high school administrator serving as chair of the assembly committee on education, joined with the president pro tem of the state senate, George Miller, to sponsor Assembly Concurrent Resolution 88, calling for the Liaison Committee to prepare such a master plan and to report back on it seven months later at the opening of the 1960 session. Operating through Dean McHenry, UC's representative on the master plan committee, Clark Kerr zealously guarded UC's prerogatives, while at the same time agreeing to help the state colleges emancipate themselves from the state board of education and form their own system. At Kerr's suggestion, the chair of the master plan survey team was neither a UC nor a state college figure but Kerr's close friend from the private college sector, Arthur Coons.

When deliberations were complete, A Master Plan for Higher Education in California, 1960–1975, was submitted to the Liaison Committee. It was a masterful compromise that represented as far as Kerr was concerned victory for UC. Under the plan, the top one-eighth (12.5 percent) of all graduates of public high schools in California would be eligible for admission to UC. The top one-third (33.3 percent) would be eligible for admission to a state college. All other students, whatever their grade point average, even if they had failed to graduate from high school, were eligible to enter a community college, for either vocational training, which was established as an exclusive community college prerogative, a terminal associate of arts degree, or lower division credits that could be transferred to either UC or a state college. Thus the state's eighty two-year community colleges, within commuting distance of 80 percent of the population of the state, could offer not only vocational education but a safety valve for late starters, even high school dropouts, who could use these local institutions to complete the first half of their educations.

The state colleges, moreover, would be reorganized as a multi-campus California State College system—later designated the California State University—under its own board of trustees, with a president on each campus, who reported to a chancellor of the entire system. This new entity would be authorized to offer graduate work leading to the master's degree, not only in education but in engineering, the sciences, the social sciences, and the humanities, especially as geared toward teaching careers. The Ph.D. would remain the prerogative of UC, although a joint UC-CSU doctorate could be arranged for candidates in the field of education, if circumstances warranted it. The UC faculty was formally charged with research; the CSU faculty, with teaching (twice the load of courses), although the state college faculty could conduct and be compensated for instruction-oriented research of relevance to courses being taught.

Kerr, McHenry, and the rest of the UC community would have preferred that this arrangement, this master plan, be voted on by the people of California as a constitutional amendment, but Governor Pat Brown—wary of the political risks involved in the constitutional amendment process—preferred to go the legislative route. Calling for the implementation of the master plan through statute, the Donohoe Act passed the assembly and senate and was signed by Governor Brown on 26 April 1960. California was defining itself as a statewide program of higher education with room for everyone, from A students to late bloomers. By preserving the doctorate for UC, Kerr and the regents had preserved not only the primacy of UC as the first tier in this new system, but also its ongoing ability to do the kind of research in pure science and engineering for which the Department of Defense would offer contracts. Whether Kerr recognized it or not, Berkeley and, to a lesser extent, UCLA were even more fixed in place as Cold War campuses.

As in the case of all victories, further obligations were acquired. California taxpayers, for one thing, must continue to see the benefit of a publicly supported institution, UC, to which their offspring had only a 12 percent chance of admission. In November 1958 voters had passed Proposition 3, authorizing $200 million in state bond issues for UC and state college construction, which suggested that the majority of Californians were buying into the system. By the end of the 1960s, there would be toward a quarter of a million students in the state college system, and this growth would continue to constitute a formidable and continuing political challenge to UC in terms of legislative and taxpayer support. Those taxpayers whose offspring were admitted to UC would have to be assured that their sons and daughters would be adequately taught and cared for, including housing, and not just processed by graduate teaching assistants and left to scramble for living arrangements. Not only would the state college system have to offer, by definition, a quality learning experience in the classroom, UC would also have to find ways of doing this as well, lest disgruntled parents express their dissatisfaction to legislators.

The multiversity, as Clark Kerr defined it, was a concept intended to help defuse such resentments. Kerr advanced the concept of the multiversity in the prestigious venue of the Godkin Lectures at Harvard, delivered in Sanders Theater in three increments on 23, 24, and 25 April 1963 and subsequently published by Harvard University Press as *The Uses of the University* (1963). He based each lecture on a key metaphor or assumption: the idea of a multiversity, the realities of the federal grant university, and the future of the city of intellect. There have been few such exalted claims for the primacy of the university in American society as that expounded by Kerr, a Quaker *pontifex maximus* in the secular city of intellect.

In his first lecture, "The Idea of a Multiversity," Kerr took an explicit departure from the inaugural lecture, "The Idea of a University," given as a series of addresses in Dublin in 1852 by John Henry Newman when Newman was endeavoring to establish a Catholic university there and later (1873) published as the title essay of a respected Victorian classic. Newman's idea, Kerr argued, drew its strength from a concept of the university as academic cloister that could be traced back to the Middle Ages. Even as Newman was lecturing, however, German universities were advancing a new model—the research university—intended to replace the fashioning of students into learned gentlemen with a focused program of research and graduate instruction intended to advance knowledge and to train knowledge professionals. This model, imported to the United States via Johns Hopkins, led to the emergence of the American research university between the 1880s and the 1920s. And now, Kerr announced, was arriving the multiversity, a vast conglomerate of research enterprises. Newman's university, Kerr argued, "was a village with its priests." The German university "was a one-industry town—with its intellectual oligarchy." The multiversity Kerr defined as "a city of infinite variety." As in every city, "there are many separate endeavors under a single rule of law."[6] In the older model, the professor was primarily a teacher. In the German model, he became a researcher who taught. In the multiversity, the professor became an academic entrepreneur embarked upon many tasks, with research accorded primacy.

The single dominant energy source for the multiversity, Kerr stated in his second lecture, was the federal government. Although he was willing to struggle in this lecture with some of the ambiguities involved, Kerr could basically find no other way out. The federal government and the multiversity had entered into a partnership that was in the process of becoming the dominant partnership of an information-based society. The Second World War had begun this process. The GI Bill had continued it. And an array of government programs and grants had finalized its development. While Kerr expressed some doubts regarding the divided loyalty of faculty members receiving government grants, he spent no time whatsoever agonizing over the defense orientation of so much of this federal research. He was, after all, speaking as the president of the university that had contributed substantially to the creation

of the atomic and hydrogen bombs. So discerning in so many instances, Kerr chose
not to judge whether or not the fusion of the university to defense-related research
was harmful to the university as an institution.

In his third and final lecture, Kerr described the multiversity as Ideopolis, City
of Intellect. Soon, Kerr prophesied, three metropolitan regions would emerge
from the amalgamation of these multiversity cities: one on the East Coast, one in
Chicago and the Big Ten universities, and one in California. Kerr was announcing
something that approached a transfer of sovereignty from government to the multiversity, or at least a partnership so close, so dominated by and channeled through
the multiversity, as to constitute a redefinition of society. One must struggle to find
comparisons for the sweeping role Kerr was advocating for the City of Intellect, the
multiversity—nothing less than the improvement of society through research across
a wide front: research, pure and applied, into every aspect of society, not just its
defense. The multiversity would make life better for everyone, not just the military
and the college crowd.

Still, there were unanswered questions, given the fact that the City of Intel-
lect, like the world itself, was divided between two competing systems, which is
to say, was in a condition of Cold War. In the final paragraphs of his third lecture,
Kerr engages—at long last—the defense issue, making a distinction between the
Communist-dominated City of Intellect and the City of Intellect in the Free World.
They were different, true, but they were also alike in their respect for rational and
scientific inquiry. These differing but overlapping university cultures of East and
West, these congruent Cities of Intellect, could conceivably form a common ground
for peace. His Quakerism surfacing, Kerr allowed himself to hope that "the intellect,
and the university as its most happy home, can have great potential roles to play in
the reconciliation of the war between the future and the past, and the solution—
one way or the other—of the war between the ideological giants who now rend the
world with their struggles."[7] The Cold War multiversity, in short, could not only
offer research for a better life through a thousand practical applications and help
secure the defense of the free world, it constituted as well a bridge of intellect, an
overlapping territory, that might very possibly serve as a common ground (a Quaker
meeting hall) for peace. It was a tenuous argument, but the very fact that Kerr felt
compelled to make it—to reconcile his Quakerism with his Cold War campus
leadership—constituted perhaps his most ambitious claim for what the multiversity
was capable of bringing about: its self-extinction as a Cold War campus.

Until that day of deliverance, however, Kerr was devoting himself to the creation
of a multi-campus multiversity in which some of the more traditional undergraduate experiences and relationships, such as he had himself experienced at Swarthmore, could be institutionalized. UC was already a multi-campus institution, with a
medical campus in San Francisco, built around the Toland Medical College (1864)
acquired by UC in 1873; a campus at Davis near Sacramento, founded in 1905 as the
University Farm to back UC's agricultural program; a campus in Riverside, opened

in 1907 as the Citrus Experiment Station; Santa Barbara College (1909) acquired by legislative fiat in 1944; and, most conspicuously, UCLA, founded in 1919 with the acquisition of the Los Angeles State Normal School (1881). In the 1950s, Riverside (1954), Santa Barbara (1958), and Davis (1959) were designated general campuses authorized to offer undergraduate and graduate programs leading to the Ph.D.

Whatever the difficulties involved, and there were many, given Berkeley's long dominance, UCLA was en route by the 1960s to its long-sought parity with Berkeley as a flagship campus. UC Davis, already possessed of a strong academic and institutional identity, made the transition to a general campus in the 1960s—law, medicine, and veterinary science being added to its already world-renowned animal husbandry and agricultural programs, including the growing field of oenology—with great success. Riverside and Santa Barbara, by contrast, were slower to gear up for campus status. Inland Riverside suffered from a serious smog problem through the 1960s. Santa Barbara, an easygoing party school, suffered a form of culture shock as its small (2,380) student body and faculty adjusted to the more demanding UC system. As president of UC, Clark Kerr guided the transition of UC San Francisco from a medical facility focusing on treatment and the training of practitioners to a medical facility undertaking federally sponsored advanced research. As equitably as possible, Kerr advanced the causes of the newly designated general campuses, appointing effective administrators as chancellors, visiting each campus personally, supplementing the library budgets of UC Berkeley and UCLA to serve as backup libraries for the developing campuses in their regions. Under the direction of the renowned Lawrence Clark Powell, university librarian from 1944 to 1960—a tireless bookman with a doctorate from the University of Dijon, a library degree from Berkeley, a flair for writing, a love of jazz, Mozart, and sports cars, and a genius for library promotion and collection development—the UCLA library had by 1960 achieved national rank.

To serve as chancellor at UCLA, Kerr appointed Franklin Murphy, M.D., chancellor and former dean of medicine at the University of Kansas. Serving from 1960 to 1968, Murphy—an upwardly mobile midwesterner fitting perfectly into the upper echelon of an upwardly mobile midwestern city—had become by the end of the decade, as many put it, Dr. Clout. Murphy came to UCLA at a time that the City of Angels was itself coming into its own, and he skillfully positioned UCLA to serve as the cutting edge and embodiment of that new maturity. An avid art collector, he turned the campus into a modern sculpture garden and was named a trustee of the National Gallery of Art in Washington. An erudite bookman, he built a magnificent new University Research Library, opening in 1964 with seats for fifteen hundred readers and shelving for 750,000 volumes. Altogether, Murphy built thirty-one new buildings during his tenure. Operating through deans and department heads, Murphy recruited talented faculty members, senior and junior, from Europe and Latin America as well as the United States. An experienced medical administrator, Murphy helped propel the UCLA medical school and hospital complex into the front ranks of American medicine. Within the decade, UCLA found itself transformed from a commuter school with a regional reputation into one of the leading universities of the nation. The chemistry department alone had two Nobel laureates by 1966. When Murphy arrived at UCLA, the enrollment was seventeen thousand. It had passed twenty-nine thousand by 1968. While Berkeley and other UC campuses were frequently paralyzed by demonstrations or other forms of dissent throughout the 1960s, UCLA remained virtually untouched by such disturbances. The Super Chief (another one of his names) rarely missed a football game, spending most second halves pacing up and down behind the team bench, especially if UCLA was trailing. Gregarious and diplomatic, dapper in his trademark blue blazer and gray flannel slacks, Murphy became the oligarch's oligarch, community leader and confidante to the movers and shakers who were boosting Los Angeles by its bootstraps.

To the chancellorship of UC Berkeley, Kerr appointed Glenn Seaborg, professor of chemistry and associate director of the Radiation Laboratory, a UCLA graduate (1934) with a Ph.D. from Berkeley (1937) and a Nobel Prize in chemistry (1951). Forty-five at the time of his appointment in 1958, living in suburban Lafayette with his wife and six children, Seaborg turned out to be an extraordinarily effective chancellor. Seaborg's brief tenure in that office, before being called to Washington by President Kennedy in 1961 to chair the Atomic Energy Commission, constituted a brief golden age, a calm before an impending storm. Easy of manner, impeccably credentialed as an academic, Seaborg enjoyed the respect and goodwill of the UC Berkeley community. He administered the campus—twenty-two thousand students, sixteen hundred faculty, seven of them Nobel laureates as of 1960, a staff of six thousand, an annual operating budget of $50 million—with the help of three part-time vice-chancellors: philosopher Edward Strong, a future chancellor, literary scholar James D. Hart, and psychologist Alex Sherriffs, their time consumed with some sixty-two building projects totaling $129 million in construction costs. As in the case of the other UC campuses, hiring was in full swing, and Berkeley was bringing on board a crop of promising new faculty, such as future chancellor and Smithsonian secretary Ira Michael Heyman, professor of law and planning, who joined such luminaries as Mark Schorer, Henry Nash Smith, and Josephine Miles of the English department, Travis Bogard and Fred Harris in theater, Henry May in American history, Eugene Burdick in political science (Burdick also served as special assistant to Kerr), and Roger Sessions and Ernest Bloch in music, plus all the Nobels and members of the various academies in engineering and the sciences.

In a manner impossible for the more reserved Clark Kerr, Seaborg was popular with the press, although there could be glitches, as when UC housing officials barred a blind undergraduate because she wanted to live in the dorm with her seeing-eye dog. Very publicly and to the press's satisfaction, Seaborg chewed out the bureaucrats. Seaborg's key crisis, however, was athletic: the breakup of the trouble-ridden Pacific Coast Conference, reformed in June 1959 as the Athletic Association of Western Universities, dominated by the Big Five—Cal, UCLA, USC, Stanford, and Washington—all this handled expertly by Seaborg and Professor Frank Kidner.

Seaborg loved athletics and attended as many events as possible. In the fall of 1958, Don Bowden, a Berkeley undergraduate, became the first American to break the four-minute mile. The next year, coached by Pete Newell, the Cal Berkeley basketball team won the NCAA national championship. In later years, somewhat wistfully, Clark Kerr stated that Glenn Seaborg, had he stayed on as chancellor at Berkeley, would have been able to handle the disruptions of 1964.

As president, Kerr was in the process of planning three new campuses: San Diego (1959), built around the Scripps Institution of Oceanography (1912); Irvine (1965), located on the Irvine Ranch in western Orange County; and Santa Cruz (1965), on the former Cowell Ranch on a two-thousand-acre site overlooking Monterey Bay. The development of these three campuses, together with the upgrading of Riverside and Santa Barbara, and the further expansion of Davis, constituted the single greatest achievement of Clark Kerr's presidency: the realization of a nine-campus university, with strong local identities and administrative authority. In ethos, ambience, architecture, and physical setting, each campus embodied an implicitly utopian statement of differing California possibilities. Berkeley was already the classical city of learning on a hill, and UCLA celebrated the Mediterranean metaphor that was at the core of the Southern California identity. The medical campus atop Parnassus Heights in San Francisco bespoke the urbanism of California's first important American city. Davis vividly evoked the state's long association with agriculture. Set beside the Pacific, Santa Barbara could not help but embody California as coastal resort. In its development the Santa Barbara campus had to struggle with this resort metaphor, ultimately domesticating it as a university with a special sensitivity to aesthetics, the arts, philosophy, and religion. Riverside, like Davis, had origins in agriculture, in this case citrus, but the great orange groves that once swept from Riverside to the sea were no more, and the city of Riverside itself seemed to have been left behind by time, a Victorian enclave centered on the Mission Inn. Yet UC Riverside staked a claim for UC in the gritty Inland Empire, thereby conferring on an elite university a populist connection that accrued to its political advantage.

Kerr had definite ideas regarding planning considerations for each campus. Each campus had to be located in a beautiful place as well as have an academic focus. Situated on the bluffs of La Jolla overlooking the Pacific, San Diego would reflect California's long relationship with the sciences. It would be a Caltech sort of a place, building on the established identity of the Scripps Institution of Oceanography as a science-oriented center for advanced research. UC San Diego would recruit senior professors with proven track records and promising graduate students. (The strategy worked. In two short decades, UC San Diego ranked among the top ten science campuses in the nation.) Set in Orange County, the center of a master-planned development of the Irvine Ranch, UC Irvine would reflect the university as planned community. For inspiration, Kerr turned to one of his favorite books as an undergraduate: *Der isolierte Staat* (1863), a pioneering treatise by Johann Heinrich von Thünen on the planning of a model city through a series of interrelated concentric circles proceeding outward from the central city to industrial zones, to housing, to agriculture. Working with architect and planner William Pereira, Kerr created for Irvine a comparable scheme with central academic buildings radiating outward to interconnected structures grouped around the major disciplines, ringed by two tiers of parking, with rings of residence halls, fraternities, sororities, and playing fields in between the parking lots. Once built, UC Irvine reflected in its rhythms of decon-struction, decentralization, and interconnectedness the rise of Orange County as a comparably decentralized yet interconnected suburban metropolis.

In his Godkin Lectures, Kerr frankly discussed a conspicuous deficiency in the developing multiversity: its tendency to downgrade undergraduate teaching, indeed, to neglect undergraduates in favor of research and doctoral programs. In the extensive two-volume memoir published shortly before his death, Kerr states that he and his good friend Dean McHenry, professor of political science at UCLA and Kerr's special assistant, were in the aftermath of Kerr's Godkin Lectures plan-ning a counter-revolution against this tendency. While chancellor of Berkeley, Kerr had embarked upon an ambitious program of dormitory construction in the par-tial belief that such structures could perhaps evolve into something resembling the house system at Harvard and the concurrently developing college system at Yale. That was Kerr's hope for Irvine as well, although, as in the case of Berkeley and UCLA, there would be no mandated residential program in the dormitories, and fraternities and sororities would be welcomed. A multi-college system, however, was planned for UC San Diego as it grew and accepted undergraduates, who would be divided into thematically related interdisciplinary colleges offering distinctive pro-grams of instruction and residence.

President of the largest and most prestigious land grant research university in the nation, its flagship campuses fueled by defense-related federal dollars, Kerr could never forget the intimacy of Swarthmore, and the intellectual, psychological, and moral formation he had received there. Nor could McHenry forget the collegial intimacy of Williams, where he had taught for five years. Could such an experi-ence be replicated at UC? At some point in the late 1950s, Kerr and McHenry grew increasingly preoccupied with this notion, and the counter-revolution it expressed. At first, it seemed that such a college could be formed in San Francisco, perhaps in the Presidio, given the fact that UC San Francisco had been authorized in 1960 to create an undergraduate college emphasizing the biological sciences, but the UCSF medical campus declined to spin off a full-fledged undergraduate college. When the regents formally approved Kerr's proposal, his and McHenry's plans grew even more ambitious: the creation of a cluster of residential and instructional col-leges on the Oxbridge model, as was being pursued in Southern California by the Claremont Colleges.

Ever on the lookout for beautiful properties, Kerr turned his attention to the sce-nic mountains of the Coastal Range on the western edge of the San Francisco pen-insula between San Francisco and San Jose. Runoff from such a campus would seep into San Francisco's reservoir lakes, it was discovered, and such a campus would be too close to Stanford to develop its own identity. The thoughts of the regents and Kerr next turned to San Jose. Governor Brown favored Evergreen, a hillside community east of San Jose, but the regents visited the site on a very hot day, and as the sun beat down upon them from the west, Evergreen seemed more an *Arabia Deserta* than a nurturing site for a UC campus. Their attention next turned to the Almaden Valley west of San Jose, and it soon became the regents' and Kerr's first choice. Between seventy and eighty parcels, however, would have to be assembled for a campus, and this could take years. Smog, moreover, was proving a problem, given the growth of the region, fueled by the rise of the electronics and aerospace. And so thoughts turned further southward to the Cowell Ranch on the Santa Cruz peninsula.

In later years, Kerr would reflect wistfully on the San Jose option, now that San Jose was the third-largest city in the state and the de facto capital of Silicon Valley. A UC San Jose would have played a part in this evolution. Its faculty would have flourished as inventors and consultants. Faculty and staff spouses would have found employment in its economy. Proximity to San Jose and the multi-centered suburban metropolis radiating from Sunnyvale would have kept UC San Jose connected to the challenges and disciplining forces of urbanism. UC and Stanford had been founded in exurban circumstances, but they had developed strong connections to San Francisco, and in each case stimulating communities and spin-off industries had grown up around them. The city-centric synergy characteristic of UC San Francisco and UCLA was flourishing from the first at UC San Diego, and an exurban or sub/urban connection was showing strong signs of development at Davis and Irvine.

Instead of a city, the regents were settling upon a beautiful but remote site sealed off by a mountain range, connected to the rest of California by the winding and woefully inadequate Highway 17, one of the most treacherous roadways in the state. These redwood-girded slopes by the shores of the sundown sea were beautiful, too beautiful perhaps, Kerr would later suggest, too escapist for serious academic work. Here was a dilemma a hundred years in duration: whether Californians had a tendency to substitute scenery for serious thought—indeed, whether a first-rate culture was possible in such Arcadian settings. Critics of California frequently leveled one or another version of this charge, but even Californians worried about it subconsciously or even explicitly in novels, poems, and other forms of imaginative literature.

Then there was another issue, discernible only to the most perceptive at the time: namely, that significant sectors of American society, including many of the undergraduates of California and the faculty who taught them, were on the verge of a rebellion against a full spectrum of political, sexual, and cultural constraints. This rebellion would soon bring Berkeley to the brink. It would also cause such an established institution as Stanford intermittent periods of disquiet. To establish an undergraduate-oriented utopia beneath the isolated redwoods of Santa Cruz County—placing an experimental, hence volatile, cluster of colleges in a void, its only quasi-urban influence nearby being a onetime lumbering capital turned fading Coney Island, which did not want the university there in the first place—was to take a chance that things would turn out not exactly as expected. It could turn out to be

Oxbridge on the Coast, as planned. Then again, it could become a Teddy Bears' Picnic for college kids and faculty—or even something worse. Neither Kerr, McHenry, nor the regents could be expected to read the tea leaves.

At Kerr's recommendation, the regents appointed McHenry chancellor of UC Santa Cruz, expected to open in the fall of 1965 as a cluster of colleges. At the beginning of his Godkin Lectures, Kerr had wrestled with the non-utilitarian purity of John Henry Newman's ideal and had returned to it in conclusion. Newman presented a challenge that would not go away: the notion that higher education, especially for undergraduates, had as its goal intellectual and social formation (moral formation would follow, Newman hoped) and employed as its primary teaching technique a personalized explication of great texts. In creating UC Santa Cruz, Clark Kerr was doing his best to reform the multiversity—which tended to neglect undergraduate teaching in favor of graduate instruction and research—and the Cold War campuses the multiversity had created. Kerr was returning forward, back to the future, to the same medieval ideal that had shaped Newman himself at Trinity and Oriel. The very architecture and groupings of the UC Santa Cruz colleges, upon Kerr's explicit recommendation, were modeled upon the medieval French city Aigues-Mortes, a walled enclave surrounded by forests.

In the fall of 1965, Cowell College, the first of nine residential colleges, opened its doors to students. Kerr and his wife Kay were on campus for the occasion, dining with students and faculty in the field house which was serving as the first dining hall, visiting after dinner in the trailers in which students were living pending the completion of construction. "It was a beautiful evening," Kerr later remembered, "with warm breezes blowing in from the ocean. There was a full moon. The students welcomed us with such enthusiasm and expressions of appreciation for what we were doing for them. Some wrote poems for us. It was for Kay and me one of the greatest evenings of our lives."[8]

Four years later, in June 1969, Kerr accepted an invitation from these same students, the first graduating class of the new campus. In four short years, however, things had changed dramatically. As he sat on the stage alongside McHenry during commencement, Kerr could feel a palpable hostility in the air. Some students made expressions of contempt as they came onstage to receive their degrees. Some went so far as to throw their diplomas at Kerr or McHenry. Still another group seized the stage and hijacked the commencement through a form of guerrilla theater. Their leader harangued Kerr and McHenry for creating Santa Cruz "as a capitalistic-imperialist-fascist plot to divert the students from their revolution against the evils of American society and, in particular, against the horrors of the Vietnam War." The guerrilla theater students then proceeded to honor Black Panther leader Huey Newton, jailed on charges of murder, with an honorary degree. They then asked the audience to rise in appreciation of all that Huey Newton and the Black Panthers had accomplished. Most of the students rose, but not their parents. To Kerr's horror, virtually the entire faculty—with the conspicuous exception of Kenneth Thiemann, the provost of Crown College—rose as well. Taking to the rostrum, Kerr threw away his prepared text and spoke movingly about his and McHenry's Santa Cruz dream, dating back to their time together as graduate students at Stanford and continuing across their long careers at UC. He was against the war as well, Kerr stated, but such behavior as he had just witnessed seemed contrary to the high ideals the students professed to hold. "I then sat down," Kerr said of the occasion. "Several years passed before I visited the campus again. What most impressed me was how such a high proportion of the faculty had stood on their feet to applaud the students who were attacking the campus the faculty had by then created. It was one of the worst afternoons of my life."[9] There would be even worse afternoons to come. One thing, however, was certain. No one would ever mistake UC Santa Cruz for a Cold War campus.

Two months before Pearl Harbor, San Francisco developer Henry Doelger (left) reviews plans with furniture store owner Charles Redlick (center) for a model home on 38th Avenue in the Sunset District that served in the postwar era as a prototype for the development of southwestern San Francisco and Daly City. *San Francisco History Center, San Francisco Public Library.*

Mass production techniques perfected in 1944–1945 by homebuilders Fritz Burns and Henry J. Kaiser allowed for the rapid development of the San Fernando Valley in the postwar era. *Los Angeles Examiner, Regional History Collection, University of Southern California.*

Just as the Bing Crosby song had predicted as the war drew to a close, thousands of Californians and newcomers to the state were choosing to make the San Fernando Valley their home. *Dick Whittington, Regional History Collection, University of Southern California.*

By February 1952 residents of the new Lakewood suburb near Long Beach were shopping at a windowless, fluorescent-lit May Company department store whose escalators were capable of moving 8,000 people per hour. *Los Angeles Examiner, Regional History Collection, University of Southern California.*

To serve the growing San Fernando Valley and other California suburbs, the Division of Highways embarked upon an epic of freeway construction. *Los Angeles Examiner, Regional History Collection, University of Southern California.*

Walt Disney wanted Disneyland to evoke the past, present, and future of suburban development across the nation. *Los Angeles Examiner, Regional History Collection, University of Southern California.*

Landscape architect Thomas Church envisioned suburban California as developed garden. *Carolyn Caddes, Bancroft Library.*

For the university he was building atop Alcalá Heights, Bishop Charles Buddy (left) preferred a historically oriented architectural metaphor, San Diego as Spanish Renaissance city. *San Diego Historical Society.*

Still, Tiki too had its adherents, among them the Barnaby Conrads, arriving for an evening at Trader Vic's, San Francisco, shrine of Tiki in Northern California. *Bancroft Library.*

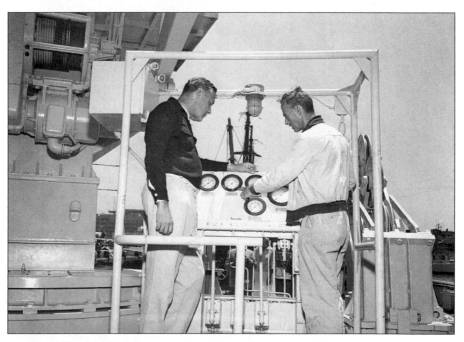

Roger Revelle (left) of the Scripps Institution of Oceanography envisioned San Diego as an epicenter of scientific research. *San Diego Historical Society.*

Investor-entrepreneur C. Arnholt Smith (center) wanted to develop San Diego into a ranking American city with a high-rise skyline. *San Diego Historical Society.*

Posing for a publicity photo for *Only in San Francisco* (1961), *Chronicle* columnist Herb Caen provided the city with a narrative of itself as Baghdad by the Bay that lasted for a half-century. *Doubleday and Company, San Francisco History Center, San Francisco Public Library.*

With a grateful UN Ambassador Henry Cabot Lodge as backup, Mayor George Christopher (center) in September 1959 rescued the hitherto disastrous visit of Soviet Premier Nikita Khrushchev to the United States, thereby confirming the reputation of San Francisco as Everyone's Favorite City. *News-Call Bulletin, San Francisco History Center, San Francisco Public Library.*

Posing on Fisherman's Wharf, symphony maestro Pierre Monteux divided his time between San Francisco and Paris, thus reinforcing San Francisco's sense of itself as the most European of American cities. *RCA Victor Records, San Francisco History Center, San Francisco Public Library.*

Resplendent in white tie and tails in the Garden Court of the Palace Hotel, writer Lucius Beebe found San Francisco a refuge from the twentieth century. *Holiday, San Francisco History Center, San Francisco Public Library.*

Decorated in Victorian splendor, the historic offices on Montgomery Street of attorney Melvin Belli served as a fixed stop for Grayline tours of San Francisco. *Holiday, San Francisco History Center, San Francisco Public Library.*

Lawrence Ferlinghetti and the other poets of the City Lights circle in North Beach found bohemia and political dissent in a city emerging as the capital of an Alternative America. *Larry Keenan Jr., The Bancroft Library.*

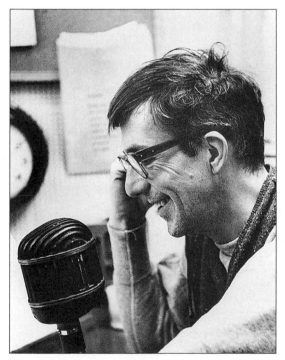

Beloved by morning commuters, KSFO disc jockey Don Sherwood was hip to Zen, existentialism, cool jazz, and zany humor as he helped pioneer a new wave of subversive comedy. *San Francisco History Center, San Francisco Public Library.*

A woman of influence, vision, and will, Dorothy Buffum Chandler dreamt of upgrading metropolitan Los Angeles through the creation of a performing arts center atop Bunker Hill. *Times-Mirror, Regional History Collection, University of Southern California.*

Such a facility, Chandler believed, would unite the city and symbolize its coming of age as a cultural force. *Welton Becket and Associates, Herald-Examiner, Los Angeles Public Library.*

So too did Paul Williams's signature structure at the Los Angeles International Airport herald the City of Angels as Super City, Metropolis of the Future. *Los Angeles Examiner, Regional History Collection, University of Southern California.*

Starting with *The Martian Chronicles* (1950), writer and urban theorist Ray Bradbury used science fiction to interpret the losses and gains of development. As a planner, Bradbury recommended that Los Angeles County boost itself even further into the future through a network of monorails. *Palms-Rancho Park Branch, Los Angeles Public Library.*

Will and Ariel Durant
considered Los Angeles the
perfect place from which to
contemplate and chronicle
for a popular audience the
rise and fall of civilizations.
Herald Examiner Collection,
Los Angeles Public Library.

Officially welcoming the
Dodgers to Los Angeles
in ceremonies on the
steps of City Hall, Mayor
Norris Poulson (left)
presents Dodgers owner
Walter O'Malley with
a replica of home plate
signed by the city council.
Or was it a replica of
the Stone Tablets, as
O'Malley's non-negotiable
conditions for bringing the
Dodgers to Los Angeles
were derisively called?
Los Angeles Examiner,
Regional History
Collection, University of
Southern California.

The Arechiga family remained unimpressed. It took a phalanx of sheriff's deputies to remove the Arechigas from their homes at Chavez Ravine, the future site of Dodger Stadium. *Los Angeles Examiner, Regional History Collection, University of Southern California.*

In November 1961, pitcher Don Drysdale enjoyed the comfort of one of the 47,964 seats and the uninterrupted sightlines of the newly completed Dodger Stadium. *United Press International Photo, Regional History Collection, University of Southern California.*

Keeping the City of Angels safe and the LAPD on the cutting edge were the lifelong passions of Police Chief William Henry Parker, who was in a rare good mood one morning in August 1954 as he accepted the keys to a fleet of newly purchased Ford patrol cars. *Art Streib Photographers, Regional History Collection, University of Southern California.*

Jack Webb (second from right) was so convincing as LAPD Sergeant Joe Friday on the long-running television series *Dragnet*, Chief Parker asked him to help interview prospective candidates for the police academy. *Los Angeles Herald-Express, Regional History Collection, University of Southern California.*

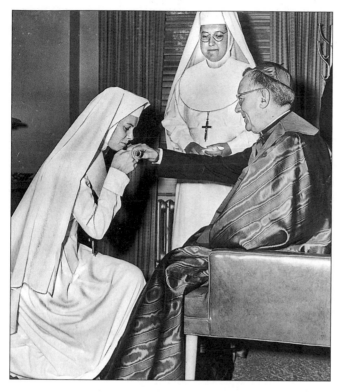

Accustomed to deference, Los Angeles archbishop James Francis Cardinal McIntyre ran a tight ship. *Los Angeles Examiner, Regional History Collection, University of Southern California.*

Too tight a ship, complained a lowly curate, William DuBay, who sent a fourteen-page telegram to Pope Paul VI calling for the Cardinal's removal. *Los Angeles Herald-Examiner, Regional History Collection, University of Southern California.*

Honeymooning off the coast of Catalina in August 1954, California governor Goodwin J. Knight had dreams of the presidency. Soon, however, the Republican center would collapse, and by mid-1958 Knight was finished politically. *Los Angeles Examiner, Regional History Collection, University of Southern California.*

Knight's successor, Democratic governor Edmund G. (Pat) Brown, loved to fish in the mountain streams of the Sierra Nevada. *Bill Knight, Los Angeles Evening Mirror-News, Bancroft Library.*

What equally thrilled the governor, following the passage of Proposition 1 in November 1960, was the prospect of a State Water Project that would impound and channel the runoff waters of Northern California now flowing wastefully into the sea. *Ken Whitmore, Bancroft Library.*

The runaway water development of California, argued conservationist David Brower and a small group of anti-growth activists, was a self-fulfilling prophecy. More water meant more people, and more people meant more water projects. *Tom Turner, Bancroft Library.*

At a time of unprecedented affluence, many young Californians of the Silent Generation, in the suburbs especially, enjoyed the use of personal automobiles, necessitating the construction of parking lots at high schools and colleges. *Associated Press, Regional History Collection, University of Southern California.*

To educate this rising generation, Bakersfield assemblywoman Dorothy Donohoe co-sponsored legislation creating a master plan for higher education. *Los Angeles Examiner, Los Angeles Public Library.*

At the apex of this higher educational system stood the University of California, whose president Clark Kerr proclaimed an impending role in American society for a comprehensive institution he called the multiversity. *Steven Marcus, Bancroft Library.*

For aspiring writer Joan Didion, Class of 1956, the University of California at Berkeley represented California's best idea of itself. *Dominick Dunne, Bancroft Library.*

As of March 1950 Dianne Goldman (later Feinstein) was a junior at the Convent of the Sacred Heart in San Francisco, competing for the title of Rodeo Queen of the Grand National Junior Livestock Exposition and Arena Show. Feinstein later graduated from Stanford, Class of 1955, where she lay down the foundations for a future political career by winning election to the student body vice presidency. *The Call-Bulletin San Francisco History Center, San Francisco Public Library.*

The MRS, however, remained an attractive degree for the women of the Silent Generation, as evident in late May 1955 when some fifty UCLA senior coeds happily announced their engagements in annual ritual by parading through a ring of pansies. *Los Angeles Examiner, Regional History Collection, University of Southern California.*

In November 1961 President John F. Kennedy dropped by the Questionettes'
Courante Ball at the Beverly Hilton Hotel to pay his respects to the debutantes.
Nat King Cole provided the introductions. *Associated Press, Regional History
Collection, University of Southern California.*

Since the 1930s, at nightclubs like the Downbeat, African American Los Angeles
had been enjoying great jazz, a genre through which the community defined itself.
Shades of LA Archives, Los Angeles Public Library.

Cooled down and cerebral, the Dave Brubeck Quartet took jazz mainstream, making of it a point of identity for the college generation. *Dave Brubeck Archives, University of the Pacific.*

Embarking aboard the Italian liner *MV Saturnia* for a European vacation, writer Christopher Isherwood and his partner Don Bachardy were by October 1955 pursuing a relationship that would eventually elevate them, according to Armisted Maupin, to the rank of First Couple of Gay America. *Regional History Collection, University of Southern California.*

Dissent was in the air, as evident in these pickets gathered in Union Square, San Francisco in February 1960 to protest the scheduled execution of Caryl Chessman. *Bancroft Library.*

An actor with a lively interest in politics by the name of Ronald Reagan was as of June 1958 serving as a spokesman for General Electric. An impending age of dissent would send Reagan to the governor's office in Sacramento and the Oval Office in Washington, DC. *Los Angeles Examiner, Regional History Collection, University of Southern California.*

9

Freeways to the Future

An Epic of Construction on Behalf
of the Automobile

IN September 1958, in the capital city of Sacramento, the Division of Highways of the Department of Public Works submitted to the Joint Interim Committee on Highway Problems of the California legislature *The California Freeway System*, a retrospective report and master plan for future construction. Impressively illustrated, the thirty-seven-page document constituted a past, present, and future definition of California through its freeway system. Like two other such government documents in this period—*The California Water Plan* (1957) and *The Master Plan for Higher Education* (1960)—*The California Freeway System* represented a species of quasi-utopian planning in its comprehensive vision of the entire state unified and brought to new levels of efficiency and pleasure, in this case through a statewide grid of harmoniously interconnected roads, highways, and freeways, either existent, under construction, or slated for development. The report appeared, moreover, as the Division of Highways was completing the first decade of a multi-billion-dollar epic of freeway construction that had begun in the late 1940s and would continue for nearly a half century.

In its sheer faith in freeways as a defining element of California as emergent mega-state, the report, like so much else in this era, constituted a triumph of modernist planning as well as a testimony to the fact that Californians had long since wedded themselves to the automobile as fact and symbol of their way of life. While the more settled societies of the East and Midwest had adapted to the automobile, California—in its distances, its population growth, its postwar suburban explosion, its expectations for personal mobility and on-demand gratification—seemed to many observers to be in the process of being literally re-created socially, culturally, and spatially by automobiles and freeways. By the 1920s, the automobile was showing its capacity—very dramatically in the case of Southern California—to alter street usage, building types, and the larger architectural environment. Photographs from the era document the influence of the automobile as it transformed such Los Angeles roadways as Vermont, Wilshire, Fairfax, Western, Hoover, and Figueroa into commercial arteries, while at the same time upgrading the auto court into the motel and re-creating the restaurant, the laundry/dry cleaner, the movie theater, even the bank, into drive-in facilities. Drive-to markets—some of them expanded into multi-store retail complexes destined to morph into shopping centers in the postwar era—were emerging across the nation, and nowhere more noticeably than in Los Angeles in such places as Westwood Village, the Farmers Market on Fairfax, the Mission Motor-Inn Market on Sunset, the Beverly Open-Air Market on Beverly, and the Plaza Market on Pico. Equally automobile-oriented were Bullock's department store (1929), the Pellissier Building (1930–31), and the pioneering Ralph's supermarket (1928) on Wilshire.

In 1896, almost simultaneously with the invention of the automobile, California state government took the first steps toward a statewide roadway system with the issuance of a report calling for standards for road construction and other related matters. In 1910 voters approved an $18 million bond issue for roadway improvement. Established in August 1911, a three-person California Highway Commission called for surveys, plans, and construction of a statewide highway system based on two highways from Mexico to Oregon, one on the coast, the other through the interior, from which connections would be made to every county seat in the state. A year later, construction began on historic El Camino Real, beneath a stately stand of eucalyptus trees in Burlingame, San Mateo County, establishing the first increment of this system. Just as El Camino Real had defined Spanish California, it was pointed out, so too would this new highway system define, eventually, the twentieth-century state. By 1925, just eight years into its statewide program, California stood criss-crossed by a 6,400-mile network of highways, the majority of them paved, augmented by paved and unpaved county roads.

Initially known as automotive parkways in New York state, where they were first developed in the mid-1920s, freeways were roadways uninterrupted at grade, allowing for continuous, unbroken traffic. In Germany, where they were perfected as a genre in the 1930s, they were known as *Autobahnen*. The automotive freeway came to California just before World War II. On 30 December 1940, a caravan of more than four hundred automobiles, led by E. Raymond Cato, chief of the Highway Patrol, traveled north on the newly completed Arroyo Seco Parkway to the Fair Oaks Avenue exit to dedicate the structure. With the assistance of Sally Stanton, queen of the 1941 Pasadena Rose Festival, Governor Culbert Olson cut a ribbon of roses stretching across the parkway linking Los Angeles and Pasadena. Two days earlier, in a preliminary ceremony, Chief Tahachwee of the Kawie Indians passed a peace pipe to Frank Clark, director of public works for the state. Amid the beating of tribal drums, Chief Tahachwee formally transferred the rights of his people to the Arroyo Seco and blessed the completed parkway. In his dedication address, Governor Olson extolled the $12 million parkway as a model of things to come. Already, the governor pointed out, the California Highway Commission had designated 91.4 miles of state highways for freeway development. Work was under way on a Cahuenga Freeway leading from Hollywood into the San Fernando Valley, and plans were being developed to convert the Bayshore Highway between Palo Alto and San Francisco into a freeway and to construct a similar freeway between Oakland and San Jose in the East Bay. Automotive traffic in California, the governor predicted, would be increasing by 25 percent over the next ten years, and California would have need of a swift and safe freeway system. During 1939, in Los Angeles County alone, the governor pointed out, 962 people had been killed on the road and 23,898 injured. Freeways would reduce such statistics.

During the war years, the heavy trucks and other vehicles of the armed forces and supporting industries pounded the highways of California mercilessly. Construction of highways was brought to a virtual halt, although in metropolitan Los Angeles, three federally funded projects continued: an extension of the Arroyo Seco Parkway into the downtown; a 3.7-mile freeway serving Terminal Island requested by the Navy and begun in 1940; and a 3.5-mile segment of the Ramona Parkway (renamed the San Bernardino in 1954) crossing over the Los Angeles River at Aliso Street and ending in Boyle Heights.

Throughout 1943 and 1944, state government and the private-sector freeway lobby continued to envision a postwar California actualized by freeways. As early as the legislative session of 1943, Governor Earl Warren successfully urged the legislature to appropriate $12 million for highway planning in the postwar era. The 1943 legislature also reorganized the State Highway Commission, adding Charles H. Purcell, the state director of public works, as an ex officio member and chairman, thus creating Purcell, in his fusion of commission and administrative power a highway czar, a Robert Moses for California. Also in 1943, on a local level, the Los Angeles County Regional Planning Commission issued a comprehensive and visionary report, *Freeways for the Region*, that summarized, intensified, and took forward a decade of freeway planning by Los Angeles County. In 1946 the Automobile Club of Southern California, the California State Automobile Association, the California Chamber of Commerce, the League of California Cities, and the County Supervisors Association of California formed a joint California Major Highway Development Committee that began to lobby for an expanded postwar program. In November that year, the state Highway Division—at the request of legislators being lobbied—issued a call for a $680 million highway/freeway construction program in the first decade of the postwar era. The federal Highway Act of 1944, meanwhile, guaranteed California $67 million in federal funds for highway construction in the first three years of the postwar era. With the end of the war in August 1945 came the end of gas rationing, and statewide traffic increased by 25 percent within the year. In the first half of 1946, automobile use jumped 53 percent over 1945.

Clearly, an ambitious program of postwar highway and freeway construction was impending. But how to pay for it? No one was worrying more about this problem than State Senator Randolph Collier of Yreka, a Republican representing a district adjacent to the Oregon border and longtime chair of the state transportation committee. Collier's concern came from his conviction that the northern regions of California, including his own district, would have to be integrated through freeways and expressways with the rest of the state if they were ever to experience their desired levels of economic and social development. In 1945 Collier, urged on by Governor Warren, introduced Senate Concurrent Resolution 27, establishing a joint fact-finding committee on highways, streets, and bridges to take a comprehensive look at the entire question of construction needs, costs, and revenues.

Out of these and other deliberations emerged the Collier-Burns Highway Act of 1947, raising the gas tax from 3 cents to 4.5 cents per gallon and registration fees for automobiles from $3 to $6 per year, along with an increase in weight taxes for trucks. Revenues were to be put into a Highway Trust Fund to finance construction planning and development. Oregon, Colorado, and New Mexico pioneered such a concept in 1919, and by 1929 every state in the nation had such a program, including California, which had established its first gasoline tax in 1923. The Collier-Burns Highway Act was passed by the legislature and signed by Governor Warren in June 1947. The act made possible the epic of highway/freeway construction that unfolded across the next two decades.

The 1950s witnessed the act expanded and augmented with federal funds as California automobilized its society. As of September 1950, the state was spending nearly $100 million a year on its highway program. By 1962 the Division of Highways was spending $633.5 million annually. How did California get there? By raising taxes. In 1953 the state passed the Lincoln Highway Act, raising the gasoline tax from 4.5 cents to 6 cents per gallon and the diesel tax from 4.5 cents to 7 cents. Other highway-related taxes, with the exception of those on buses and rental trucks, were raised by the proportionate 33 percent. The increases mandated by the Lincoln Highway Act were supposed to be reduced at the end of two years, but subsequent legislation sustained these levels indefinitely and, in 1963, granted another 1 cent increase, bringing the gas tax to 7 cents a gallon.

Federal highway taxes, meanwhile, were being increased to 2 cents per gallon in 1951, 3 cents per gallon in 1956, and 4 cents per gallon in 1959. In 1956, building upon concepts first advanced in the Federal-Aid Highway Act of 1944, augmented by the Federal-Aid Highway Act of 1952, Congress passed and President Eisenhower signed the Federal-Aid Highway Act of 1956, more commonly known as the National Interstate and Defense Highways Act of 1956. The act called for the creation by 1972 of a 41,000-mile interstate highway system, with the federal government paying 90 percent of construction costs from a highway trust fund dedicated exclusively to this program. Few acts in American history have had such a profound effect on American society than this act envisioning the entire nation unified through a freeway/express-way system. By the end of 1957, federal aid was accounting for 29 percent of the street, road, and highway dollars being spent in California. Constructed through the 1960s and 1970s, the interstate system represents the third chapter—a 2,100-mile chapter—of freeway development in California, with the San Diego, Golden State, Santa Monica, San Bernardino, Foothill, and San Gabriel River freeways built with federal funds.

In 1951 State Senator Collier commissioned from the Division of Highways a survey that documented California's eleven thousand miles of highways and freeways as woefully inadequate for future needs. This report led to the Lincoln Highway Act of 1953 and to Senate Concurrent Resolution 26 during the 1957 legislature commissioning even more comprehensive twenty-year master plan, *The California Freeway System* (1958), prepared with the assistance of the Institute of Transportation and Traffic Engineering at UC Berkeley. To review this report nearly a half century after it was issued is to re-experience a generation's faith in what the automobile and freeways could bring to California in social, economic, and cultural terms. It envisions the entire state, including the sparsely settled far north, the eastern side of the Sierra Nevada, and the desert regions of the southeast, unified through an integrated freeway grid. In 1959 the report led to legislation classifying more than twelve thousand miles of highways as state freeways and calling for a continuing program of planning and construction under the jurisdiction of the California Highway Commission, which was upgraded to a semi-autonomous governmental entity along the lines of the University of California.

The California Freeway System resulted in Senate Bill 480, introduced by State Senator Collier, calling for a $10.5 billion freeway/expressway construction program across the next twenty years. Signing the Freeway and Expressway Act of 1959, Governor Edmund G. (Pat) Brown described the occasion as momentous. In one sense, however, the bill, as notable as it might be, could also be seen as an effort to upgrade, further systematize, and project forward a program upon which California was already embarked. One freeway, the Arroyo Seco, had been completed by 1941, and three others—Terminal Island, the Hollywood, the Ramona—were under construction. All in all, metropolitan Los Angeles County had some 613 miles of freeways planned by February 1946. To survey the *California Highway and Public Works* magazine of the Division of Highways from the late 1940s forward is to encounter through maps and photographs a growing network of freeway sinews expanding through the population centers of the state as segment after segment of completed freeways are brought online by construction contractors. Aerial photographs depicting freeways cutting through cities, suburbs, and agricultural regions, to include bean fields rapidly en route to becoming suburbs, are especially evocative of this growing network. By September 1950 California had fourteen thousand miles of state highways serving an estimated 10.875 million people driving 4.58 million motor vehicles. A 1952 map depicting freeway construction progress in the Los Angeles metropolitan region demonstrated the ambition of District 7 plans as seven freeways, including a connection between a proposed Harbor Freeway and the existing Arroyo Seco Parkway, began to define themselves as a network linking Los Angeles, Orange, San Bernardino, and Ventura counties.

The building of freeway-related bridges, meanwhile, was proceeding apace under the direction of chief bridge engineer F. W. Panhorst, a University of Illinois–trained specialist in naval architecture and bridges, who had played an important role in the construction of the San Francisco–Oakland Bay Bridge in the prewar era. Under construction since March 1953, the upper deck of the Richmond–San Rafael Bridge across the northern portion of San Francisco Bay was ready by September 1956. More of a causeway than a bridge, a freeway across the water, the Richmond–San Rafael Bridge linked Marin County directly to Contra Costa County in the northeast Bay Area and the San Joaquin Valley beyond. Governor Knight made a specialty of being on hand for freeway and bridge dedications throughout the mid-1950s and used each occasion to comment upon how well California was doing in its freeway program and how this program embodied the future of the state.

The district maps, meanwhile, being published in *California Highways and Public Works*, especially the maps for District 7, Metropolitan Los Angeles, and District 4, the San Francisco Bay Area, were growing denser and denser in their interconnected black lines of freeways completed or under construction, their dotted lines of freeways budgeted, and their smaller lines of freeway routes being planned. As of 1958, for example, District 7 freeways in various stages of completion, construction, or planning included the Santa Ana, the San Diego, the Laguna, the San Bernardino, the Glendale, the Long Beach, the Ventura, the Riverside, the Santa Monica, the Temescal, the Hollywood, the Golden State, the Pasadena, the Harbor, the Colorado, the Foothill, the Artesia, the Riverside, the Ojai, and the Pacific Coast: each of these thoroughfares facilitating automotive traffic into, from, or through innumerable communities whose economic well-being and spatial forms were either growing up in response to the freeways or being powerfully adapted to them. Nineteen sixty-two witnessed the completion of the Bayshore Freeway from San Francisco to San Jose in January and the Santa Monica Freeway from Santa Monica to downtown Los Angeles in October. Both freeways unified their regions by following and augmenting historic pathways: in the case of the Bayshore, the north-south El Camino Real of the Mission era; in the case of the Santa Monica, the ancient Native American east-west pathway between the village of Yang-Na and the Pacific Ocean, expanded as a cattle trail in the Spanish, Mexican, and frontier American eras and later providing the axis for Wilshire Boulevard. Planning was under way that year as well for the Junípero Serra Freeway linking San Francisco and San Jose north and south along the San Francisco peninsula past the Crystal Springs Reservoir, the campus of Stanford University, and the hills of Los Altos, one of the most beautiful stretches of freeway in the state. By October 1962 the California Highway Commission had passed the halfway mark in the adoption of routes for the 12,241-mile master plan signed into law in 1959.

Who were the civil servants responsible for the design, contracting, and monitoring of this epic program? They were engineers: young, middle-aged, and late middle-aged, white men in the main, although the Division of Highways did have one female engineer as of 1955, Marilyn Jorgenson, a 1948 graduate in civil engineering from the University of Minnesota, busy working on a section of the San Diego Freeway near Venice. (By January 1963 Jorgenson would have seven female engineer colleagues in District 7.) Standards had been set for the division in the prewar era by the formidable Charles Purcell, a 1906 graduate in civil engineering from the University of Nebraska. In 1921 Stanford sociologist Thorstein Veblen published his pathbreaking *The Engineers and the Price System*, in which he predicted that engineers would be to the twentieth century what lawyers had been in the nineteenth and businessmen in the fin de siècle: the energizers, actualizers, and moderators of society. Purcell embodied the Veblen model. He began his career building bridges in Wyoming, followed by a stint with the Guggenheim Corporation in Peru. He then returned to the United States for stints with the Oregon Highway Department and the federal Bureau of Public Roads before being named by Governor Clement C. Young state highway engineer of California in February 1928. Many talents went into the design and construction of the San Francisco–Oakland Bay Bridge, opened to traffic in November 1936, but no one played a more important role than its director, starting from the moment the governor appointed Purcell a member and secretary of the San Francisco–Oakland Bay Bridge Commission. In January 1943 Governor Earl Warren named Purcell director of the entire Department of Public Works. In 1950 Warren appointed Purcell chairman of the Highway Commission as well. No civil servant had ever held such authority in California.

Following the war, Purcell sparked the revitalization of the Division of Highways. Due to the draft and other war-related causes, only nine hundred engineers were on duty by December 1945. That figure stood at twenty-five hundred engineers and a support staff nearing five thousand by 1951. In the late 1940s and early 1950s, the Division of Highways had two types of engineers: those who had entered just before or after World War I, in which many served as engineering officers and now, like Purcell, were nearing retirement; and those who had entered just after World War II, veterans as well, then in their thirties and forties. Typical of the late-middle-aged group, to take one example, was district engineer Milton Harris, an Oregon State graduate who had served as an Army first lieutenant of engineering during World War I and was recalled in 1942. As a lieutenant colonel with the Allied military government, Harris served as traffic engineer for the city of Rome and was decorated by the Italian government and the Vatican. Military service had accustomed the engineers of the Division of Highways to large-scale engineering efforts and sharpened their mobilizing skills.

The engineers at their drawing boards—in the Division of Highways headquarters in an elegant five-story Art Deco building in Sacramento or in one or another of the eleven district offices—or out on construction sites conferring with contractors seemed almost paramilitary in their uniform dress: double-breasted suits and rimless glasses for the middle-aged; crew cuts, horn-rimmed glasses, and short-sleeved white shirts for younger engineers, an array of pens and pencils popping up from their breast pockets. In an age of conformism, they were model conformists, working in a standardized environment, paid at standardized rates, motivated by the same retirement package, living in tract housing, driving similar makes of automobiles, barbecuing in comparable backyards on the weekends. From another perspective, they can be seen as engineering alchemists, turning one California into another

via highway, freeway, and expressway construction, and doing so with an evangelical zeal born of their profession and of their belief in freeways and in California's
future.

Speed was their concern, but so was safety. In dedicating the Arroyo Seco Parkway, Governor Olson had cited safety as an important benefit of freeway design. In
the years that followed, the freeway lobby made frequent reference to the safety factor. Freeways were intended, they argued, to replace such dangerous state highways,
with their high crash and casualty rates, as "Blood Alley" in the San Joaquin Valley
(Highway 152 between Highway 99 and Gilroy) or "Slaughter Alley" in Southern California (Highway 101 between San Diego and San Clemente). An August
1954 report by the engineering department of the Automobile Club of Southern
California was optimistic. The forty-five miles of completed freeways in metropolitan Los Angeles, the report stated, had reduced traffic deaths from 4.65 per 100
million vehicle miles to 2.03. Nevertheless, population growth and the introduction
of millions of new drivers onto the demanding freeways qualified such optimism.
By 1959 the population of California stood at fifteen million, with more than seven
million registered automobiles and seven million licensed drivers, more autos and
drivers than any other state. Racking up sixty-four billion miles in 1958—the equivalent of all the driving in eighteen other states combined—3,510 persons had been
killed and 135,565 injured.

Design engineers at the Division of Highways were struggling against a rising
tide of accidents throughout the decade. Some measures were obvious: A 1947 law
required registered motorists to carry insurance; a 1949 law mandated driver education in high schools; a 1960 law established a speed limit of sixty-five miles per hour
for automobiles, forty-five miles per hour for trucks. By 1959, nearly twenty-five hundred Highway Patrol officers were cruising the eighty-one thousand miles of streets,
highways, and freeways of the state, enforcing safety. Other challenges related to
the design and construction of the freeways themselves. How wide should traffic
lanes be, for example? The *Autobahnen* of Germany required fourteen feet. A cautious Massachusetts was demanding a width of twenty to thirty feet. The engineers
of California struggled with this issue throughout the 1930s before deciding on a
twelve-foot width. Another design challenge was pavement markings to differentiate
lanes. Experiments continued on various techniques until a successful solution—
pavement dots that emitted a rumbling noise when crossed—was decided upon.
While such dots were expensive—$800 per mile to install as of 1964, as opposed to
$100 per mile to paint a stripe—they came increasingly into use.

Also related to the lane problem was the matter of trucks on freeways, with their
tendency to drift from lane to lane or, even worse, to jackknife into adjacent lanes
and cause catastrophic collisions. Throughout the decade, freeway advocates waged
a losing battle to banish trucks from freeways altogether. The all-powerful trucking
industry beat back all such efforts. The width of shoulders for disabled vehicles
was another related problem. Over the decade, shoulder width was consistently
increased.

While roadkill remained a minor nuisance, unless the animal happened to be a large deer, many pedestrian deaths occurred on freeways during this period, beginning with the death in 1948 of Richard Mehling, fifty-seven, who cut a hole in the Cyclone fence along the Ramona Freeway to facilitate his walk to work. Mehling's death anticipated a recurring problem. By 1960 14 percent of fatal freeway accidents involved pedestrians: people with car trouble walking along the outer lane, hitchhikers now and then, but mostly people trying to cross a freeway on foot for one reason or another and becoming human roadkill. One early solution in urban areas was to construct tunnels under freeways, but these tended over time to become danger zones filled with trash or sexual predators. When it came to bridges over freeways, youngsters and teenagers made a sport of walking across their rails, which led to Division of Highway engineers narrowing and rounding them, even installing spikes along the surface. Misbehaving youngsters also had a tendency to drop things on cars below, trying to break windshields. Eight-foot fences across bridges, while unsightly, solved this problem in urban areas, where it was most intense.

Then there was the question of median divides to prevent cars from jumping lanes into oncoming traffic and causing head-on collisions. The first concrete barrier was erected in 1946 on Grapevine Grade (State 99), intended to prevent runaway trucks from crossing into oncoming traffic. Other concrete median divides followed. By 1952, however, concrete barriers had fallen out of fashion. While such barriers might help stop cars or trucks from jumping lanes, the Division of Highways determined, they also increased accidents for drivers losing control of their lanes and running into the median barrier. The death rate from such accidents had increased by 10 percent. A 1957 report by the Division of Highways advocated a variety of solutions, including a steel cable chain-link barrier that, while increasing safety, had aesthetic problems and was not universally adopted. Another problem related to oncoming traffic was glare, which surfaced as a problem as early as the Arroyo Seco. The first solution was to emplace large plants in the dividing strip, but these plants did not prosper under the fifty-mile-per-hour winds created by opposing lanes of traffic. A low fence alternating with plants was then tried, but the problem was never fully solved.

Signage remained a problem—in many ways *the* problem—through the 1950s. Motorists traveling at high speeds had to be able to read freeway signs quickly and accurately if they were to negotiate the system. That meant something as fundamental as reading the alphabet. Initially, capital letters were exclusively employed before a return in 1949 to a traditional use of capital and lower-case letters. Signage on the Arroyo Seco Parkway had been found to be too small. By 1948 the Division of Highways had begun to demand large overhead signs that could be seen from all lanes of traffic, were not obliterated by glare, and were properly lit at night. After some experiment, a background color of green was chosen. By 1956 statewide standards for signs and light fixtures had been formulated. When not caused by drunk driving or other form of impairment, mistaken entries—the wrong-way driving up exit lanes into head-on collisions, a major cause of traffic deaths—could only be stopped by effective signage. By the mid-1960s an evolved wrong-way sign and arrow system had cut the number of fatal accidents due to wrong-direction entries by 50 percent. Still, as late as 1965, the Division of Highways was dealing with the fact that 25 percent of all freeway accidents was occurring at off-ramps, with inadequate signage remaining the main problem.

The challenge of designing freeways—entrance and exit angles, grade banking, signage, overpasses, underpasses—constituted an art form growing in complexity. While little of this was unique to California, the scale and the social and psychological significance of freeways as a component of California culture were, especially in Southern California, where the freeway was emerging as a founding and defining event in a rapidly developing suburbanized society. As in the case of all great engineering on such a monumental scale, the freeways bespoke the values and technology, the options and choices, the sheer drama, of the brave new world Californians were creating.

Freeway interchanges were especially compelling as architecture. There were fourteen iterations of exchanges, growing in complexity from two variations of the simple diamond exchange, two variations of the ramp, the bridged rotary, the trumpet interchange, an elongated clover leaf, two variations of the two-quadrant clover leaf, and a full clover leaf with five variations, culminating in the four-level exchange. Each of these variations, growing in complexity like cells combining to form organisms, like flowers bursting into bloom, prompted biological and/or botanical comparisons. By the end of 1954, a triumphant four-level interchange had risen in downtown Los Angeles where the Harbor, Hollywood, Santa Ana, and Arroyo Seco/Pasadena freeways intersected. Here was not only a utilitarian solution to four converging freeways but an heroic example of architecture and engineering in motion, at once defining and celebrating the society it served.

When prodigious federal funds became available after February 1956, there was constructed the greatest freeway of them all, Interstate 5, running through the interior of California from Mexico to Oregon, just as had been initially envisioned in the Hiram Johnson years. The first formal study of the Westside Freeway, as it was then called, was made in 1950 when the legislature allocated money to investigate the feasibility of a toll road between Los Angeles and San Francisco. A full plan was revealed in November 1958, and the program moved toward construction in the early 1960s. When it was finished nearly two decades hence, Interstate 5 stood as a monument to the freeway as a genre and to the Cold War energies of the Defense Highway Act of 1956, intended to unify the nation in case of foreign invasion. From a post–Cold War perspective, a Cristo fence of freeway engineering ran up the Central Valley, providing California with a third spine between the Sierra Nevada and the coastal ranges. The fact that the California Aqueduct, moving water from north to south, ran parallel to I-5 only compounded the reality and the symbolism of the structure. Here, as in the roadways and aqueducts of ancient Rome, was the engineering language of empire. A French- or Japanese-style high-speed train along the same axis would have completed the picture—and would have been facilitated by economies of concurrent construction—but the Californians of that era were thinking cars and freeways, not public transit.

Such structures, so powerful as engineering, by a dialectic of opposites, technology and the garden, demanded aesthetic response and embellishment. Freeways were initially given poetic-evocative names, drawn from historic, literary, or geographical sources: the Cahuenga, the Bayshore, the Redwood, the Ramona, the Cabrillo, the James Lick, the Nimitz. In the second phase of development, freeways tended to take on the names of their destinations—the Hollywood, the Long Beach, the Santa Ana, the San Bernardino—as in August 1954 when the Arroyo Seco Parkway became the Pasadena Freeway. In the third phase of development, freeways were to become known primarily by their numbers—the 10, the 5, the 880, the 101—for they were now part of an integrated state grid, scheduled for integration into an interstate system.

Ever since the 1890s, roadway beautification had been a goal of state and county government. In 1918 the Highway Commission established an arboreal nursery near Davis as a source of trees and shrubs for landscaping. Although experimentation was needed to see which plants and shrubs could survive, the Arroyo Seco Parkway was eventually landscaped with more than four thousand plants of forty-seven varieties, forty-two of them native species. In time, the parkway was planted with more than ten thousand plants—wild lilac, fremontia, catalina and holly cherry, barberry, poppies, wild roses, manzanita, blue sage, snapdragons, fuchsias—designed to bloom in sequence across the year in hues of yellow, orange, green, purple, and blue. The Arroyo Seco, in fact, functioned as an horticultural testing ground for the developing freeway system. In this regard, the oleander was destined to do yeoman service as a median barrier. A Mediterranean plant, the Levantine oleander could endure both drought and rain, as well as the winds created by freeway traffic. Its leathery leaves were poisonous, but no one seemed interested in crossing a two- to three-lane freeway to munch on oleander leaves in contrast to the fruit trees that were used for a while, until a woman was struck and killed crossing a freeway to pick pomegranates planted in the median strip. Stabilizing the embankment landscape and reducing fire hazards as well was the ice plant, an imported succulent, dense and persistent, or sturdy ivy of the English or Algerian varieties, or even in certain cases—the Santa Ana and the Hollywood, for example—grassy lawns. And beyond these embankments—defining and stabilizing ridge lines, acting as windbreaks, sometimes used on medians in certain shrub-like varieties—were those California stand-bys, acacias and eucalypts, the latter imported into the state in the late nineteenth century from Australia and New Zealand.

During the 1950s Mervyn Blacow, senior landscape architect for the Division of Highways, supervised a continuous program of landscape design and planting, further empowered in 1957 when the legislature passed a law allowing highway tax funds to be used for aesthetic design and/or improvement and the landscaping and planting of freeways and overpasses. Governor Pat Brown was personally committed to this effort. In January 1960 Brown requested the Division of Highways to draw up a scenic highway/freeway program for the entire state. Released in March 1963, *Preliminary Plan for Scenic Highways* called for an expanded program of beautification and the integration of freeways into the statewide park and recreational program. In June 1963 the legislature passed a Scenic Highways Act, first introduced by State Senator Fred Farr of Monterey, mandating a comprehensive program of aesthetic landscaping and design. One result of this legislation was the design by San Francisco architect Mario J. Ciampi of a series of breathtaking bridges and interchanges along the north-south Junípero Serra Freeway (280) down the San Francisco peninsula. Ciampi's bridge over San Mateo Creek for I-280 would eventually rank as one of the most beautiful public structures in the state.

Not everyone, however, was buying into the freeway program. Almost from the beginning, there emerged a paradox. As the population of California grew, it was rapidly being served by new freeways, which in turn facilitated further growth. Yet these new freeways also could impinge directly upon existent or emergent settlement patterns. Hence the Division of Highways found itself involved in the right-of-way business on a massive scale. The 1950s witnessed a bureaucratic and legal epic of negotiation, dislocation, property acquisition, legal maneuvering, resistance, and, when necessary, eminent domain. Right-of-way powers and procedures were anchored in prewar (1933) legislation, augmented by a 1942 court decision, *Rose v. State of California*, holding that a landowner did not have a property right in the traffic flow past his or her property. This meant that small businesses would have a tougher time stopping freeways from being constructed in front of their stores or, conversely, diverting traffic to their business site. That same year, a fully staffed Right-of-Way Department was established as part of the division. By the 1950s the department was fielding an effective team of appraisers and negotiators for the advancing system. In 1952 further legislation created a $10 million fund, augmented by federal monies in 1962, for right-of-way teams to begin purchasing land on a preventive basis so that anticipated routes could be maintained.

As early as 1939, the Division of Highways found itself in the rental business, having acquired numerous properties in advance of moving or demolition. In 1959 the legislature established a Highway Property Rental Fund that redistributed a quarter of all rental income back to the counties from which the money had come in the first place and diverted the rest to the Highway Fund. By fiscal year 1962–63, the state was deriving $12 million in yearly income from such rentals, while at the same time enduring criticism that many of its rental properties were not being properly maintained and that the state was creating temporary slums awaiting destruction.

Understandably, the state preferred removal to renting, and moving houses became a profitable business, especially in Southern California. Buildings that could not be removed were demolished and sold for salvage. Condemnation remained a last resort. The Division of Highways, in fact, had a relatively low condemnation rate through the 1950s, given the gigantic nature of its enterprise. Impressive as well was the low number of legitimate complaints of price-gouging by the state. The Coro Foundation of San Francisco went so far as to praise the state for its right-of-acquisition program for the Bayshore Freeway. By 1963 the California Farm Bureau Federation was lauding the Division of Highways for being the most fair of all state agencies to deal with in matters of enforced land acquisition. Nor did environmental concerns, so pressing in a later era, surface with any noticeable force during the construction-friendly 1950s, with one exception: the temporary but ultimately unsuccessful resistance by environmentalists against a 1952 plan to run State 101, expanded to four lanes, through Humboldt Redwood and Prairie Creek state parks in Humboldt County.

Urban-based resistance, however—in San Diego, Long Beach, Beverly Hills, and San Francisco—had a sharper focus and intensity, although only in the case of the Great Freeway Revolt in San Francisco, as this saga was eventually called, did there arise a more broadly based hostility to what the freeway movement was doing to cities. And no wonder! The comprehensive program for freeway development in San Francisco issued by the Division of Highways in June 1949 was so egregious that even the most ardent supporter of freeways might begin to have doubts. Plans called for a Bayshore Freeway to move from the San Francisco Bay Bridge down the peninsula to San Jose. This cannot, in retrospect, be seen as controversial; nor did it generate any controversy. Other plans, however, called for an elevated Embarcadero Freeway to move from the Bay Bridge along the waterfront; a Golden Gate Freeway to link the Embarcadero Freeway with the Golden Gate Bridge; a Park Presidio Freeway to move from the Golden Gate Bridge through Golden Gate Park to link up with the Bayshore; a Junípero Serra Freeway to move south from Golden Gate Park down the western edge of the peninsula to San Jose; a Panhandle Freeway to move through Golden Gate Park and connect with a Central Freeway in the Civic Center; and, finally, a Mission Freeway to connect from the Central Freeway to a crosstown Southern Freeway. While the proposed Junípero Serra Freeway, moving traffic like the Bayshore to and from San Francisco, might be easy to understand and accept, the prospect of crisscrossing the relatively small (46.38 square miles), densely developed, and fragile fabric of a city based on an 1847 grid with seven crosstown freeways was bound to cause controversy.

The Embarcadero Freeway provided the flashpoint and focus for resistance, although when the first public hearing was held in San Francisco on 20 January 1954 not much debate or opposition seems to have surfaced, given the rather bold proposal to run a double-decked elevated freeway across the northern edge of the city, sealing off significant parts of the downtown from the waterfront. Perhaps this was because the wharves themselves had since the 1920s been sealed off from view by a phalanx of facades designed by the noted architect Willis Polk. At one point, it was even argued that the view of the Bay from an automobile on the upper deck of the Embarcadero Freeway would actually increase scenic opportunities. Within time, however, opposition to the Embarcadero Freeway gained momentum. It was a case of high provincial San Francisco versus Baghdad. High provincial San Francisco—the chamber of commerce, the Harbor Commission, the Downtown Association, Mayor George Christopher, and the *Examiner*—favored the project. The *Examiner* editorialized that while the Embarcadero Freeway cut off some views, the city still had more than an ample number of scenic waterfront sites at Aquatic Park, the Marina Green, Lincoln Park, and Land's End. *Examiner* columnist Dick Nolan argued that San Francisco had long since lost its view of the harbor from Market Street. With its concern for San Francisco as a unique place—its picturesque architecture and skyline, its European charm, its mosaic of atmospheric neighborhoods—Baghdad San Francisco, led by Scott Newhall's *Chronicle*, opposed the Embarcadero with a vengeance through editorial and column commentary and sensationalized reporting.

In June 1956, after construction begun, the Blyth-Zellerbach Committee retained the architectural firm of Skidmore, Owings & Merrill to explore the feasibility of having the Embarcadero Freeway go underground in front of the Ferry Building. SOM reported that this would cost an additional $4 million. Not wanting the Ferry Building to be blocked, the state Parks Commission announced that if such an underpass were built, it would contribute $2 million for a Ferry Building plaza park. A reluctant Mayor Christopher, who in January had argued vociferously at a public meeting against any delays, ordered a halt to construction so the matter could be studied. A second study claimed that the underpass would cost $14.5 million or more. This was out of the question, Christopher decided, and construction recommenced. State Senator Randolph Collier of Yreka, warning that San Francisco was endangering its entire freeway program, proposed that the Embarcadero Freeway be painted and covered in ivy to make it less of an eyesore. Another proposal was to sheath it with marble.

Two high provincial politicians, Supervisor William Blake and State Senator Eugene McAteer, were won over by arguments from neighborhood activists that their neighborhoods would be destroyed to benefit people passing through San Francisco and began rapidly moving in an anti-freeway direction. Blake persuaded a majority of the board of supervisors, and McAteer, a Democrat, planning to run for mayor, advanced the argument in Sacramento. Even city planning director James McCarthy, who reported to Mayor Christopher, was diplomatically aligning himself with the anti-freeway forces. Almost on a daily basis, meanwhile, the *Chronicle* was lambasting the freeway even as it was rising along the Embarcadero. While the Embarcadero Freeway did open in 1957, it remained incomplete and was never connected to the Golden Gate Bridge, which represented a victory of sorts for Baghdad.

When it came to the proposed crosstown Western Freeway, moving from the Golden Gate Bridge through Golden Gate Park to link with the Bayshore, the anti-freeway forces, solidly led by Supervisor Blake, were fully victorious. In June 1956 Blake introduced a successful resolution to withdraw the Western Freeway from the city's traffic plan. Mayor Christopher vetoed the measure, but even the iron-willed Christopher knew that support for such a freeway was waning. More than

ninety-seven organizations had testified against the project by 1959. In July 1961 the
board of supervisors vetoed the project once and for all in a unanimous vote that
precluded a veto. In the months that followed, yet another freeway being proposed
by Sacramento—this one along Sunset Boulevard through Golden Gate Park—was
also unanimously rejected.

When it was finally over, by 1968, none of the crosstown freeways had been built,
and the Embarcadero Freeway stood a truncated edifice, serving little purpose,
destined to be torn down before the end of the century and replaced with palm
trees, landscaping, and antique streetcars. From this perspective, the Great Freeway
Revolt was a total success. Even Sacramento got the message, with Governor Pat
Brown convening a statewide Conference on California's Urban Areas and the State
Highway System in 1960 and State Senator Collier introducing Senate Bill 1335 in
1961, calling for a free and open exchange between the Division of Highways and
local governing bodies during the planning period for future freeway development.
Not only did Baghdad San Francisco win the freeway battle, keeping the city free
of crosstown behemoths, its victory precipitated a long-term shift in political power
from the downtown to the neighborhoods and from large-scale organizations, public
and private, to smaller, neighborhood-oriented, highly skilled and motivated activist groups.

Southern California, meanwhile, was facing its own automobile-related challenge—
smog—although it would take more than a decade to isolate automobile exhaust as
a major cause of the problem. The term *smog*, a combination of *smoke* and *fog*, was
coined in 1905 by physician Harold Antoine des Voeux of the Coal Smoke Abatement Society of London to describe the deadly combinations of stagnant fog and
smoky coal emissions, concentrating sulfuric acid in fog droplets, that frequently
enveloped London with deadly effect. Factory emissions as well as domestic coal
smoke could prove equally toxic. In December 1930 industrial smog killed sixty-
three in the Meuse Valley of Belgium. In October 1948 smog covering Donora,
Pennsylvania, killed twenty and made more than 40 percent of the population ill,
10 percent of them seriously. In December 1952 another killer smog caused an estimated four thousand deaths in London. A similar attack the following year in New
York City led to two hundred deaths.

While metropolitan Los Angeles never experienced such deadly attacks, it
became the poster city in the postwar era for the smog crisis precisely because it
was so automobile-dependent and because its smog problem remained so chronic.
Temperature inversions—warm air holding colder air in place—stabilized smog
over cities; and in no other American city were such inversions more common than
in Los Angeles. As early as 1542, sailing into San Pedro Bay, Juan Cabrillo noticed
how the smoke from Native American fires, hanging in the air, stretched horizontally across the Los Angeles plain. Indeed, the Native American name for this plain
was the Valley of Smokes. If such were the case when only a few thousand Indians
lived in the region, it was not surprising that by the early 1940s Los Angeles was

experiencing serious atmospheric problems as cool air blew in from the Pacific 250 days a year and was stabilized by warmer air above and the near-complete ring of mountains surrounding the plain. Pollutants of various sorts — rising into the layer of cold air, which could reach an inversion level of as low as 500 feet—were then warmed by the sun into a noxious photo-chemical brew. Thus Los Angeles was being victimized by its very attributes of site and climate.

Los Angeles experienced its first smog attack in July 1940, followed by a second attack in September 1942. A third attack—brought on, it was later determined, by increased automotive traffic during a streetcar strike—came in July 1943 and reappeared in September. The smog attack of 8 September 1943, subsequently known as Black Wednesday, brought the city to a standstill. A fourth attack came in September 1944, blanketing the downtown; a fifth in October and a sixth in December of that year. While these attacks were described as smog, they were not traced back to the automobile by city health officials, for whom wartime aviation gasoline refineries and a synthetic rubber plant were considered the primary suspects. Nor did the automobile emerge as a primary culprit after the war, as health officials continued to cite locomotives, diesel trucks, burning dumps, lumberyard incinerators, and asphalt plant and oil refineries as the major culprits. The smog problem continued through the 1940s, with oil refineries and other processing plants dumping some eight hundred tons of sulphur dioxide and one hundred tons of metallic oxides into the air by 1949, causing eyes to water and moviemakers to cancel plans for outdoor shoots. In 1950 the Dutch-born Caltech biochemist Arie Haagen-Smit created smog in a test tube and scientifically described it as a compound of carbon monoxide, nitrogen oxides, acid aerosols, and, as he later determined, up to two hundred other chemicals brought into interaction by ozone and sunlight in a process of photo-chemical formation. While Dr. Haagen-Smit continued to cite the usual suspects along with the automobile, his research constituted a tipping point, however understated, in the willingness of scientists and health officials to rank automotive exhaust as a leading cause of the problem.

The Los Angeles establishment was reluctant to acknowledge, much less engage, a problem that constituted such an affront to the identity of the city and a public relations disaster. It took until November 1953 for the Los Angeles Chamber of Commerce openly to admit that the city had a major issue with smog, much less begin to zero in on the automobile as the predominant cause. In early November 1953, Los Angeles endured yet another smog attack, but automotive exhaust continued to remain tucked away among a variety of other causes. A year later, across eighteen days in October and November 1954, in the worst attack ever, an especially heavy blanket of smog lay intermittently over the metropolitan region. Three babies died from respiratory causes, and their parents threatened to sue the city; a child went temporarily blind; a middle-aged woman attempted suicide, her husband claimed, because of smog-induced headaches. In Pasadena, a Citizens Anti-Smog Action Committee demanded a grand jury investigation of the crisis at a rally in the civic auditorium where angry protesters waved signs such as SMOG HAS CHANGED SAN

GABRIEL VALLEY TO DEATH VALLEY. Another group called for the National Guard to be brought in. At the weekly meeting of the Optimists Club in Highland Park, attendees wore gas masks in serio-comic protest and were covered in *Life* magazine. While Governor Goodwin J. Knight, running for reelection, called for the shutting down of twenty-five oil refineries in the region, and the 1.5 million backyard incinerators in Los Angeles County were also cited, the exhaust emitted by more than two million automobiles—for the first time—also came in for an equal share of the blame.

Whatever the cause, the problem persisted. Between 1955 and 1960, metropolitan Los Angeles, by now the third-largest metropolitan region in the nation, experienced thirty-nine first-level smog alerts. Smog abatement programs, fortunately, were growing more comprehensive. In October 1947 Los Angeles County established an Air Pollution Control District, the first of its kind in the nation. Almost immediately, the district went after factories and refineries. It was, however, a program of persuasion and continuing research as opposed to rigorous enforcement through penalties. Yet the automobile was coming into focus. In early 1953 Los Angeles County Supervisor Kenneth Hahn formally inquired of Detroit automakers whether or not they were putting resources behind the effort to mitigate emissions. Detroit's response was inconclusive, but the question had been asked. In 1955 the Air Pollution Control District established a Motor Vehicle Pollution Control Laboratory with federal funds made available under the Federal Air Pollution Control Act of 1955.

Finally, in July 1956, a private organization, the Air Pollution Foundation of Los Angeles—noting that air from refineries seemed never to be carried into the western or northern portion of the Los Angeles Basin, where the smog problem was the most serious—identified the automobile as the co-equal, if not exclusive, cause of smog alongside industrial pollution. Still, to name the automobile as a primary contributor was not the same thing as bringing Detroit to its knees, and by 1960, after nearly a decade and a half of abatement efforts, industrial and automotive emissions were each day pouring some two thousand tons of smog-forming pollutants into the atmosphere. Anti-smog activism was on the rise, however, and some progress was being made. In 1959 the legislature ordered the state Department of Public Health to study and set quantitative limits on any and all pollutants being emitted by motor vehicles and to test and promote emission-reducing technologies. The next year, the legislature created a state Motor Vehicle Pollution Control Board to enforce the limits being determined by the Department of Public Health. Still, as of 1960, Los Angeles was experiencing 1,114 deaths above the normal rate during the heavy smog months from March to September, and city health department statistics showed statistics that Los Angeles had the highest rate of deaths from respiratory diseases nationwide. Chemical compounds from automobiles—10,000 tons by 1964, emitted from some 3.5 million exhaust pipes—were shrouding the Los Angeles Basin in gray smog banks, acrid and miasmic, testifying to the price Southern Californians were paying, and were perhaps willing to continue paying, for the convenience and freedom of the automobile.

The automobile and the freeway, in short, whatever the trade-offs, had become fixed components of California culture and would remain so for the rest of the century. Hence the difficulties faced—as early as the mid-1920s—by advocates of rapid transit: which was ironic, given the fact that the entire Los Angeles Basin had been metropolitanized, exurbanized, and suburbanized at the turn of the century by the Big Red Cars of the Pacific Electric Railway, one of the most effective rapid transit systems in all of modern transportation history. That system remained alive and well in the prewar era, but in downtown Los Angeles streetcars were coming increasingly in conflict at grade crossings with the automobile. The often-repeated claim that General Motors conspired to rid the region of the Big Red Cars is mere folklore, but like most folklore it embodied a truth. In the long run, the automobile did rid the region of its public transit system.

Still, rapid transit continued to have its advocates for the next four decades— indeed, for the rest of the century. Los Angeles's ongoing self-discovery as a city can be plotted through the visionary, even utopian, public transit plans that were commissioned, researched, written, discussed, and rejected in favor of the automotive option. As early as 1924, in one of the first important planning documents of the period—A Major Traffic Street Plan for Los Angeles, issued by the Los Angeles Traffic Commission—public transit continued to be advocated by a consulting team that included Frederick Law Olmsted Jr.; yet the dense boulevard-and-parkway system radiating from the Central Business District betrayed the more compelling automotive orientation of the report. Commissioned by the City Council of Los Angeles and the Board of Supervisors of Los Angeles County, the Report and Recommendations on a Comprehensive Rapid Transit Plan for the City and County of Los Angeles (1925) was prepared by the highly respected Chicago engineering consulting firm of Kelker, De Leuw and Company. Drawing upon the transit and traffic solutions of Boston, New York, Philadelphia, and Chicago, the report called for an integration of street cars, interurban electrics, elevated lines, subways, and buses in conjunction with the automobile as the long-range solution for traffic and transit in Los Angeles, city and county. The very strength of the Kelker, De Leuw report, however—its reliance upon the tested traffic and transit solutions of the densely developed cities of the East and Midwest—was its weakness; for the Chicago consultants were, in effect, pointing to a paradigm of Los Angeles as a traditionally developed city at a time when many Los Angelenos had other options in mind. The very next year, Los Angeles voters rejected a proposal to build four miles of elevated railway in the heart of the city because it seemed too traditional, too reminiscent of the older cities of the East.

Issued by the county in 1939, when the forthcoming freeway era was already in sight, A Transit Program for the Los Angeles Metropolitan Area creatively advocated the integration into freeways of bus lanes and center-divide fixed-rail systems. In the long run, some of these proposals—further refined and advocated in the joint state and local Rail Rapid Transit report (1948) and the Preliminary Report on Rapid Transit for the Los Angeles Area (1950) issued by the Assembly Interim Committee on Public Utilities and Corporations—were put into effect. Yet the combining of freeways with public transit had to fight an uphill battle. As the freeway system began to develop in the 1940s, a social division began to assert itself. Public transit, like renting, became associated with the less affluent and the non-white; and the family automobile, like the family-owned home in the suburbs, suggested a more successful and, by implication, more white lifestyle.

At this point, a species of imaginative and self-deceiving futurism began to attach itself to public transit planning, especially in metropolitan Los Angeles, through an advocacy of monorail. Even as metropolitan Los Angeles was grappling with its traffic problems through the building of more and more freeways, which were in turn creating more and more traffic, it was also flirting, subliminally, with a Buck Rogers notion of subways in the skies. The 1950 assembly plan had suggested a monorail system running along freeways as a serious option along with express lanes for buses. Within two weeks of each other, in December 1953 and January 1954, two reports to the Los Angeles Metropolitan Transit Authority by consulting engineers based locally and in New York came out enthusiastically in favor of monorail as the solution to the rapid transit needs of the region. Coverage of these reports was illustrated by futurist depictions of monorails speeding throughout the region, with frequent references to the short-line monorail already being planned for Disneyland. The noted futurist and science fiction writer Ray Bradbury, a self-taught planning consultant, entered the discussion with an even more visionary proposal that the entire region be linked via a monorail grid.

In July 1967 a non-profit organization headquartered in Los Angeles, the Citizens Advisory Council on Public Transportation, issued an almost equally futurist report, *Improving Public Transporation in Los Angeles*, that looked to such avant-garde solutions also under consideration in Japan and France as the tracked air-cushion vehicles being developed on the hovercraft principle, propelled by linear induction motors over concrete roadbeds. Even more futurist proposals included a tube flight train that would propel vehicles through steel or concrete tubes by means of gigantic turbo fans or gravity vacuums. From one perspective, Bradbury and the consultants to the Citizens Advisory Council were imagineering, to use a term later coined by Disney designers developing theme parks. But such a recourse to futurism could also be seen as a form of escapist dream-wish: a science fiction fantasy on the part of metropolitan Los Angeles—and perhaps other parts of California as well—to find some release from the knowledge that the system they were building might itself one day, like a shrinking universe, implode back upon itself into gridlock.

In the Bay Area, on the other hand, the planners involved in creating the semi-futurist Bay Area Rapid Transit System were optimistic regarding the ultimate success of their project. Planning for BART had been authorized by the state legislature in 1951, and in a January 1956 report, finalized in December 1957, the consulting firm of Parsons, Brinckerhoff, Hall, and Macdonald of New York presented to the legislature a plan calling for the integration of the entire Bay Area by a system of electrically driven high-speed, aerodynamically designed light rail cars that would in its first phase move north and south along each side of the Bay and eastward in to Walnut Creek in Contra Costa County. In a second phase of construction, BART, having already crossed the Bay from San Francisco into Marin, would continue north toward Novato and southward on both sides of the Bay to San Jose. Subsequent phases of construction would advance BART northward to Santa Rosa and Napa, east-west between Petaluma and Fairfield, east-west into Brentwood and Livermore, and southward to Los Gatos below San Jose, looping back to Palo Alto through western Santa Clara County. There would also be built, in subsequent phases, three more crossings across San Francisco Bay, one between San Francisco and Oakland via an underwater tube and causeway crossings between San Mateo and Hayward, continuing out to Livermore in Alameda County, and from Redwood City into Fremont in western Alameda County.

It was an audacious concept: the unification of the entire Bay Area, north and south, east and west, through one rapid transit system to be financed and administered according to a scenario laid down by the Stanford Research Institute in a March 1956 report. The organization, financing, and construction of the proposed BART system would, in one way or another, consume the rest of the century and, for one reason or another, would never be fully realized. BART never crossed the Bay into Marin, never reached Santa Rosa to the north, never ran south to Los Gatos via the San Francisco peninsula. Yet in social and cultural terms, the advancement of such a project, however abbreviated its final form, underscored the social and cultural differences between the Bay Area and metropolitan Los Angeles. In transportation terms, the San Francisco Bay Area did not invent itself through the automobile but through the railroad, the ferry boat, the seaborne freight barge, and horse-drawn transportation. By the time the automobile became a factor, San Francisco and its hinterlands had already achieved significant densities and psychologies of place.

Metropolitan Los Angeles had in transit terms been brought into being in the late nineteenth and early twentieth centuries through the interurban electric streetcar and was in the process, before the advent of the automobile, of developing a psychology of place similar to that of the Bay Area. Not only did the automobile overwhelm the Big Red Cars, however, it also fused to the psychology of place a new sense of motion and social experience. Riding the interurban Big Red Cars or the intra-urban Yellow Cars of Los Angeles was a communal experience. In the automobile, by contrast, the nuclear family on a Sunday drive to the mountains or the beach alternated with the solo weekday commute of one individual to and from suburb to job site. Place—where one lived or where one worked—began increasingly to be perceived in terms of the attached motion, automotive and solipsistic, of the commute involved. The freeway institutionalized this relationship.

The freeway moved an individual from one place to another, but the time spent in motion in an automobile was budgeted time, standardized time, recurrent time, an accepted mode of life for parts of each day, week, month, year. Freeways could be dangerous, but they could offer solace and relief as well. In *Play It as It Lays* (1970), Joan Didion depicts her heroine cruising the freeways in times of stress as a mode of existential encounter, a ritualized way of coping with the flux and confusion of life, a mode of therapy.

In *Los Angeles: The Architecture of Four Ecologies* (1971), the English-born social critic Reyner Banham describes the freeways of the Southland as an autonomous environment, Autopia, a fixed ecology along with the suburbanized seashore (Surfurbia), the foothills, and the sprawling city itself (the Plains of Id). The society sustained by Autopia took as its fundamental premises motion, private freedom, and public discipline as far as traffic laws and procedures were concerned. Banham was intrigued by the collective freeway knowledge of the region, not just the individual maps in millions of individual minds but the collective ability to handle on any given busy freeway interchange a complexity of data and a multiplicity of choices. In Southern California, David Brodsly observes in *L.A. Freeway: An Appreciative Essay* (1981), one knew where one was, one fixed one's place, spatially, socially, and psychologically, in terms of freeway references. The Harbor Freeway (110), for example, delineated poverty and color to its east, and the San Diego Freeway (405) erected a barrier wall of whiteness and privilege for its west. From this perspective, the freeways of the region were social as well as spatial signs. Freeways unified the region, but they also divided it across barriers that would prove increasingly troublesome in a later era.

Radio reporter Paul Pierce intuitively understood the pervasive presence and influence of the freeway in the life of metropolitan Los Angeles. KMPC radio station owner Gene Autry put Pierce on the freeways for some fifty thousand miles a year, covering on live radio via his transmitter traffic patterns, smooth or blocked; weather and visibility, from sunshine to fog; accidents, from minor to tragic, ranging from a stalled car in a center lane to the jackknifing of a big rig—with its cargo strewn across the roadway, bales of hay, concrete blocks, lumber, even live cattle. Pierce covered the moods of the freeway system across a twenty-four-hour sequence: friendly, leisurely, hostile, or anxiety-ridden at differing times of the day in various conditions. He was sensitive to the beauty of a nighttime river of light of steadily moving traffic or the pre-dawn magic of passing the newly constructed pavilion of the Los Angeles Music Center and the nearby steel-and-glass elegance of the Department of Water and Power headquarters, or catching a glimpse of the rise of City Hall tower above the skyline, all this caught as night yielded to the light and urgency of the morning. When a new freeway was dedicated, Pierce was on hand, interviewing the politicians, along with Miss Orange County or Miss Seal Beach or Miss Garden Grove.

The introduction of radios into automobiles had long since privatized car interiors into entertainment centers, but they had also linked individual drivers to a community of live coverage. The majority of Pierce's listeners were themselves driving on freeways as they listened to his reports, grateful when he could point out a problem they could potentially avoid. After 1958 station KMPC also kept a helicopter in the air, monitoring traffic in this manner, and the so-called sig-alert alerting listeners to traffic problems became a fixed component of freeway culture. As he drove, Pierce monitored multiple police radio receivers to gain information not just on traffic patterns but on fleeing suspects. Covered on live television from helicopters, such high-speed chases would eventually become a staple of news coverage throughout the region.

By the late 1950s, freeway engineers from Japan, Switzerland, Denmark, Sweden, Australia, New Zealand, South Vietnam, and India were coming to California individually or in delegations to study its emergent freeway system. They were interested in technical questions primarily, but they were also concerned with economic and social impacts and, some of them, with cultural issues. What sort of society were these freeways creating? What would be their lasting impact? Were they making California a better place? Would they endure across the centuries? Or would they someday be absorbed into the very cities they were now serving or be recycled as electronic and digital pathways? Or would they be abandoned as unuseable relics of a bygone era, pyramids to gods no longer worshipped? At some far distant point in the future, the science fiction writers of California would soon be suggesting, the survivors and archeologists of future time, contemplating the freeways, would lament the loss of a society capable of building such structures. More optimistically, they would marvel at the energy, creativity, and resources of that long-ago era and the hopes and way of life embodied in its engineering.

10

Mare Nostrum

The State Water Project

A S Election Day, 8 November 1960, approached, first-term governor Pat Brown was busy persuading the voters of California to pass Proposition 1, authorizing a $1.75 billion bond issue for the construction of a seven-hundred-mile State Water Project—dams, reservoirs, aqueducts, tunnels, hydroelectrical and pumping stations—to be built across the next two decades. All things considered, Proposition 1 was asking for the most ambitious water storage and distribution system in the history of the human race, and as such it was a tough sell, even for such a masterful salesman as Brown. The magnitude of the project, moving the waters of the north southward into Southern California, clashed headlong with the sectional feeling that continued to characterize the state. Nowhere, for example, was opposition to Proposition 1 stronger than in Brown's hometown of San Francisco, where the *Chronicle* lambasted the proposal almost daily as a water-grab by the Southland, depicting Brown in one cartoon as a bespectacled octopus asking a voter to sign a blank check. Given the high self-regard of the Bay Area, and the water-sufficient success of the Hetch Hetchy and East Bay Utility systems, the opposition of the *Chronicle* made a certain sense, as did the wholesale endorsement of the measure by the *Los Angeles Times*, whose readers desperately needed the water.

But why was the California Labor Federation so opposed to a measure that would precipitate a construction boom? The answer further underscored the deep fault lines that ran beneath the state in matters ideological as well as seismic. Why, the Labor Federation was asking, should the working people of the state underwrite a project that would represent such a water windfall to the corporate landowners of the lower San Joaquin, entities such as the Kern County Land Company, the Southern Pacific Land Company, and the land-rich oil companies, not to mention the vast Tejon Ranch, owned in part by the *Los Angeles Times*?

Despite the flood control aspects of the proposed project, only two of the counties of Northern California were supporting the measure: Butte, where one of the key elements of the project, the Oroville Dam on the Feather River, would be located, and Yuba, where during the Christmas season of 1955 a levee had collapsed and flooding had killed thirty-six people and destroyed four hundred homes. All in all, flooding that year, the greatest of its kind on record, killed sixty-four people, inundated a hundred thousand square miles, and caused more than $200 million in property damage. Yet even the flood control aspects of the project, centered on the proposed damming of the Feather River at Oroville, were not enough to convince— at least not immediately—a majority of voters in the northern counties.

Even the Metropolitan Water District of Southern California was in opposition, fearing that the project would weaken its claims to Colorado River water being contested in the Supreme Court by Arizona. Believing that Los Angeles County was already bearing a disproportionate share of running the MWD system, the Los Angeles–dominated MWD board was also objecting to a provision in the Burns-Porter Act of 1959 behind Proposition 1 that obligated Los Angeles users to help pay for a proposed East Branch Aqueduct serving San Bernardino County. On a more paranoid level, the MWD board had fears that, given the protective county-of-origin law passed by the legislature in 1931 and subsequently updated, the counties of the north, even after the State Water Project was built, could turn off their spigots on the basis of local need. As was the case in the other ballot issue claiming the governor's attention, the race between Richard Nixon and John F. Kennedy, the outcome for Proposition 1 was too close to call.

In heroic terms, Proposition 1 represented the fulfillment of nearly eighty-five years of vision and planning and local construction as California irrigated itself, metropolitanized itself, suburbanized itself, invented itself through water. In another sense, however, the very fact that Proposition 1 was on the ballot—urging voters to put aside sectional and political differences and to establish the water infrastructure of an impending mega-state—was due to Pat Brown. Unlike the statewide freeway system, the statewide water proposal had languished in political limbo during the postwar era, and Brown had vowed in that opaque blend of high-minded duty and self-regard characteristic of elected officials that he would get the State Water Project up and running as the signature achievement of his governorship. What about school construction? What about higher education? What about freeways? Legislators and other interest groups had been asking such questions throughout the first half of 1959 as Brown lobbied incessantly in the legislature on behalf of the Water Resources Development Bond Act (Burns-Porter) authorizing the bond issue that would pay for the first phase of construction. And, it was further argued, did not the state first require a constitutional amendment establishing local and statewide prerogatives regarding water so that, among other imagined catastrophes, the northern counties would not be drained dry as the City of Los Angeles had drained dry the Owens Valley?

Skillfully, Brown sidestepped these issues as he lobbied, legislator by legislator, on behalf of the Burns-Porter bill. Such questions could be negotiated, Brown argued, as part of an ongoing process. To negotiate all differences down to the final dotting of all i's and the crossing of every t was to continue the filibuster that had kept California paralyzed as far as statewide action for water was concerned. The constitutional amendment alone, which would have to go to the voters, had been enough to stymie any thought of a statewide water system during the administrations of Earl Warren and Goodwin J. Knight. Put it back in a conference committee, and it will die. If San Francisco or Los Angeles had become bogged down in such a manner, paralyzed by anticipated difficulties, there would have been no Los Angeles Aqueduct, no Hetch Hetchy, hence no metropolitanization of these two great cities. Keep the bill alive! Keep it moving! It was time for California to step up to the plate.

Personable, accommodating in his lobbying style, rolling out the pork barrel when necessary, Brown played the key role in getting Burns-Porter through the senate and the assembly devoid of what he considered debilitating amendments, empowered by the fact that he was the first Democratic governor since 1888 to enjoy a solid majority in each house and in the gubernatorial election had beaten his Republican opponent William Knowland by a whopping million-vote plurality. The final passage of the Burns-Porter Act in June, however, also represented a triumph of gubernatorial persuasion that cannot be detached, finally, from the power of Brown's arguments as well as the skill with which he made them. The Burns-Porter Act, signed by Brown on 10 July 1959, mandated the comprehensive and final integration of California through water engineering. Like the Collier-Burns Highway Act of 1947 financing freeway construction or the Donohoe Act of 1960 calling for a master plan for higher education, the Burns-Porter Act constituted a high point of postwar thought and action in the matter of what Californians, the majority of them at least, wanted their state to be: a modernist commonwealth, a triumph of engineering, a mega-state embracing growth as its first premise. As far as Brown and millions of other Californians were concerned, the waters flowing down the undammed rivers of California to the sea—which was to say, 40 percent of the runoff water in the state—were wasted waters that could otherwise be used to enable continuing development.

And that was the case Pat Brown was taking to voters a year later as Proposition 1 with all the energy, sincerity, charm, and occasional blarney at his command. California had a destiny, Brown told the voters, and that destiny was to grow, and the State Water Project would make it possible. Traveling up and down the state in the company of Ralph Brody, his chief water adviser, and Harvey Banks, his director of water resources, at his side to answer technical questions, Brown had a number of sources of opposition to overcome that had recently faced him in the more private back rooms and corridors of the capitol in Sacramento and were now being put forth by, among others, the Committee for Sound Water Development, with dual headquarters in San Francisco and Los Angeles: objections technical, objections political, objections appealing to local fears, objections to agribusiness, which would benefit, it was argued, unfairly from the project, financial objections that even $1.75 billion would not cover the cost of such a project. The true cost of the project was closer to $4 billion, $2.5 billion of it in the first phase alone, but such a sum was a political roadblock and was kept on the q.t. Even the openly acknowledged $1.75 billion figure represented the nation's single largest state bond issue to that time. A number of other objections were also legitimate. Until northern water would be needed by Southern California, Central Valley agribusiness interests such as the Kern County Land Company and the oil companies, not to mention the Times-Mirror Corporation, majority stockholder in the Tejon Ranch, would have an opportunity to purchase surplus water (for nearly two decades, as it turned out) at highly subsidized prices. Further financing, moreover, meaning further bond issues, would be necessary for the project, as envisioned, to be completed.

Brown finessed these questions as they surfaced, arguing, for example, that the project would eventually be on a sound user-supported fiscal basis, paying for itself. In the meantime, tax revenues from tideland oil drilling could be used to help finance it. Besides, the financial gurus at Dillon, Reed had given their approval. And as far as cutting off local needs was concerned, the Davis-Grunsky Act, another Brown-backed creation, was authorizing $130 million for local water projects for purposes of storage, conservation, flood control, wildlife enhancement, and recreation (including the five small man-made storage and recreational lakes being demanded in Plumas County by Assemblywoman Pauline Davis, otherwise known as Pauline's Puddles). And one more point, Brown continued, the Federal Bureau of Reclamation would be helping to pay for the San Luis Dam, and the Army Corps of Engineers would be paying for 22 percent of the construction costs of the Oroville Dam, exclusive of the cost of power facilities.

Still, it was a stretch, a Wizard of Oz performance from behind the green curtain, and Brown knew it and confessed as much, in his off-hours. He went to bed on election night thinking that he had lost. It took twenty-four hours to count the ballots. Proposition 1 won by fewer than 174,000 votes, less than three-tenths of 1 percent of the 5.8 million votes cast. As far as water was concerned, California was still a divided state, with only the two northern counties in the support column—and flood-ravaged Yuba County begrudgingly at that, by a mere 294 votes. The South Coast, from Santa Barbara to San Diego, where the majority of people lived and water was most needed, had tipped the scale. Even the Metropolitan Water District had at the last minute dropped its opposition and would soon be negotiating an increase in its allotment.

As Pat Brown had so effectively argued in his sometimes roundabout way, American California had invented itself through water. Although the governor never fully amplified his thesis—this was politics, after all, not a history class—there was plenty of history on hand to bolster his contention. The basic technology of the Gold Rush—moving water to, through, or across land—morphed into the technology of irrigation that transformed California into an agricultural state by 1879. This technology of dams and aqueducts metropolitanized Los Angeles and the San Francisco Bay Area in the early decades of the twentieth century. But what about statewide water thinking? Where had that bold idea come from? Who were the visionaries who first advanced the statewide project that Pat Brown—perhaps the most notable water visionary of them all, in terms of results—had brought to political completion? Proposition 1 and the State Water Project it enabled represented a culmination of nearly a century of envisionment and planning. All this effort was brought to completion and politically implemented in the 1950s. The construction of the State Water Project would occupy California for the next quarter century. But without the ninety years of dreams and plans that preceded it, culminating in the politics of the 1950s, it would not have existed in the first place, or at least not existed with the breadth and scale it showed upon its completion.

In the first phase of thinking it had been Barton S. Alexander (1819–78), lieutenant colonel in the Army Corps of Engineers, more commonly accorded his brevet rank of brigadier general from the Civil War, awarded him for organizing the defenses of Washington, D.C., who laid down the foundations for the statewide water engineering of California. Every inch the West Point–trained military engineer, commanding and self-confident, Alexander arrived in California following the War as senior Army engineer on the Pacific and immediately established himself as the leading authority in water management and flood control. In 1873 the Congress, President Ulysses S. Grant, and the Corps ordered Alexander to make an irrigation survey of the Sacramento and San Joaquin valleys, the first study of its kind. Alexander's *Report of the Board of Commissioners on the Irrigation of the San Joaquin, Tulare, and Sacramento Valleys of the State of California* (1874)—integrating, as it did, the northern, central, and southern portions of the state was the first state-wide water plan. Alexander's linkage of flood control in the north to the movement of water southward via a two-hundred-mile aqueduct running along the west side of the San Joaquin Valley anticipated a major feature of the State Water Project.

Alexander's field assistant in the Sacramento/San Joaquin survey, William Hammond Hall—a young and equally brilliant civilian engineer attached to the Corps of Engineers—never forgot the power of Alexander's brilliant integration of the waterways of California into one north-south system for purposes of irrigation, urbanization, and flood control. Which is exactly what Hall called for as California's first state engineer, serving from 1878 to 1889, in the three foundational studies— *Physical Data and Statistics of California* (1886), *Irrigation Development: History, Customs, Laws, and Administrative Systems Relating to Irrigation, Water-Courses, and Waters in France, Italy and Spain* (1886), and *Irrigation in [Southern] California* (1888)—issued by Hall while in office. To read these studies today, together with Hall's other memoranda and reports, is to appreciate the powerful and prophetic presence of a highly developed civil servant, even if, as in Hall's case, the civil servant was thinking out ahead of what politics could deliver. The very juxtapositioning by Hall of California, a sparsely developed frontier province, with European and Asian civilizations sustained by water-related public works in ancient and modern times was more than a flattering comparison. It was an act of cultural invocation and prophecy on behalf of a beleaguered civil servant whose vision went far beyond the concerns of the legislators to whom he reported. Not content merely to ignore Hall's recommendations, they went so far as to bring him up on charges (Hall was exonerated) of spending too much money, and improperly at that, on his surveys.

So too did the equally visionary proposals in 1919 of another Corps of Engineers officer, Lieutenant Colonel Robert Bradford Marshall, chief hydrographer of the United States Geological Survey, go unrealized. A thirty-year veteran of the USGS, Marshall knew California from a theoretical and field perspective. In his *Irrigation of Twelve Million Acres in the Valley of California* (1919), a non-governmental report published by the California State Irrigation Association, Marshall advocated a statewide system based on the damming of the upper Sacramento River, a flood-control infrastructure in the lower Sacramento Valley, a delta infrastructure designed to protect against the intrusion of saltwater and to wheel water to East Bay cities, and the running of two aqueducts down the Central Valley, reclaiming some twelve million acres for agriculture. Even more boldly, the Kern River would be redirected southward into Southern California via a tunnel through the Tehachipis. Electrical generation plants along the project, together with user fees, Marshall argued, would eventually put the entire system on a self-sustaining basis. Retiring from the Army, Marshall advocated his plan ceaselessly and sought election as a state senator from Stanislaus County in the upper San Joaquin Valley in an effort to leverage his ideas. Bits and pieces of Marshall's plan made it in 1922, 1924, and 1926 onto the ballot but were rejected. Marshall lost his voice proselytizing and was forced to speak through an amplifier, and in the end he retired to his ranch near Modesto, awaiting a better day.

Enter the federal government, specifically the Bureau of Reclamation, established in 1902 during the first term of Theodore Roosevelt. From the beginning the Reclamation Service, as it then was, pursued a program of social engineering through water. Inspired by a philosophy of proto-Progressivism, the service sought to bring as many people as possible to a sustainable life on irrigated lands. Hence it set a 160-acre per individual limit for land grants receiving reclamation water, although related family members could amalgamate 160-acre grants and the service could, upon review, expand the 160-acre limitation if it judged that more acreage was needed to make a farm sustainable.

While frontier American California had small farm units in and around the Mother Lode and the Bay Area during the Gold Rush and would witness a resurgence of smaller sustainable ranches during the citrus boom of the 1880s in Southern California, its fundamental land use patterns, dating from the Spanish and Mexican eras, had been in sprawling and frequently indeterminate aggregates. As far as land use patterns were concerned, the central dynamic of nineteenth- and early twentieth-century California was the process whereby landholdings became larger and larger, and agriculture became agribusiness.

Two legal acts, however—a court decision and a law—set opposite forces in motion. In *Lux v. Haggin* (1886), the California Supreme Court ruled that mere ownership of property did not automatically confer riparian rights to the water.

Patterns of prior use were also relevant. *Lux v. Haggin* did not represent a victory for small farmers. The two contestants in the case, after all, were gigantic land companies. Yet the state supreme court had qualified the English common law doctrine of riparian rights (whoever owns the land owns the water flowing through it), and this qualification represented, as far as irrigation law was concerned, an intrusion of the camel's nose into the tent. The next year, the state legislature passed the Wright Irrigation Act of 1887, sponsored by State Senator C. C. Wright from Modesto. The Wright Act stated that individual farmers could join together to create irrigation districts that were semi-governmental entities. These districts could appropriate water for use within the district, even if such water had previously been running through someone else's property. Hence, through federated irrigation, smaller farm units could make a comeback. After 1902 the Reclamation Service was projecting an even bolder program: the use of public resources to create public water projects to irrigate public lands, which would then be privatized into family farm units. Hence the subversive nature, as far as agribusiness was concerned, of the Reclamation program. Acreage limitation, agribusiness argued, represented social engineering of the worst sort, and, worse, it was being pursued with a moral resolve verging on the messianic.

Reclamation encouraged Californians to regard their water resources from a statewide perspective, especially when such a perspective was being advocated by the charismatic Elwood Mead, commissioner for reclamation from 1924 to 1936. A professor of rural institutions at the University of California from 1915 to 1924, Mead had ceaselessly advocated a program of statewide water development, intended to settle as many people as possible on the land through reclamation. Mead's advocacy must be given great credit for the allocation in 1921 by the California state legislature of $1 million to investigate the possibilities of a statewide water plan and in 1927 to pass the Feigenbaum Act granting the state the right to appropriate any and all unappropriated waters for statewide purposes. The legislature went so far as to reestablish the office of state engineer, which it had disestablished in pique against William Hammond Hall.

Working on the statewide survey was yet another distinguished civil engineer/ civil servant, Edward Hyatt, the son of a highly successful state superintendent of public instruction. Finishing two degrees in civil engineering at Stanford, followed by a stint in the private sector with San Joaquin Light and Power, Hyatt entered state service with the Highway Commission, transferred to the Water Commission, and in 1927 was appointed state engineer and chief of the Division of Water Resources of the Department of Public Works. As state engineer, Hyatt bore major responsibility for the *Report to State Legislature of 1931 on State Water Plan* (1930), the planning blueprint for the Central Valley Project, one of the most ambitious public works programs in American history. The Hyatt Plan, further elaborated in *Bulletin No. 25* (1930), called for a $158 million statewide system for irrigation, flood control, hydroelectrical generation, navigation enhancement, and protection against saline encroachment in the delta. Roughly two-thirds of all precipitation and snowpack meltoff occurred in the northern Sacramento Valley watershed, and approximately two-thirds of the irrigable land in the state lay to the south in the San Joaquin Valley. The Central Valley Project was intended to bring northern water to southern land and in so doing to make California an even more coherent state. One cannot overestimate the dazzling scope of this 1930 proposal, advanced in careful language by the professorial Hyatt, conservatively dressed in a three-piece suit, surveying the world from behind owlish tortoise-shell glasses: the organization into one water delivery system of two major dams (Shasta in the north, Friant northeast of Fresno), thirty-eight reservoirs, 350 miles of canals, scores of siphons, tunnels, and bridges, twenty-eight hydroelectric power plants, power transition lines, and pumping plants. Surveying the Central Valley Project from the vantage point of 1948, UC Berkeley economist Paul Taylor considered it "the greatest and most complex reclamation project on the continent...exceeding the federal investment in the Tennessee Valley and approximating the cost of developing the first atomic bomb."[1]

As a state enterprise, the Central Valley Project would not be subject to the 160-acre limitations demanded by the Reclamation Act of 1902, or at the least Hyatt was leaving the question moot, and that was the main reason, perhaps, that Hyatt's proposal received such an enthusiastic reception in the legislature. Agribusiness—which is to say, the land monopolists—were especially delighted. In rapid order, a mere two-plus years from the time Hyatt's report was officially received, the legislature passed and Governor James Rolph signed the Central Valley Act of 1933, placing a $170 million bond issue on the ballot for a special election on 19 December 1933, the nadir year of the Great Depression. The bond issue passed, barely—459,712 in favor, 426,109 against—in part because the voters considered it a stimulus to the economy and because the Bay Area, where water deliveries would be made by the project, stood to gain as well. (Los Angeles, outside the proposed delivery system, rejected the measure two to one.) But the bonds failed to sell on Wall Street, and by 1934 Hyatt, the California congressional delegation, and other relevant California officials were in negotiation with Congress and the Secretary of the Interior to have the Bureau of Reclamation take over the Central Valley Project. Already, in the bond issue passed by the voters, mention of such assistance from the federal government in finance and construction had been made. Through legislation and executive action, the Bureau of Reclamation assumed responsibility for the Central Valley Project in 1937 as part of President Franklin D. Roosevelt's job-creating New Deal, and in September 1938 Reclamation awarded a $36 million contract to the twelve-company Pacific Constructors, Inc., to begin work on Shasta Dam, the cornerstone of the system.

Shasta Dam was to the Central Valley Project what the Boulder/Hoover Dam was for the Boulder Dam Project: the bulwark, the cornerstone, the founding premise. The Shasta Dam on the Sacramento River north of Redding represented a New Deal construction epic of monumental proportions. From 1938 to 1945—machinery moving overhead on cables, concrete pouring from great receptacles, steelwork and scaffolding disappearing under its flow—synchronized teams of men in hard hats, under the direction of construction chief Frank Crowe, erected in sight of Mount Shasta a dam half again as vast as the Great Pyramid, its spillways three times the fall of Niagara, the second-largest dam in the world after Boulder/Hoover.

Another Reclamation project, meanwhile, the All-American Canal, was inching its way from the Imperial Dam on the Colorado River, part of the Boulder/Hoover project, across the Colorado Desert into the Imperial Valley: eighty miles, gravity-driven, bringing the waters of the Colorado to more than 630,000 acres. While not of the scale of Shasta Dam, the All-American Canal, completed in 1940, was also the fulfillment of longtime water dreams and planning and as such part of the ongoing invention of California through water. Geologist William Blake had called for the canal in 1853, and Dr. Oliver M. Wozencraft, an Indian affairs commissioner who also had big ideas about a transcontinental railroad, personally lobbied for the canal in Congress in the early 1860s. The California Development Company had accessed the waters of the Colorado in 1901 via a hastily scraped canal through Mexico, turning it north into the Imperial at the last moment. The canal flooded from 1905 to 1907, creating the Salton Sea, and was only repaired by the heroic (and uncompensated) efforts of the Southern Pacific Railroad. An improved Inter-California Canal continued as a water lifeline into the 1930s, despite the fact that an All-American Canal had been promised as early as 1924 as part of the Colorado River Compact. By 1940 the All-American Canal was complete, and by 1942 it was providing the entire Imperial Valley with its water.

So too was the vast network of the Metropolitan Water District under construction during the 1930s, bringing the waters of Lake Ellwood Mead impounded by the Boulder/Hoover Dam to Southern California via the Colorado River Aqueduct: to Lake Havasu behind Parker Dam on the Arizona-California border and from there to storage reservoirs within the district for distribution via 150 miles of feeder lines to member cities. Combine the All-American Canal, the Colorado River Aqueduct, and the dams and distribution systems of the MWD with the previously completed (1913) Los Angeles Aqueduct from the Owens Valley, together with the San Diego Aqueduct that would eventually (1947) be bringing the waters of the Colorado River to San Diego, and you have a unification of Southern California through water that over time would create a market, hence economic and political pressure, for the waters of the north being concurrently organized through the Central Valley Project, which itself was connected to the Hetch Hetchy system of San Francisco and the West Bay and the East Bay Utility District. California, in short, was organizing itself via a number of major water systems—north, south, and central—that would soon be demanding statewide convergence.

Shasta Dam was ready by 1945. Water delivery from the Central Valley Project, delayed by wartime shortages, began in 1951 after half a billion dollars of construction across fourteen years. The final statistics of the Central Valley Project were truly impressive: twenty dams and reservoirs, five hundred miles of canals serving three million acres of farmland and 2.5 million city dwellers, its eleven power plants

annually generating 5.6 billion kilowatt hours of electricity. And yet, as this behemoth was coming online, this organization of the Great Central Valley through
water, there was a problem—the 160-acre limitation imposed by the Reclamation
Act of 1902—which caused the CVP to divide Californians as much as unite them.
Two opposing Californias were clashing: the California offering renewal, a second
start, to ordinary citizens—those displaced by the Great Depression, returning veterans wanting to get a start in agriculture—and the California of land monopoly
that had been developing since the mid-nineteenth century, subsuming the land
monopolies of the Spanish and Mexican eras, creating vast landholdings in the Central Valley, north and south. Conflict over this question constituted a core element
of economics and politics in nineteenth- and twentieth-century California: the family farm versus agribusiness, a civilized yeomanry living on the land versus corporate
ownership farming vast acreages with advanced machinery and hired help.

And so, as the Central Valley Project came under construction and the prospect
of its water and electricity came into view, lobbying and counter-lobbying ensued.
In 1936, as California began its lobbying for a federal takeover for the CVP, the
160-acre provision was endorsed. It fit into the mood of the Great Depression and
the New Deal. Yet even then, the Madera Irrigation District openly objected. By
1944, as Shasta Dam neared completion, the debate surfaced as a pivotal point of
conflict in the internal politics of California and the external politics of California
in relationship to the federal government. On the one hand, President Roosevelt,
Secretary of the Interior Harold Ickes, and officials from the Bureau of Reclamation had been making statements that the acreage limitation would be enforced in
California. Resistance in the San Joaquin Valley—where, as of 1944, 4 percent of
the landowners owned 53 percent of the irrigable land—was immediate. Representing the growers, Congressman Alfred J. Elliott, a Democrat, brought to the floor of
the House an amendment to a rivers and harbors bill exempting the Central Valley
from acreage limitation. The amendment passed in the House and was supported
in the Senate by Republican Hiram Johnson and Democrat Sheridan Downey of
California, but was resisted by such old-line Progressives as Robert M. La Follette Jr.
of Wisconsin and Carl Hatch and Dennis Chavez of New Mexico, and because of
their opposition the entire rivers and harbors bill failed. In the following Congress,
the Eightieth, the six senators from California, Colorado, and Texas, including
Senator Downey and the newly appointed William F. Knowland, tried for acreage
exemptions in three projects, but the bill never made it out of committee.

Back in California, the two sides on the acreage question squared up against each
other: the California Farm Bureau Federation, the state chamber of commerce, the
California Irrigation Districts Association lining up against such pro-acreage groups
as the California Grange, the AFL-CIO, the Veterans of Foreign Wars, the American Veterans Committee, the Catholic Rural Life Conference, and other Christian and Jewish groups, augmented nationally by the National Farmers Union and
the American Legion. A frustrated Senator Downey went so far as to write a book,
They Would Rule the Valley (1947), making extensive arguments against acreage

limitation. Agribusiness, meanwhile, was trying another ploy, transferring the San Joaquin Valley dams of the Central Valley Project to the Army Corps of Engineers under the Flood Control Act of 1944: to use flood control, in other words, and the reservoirs created by such Corps of Engineers dams as Folsom and New Melones, as a source of water that could be distributed with no acreage limitations. Governor Warren put himself behind such a recommendation.

As the wrangling continued, and the engineering dams remained only future possibilities (Folsom coming online in 1955, New Melones in 1978), San Joaquin Valley agribusiness—prompted by new markets for California fruit, wheat, cotton, and produce—began digging deeper and deeper into aquifers to pump groundwater. As of the early 1930s, agribusiness was taking water from an average of fifty-five feet below the surface. By the late 1940s and early 1950s, depths had tripled or quadrupled. In many places land surfaces would sink up to thirty to forty feet as emptied aquifers—nature's storage tanks, replenishable by rain—collapsed and were lost forever. It was as if agribusiness were punishing the land itself for Reclamation policies or at the least practicing a species of non-sustainable agriculture that was destroying the land for quick profits. Subsided land, if not under irrigation, had a tendency to flake into dry dust, and blinding dust storms became increasingly frequent in the affected areas of the San Joaquin.

There had to be a better way. In 1945 the legislature commissioned the Division of Water Resources of the Department of Public Works to make a statewide investigation of all water resources in California and, by implication, to establish a statistical platform for a statewide water plan. In one sense, such a plan already existed, in that the report of the Division of Water Resources to the legislature of 1931, which resulted in the Central Valley Project, also suggested the construction of a canal that would deliver the waters of the Kern River to southern Kern County and perhaps take them even further south through the Tehachapis via a tunnel. Since the already existing Los Angeles Aqueduct, moreover, had its beginnings in Inyo County to the north and continued into Los Angeles, such a transmission from north to south around the Tehachapis was already occurring. All that was required, in planning terms at least, was to cross the Tehachapis and make a connection with the Metropolitan Water District distribution system fed by the Colorado River Aqueduct, then continue south via aqueduct to San Diego. All this was implied in the map submitted to the legislature in 1931, which even bore the title *The State Water Plan of California*.

Fortunately, the state engineer who prepared the Central Valley Project report, Edward Hyatt, remained on hand as of 1945 to push that plan forward even further. Nearing retirement, Hyatt worked closely with assistant state engineer Arthur (A. D.) Edmonston, who succeeded Hyatt in 1950 and pushed the plan to conclusion. Across the next six years, under Edmonston's direction, the Division of Water Resources issued a State Water Plan in three reports: *Water Resources of California* (1951), *Water Utilization and Requirements of California* (1955), and *The California*

Water Plan (1957). In addition, Edmonston also proposed in a separate report in 1951 the flood-control-oriented Feather River Project that would serve as the initiating element of the statewide plan: a first installment scheduled to jump-start the system out of existing state and federal revenues. The three reports built on each other's complexity. The 1951 report asked and answered the question: What do we have in terms of precipitation, snowpack, unimpaired stream flows, flooding, and water quality? The 1955 report asked and answered: What will be the water and hydroelectrical needs for California for the next half century? Appearing the year of Edmonston's death and dedicated to his memory, the 1957 report answered the question: What kind of statewide water system could meet these future needs?

As such, *The California Water Plan* of 1957 is to be placed alongside *The California Freeway System* (1958) and *A Master Plan for Higher Education* (1960) as a high point of the re-invention of California of the 1950s through governmental action. Setting forth the most ambitious statewide water program in American history, comparable to the greatest of federal projects, *The California Water Plan* ranks as a public works planning document of national importance. A later generation—more oriented toward the earth that was moved as opposed to the earth-movers, more oriented toward the idea of nature and wilderness as opposed to society and settlement, more oriented, in short, to the ambiguities and trade-offs of water engineering as opposed to the growth and benefits it makes possible—cannot be expected to appreciate *The California Water Plan* on such terms, embodying, as it did, a philosophy of triumphant use. The very ambition of the document can be seen as a species of hubris, doomed to failure at some distant point, an onerous installment toward the Cadillac Desert, as environmental writer Marc Reisner would later describe it. Defenders of the plan and the society it would bring about, on the other hand, can be moved by what they consider its imaginative and implied moral force, its vision and advocacy, and can laud the report on four counts: first, it was researched, envisioned, and written; second, it was negotiated through the legislative process; third, it was approved by the voters, who agreed to pay for it; and fourth, it was in rapid order brought into existence. Like any other good planning document, *The California Water Plan* was open-ended and in play, to be updated at regular intervals. Yet the major outline of what it was proposing stood clear: a statewide system, heroic in magnitude, of dams, reservoirs, pumps, pipes, aqueducts, canals, tunnels, siphons, and hydroelectrical generating plants. The first phase of this plan, centered on the upper Feather River, the Oroville Dam in Butte County (the highest earth-filled dam in the world), the lower Feather River, and the Sacramento, was sent to the legislature by Edmonston in 1951 as a flood control project, updated in 1955, and sent to the Bechtel Corporation for outside review. Bechtel declared the engineering sound but increased the cost of certain aspects of the project by 3 to 9 percent. Even with Bechtel's approval, however, the Feather River Project might have languished in the legislature, given the contentiousness of all water issues, but for the catastrophic flooding of December 1955 and early 1956 with its widespread destruction and more than sixty deaths. The following year, the legislature approved an initial outlay of

$25.2 million from state revenues to get the project started by rerouting Highway 70 and the lines of the Western Pacific Railroad, together with the construction of two out of five water tunnels.

Governor Goodwin J. Knight, meanwhile, was consolidating all state water agencies into a single Department of Water Resources, which began functioning in July 1956 under the direction of Harvey O. Banks, then serving as state engineer following Edmonston's retirement, yet another Stanford-trained civil engineer, with a lieutenant colonel's reserve commission in the Army Corps of Engineers. On 1 June 1957 Banks joined Governor and Mrs. Knight and Walter Schulz, chief engineer for the project, and some five hundred other celebrants for a twenty-two-car train ride from Sacramento to the dam site for groundbreaking ceremonies, followed by barbecue. In his remarks, Governor Knight stressed the Feather River Project as the beginning of a seven-hundred-mile long State Water Plan, although at the time Knight had no idea how such a plan could be negotiated through the legislature or financed without the prior passage of a constitutional amendment. From this perspective, the beginning of construction on the Feather River Project was a jump-start verging on a bluff. Knight wanted the statewide water plan, but he was also harboring presidential ambitions, and he knew that contention over the plan would inevitably erode his popularity within the state, hence deprive him of his power base.

The impasse faced by Knight on the issue of a water-related constitutional amendment throws into relief the breakthrough nature of the Burns-Porter Act, its near-miraculous passage by the legislature under the urging of Governor Brown, and its ultra-narrow approval by the voters in November 1960. As attorney general from 1950 to 1958, Brown had sided with the 160-acre limit out of Democratic sympathy for the little guy, but he also believed that if California continued to resist the limit, as the previous attorney general Frederick Howser had been doing, or to continue to subvert it, as was the common practice among agribusiness, Reclamation would become increasingly skittish about extending the Central Valley Project southward or undertaking any new efforts. This conundrum led Brown, over time, to the position: Why not have California assume the dominant responsibility for its own statewide project, hence avoid the acreage question altogether? By definition, such a proposal represented a massive subsidy by the taxpayer of agribusiness and suburban developers, and objections to such subsidies by labor, veterans, and various small-farmer interests would form the core of opposition when it went before the voters. On the other hand, Brown was a New Deal Democrat with an over-riding faith in the social benefits of public works and a politician looking for a long-term legacy, with an instinctive desire to have California grow into a mega-state. Burns-Porter allowed Brown to bypass the necessity for a constitutional amendment that had brought his predecessor Goodwin Knight to an impasse. It could very well have been titled the Burns-Porter-Brown Act, given the governor's personal involvement in its formulation and passage. State Senator and President Pro Tem Hugh Burns, a Democrat from Fresno, and Assemblyman Carley Porter, a Democrat from Compton in Los

Angeles County, chairman of the Assembly Water Committee, were from the beginning firm allies of the governor. They even looked like the governor. Nearly everyone
in the legislature in the 1950s, in fact, looked that way: male, white, middle-aged,
bespectacled, suit, tie, white shirt, hair pomaded and slicked back, the majority of
them Democrats, but Republicans featuring the same mid-American look. The legislative infrastructure for the mega-state being created in the late 1940s, 1950s, and
early 1960s was being assembled by legislators such as these: middle-aged, middle-
class men of similar backgrounds, career politicians, no better and no worse than
their counterparts in the chambers of commerce, the Rotaries, the Elks, Moose, or
Masons, or the local veterans groups from whence they came. Hugh Burns—past
Exalted Ruler of the Fresno Elks, chairman of the board of the Sequoia Savings and
Loan Association, partner in the insurance firm of Sullivan, Burns and Company,
president of Bankers Acceptance Corporation, each a Fresno company—had played
an important role in passing the Collier-Burns Act of 1947 that was now crisscrossing
the state with freeways. Assemblyman Porter—an Elk, a Moose, a Rotarian, a Red
Cross chairman, a Boy Scout commissioner, a president of the local junior college
board—had turned from teaching high school and junior college to the cemetery
business to politics. First elected to the legislature in 1949, Porter made a specialty of
water, representing as he did the water-hungry suburban communities of Lynwood,
Paramount, Bellflower, Downey, and Compton.

Legislators such as these, ordinary politicians, managed to pass a remarkable series
of water-related measures in rather short order, a number of them conservationist
in orientation. Burns-Porter reaffirmed the series of county-of-origin and watershed-
of-origin acts that since 1931 had been protecting local water sources from being
disastrously depleted, as had happened to the Owens Valley via the Los Angeles
Aqueduct. The Delta Protection Act of 1959 passed in tandem with Burns-Porter
mandated programs confronting the intrusion of saline bay waters into the delta
as part of the statewide program. The Davis-Grunsky Act of 1960 mandated a statewide program of financial assistance to local public agencies for the development,
control, and conservation of water resources, the expansion of recreational opportunities, and the enhancement and protection of fish and wildlife resources keyed
to recreation. Its provisions created Antelope Lake in Los Angeles County, finished
in 1964, the first major reservoir ever built in California exclusively for recreation
and fish and wildlife enhancement. The Davis-Dolwig Act of 1961 expanded these
programs by setting up mechanisms for financing recreational facilities and fish and
wildlife enhancement projects and mandated that such projects be a required part
of the State Water Project.

And so the call went out from the Department of Water Resources: The state is hiring engineers for its newly reorganized divisions of resources planning, of operations
and maintenance, design and construction. Those answering the call included a
number of seasoned veterans but tended in the main to come from engineers and
other professionals who had attained their degrees in the 1950s and early 1960s,

eager to accelerate their careers in, it was advertised, the biggest single water project in world history. By the mid-1960s, with as many as fifty major construction contracts under way, the Department of Water Resources staff numbered approximately 4,480, with 2,250 of them alone in design and construction. On 12 October 1961, a hard-hatted Pat Brown, a look of absolute glee on his face, pushed down the lever to dynamite the first earth at Oroville Dam. On 18 August 1962, President John F. Kennedy joined Brown to push down the handles and dynamite the earth at dedication ceremonies for the San Luis Dam and Reservoir. That year as well, the first water deliveries were made via a partially completed South Bay Aqueduct to the Alameda County Water District and the Alameda County Flood Control and Water Conservation District Zone 7.

When the Metropolitan Water District lost its case against the state of Arizona in 1963 and was forced to set new limits on its intake from the Colorado River via the Colorado Aqueduct, it secured an increase of two million acre-feet from the State Water Project to continue to service its Southern California constituency. Eventually, some 70 percent of all State Water Project deliveries would be going to urban and suburban users, making possible the explosive growth of Southern California in the final decades of the twentieth century. By this time, Pat Brown was living in Los Angeles, having been denied a third term by Ronald Reagan. Turning the tap in his home, the former governor could draw upon northern water that had come south via the 440-mile aqueduct named in his honor.

IV

ART AND LIFE

11

Provincials, Baghdaders, and Beats

Literary San Francisco in the 1950s

THE 1950s witnessed a revival of prose and poetry in San Francisco. In the Fall 1957 *Evergreen Review*, poet and critic Kenneth Rexroth went so far as to describe the era as a San Francisco Literary Renaissance comparable to the flourishing of letters in the city in the 1860s and fin de siècle. Time has qualified Rexroth's assessment but not wholly dismissed it, if one is to judge from the steady stream of biography, critical editions, commentary, and college and university courses dealing with the San Francisco writers of the postwar period, especially the Beats. Yet the Beats were only part of the San Francisco literary scene, and even within their numbers there were groupings and divisions. Non-Beat writers, meanwhile—Provincials, most notably, from an earlier era, together with Baghdaders who had recently colonized the city—were active as well. A few of these Baghdaders would achieve above-average reputations and remain productive for the rest of the century. Provincials, as might be expected, tended to write about San Francisco as subject matter and occasion. Baghdaders and Beats, by contrast, sometimes wrote about San Francisco and at other times ignored it completely. Yet for all three groups the city provided a matrix for living and writing that affected their work; and they, in turn, contributed to the cumulative culture and definition of the city. The Provincials, experiencing the passing of prior definitions, turned to history for corroboration. Baghdaders devised new definitions, and the Beats—who had subsumed and co-opted the radical and bohemian traditions of the city—forecast an impending era of political dissent, sex, drugs, and rock 'n' roll.

The Provincial wing of literary San Francisco remained vital through the first half of the twentieth century. Provincials constituted a third of the writing community: the lesser known third, true, an obscure third even, but a third nevertheless connected directly to the nineteenth century. The re-founder of the Provincial tradition, Frank Norris, was paradoxically a major and bestselling American talent, which cannot be said of any of his successors. Before his untimely death in 1902 at the age of thirty-two, Frank Norris, more than any of his contemporaries, had reestablished the San Francisco literary tradition in the fin de siècle. Jack London was important, and so was Ambrose Bierce; yet neither of these writers—however popular in his time and later revered by literary historians—was a San Franciscan as a matter of choice or daily living. Living in Sunol in Alameda County, Bierce ignored San Francisco other than to lambaste it, and London, living in Sonoma County or traveling the world, set only a small part of his work in the city of San Francisco proper, never talked much about the place, and when he did showed something resembling Bierce's ambivalence. Frank Norris, by contrast—and this despite his residence in New York while writing *The Octopus* (1901)—came of age in San Francisco as a writer, covered San Francisco as a reporter for the *Wave* in the 1890s, set such still-read fictions as *Moran of the Lady Letty* (1898), *McTeague* (1899), *The Octopus*, and the posthumously published *Vandover and the Brute* (1914) in San Francisco and in *Blix* (1899) made a triumphant return to the city where he hoped to spend the rest of his career. No other writer of his generation depicted San Francisco with such success; and no writer or working critic of his era praised San Francisco more explicitly as a subject and mise-en-scène for fiction.

With Norris's death, a number of talented writers who knew him and were of his tribe became keepers of the flame. Like Norris, they blended an abundance of naturalistic proto-cinematic detail (Norris spoke and read French fluently and had deliberately sought to imitate the naturalism of Emile Zola, including Zola's ability to suggest the magnetism of sexual attraction), mitigated by a taste for picturesque social types and situations, flashes of Dickensian whimsy, and a belief in the psychic and paranormal. Two of the finest novels ever set in San Francisco—*The Heart Line* (1907) by Gelett Burgess and *The Day of Souls* (1910) by Charles Tenney Jackson— reprise Norris in story, tone, and technique to such a degree as to constitute a form of self-conscious tribute, especially from Burgess, who had been a staff member with Norris on the *Wave* in the 1890s and a fellow member of Les Jeunes, a coterie of young San Francisco writers who, briefly, put out a somewhat precious publication called the *Lark*. As in the case of Norris's own novels, *The Heart Line* is at once fascinated and repelled by social life in San Francisco, with its blend of bohemianism and effete privilege. Charles Tenney Jackson, by contrast, was a more hardscrabble kind of writer: an Army brat raised in a series of Great Plains forts, a veteran of the Spanish-American War, a Chicago-trained newspaperman who had come to San Francisco after being fired, serving as editor of the *Modesto News* while writing novels on the side. Burgess's *The Heart Line*, as might be expected, blends the society of the Western Addition and Pacific Heights with the bohemia of Telegraph Hill, North Beach, and the cocktail route along Kearny Street, while Jackson's *The Day of Souls* is set in saloons, bookie joints, and smoke-filled rooms packed with scheming politicians; yet each novel is totally Frank Norris in its sense of the city as a commanding presence, its vivid array of characters, its power of attraction between men and women.

Another surviving Norrisite, Charles Caldwell Dobie, who in 1928 wrote for the *American Mercury* one of the first and still relevant essays on Norris and kept on in the mode of his master until his death in 1943. Born in San Francisco in 1886, Dobie resembled Norris in his upper-class demeanor and taste for social life, although Norris, the son of privilege, attended UC Berkeley and Harvard, while Dobie, due to family setbacks, had been forced to forgo high school and enter the marine insurance business. Still, like Norris, Burgess, and Jackson, Dobie learned to write well, achieved a national reputation in the 1920s when H. L. Mencken began to publish his short stories in the *Smart Set*, and like Norris became an active member of the Bohemian Club. A lover of the picturesque, Dobie set many of his stories, gathered in 1935 as *San Francisco Tales*, in Chinatown as well as the French, Italian, Spanish, and Greek neighborhoods of the city. Like Norris, Dobie could deal with the buried past, the psychologically and socially suppressed, racial conflict, and sexual taboos. In *San Francisco: A Pageant* (1933), Dobie achieved the most effective evocation since Frank Norris of the many moods and places of the city.

While no new Frank Norris appeared on the scene following his untimely death, his brother and sister-in-law, Charles Gilman Norris and Kathleen Thompson Norris, each pursued San Francisco–based fiction with the amplitude that would have characterized Frank Norris's career had he lived. Kathleen Norris was by the 1930s the best-selling and highest-paid writer of fiction in the United States; and her husband Charles, who managed her career, also found time to turn out a steady stream of novels in the naturalistic mode favored by his brother, each of them set in San Francisco. Neither Kathleen nor Charles Norris has received the critical attention each deserves. Most literary critics, uneasy with best-selling authors in general, tend to find Kathleen Norris's novels and short stories, many of them initially published in popular magazines, prosaic, formulaic, and conventional. Similarly, Charles Norris's novels have been found to be almost elephantine in their documentary omnivorousness, hence cumbersome and deficient in dramatic effect. Yet the fiction produced by this couple abounds with atmospheric depictions of San Francisco, implicitly inspired by Frank Norris, from the 1910s through the 1930s, while chronicling the efforts of recognizable people to deal with the challenges of ordinary life.

Like their brother and brother-in-law, whose last novel, *The Octopus*, was as much a political, philosophical, even theological tract as it was storytelling, Kathleen and Charles Norris wrote thesis novels dealing with many of the significant problems of the day. Appearing between 1916 and 1944, Charles Norris's fiction dealt in a broadly sociological manner with such topics as the art world, society, university life, marriage and divorce, working women in the downtown, the steel industry, the stage, birth control, sexual incompatibility, agriculture, and the San Francisco strike of 1934. Kathleen Norris wrote fiction for women about women dealing with the important issues of life: love, marriage, birth control, career versus homemaking, and other aspects of domestic life. As a young woman she had worked as a society reporter for the *San Francisco Daily Morning Call*, and the best of her seventy-five novels abound in period detail of San Francisco life among all the classes, including the Irish Catholic working people of the Mission district.

The settings and themes of San Francisco–based popular fiction in this period constituted a mental and imaginative map of the city and its residents. First of all, there is the question of whether one should be in San Francisco at all, if one had serious ambition, artistic, literary or otherwise. The young women of Rose Wilder Lane's *Diverging Roads* (1919) each turn down the San Francisco options of arty bohemianism or bourgeois respectability and leave the city for careers in the East as newspaper reporters. The heroine of Ruth Comfort Mitchell's *Strait Gate* (1935) becomes an aviatrix, while the lesbian protagonists of the minimalist classic *We Too Are Drifting* (1935) by Gale Wilhelm become trapped by indecision about what to make of their lives. In her memoir *Laughter on the Hill: A San Francisco Interlude* (1945), Margaret Parton describes her San Francisco experience as just that, an interlude, living on Telegraph Hill and flirting with a bohemian lifestyle before acquiring her chops as a newspaperwoman at the *Call-Bulletin* as a cub reporter paid $24 a week, transferring to the *Examiner* for even more training, then lighting out for the East. Even the hero of Oscar Lewis's *The Uncertain Journey* (1945) must leave San Francisco to pursue his artistic goals—and this coming from one of the most successful and civic-minded writers in the city.

From the fin de siècle, Society with a capital S and class stratification accentuated by uncertainties regarding the provincial status of the city and the ambiguous origins of many of its elite asserted itself as a local concern beyond the ordinary. All elites are obsessed with status, but in San Francisco—insecure, yet affluent and stylish—social maneuvering had long since become a blood sport. Hence, not surprisingly, popular fiction found settings, topics, and characters aplenty in Society in the prewar and postwar period. The best of such novels is *Proud Flesh* (1924) by Lawrence Rising, a richly detailed and textured novel in the manner of Frank Norris centered on the powerful attraction across social barriers between Fernanda Borel, a socially prominent third-generation San Franciscan, and Patrick O'Malley, an Irish-American of lesser origins. The presence of Frank Norris can be felt throughout *Proud Flesh* in its detailed descriptions of city life and the sexual magnetism between its protagonists. Wallace Irwin, a friend of Frank Norris, had gone to Stanford in the 1890s, become editor of the *Overland Monthly*, and lived in San Francisco until he moved to New York in 1902. Irwin kept his connections with the city, however, the Bohemian Club especially and the Stanford circle revolving there around Herbert Hoover; and he set many of his best novels—*Blooming Angel* (1919), *Lew Tyler's Wives* (1923), *Lew Tyler and the Ladies* (1928), and *The Days of Her Life* (1930)—in San Francisco. Irwin's plots deal with the struggle for love, wealth, and social distinction. In the novels of Gladys Johnson—*Desire* (1929), *Late September* (1932)—women negotiate their way through the same complexities. In the 1930s, as might be expected, depictions of upper-class life and class stratification acquired an edge. Charles Norris's *Zest* (1933) contrasts the preoccupations of social elites with the struggles of the underclass. The heroine of Morris Hull's *Cannery Anne*

(1936) and the hero of George Albee's *Young Robert* (1937) are idealized proletarians. Albee's hero, an aspiring writer from the wrong side of the tracks, is tragically shot to death during a labor demonstration.

The best San Francisco fiction from this period—indeed, the only genre in which such fiction attained acknowledged literary distinction—is the crime novel, the detective story, and the mystery. Jack Boyle, author of *Boston Blackie* (1919), an anthology of previously published short stories harmonized into a continuous narrative, was a onetime San Francisco newspaperman with an opium habit acquired (as relief from overwork, he claimed) in the opium dens of Chinatown. Boyle turned to crime to support his habit and did two, possibly three, prison terms for bad checks and armed robbery. Written while Boyle was in prison and published in the *American Magazine, Redbook*, and *Cosmopolitan*, the Boston Blackie stories revolve around a gentleman safecracker, Boyle's alter ego, who reforms himself and turns detective with the assistance of his wife and crime-solving partner Mary. The salient characteristic of the Boston Blackie stories is not their San Francisco setting, which is sketchy, but Boyle's tense, laconic, staccato prose and dialogue that with a significant boost from another San Francisco–based mystery writer, Dashiell Hammett, would establish a new genre, the hard-boiled detective story.

Like Boyle, Hammett—a tubercular Pinkerton detective and advertising manager for a jewelry company—shook the dust of San Francisco from his feet as soon as other opportunities beckoned. Both spent significant time in Hollywood (fourteen Boston Blackie films were made between 1919 and 1949), although Hammett would experience a lifelong writer's block after 1934. His best writing had been done in San Francisco, and his Hollywood fame would come from director John Huston's 1940 version of *The Maltese Falcon* (1929) for Warner Brothers. If Frank Norris invented the San Francisco of the 1890s as literary mise-en-scène, Dashiell Hammett performed the same service for the 1920s and 1930s, establishing a mood, an iconography, a social complexity, solidly based in place, that would flourish in fiction and film for the rest of the century and remain a fixed element of the San Francisco identity. *The Maltese Falcon* was one of those few novels—John Steinbeck's *Grapes of Wrath* (1939) was another—to stimulate a film of equal achievement, and it was the film as well as the novel that so appealed to Baghdad San Franciscans, for whom Hammett's world of desperate characters, tough-talking cops, treacherous women, mysterious motivations, and real places—the actual restaurants, apartment and office buildings, hotels, banks, Hall of Justice, DA's office, newspapers, and nighttime foghorns of the city—suggested the magic of Baghdad San Francisco where they had chosen to live.

Each Thanksgiving and Christmas, Charles Caldwell Dobie, a lifelong bachelor living in the Bohemian Club, would dine in the home of Gertrude Atherton, who, born in 1857, lived and wrote into the postwar era, the most formidable surviving Provincial of her time. Before her death in 1948 at the age of ninety-one, Atherton did some of her best writing, pecking out on her upright typewriter the memoirs *Golden Gate County* (1945) and *My San Francisco: A Wayward Biography*

(1946)—her fifty-fifth and fifty-sixth and final books—in an eyrie apartment atop her daughter's home on Green Street. While concerned with the Provincial past, mixing reminiscences from as far back as the 1880s with present-tense observations, Atherton ends *My San Francisco* with a reverie regarding the city below, from sundown to sunrise as seen from the Top of the Mark, that constitutes one of the notable set pieces of its kind and a tribute to a writerly relationship to San Francisco as mystic and transformed city so powerfully explored by George Sterling and later to be taken up by Herb Caen and the Baghdaders.

Wartime and the postwar era witnessed the passing of many Provincials and the survival of a few. Peter B. Kyne, author of twenty-five novels and hundreds of short stories in the Cappy Ricks series, born in San Francisco in 1880, serving in the Spanish-American War, had, like Charles Caldwell Dobie, spent his final years living in the Bohemian Club before dying in 1943. Charmian (Mrs. Jack) London died at Glen Ellen in January 1955, age eighty-four, nearly a half century after Jack's departure. Idwal Jones, historical novelist, food and wine writer and historian, having long since moved to Southern California to write for the movies, passed on in November 1964. During the 1920s and 1930s, Jones and his wife's flat at the corner of Hyde and Greenwich, with its stunning Bay views, was one of the epicenters of the flourishing bohemia of that era. With the end of Prohibition in 1933, Jones played an important role as a wine and food writer in re-educating Americans to the wines they had been so long denied.

By the late 1950s, a widowed Kathleen Norris was living in the El Driscoll Hotel in Pacific Heights, where San Francisco ladies of a certain standing were accustomed to spend their retirement years. She remained active in Republican affairs and was busy writing her autobiography, *Family Gathering* (1959). Norris ends *Family Gathering* as Atherton ends *My San Francisco*, standing before a window with a view of the Bay on a late December afternoon, looking back on her life, its variety and achievement, her children, grandchildren, and the books she had written, all of them so profoundly connected to the city. Norris lived on until 1966, among the last—but not the last—of the surviving Provincials to make it into the postwar era.

Miriam Allen De Ford was alive and well and would survive into the early 1970s, living in two book-crammed rooms at the Ambassador Hotel at the corner of Mason and Eddy and continuing to write—novels, short stories, non-fiction—as she had been doing since her arrival in San Francisco in 1920 after attending Wellesley and Temple and doing graduate work at the University of Pennsylvania. De Ford played some bit parts in Hollywood, worked as an insurance claims adjuster, them moved to San Francisco to marry the Socialist writer-scientist Maynard Shipley, a good friend of Jack London's and the poet George Sterling's, joining her husband in the long campaign to free Tom Mooney and Warren K. Billings, railroaded into San Quentin for the Preparedness Day bombings of 1916.

And Oscar Lewis—historian and novelist, born in San Francisco in 1893, the son of a prosperous architect-developer and his piano-teacher wife, and raised in the Sonoma County town of Sebastopol—was still alive and would remain very much so until his departure in July 1992 at the age of ninety-nine, frail but energetic until the last five bedridden years in his flat on Union Street (with yet another beautiful view of the Bay from his bedroom) and continuing to write as he had been writing since selling stories to *Boys' Magazine* while still in high school and during his one year at UC Berkeley, living by his pen since he left UC Berkeley in 1912 to become a full-time writer, selling his stories to *Smart Set* and other magazines. Lewis interrupted his writing career to serve in a UC-sponsored ambulance squad on the Western Front, then returned to the Bay Area, first to Berkeley and then to San Francisco to support himself (almost completely) by freelance writing, publishing history and fiction with Alfred A. Knopf while holding down a part-time position as secretary of the Book Club of California. Lewis's books sold, and he did well, and his wife eventually inherited real estate, and so there was a certain prosperity to Lewis, who had been born that way, after all, into prosperity and had remained productive all of his long life. Until his final years, Lewis, a Tory bohemian of the prewar San Francisco style, given to bow ties and good tailoring, could be found on a weekly basis in the Cartoon Room of the Bohemian Club, a pre-luncheon Manhattan at the ready, discussing books and writing in a soft and understated but pertinent way with club mates George Stewart and James D. Hart of the English department at UC Berkeley or in the evenings attending meetings of the Roxburghe Society of book collectors or merely browsing of an afternoon at Charlotte Newbegin's or John Howell Books, or Richard Hilkert's Dickensian bookstore on Hayes Street—a white-haired figure from another era, almost preternatural in his constant calm and good humor.

San Francisco was a book-collecting as well as book-publishing town, as might be expected from its self-conscious care for culture dating to the isolation of the frontier period when it had been an isolated maritime colony. San Franciscans revered the art of printing and the book and supported them at Holmes at Third and Market and McDonald's on Eddy in the Tenderloin, where only the ancient proprietor, an Ichabod Crane figure in vest, arm bands, and green eyeshade, could tell you the precise location of any one of the hundreds of thousands of books in stock. The Emporium, the White House, and Brentano's in the City of Paris maintained comprehensive bookstores. The genteel and spinsterish Charlotte Newbegin served the carriage trade from her establishment on Post, later moved to Tillman Place. Paul Elder & Company, on Post as well, was more than a bookstore; it was an institution with its roots going back to the 1890s when Paul Elder Sr. started as a clerk at Doxey's bookstore in the Palace Hotel before opening his own establishment in 1898 on the mezzanine of the Mills Building. After many moves, Paul Elder & Company settled finally in 1948 at the corner of Stockton and Sutter, taking with it at all times its luxuriant Craftsman-Gothic bookcases and interiors designed by Bernard Maybeck. The bookstore had long since become an institution—a distinguished fine press publishing house as well as a purveyor of paintings, statuary, and Asian objets d'art— presided over by the UC Berkeley–educated Paul Elder Jr., an accomplished cellist in the Bohemian Club orchestra, who had learned the book trade, new, used, and antiquarian, during a New York apprenticeship in the 1920s.

Elder Jr.had served in the war, as had Warren Howell of John Howell Books on Post near Powell, who won a Bronze Star with Combat Cluster as a naval lieutenant in the Pacific. Howell's naval service included stints in Washington on the staff of the chief of naval operations, Admiral Ernest J. King, and as flag secretary to Rear Admiral Richmond Turner, commander of amphibious forces, Pacific Fleet. These assignments were typical of Howell, being so highly connected, knowing everyone, even in the Navy. As a young man, Howell had been forced to leave Stanford because of the Depression and join his father at John Howell Books as an apprentice and office assistant. The loss of Stanford and the uncertainty of those Depression years had affected him deeply. In compensation, Howell crafted for himself the persona of an impossibly patrician figure, impeccably tailored, surveying the world over half-glasses, a member of the Pacific Union and Bohemian clubs, a lover of social life, leading the parade of debutantes each year after the war, resplendent in white tie and tails, at the annual Cotillion in the Palace Hotel, yet a workaholic as well, commonly putting in ten- to twelve-hour days, including Saturdays, when he would exchange his three-piece suit for a gold-buttoned blue blazer with gray flannel or cavalry twill slacks. Under Warren Howell, John Howell Books became a shrine to San Francisco projected internationally through the antiquarian book trade: a narrow but deep store, packed bookshelves of well-selected and impressively bound volumes rising on either side to the ceiling, and in the distance, glimpsed sitting at his desk in a pool of lamplight, the presiding bookseller Warren Howell, examining a volume, marking its price on the inside cover with soft pencil, keeping an eye all the while on the young and under-paid apprentices in his over-staffed establishment, from whom would come, when they went out on their own, as they invariably did, the antiquarian book-trade professionals of the next era. Like Paul Elder Sr. and John Howell in an earlier era, Warren Howell was also a notable publisher of bibliography and regional history, elegantly designed and produced by the noted San Francisco printer Lawton Kennedy.

Howell's good friend and fellow antiquarian the English-born David Magee was equally erudite, respected, and successful; yet Magee cultivated a more informal demeanor and style, greeting his guests with a scotch and soda if the hour were right (and frequently when it was not) on one of two floors at his establishment on Post, discussing books as if he were an Oxbridge don conducting a tutorial. A graduate of Lancing College, Sussex, where he had played on the cricket team, Magee had gone up to London in the 1920s to learn the antiquarian trade and, arriving in San Francisco, served a period of time with John Howell Books before launching his own enterprise. While Howell's style was stentorian and majestic, Magee—who had in his London days published a comic novel in the style of P. G. Wodehouse—was quick, alert, chatty, and facetious in the Bertie manner, yet remaining elegant as well, as befit the grandson of an Archbishop of York and a man who had known London in the 1920s.

Howell and Magee's local customers tended to belong to the Roxburghe Club, founded in 1928, or the Book Club of California, founded in 1912. While the Roxburghe Club had no permanent quarters, meeting for monthly dinners and presentations in the Sir Francis Drake Hotel, the Book Club maintained rooms and a library on the fifth floor of 312 Sutter, where convivial get-togethers were held each Monday at the cocktail hour. Members of the Book Club were derived from the book-collecting community, including Francis V. de Bellis, a noted collector of Italian Renaissance books and manuscripts. The Book Club pursued an ambitious program of publishing fine press and scholarly books, such as its ever-useful *Bibliography of the History of California, 1510–1930* by Robert Ernest Cowan and Robert Granniss Cowan (1933), designed by the eminent San Francisco printer John Henry Nash.

A notable academic librarian of the city, William J. Monihan, was, in a personal sense, stone-cold broke, having taken a vow of poverty as a Jesuit before going on to library school at Columbia. Returning to San Francisco, Father Monihan assumed direction of the Richard J. Gleeson Library at the University of San Francisco, named in honor of a beloved Jesuit bookman of an earlier era. Monihan embodied the transforming power of books and libraries to generations of students at the university and to the Bay Area book community, for whom he would organize a symposium each August, bringing to the city internationally known scholars from Europe and elsewhere for three days of lectures, discussions, presentations, and festive dinner gatherings in one or another landmark or club venue. Through assiduous collecting and astute fundraising, Monihan developed the Countess Mary Bernardine Murphy Donohue Rare Book Room, named in honor of its deceased benefactor, a papal countess from Los Angeles, into an internationally respected collection of English Recusant literature, Catholic Literary Revival writers, Oscar Wilde, Robert Graves, and fine press books. Monihan also secured for the Gleeson Library the state-owned collection assembled by Adolph Sutro in the late nineteenth century, containing among other items the most ambitious gathering of incunables of its era and a notable collection of medieval Judaica, including manuscripts from the school, perhaps even the hand of the great Sephardic teacher Moses Maimonides.

Such figures embodied a Provincial genteel tradition in its bookish mode during a time when, across the city in North Beach, the poets and writers hanging out at Lawrence Ferlinghetti's City Lights Books had an entirely different agenda in mind, as did the Baghdaders, who in their own more conventional way were forging new definitions for the city. Which is one reason, perhaps the primary reason, Provincial San Francisco was so interested in history during this period: as a way of shoring up its identity in the face of the changes that were everywhere. A sense of San Francisco as a city brave and defiant and exuding panache during the Earthquake and Fire of April 1906, rather than a mismanaged catastrophe as would be proven a hundred years later, became a fixed point of reference for Provincial San Francisco, the staple of annual commemorative speeches, and pervades two studies—*The Earth Shook*, *the Sky Burned* (1959) by William Bronson and *The Damndest Finest Ruins* (1959) by Monica Sutherland—of the postwar period. These two histories were but part of an absolute cavalcade of San Francisco historiography, amateur and professional, non-fiction and fiction, that began in the 1930s and continued across the next three decades. In 1933 novelist Ruth Comfort Mitchell, a native daughter now living in the Santa Clara Valley, published *Old San Francisco*, a four-novella saga boxed and sold as a set. Oscar Lewis's *The Big Four* (1938), a study of the railroad era, remained in print for fifty years. Writing in *California Classics* (1971), UCLA librarian and critic Lawrence Clark Powell considered Lewis's historical novel *I Remember Christine* (1942) among the half-dozen best works of fiction with a San Francisco setting.

The postwar 1940s witnessed a plethora of such efforts, as writer after writer sought to evoke and define the frontier and Provincial heritage of the city. During the war Evelyn Wells had produced *Champagne Days of San Francisco* (1943). Gertrude Atherton's *Golden Gate Country* (1945) and *My San Francisco* (1946) were largely first-person memoirs of the times she had lived through and the figures of Old San Francisco—Mark Twain, Bret Harte, Ambrose Bierce, George Sterling, James Duval Phelan—she had known personally. Former Marine Captain William Martin Camp chronicled the port in *San Francisco: Port of Gold* (1947) at a time when it was in the full flush of its wartime expansion and success. (Unfortunately, Camp himself was experiencing financial difficulties and perhaps some form of postwar trauma and committed suicide shortly after publication of this book.) In 1948 Robert O'Brien published *This Is San Francisco*, a collection of the meticulously researched historical columns he had been writing for the *Chronicle*. More comprehensively, John Bruce, city editor of the *Chronicle* and former city editor of the *Call-Bulletin*, issued his ambitious history of local journalism, *Gaudy Century* (1948). In 1949 Julia Cooley Altrocchi—a Vassar graduate married to a professor of Italian at UC Berkeley (she also wrote articles on European topics for *Atlantic*, *Harper's*, and the *Yale Review*)—followed up her *Snow Covered Wagons* (1936), a blank-verse narrative of the Donner Party, with *The Spectacular San Franciscans*, a vivid portrait of social life since the Gold Rush. All this history writing by Provincials must in some way be put into the context of a reverence, a nostalgia, for the past, now that there had been a world war and things were changing and would never be the same.

The 1950s witnessed a cavalcade of history writing empowered by an admixture of scholarship, anxiety, and nostalgia. In 1951 Idwal Jones published *Ark of Empire*, a history of the Montgomery Block (1853) that functioned from the 1870s onward as a complex of artists' studios. Ground zero of the fin-de-siècle bohemian tradition (Coppa's restaurant was a few doors away), the Montgomery Block was unfortunately heading for demolition by the end of the decade, and thus Jones's evocation of what the Block had meant to San Francisco functioned as an anticipated elegy to a structure built solidly of granite, resting on deep redwood piles, but nevertheless vulnerable, like Provincial San Francisco itself, to change. The literary tradition of San Francisco in its frontier phase had in times past been solidly covered in longtime *Argonaut* editor Jerome Hart's *In Our Second Century* (1931), in UC Berkeley professor George Stewart's *Bret Harte* (1931, and in Mills College professor Franklin Walker's *San Francisco's Literary Frontier* (1939), another of the books about the West personally solicited by Alfred A. Knopf on one or another of his trips to California. In 1952 *Chronicle* literary critic Joseph Henry Jackson published *The Western Gate*, an anthology of one hundred years of San Francisco writing, as part of a city and county literary series being issued by Farrar, Straus & Young.

An omnivorous and energetic book reviewer, literary critic, and cultural historian, the Clifton Fadiman of San Francisco, Jackson earned a national reputation in publishing circles as a gatekeeper, either in the *Chronicle*, where he had been reviewing since 1931, or on his weekly radio program. A tall, angular, and very civil man, the descendant of seventeenth-century English immigrants, a graduate of Lafayette College and an Army lieutenant in the First World War, Jackson—like Oscar Lewis—asserted by his very presence that the career of a man of letters, to one degree or another, was possible in the Bay Area. Writers promoting their books were thrilled to lunch with Jackson at the men-only English Grill in the St. Francis Hotel, or the Mural Room if the writer were female. A review by Jackson sold books. A photograph from the period—taken by Max Yavno for Herb Caen's *The San Francisco Book* (1948)—depicts Wallace Stegner, William Saroyan, Oscar Lewis, George Stewart, C. S. Forester, and Kathryn Forbes happily chatting at one of the frequent gatherings of literary folk Jackson would host in his Berkeley home. In 1953 Jackson published an extended essay, *My San Francisco*, in which he extolled the civility of the San Francisco way of life. When Jackson, taping a review, expired from a heart attack at the age of sixty-one in the studios of KNBC, he exited local history as the most influential Bay Area critic of his kind in the twentieth century.

The effort to chronicle the literary traditions of the city continued with Oscar Lewis's *Bay Window Bohemia* (1956), a rich evocation of the 1890–1915 period that, even more than the post–Gold Rush era, witnessed a flourishing of local writing. By this time, the mid-1950s, the San Francisco history machine—whether powered by academic ambition or Provincial nostalgia or a combination thereof—was in high gear. During this period as well, the productivity of the San Francisco historians who would dominate the next forty years began to assert itself. At the University of San Francisco, Jesuit historian Peter Dunne had found an equally ambitious Jesuit successor, John B. McGloin, who would continue Dunne's work of mapping the extensive contours of Catholic California, as well as writing a history of San Francisco. At UC Berkeley, San Francisco native James D. Hart—joined in San Francisco by amateur historian George Harding, an accountant at Pacific Telephone—was conducting studies in printing and publishing history that would result in a number of books. Richard Dillon, meanwhile, librarian of the Sutro, was at the beginning of his prolific career as an historian of California and the Far West, as were two other scholar-librarians, James de Tarr Abajian at the California Historical Society and Dale Morgan at the Bancroft. The tradition of literary retrospective, meanwhile, continued with Mrs. Fremont Older's *San Francisco: Magic City* (1961), a memoir impossible to dismiss as mere nostalgia, given the fact that Cora Miranda Baggerly Older, now eighty-six, had lived through the decades of the fin de siècle—one of the most beautiful women in the city, residing with her husband, *Bulletin* editor Fremont Older, in a suite in the Palace Hotel, the two of them constantly entertaining prominent writers and journalists and VIPs passing through—and she remembered everything.

This quality of living memory, reinforced by scholarship, was characteristic as well of the historian and preservationist C. Albert Shumate, second only to Oscar Lewis as an historical writer who was also an historical personality in his own right. Living in a house on Scott Street his grandfather had built in 1870, Shumate—the son of a politically prominent physician and owner of drugstores—had taken an M.D. at Creighton University and completed a residency in dermatology at Columbia before returning to San Francisco. After a decade of being on the town and a stint in the Public Health Service during the war, Shumate rose to clinical professor of dermatology at Stanford, with a flourishing private practice, together with involvements in numerous historical and preservationist activities. Each year, Shumate would sponsor a reception at his Scott Street home, which contained his extensive collection of California books and art, in honor of La Favorita, a young lady descended from a founding Spanish family who would preside over birthday festivities for the city—a San Francisco version of a Rose Queen. All these activities would have been sufficient to place Dr. Shumate at the center of the Provincial city, which they did; yet he was also an indefatigable researcher and gifted writer, producing eleven books and sixty-nine articles and pamphlets on San Francisco or California history.

Two high points of Old San Francisco's self-definition came, as might be expected, from Provincial San Francisco itself, through Samuel Dickson and, paradoxically and outrageously, the flamboyant Baghdader Lucius Beebe. Dickson began writing scripts for the *Streets of San Francisco* series in 1932, and was by the 1950s still having his vivid and detailed vignettes read on the air by announcer Budd Heyde each Sunday morning and evening on radio station KNBC, sponsored by Rickey's Restaurants. As Dickson's scripts accumulated (2.5 million words by the mid-1950s), Stanford University Press issued them as books—*San Francisco Is Your Home* (1947), *San Francisco Kaleidoscope* (1949), *The Streets of San Francisco* (1955)—combined into the omnibus volume *Tales of San Francisco* (1957). Born in San Francisco in 1889, of Bavarian Jewish descent (having changed his name from Dinkelspiel during World War I, when aggressively German last names were proving a liability), Dickson married into a well-heeled and socially prominent Burlingame family, having met his wife at the debutante cotillion at the Palace Hotel. Moving to San Mateo County, where he remained comfortably ensconced for the next sixty years, Dickson found his métier as an historian. All things considered, Dickson's writings, especially as represented in the cumulative 1957 volume, constituted an apogee of Provincial San Francisco's nostalgic conception of itself.

The co-existence of so many Provincials, Baghdaders, and Beats in one small city across a short period of time centered on the 1950s testified to the complexity of San

Francisco. Few other cities in the country, outside of New York, could show such divergence, underscoring the complexities and contradictions of the postwar era and the very nature of urbanism itself. Baghdad writers can be grouped in three categories: those who chose to live in the Bay Area, some of whom arrived with established reputations but continued to write about someplace else; those who came to the Bay Area because they were attracted by its political culture and would write intermittently about San Francisco; and writers who came to San Francisco and began to engage the city. Ensconced atop Twin Peaks, Erskine Caldwell remained aloof from local life, keeping his focus on Tobacco Road and the demimondes of elsewhere. Ernest Gann, a onetime pilot for American Airlines, kept his eyes on Hollywood and the sky, although in *The High and the Mighty* (1953) the San Francisco airport is the desired goal of a troubled flight from Honolulu. English expatriate C. S. Forester, while sociable, kept his focus on Horatio Hornblower and related English subjects. Oakley Hall lived on Macondray Lane in a home that had been once inhabited by California poet laureate Ina Coolbrith. After a series of San Diego novels, Hall was concentrating on the Arizona frontier, the mise-en-scène of his existential western *Warlock* (1958). and would only return to San Francisco subjects and settings in the 1990s. The setting and themes of Evan Connell's fiction, beginning with *Mrs. Bridge* (1959), were Kansas City and the Midwest. Although Ernest Gaines had been raised since age fifteen in Vallejo, had graduated from San Francisco State College in 1957, and maintained a flat on Divisadero Street at the epicenter of the African American community, his heart and soul, and his writing, remained with the rural black folk of his native Louisiana. The English department at San Francisco State had on its faculty Walter Van Tillberg Clark, who wrote westerns set in Nevada, and comic writer Mark Harris, whose settings and subjects were all over the map. Although the protagonist of Harris's *Wake Up, Stupid* (1959) teaches at San Francisco State, he is trying to get his play produced in New York so he can split to the East. Arriving in San Francisco in 1960, Herbert Gold continued to set his fiction in Cleveland but would soon turn to his adopted city for setting and subject matter.

Two novelists from opposite ends of the social spectrum were especially attracted by the left-liberal culture of the Bay Area. A working-class social and political activist, busy with a full-time job, children, and housework, Tillie Olsen was admitted to the Stanford Creative Writing Program in 1955 despite her lack of a college degree. Olsen's *Tell Me a Riddle* (1962) made the Ten Best Books of the Year list of *Time*. Despite her local political involvements, Olsen belonged to the larger world of emergent feminist fiction; and despite her new-found fame, she remained that rare American phenomenon: a working-class writer writing about working-class people even after fame found her. Kay Boyle, by contrast, was to the manner born. A former European correspondent for the *New Yorker*, living in Paris through the 1930s, later married to an American diplomat, Boyle belonged to the International Left in its upper-register dimensions. Moving to San Francisco in 1963 after the death of her husband to accept a professorship at San Francisco State, Boyle, like another San Francisco–based writer, Alice Adams, reconsolidated herself locally as an iconic figure fusing feminism, leftism, high taste, and a certain presence bordering on hauteur, emanating from a sense of caste, of having one's origins in a larger world beyond San Francisco. The Virginia-born Alice Adams, a graduate of Radcliffe, living in the Bay Area since the 1940s, when her then-husband was at Stanford, while less political than Boyle, shared the same upper-register feminist style and was widely admired by younger women writers. While her early short stories were set in and around Chapel Hill, North Carolina, where her father taught Spanish litera-ture, Adams also set many of her short stories in San Francisco, albeit in a sketchy manner, since the focus of her writing was not a Balzacan abundance of detail but elliptical dialogue and the upper-bourgeois aperçu.

San Francisco of the wartime and postwar era was not lacking explicitly detailed and interpretive novels written by San Franciscans, non–San Franciscans looking for local color, temporary San Franciscans or, in the case of Niven Busch, a Baghdad insider. In *Home Is Here* (1941), Sidney Meller, a local, told the story in full detail of an Italian family living atop Telegraph Hill in the pre–World War I era, deciding whether or not to return to Italy. In *King of This Hill* (1945), Nathaniel Meserve, a local passing through, told the story of three returning GIs batching it together atop Telegraph Hill en route to their long-range identities. Details of local life are also characteristic of Margaret Cochran Shedd's *Return to the Beach* (1950), the story of a middle-class family struggling with the impending death of a son, and Vicki Baum's three-generational saga *Danger from Deer* (1951). Each of these writers—the one a well-known Hollywood screenwriter, the other an unknown local—employs San Francisco settings to corroborate emotional and psychological states. Abundantly detailed as well is local writer Evelyn Wells's *The Gentle Kingdom of Giacomo* (1953), a novel set in the flower-growing regions of the Santa Cruz peninsula and the floral stores of San Francisco. Born and raised in San Francisco, a graduate of Stanford, married to a Podesta connected to the leading florist of the city, Podesta Baldocchi, Wells knew firsthand the floral industry and the people she describes.

The hero of *Walk Toward the Rainbow* (1954) by San Franciscan John Bell Clay-ton is a trust-funder struggling with a booze and Seconal problem, tenuously under control, who returns to his native city in an effort to rebuild his life and writing career. Clayton's novel abounds in ample and precise detail regarding the city and concludes with a four-page threnody blending Frank Norris, Provincial, and Bagh-dad motifs. In *A View of the Bay* (1955), the Stanford-based novelist Richard Scow-croft pulls off a partially realized San Francisco novel of manners, centered on a delayed adjustment of a veteran to civilian life, in which the central protagonist continually fantasizes fleeing the Bay Area for Tahiti. In *Young Mr. Keefe* (1958), the Los Angeles–based novelist Stephen Birmingham deals with the problem of adjust-ment from the Korean conflict, booze, marriage, and divorce, some of it in a Pacific Heights setting.

Three of the most ambitious San Francisco–set novels of the period were by a Baghdad insider, Niven Busch. A former editor at *Time* and staff writer for the *New Yorker*, Busch had done well enough as a Hollywood screenwriter—among his credits were *The Postman Always Rings Twice* (1946) and *Duel in the Sun* (1946), based on his novel of the same name—to buy himself a cattle ranch in Hollister south of the city and a Pacific Heights pied-à-terre. Socially ambitious in a John O'Hara sort of way—a Princeton dropout, a Republican, and an Episcopalian— Busch soon became a fixture in social circles and a charter member of the Algon- quinish circle formed by Herb Caen meeting for literary lunches at Trader Vic's. Having soaked up the mise-en-scène of Pacific Heights and the founding families liv- ing there, Busch embarked upon a trilogy of novels dealing with upper-register San Francisco, separate in story but overlapping in theme and setting. *California Street* (1959) was centered on a newspaper family, *The San Franciscans* (1962) on a banking family, and *The Gentleman from California* (1965) on a San Francisco–based Repub- lican senator who wins the presidential election of 1972. *California Street* had just enough connection to the de Youngs of the *Chronicle; The San Franciscans* had just enough connection to the Tobins of the Hibernia Bank; and *The Gentleman from San Francisco* was prophetic enough of Ronald Reagan to make it all very interest- ing in local terms. A Baghdader, Busch displayed an informed appreciation of Old San Francisco, although it was a Baghdad appreciation of the founders as ruthless and disreputable as opposed to the revered figures of Provincial memory.

When it came to non-fiction, San Francisco and the Bay Area was an almost completely Baghdad affair. Herb Caen was at the top of his game during these years, premier columnist and man-about-town. In 1957 Caen produced a best-selling guide to the restaurants and hot spots of the city. By the early 1960s, another *Chronicle* columnist, Charles McCabe, modeling his columns on the essays of Montaigne, was producing literate effusions on a wide variety of topics. McCabe began each working day by wending his way down from his Telegraph Hill apartment to Gino & Carlo's bar on Green Street in North Beach, where he reviewed his mail while sipping away at no more than five Rainier ales, his morning limit. Another *Chron- icle* columnist, Allan Temko, had already written a definitive study of Notre Dame Cathedral and was commenting on architecture and the built environment with a literary skill equal to McCabe's.

Through Charles McCabe, *Chronicle* editor Scott Newhall met and subse- quently hired as a columnist Lucius Morris Beebe, a Baghdader who had moved from New York to Nevada in 1949 and began writing for the *Chronicle* in 1960. As in the case of all dandies, it is difficult to decipher Lucius Beebe beneath the flam- boyant pose; for Beebe was a devoted writer as well as a poseur and was in his own way acting out a statement of rejection regarding modern life and values that linked him simultaneously to Old San Francisco and to Baghdad. Clifton Fadiman once said of Beebe that he had "successfully evaded the twentieth century by the simple expedient of never emerging from the nineteenth."[1] A staunch Republican, Beebe said that he considered Calvin Coolidge a liberal. How much of this was pose on Beebe's part, how much the result of historical analysis and conviction, how much just good fun—or how much of this was a viscerally felt rejection of modernity and a nostalgic attraction to the imagined Right of a bygone era—remains a mystery;

but the need for a flamboyant persona, a pose, also links Beebe, a homosexual, with other gay performers forced to the margins of that closeted era.

Born in 1902 in Wakefield, Massachusetts, to a venerable Boston mercantile and banking family, Beebe graduated from Harvard (after being expelled from Yale) and spent two post-graduate years there doing a master's degree in English under the renowned John Livingston Lowes. He thereupon decamped for New York City, where he wrote social commentary for the *New Yorker*, followed by a column covering café society for the *Herald Tribune*. Beebe liked to carouse about town into the wee hours, as often as possible in white tie, and sleep late. His distinction during these years was to make the Ten Best-Dressed List in 1937 and in 1938 to publish the best-selling *High Iron*, the first of his many railroad books; for in the drama of nineteenth-century railroading Beebe had discovered an objective correlative for all that he felt was lacking in modern life.

In 1949, having come into his inheritance, Beebe moved to Virginia City, Nevada (population 350, twenty saloons), where there were no state income or inheritance taxes. There as well, in the company of his longtime partner photographer Charles Clegg, who would co-author seventeen of Beebe's thirty-three books, Beebe spent the next seventeen years, acting out a scenario of himself as the last survivor of the railroading Age of Silver in the Far West, living, alas, in a depleted and forlorn present. Beebe and Clegg decorated a Virginia City mansion in high Victorian style. They purchased a private railroad car, staffed it with a butler and decorated it with antiques, in which they visited the Bay Area and the East. Their 185-pound St. Bernard, T-Bone, was known to nibble on steaks and pate de foie gras, and when T-Bone departed this life, he was succeeded by the equally formidable and lucullan T-Bone Towser, who had the same tastes. Purchasing the *Territorial Enterprise* in 1952, Beebe and Clegg drove its circulation from fifty to fifteen thousand by covering local events as if they were world-shaking—the efforts of a local priest, for example, to close a bordello opposite the parish school—and by evoking constantly the vigor and gusto of nineteenth-century Silver Age Nevada. What made Beebe a San Franciscan, aside from his winter home in Hillsborough and his frequent appearances in the city, was his *Chronicle* column covering the mores and institutions, the hotels and restaurants, the wine and cuisine, any and all surviving elements in the city that would remind readers of San Francisco's colorful past. A photograph in *Holiday* for April 1961 of Beebe, resplendent in top hat, white tie, tails, and silver-tipped cane in the glass-domed inner court of the Palace Hotel, said it all: the history, true, but the nostalgia and fantasy as well, the harkening back to a glorious past that was by definition a judgment on the slippery and uncertain present.

The rise of Bay Area universities in the postwar era brought to the region a number of noted academics and men of letters, diversely active in fiction, biography, history, and criticism: Wallace Stegner and Albert Joseph Guerard at Stanford; Mark Schorer, Thomas Parkinson, and the novelist and cultural critic Eugene Burdick at UC Berkeley. In this period as well, the English department at San Francisco State was flourishing, not only with fiction writers and poets but with literary critic

Leonard Wolf and semanticist S. I. Hayakawa, whose *Language in Thought and Action* (1949) was attaining the status of an academic classic. The city of San Francisco even enjoyed the presence of its own resident philosopher, the neo-Aristotelian Mortimer Adler, director of the Institute for Philosophical Research in the Whittier mansion in Pacific Heights, where under Adler's direction a core of researchers were preparing the Synopticon, a guide to the great ideas as found in the Great Books series Adler had helped edit for the Encyclopedia Britannica.

All such academics and writers tended to be Baghdaders who had deliberately chosen to come to the Bay Area and throw themselves into the local mix. Mark Schorer, for example, made frequent appearances on radio and television and belonged to the Trader Vic's roundtable. A talented jazz pianist, S. I. Hayakawa loved a party and could frequently be found at one, hunched over the piano. Eugene Burdick and Allan Temko were tireless in their efforts to cover the region for national publications. In his *San Francisco: A Profile with Pictures* (1959), Barnaby Conrad, Baghdader par excellence, achieved a lyrical and lightly triumphant love song to the city. A Yale man, Conrad had moved to San Francisco after serving in the consular corps in Spain during the war. While in Spain, Conrad fought bulls as the California Kid and wrote the best-selling novel *Matador* (1952), based on the life of the great Manolete. Conrad had met Caen at Yale, when Caen was in training as an Army Air Forces public relations officer, and the two of them became fast friends. A lover of nightlife, Conrad opened El Matador, a Spanish-style drinking establishment on Broadway in North Beach, through which poured a cavalcade of visiting celebrities, whose witticisms were reported on the next day by Herb Caen.

To appreciate the relevance to the definition of Baghdad of Conrad's *San Francisco: A Profile with Pictures*, one only has to contrast it with the equally detailed *The Face of San Francisco* (1960) by local journalist Harold Gilliam, with photographs by Phil Palmer, published a few months later. Gilliam's guidebook is a tour de force of scholarly reportage, augmented by Palmer's black-and-white photo-realism. Comprehensive and complete, it presents the city with an evenhanded conclusiveness almost documentarian in tone, as does *Chronicle* newsman James Benét's *Guide to San Francisco* later in the decade. Conrad, by contrast, celebrates San Francisco as Baghdad by the Bay. Like Herb Caen, he re-perceives the city, making its sights and sounds and daily activities—buying flowers from a sidewalk flower stand or fresh crab on Fisherman's Wharf, lunching at the sidewalk café outside Enrico's on Broadway, sailing on the bay, the parade of debutantes at the Cotillion, the newspaper photographers in white tie and tails covering opening night at the opera, a North Beach artist painting a nude model, bocce ball in Golden Gate Park, pigeons in Union Square, a poetry and jazz performance at the Cellar on Green Street in North Beach, a heady discussion of existentialism in a nearby café—all seem magical because they have been transformed by the Baghdad vision.

Harold Gilliam also covered the working life of the waterfront, which could be atmospheric, true, when encountered in Dashiell Hammett or in a film noir, but was also a prosaic workaday place, where one might encounter the decidedly non-Baghdadian Eric Hoffer. In political terms, the preponderance of Baghdad San Francisco was left-liberal. Eric Hoffer was decidedly not a left-liberal, although exactly how he can be defined remains problematic. A figure from the Old Left, anchored in working-class realities, or a figure from the Old Right, anchored in the Jeffersonian isolationism of the Early Republic, or some idiosyncratic combination thereof—Hoffer was all this and more. Born (1898) in New York to Alsatian immigrants (he spoke with a German accent throughout his life), Hoffer went mysteriously blind as a child following the death of his mother and stayed blind until he was fifteen, cared for by an Alsatian woman who taught him English. Moving to Los Angeles in 1920, he spent a decade there working as an odd-jobs man and in the 1930s went into the fields as a migrant worker, reading incessantly, before settling in San Francisco, where he joined the Longshoremen's Union, worked on the docks, and continued to read and take notes, eventually accumulating some 130 notebooks. Living in a room on McAllister Street near the public library (a bed, two chairs, a phonograph, a 78 recording of Beethoven's Ninth), Hoffer composed his first book during the waterfront strikes of 1946 and 1948 in longhand on a plywood plank stretched between two chairs. He submitted *The True Believer* (1951), a study of mass movements, to Harper & Row as a handwritten manuscript. It was the first of nine books he published with Harper & Row, each of them written in an aphoristic style modeled on Montaigne and Pascal.

Hoffer's relationship to San Francisco was paradoxical. On the one hand, the city gave him a steady job, union protection, a library card, a room in which to live and write, Golden Gate Park through which he would walk three miles to the ocean while ruminating on what he had read, and inexpensive eateries such as Schroeder's, the Palm Garden, and Tommy's Joynt, where he could dine on old-fashioned German food. San Francisco would put him on its public television station, leading to a nationally broadcast series of interviews by Eric Sevareid on CBS, which helped earn him an adjunct professorship at UC Berkeley and, in the Johnson administration, the Presidential Medal of Freedom, the nation's highest civilian honor. But while Mayor Joseph Alioto might invite Hoffer to speak at his inauguration, the preponderance of left-liberal opinion in San Francisco by the 1960s had engendered extraordinary hostility against a conservative social philosopher who remained a working longshoreman until his retirement in 1967 and dressed like one—flannel shirt, flat white cap, Big Ben pants, heavy shoes—even on formal occasions, and had no qualms taking on in an outspoken, sometimes bellowing manner the assumptions and shibboleths of the 1960s.

In his own way, Eric Hoffer was a bohemian, and bohemianism had remained a flourishing tradition in San Francisco since the 1860s. In the aftermath of the Earthquake and Fire of April 1906, the bohemian community of San Francisco—centered on Coppa's restaurant on Montgomery—relocated itself to Carmel for a decade or so, then reconsolidated itself in San Francisco around such figures as George Sterling and Henry Lafler. Described by his good friend Jack London as the Uncrowned King of Bohemia, poet George Sterling was adopted by the Provincial establishment as a living symbol of literary achievement. At the Panama-Pacific International Exposition of 1915, Sterling's name was carved above an entrance gate alongside the names Shakespeare, Spencer, and Milton. Businessman Thomas Barbour underwrote Sterling's room and board at the Bohemian Club. A visit with Sterling became a requirement for any literary personage passing through the city. When he took his own life by cyanide in his rooms at the Bohemian Club in November 1926, his friend Idwal Jones said that it was like a unicorn dying. Mayor Rolph wanted him to lie in state beneath the rotunda of City Hall, but Sterling's family vetoed the idea.

With its sweeping views and available housing stock, Telegraph Hill above North Beach served as epicenter of bohemia in both the pre- and post-1906 era. In the immediate aftermath of the Earthquake and Fire, poet-newsman Henry Anderson Lafler, turning developer, used scrap lumber to build a number of low-cost, live-work bungalows atop the hill. By the mid-1920s, an integrated series of these homes, known as the Lafler Compound, clung to the side of Telegraph Hill like the lama-series of Tibet or the monasteries of Mount Athos. There, until Lafler's death in an automobile accident in January 1935, the bohemia of San Francisco remained centered.

Below Telegraph Hill was North Beach, a densely settled littoral of two- and three-story flats running between Telegraph and Russian hills from downtown to the Bay, overwhelmingly Italian in population and ambience since the 1890s, as J. B. Monaco's photos from the early years of the twentieth century reveal, a picturesque Little Italy. The first wave of Italian immigrants in the 1880s included many who were merely looking San Francisco over, reserving the option of returning to Italy, and even if they did not return, vigorously maintaining their Italian language and loyalty to their homeland. Indeed, it would be difficult fully to determine whether the grizzled retirees sitting in the sunshine on the benches surrounding Washington Square were, as far as their own sense of time and place was concerned, living back in Italy or in San Francisco. North Beach had its own Italian-language newspaper, *L'Italia*, an Italian-language bookstore, A. Cavalli & Co., its own array of ethnic grocery stores, delicatessens, and restaurants. North Beach made its living on Fisherman's Wharf, with its fleet of seven hundred craft, serviced by some twenty-five hundred fishermen, together with hundreds of others processing and shipping fish on the wharf itself. Other North Beach men worked in the garbage industry for the employee-owned Sunset Scavenger or Golden Gate Disposal, with each scavenger owning shares, while working the trucks. Hard-working and financially prudent, they invested their earnings in apartment buildings in North Beach and the nearby Marina district—where Joe DiMaggio's parents had moved before the war—and many of them retired as wealthy men.

The Italian community of North Beach was tightly knit, conservative, Republican, anchored in family and property. Large families grew up in single flats, the young people not leaving home until they married. The Italian word for the ethos governing North Beach is *campanilismo*, the spirit, the situation, of being near the campanile, with people from the same province, the same town, even the same village resettled together. In the case of North Beach, the campaniles consisted of the spires of St. Francis Church (1849) at Columbus and Vallejo, the oldest church and proto-cathedral of the city, and the more recently constructed (1922) Sts. Peter and Paul on Filbert facing Washington Square, a white wedding cake of a church, with a parish school on the top floor, a gymnasium in the basement, and an adjacent boys' club, all of it staffed by priests, brothers, and sisters of the Salesians, an order founded in Italy in 1859 for the education of youth and missionary work abroad. The Salesian Boys' Club there ran an ambitious athletic and academic program intended to insert young men into the political and legal establishment of the city. By the 1950s numerous judges, commissioners, and city and state officials, together with a host of prominent lawyers and businessmen, were North Beach natives and graduates of the club: Joseph Lawrence Alioto, for example, born in 1916 to a fishing and fish-processing family and raised in the family home on Beach Street. Graduating in 1940 from the law school of Catholic University, where he acquired an expertise in monopolies and trusts, Alioto served in the Pentagon during the war as a civilian intelligence expert, tracing concealed ownership linkages among Allies and belligerents. By the 1950s he had emerged as a man of the hour, a member at various times of the board of education and the redevelopment commission, a frequent speaker, a future mayor of the city.

The ambience created by North Beach and its Mediterranean traditions—if not the conservative politics—motivated poet Kenneth Rexroth to move to San Francisco in 1927 as a place to lead the literary life; and it was around Rexroth, prior to the emergence of the Beats, that the San Francisco Literary Renaissance organized itself. Rexroth was a philosophical anarchist, and the radical strain in Bay Area literary traditions had attracted him as much as the Mediterranean atmosphere. In the pre-Earthquake period, bohemia had its left and right wings, with George Sterling and Jack London—Socialists belonging to the Bohemian Club—having a foot in each camp. In the post-Earthquake era, the Tory bohemianism as represented by the Bohemian Club became increasingly confined to its own culture, while anarchism of the romantic variety dominated bohemian circles. In the 1930s Marxism made its appearance, not only in literary circles but in the maritime unions for which Rexroth had worked as an organizer following his arrival in San Francisco. The Second World War brought a new generation of non-conformists to the West Coast, many of them, such as William Everson, assigned to the conscientious objectors' Camp Angel in Waldport, Oregon, but free to hitchhike to the Bay Area when on pass from their work in the Forest Service. The camp issued its own review, the *Illiterati*, dedicated to a warless society, and a related publication, *Circle*, was published in Berkeley between 1944 and 1948, featuring such writers as Rexroth and Henry Miller (recently moved to the Coast) and poets William Everson, Josephine Miles, and Philip Lamantia. In 1946 the *Circle* circle created the Pacifica Foundation, and in 1949 the foundation put listener-supported radio station KPFA-FM on the air under general manager Lewis Hill, a Stanford-educated conscientious objector. Rexroth reviewed books for KPFA-FM. For the rest of the century, KPFA-FM would function as a radio version of the *Village Voice* for the San Francisco Bay Area: dissenting, frequently radical (but anti-Communist), always worth listening to, even by those who did not share its opinions.

Another crucial arrival, in April 1951, was that of Lawrence Ferlinghetti, a man of impeccable Baghdad credentials: an Eagle Scout as a teenager; a graduate of Mount Hermon prep school; a member of Sigma Kappa at the University of North Carolina, Chapel Hill; a decorated veteran who had enlisted in the Navy before Pearl Harbor, won a commission, and commanded a sub-chaser in the Normandy invasion, followed by service as a navigator in the Pacific. Released from the service, Ferlinghetti worked briefly in advertising, then used his GI Bill to take an M.A. in English at Columbia under Mark Van Doren, with a thesis on the relationship between John Ruskin and J.M.W. Turner (Ferlingetti was himself an aspiring painter), prior to going on to the Sorbonne for a Ph.D. in literature, with a dissertation, written in French, on the city as symbol in modern poetry.

There was much in Ferlinghetti, in short, that would have propelled him into a standard postwar academic career, except for the fact that he had been deeply affected by a visit to Nagasaki shortly after the bombing. "So that made me an instant pacifist," Ferlinghetti later stated. "I mean, I had been a good American boy, a Boy Scout, an Eagle Scout, and a skipper of a sub-chaser at Normandy. This completely changed my world view."[2] Other influences on Ferlinghetti included his experiences of Greenwich Village during his Columbia days, his reading of Henry Miller's *The Colossus of Maroussi* (1941) while on a visit to Majorca, his interest in the urban context of modern poetry, and his residence in Paris, a city that, like New York and the other cities he had experienced through travel and literary analysis, had led him to expect more from an urban environment than a mere delivery of goods and services.

And so, in early 1951, taking the Union Pacific California Zephyr out to San Francisco, Lawrence Ferlinghetti decided to move to San Francisco. Following his marriage in April 1951, he moved with his wife into a flat on Chestnut Street near the California School of Fine Arts. Within four years, Ferlinghetti would stand alongside Rexroth at ground zero of the San Francisco Literary Renaissance. It happened rapidly. Setting up a painting and writing studio in the Audiffred Building on the Embarcadero, Ferlinghetti began work on translations from the French of the poetry of Jacques Prévert and on the novel *Her*, eventually published by New Directions in 1960. Keeping up his New York connections, Ferlinghetti wrote art criticism for the *Art Digest* at a time when painting in San Francisco was at a highpoint unmatched since the nineteenth century. Joseph Henry Jackson invited him to write book reviews for the *Chronicle*, and Ferlinghetti began to participate in the workshops for aspiring poets given by Kenneth Rexroth in his spacious second-floor flat at 250 Scott Street on the edge of the Fillmore. There Ferlinghetti met such other aspiring poets as Kenneth Patchen and Philip Lamantia and the UC Berkeley literary critic Thomas Parkinson, who would eventually issue the first important anthology of the Beats.

Still, freelance criticism, translations, even a developing practice as a poet, represented a precarious hold on San Francisco. Ferlinghetti was on the lookout for a
way of remaining in the city on a more settled basis. His Sorbonne doctorate might
have led to an academic career, and Ferlinghetti had tried teaching, briefly, at the
University of San Francisco, but the Jesuits had not renewed his contract after he
had lectured on homosexual themes in Shakespeare's sonnets. What to do? Ferlinghetti was at the time contributing to yet another literary magazine, *City Lights*,
edited by New York émigré Peter Martin, the son of a famed Italian anarchist, Carlo
Tresca, who had been assassinated in 1943. When Martin told Ferlinghetti that he
was looking at the possibility of starting up a bookstore in North Beach, Ferlinghetti
matched Martin's initial investment of $500, and the two of them became co-owners
of the City Lights Bookstore at 261 Columbus, with the editorial offices of the *City
Lights Review* on the second floor. Shigeyoshi Murao, a Japanese-American from
Seattle, with a wide-ranging knowledge of contemporary literature, volunteered to
work as clerk for free until he could be paid. When Martin returned to New York a
year later to open another bookstore on the Upper West Side, he sold his interest to
Ferlinghetti, and Murao became manager and, in time, co-owner.

At the Sorbonne, Ferlinghetti had analyzed the relationship between poets and
cities. He now set about creating such a nexus in San Francisco, centered at City
Lights. First of all (and this was Martin's idea), City Lights would sell only paperbacks, which were coming into vogue. That meant that the books for sale at City
Lights were affordable. Second, the paperbacks for sale would by and large be connected to the avant-garde in its European, North American, and Latin American
dimensions. Third, business hours were long, and browsing was encouraged. (For an
entire generation of readers, standing before the bookshelves of City Lights, browsing, constituted a form of education, a window on the world of the avant-garde.)
Fourth, beginning with his own *Pictures of the Gone World* (1955), Ferlinghetti
determined to expand the City Lights tradition into a publication program, City
Lights Books, a New Directions, a Grove Press, for San Francisco, even more daring than its New York counterparts. Last, combining all these elements, including
the emergence of City Lights as a place to hang out, Ferlinghetti fostered a sense of
community between poets and San Francisco, reflecting the literary patterns he had
studied at the Sorbonne. Over the next decade and more, there would be numerous
photographs taken of individual poets, groups of poets, and even larger gatherings
of poets spilling out across the sidewalk onto the street in front of City Lights. An
appearance in such a photograph constituted a form of recognition as well as proof
of community. Provincial San Franciscans gathered at the Roxburghe Club or the
Book Club of California or browsed at Paul Elder and John Howell Books. Avant-
garde San Francisco had the more loosely defined but comparably meaningful community of City Lights.

The physical fabric of North Beach and its preexisting tradition of bohemianism
served to consolidate and nurture the City Lights movement, as it might be called,

whether considered from its diversely recognized Literary Renaissance, Black Mountain, New York expatriate, or Beat dimensions. North Beach was a densely developed myriad of flats and apartments reminiscent of an Eastern city. When younger Italian families began to move to the more upscale Marina or to the suburbs, North Beach had a steady supply of flats and apartments available for rent at reasonable rates, together with a supportive infrastructure of grocery stores, coffeehouses, bars, and family-style (Italian, Basque, and nearby Chinese) restaurants, where aspiring artists could keep body and soul together inexpensively. Certain venues—Vesuvio's, Tosca's, 12 Adler Place, the Co-Existence Bagel Shop, the Coffee Gallery, the Cellar, where poetry and jazz sessions were held, the Place on Upper Grant, Gino & Carlo's—became fixed points of reference in the interconnected spaces sustaining the necessary amounts of company-keeping, conversation, and hanging out, characteristic of any urban-bohemian movement. The Dante Billiard Parlor around the corner on Broadway—pool tables, drinks, make-your-own sandwiches—attracted a late-night mixed bohemian and café society clientele, while across the street at Barnaby Conrad's El Matador, Baghdad and café society hung out. Also of use, especially for New Yorkers homesick for Times Square, were the 24/7 Foster's and Manning's cafeterias of the city, where one might linger over coffee, alone or in groups, at any odd hour, talking, writing, as did Allen Ginsberg, who sketched out crucial notes for the Moloch section of *Howl* in Manning's cafeteria on Powell Street.

Every now and then, William Saroyan, a bohemian from the old days, would breeze into town, but only for visits. Saroyan would soon be dividing his time between Paris and Fresno, although he could never fully detach himself from the town in which he had first experienced the time of his life. As far as literary personalities were concerned, the mantle of bohemia had passed from George Sterling to Henry Lafler to William Saroyan, and it was now passing to novelist and non-fiction writer Herbert Gold. Like Rexroth and Ferlinghetti, whom he resembled in work ethic and steady focus, Gold was not a Beat. His review of Jack Kerouac's *On the Road* (1957) in the 6 November 1957 issue of the *Nation*, written when Gold was living in New York, represented a savage putdown of Kerouac's whole attitude and spontaneous bop writing style. (Gold was equally dismissive of Ginsberg's *Howl*.) Gold was, rather, a Baghdad bohemian, a Cleveland-born, Columbia-educated New York writer who chose San Francisco as a place for life and writing for much the same reason that Rexroth and Ferlinghetti had chosen the city: because it combined elements of Europe and New York in a congenial setting. *Fathers* (1967)—the first notable novel Gold produced in his studio on Russian Hill over the Broadway Tunnel—was not about San Francisco at all but was, rather, a quintessential novel of the East Coast Jewish immigrant experience. Bohemian in his love of socializing and literary company, Gold also moved with ease in café society and related Baghdad circles. He was, however—and this distinguished him dramatically from the Beats—disciplined and focused and constantly productive as novelist, travel writer, foreign correspondent (the Biafra rebellion, numerous crises in Haiti), and chronicler of the bohemian way of life across Europe and the United States.

Gold was, in short, a professional and something of a formalist, which is to say he had a decidedly non-Beat approach to his craft, as did Rexroth, at least in Rexroth's re-workings of classic Chinese and Japanese poems. Equally disciplined were such academic poets as Josephine Miles of UC Berkeley and Yvor Winters of Stanford. The first woman to win tenure in the English department at Berkeley and a member of the American Academy of Arts and Sciences, Miles was a well-known scholar of poetic syntax and vocabulary, and her published poetry reflected such awareness. At Stanford, Yvor Winters was writing poetry of even more intense formalism and, as critic and teacher, was doing his best to promote a rationalist ethos for American verse. Two other Stanford poets, Winters's wife Janet Lewis and Melville scholar Helen Pinkerton, a Harvard Ph.D., were likewise loyal to meter, form, and tempered rhetoric. Although he moved to San Francisco in 1960 and spent years teaching at UC Berkeley, Winters's student, the English-born, Trinity College, Cambridge-educated Thom Gunn, with his controlled imagery and precision, can also be considered an affiliate of the Stanford School. W. H. Auden was on hand in 1954 for the dedication of the Poetry Center at San Francisco State College, giving an early version of his classic essay "The Hero in Modern Literature" as an inaugural address. Founded by English professor Ruth Witt-Diamant, a Baghdader from the East, the center brought to San Francisco many of the notable poets of the era for readings—among them, Louise Bogan, William Carlos Williams, Richard Wilbur—and fostered the careers of such locals as Charles Olson, Robert Creeley, Michael McClure, and Ron Loewinsohn. Although Allen Ginsburg wrote the preface to Loewinsohn's first book, *Watermelons* (1959), Loewinsohn's poetry was closer in style and technique to the objectivist poetry of another future San Franciscan (arriving in 1967), George Oppen, who would win the Pulitzer Prize in 1969. The Bay Area, in short, had an abundance of poets who would not in any way consider themselves Beats.

In his classic anthology *The New American Poetry, 1945–1960* (1960), Donald Allen divides the poets of the Bay Area into five distinct groups: Black Mountain, San Francisco Renaissance, Beats, New York poets, and such younger locals as Gary Snyder, Philip Whalen, and Michael McClure. The New York category is especially intriguing, given the range and variety of New York City poets and writers living and working in San Francisco in various stages of temporary sojourn or exile. Muriel Rukeyser lived in San Francisco from 1945 to 1954, teaching at the California Labor School and making friends with Rexroth, Olson, and Duncan; yet her poetry from the period shows no discernible sea change. Rukeyser remained a New York poet, although one poem from the period, "Foghorn in Horror," draws upon a San Francisco setting and imagery.

New York poet Weldon Kees—whom California poet Dana Gioia, among others, considers the great unacknowledged poet of twentieth-century America—arrived in San Francisco from New York in November 1950, looking for a new start. A bad career move, as it turned out. Whatever demons were bedeviling Kees in New York, removing himself from the established circles, outlets, and connections of New York represented a risky proposition. In New York, the native Nebraskan—by turns a jazz pianist, a librarian, an aspiring playwright, poet and writer of short stories, a book and music critic for the *New Republic* and *Time*, a scriptwriter for the Paramount News Service, and an abstract expressionist painter—had managed to keep body and soul together, move in impressive company, and have his poetry published in the *Partisan Review* and the *New Yorker*; but in San Francisco—to which he had fled to escape what he considered the soulless competitiveness of New York—it was as if Kees, as far as poetry was concerned, had dropped off the edge of the planet. A talented painter who had had a number of art shows in New York, including one at the Whitney, Kees was given a solo exhibition at the California Palace of the Legion of Honor. He reviewed film weekly on KPFA-FM with aspiring Berkeley critic Pauline Kael and mixed in well with the North Beach bohemia and even managed to co-author with a Langley Porter Clinic psychiatrist an academic study of non-verbal communication. Kees's third book of poetry, however, was turned down by more than a dozen New York publishers before it was brought out by a small private press in San Francisco.

Was it because Kees was no longer on the scene in New York? It could not have been the fact that his poetry had changed since his removal to the Coast. At least half of the poems he had submitted had been written in New York, and Kees had not changed his writing style. His wife began to drink heavily, and they divorced. Kees was drinking heavily as well and abusing prescription drugs. Hanging out in North Beach—a dapper Howard Hughes look-a-like in coat and tie with a pencil-thin mustache and slicked-back hair, not looking at all like a bohemian—Kees threw his efforts into a serio-comic revue, *The Poet Follies of 1955*, in which he wore a derby and played piano, and Lily Ayres, a literarily inclined stripper at the El Rey Burlesque in Oakland (reputed to be supporting her husband through medical school), appeared as Sarah Stripteasdale, reciting from T. S. Eliot. It was all very San Franciscan, an anticipation of the English revue *Beyond the Fringe* (1961), perhaps, or even more grandiloquently, an early instance of performance art. But was it enough to have justified a move from New York? Was this the new beginning Kees was so desperately seeking?

Sinking his money into the refurbishment of a pre-Earthquake building in the Mission district, which he renamed the Showplace, Kees hoped to produce serious one-act dramas, including his own play "The Waiting Room." When the fire department declared the building unsafe shortly before opening night, the venture went under, with Kees responsible for the unpaid lease. He began to talk of suicide or disappearing into Mexico like Ambrose Bierce. On 19 July 1955, the California Highway Patrol found Kees's 1954 Plymouth Savoy abandoned on the north side of the Golden Gate Bridge, the keys in the ignition. No body was ever found, and there was no suicide note, but Kees was considered dead, although rumors surfaced of sightings in New Orleans and Mexico.

In its origins and obsessions, its cast of characters and its long-term resolutions, what literary history calls the Beats was predominantly a New York movement, a road

show in the provinces by actors anxious to make it back to Broadway. Within this
New York influence, the Beats represented a decidedly Columbia movement, the
alma mater of Jack Kerouac and Allen Ginsberg and so many others, and as such
brought to San Francisco the spirit of Columbia professor Mark Van Doren, who
instilled in his students a sense of literature as the One Important Thing, as long as
it remained connected to life. Thomas Merton, a proto-Beat from Columbia who
became a Trappist monk in search of beatitude (Jack Kerouac's definition of *Beat*),
absorbed that message from Van Doren in the late 1930s and in 1941 fled to the
Abbey of Gethsemane in Kentucky as a means of finding God and maximizing his
talent. As a poet, a pacifist, a student of Zen still capable of a riff or two on the bongos, Merton saw himself as a corresponding member of the City Lights movement,
especially in its pacifism, and when he was passing through San Francisco in May
1968 en route to Asia, his last journey beyond monastery walls, Merton headed for
City Lights and spent the afternoon with Ferlinghetti, talking poetry and pacifism
over espresso at Enrico's sidewalk café on Broadway.

In the early 1950s, a group of WASP prep school and Ivy League graduates—
among them, George Plimpton, Irwin Shaw, Peter Matthiessen, and Terry Southern, joined by two older writers of the same ilk, John P. Marquand and William
Styron, musician Peter Duchin, and an assortment of Radcliffe, Vassar, and Smith
graduates—decamped for Paris, where they established the *Paris Review* and enjoyed
the literary life. Likewise did a group of middle-/lower-middle-class aspiring poets
and writers, even an ex-con, ethnic Jews, Italians, French Canadians and the like,
decamp for San Francisco for approximately the same reasons: to get away, to party,
to write, to experience something different, but always keeping New York as a fixed
point of reference, the once and future place. The very term *Beat* originated in
New York, first used in 1944 by Times Square hustler Herbert Huncke, who took the
term to junkie writer William Burroughs, a Harvard man, who took it to Columbia
freshman Allen Ginsberg, who took it to Columbia dropout Jack Kerouac, who
refined and annotated the term across the next decade, seeking to upgrade its street
origins with overtones of beatitude and spiritual quest. The breakthrough statement
of the Beat movement was a novel set entirely in New York: *Go* (1952) by John Clellon Holmes, another Columbia man drawing upon his association with Kerouac,
Ginsberg, and their mutual friend from Denver, Neal Cassady. The success of *Go*
prompted another formative statement by Holmes, "This Is the Beat Generation,"
published in the *New York Times* in November 1952.

While poets Kenneth Patchen and Gregory Corso were not Columbia men,
they were quintessential New Yorkers, each of them being formed by the ethos of
Greenwich Village, and Corso, who was born in the Village, being further refined
by the reading he did while serving a three-year sentence at the state prison in Dan-
nemora, New York, for armed robbery. Allen Ginsberg wrote *Howl* in Berkeley and
San Francisco and first read it publicly in San Francisco; yet its content, style, and
story line, its Jewish imagery and literary forms, render it in every possible way a
New York production. The very world that Ginsberg evokes—of hipsters, frustrated

Jewish intellectuals, urban junkies, late-night rap sessions in Times Square coffee shops, bebop joints, psychiatric wards—is not a recognizably California landscape. Ginsberg's one expressly Bay Area poem, "In a California Supermarket," from the same period, is filled with imagery ambivalent to California. All things considered, Ginsberg sojourned in California in 1955 and 1956, on and off. But gritty New York, not the pastel city by the Bay, was his true turf.

The entire episode of *Howl*—from its first reading to its trial for obscenity—is one of the best-known episodes in the twentieth-century history of attempted censorship. It was also, as far as San Francisco was concerned, an interplay of Provincial, Baghdad, and Beat values. The very genre that *Howl* represented, a publicly declaimed jeremiad, was initially established by Rexroth, a longtime resident of San Francisco with extensive connections to the Provincial establishment and as such a civic and literary principle distinct from the Beats. Rexroth also established the genre of public performance of poetry to jazz accompaniment, most notably in his sweeping jeremiad "Thou Shalt Not Kill," a euology for the Welsh poet Dylan Thomas, who succumbed to alcoholism in November 1953. From Rexroth's perspective, it was not the booze that killed Thomas, but the very same corporate capitalist military/industrial culture—led, as Rexroth put it, by the sons of bitches in Brooks Brothers suits—that had wiped out practically every major American poet of the twentieth century. "Thou Shalt Not Kill" constituted an outspoken denunciation from the Left during an era of Cold War McCarthyism and was especially effective when Rexroth read it to jazz as part of the Cellar series of poetry and jazz readings he had organized, some of them released as LPs by Fantasy Records. By combining jazz and poetry, Rexroth was emphasizing poetry as a flexible and open-ended idiom, declamatory and spontaneous in the manner of Walt Whitman and jazz, yet possessed as well of an inner logic and discipline.

Howl made its debut as spoken word at a reading at the Six Gallery in the Marina on 13 October 1955. Organized in part by Ginsberg, the evening was emceed by Rexroth and featured, in order of recitation, readings by Philip Lamantia, Michael McClure, Philip Whalen, Ginsberg, and Gary Snyder. The reading of *Howl* by Ginsberg turned the evening into the Pentecost of the Beat movement: a moment of revelation and empowerment—sudden and swift, as from an unseen but transforming force—that, as McClure would later put it, convinced each person in the audience of some seventy-five disciples that things would never be, could never be, the same. Jack Kerouac had declined to read from his own work in progress, *Mexico City Blues* (1959), out of fearfulness, but, swigging red wine from a jug, Kerouac led a chant of "Go!" as Ginsberg (who had also imbibed to bolster his courage) ended each declamatory line of a poem that, like Rexroth's "Thou Shalt Not Kill," indicted contemporary civilization for the destruction of the best minds of a generation, visualized as the Canaanite god Moloch being fed sacrificed firstborn children. Interestingly enough, as far as the interaction of Provincial and Beat realities were concerned, Ginsberg had first envisioned the temple furnace of the devouring god Moloch when, looking out the window of a Nob Hill apartment at night, he beheld the Sir Francis Drake Hotel at Powell and Sutter ablaze in light. Leaving the apartment, Ginsberg wandered down Powell Street obsessed by his vision and sketched out the Moloch sequence over coffee in Manning's cafeteria.

On either the night or the morning following the Six Gallery reading, Ferlinghetti sent Ginsberg a telegram, greeting him as Emerson greeted Whitman upon receiving a copy of the 1855 edition of *Leaves of Grass*, at the beginning of a glorious career, and offering to publish *Howl* at City Lights. The forty-four-page *Howl and Other Poems* (1957) appeared as publication number 4 in the Pocket Poet Series of City Lights Books, following Patchen's *Poems of Humor and Protest* (1954), Ferlinghetti's own *Pictures of the Gone World* (1955), and Rexroth's *Thirty Spanish Poems of Love and Exile* (1955). Ferlinghetti had the volume printed by Villiers Publications in England with an appreciative foreword by William Carlos Williams. When the second shipment of *Howl and Other Poems*, letterpressed and saddle-stitched, reached San Francisco in March 1957, however, Chester McPhee, the Provincial politico heading the United States Customs Department, ordered the books impounded on grounds of obscenity. Anticipating such a reaction, Ferlinghetti had already been in touch with the American Civil Liberties Union, which promised its support. Boldly, Ferlinghetti printed an identical version of *Howl and Other Poems* in a photo-offset edition; locally issued, it was beyond the jurisdiction of Customs, and put it on sale. In a *Chronicle* op-ed piece, Ferlinghetti thanked McPhee for making *Howl* a best-seller.

At this point, the controversy over *Howl*, which had many dimensions, also squared off as a confrontation between the Beats and their Baghdad allies and the Provincial establishment. Had not the Provincials provoked the matter, the issue would have remained moot. The United States attorney, after all, had already declined to prosecute *Howl* in federal court. But Captain William Hanrahan of the juvenile division of the San Francisco Police Department, deciding to provoke the situation further, sent two of his officers to City Lights Bookstore with warrants for the confiscation of *Howl* and Ferlinghetti's arrest. City Lights clerk and manager Shigeyoshi Murao, on duty that night, was also arrested but was later dropped from the indictment on the basis that there was no evidence that he had any prior knowledge of the content of the poems.

Held in the municipal court of Judge Clayton W. Horn, the *Howl* trial represented a case study of opposing San Francisco cultures. At first glance, Judge Horn—a churchgoing Christian who had recently sentenced five female shoplifters to see the movie *The Ten Commandments* (1956) and write essays regarding the importance of the commandment, "Thou shalt not steal"—would seem to have been a bad luck draw for the defense, as was the lead prosecutor, assistant district attorney Ralph McIntosh, an up-from-the-ranks civil service Provincial who had put himself through night law school while working as a linotype operator and prided himself on his successful prosecution of cases involving pornographic movies and nudist magazines.

Totally outmaneuvered by the lead defense attorney Jake (the Master) Ehrlich, backed by ACLU counsel, McIntosh hammered away on a word-by-word basis at the alleged obscenities in Ginsberg's text. Putting a phalanx of blue-chip literary scholars and critics on the stand, Baghdaders all—among them, Mark Schorer, Thomas Parkinson, Eugene Burdick, and Leo Lowenthal of UC Berkeley, Ruth Witt-Diamant of the Poetry Center at San Francisco State, Kenneth Rexroth, and *Chronicle* book editor William Hogan, together with publisher James Laughlin of New Directions and Donald Allen of the Grove Press—Ehrlich eviscerated McIntosh's arguments, if and when they ever managed to surface against the smooth and informed assertiveness of Ehrlich's highly credentialed witnesses.

In rebuttal, McIntosh put two members of the English department at the Jesuit University of San Francisco on the stand: David Kirk, whom Ehrlich outmaneuvered in a debate on Dadaism, and composition instructor Gail Potter, whose testimony was so weak, drawing laughs from the audience, Ehrlich let it pass without cross-examination. In his summation, McIntosh faced Judge Horn, one Provincial to another, and argued that San Francisco would be in dire danger if smut such as *Howl* were allowed on the streets. Jake Ehrlich, by contrast, ever the Master, drawing upon the expert testimony he had orchestrated and his own genius for summary argument, advanced the notion that even if individually obscene words had been used in *Howl*, they had not been used for pornographic purposes but to underscore, through the mysterious alchemy of poetry, dark and desperate states of consciousness.

In a number of rulings during the trial, Judge Horn had shown a solid grasp of intellectual and legal distinctions relevant to literary creation. In the two weeks that he took to reach his decision, Horn read Joyce's *Ulysses* and the landmark decision allowing it to be distributed in the United States. Horn's written decision, declaring that *Howl* met a minimum level of redeeming social importance and was hence protected by the First and Fourteenth Amendments and the constitution of the State of California, was destined to dominate obscenity law in the state for the half century to come and is given credit by literary historians for enabling the subsequent publication of D. H. *Lawrence's Lady Chatterley's Lover* and Henry Miller's *Tropic of Cancer*. Two Provincials, Judge Horn and Jake Ehrlich, showed themselves more than capable of appreciating the nuances of literary discourse, and this represented a saving of face for Provincial San Francisco. But it was equally a Baghdad victory, as evidenced most dramatically in the smooth and compelling discourse of Mark Schorer. Were one inclined to give habitation and a name to the passing of one San Francisco and the arrival of another, the *Howl* trial might very well serve such a purpose, especially given the fact that Judge Horn had so compellingly grasped the point of the Baghdad argument and had proven sympathetic. Soon, the Beats would be gone, most of them at least, but not Lawrence Ferlinghetti and what he represented and Baghdad and what it represented: the de-provincialization of a Provincial capital and, behind that, the continuing de-provincialization of California itself.

12

Big Sur

The Search for Alternative Value

FROM the beginning of American California, certain places stood for more than just themselves, however important they were as regions of the state. Within this category, three localities—Big Sur, Marin, and the South Coast, extending into its desert backcountry—proved especially vibrant at mid-twentieth century in the search for alternative value and hence became metaphors as well as geographical designations. In various ways and in various degrees of admixture, these places stood for art, rebellion, contemplative value, and transcendence, and were cited as such. Nature and previous experience structured these identities. Other Californians, beginning with the First Californians, had been in these places in times past and experienced similar transformations. Personal experience and the projections of art, literature, psychology, philosophy, and theologized aesthetics reinforced these regional metaphors at mid-century, enriching the larger California identity. Eighty or so years earlier, the romanticized Franciscan missions along El Camino Real had served a similar purpose. Now it was the turn of the environment itself to symbolize the search for higher value.

The story begins in Big Sur. South of Monterey—taking an almost symbolic point of departure at the Carmel River just below Mission San Carlos Borroméo (1770)—Big Sur extends for sixty-five miles of wild coast. Almost uninterruptedly, the mountains of the Santa Lucia Range rise abruptly from the Pacific, their granite cliffs sealing off the region from maritime traffic. Point Sur is one of eight promontories along the coast that together with five landings constitute breeches in the granite coastal wall sealing Big Sur off from the sea. In the Big Sur itself, deep redwood canyons and creeks cut laterally, east-west, and offer natural pathways for human settlement. The largest of these canyons, the Big Sur, gave its name to the region. The Spaniards explored Big Sur and named its rivers and creeks. Occasionally they entered the region to retrieve runaway Indians or to capture a grizzly bear to match against bulls in a barbaric form of local entertainment; but in general the Spaniards avoided the Big Sur, as did the Mexicans, although two land grant ranchos were bestowed during the Mexican period: the San José y Sur Chiquito to Marcellino Escobar and El Sur Rancho to Juan Bautista Alvarado. These ranchos, however, remained undeveloped. Escobar, legend has it, lost his property in a dice game with soldiers from the Presidio of Monterey; and in the 1830s or 1840s Alvarado either gave or sold El Sur Rancho to his uncle by marriage, the English-born Juan Bautista Rogers Cooper. In the 1850s Cooper used the property as a site for offshore smuggling operations into the Big Sur River (El Rio Grande del Sur) designed to avoid the heavy American customs charges at Monterey.

In the 1870s and 1880s, a handful of homesteaders took up claims in Big Sur: Michael Pfeiffer and his French-born wife Barbara, for example, who began a multi-generational family of Big Sur residents; or David Castro, married to Amadia Vasquez, first cousin to the well-known bandit Tiburcio Vasquez; the Partington and Anderson brothers; Gabriel and Elizabeth Dani, the Harlans, the McQuades, the Posts, Tom Slate, Charles Bixby, John William Gilkey, and Sam Trotter, among others. There were only a few of them, and they lived in isolation, their children and children's children intermarrying with other Big Sur offspring. Thus was created an Homeric world, remote (serviced since 1881 from Monterey by a narrow and winding wagon road), sparsely settled, elemental in detail. Families survived on subsistence farming and the running of a few cattle and were intermittently violent, as Dr. John Roberts, the first physician to service the region, was discovering by the late 1890s, when feuds over land or women flared forth into abduction, suicide, assaults, or other forms of mayhem.

The migration of Bay Area artists to Carmel-by-the-Sea, starting in 1904 and picking up momentum after the destruction of San Francisco by earthquake and fire in April 1906, founded a literary and artistic colony on the northern edge of Big Sur. Established in 1903 by real estate developer James Franklin Devendorf and San Francisco lawyer Frank Powers, operating as the Carmel Development Company, Carmel-by-the-Sea and the nearby Point Lobos constituted the northern march or borderland of Big Sur. Despite its geographical position, Carmel-by-the-Sea was primarily an extension not of the wild, even Homeric, Big Sur but of the academic and urban bohemian culture of the Bay Area. Faculty from UC and Stanford were among the first to buy lots and build cottages in the development centered on Ocean Avenue, bringing with them a regard for art and intellect fused with middle-class values and manners. Building a home there in the summer of 1905, aspiring poet George Sterling, thirty-six, embodied the urban bohemianism that accounted for the most colorful aspects of the early years of the settlement and, tamed and subdued, would eventually fuse with the faculty culture to create an upper-middle-class enclave of permanent and summer residents who savored the local confluence of setting, scenery, and the arts.

In its early years at least, this bohemianism—in its free-thinking, sexual promiscuity, and unconventional lifestyles; its haphazard finances, leftist politics, and philosophical pessimism—clearly differentiated itself from the proprieties of the co-existing academic culture. More than any other bohemian, George Sterling helped set the tone. Emigrating to the Bay Area from his native Sag Harbor, this onetime candidate for the Roman Catholic priesthood had gone to work for his uncle, real estate developer Frank C. Havens, and had married his stenographer, Caroline (Carrie) Rand, a statuesque Gibson girl whose equally beautiful sister Frank C. Havens had already married. Thus was set in motion a respectable scenario for Sterling and Carrie, cozily ensconced in their new home in Piedmont, a picturesque enclave in the hills of Oakland, to live happily ever after as George, with his uncle's guidance, prospered in real estate development.

But George Sterling had other ideas. He wanted to be a poet. Commuting by ferry back and forth between San Francisco and the East Bay, Sterling composed poems, and in his off-hours he assiduously built his vocabulary and studied a rhyming dictionary. He also began to submit his verse to the scrutiny of poet and short story writer Ambrose Bierce, who guided Sterling in the direction of rhyme and formal stanzas, syntactical correctness, and a verbal formality verging on archaism. As Sterling began to publish his poetry locally, he also began to pursue a double life as a hard-drinking bohemian and chronic philanderer. He began, in short, to act out the stereotype of the poet as free-thinking sensualist. In Sterling's case, the more he reached for great poetry—and the more great poetry eluded him—the more free-thinking, hard-drinking, and promiscuous he became.

With San Francisco in ruins, the writers and would-be writers of the city and its East Bay affiliate, centered in Piedmont, began to look southward to Carmel-by-the-Sea. Within a few years, a loosely organized colony had established itself on the northern border of Big Sur. Carmel was not a formally organized community, nor was it particularly stable. Its members came and went, depending upon writing assignments and the errant and aberrant vagaries of their personal lives. George and Carrie Sterling constituted the nucleus of this moveable feast, entertaining their friends in the spacious living room of their rustic Arts and Crafts cottage or bringing them down to the beach to barbecue mussels and abalone. Most of the notable names associated with Carmel-by-the-Sea—poet Joaquin Miller and satirist Ambrose Bierce, aged veterans of the post–Gold Rush literary frontier, or the young novelist and short story writer Jack London—were merely visitors, although London, a close personal friend of Sterling's, did portray the Carmelites in his novel *The Valley of the Moon* (1913), and hence became permanently associated with the settlement. Living in nearby Monterey was another survivor of the frontier era, poet and essayist Charles Warren Stoddard, and a much younger talent on the rise, artist Charles Rollo Peters. Prior to his arrival at Carmel, Upton Sinclair, author of the best-selling novel *The Jungle* (1906), had established his own art colony, Helicon Hall, in Englewood, New Jersey, but it had been destroyed by fire. Also on hand, at various times, were other younger writers headed for a measure of fame, such as poet William Rose Benét, literary historian Van Wyck Brooks, a Harvard graduate, on the faculty at Stanford, and the recent Yale graduate Sinclair Lewis, a silent and awkward young man, developing his skills by devising plots, some of which he sold to Jack London. Artist members of the colony included the Mexican-born, Paris-trained Xavier Martinez, a member of the Piedmont Crowd, and Arnold Genthe, a pioneer in color photography. These and others brought to Carmel-by-the-Sea a condensed version of aesthetic Northern California in the early 1900s: an admixture of athletic environmentalism, an Arts and Crafts preference for woodsy localism, a political tilt to the left, a tendency to spiritualism and parapsychology, and a conviction that California—meaning the San Francisco Bay Area and now Carmel—was destined to emerge as a national nursery of the arts.

In the midst of their work schedules, the Carmelites had fun. Their swimming and beach parties were legendary, as were their abalone roasts and the songs they composed together as they beat tough and sinewy abalone steaks into edible submission. They created for themselves aesthetic environments, including an array of cozy and charming cottages, cabins, and related work spaces. Mary Austin, novelist, essayist, playwright, did her writing in a tree house behind her cabin. In 1910, under the leadership of Herbert Heron, they founded the Forest Theater, an outdoor amphitheater where they produced elaborately costumed historical plays and pageants. But there was another side to the colony as well, one noted explicitly by Jack London and Van Wyck Brooks, among others; and that was an underlying tension, a morbidity even, among so many of the residents. A number of the Carmelites drank heavily, which can be seen as part of the artistic lifestyle, but nevertheless gave rise to periods of anxiety and lassitude born of hangovers. Then there was the matter of the promiscuity that caused Carrie Sterling such stress, although this is more difficult to document. For all their gaiety, the Carmelites felt the limitations of their own provincial bohemia and the larger ambiguities of the fin de siècle, with its underlying sense of defeat and impending disaster. Sojourning among the Carmelites, Saxon and Billy Roberts, the working-class protagonists of Jack London's *The Valley of the Moon*, are taken aback by the pessimism frequently cropping up in the conversation of poet Mark Hall, based on George Sterling, against whom Billy Roberts debates in favor of a simple acceptance of life's challenges and pleasures. In his memoir of Carmel, Van Wyck Brooks would be even more explicit. George Sterling, Brooks remembered, "had precisely the aspect of Dante in hell." Brooks blamed California in general for the universal malaise on the part of "others who had come from the East to write novels in this paradise [and] found themselves there becalmed and supine. They gave themselves over to day-dreams while their minds ran down like clocks, as if they had lost the keys to wind them up with, and they turned into beach-combers, listlessly reading books they had read ten times before and searching the rocks for abalones. For this Arcadia lay, one felt, outside the world in which thought evolves and which came to seem insubstantial in the bland sunny air."[1]

Jack London was especially sensitive to the undercurrents of pessimism among the Carmelites, especially their interminable discussions of suicide, because he himself was struggling with the same demons. All things considered, it is surprising just how many Carmelites, over time, did take their own lives, beginning with aspiring poet Nora May French, who swallowed a fatal dose of cyanide in the early morning hours of 14 November 1907. French's suicide and the strained ceremony of scattering her ashes from Point Lobos, with two rival lovers glaring at each other from opposite ends of the burial party, served as the dramatic prologue to the death of London himself on 22 November 1916 under ambiguous circumstances. Divorced and despairing, Carrie Sterling swallowed cyanide in Piedmont on 17 November 1918 with Chopin's "Funeral March" playing on the gramophone. Then, in the aftermath of World War I, in Germany, came the bizarre death of poet Herman Scheffauer, Carmelite and Bohemian, who, after fatally stabbing his mistress and slashing his wrists and throat, jumped to his death from a high window.

Sterling coped with his demons—alcoholism, satyrmania, despair over not evolving into a first-rate poet—through the communitarian rituals of Carmel life: the swimming parties that afforded him an opportunity to display his Grecian physique, the abalone roasts on the beach, gatherings before the great fireplace in his living room, or quiet hours of composition in the grove behind his cottage, which he adorned with the horned skulls of cattle and deer so as to create a chthonic shrine to ancient deities. Still, Sterling's demons were surfacing, not only in the drinking and philandering but in his remorseless hunting of small game throughout the region, way beyond the requirements of either sport or table, as if he were seeking to extinguish life itself in an orgy of shooting furry little creatures. In the early morning hours of 16 November 1926, Sterling swallowed cyanide in his room at the Bohemian Club, leaving behind the charred remnants of a poem he was writing earlier in the evening, from which could be deciphered the lines

> Deeper in the darkness can I peer
> Than most, yet find the darkness still beyond.

Not for Sterling, the onetime seminarian, would there be the consolations of Catholicism that were solacing two other Carmelites, Charles Warren Stoddard and Michael Williams. Stoddard might be, in one dimension of his nature, an aged homosexual, drinking too much in his loneliness, dreaming of the beautiful brown boys on the beaches of the South Pacific, where he had sojourned forty and more years earlier. But Stoddard was also a sincere convert to Catholicism, a onetime professor of literature at Notre Dame and the Catholic University, who had written sensitively of his conversion experience. Being close to Mission Carmel, as he was, where Father Junípero Serra was buried, Stoddard at least had the consolations of Catholic California, which in its resonances and reverberations continued, as they had done in the past, to calm his troubled heart. Michael Williams, a recent San Francisco newsman who had drifted away from his faith, was experiencing something similar due to being in the same proximity to Mission San Carlos Borroméo at the mouth of the Carmel River: a quickening of his lapsed Catholicism through visits to the mission and to Serra's grave there and a reading of the autobiography of St. Thérèse of Lisieux, the young French cloistered Carmelite nun—a true Carmelite, Williams came to believe—who had determined before her death in 1897 from tuberculosis at the age of twenty-four that her vocation, her destiny, was to love God in ordinary things. Here was the true Carmel connection, Williams became convinced, between the mystical mountain in the Holy Land, associated with the prophet Elijah, taken by the sixteenth-century Spanish Carmelite saints Teresa of Ávila and John of the Cross as a symbol of spiritual ascent. Williams returned East, where he belonged, and in 1924 founded the lay Catholic journal *Commonweal*, destined to exercise influence on American Catholicism for the rest of the century.

This was a Carmel of a different sort: the Carmel of Israel and California, Old Testament and New, conjoined, toward which George Sterling might look with nostalgia and regret, especially in conversations with Stoddard and Williams, prompting recollections of the years that he had spent at St. Charles College seminary in Maryland under the tutelage of the priest-poet John Bannister Tabb, a member of the faculty, from whom Sterling first glimpsed the possibilities of the poetic vocation. A prodigal son half-choosing his exile, Sterling sought redemption through poetry. *The Testimony of the Suns* (1903) possessed a cosmic, mystical element, however overwrought, an orientation that continued in the main effort of his Carmelite years, *A Wine of Wizardry* (1909), initially published with elaborate illustrations in William Randolph Hearst's *Cosmopolitan* magazine. There was more than astronomy to these poems. There was an effort on Sterling's part to achieve a Lucretian connection to the universe. Neither Sterling's intellect nor poetic talent, however, could quite get him there, but he dreamt nevertheless of making a voyage outward through poetry to distant galaxies and suns and there experiencing, simultaneously, the power and the indifference of the cosmos.

He had been trekking, meanwhile, tentatively, southward into the northern edges of the Big Sur on long rambles that were at once escapes from the thickening texture of Carmel and a search for new imagery. In time, the poetic harvest of these rambles would manifest itself in the poems gathered into *Beyond the Breakers* (1914) and *Strange Waters* (1926), which appeared the same year as Sterling's *Robinson Jeffers: The Man and the Artist*, a pioneering appreciation and assessment. Generously, but with some despair, Sterling beheld in Jeffers the poet he himself had failed to become.

Taking up residence in Carmel with his wife Una in December 1914, Robinson Jeffers brought with him an emerging poetic talent and an independent income. Shortly after his arrival in Carmel-by-the-Sea, Robinson and Una Jeffers traveled down the coast by horse-drawn mail stage to Pfeiffer's Resort in Big Sur. In the course of the trip, Corbett Grimes, driver of the mail stage, a garrulous young émigré from England, regaled his passengers with lurid tales of every murder, suicide, sexual scandal, or instance of mayhem connected to the canyons, beaches, points, and cabins along the way. Grimes's narrative of elemental and near-mythic mayhem dovetailed with the damp and foggy grayness of the weather, the perilous cliffs and crashing surf in the near distance, the cry of seabirds overhead, the forested canyons disappearing into the mountainous distance. This experience provided

Jeffers—whether he knew it exactly then or not, for he would make further trips into the region—with the setting for his life's work. Across some thirteen years of prodigious production—from the publication of *Roan Stallion, Tamar, and Other Poems* (1925) to the publication of *The Selected Poetry of Robinson Jeffers* (1938) by the Modern Library—Jeffers achieved a national literary reputation and affixed to Big Sur a meaning it would never lose.

Like John Muir—another Californian of national reputation who also transformed a region of California imaginatively—Robinson Jeffers came from a strong Calvinist background. His father was a distinguished Presbyterian minister and professor of the Old Testament at the Western Theological Seminary in Pittsburg, Pennsylvania, where Robinson Jeffers was born in 1887. Within the context of California types, Jeffers was a Pasadenan, the city to which his family moved in 1903, the same year that Jeffers entered the nearby Occidental College. From his Calvinist birthright, Jeffers, like Muir, absorbed a lifelong preoccupation with sin, suffering, atonement, salvation, and transcendence: however transformed—again, as in the case of Muir—these preoccupations might become once he had drifted away from formal Christianity. Also Pasadenan was Jeffers's upbringing in an atmosphere of bookish erudition. He knew the scriptures, as might be expected from the son of a professor of the Old Testament, and was reading classical Greek at an early age. From scripture and from the classics Jeffers early in life absorbed an emotional and scholarly relationship to myth: to those primal narratives of Greeks and Hebrews alike through which the cosmos was explained and fundamental meanings set forth. Pasadenan in Jeffers as well was his love of the outdoors, as evident in the long rambles he would take in the San Gabriel Mountains outside the city. Love of nature led to an interest in natural science: geology and biology, emerging from Jeffers's love of the mountains, but also an abiding interest in astronomy, so flourishing in the researches being conducted by George Ellery Hale atop Mount Wilson overlooking Pasadena, where there would soon be put into operation an observatory equipped with the largest telescope in the world.

In the early 1900s, a significant number of scientists, astronomers most notably, were the children of Protestant ministers, as if the cosmic focus of one generation, expressed through religion, were now being transmitted to the next generation via the rising profession of science. Which again puts Robinson Jeffers into context; for this Pasadenan—a graduate of Occidental, erudite in scripture and the classics, well traveled in Europe on trips with his parents, an outdoorsman, muscular and athletic—turned to the most universal of sciences, medicine, as his chosen profession, enrolling in the medical school of USC after a period of graduate study there in literature, followed by further study in humanities at the University of Zurich. How Pasadenan it would have been had Robinson Jeffers become a physician, perhaps even a research scientist, following in this generational trend!

Two factors, however, poetry and sex, were thwarting this scenario. As a graduate student in literature at USC, Jeffers fell in love with a married woman, Una Call Kuster, with whom he shared a love of Wordsworth. Una began talking of divorce from her lawyer husband and was sent east to relatives to think it over. Jeffers's parents were equally disturbed and sent him off to Europe. Jeffers, meanwhile, was contemplating not only marriage to another man's wife but a new profession entirely, poetry, which led him to leave the USC School of Medicine after three years and enroll in the forestry program at the University of Washington so as better to prepare himself for a career as a forester and poet of the outdoors. A period of sexual *Sturm und Drang* ensued (in which Jeffers became for a while an early version of a Southern California beach bum) before Una obtained her divorce, and she and Jeffers were able to be married in Tacoma in August 1913.

Also relevant to Jeffers's developing talent was his extensive reading of Freud, Jung, and Havelock Ellis in response to religious doubts and sexual tensions. Science, studies in comparative religion, myth, and abnormal psychology, and, between 1914 and 1918, the senseless slaughter of the First World War each reinforced in Jeffers an already evolving disbelief in traditional Christianity. Across eight years of experience, meditation, and composition, Jeffers found his answer. This process of discernment had a physical component, the building by Jeffers personally of Tor House and Hawk Tower from local granite stones, prompting meditations on what Jeffers would later call the mysticism of stone. The local granite Jeffers was assembling, stone by stone, in the creation of his oceanside residence and writing studio, where he would live for the rest of his life, embodied for him the trans-human objectivity and permanence of the physical universe in comparison to human life. Jeffers was traveling down a well-worn California path, anchored in the aesthetic geology of the 1860s and 1870s; the biology-oriented naturalism of the 1890s so evident in Jack London, Frank Norris, and, later, John Steinbeck; the Darwinian philosophizing of Joseph Le Conte at Berkeley and David Starr Jordan at Stanford, each of them seeking an ethical upgrade for the survival of the fittest; and the environmentalism of the Sierra Club and similar organizations. What John Muir beheld in the glacial formation of the Sierra Nevada, nature at once scientifically measurable as well as symbolic, Jeffers saw embodied in Carmel granite in an eclectic blend of pre-Socratic, Lucretian, neo-Platonic, scientific, and poetic insights. In pre-Socratic terms, Jeffers was seeking the ultimate stuff and process of the universe, local and cosmic. Like Lucretius, Jeffers advocated resignation to a world that was material and winding down. Like the neo-Platonists, he sought to unify the confusion of things into one coherent and transcendent scheme. From the perspective of contemporary astronomy—most notably, the theories of Albert Einstein, verified by Edwin Hubble, regarding the origins, unity, and expanding nature of the universe—Jeffers wanted to anchor that unity solidly on a foundation of modern science. And finally, as a poet, he derived from the mysticism of stone an imaginative respect for the non-human Otherness of the cosmos.

Van Wyck Brooks believed there was something atavistic, nihilist even, to Jeffers's way of thinking. Modern culture, indeed humanistic culture in general, meant nothing to Jeffers, Brooks noted. Tor House and Hawk Tower represented for Jeffers a kind of Stonehenge, an emblem of total retreat into an imagined primordialism on the part of a neo-Calvinist eager to escape the inescapable; which is to say, to escape the burden of sin so evident in all human history. Christian theology put human beings at the center of creation as its highest form of conscious and rational develop-ment; indeed, Christianity postulated that Divinity itself had become man. But what if the opposite were true, as Jeffers had come to believe? What if human beings— in their arrogance, their pride, their destructiveness, their delusional conviction of their own grandeur—constituted an affront, and not a culmination, to the cosmos? Where did that leave the human species? And what was to be done about it?

Pain and suffering, Jeffers decided, could deconstruct human arrogance and realign human nature with the cosmos. While he was building Hawk Tower, Jeffers was working on three poems—"Tamar," "Roan Stallion," and "The Tower Beyond Tragedy"—that constituted a working out of these developing assumptions. Tamar, for one thing, was a Big Sur girl gone bad of cosmic proportions: the seducer of her brother, her lover, and her father and the destroyer of all three. In her monstrosity, Tamar is totally mythic, although presented in a psychologically realistic manner and in a recognizable Big Sur setting. Her destruction of herself and others goes beyond sin as defined from a Judeo-Christian perspective. Tamar is, rather, a mythic presentation of the destructive force at the core of human nature itself. Destroying herself and others, Tamar breaks the mold of her own and their humanity; and that is the point of the poem philosophically, as far as Jeffers is concerned. "Humanity," he would soon be writing in "Roan Stallion,"

> is the start of the race; I say
> Humanity is the mold to break away from, the crust to
> break through, the coal to break into fire,
> The atom to be split.

In the narrative poems to come, Jeffers created even more Big Sur residents to be broken, as any redaction of the plots of the narrative poems soon reveals.

In "Roan Stallion," a retelling of the Pasiphae myth, a Big Sur ranch woman by the name of California—of Native American, Hispanic, and Anglo descent, like California itself—abused by a much older husband, becomes enamored of a great roan stallion to which she is attracted (without sexual contact) as if to the Life Force itself, riding him wildly by night. She executes the stallion, however, with rifle fire when he tramples to death her husband when her husband tries to beat her. After the execution, California turns to her daughter with "the mask of a woman/Who has killed God." In "The Coast-Range Christ," Jeffers's next long narrative poem, Peace O'Farrell, another young ranch wife married to an abusive older husband, unsuccessfully tries to seduce David Carrow, a young Christian idealist hiding out in the Big Sur to avoid the draft. Scorned in her efforts, Peace O'Farrell informs the sheriff where Carrow is hiding, shoots him with a revolver to prevent his escaping, and claims that he tried to rape her. Carrow's father thereupon kills his son, Peace's husband hangs himself, and Peace herself takes up with a deputy sheriff. In "The Women at Point Sur," the Reverend Dr. Barclay, a Christian minister, succumbing to the temptation of lust and power, consorts with an Indian servant girl, rapes his own daughter, who commits suicide, and wreaks various forms of havoc on assorted ranch hands before wandering into the mountains to die. In "Cawdor," Fera, the young wife of another aging rancher, attempts to seduce her stepson Hood; when she fails, she tells her husband Cawdor that Hood tried to seduce her—a retelling of the Potiphar story in the Old Testament. Falling into a rage, Cawdor murders his son. Later learning the truth, he gouges out his eyes like Oedipus, lest he be forced to gaze upon such a fallen and perverse world.

And so go the plots of these and the other long narrative Big Sur poems of Jeffers high creativity, so many of them concerned with an older abusive husband and a younger sexually aggressive wife, each of them abounding in catastrophic destruction. Some future biographer of Jeffers will elucidate the predominance of abusive older men and sexually frustrated younger wives in these poems, together with the explicit attacks against Christianity. In "Dear Judas" Jeffers reverses the roles of Jesus, a prophet promising too much, and Judas, an everyman betrayed into belief. Even such a seemingly religious poem as "The Loving Shepherdess" contains within itself an anti-Christian statement in that the heroine, the pregnant shepherdess Clare Walker, represents a level of self-sacrifice beyond Christianity itself.

Such a rejection of Christianity demanded that Jeffers come up with a counter point of view: not necessarily in the form of a fully coherent philosophy, since Jeffers was a narrative poet, probing reality through story as opposed to consistent thought. At the very beginning of his poetic maturity—in "The Tower Beyond Tragedy," a reworking of the Aeschylus *Oresteia* trilogy, chronicling the fall of the House of Atreus, Jeffers began the construction of his answer along with his construction of Tor House and Hawk Tower. Annihilated through suffering, Orestes finds in the stones of Mycenae the fact and symbol of his release. As Orestes puts it, he has "fallen in love outward," which is to say, he has projected himself into a Lucretian connection with the non-human universe as embodied in stone. With such a connection, he will build for himself a tower beyond tragedy: an Archimedean point from which he, thoroughly crushed by suffering, broken, might extricate himself from the delusions of human existence. Very soon, Jeffers would be calling this philosophy Inhumanism, and toward the end of his career, in Part II of *The Double Axe* (1948), he would designate his central protagonist the Inhumanist.

Scholarly critics of Jeffers—the majority of them from California, where Jeffers's poetic lamp continues to burn bright even after his national reputation has receded— have explicated Inhumanism from numerous perspectives. Seeking transcendence, they point out, mystics of every epoch, tradition, and clime have sought connection with an Ultimate Reality purged of contingency. Even more, however inconsistently, Jeffers was pushing himself to that point of perception when science leads to philosophical, even theological, questions regarding the origins and nature of the universe. From this perspective, Jeffers was not an atheist, nor even a materialist, but a philosophical poet in search of transcendence through an identification with a non-human universe that was material but possessed of consciousness. In "Rock and

Hawk," depicting the alighting of a falcon on a stone, Jeffers offered his most pithy presentation of the mystery he was exploring:

> Fierce consciousness joined with final
> Disinterestedness;
> Life with calm death; the falcon's
> Realist eyes and act
> Married to the massive
> Mysticism of stone...

The stone—material, near-permanent, yet the result of geological forces—is the universe from one perspective; and the falcon—aware with ferocious purity of what it should be properly aware of—is the universe in its struggle for appropriate intelligence, so in contrast to the arrogant misuse of intelligence by the human race.

Two lesser figures—Ella Young, an Irish poet and Celtic mythologist; and the psychiatrist, anthropologist, linguist, and Big Sur rancher Jaime de Angulo—also added to the growing complexity of Big Sur interpretations. Ella Young's vision of Point Lobos as the epicenter of spirit in America, the setting for a second Celtic Twilight, was the most fragile and evanescent, except that it dovetailed with the influence of the Irish Literary Renaissance on Robinson Jeffers, with Una Jeffers's deep identification with everything Celtic, and the Jefferses' own identification of Big Sur with western Ireland. In her memoir of Una Jeffers, Edith Greenan recounts evenings in Tor House following dinner with Robinson Jeffers reading aloud before the fire from the poets and playwrights of the Irish Literary Renaissance, while guests sipped Angelica from tumblers. Una herself was wont to dress in quasi-medieval Celtic attire on these and other occasions, the general impression of antique Irishness she was creating reinforced by the style in which she dressed her hair by circling two thick braids atop her head. Robinson Jeffers, for his part, was fully aware of the Irish Literary Renaissance, also known as the Celtic Twilight, as a model for what he was doing on behalf of Big Sur: exhuming old and frequently lost legends, imposing narrative on landscape, liberating a silent people into literary expression. The western Irish coast and Big Sur had many similarities of seascape, landform, and weather and offered the same resistance to human habitation. The Jefferses spent the year 1929 living in the west of Ireland, where Robinson Jeffers composed the revealing poems of Descent to the Dead (1931).

Thus the relevance, however fragile, of Ella Young's visits to Carmel-by-the-Sea, Point Lobos, and Big Sur between the mid-1920s and the mid-1930s when she was lecturing at UC Berkeley in Celtic studies, thanks to a ten-year chair endowed for her by Carmelite Noel Sullivan in honor of his uncle James Duval Phelan, former mayor of San Francisco and United States senator. Tall, majestic, as distinctively beautiful in her youth as her good friend Maud Gonne, with whom William Butler Yeats was so enamored, Ella Young seemed a figure stepping forth from a medieval manuscript in the library of Trinity College, Dublin. (Like Una Jeffers, Young favored an antique Celtic mode of dress.) In the most fundamental aspect of her character and personality, Young was a poet given to the acting out of her poetic vision, which in her case had been formed in the west of Ireland, where she had lived and studied Gaelic following her graduation from the Royal University, and by Theosophy, that mélange of mystic theories and metaphors that during the same period was also attracting William Butler Yeats and George Russell. Under these influences, Ella Young became a minor but respectable poet of the Celtic Twilight, an anthologist of ancient Irish folktales, and a student of Celtic mythology, who more than half believed in the reality of the myths she was studying. Until the Irish Society intervened, she was almost denied admission to the United States in 1926 when she suggested to her examiners at Ellis Island that she believed in fairies.

Yet Ella Young was also, like her Dublin flatmate Maud Gonne, a revolutionary patriot, a member of Sinn Féin since 1912, a founding member of the underground movement Cumann na mBan and as such active in the Easter Rising and the war of independence. When civil war broke out following the establishment of the Irish Free State, Young was arrested by the Free State for running guns to the Republicans and imprisoned. This experience persuaded her to leave Ireland for the United States and, eventually, to sojourn in Carmel-by-the-Sea, where she was befriended by, among others, Robinson and Una Jeffers, the Carmel artists Ireland-born John O'Shea and his wife Molly, and Noel Sullivan, a wealthy scion of the Phelan-Sullivan clan of San Francisco. Taking up the lectureship Sullivan endowed for her at UC Berkeley, Young divided her time between Berkeley and Carmel for the better part of a decade, part of the Sullivan-Shea circle. Her presence there afforded the Jefferses with a living connection to so many of the great figures of the Irish Literary Renaissance.

Young, in turn, reinforced through conversation and lectures the parallels between Big Sur and the west of Ireland. For such a Celtic Twilight figure as she was, Young adored the United States, California especially. "Ireland," Young believed, "was a white unicorn!" England, "a heavy-flanked bull: too long stall-fed." America, by contrast, was "a tawny lioness, beautiful, alert, and sinewy-muscled." This is the way that Ella Young spoke, elliptically, in metaphor, and hence was the way she spoke to Big Sur resident Rosalind Sharpe Wall, who was taking Young's course at Berkeley, when she told Wall that she had come to the United States when the "Guardians of Ireland had changed" and that "Point Lobos was a sacred place, one of the most powerful in all of America." Point Lobos, Young reiterated on a later occasion, "is the center of psychic force for the entire Pacific Coast. There are other sacred mountains, other sacred places, but this is the most powerful." There were sea spirits at Point Lobos, she claimed, and fairies, although not as many fairies as there were in Ireland—yet stronger fairies, stronger spirits on Point Lobos and the Big Sur to the south than in Ireland. There was a connection between these Celtic-like entities and the long-ago Native Americans of the region. "The Indians hold the magic of America," Young asserted. "When America taps this magic that the Indians had, then we will have great poetry, great music, great singing. This is also true of Lobos.

When the force of Lobos is released, a great thing will happen in America—but Lobos is not ready to make friends yet."[2]

An equally eccentric Jaime de Angulo, meanwhile, was also probing the Native American meanings of Point Lobos and Big Sur, albeit from the perspective of anthropology and linguistics as opposed to vatic utterance. Still, were one to encounter de Angulo during his early Carmel and later and longer Big Sur sojourns, comparisons to Ella Young might not seem that far-fetched. Like Young and so many other permanent and semi-permanent Carmelites, in fact—de Angulo was an eccentric, a poseur even, however sincere the assumptions behind the pose. Long-haired, dressing whenever possible as a vaquero, cutting his meat with a long knife tucked into his belt, earning his living as a Big Sur rancher while carrying on pioneering work in Native American anthropology and linguistics, Jaime de Angulo bore witness in lifestyle and scholarship to his belief in the continuing relevance of Native American and Hispanic traditions, not just for Big Sur but for all of California and the entire Southwest.

Again, as in the case of Ella Young and Ireland, there is a Robinson Jeffers connection. As Lawrence Clark Powell first pointed out, Jeffers deployed in his narrative poems a host of Indian and Hispanic-Indian figures—ranch hands, herdsmen, cooks and other household servants, upright wives or mistresses, frequent observers of white folly. While remaining minor, such characters nevertheless anchor the action in a matrix of historical setting, the Native Americans and the Spanish-Indian past. The Native American peoples of the Big Sur constituted the true prehistory and the present-tense ghosts of the region: a notion corroborated by Alfred Kroeber in his classic *Handbook of the Indians of California* (1925). The Esalen of the region, Kroeber points out, were already a near-vanished people by the time Spaniards were reconnoitering the coast of California in the early sixteenth century. In ancient times, the Esalen belonged to a much larger linguistic group that roamed the region but was eventually reduced to between five hundred and one thousand living on the Big Sur coast. To the north of the Esalen were the Rumsen Costanoans of Monterey, also called the Carmelenyos, due to their absorption into Mission San Carlos Borroméo. Even in Native American times, then, Big Sur was sparsely settled. Yet legend kept alive the memory of these peoples, including a folkloric belief that Native Americans had acquired and hidden a cache of gold, which fed into Robert Louis Stevenson's use of Point Lobos as the setting for *Treasure Island*.

While Ella Young might dream of fairies and other spirits inhabiting Point Lobos and the regions to the south, Jaime de Angulo—as is evident in his two 1922 novellas, *Don Bartolomeo* and *The Lariat*—was concerned with recovering the Native American and Hispanic past of the region. Born in Paris in 1887 of wealthy Spanish expatriate parents, educated by the Jesuits but turning to lifelong disbelief, de Angulo used part of his inheritance to emigrate to Colorado at age eighteen to acquire the skills he would need to become a rancher in the American West, the calling that he had improbably chosen. Gaining experience as a cowboy in Colorado and Honduras, where he also studied banana farming, de Angulo—again

with financial assistance from his father—returned to the United States, this time
to California, where he found himself in San Francisco just in time for the destruction of the city in April 1906. Resuming his education, de Angulo chose medical
school as offering the broadest kind of education in the sciences and enrolled in the
Cooper Union Medical School in San Francisco (later incorporated into Stanford
University) before transferring to Johns Hopkins, where he took his M.D. in 1912. By
that time—thanks in part to reading *Ancient Society* (1877) by Lewis Henry Morgan
and *The Mind of Primitive Man* (1911) by Franz Boas, under whom Alfred Kroeber
had studied at Columbia—de Angulo determined upon a scientific career and set up
his own research laboratory in Palo Alto, where he conducted research in genetics.

At this point de Angulo, along with other Stanfordites, began to vacation in
Carmel-by-the-Sea with his wife Cary, a Vassar graduate and de Angulo's fellow
medical student at Johns Hopkins. These sojourns in Carmel-by-the-Sea, still a
relatively undeveloped settlement, touched something deep within de Angulo: his
Spanish descent, for one thing, his youthful dreams of becoming a rancher in the Far
West, his actual experiences as a cattleman in Colorado and Honduras. In Carmel
de Angulo was first glimpsed riding about on horseback dressed in the vaquero costume that would become his lifelong attire, save for the years he spent in uniform
as an Army medical officer during World War I, or the respectable tweed suits he
wore when lecturing at Berkeley in the 1920s, or the dresses and other female attire
he featured as a cross-dresser in Berkeley and San Francisco doing anthropological
fieldwork in the role of women in contemporary society.

Jaime de Angulo was an eccentric, to say the least. He was also a brilliant field
researcher in Native American linguistics at a time, as his biographer Wendy Leeds-
Hurwitz points out, when anthropology was still an informal enterprise bringing
academically trained professionals with university appointments into collaboration
with talented amateurs. By 1914 de Angulo was ranching near Alturas on the Pit
River in Modoc County while beginning to observe the habits and language of the
Achumawi people and writing up his observations. The following year, de Angulo
relocated his ranching efforts to a homestead in Big Sur, personally driving a herd of
eighteen horses south from Alturas. For the next thirty and more years, de Angulo's
ranch in Big Sur—Los Pesares (the Sorrows) he called it—remained an anchor-
age point as his idiosyncratic career took him to service as a medical officer in the
United States Army, where he specialized in psychiatry, treating the shell-shocked.
At UC Berkeley, de Angulo taught summer courses in anthropology and psychology. In Modoc County, he continued and formalized his studies of the Achuwami.
In Oaxaca, Mexico, he researched indigenous languages. In Zurich, he studied
with Carl Jung. (De Angulo's divorced first wife, Cary, was working as Jung's secretary.) Then back to Berkeley, where he lived with his second wife, Nancy Freeland,
another Vassar graduate, whom he met when she was running a bed and breakfast in
Carmel. Then on to Taos, where the de Angulos moved in the Mable Dodge Luhan
circle. Then back to California, where he did further field work among the Karok
and Shasta. Then once again to Europe, where he studied the prehistoric caves in

the south of France. Then back to Big Sur, where a tragic accident curtailed his scientific career, exacerbated his alcoholism, and turned him into a near-recluse. Driving in Big Sur that summer, de Angulo veered off a cliff on Highway 1. His twelve-year-old son Alvar was killed instantly, and de Angulo spent more than twelve hours pinned under the wreckage before being rescued. Even with this catastrophe, however, de Angulo managed for two years, 1937 and 1938, to revive his researches into Chinese, yet another language he had mastered, and begin the manuscript of a book, *What Is Language?* in summary of his life's work.

What is one to make of such a life, by turns so brilliant and productive and scattered, wasted even, masked behind a vaquero persona that had become more than a pose, marred by alcoholism and anti-social behavior? Subsequent evaluation of his work by scholars has testified to de Angulo's skills as a field researcher in linguistics. On a less technical level, de Angulo's English-language redactions of Native American stories and myths, which he read over Berkeley radio station KPFA-FM with great success in 1949–50 just before his death from cancer, made of him a quasi-cult figure to the Beat generation of the 1950s, beginning with poet Robert Duncan, who served as his secretary. So too have de Angulo's two novellas of the Big Sur, *Don Bartolomeo* and *The Lariat*—written in the 1920s in competitive response to D. H. Lawrence, whom de Angulo had known at Taos—since their reissue in *A Jaime de Angulo Reader* (1979) steadily impressed a new generation with their depictions of Native American and Hispanic Mestizo culture, together with their Laurentian themes of eros on the Hispanic frontier.

But it was as a presence, a persona, an emblematic poseur if you will, that Jaime de Angulo exercised his influence on the 1950s. Henry Miller would later write that of all the people he met in Big Sur, he most regretted not doing a full length portrait of Jaime de Angulo, so expressive did this Euro-Californian seem of Big Sur values. Even before he knew the precise details of de Angulo's life or had read any of his writings, poet Gary Snyder would later observe, he already felt the mediating presence of de Angulo in Big Sur as an avatar of a message contained within the region. For Snyder and others, de Angulo embodied values they believed themselves to be seeking: an escape from the conventional and the discovery of *dharma* on the Big Sur coast.

The arrival of Henry Miller in the spring of 1944 signaled the emergence of Big Sur as an artists' colony and epicenter of dissent. Prior to his move to Big Sur, the life of Henry Miller constituted an epic acting out of resistance to what just before the Second World War he had termed the Air-Conditioned Nightmare of contemporary American life in a book that could not be published in wartime, lest Miller and his publishers be brought up on charges of sedition. As man and artist, Miller represented a paradox of Yes! and No! affirmation and dissent, pursued, acted out, talked about, written about, simultaneously and without cessation. On the one hand, Miller saw himself as a new Walt Whitman, a Yea-Sayer to life and the human condition. Yet Miller also pursued a lifetime program of Saying No. More than any of his contemporaries who are still read and remembered, Henry Miller refused to make peace with American life.

Before his arrival at Big Sur, Miller's life constituted one long Brobdingnagian rejection of bourgeois respectability: the rebelliousness and near-delinquency of his boyhood and adolescence in Brooklyn in the early 1900s, his aversion to steady employment as a young man, his rejection of a college education, his avoidance of the draft during World War I through a hasty marriage and fatherhood, his unconventional friends and associates, his sexual adventurism, his bizarre obsession with his second wife (a taxi dancer, would-be actress and part-time prostitute), together with his willingness to chronicle this sado-masochistic relationship in sexually explicit terms, his expatriation to Paris in the 1930s and his survival there as a moocher of legendary proportions. Even as regards literature, to which he dedicated his life, Miller showed contempt for the rules, not only in terms of the sexually explicit material that would keep him confined to avant-garde Paris publishers, his books banned in the United States, but in terms of the very requirements of literature for form and coherence. Miller preferred, rather, to plunge himself into a free-associative narrative present, the literary equivalent of his conversational harangues, moving from topic to topic with the compulsion of an autodidact exploding in a super-nova of random learning.

And yet, despite all this—the great barbaric yap of his life, which he modeled on Whitman but which Whitman himself would most likely consider to be somewhat over the top—a measure of calmness, serenity even, entered Henry Miller's life following his move to Big Sur, if one is to judge from the memoir of the fifteen years he would spend there, *Big Sur and the Oranges of Hieronymus Bosch* (1957). Miller had ended his years of European expatriation with a visit to Greece and the Greek islands in the summer of 1939, hosted there by his good friend Lawrence Durrell. There, in that distinctive landscape, on Corfu especially, a calming attraction to the contemplative life seeped into Miller's turbulent soul, or so he tells us in *The Colossus of Maroussi* (1941). The thought of moving to Greece permanently, quieting down his life, devoting himself to deeper things, seized hold of Miller. But war was on the horizon, and so Miller returned to the safety and stability of the United States, touring the country by automobile and excoriating it as the Air-Conditioned Nightmare before settling down in Los Angeles, temporarily, on mooched resources, then moving on to Big Sur, again on someone else's dime.

As far as such a discovery is possible to human beings, Miller opined, he had found a kind of paradise at Big Sur. He remained broke, as ever, living in a borrowed house, unashamedly begging for assistance in letters to the editor and billboard notices posted in literary venues. Not until the early 1950s would he be able to access accrued royalties from his Paris publisher. Yet for seven years Miller enjoyed a happy third marriage and two beautiful if rambunctious children from that union, followed by a fourth marriage when his third wife left him for another man, as would his fourth wife, an embarrassment, alas, for the most celebrated erotic writer of his era. Still, Miller found a patron who rented him a cabin for ten dollars a month and, later, another patron who provided him with an even more accommodating home, which he could pay for once his royalties came through, and he was thus able to work, more or less steadily, on the *Rosy Crucifixion* trilogy (1965) based on his life through the 1920s, together with other literary projects. Thanks to these Big Sur years and to the publishing courage of New Directions, Miller was able to make the transition from an underground writer whose books had to be smuggled into the United States to a canonic if controversial American author.

The oranges referred to in the title of Miller's Big Sur narrative are the shiny oranges on the trees of Paradise depicted in the left panel of Hieronymus Bosch's early sixteenth-century triptych *The Millennium*. All things considered, Miller found a paradise of life, love, work, and place in Big Sur. Breaking daily stints at his typewriter with long walks along Partington Ridge, sitting outside his cabin at sunrise and sunset, Miller felt as much at peace with himself as he had ever felt in his life. Miller especially enjoyed the informed community of artists and aspiring artists developing in the area that spontaneously took him as its central point of reference: artist Emil White, for example, a Polish-Jewish refugee who lived down the road on Highway 1 and acted as factotum, gatekeeper, and designated substitute seducer of the women who came to Big Sur to seduce Henry Miller and found him, temporarily, a happily married man. Other members of the Miller circle included the sculptor Franz Sandow; Gilbert Neiman, busy translating Lorca; silk-screenist Bezalel Schatz, with whom Miller collaborated on an illustrated book; his housing patrons, artists Lynda Sargent and Jean Wharton; and sculptor Beniamino Bufano—but definitely not Miller's neighbor Nicholas Roosevelt, TR's equally patrician and Republican cousin, a retired *New York Times* editor, who thoroughly disapproved of Miller's books, friends, and lifestyle. Miller himself was not so positive about the dropouts, the seekers, the conscientious objectors, and, following the war, the veterans with wounded sensibilities who were increasingly showing up at Partington Point to make personal confessions and declarations of their angst and alienation, considering Miller the very embodiment of the rejection of American life that they themselves were experiencing. Miller had come to Big Sur to simplify his life and not to become the guru to those in pain from wartime anguish or the high priest of sexual liberation. Nonetheless, postwar dissent did have a tendency to consolidate itself on Henry Miller of Big Sur, man and symbol, whether Miller liked it or not.

The quest for alternative value also involved the South Coast and its desert hinterlands. Even as Henry Miller was fleeing Europe in 1939, there were also fleeing to Southern California three other expatriates, Englishmen—Aldous Huxley, Christopher Isherwood, and the lesser known Gerald Heard—who would also become iconic figures of quest and dissent. Their arena would be Southern California, with its existing tradition of religious experimentation; and their quest would also fuse similar elements of religious, political, and sexual liberation, organized in their case around the Hindu tradition of Vedanta.

In 1929 Swami Prabhavananda, a Hindu monk of the Ramakrishna Order, then in his mid-thirties, founded the Vedanta Society of Southern California, eventually located in a three-building Spanish-style compound at 1946 Ivar Avenue in Hollywood, premises donated by a supporter of the society who had become a Vedanta nun. As one of the six classical traditions of Indian philosophy, Vedanta postulates the ultimate reality of Brahman or the Self. From Brahman, the Absolute, proceeds the material universe in all its mutability and diversity. Yet the world of appearances is by definition shifting and ambiguous. The challenge thus becomes: How does one move from shifting appearances to Brahman, to the Self, to the Absolute? Through study of the Upanishads, for one thing, the final sequence of the Veda, and by an exploration inward via asceticism and meditation to discover the self within. Purged of illusion, that inward self, once encountered, opens a pathway to Brahman, that transcendent Self from which emanates—whether as reality or illusion—the physical and human universe. Thus Vedanta parallels the Western tradition of Platonism, neo-Platonism, and classic Christian mysticism in its search for a transcendent One beyond creation or, in Christian formulation, a Godhead of pure and absolute Being. Vedanta, in short, was not a crackpot cult sprouting in the pan-fertile soil of Southern California. It was, rather, a missionary venture of high Asian thought planted, however fragilely, in a new and eclectic landscape.

Also active in Southern California, based out of Ojai in nearby Ventura County, was the highly regarded teacher Jiddu Krishnamurti. Born in 1895 to a Brahmin family, Krishnamurti came under the influence of the Theosophical Society through his father, an official in the colonial government, who had leavened his orthodox Brahmin Hinduism with an interest in Theosophy, an eclectic blend of Hindu and Buddhist beliefs. A communitarian as well as mystical movement, the Theosophical Society in 1897 established at Point Loma south of San Diego a community that lasted until 1942. Around 1910 leaders of the Theosophical Society discerned in the teenager Jiddu Krishnamurti the long-expected World Teacher and established an auxiliary organization, the Order of the Star, to prepare for his ministry. The problem was: Krishnamurti, as he came to maturity, thanks in part to his English education, began to have doubts regarding the necessity for a World Teacher. By August 1922, living with his tubercular brother in a secluded valley near Ojai in Ventura County on a property owned by the Order of the Star, hoping for a cure in the Southern California climate, Krishnamurti grew even more doubtful. When his brother died in November 1925, Krishnamurti renounced the very concept of a World Teacher in favor of a pathless way to the truth that each individual must negotiate on his or her own terms. Krishnamurti soon developed into a world-renowned freelance teacher and prolific writer, proclaiming a personalized path to enlightenment through study of the philosophical traditions of Asia, meditation, compassion, self-discipline, and an acceptance of suffering. Like Swami Prabhavananda, Jiddu Krishnamurti was an exotic in the religious landscape of Southern California, but he was not a crackpot. Krishnamurti became, rather, a respected figure on four continents.

Krishnamurti was also, like Swami Prabhavananda, a pacifist, only more out-spoken than the swami; so much so, in fact, that he earned investigation by the FBI as World War II approached and prudently decided to remain silent on issues of war and peace until the war was over. Pacifism, in significant measure, brought Huxley, Heard, and Isherwood to Southern California (and Henry Miller as well, for that matter): a despair at the suffering that was about to be unleashed on Europe, together with a desire to escape the conflict. Their flight to the United States would earn for each of these men, Isherwood especially, who was younger and eligible for service, the resentment of those who had remained behind to fight for England and would also cause each of these expatriates a measure of guilt and disquiet over sitting out the war in safe and sunny Southern California as German bombs and rocket bombs rained down on the homeland.

Aldous Huxley, Gerald Heard, and Christopher Isherwood had their differences in terms of age, talent, and sexual persuasion, but they also had much in common, aside from their Englishness. Each came from an established background, Huxley especially, being as he was the great-grandson of Dr. Thomas Arnold, the noted headmaster of Rugby, the great-nephew of Matthew Arnold, the poet and educator, the nephew of the novelist Mrs. Humphrey Ward, and the son of Thomas Huxley, biologist and philosopher of science. As his longtime friend and biographer Sybille Bedford points out, Aldous Huxley belonged to that genre of upper-middle-class English families—the Trevelyans, the Macaulays, the Arnolds, the Wedgwoods, the Darwins—who did much of England's thinking during the nineteenth century. Aldous's younger brother Julian would in time become a biologist and higher civil servant almost as noted as his father. Aldous himself developed into one of the most respected and prolific novelists and essayists writing in English in the twentieth century. Heard and Isherwood, by contrast, came from slightly lower on the social scale in a society in which class distinctions were paramount. Heard was the son of an Anglican clergyman and Isherwood the son of a Sandhurst-trained Army officer from the Cheshire squirearchy, destined to lose his life at the battle of Ypres. From this class, however—clergymen, barristers, military officers, country squires—had also come a host of creative intellectuals, writers, and poets of every sort during the Victorian and Edwardian eras, and Heard and Isherwood were part of this milieu. All three were Oxbridge-educated. In the world of letters, Huxley and Isherwood would over time earn decidedly more significant reputations; yet Isherwood wrote slowly, deliberately and with some difficulty, while Huxley—despite a boyhood bout of *keratitis punctata* that would leave him blind for eighteen months and severely short-sighted for the rest of his life—wrote and published steadily across a lifetime, from 1916 to his death in 1963, as did Heard, writing more than forty books before his death in 1971.

In a number of regards—Asian-oriented mysticism, communal living, the belief that a better age was dawning, drug usage, and the search for sexual liberation— Huxley, Heard, and Isherwood, like Henry Miller up north at Big Sur, seemed con-nected to, even prophetic of, the counter-culture of the 1960s and 1970s. Was this because they helped create this era or merely that they anticipated it; or was their anticipation a necessary part of the process? The Southern California pilgrimages of Heard, Huxley, and Isherwood seem in retrospect both to anticipate the future and, because they wrote about it so well and were read by so many, to make the future happen.

Long before their arrival in Southern California, Huxley, Heard, and Isherwood were at odds with English life, or, to put the matter more positively, they were in search of a less constricted existence: a quest they shared with, among others, Huxley's good friend D. H. Lawrence and Henry Miller's good friend Lawrence Durrell. An independent writer, supported by a long-term contract from the London publishing firm of Chatto & Windus, Huxley lived abroad, in Tuscany and Sanary in the south of France, for most of the 1920s and 1930s. Isherwood spent most of the 1930s in Europe, centered on Berlin. All three were utopians. Heard lived in Ireland from 1919 to 1923 as the executive assistant to agrarian reformer Sir Horace Plunkett, then trying to introduce cooperatives into Irish agriculture. Italy and the south of France, indeed the Mediterranean in general, bespoke to Huxley cultures that had achieved deeper connections to art and the imaginative life as well as more pleasant places to live in terms of weather, terrain, housing, cuisine, and the rhythms and protocols of daily life.

At the same time, however, Huxley's utopianism was even more fundamentally expressed by his quarrel with contemporary culture, so evident in his dystopian novel *Brave New World* (1932), which launched Huxley into a thirty-year opposition to the totalitarian direction he believed society was taking in its misuse of science and technology, its ignorance of perennial philosophy as evident in the great philosophical and mystical traditions of Europe and Asia, its failure to appreciate art and the humanistic tradition, and, most of all, its disregard of human life through state-sponsored violence and a misappropriation of planetary resources, food and water especially.

Gerald Heard was an out-and-out utopianist across a cavalcade of books that make and remake with minor variation a reiterated anthropological and historical argument. In *The Ascent of Humanity* (1929), *The Emergence of Man* (1931), *Social Substance of Religion* (1931), *The Source of Civilization* (1937), and the summarizing (finally!) *The Five Ages of Man* (1963), Heard mapped out and elaborated upon the evolution of the human species through successive stages of pre-individualized group consciousness, proto-individuality, and individuality through successive stages (monastic, humanistic, revolutionary), climaxed by the contemporary development of a group consciousness that did not obliterate the individual. Each of Heard's studies constituted a different take on this process—psychological, social, religious, political—although his basic perspective remained anthropological and historical, and his basic theme remained the evolution of human consciousness to higher planes and the social causes and consequences thereof.

In the 1930s Isherwood's utopianism consisted in a flirtation with Communism common among the bright young Cambridge men of his generation, a flirtation that would later have Isherwood interviewed by the FBI regarding, among other topics, his friend the escaped double agent Guy Burgess, with whom Isherwood had for some three years shared a lover. By 1939, however, Isherwood's utopianism was basically personal, which is to say, an effort on his part to live the homosexual life as openly as possible, which is why he so felt at home in Weimar Berlin and, later, Rugen Island in the Baltic Sea off the coast of Pomerania, where an informal homosexual circle briefly established itself. Heard, for his part, was homosexual but would more or less remain in the closet for his lifetime. Huxley lived, discreetly, in an open marriage in which his wife Maria, herself bisexual, selected suitable paramours for her husband.

Another kind of utopianism, pacifism, brought Huxley and Heard to Southern California. In the fall of 1935, both Huxley, living in Sanaray, where he was working on *Eyeless in Gaza* (1936), and Heard, who was making his living as a university lecturer and science commentator for the BBC, were active in the Peace Pledge Union being organized in London, a movement having as its goal a personalized statement by millions, it was hoped, that they would refuse to participate in any future wars. Over the next two years, thanks to their mutual work for the Peace Pledge Union, Huxley and Heard—two pacifist polymaths writing and lecturing for a general as well as a highbrow audience—became good friends. From this period as well—since almost everything Huxley thought or lived through he wrote about—came Huxley's *An Encyclopaedia of Pacifism* (1937), setting forth the strongest possible case for the anti-war movement. Arguments were one thing, however, the certainty of war another. Although neither Huxley nor Heard ever came out and plainly said it, by 1937 they were seriously thinking of fleeing to safety from a Europe on the verge of catastrophe. In March 1937 Gerald Heard and his partner, the independently wealthy Christopher Wood, joined Aldous and Maria Huxley and their son Matthew on the SS *Normandie* for a trans-Atlantic voyage of emigration to the United States. Arriving in New York on 7 April 1937, the group, minus Christopher Wood, who was traveling separately, took an automobile journey of five weeks across the United States, spending part of the summer at Frieda Lawrence's ranch in Taos, followed by a cross-country lecture tour in November and December on behalf of the peace movement, followed by a decision in February 1938 to settle permanently in Southern California, where Huxley went to work as a screenwriter for Metro-Goldwyn-Mayer and began the Los Angeles novel *After Many a Summer Dies the Swan* (1939).

Huxley's good friend Anita Loos, author of *Gentlemen Prefer Blondes* (1926), which Huxley (along with George Santayana) greatly admired, secured for Huxley his first screenwriting job at MGM. Like so many other émigrés, Huxley did well in Hollywood, although his scripts were rarely translated directly to the screen. Still, it flattered the studios to have such a respected man of letters with an English accent working on such ambitious films as *Madame Curie* (1944) and *Jane Eyre* (1944). Even Walt Disney, in the summer of 1945, secured Huxley's services for an early treatment of *Alice in Wonderland*, which was, after all, based upon an English classic. For his second assignment, *Pride and Prejudice*, Huxley felt reluctant to accept what he considered his lavish salary of $1,500 a week, given the sufferings being endured by the British people. Take the money, Loos advised Huxley, and send part of it home. Loos and the Huxleys formed their own social circle, which included, among others, Charles Chaplin, Paulette Goddard, Greta Garbo, Igor Stravinsky, and Bertrand Russell. The circle would meet for gala evenings at Loos's home in Santa Monica or for Tuesday lunches at one or another of the vegetarian restaurants at the Farmers Market in the Fairfax district.

Shortly after settling in Southern California, Gerald Heard met Swami Prabhavananda, whom he introduced to Huxley. Heard and Huxley also established contact with Krishnamurti in Ojai. Heard's historical monographs demonstrate his mastery of Western theology and mysticism, and in *The Perennial Philosophy* (1945) Huxley even more vividly demonstrated his mastery of classical and Christian ascetical thought, together with an ability to align these traditions to comparable stages and concepts in Asian thought. While they respected Swami Prabhavananda, Heard and Huxley ultimately favored the open-ended, eclectic approach of Krishnamurti over the more formal teachings and practice of the Vedanta Center, although they remained connected there as well. An open-ended, syncretic approach to the contemplative life characterized the program at the Trabuco College of Prayer established by Heard in the early 1940s in an Italianate brick compound in a remote canyon in the Santa Ana Mountains.

Christopher Isherwood, meanwhile, spent the first half of 1938 traveling in China with W. H. Auden, a trip resulting in the co-authored travel book *Journey to War* (1939), the war that brought Isherwood and his fellow pacifist Auden to New York in late January 1939. Auden settled in New York. Isherwood, however, did not like New York. It was, he wrote his English publisher John Lehmann a "nervous-breakdown expressed in terms of architecture."[3] He was accepting, instead, an invitation from Gerald Heard and Aldous Huxley to explore possibilities in Hollywood. Arriving in Los Angeles in mid-May 1939 after a cross-country Greyhound bus ride in the company of his current attachment, Isherwood first encountered "the theatrical impermanence" of the city where he would spend the rest of his life. "I love California more than ever," Isherwood would be writing Lehmann by 26 December 1940. "It is without nostalgia or regret or apprehension of the future—you are free here, you can be anything you make yourself."[4]

What Isherwood set out to make of himself was a screenwriter, a draft-exempt pacifist, a Vedanta mystic, and, in time, one of the most iconic gay men of his generation. Earlier in the decade, Isherwood had worked as a screenwriter specializing in dialogue at the Gaumont-British studio in London on the film *The Little Friend*, being directed by the Viennese-born Berthold Viertel. an experience upon which Isherwood would base his well-received novel *Prater Violet* (1945). Through Berthold Viertel and his wife Salka, a Polish-born actress and screenwriter for Greta Garbo, Isherwood was introduced to the émigré circle that met on Sundays at the Viertel home in Santa Monica Canyon, where Isherwood's fluent German made him a de facto member of the émigré community. Another member of that community, Gottfried Reinhardt, son of the legendary producer-director Max Reinhardt, introduced Isherwood to MGM, where in May 1940 Isherwood signed a one-year contract, doing most of his script discussion in German with his fellow émigrés. Across the next four decades Isherwood derived a significant part of his livelihood from screenwriting and, given his highly social nature, became a popular member of the film community. Isherwood's detailed diaries from this era would ultimately constitute a Who's Who, a fragmented saga, of filmdom and film folk in the golden age of the studios.

In early conversations with Heard and Huxley, moreover, Isherwood consolidated his pacifism. Having lived for most of his adult life in Italy and France, Huxley had over time turned himself into a quasi-stateless person. (His pacifism, moreover, prevented him from becoming an American citizen when he applied for citizenship following the war.) For his part, Heard had not lived in exile like Huxley but, as far as England was concerned, had gone into an exile within, a psychological statelessness, fueled by pacifism. As late as July–August 1941, at a time when only Great Britain and Greece were actively opposing Nazi expansion, Heard conducted a month-long pacifist seminar at La Verne College in cooperation with the Friends Service Committee. During the same period, Huxley researched and wrote *Gray Eminence* (1941), a biography of the Capuchin priest Father Joseph, who became the gray eminence behind Cardinal Richelieu and whose allegedly good intentions, Huxley contended, helped unleash the fury of the Thirty Years War. Moral of the story, Huxley argued: War can never be resorted to, for whatever purposes. Still, for all the English living in Southern California, whether explicitly pacifist or not, expatriation remained a delicate matter after war broke out in September 1939, the British nearly lost their army at Dunkirk, Hitler prepared for invasion, and the Battle of Britain was fought in the skies over southern England. As early as June 1940, Conservative MP Major Sir Jocelyn Lucas rose in Parliament to call for an investigation into why Auden, Isherwood, and others (actor James Mason had applied for and received conscientious objector status) were sitting out the war in the United States. Even Isherwood's English publisher John Lehmann was critical. Chafing under such attacks, composer Benjamin Britten, a registered conscientious objector, returned to England in 1941 to show solidarity with the war effort. And as far as the German-speaking émigré community was concerned, many of them had in one way or another served in World War I and backed the British resistance to Nazi Germany. Isherwood shocked the émigré community when a letter from him to an English friend got into the press alleging that the German émigrés of Los Angeles would "gladly sacrifice the entire British Army to make Berlin safe for nightlife."[5]

As a registered permanent resident of the United States, moreover, Isherwood was now eligible for the draft, and following Pearl Harbor being drafted was a real possibility. Already, Isherwood had been flirting with the idea of volunteering for a Quaker ambulance unit. On the other hand, Isherwood could claim conscientious objector status, but even if such a status were granted, he would be placed in a conscientious objector camp. A more total exemption—since Isherwood was most likely not 4-F, physically unable to serve—would be a 4-D exemption as a theological student. Although he had what he considered a religious nature, and for some time had been feeling the need for some form of religious development, Isherwood loathed Christianity. Gerald Heard had introduced him to Swami Prabhavananda, and the swami had begun, tentatively, to instruct Isherwood in meditation. Full membership in the Vedanta Center as a postulant would offer Isherwood 4-D status. Formally accepted aspirants to the Ramakrishna Order, however, were expected to observe celibacy, and Christopher Isherwood was decidedly not a celibate.

It would be too easy to say that Isherwood was attracted to Vedanta because he wanted to avoid the draft. For some months, he had been in discussion with Swami Prabhavananda regarding the omnivorous sexuality that was proving such a barrier, Isherwood believed, to his spiritual growth. Isherwood's attraction to Vedanta, while compromised, was genuine; and when Isherwood broke up with his partner in February 1943, he moved into the Vedanta Center as a postulant. By this time, ironically, the draft age had been lowered, and Isherwood was for all practical purposes exempt. At the center, Isherwood lived a monastic life—a vegetarian diet, meditation, sexual abstinence—although he was given leave on weekends to work at MGM or to dine with such friends as Tennessee Williams, who had called upon him at the center with a letter of introduction, or to attend the Viertel Sunday soirees in Santa Monica. A sometime member of that circle, Greta Garbo, also visited Isherwood at the center, flirting slightly with the swami and "telling him how dark and mysterious his Indian eyes were." While at the center, Isherwood helped Swami Prabhavananda edit *Vedanta and the West*, a bimonthly magazine, and, more important, served alongside the swami on what became the standard translation of the Bhagavad-Gita, with Isherwood polishing the swami's literal translations from the Sanskrit.

As attracted as he was to Vedanta and the Ramakrishna Order, celibacy remained an arduous requirement, which Isherwood struggled to observe, unsuccessfully as it turned out, toward the end of his residence there. In August 1945, following the surrender of Japan, Isherwood moved out of the center, although he continued to work with the swami on further translations. After a number of relationships, Isherwood in 1953 formed a long-lasting partnership with UCLA student Don Bachardy, thirty years his junior. Even among Isherwood's most sympathetic friends, the partnership with Bachardy initially caused some disquiet; but as Isherwood and Bachardy remained a couple, living together in a jointly owned home on Adelaide Drive in Santa Monica Canyon —with Isherwood resuming his career as a novelist and Bachardy gaining a reputation as an artist—the pair became by the late 1950s an accepted duo, treated almost matter-of-factly, as just another couple, by the Los Angeles press. Hollywood had long since supported an active homosexual community at every level of the industry, yet Hollywood homosexuals tended to remain in the closet. Isherwood, by contrast, dealt openly with homosexual themes in his fiction and lived openly with Bachardy. As the gay rights movement developed,

Isherwood's writings became increasingly important to gay and lesbian America, and Isherwood and Bachardy became, as gay chronicler Armisted Maupin would later describe them, the First Couple of Gay America.

In the early 1950s there emerged in Huxley and Heard yet another orientation destined to become a trend in a later era: drugs—mescaline initially, first taken by Huxley and Heard in May 1953, followed by experiments with lysergic acid diethylamide (LSD), first ingested by them in December 1955. Huxley wrote about these experiments in *The Doors of Perception* (1954) and *Heaven and Hell* (1956), titles taken from the English visionary poet William Blake, who required no pharmaceutical encouragement, it must be said, to make contact with either heaven or hell on earth. Huxley's and Heard's turn to pharmaceuticals in 1953, however, can be linked to a conviction in each of them that as far as the contemplative life was concerned they had reached an impasse. As scholars of mysticism, East and West, Huxley and Heard were fully aware that in the final stages of ascetical assent, mystics made contact with transcendent reality, the One, the Ultimate. Yet Huxley and Heard, and Isherwood as well, for all their scholarship, for all their brilliance, were not true mystics but were, rather, contemplative savants, very much enmeshed in the world and the flesh. Just prior to the war, Heard had been meditating up to six hours a day, but now, as his friends were noticing, he seemed less ascetic, less at war with his sexual identity. In late 1944 Heard turned his Trabuco College of Prayer over to the Vedanta Center. The Huxleys spent the years 1943 through 1947 dividing their time between Beverly Hills and the Mojave Desert, where they established a quasi-hermitage near the ruins of the Llano del Rio Cooperative Colony founded by Socialist Job Harriman in 1914 after Harriman, just barely, had lost his bid to become mayor of Los Angeles. By 1947, however, the Huxleys were back full-time on Doheny Drive in Beverly Hills and were on the verge of resuming their traveling life: to New York in September by automobile, their first absence from California since 1938, then back to New York the following June, followed by a voyage to Europe on the SS *Queen Mary*. His eyesight remarkably improved by therapy techniques being advocated by the New York oculist W. H. Bates, Huxley was resuming the good life of a respected and well-paid Hollywood screenwriter and sage in the larger republic of letters. At the same time, Heard was evolving into a clubbable English intellectual with excellent Southern California connections, and Isherwood was reclaiming his reputation as a writer.

Mescaline and LSD, then, offered Huxley and Heard a fast track forward to a continuation of their mystical quest. Mescaline, as Huxley would soon be arguing, was an essential component of Native American religious rites in the Southwest. His and Heard's experiments, moreover, were under the supervision of Humphrey Osmond, a Canadian M.D.-psychiatrist with extensive experience in drug therapy. Following the death of his wife Maria from cancer in February 1955, Huxley, after much study and consultation, took LSD along with Heard and uranium dealer Albert Hubbard, another Englishman sojourning in Southern California, with Bach's B minor Suite playing on the hi-fi. Isherwood and Bachardy experimented with *majoon* and *kiff* on a trip to Tangier in October 1955, after Isherwood had tried mescaline in London, but kept quiet about it. For both Isherwood and Bachardy the Tangier experience was a bad trip, with Bachardy growing paranoid and Isherwood feeling claustrophobic, unlike, he noted in his journal, the usual rhapsodic reports of mescaline users. Had Huxley's drug sessions and the ones that followed been discreet and private experiments, they might have been of minor historical importance. But as he did with everything else—the improvement of his eyesight, for example, which Huxley chronicled in *The Art of Seeing* (1942)—Huxley soon mastered the scholarship of mescaline and LSD, linked their results to classic mystical states in Asian and Western traditions, wrote about them in two books soaked in scholarship and literary analogy (not only William Blake but *The Tibetan Book of the Dead*), and lectured on the topic before professional and lay audiences, all this in the midst of the Eisenhower era. In the world of letters Aldous Huxley was a colossus. That colossus was now an open apostle of mescaline, peyote, and LSD: if taken by the right people, of course, and approached in the right spirit. A revolution, a crusade, was launched.

Another English expatriate with mystical ambitions, Alan Watts of Marin County, joined the movement. Huxley's advocacy of LSD led Watts to his own experimentation with the drug while a visiting scholar at Harvard in the early 1960s, under the supervision of faculty members Timothy Leary and Richard Alpert of the Harvard Center for Research on Personality. So too did Watts write of his experiences in *The Joyous Cosmology: Adventures in the Chemistry of Consciousness* (1962). Watts, however, was not a Vedantist nor even vaguely South-Asian Indian in his mystical attractions. He was, rather, a Nipponophile Zen Buddhist active in Buddhism since his teenage years.

Like much of India, Southern California was sun-drenched, semi-arid, scarce in its native vegetation, and the Hindu tradition fit into the landscape. Big Sur, the Monterey peninsula, and the Bay Area, by contrast, were wet and maritime in weather, stately in trees and flora, more island-like—English, Irish, Japanese—in topography and ambience. In such an environment, the Zen traditions of Japan, together with an identification with Tibet in the case of Big Sur, arose almost spontaneously. From the late nineteenth century onward, a certain kind of Zen metaphor, however fragile, a repose, a mystic quiet, exercised its influence in the art, architecture, and aesthetics of the region. In the postwar era this inclination was surfacing in full force—in Alan Watts, in the best of the Beat poets, in architecture, cuisine, garden design, and lifestyle—so much so that by the mid-1950s Alan Watts would be celebrating the rising Asian-fusion culture of the Bay Area.

If that were the case, then Watts and his friends were building upon a latent identity. Along with the rest of the nation, San Francisco found itself enamored with the aesthetics of Japan, from the success of the Japanese Pavilion at the Centennial Exhibition in Philadelphia in 1876 onward. Bay Area painter Theodore Wores spent much of the 1890s in Japan, painting its places and people, and was decorated by the Japanese government for his efforts. Wores's interest in Japanese culture was shared by many of his fellow members of the Bohemian Club. In September 1892, as part of their annual summer encampment in the redwoods, the Bohemians built a seventy-foot-high plaster replica of the renowned Daibutsu (great Buddha) statue of Kamakura, Japan, in Sequoia Canyon at the base of Mount Tamalpais. There, in a circular space some three hundred feet in diameter, Bohemians vested in white kimonos and carrying lighted torches conducted a Cremation of Care ceremony attended by some two hundred club members. These Buddha Jinks, as the ceremony was called, integrated music, choral singing, pageantry, and the spoken word in a distinctive outdoor performance that became an annual feature of the club's midsummer encampment. As part of the ritual, celebrants vested as Buddhist priests recited poetry linking the enlightenment of the Buddha under the banyan tree with a comparable search for *satori* beneath the redwoods and madrones of Sequoia Canyon.

The president of the newly established Stanford University, David Starr Jordan, an ardent Nipponophile, traveled to Japan in 1900 and 1911, making a special effort to recruit Japanese students. Thanks to Jordan's efforts, Stanford ranked second only to Harvard as the university of choice for Meiji-era students eager to sharpen their professional and technical skills. Ever since the American acquisition of the Philippines, Jordan had been outspoken in his evocation of the United States as an Asia/Pacific power with the San Francisco Bay Area, including Palo Alto, as its Asia/Pacific capital. In October 1905 Jordan joined San Mateo attorney Henry Pike Bowie to form the Japan Society of Northern California, which launched a busy schedule of lectures, exhibitions, study-travels, and other cultural activities. In 1904 the New York City–based poet and art critic Sadakichi Hartmann published his pioneering study *Japanese Art*. Born in 1867 on the island of Desima in Nagasaki harbor and raised by his German father in Hamburg following the death of his Japanese mother, Hartmann played an important role in introducing Japanese aesthetics to an American audience. In 1916, in the course of a visit to San Francisco, Hartmann published locally his *Tanka and Haiku: Japanese Rhythms*, later reissued in New York, introducing these literary forms to an American audience. Throughout the twentieth century, San Francisco strengthened and expanded its Asia/Pacific connections through such enterprises as the American-Hawaiian Steamship Company (its president Roger Lapham would in 1944 become the mayor of the city), the trans-Pacific freight and passenger traffic of the Dollar and Matson lines, the trans-Pacific flights of the Pan Am Clippers, the Asian spice import trade of Schilling and Company, the Asia/Pacific import-export business of Wilbur-Ellis, imported art and furniture in Gump's department store, and the Tokyo operations of the San Francisco–based Bank of America.

Many scholars in the academy considered Alan Watts's studies of Zen Buddhism a species of Gump's decoration. Watts did not possess a university degree. He began the study of Zen Buddhism, rather, while a student at the King's School attached to Canterbury Cathedral, where he received a Public School education in classics, greats, choral music, and liturgy intended for young men heading toward the

Anglican priesthood. Working in a London printing house and, later, a London bank when the Depression precluded university, Watts came under the influence of Nigel Watkins, who owned and operated a bookstore on Charing Cross Road specializing in Asian mysticism and related subjects. Watkins and his aged father, a Theosophist, served as Watts's bibliographers and tutors on Buddhism, comparative religion, and mysticism and guided his attendance at sessions being offered by various teachers. Watts also came under the influence of barrister Christmas (Toby) Humphreys, a learned member of the Buddhist Lodge of London, which Watts had joined in 1931. In 1936, when the World Congress of Faiths was meeting at the University of London, Watts met and enjoyed formative conversations with Jiddu Krishnamurti and the legendary scholar of Zen Buddhism D. T. Suzuki. Rapidly, in an early example of his writing fluency, Watts produced his first book, *The Spirit of Zen* (1936), based on these conversations.

In 1938 Watts married an American, Eleanor Everett, whose mother was at the center of Buddhist circles in New York. Shortly thereafter, the couple emigrated to the United States. Watts and his wife became parents of a daughter in November 1938, which would not have exempted him from service in the United Kingdom, nor would it exempt him from American service, once the United States passed a draft law in the summer of 1940. Watts's eligibility for the draft became even more likely after Pearl Harbor. In any event, Watts put aside his Buddhism and recovered his Anglicanism sufficiently to discern a vocation to the Anglican priesthood. Enrolling in the Seabury-Western Theological Seminary in Evanston, Illinois, as a candidate for Anglican orders, hence eligible for 4-D status, Watts was ordained for the Diocese of Chicago in 1945 by Bishop Wallace Conkling, who had accepted Watts's writings as the equivalent of a bachelor's degree.

Watts spent four years as university chaplain at Northwestern, his Anglicanism expressed in such titles as the *Theologicala Mystica of St. Dionysius* (1944), a translation from the Greek; *Behold the Spirit: A Study in the Necessity of Mystical Religion* (1948); and *Easter: Its Story and Meaning* (1950). Yet these studies, ostensibly if liberally Christian, were strongly comparative, and expressed a high regard for Asian traditions. Now that the war was over, Watts was rediscovering his Buddhist self. After an extramarital affair, he formally stated in writing that he had always believed in free love. His wife received a church annulment. In 1950 Watts resigned from the Anglican priesthood and moved back to New York, where he hung out for a while with a circle centered on mythographer Joseph Campbell before heading west in the spring of 1951 to San Francisco to serve as professor and dean of the newly established American Academy of Asian Studies. Augmented from Cal and Stanford, the academy faculty was impressive, yet its finances remained tenuous. Tired of fundraising, Watts resigned in 1955 to pursue a freelance career.

His first book following his resignation, *The Way of Zen* (1957), was a bestseller and remained a steady seller for the rest of his life. *The Way of Zen* became, in fact, one of the formative books of the 1960s as well as launching Watts into a freelance career as a writer, radio and television personality, and grant recipient (from the

Bollingen Foundation for study at Harvard), visiting lecturer at colleges and universities, and all-round public personality. No single figure, it can be argued, did more to promote Zen Buddhism to a popular audience than Alan Watts, who fused his knowledge of Zen with linguistics, psychotherapy (Watts studied with Jung in 1958 at the C. G. Jung Institute in Zurich), and experiments with LSD at UCLA and Harvard in the early 1960s, together with ongoing interests in Chinese calligraphy, Japanese architecture, urban and landscape design, and cuisine, especially as exemplified by the sacred and imperial city of Kyoto, to which Watts made four lengthy pilgrimages. Watts continued his commitment to free love and open marriage, which he described as erotic spirituality. He married two more times and had four more children. He considered his way of life a form of bohemian sensualism, which unfortunately included a growing problem with alcohol.

Take any aspect of the social and cultural revolution of the 1960s and 1970s and it can be read back into one or another of Watts's interests, books, and pursuits, to include modifications of dress, as a bearded Watts began to attire himself domestically in Japanese kimonos and other eclectic variations of Asian attire, including headbands. Whether based out of his Sausalito houseboat or his Zen retreat in a misty canyon at the base of Mount Tamalpais, Watts flourished at the center of a circle of like-minded friends resembling Henry Miller's in Big Sur of artists and aspiring artists, philosophers and aspiring philosophers of every sort, the accomplished and the wannabes, all boon companions of Alan Watts, the majority of them oriented in one way or another to a Zen Buddhist way of life or, at the least, admiring of Watts's writing and lifestyle and being more than willing to stay up late with Watts into the dawn, burning incense, intoning Buddhist chants, dancing ritual Buddhist dances.

Watts's circle included one of his fathers-in-law, Gavin Arthur, the grandson of President Chester Arthur. A locally known astrologer and gay activist, Gavin Arthur belonged to Beat circles in San Francisco, where he was living as resident guru in a rambling East-West House in Japantown along with aspirants such as Gary Snyder and Philip Whalen, interested in a serious study of Buddhism. As an astrologer, Arthur fused astrological, sexual, and Buddhist insights, as evident in his *The Circle of Sex* (1966), for which Watts wrote the introduction. Watts was also friendly with record executive Henry Jacobs, who encouraged him to tape his lectures for commercial sale, and Jacobs's Japanese wife Sumi, daughter of the respected Zen teacher Sabro Hasegawa. Sumi Jacobs dressed in a kimono whenever possible, was a master of Japanese cuisine, and on weekends gave haiku performances with Watts that attracted Zen aficionados from around the Bay Area. Near Watts's montane retreat in Mill Valley lived another friend, the noted Japanese artist Noriko Yamamoto.

Watts loved Big Sur, as might be expected, and saw in it the essence of the mystic landscape and was a frequent visitor to the newly established Zen spa at Esalen, where he would die in his sleep from heart failure after a particularly exhausting lecture tour. Watts admired Henry Miller, whom he described as "a bohemian of the European style, with the same atmosphere of bright color, wine, cheese, good bread, sunlight, and women of passion and intelligence. Henry seems to live inside a painting by Matisse."[6] Although a frequent visitor to Partington Ridge, however, Watts could not permanently settle in Big Sur. He required, rather, the accessibility of Marin County to the public television stations, the FM radio outlets, recording studios, conference facilities, even the airport of San Francisco, all so necessary for him to make a living.

Zen insights and resolutions pervaded every book Watts wrote following the publication of *The Way of Zen* in 1957, including his best book of this sort, *Beyond Theology* (1964), an effort to progress through classical Judeo-Christian theology to Zen Buddhism. Watts dealt with sexual liberation in *Nature, Man, and Woman* (1958), *Psychotherapy East and West* (1961), and *Erotic Spirituality* (1971), among other titles. Watts's sexual theories moved in the direction of the free love that he himself practiced and had first justified in his resignation from the Anglican priesthood. Jung helped Watts reinforce his previously held theories of mythic patterns and consciousness. Zen taught Watts that ego—the self, personhood—was an illusion and was, rather, only one of the infinite and shifting manifestations of a Final Reality that was definitely not a personalized or tri-personalized Godhead but a source of existence resisting definition. Psychologically, in short, Watts preached a form of transcendent pantheism: a belief that all was one, and all was holy, that pointed toward the environmental movement of ensuing decades. On the other hand, if he, Alan Watts, were only an illusion, as Zen taught and as Watts wrote repeatedly, then why this burden of consciousness, this isolation of self, that so afflicted him? Why this terror of death, this dissolution of self, this loneliness, assuaged, however briefly, by sexual communion? For all his bohemian sensualism, discussions of death account for some of Watts's most compelling writing; and hence arose his interest in psychedelic drugs as a way of escaping the burden of self, of making an end run around phenomena and achieving a more direct connection with transcendent realities. Already struggling with a booze problem, however, Watts did not become a steady LSD user. Once you have heard the message, he opined, hang up the telephone!

When, in *Beat Zen, Square Zen, and Zen* (1959), published by City Lights, Alan Watts described the orientation of the Beat poets to Zen he was at once acting as an observer and helping to fashion a movement. A number of Beat poets were in the process of making an enduring connection with Zen. As an undergraduate in the late 1940s at Reed College in Oregon, Gary Snyder roomed with Philip Whalen and was friendly with Lew Welch. When the three aspiring poets reconvened in San Francisco in the early 1950s, they formed a Reed College contingent that would soon be augmented by poets migrating to San Francisco from Black Mountain College in North Carolina, which closed its doors in 1956.

As graduates of Reed, Snyder, Whalen, and Welch were each well schooled in formal poetics and the High Modernist tradition—structured, allusive, ironic, detached, highly controlled, imagist in orientation—as practiced by Ezra Pound, T. S. Eliot, Wallace Stevens, and William Carlos Williams, who visited Reed and praised their work. San Francisco and Zen Buddhism, however, changed each of them. Whalen introduced Snyder to Zen in the early 1950s when the two of them were rooming together in an apartment on Montgomery and Green. The two later moved into the East-West House and were soon spending long periods of study in Japan. Whalen also experimented with peyote, which he believed expanded his poetic consciousness. The result for Whalen was a radical breakthrough from High Modernism to a more open-ended verse—colloquial, concrete, each poem seeking its own form—as evident in such enduring poems from the period as "Sourdough Mountain Lookout," based on Whalen's experiences as a fire watcher atop a lookout tower in the Cascades, and "A Dim View of Berkeley in the Spring," a meditation on UC Berkeley fraternity boys playing volleyball. Living and studying in Japan from 1958 to 1971, Whalen eventually became a Zen monk and spent the rest of his life at Zen centers in San Francisco and New Mexico, rising to the rank of abbot. Lew Welch, meanwhile, after time as an advertising copywriter in New York and Chicago—which, it can be argued, gave added precision to his writing—steered a similar path toward colloquial simplicity and precision under the influence of a developing Zen Buddhist aesthetic. The practice of Zen, moreover, helped center and calm Welch, who had already suffered a nervous breakdown, although he remained manic and hard-partying and would eventually, in 1971, carrying a rifle, disappear into the wilderness from Gary Snyder's house in Nevada County, his body never found.

Even the Black Mountain College coterie, centered on poet Jack Spicer, was showing by the late 1950s strong signs of Zen Buddhist influence in poet Joanne Kyger, formerly a student at UC Santa Barbara, where she had studied with Hugh Kenner, archpriest of High Modernism. In January 1957, just short of her degree, Kyger moved to San Francisco in the company of her Siamese cat and joined the Black Mountain College circle. Attractive and well-bred—more a UC Santa Barbara sorority girl in demeanor than a Beatnik chick—Kyger became resident muse to the significantly gay Black Mountain circle hanging out at the Place, a writers' and poets' bar in North Beach. She was also developing, partly under the influence of Zen, into a poet of sparse effectiveness and had her first reading at the Bread and Wine Mission in 1959, before moving to Japan with Gary Snyder, whom she married there in 1960, the two of them traveling to India with Ginsberg as *dharma* bums on pilgrimage.

In introducing Gary Snyder to Zen, Philip Whalen performed a service to American letters. Over the next half century, Snyder, thanks in part to his absorption of Zen Buddhist insights and practices, developed into one of the most respected American poets of his generation. For the time being, Gary Snyder—born in San Francisco in May 1930, raised in Washington and Oregon in poor but self-respecting circumstances, graduating from Reed College in 1951 with a degree in anthropology and literature—was just another aspiring poet drifting into the Bay Area in the early and mid-1950s, part of a rising generation exercising and consolidating its developing powers. Mountaineering, outdoor employment, foreign travel as a merchant seaman, the study of Chinese and Japanese, and Zen each played a part in the emergence of Snyder as poet. As a teenager, he belonged to Mazamas, a mountain-eering club in Portland, and had climbed a number of peaks in the Pacific North-west, including Mount Rainier. Snyder hitchhiked to New York in the summer of 1948, secured his seaman's papers from the Marine Cooks and Stewards Union, and worked a voyage to South America. He spent the following summer on a trail crew for the United States Forest Service in southwest Washington, the summer of 1952 as a lookout at Crater Mountain in the Mount Baker National Forest in the Cascades of southwestern Washington, and the summer of 1953 as a lookout on Sourdough Mountain in that same venue. Snyder worked the summer and fall of 1954 as a lum-berman tree-climber in Oregon and the summer of 1955 working on a trail crew in the Yosemite National Park and backpacking in the Minarets and headwaters of the Kern. Physically, Snyder was muscular, compact, not overly tall, and in top physi-cal condition. Following graduation from Reed, he began the study of East Asian languages at Indiana University for a semester and continued these studies from 1953 to 1955 as a graduate student in the Department of East Asian Languages at UC Berkeley, where he laid down solid foundations in Chinese and Japanese.

Snyder's study of Zen Buddhism, meanwhile, continued through the 1950s as well. In May 1956 he traveled by freighter to Kyoto to live in Zen Temple Shokoku-Ji and study under the renowned teacher Miura Isshu Roshi, followed by a climbing and backpacking trek through the Northern Japanese Alps. He returned to Kyoto in 1959 to study under Oda Sesso Roshi at the Daitoku-Ji monastery for a second period of formation. Snyder spent most of the 1960s in Japan, studying with various masters. His life as a merchant seaman, meanwhile, continued with an eight-month voyage, from August 1957 to April 1958, as an engine room wiper on the SS *Sappa Creek*, which took him to the Persian Gulf, Italy, Sicily, Turkey, Ceylon, the Pacific Islands, and Hawaii. In the midst of each of these engagements, Snyder continued his studies in Chinese and Japanese and embarked upon a translation of the poetry of Kanzan, the seventh/eighth century hobo-hermit Chinese poet who wrote under the name of Han Shan (Cold Mountain) and was revered by the Zen painters of a later era for his ability to express so much with so few words. Snyder also kept throughout the 1950s a journal chronicling his life in precise, almost telegraphic, entries that seem, when read, poems in the making, or at the least prose codas to the poems he was busy writing, drawing upon the same experiences.

Gary Snyder made his debut as a poet with *Riprap* (1959) and *Myths & Texts* (1960), in poems that in their verbal simplicity seem to be occurring naturally, even to be writing themselves. Native American and Zen studies had led Snyder to the belief that language was a living thing, a wild thing, embedded in nature, which spoke through words in the same way that it spoke through waterfalls or flowers. The poet was a kind of naturalist, liberating the words, the language, the symbols residing in natural entities, as essential to their substance as any molecular structure. Poetry was not a performance. It was, rather, a liberation of what nature wished to say, hence a discovery through language of natural meanings and solutions. The word *riprap* suggested the laying down of stones in place as in the construction of a forest trail: the discovery, that is, of intersections and edges that already fit. "Lay down these words," Snyder exhorts in the title poem of *Riprap*,

> Before your mind like rocks
> placed solid, by hands
> In choice of place, set
> Before the body of the mind
> in space and time...

An admirer of the poetry of Robinson Jeffers, for whom granite embodied the transcendent otherness of creation, Snyder was calling for the very stones to speak and for human beings to learn how to listen. In Snyder's poem "John Muir on Mt. Ritter," Muir, speaking in the first person, finds himself caught halfway up the face of a granite wall, unable to discern his next move, fearing to fall to the glacier below, then experiencing, in a rush, an affinity with the stone and letting it speak to him, instructing him how to extricate himself from danger.

The Zen-oriented rock climbers of Camp 4 in the Yosemite understood the poem immediately. Following in Muir's footsteps, a generation of climbers spent the 1950s and 1960s scaling the granite walls of the Yosemite and bringing the art and science of rock climbing to new levels of technical perfection. In July 1957 three climbers from Southern California—Royal Robbins, Jerry Gallwas, and Mike Sherrick—made the first ascent of the two-thousand-foot high Half Dome. Fifteen months later, on the morning of 12 November 1958, another party of three—Wayne Merry, George Whitmore, and Warren Harding —surmounted the three-thousand-foot face of El Capitan, with Harding first over the summit. Between 1957 and 1970, the climbers of Camp 4 made more than three dozen first ascents throughout the greater Yosemite. The poetry of Gary Snyder can serve as a gloss on the existential mountaineering of these Camp 4 Silent Generation climbers, who while devoid of the rhetoric of either Zen or existentialism were writing poems of action on sheer walls of granite. So too would another Yosemite climber, Glen Rowell, turning to photography, embark upon a photographic career paralleling Snyder in Zen-still, Zen-accurate depictions of topography, weather, flora, and fauna, and, in the case of Rowell's photo-essays on Tibet, the documentation of Zen California's objective correlative and Ultima Thule.

Camp 4 was a commune of sorts, or at the least a community of rock climbers lasting for more than a decade. The search for alternative value almost invariably led to some form of formal or informal communal response. In Carmel, an art colony had formed around George Sterling and Robinson Jeffers; and bohemian circles had coalesced around Henry Miller at Big Sur and Alan Watts in Marin. The Vedanta Center in Los Angeles and Krishnamurti's establishment in Ojai were each highly communitarian. The Vedanta Center, in fact, was formally organized as a monastic enclave, as was Gerald Heard's Trabuco College of Prayer in the

Santa Ana Mountains. Each of these movements, moreover, contained within itself a strong element of utopianism edging into social expression. To this impulse can be traced—in various modes and degrees of organization, plausibility, and legitimacy— a number of disparate communitarian responses to alternative value founded in this era. The Trappist and Camaldolese monasteries at Vina and Big Sur and the Zen Center of San Francisco represented traditions going back for thousands of years. Esalen, Scientology, and the Church of All Worlds, by contrast, were creations of the 1960s. Yet each of these movements—however historical, however eccentric, bizarre even—pointed forward to the social experimentations of the 1960s and 1970s that, for better or for worse, became so much part of the California scene.

Roman Catholic contemplative monks, Cistercians of the Strict Observance— more commonly known as Trappists, from the Abbey de la Trappe near Montagne, France, where their reform movement began in the mid-seventeenth century— established themselves in 1955 in Vina, Tehema County, on land once part of the Stanford Ranch. Their monastery, Our Lady of New Clairvaux, was a monastic colony of the venerable Abbey of Gethsemani in Kentucky founded by French monks in 1848. The California colony attracted recruits, expanded its plant, and brought into operation an extensive, well-run agricultural enterprise. A guesthouse opened, welcoming individuals wishing a time of silence and prayer. Three years later, in 1958, four Italian hermit-monks belonging to the Abbey of Camaldoli in the Tuscan-Romagnese Apennines of central Italy, where their reform of Benedictine monasticism dated to the early eleventh century, looking to make an American foundation, were scouting the Big Sur for possible sites. To their delight, Harry John, a wealthy brewer and Roman Catholic layman, offered the four hermit-monks a property in the Santa Lucia Mountains of Big Sur, where they founded the New Camaldoli Hermitage. Thus by 1960 two of the most austere and contemplative orders of the Roman Catholic Church had solidly established themselves in California, with the New Camaldoli Hermitage of Big Sur eventually growing to more than twenty hermit-monks, who fit quite easily into the ethos and milieu of Big Sur as a seedbed of alternative value.

The long-established Dominican Priory of St. Albert in Oakland, meanwhile, was nurturing the poetic talent of William Everson, now a member of the order under the name of Brother Antoninus, in honor of the fifteenth-century founder of the Dominican Convent of San Marco, Archbishop of Florence, and patron of the arts. Between 1951 and 1969, Brother Antoninus, helped on by studies in Jung and encouraged by his fellow Dominicans, an order known for its love of the arts, produced a torrent of poetry blending fleshly and spiritual themes, brought together in such volumes as *The Crooked Lines of God* (1959), which included "Annul in Me My Manhood," a high point of American Catholic poetry, and *The Hazards of Holiness* (1962), containing the equally impressive "A Frost Lay White on California."

Established in the early 1950s, the American Academy of Asian Studies and the East-West House in Japantown represented the first communal responses in San Francisco to the Zen movement. In 1962 a San Francisco Zen Center was established

under the direction of Shunryu Suzuki Roshi, author of the classic *Zen Mind,
Beginner's Mind* (1970). As a Buddhist *sangha*, or teaching monastery, the center
was based on the Soto Zen tradition established by Dogen Zenji in thirteenth-cen-
tury Japan and—augmented by the Green Gulch Farm in Marin County and the
Tassajara Zen Mountain Center in the Ventana Wilderness inland from Big Sur—
would eventually develop into one of the largest Buddhist *sanghas* outside Asia.

The best-known California establishment based on alternative values remains the
Esalen Institute, founded in 1962 by two Stanford graduates, Michael Murphy and
Richard Price. Located on twenty-seven acres of Big Sur coastline nine miles north
of Lucia, the Esalen Institute—through its therapeutic programs, largely based on
Gestalt theory, admixed with Zen, augmented by a publishing program—has long
since been considered a driving force behind the counterculture and the human
potential movement that has so powerfully affected the social psychology of America
since the 1960s. Michael Murphy initially intended to major in pre-med at Stanford;
but, wandering one day by accident into a lecture on comparative religion by Professor Frederic Spiegelberg, an expert on Eastern religions, he experienced a *metanoia*,
a change of heart and direction that led him to resign from his fraternity, take a leave
of absence, and spend a year and a half in an ashram in India: all this in the early
1950s, when such behavior was a decade and more before its time. Returning to
Stanford, Murphy graduated in psychology, followed by a two-year stint in the Army,
followed by another stint of study in India. Rick Price had studied briefly in the
newly established social relations program at Harvard, dropped out, was commissioned in the Air Force as a psychological testing officer, became part of the North
Beach scene while still in uniform, married an Asian woman in a Japanese Buddhist
ceremony at the Soto Zen Temple in San Francisco (later annulled), continued studies with Spiegelberg and Watts at the American Academy of Asian Studies, suffered
a severe psychotic episode in a North Beach bar while still on active duty, and was
taken by police to Letterman Army Hospital in San Francisco. Price later recovered
at his parents' expense at the Institute of Living in Hartford, Connecticut. According
to the practice of the day, he received some fifty-nine insulin shock treatments, ten
electroshock treatments, and continuing doses of phenothiazines, therapies that left
him physically devastated though technically healed. Price returned to California
convinced that there had to be a more civilized mode of therapy, integrating the
insights of Zen and the most advanced notions of Western psychology.

This was exactly the program, in general terms, on Murphy and Price's minds,
when they leased from Murphy's grandmother the Big Sur property, with hot
springs, that his grandfather Dr. Henry Murphy had purchased in 1910 from Thomas
Slate, who had homesteaded the property in the early 1880s. A Salinas physician,
Dr. Murphy had hoped to develop a European-style health spa centered on the local
hot springs. Some hotel rooms were built, together with a restaurant. Prior to the
lease of the site to Murphy and Price, it had functioned as a gay resort, which is how
Jack Kerouac describes it in *Big Sur* (1962). The notion of psycho-sexual liberation
associated with a gay resort carried over into Esalen's well-publicized program of

therapy. (Henry Miller, the iconic avatar of sexual liberation, made guest appearances.) The Esalen program, in point of fact, subsumed unto itself many of the important alternative quests of the 1940s and 1950s. Michael Murphy had come under the influence of Vedanta; Rick Price was largely influenced by Zen Buddhism; and Alan Watts, Gerald Heard, and Aldous Huxley served as consultants.

The program of healthy living upon which Huxley based his advice to Esalen can be gleaned from Huxley's last novel, *Island* (1962). Huxley rescued the solitary manuscript of *Island*, just barely, from the Bel Air fire of May 1961 that destroyed his home on Deronda Drive and incinerated his personal library and archive dating back to the First World War when Huxley was serving on the faculty of Eton. It was as if Huxley were rescuing the work of a lifetime. *Island* represented a last will and testament. Over the years, Huxley had created a string of notable dystopian novels, most recently *Ape and Essence* (1948), a portrayal of Southern California as a Planet of the Apes nightmare millennia after a nuclear war has destroyed human civilization. In *Island* Huxley set forth an alternative scenario, a society serving "human potential," a term Huxley coined on behalf of Esalen. The island society at the center of the novel is a utopia in the seas off Sri Lanka that in every phase—family, sexuality, attitudes toward life and death, community values, educational programs, the employment of science and mysticism—represents a society based on a fusion of the best possibilities of Asia and the West. Wealth and resources are equitably distributed. Children belong to their parents but also to the larger community as well. Nature and animals are regarded as sacred and used with respect. Family life is communal through the extended family and child-rearing less claustrophobic and tyrannical. Sexuality is as far as possible freed from guilt and related hangups, but remains centered on love, procreation, and mutual respect. Education is physical as well as intellectual and keyed to all phases of life. When appropriate, mind-altering drugs are used for psychological growth or therapeutic purposes. *Island*, in short, not only forecast the program at Esalen, which would soon be drawing upon some of the most innovative psychologists and therapists in the nation, but pointed in the direction of numerous communes destined soon to spring up in California and across the country in the years to follow.

Island also suggests the parallel influences of science fiction writers L. Ron Hubbard and Robert Heinlein: certainly not thinkers of Huxley's status or achievement, far from it, but writers nevertheless sharing Huxley's faith in science linked to mystical value. Following naval service in World War II, Hubbard, a now-and-then Los Angeleno since the 1930s, began to interest himself in the application of science—Dianetics, Hubbard called these techniques—to mental health therapy. Dianetics consisted of a program of introspection, supervised analysis, and scientific measurement designed to clear the mind of negative forces. *Dianetics* (1950), Hubbard's first book outlining the program, sold 150,000 copies in its first year of publication. Huxley knew L. Ron Hubbard and had at least an open mind regarding Dianetics. By 1952 Hubbard was busy expanding Dianetics into an applied religious philosophy he called Scientology. Shortly thereafter, Hubbard further recast Scientology as a religion, setting the stage for a half century of controversy as Scientology struggled to attain the legal status of a recognized religion. Ten years later, from another former Navy officer and intermittent Californian, science fiction writer Robert A. Heinlein, came the novel *Stranger in a Strange Land* (1961), the story of a Christ-like figure raised on Mars returning to Earth and spreading a higher consciousness before being martyred. The themes of *Stranger in a Strange Land*, a perennial best-seller—especially those regarding communal sexuality, parapsychology, the mind-body relationship, and a neo-pagan mysticism of nature and natural science—seeped into the alternative culture movements gaining momentum by the mid-1960s and inspired as well the founding of a neo-pagan Wiccan religious group calling itself the Church of All Worlds. Science fiction, in short, had by the 1960s gained a prophetic momentum, a mysticism or pseudo-mysticism of science edging into religious practice, however peculiar.

Even Jack Kerouac can be considered within this religious context. *On the Road* is replete with religious or quasi-religious references, by turns Buddhist or Roman Catholic, beginning with the very name of Kerouac's narrator, Sal Paradise, and continuing through multiple scriptural echoes, references to Catholic theology and practice, and a furtively expressed evocation of the Holy Family in flight to Egypt when Sal Paradise assumes the care of a young Mexican American woman and her child, supporting them in the fields as a wandering harvest worker. The Holy Family theme, occurring a number of times in Kerouac's fiction, reflected his lifelong guilt over abandoning his first wife and repudiating paternity of their daughter, his only child. Even when Kerouac was at his most Buddhist, as in *The Dharma Bums* (1958), a novel centered on the Gary Snyder–like figure of Japhy Ryder, he had frequent recourse to Roman Catholic imagery. Kerouac dedicated *The Dharma Bums* to Han Shan, the vagabond Chinese poet Snyder translated; and in one memorable sequence Kerouac called for "a great rucksack revolution" across America in which millions of young men would take to the road in the spirit of Han Shan and Japhy Ryder. The conclusion of *The Dharma Bums* lyrically celebrates Kerouac's own version of his spiritual enlightenment while on fire-watch atop Desolation Peak in the Cascades, where Gary Snyder and Philip Whalen also had had similar experiences. And yet Kerouac's narrator, Ray Smith, wants a personal God as well as Zen insights into Ultimate Reality and ends the novel with something very much resembling a traditional Christian prayer.

The Dharma Bums, then, ends on a note of triumphant acceptance of life and hope for the future. Four years later, in the novelized memoir *Big Sur* (1962), Kerouac documented the catastrophe his life had become due to alcoholism and his inability to assume the responsibilities of marriage and family. Based on his experiences at the time, as are all of Kerouac's novels, *Big Sur* depicts a landscape of despair as seen from Lawrence Ferlinghetti's cabin overlooking Bixby Creek, especially as symbolized by the wrecked automobile that lies rusting at the base of a nearby cliff. The car that once took Sal Paradise and Dean Moriarty on the road across America has become an abandoned wreck on the road to ruin now being experienced by Kerouac at a dead-end point in his life due to drinking and despair. Once again, the Kerouac narrator finds, then rejects, a woman and her child. An attack of delirium tremens induces in Smith a Dark Night of the Soul and a paranoid sense of being persecuted because he is a Roman Catholic. Yet the DTs also induce a fleeting vision of the Virgin Mary, just when it seems that, like Faustus, the Devil is coming to snatch his soul.

"Suddenly as clear as anything I ever saw in my life, I see the Cross," says Kerouac's narrator in the concluding sequence of *Big Sur*. The cross Kerouac was seeing was a cross arising from the DTs. That was obvious, but it was also the cross of Kerouac's remembered boyhood and adolescence in Lowell, Massachusetts, when he served as an altar boy at St. Jean Baptiste Cathedral (from which he would in a few years be buried) and carried that same cross in liturgical procession. The envisioned cross, the hallucinated cross, the DTs cross, was the remembered cross of Kerouac's collapsing life. But it was also related to the cross atop the newly established Camaldolese monastery-hermitage nearby, rising against the Santa Lucia Mountains of Big Sur. "I see the Cross, it's silent, it stays a long time, my heart goes out to it, my whole body fades away to it...I lie there in cold sweat," says Smith, at the conclusion of the novel, "wondering what's come over me for years my Buddhist studies and pipesmoking assured meditations on emptiness and all of a sudden the Cross is manifested to me—My eyes filled with tears—we'll all be saved...I'll get my ticket and say goodbye on a flower day and leave all San Francisco behind and go back home across autumn America and it'll all be like it was in the beginning—Simple golden eternity blessing all."

13

Silent Generation

Coming of Age on the Coast of Dreams

WORLD War II made Americans very much aware of the next generation. In the years before Pearl Harbor, Americans had shown themselves
concerned for the generation that would soon be going into uniform;
and when that young generation itself returned from the war, married, and had its
own children, it in turn re-conceptualized its own offspring as the embodiment of
its survival and its continuing hopes for life. Nowhere was this focus on youth more
apparent than in California, where so many veterans were in pursuit of the postwar
good life. Contemporary social critic Remi Nadeau claimed that Californians had
a tendency to be obsessed with their children and, if the truth be told, to spoil them
rotten. Long before the emergence of the soccer mom, Nadeau described a suburban society in which mothers, and frequently fathers, organized a significant amount
(if not most) of their free hours chauffeuring to and cheering on their children at a
ceaseless pageant of Little League, Boy and Girl Scouts, Brownies, Camp Fire Girls,
YMCA activities and related events. Suburban California children from middle-
class white families, Nadeau was noting as of 1963, were not exactly spoiled. They
merely expected more in the matter of parent-provided goods and services, and they,
however subconsciously, knew themselves as the raison d'être of their parents' lives.
Children and adolescents from such backgrounds took for granted that they would
have their own bedroom (a rarity in American life to that period), a closet full of
clothes, bicycles (cars in the last years of high school), record players, television sets,
a swimming pool in the backyard, riding lessons, even a horse for girls.

The youngest of these children were the first wave of the Boomer generation,
born since 1946, a generation being raised across the nation on Dr. Spock and all
that Dr. Spock stood for. They would be in grammar or junior high school by the
early 1960s. Their older siblings, born in the last years of the Depression or during
the war, high school students by the late 1940s and constituting the high school

and college generations of the 1950s and early 1960s, belonged to another generation entirely, the so-called Silent Generation, as first defined in 1958 by Princeton
dean Otto Butz. No theory of generations can erect a firewall from one generation to another. Overlapping and interactive influences are constant. Yet the older
brothers and sisters, the young uncles and aunts, of the Boomer generation being so
solicitously shepherded through childhood and early adolescence in California and
elsewhere throughout the nation, were distinct enough to be represented as differing
generational cohorts.

In *Generations: The History of America's Future, 1584 to 2069* (1991), historians
William Strauss and Neil Howe provided an expanded definition of the Silent Generation first offered by Dean Butz. Wedged between the GI generation who fought
World War II and the Boomers, the Silents, according to Strauss and Howe, possessed a broad band of birth dates, from 1925 to 1942 (a date more generally expanded
to 1945 to encompass the entire war era), which meant that the oldest of them overlapped with the GI generation fighting World War II. The Silent war would be
Korea, and like everything else about the Silents, it would be muted in meaning.
The Silents, Strauss and Howe argue, were caught between the can-do assertiveness
of the GI generation and the rebellious self-actualization of the Boomers. A small
generation in terms of numbers, since the birthrate fell during the Depression and
war years, Silents tended to be dominated by their elders and their younger siblings.
Growing up, the Silents absorbed the values and lifestyle of the GI generation and
came to maturity believing that, if they remained the Silents—remained orthodox,
that is, and played the game—the GI generation would bring them along and, eventually, in good time, as part of the order of things, hand the world over to them. The
good life, in short—education, career, promotion, a place in the world—came from
one's elders as a kind of gift, a rite of succession. Maturity consisted in conforming to
the norms of the GI generation and mastering its tools. The Silent Generation was
silent in part because the story of the elder GI generation overwhelmed any story
they might be tempted to tell of themselves.

In their maturity, the Silents would become facilitators between the world
according to the GI generation and the rebellion of the Boomers. In this process,
the Silents were destined to lose even further a conviction of the relevance of their
own narrative. Of all generations since the founding of the Republic, theirs would
be the only one not to produce a president. When they themselves had grown old,
Silents would watch a surviving GI, George H. W. Bush, and a Boomer, Bill Clinton, become the best of buddies.

The youth scene of postwar California into the early 1960s can be seen, if one fol-
lows the analysis of Strauss and Howe, to sustain a tension as two competing generations crowd the same territory: a generation of conformists in the Silents, teenagers
and college students between the late 1940s and the early 1960s, and a Boomer generation, self-regarding and rebellious, finishing high school and entering college in
the 1960s. In one sense, that is why the California of 1963, at the latest, often seems
to have more in common with the 1950s than it does with the post-1964 era. In the

1960s innumerable Silents would join the Boomers in the shattering of conventions; indeed, as Strauss and Howe point out, members of the Silent Generation would become the primary facilitators of the civil rights movement, the resistance to the Vietnam War, feminism, and the sexual revolution, which reinforces the notion that firewalls cannot be erected between generations.

Still, the high school yearbooks of the late 1940s, 1950s, and early 1960s yield a generational statement reaffirming the existence and values of the Silents. Such a statement is at once generic and localized. In their generic dimension, the California yearbooks from this era were identical with those from most high schools in the other forty-seven, soon to be the other forty-nine, states. Indeed, the very genre of high school yearbook—with its photographs of graduates, administrators, and faculty, its group portraits of freshmen, sophomores, and juniors, its documentation of athletics, clubs, dances, and other social events, its dedication to a revered principal or teacher or a classmate taken before his or her time—suggests the generalized and triumphant uniformity of American high school culture by mid-century. Yet the yearbooks produced by California high schools in the postwar era into the early 1960s do come from a localized time and place, and as such they reflect patterns of local life that can be read impressionistically. These yearbooks testify to the surface well-being and conformity of American life in this period. Here is a generation preserved from the ravages of World War II. Here are teenagers by and large too young for Korea and not yet knowing of a place called Vietnam. Nearly everyone is smiling, nearly all the time, which can be expected in yearbooks; yet the sheer abundance of smiling faces— caught candidly in class or in extracurricular activities—suggests the tide of well-being upon which innumerable high schools were floating through the Eisenhower years.

After a century of struggle to make itself a mainstream requirement, the American high school had come of age. Whatever the ambiguities of actual experience might be (and the 1950s were hardly exempt from noir), administrators and faculty are treated with respect and affection. In some yearbooks, even the janitors are lined up for group photos. Athletic programs are ambitious, as might be expected. In California, sports programs also include a rising tide of instruction in tennis and golf, as if to prepare teenagers for the country club. Some high schools, such as Woodrow Wilson in Long Beach, have ambitious equestrian programs, together with a riding club for those who owned horses or were willing to rent them. Gymnasiums and, in Southern California especially, swimming pools abound. Musical instruction seems universal, and even smaller high schools support a formal orchestra as well as a uniformed marching band. Theatrical productions of such standbys as *The Importance of Being Earnest, Life with Father, Harvey,* and *The Mikado,* together with such innovative selections as *Our Hearts Were Young and Gay* (the ambitious senior play at Berkeley High School in 1955) were produced and costumed and backed by school orchestras.

A number of California high schools—Sacramento, Lowell and St. Ignatius in San Francisco—were celebrating centennials by mid-decade. Others—Orange Union in Orange County, for example—were reaching the fifty-year mark. Located in a sprawling suburban campus, Woodrow Wilson High School in Long Beach—twenty-five years old as of 1951, with a portrait of Wilson in its foyer, donated and dedicated in January 1928 by Eleanor Wilson McAdoo, daughter of the late president, and her husband William Gibbs McAdoo, United States senator from California—prefigured the mega high schools of the next generation. Other comprehensive public schools on this scale were offering college prep, general, commercial, and vocational tracks to a diploma. The very integration of these tracks in the same comprehensive high schools, in fact, was making a statement about American culture in this era: that it could be kept together, anchored in a common experience via elements of a common curriculum through grammar and high school years. The successful completion of the academic track at any one of these institutions represented a one-way ticket to college. Good grades at Lowell, Sacramento, Berkeley, Beverly Hills, Hollywood, or Pasadena High School constituted an automatic admission to UC Berkeley or UCLA. Yet college-bound teenagers were also coming of age alongside those who would enter the world of work following high school; and even though divisions existed, there remained a common experience, especially in athletics, and mutual respect among young people heading in different directions. The world of work was implicitly respected in schools where future plumbers and electricians and contractors, including minorities, won varsity letters and were elected to student office. The world of work, moreover, was anticipated in future nurses and teachers clubs, and, yes, future homemakers clubs as well.

In yearbooks from this period, teenagers of the Silent Generation seem older, more mature, than their counterparts of today. Perhaps it is because the young women all seem to be wearing adult hairstyles, with the possible exception of the ponytail, or perhaps it was because females were wearing the same fashions they would be wearing in later life. While young men were showing in the late 1940s and very early 1950s remnants of the *pachuco* style in their one-button roll jackets with shoulder pads and wide lapels, or the influence of black culture in their flared Billy Eckstine collars, and even a *retardaire* hint of the late 1930s and early 1940s in their Pendleton wool shirts, the driving force of male teenage fashion through the 1950s, especially among the more affluent and upwardly mobile, was in the direction of an Ivy League look: poplin windbreakers from McGregor, khaki pants with a backside belt and buckle, brown and white saddle shoes or all-white bucks, loafers, or Clark's desert boots. Likewise did male hairstyles show the same transition from street-smart *pachuco* to suburban Ivy League as the *pachuco*-inspired ducktail or DA (duck's ass) haircut, with luxuriant side locks sweeping back to a meeting point, yielded by the mid-1950s to a modified flat-top with side fenders and by 1960 to the Ivy League austerities of the Princeton cut, short and flat against the head. Since teenagers defined themselves so aggressively by fashion, the deliberately stylized upward mobility of teen fashions in this period, together with the ubiquitous coats and ties, adult dresses and high heels, of more formal occasions, suggested something about the social aspirations of the Silent Generation, its desire for success and an adult identity.

Here was a generation that would marry early (the earliest of any generation ever, according to Strauss and Howe) and have more children earlier in life, even college-educated females, whose fertility surpassed their lesser-educated counterparts. In this regard, California yearbooks yield a paradox. Photographs from public schools reveal females moving with interspersed equality in most group scenes. Young women tend not to be huddled among themselves in most spontaneous photographs but to be participating side by side with males in whatever was happening at the moment. Such photographs bespeak a closer and more equal relationship between the sexes than is generally admitted of the period. Women, moreover, are engaged in a wide variety of varsity and intramural sports—basketball, field hockey, softball, volleyball, tennis, golf—earning varsity letters and proudly wearing their block sweaters to campus. Females also seem to participate equally and hold leadership positions in the multiplicity of clubs organized around a variety of pursuits—including math, science, chess, Latin, and agriculture—with club participants, male and female alike, posing proudly before the camera at the end of the year with their faculty adviser. Yet there seems to be—in California and elsewhere—an equally powerful preoccupation with the crowning of queens and princesses for football games, homecomings, proms, and dances. Yearbooks from the 1950s devote special sections to couples going steady, along with the usual attention paid to cheerleaders, song girls, majorettes, and flag-twirlers. Other yearbook categories, moreover—cutest, best-looking, best dancers—also bespeak a certain coy awareness of gender roles and how they would determine life after high school.

Not that every teenage female in California, or elsewhere for that matter, was buying into this scenario. At the very beginning of the postwar era, North Hollywood High School student Susan Sontag of Canoga Park, although barely into her teens, was already creating for herself a culture of assertive intellectualism that would help her develop into one of the most respected writers of her generation. The very insertion of Susan Sontag, however, into the landscape of the suburban San Fernando Valley of the late 1940s possesses a certain dissonance and irony that Sontag was herself aware of. How could such a European-style woman of letters, the very epitome of the Euro–New York avant-garde intellectual of her era, have come from such seemingly prosaic suburban California circumstances? Precisely because, it can be answered, that is where she came from and where she lived during her formative adolescence. However brief were Sontag's high school years—years of reading and self-discovery that would lead to further development at UC Berkeley, followed by the University of Chicago, followed by Harvard, followed by the Sorbonne, followed by New York and a life in letters—they cannot be declared irrelevant in the assessment of her formation, as Sontag herself would later suggest in a December 1987 memoir in the *New Yorker*, chronicling her San Fernando Valley, North Hollywood High School years.

First of all, there was the creative tension of opposites. A brilliant young Jewish girl, born in New York City in 1933 (hence a senior member of the Silent Generation), moves to Canoga Park in 1946 with her mother, stepfather, and younger sister from Tucson, Arizona, following her stepfather's release from the service. There, the precocious North Hollywood High student, brilliant and rebellious, defines herself against her environment: the indifferent teaching, the lack of role models, the general cultural wasteland, from her perspective, of the San Fernando Valley. Countless aspiring intellectuals have similarly defined themselves against their environment. Yet the Los Angeles she was encountering was at a high point of expatriate vitality. The precocious teenager was able, among other things, to attend a performance of Bertolt Brecht's *Galileo*, starring Charles Laughton, at the Coronet Theater in Hollywood; to watch the rehearsals of the Lester Horton/Bella Lewitzky Dance Company in Hollywood; to witness Stravinsky attending a performance of his own music at the Wilshire Ebell Auditorium, Ingolf Dahl conducting; to listen to avant-garde music on the Monday night Evenings on the Roof concerts sponsored by Peter Yates and his wife, pianist Frances Mullen, atop the roof of their Schindler-designed studio in West Los Angeles; and to hear classics performed by the Los Angeles Philharmonic while ushering at the Hollywood Bowl. She could hang out with the teenaged children of expatriates who knew the world and spoke other languages, a breed apart from the other kids at North Hollywood, and spend long hours browsing and trolling for books at the Pickwick Bookstore on Hollywood Boulevard, bringing home for astonishingly low prices the titles she would line up on a shelf in her room (the beginnings of the fifteen-thousand-volume private library that would one day grace her Riverside Drive penthouse apartment in New York City). Near Pickwick's, moreover, was a record store whose sympathetic owner allowed her to preview innumerable 78s, while buying only a few, and a nearby international newsstand, where an equally indulgent proprietor allowed her to browse through such publications as the *Partisan Review*, the *Kenyon Review*, the *Sewanee Review*, and other avant-garde publications. Enamored of Thomas Mann's *The Magic Mountain*, Sontag read it twice over, the second time aloud; and she and a high school friend—at his instigation—arranged to have Sunday tea with Mann himself at the Mann household on San Remo Drive in Pacific Palisades. The interview with the great writer was somewhat disappointing (Mann talked like a favorable book review of his own works, Sontag later remembered), and Mann discussed her studies at North Hollywood High as if she were attending a demanding *gymnasium* in Kaiserine Germany, yet here she was, only fourteen, having tea and cookies with Thomas Mann. Attached to this experience were, by implication, all the other fragments of high European culture she was encountering in the Los Angeles of her era. For all her precocity, Susan Sontag was still a kid, and the City of Angels was teaching her things.

The future political scientist and social philosopher James Q. Wilson, meanwhile, was coming of age at David Starr Jordan Senior High School in Long Beach and would return there twenty years later to explore how teenage Southern California had changed and remained the same. Stephen Breyer, Wilson's longtime colleague at Harvard and, eventually, a United States Supreme Court justice, prepared at Lowell High School in San Francisco, along with Bart Voorsanger, later a distinguished New York architect. Breyer's eventual colleague on the Supreme

Court, Anthony Kennedy, meanwhile, was preparing for college at McClatchy High School in Sacramento. Breyer and Kennedy would attend Stanford. Joan Didion was prepping for (she hoped) Stanford at McClatchy, the high school of choice for the Sacramento establishment. Dianne Goldman, later Feinstein, was preparing for Stanford at the Convent of the Sacred Heart in San Francisco. Also in a San Francisco Catholic high school was Joan Vivien Beatty, who would soon be painting under the name Joan Brown. Graduating from Presentation High School in 1955, Beatty wanted to go to art school, yet at her parents' insistence agreed to enroll at the nearby San Francisco College for Women, a Catholic college atop Lone Mountain conducted by the Religious of the Sacred Heart. She lasted barely a semester before transferring to the California School of Fine Arts on Chestnut Street in North Beach (after 1961 the San Francisco Art Institute), where she studied with Elmer Bischoff and Manuel Neri. Within a few years of leaving Presentation, Joan Brown was having her work exhibited at the Six Gallery and the San Francisco Museum of Art. By September 1960 she was being profiled in *Look* at work in in the studio at Mission and the Embarcadero that she shared with Manuel Neri, whom she later married. All this represented a rather rapid trajectory, perhaps, for such a recent graduate of the Convent of the Presentation, yet was testimony in its way to the determination characteristic of so many Silent young women in this era.

Another San Franciscan, Richard Serra, was working his way through UC Berkeley in the steel mills on the southern edge of the city. Of blue-collar origin, Serra did not mind the work. He expected it. And besides, there was something very basic about metal that intrigued him. At once a product of nature and industry, for example, steel was in its own way a work of art, capable of strength and form. Transferring to UC Santa Barbara, Serra majored in English in a department dominated by Hugh Kenner, a leading expert on, and exponent of, High Modernism. Could steel itself be shaped into High Modernist forms, like lines in a poem by Ezra Pound? Was steel itself a language? Such questions were implicit in steelman Serra's literary studies, although a long way off from realization. Graduating in 1961, Serra spent the years 1961 through 1964 at Yale, earning bachelor and master of fine arts degrees, but not as of yet breaking forth into sculpture. He studied painting instead, before going on to a year in Paris on a Yale Traveling Fellowship, where he spent quality time at the Musée National d'Art Moderne. Painting would hold Serra through sojourns at Yale, Paris, Florence, and Rome, where he had his first solo exhibition in 1966. That same year, he would move into sculpture, using non-traditional materials. He then moved on to molten lead, en route to sculptured steel, in which medium he would eventually produce High Modernist probes heroic in scale into geometries of space, time, and human perception.

At St. Ignatius High School in San Francisco during these years was Edmund G. (Jerry) Brown Jr., son of the attorney general of California. Founded in 1855 by Italian Jesuits, St. Ignatius High School had become by the mid-1950s a powerhouse secondary school in the long-standing tradition of Jesuit secondary schools, producing phalanxes of ambitious, verbally adroit Irish and Italian Catholic young men, heading for careers in law, business, medicine, education, public service, and the clergy, their skills honed by a philosophy and curriculum based on Latin, Greek for honors students, memorization, recitation, and debate. Brown excelled in these subjects and, along with a number of his fellow Ignatians—Baxter Rice, Bill Hogan, and Charles Gagan, also from the Class of 1955—resolved to enter the Jesuit novitiate in Los Gatos following graduation. Brown's mother, of Protestant lineage, opposed the idea and insisted that Jerry enroll at Santa Clara University instead. After a year at Santa Clara, however, Jerry Brown entered the Society of Jesus.

In Southern California, another Catholic high school student contemplating the priesthood, William Joseph Levada, a senior at St. Anthony's in Long Beach, Class of 1954, was planning to enter the seminary for the Archdiocese of Los Angeles following graduation. Born and raised in Long Beach of Portuguese and Irish lineage and educated in the Catholic school system there, with the exception of three years in Houston, Texas, where his father, a Shell Chemical Corporation executive, had been temporarily transferred, Levada—as unassuming as Jerry Brown was assuming, pious but possessed of inner steel—was at the beginning of a busy and productive life that would see him educated at the elite North American College and Jesuit-staffed Gregorian University in Rome, where he took a doctorate in theology, followed by stints as a parish priest, a seminary professor, the chief lobbyist for the Church in Sacramento, a Vatican staffer, a Los Angeles auxiliary bishop, and the Archbishop of Portland and, later, of San Francisco, followed by an appointment by the newly elected Pope Benedict XVI to the prefectship of the Congregation for the Doctrine of the Faith, the number three position at the Vatican, and elevation to cardinal.

Up in Sacramento, meanwhile, Richard Rodriguez was also experiencing both the constraints and the liberations of a Catholic high school education, in his case at Christian Brothers. Founded in seventeenth-century France for the education of non-elites, the Christian Brothers—who also conducted Sacred Heart High School in San Francisco—were sensitive, without being overly talkative about it, to the educational needs of what would later be designated young men of color, although Richard Rodriguez would be the first to resist such a categorization and would continue to do so in later years, sometimes at great personal expense. At Catholic grammar school, the young Mexican American—dark, beak-nosed, an Indio, not some wannabe Spaniard, and proud of it—was educated by his Irish-born Sisters of Mercy teachers, so he would later remember, as if he were the most precious child on earth, which is the way the sisters tended to treat everyone, to include, in some cases, the universal application of a ruler across knuckles of misbehaving boys, regardless of color. At Christian Brothers High School, Rodriguez received the same non-discriminatory treatment, he later recalled, from his classroom teachers in long black soutanes and stiff white clerical neckbands: brothers who were at once evocative of the European past and yet thoroughly American in their wit and humor, their irony even, which Rodriguez would remember throughout his lifetime. The *Gale* yearbook of Christian Brothers High for this era abounds in Mexican American names and faces, together with at least one African American student body

president, and the Brothers, Rodriguez later remembered, never separated minorities from non-minorities, even verbally. Graduating in 1963, Rodriguez went on to
Stanford, followed by a doctorate in Renaissance literature at UC Berkeley and a
distinguished career as a public intellectual and man of letters.

On the other end of the reality scale, in terms of a connection to ordinary life,
were those teenagers of the Silent Generation, three of them Oscar winners, who had
come of age as actors in Hollywood. A popular query asked, "Is there life after high
school?" For them the question "Is there life after childhood or teenager stardom?"
would seem even more relevant. Oscar winner Claude Jarman Jr. — this in 1946, for
his role as the Florida backwoods youth Jody Baxter in the film version of Marjorie
Kinnan Rawlings's *The Yearling* (1945) — found himself increasingly skeptical, for
example, of making the transition to adult roles, despite his contract with MGM
in the golden age of that studio. Born and raised in Nashville, Tennessee, Jarman
had almost accidentally stumbled into acting when he was chosen for the role from
hundreds of candidates in a public search. Jarman, then, had already experienced
a normal life before MGM and remembered it positively; and so — after starring in
another Clarence Brown–directed adaptation, *Intruder in the Dust* (1949), filmed in
Oxford, Mississippi, with William Faulkner constantly on the set, and a supporting
role with John Wayne and Maureen O'Hara in *Rio Grande* (1950), directed by John
Ford — Jarman returned to Nashville, where he finished high school and completed
a bachelor's degree at Vanderbilt. Moving to San Francisco, Jarman worked in the
insurance business and eventually became cultural affairs director for the city. Nor
could the talented Margaret O'Brien, another Academy Award winner — in 1944,
for her performance alongside Judy Garland in *Meet Me in St. Louis* — make the
transition to adult stardom, although O'Brien did finish her adolescent career with
her finest performance ever, in *The Secret Garden* (1949), in which she played an
adolescent, before failing to make the transition to more mature roles in *Her First
Romance* (1951). O'Brien's gifts were comedic, and when she did return to acting in
middle age it would be in comic support roles.

Natalie Wood, by contrast — who edged out O'Brien for one of the three lead roles
in *Rebel Without a Cause* (1955) — made the transition that had eluded other child
stars. Born Natalia Nikolaevna Zakharenko in July 1938 in San Francisco to Russian
émigré parents, Wood moved with her family at the age of four to the picturesque
Sonoma County town of Santa Rosa. Wood's film debut was even more serendipi-
tous than Jarman's, happening when director Irving Pichel chose Natasha, age four,
to play a little girl who drops her ice cream cone in an opening parade scene in the
film *Happy Land* (1943). Thrilled by this vignette, Natasha's parents — her mother
Maria, a onetime ballerina, and her father Nicholas, a would-be set designer supporting his family as a manual laborer — moved the entire family, including Natasha's
younger sister, to Hollywood and successfully laid siege to the studios for bit parts for
both Natasha and her mother. In 1946 came Natasha's first breakthrough, in Pichel's
Tomorrow Is Forever, in which, renamed Natalie Wood, she starred opposite Orson
Welles and Claudette Colbert, winning kudos for her performance and leading

to another Pichel film, *The Bride Wore Boots* (1946), and the even more dramatic breakthrough of *Miracle on 34th Street* (1947), which solidified her position as one of the two or three top child stars of the day.

In *Rebel Without a Cause* (1955), Wood not only won an Oscar for Best Supporting Actress, she successfully negotiated the transition into adult roles as signified by her appearance in such post-*Rebel* films as *The Searchers* (1956), *A Cry in the Night* (1956), *The Burning Hills* (1956), and *The Girl He Left Behind* (1956), an unprecedented four films in one year, followed by the Cold War epic *Bombers B-52* (1957) and the screen adaptation of Herman Wouk's best-selling novel *Marjorie Morningstar* (1957), in which she beat out Elizabeth Taylor and Audrey Hepburn for the lead role. The last phalanx of the Silent Generation, coming of age in the late 1950s, kept company with Natalie Wood as she moved through the decade in these and such other signature films as *Kings Go Forth* (1958), *Cash McCall* (1959), *All the Fine Young Cannibals* (1960), *West Side Story* (1961), and *Splendor in the Grass* (1961), each film so expressive of the underlying concerns, values, textures, and styles of the era.

Another Silent, Ricky Nelson, a Hollywood product, played himself alongside his brother and parents in the long-running *The Adventures of Ozzie and Harriet* radio and television series. Nelson had outside connections as well. Attending classes at Hollywood High, he experienced the music of his generation in a popular setting, and, with his bandleader father's musical scholarship, became an accomplished performer in rock, country-western, blues, and the combination of these modes that he fashioned into a signature style, beginning with his first hit, in April 1957 when he was sixteen, a cover recording of Fats Domino's "I'm Walkin'." Historians of popular music are today highly respectful of the various stylistic strands Nelson wove together for the more than two dozen hits he recorded between 1957 and 1961, together with the country rock sound he pioneered in the 1960s with his Stone Canyon Band, and are equally respectful of his acting alongside John Wayne and Dean Martin in Howard Hawks's *Rio Bravo* (1959).

Another 1950s teenager with musical tastes, Joan Baez, was doing her best to fit in at Palo Alto High School. It was not easy, however. Baez was dark-skinned, for one thing, her father being Mexican-born, her mother born in Scotland, with Joan moving toward the Mexican side of her heritage. With her thick black hair, brown skin, angular features, high cheekbones, and *mestizo* eyes, Baez found herself an exotic in the Wonder Bread world of 1950s Palo Alto. And the Baez family were strongly progressive, as that term had emerged in the late 1940s, signifying a left-liberal orientation intensified even further when Baez's parents converted to Quakerism. Although she herself never converted, Baez refused to cooperate with school air-raid drills. Ira Sandperl, a Quaker teacher, introduced her to the teachings of Gandhi and Martin Luther King Jr. Meanwhile, this shy, gawky high school junior and senior, out of step politically with the majority of her classmates, differing in appearance, given to going barefoot when she could get away with it, was discovering that sine qua non of teenage existence, peer group acceptance, through singing the songs of Odetta,

Pete Seeger, and Harry Belafonte in her self-taught soprano, accompanying herself on an inexpensive guitar she had bought and taught herself to play. In the spring of 1959, Baez sang at her high school senior prom, wearing a long white dress, in bare feet. Next stop: Boston University and the folk music scene in and around Harvard Square. By November 1962 she was on the cover of *Time*, profiled by John McPhee as the signature figure of the folk music craze sweeping the nation.

By this time, of course, Joan Baez had long since put aside any thought of completing college. And so too, from the late 1940s to the early 1960s, did successive waves of Silents, in California and throughout the nation, make the transition from high school to something else: work, the military, vocational training, further education. It was not a time when the latitude of high school years could be indefinitely prolonged into and perhaps through one's twenties. Work, marriage, military service, preparation for career: It all came early, even for those who were college bound. Part of this dynamic was demographic. The Silents were a small generation, and until the Boomers came to maturity, the Silents were necessary to fill positions and play out roles, whatever they might be, in American life.

The draft had a way of concentrating one's attention. Young men were required to register with their local draft boards when they turned eighteen, and the draft boards in turn presented millions of Silent eighteen-year-olds with their options. Enlist now or be drafted, if you were able-bodied, single, and finished with your education. Enlistment presented a number of options—Army, Navy, Air Force, Marines, Coast Guard—and a variety of programs, ranging from full terms to shorter periods of active duty, followed by five to six years of reserve. The draft by and large meant the Army, now, pronto, for two years. A college deferment postponed the draft until graduation. While in college, students who were interested had a variety of Reserve Officer Training Corps (ROTC) and other programs, leading to a commission. ROTC was intended to provide the services with junior officers and to leaven the upper-officer ranks over time with career military coming from a civilian background: men such as Richard Hearney, Stanford Class of '62, the scion of a Northern California ranching family, who rose to four stars as assistant commandant for air for the Marine Corps; or four-star Army General William Crouch, Claremont Men's College, Class of '63, who finished his career as commander of Allied Land Forces Central Europe. For those just graduated, the services maintained a variety of post-degree officer training programs that could be signed up for in advance.

College graduates who decided to take their chances following graduation were few, for the draft had a way of sweeping up one and all. An entire generation of male college graduates, then, preferred to exercise their option as enlisted men, if they were able to get into one or another of the six-months active duty programs. Others, drafted, served two years in the ranks. Yet however one served, in whatever branch of the service and whatever rank, the draft had a way of fast-forwarding the time available to come to maturity. In the case of those drafted or enlisting during the Korean War, moreover, the danger to life or limb was pronounced. Some 54,246 young men and some young women would lose their lives in that ambiguous conflict, and another 103,284 would be seriously wounded. As in the case of so much to do with the Silent Generation, the Korean War was inconclusive in outcome and was soon to be overwhelmed, if not outright erased from memory, by the Boomer war, Vietnam, that followed.

High school yearbooks from the period, especially those from large inner-city high schools, give ample treatment to vocational classes and programs. Prior to World War II, vocational training tended to be consolidated in large vocational high schools, such as the Frank Wiggins Trade School in Los Angeles, Technical High School in San Jose, and John O'Connell High School in San Francisco. At Frank Wiggins thirty-eight faculty members taught twenty-eight trades. In the post-war period, however, federal and California state legislation, programs, and funding tended to shy away from the segregation of trade and/or technical high school in favor of the comprehensive model in which young men and women acquiring vocational training would be educated alongside their peers on other tracks. Such integration prevailed as two-year colleges became increasingly involved in vocational education. In September 1949, for example, the Frank Wiggins Trade School was upgraded to the Los Angeles Trade-Technical College, offering associate of arts degrees. Junior colleges, as they were then called, dated from the efforts in the 1890s led by President William Rainey Harper of the University of Chicago and other Midwestern university presidents to persuade local boards of education to have high schools in their districts offer thirteenth- and fourteenth-grade instruction as a way of relieving pressure on four-year colleges. In California the notion was formalized by legislation in March 1907 authorizing two years of collegiate instruction on the local level. Given its distance from any four-year college, the Fresno Board of Education was first to act on the idea and was offering college-level instruction by the fall of 1910, followed by Santa Barbara in 1911, Bakersfield and Fullerton by 1913, San Diego by 1914. Most junior colleges in this first period were in Central or Southern California at distances of three hundred to five hundred miles from the nearest state university. As early as 1914, students transferring from these programs to four-year universities were showing a higher rate of academic performance than those entering directly from high school. From the beginning, the junior colleges of California—reorganized as locally governed community colleges in 1968—were based on the premise that any Californian over eighteen, however dismal his or her high school academic record, had rights of admission to the local community college, hence a second chance. Two of the most noted writers emerging from the Silent Generation in this period, Carolyn See and Joan Didion, were junior college students, albeit coming from decidedly different circumstances.

Born in 1934 to a hardscrabble Anglo-American Protestant family, Carolyn See grew up in a dysfunctional environment—a father who fled the family when she was eleven, an embittered mother who drank and who belittled and beat her, a sister with a serious drug problem, a pervasive atmosphere of shabby hopelessness—that she would later consider part of a long-established pattern in her family tree, dating back to the seventeenth century. Even WASPs of a certain lineage, See would later point out, could get goofy and sordid. Hard luck, early deaths from disease and infection, suicides, recurrent alcoholism and generalized failure could plague Anglo-America as much as any other group. In between beating and belittling her, See's mother would remark—sometimes a dozen times a day—"As soon as you hit eighteen, you're out of here."[1] Actually, See's mother, pregnant and remarried to a fellow barfly, threw her out when she was sixteen. See moved in with her father and his third wife for a year, then went out on her own, working part-time at Van de Kamp's Restaurant as a waitress in a Dutch peasant costume and lace hat, living in a $5-a-week furnished room, and taking classes at Los Angeles City College, where the tuition was $2.50 a semester. Finishing City, See transferred to Los Angeles State College, where she took a bachelor's degree, followed by a Ph.D. in English from UCLA.

Throughout her writing career, See would honestly engage the dysfunctionalism and wretchedness of her life that lasted through her thirties across two failed marriages. Although See could be satirically, even painfully, honest in her later novels—the autobiographical *Golden Days* (1986) especially—and her no-holds-barred memoir *Dreaming: Hard Luck and Good Times in America* (1995) regarding the inadequacies of City and Los Angeles State, operating out of Quonset huts on a hillside in East Los Angeles, these institutions, especially City College, managed to help leverage an impoverished and isolated young woman, who had graduated from an alcoholic and abusive mother to an alcoholic, improvident husband, into a self-sufficient life as writer and college professor.

Another noted California writer, Joan Didion, had a junior college background as well. If See had come from Anglo-American California in its downward arc, Didion—a fifth-generation descendant of a pioneering Anglo-American family that had flourished as ranchers and developers in the Sacramento Valley—represented the mirror opposite. The Didions had prospered, for one thing, in ranching and real estate. During World War II, Didion's father had served as an officer in the Army Air Corps. The Didions lived in a large home filled with mementos of a family that had been in Sacramento ever since the arrival of her great-great-great-grandmother Nancy Hardin Cornwall by wagon train in 1846. Not far from the Didion home was a nineteenth-century graveyard replete with the tombstones of collateral relatives and ancestors, and as a child, Didion was taken on a nearly ritualized tour of visits to female cousins and great-aunts who would instruct her in the family heritage. The Didions worshipped at the Trinity Episcopal Pro-Cathedral on M Street and spent the worst of the long hot Sacramento summers at Stinson Beach on the Marin County coast. As a student at McClatchy High School in Sacramento, Didion was fast friends with Nina Warren, the governor's daughter, and pledged a sorority called the Mañana Club. Her initiation was held in the governor's mansion. Didion's first novel, *Run River* (1963), draws heavily upon her established background, with its references to pioneering ancestors from the 1840s, a social connection to the Stanfords in the 1860s, a candidate for the governorship in the 1930s, the Sutter Club, duck clubs in the nearby wetlands, shopping trips to I. Magnin's in San Francisco,

Stanford, Cal, and Ivy League connections, land ownership, business success: the expected mosaic of upper-middle-class Sacramento life.

By the spring of 1952, Didion, a number of her sorority sisters from the Mañana Club, and a number of other girls from McClatchy were all planning to attend Stanford, where college-bound girls of Didion's caste were accustomed to go: Stanford, with its magical Mission Revival/Romanesque quadrangle, where undergraduate women dressed stylishly each weekday evening for dinner, waited on by white-jacketed male hashers working their way through the university, chosen, it was alleged, for their good looks. On 25 April 1952, coming home from McClatchy, Didion opened a mimeographed letter from Rixford K. Snyder, director of admissions at Stanford, informing her that the university regretted that she would not be among those admitted to the Class of 1956. "I remember quite clearly the afternoon I opened that letter," Didion would later recall. "I stood reading and re-reading it, my sweater and my books fallen on the hall floor, trying to interpret the words in some less final way, the phrases 'unable to take' and 'favorable action' fading in and out of focus until the sentence made no sense at all. We lived then in a big dark Victorian house, and I had a sharp and dolorous image of myself growing old in it, never going to school anywhere, the spinster in *Washington Square*. I went upstairs to my room and locked the door and for a couple of hours I cried."[2] Adding insult to injury, Didion was also rejected by her second choice, Cal Berkeley, not exactly rejected, but not admitted either, pending the successful completion of certain absent requirements. And so, as her McClatchy classmates took off for Stanford, Joan Didion joined the undecided, the underachieved, the rejected, the challenged, the impoverished at Sacramento Junior College, an institution designed explicitly to give the more troubled sectors of student society a second academic chance, where she punched out the requirements for admission to Cal in the spring.

For Carolyn See, Los Angeles State, however rudimentary an institution, had led to career and a better life. For See's fellow student at Cal State L.A. in this period, Myron Roberts, later the editor of *Los Angeles* magazine, the recently founded (1947) Cal State L.A. epitomized what Roberts called Off-Ramp U: a campus for upwardly mobile students, many of them holding down full-time jobs, to commute to by car, get the courses they needed for their degree, then drive down the ramp to the freeway. The same could not be said, however, for the more venerable state colleges—San Francisco (1861), for example, San Jose (1870), Chico (1889), San Diego (1897), or Fresno (1911)—institutions with nineteenth-century origins and strong relationships to local life, and architecturally respectable campuses. San Jose and Chico State, for example, were housed around Mediterranean Revival quadrangles climbing with ivy. With their developed fraternity and sorority cultures, moreover, these state colleges had a reputation for being party schools, especially Chico and San Jose, where the Spartans enjoyed the added attraction of being a ranked football power. State college students in this era by and large came from the locality, worked at least part-time in the locality, and planned to live and work in the locality following graduation. In less populous states, any number of these state colleges would have eventually assumed the rank of the state university, emphasizing career-oriented educations. San Francisco State, by contrast, had more than its share of literary and political distinction and was, in point of comparison, the City College of New York of the Bay Area, open to the many yet possessed of its own distinctive esprit d' corps. Aspiring novelists and short story writers Ernest J. Gaines '57, Gerald Haslam '63, and Anne Rice '64 had no trouble honing their skills there before (Gaines) going on to a post-graduate writing fellowship at Stanford and (Haslam and Rice) staying on for an M.A. John Handy '63 was en route to becoming one of the notable jazz saxophonists of his generation. Aspiring politicians Willie L. Brown Jr. '55 and John Burton '54 were busy honing the political skills they would eventually exercise as, respectively, speaker of the assembly and president pro tem of the state senate.

In contrast to high school yearbooks, college and university histories tend to emphasize academics, administration, and development over athletics and student life. Yet no history covering this era should ignore the joy of life, the fun, of college years in the time between Korea and Vietnam: the bonfire rallies and football games, student politics and government, campus newspapers and literary magazines, the glee clubs, choirs, and theatricals, the formal dances (a tradition that would disappear by the end of the next decade), the clubs, fraternities, sororities, and student hangouts: all this not differing from the rest of the nation yet localized and specific. At the Claremont Men's College (CMC) there was a beer bust at a different location each Friday afternoon. Just thinking about it drove President George C. S. Benson to distraction. The men of Claremont divided themselves into two social groups: the Tortugateers (Turtle Men) of Prado Dam, who dressed in outlandish wear and repaired to the nearby Prado Dam for various dissipations, and the Knickerbockers, who featured a button-down preppy style and socialized at elegant venues in coat and tie: the two sides of the 1950s, in short, Silents at once mocking the establishment, temporarily at least, while preparing themselves to join it. At the nearby Stinky's, CMC undergrads had recourse to a twenty-four-hour-a-day, seven-day-a-week jukebox, pinball, and hamburger joint. But then again, every university and college campus supported its own distinctive constellation of eateries, watering holes, and hangouts: places to congregate and have fun at a time when, short of a nuclear exchange between the United States and the Soviet Union (which was always possible), the future held infinite possibilities.

In college, as in high school, the Silent Generation was finding itself and preparing for that future. At Pomona, Richard Chamberlain '56 was acquiring his acting chops in student productions, and Andrew Hoyem '57 was acquiring a taste for poetry and the printed word that would see him develop into one of America's leading fine printers. At Whittier, Stan Sanders '63 became one of the first African American Rhodes Scholars in the history of the program, preparatory to a career in law and public service. At the College of the Pacific, George Moscone '53 was heading for law school, elective politics, and the mayoralty of San Francisco. At the University of San Francisco (USF), *Foghorn* editor Warren Hinckle '60 was acquiring his skills as a muckraking journalist by taking on the Jesuit establishment. Ming Chin '64, meanwhile, later the second Asian American member of the California Supreme Court, was preparing for law school and, through ROTC, distinguished service in Vietnam. At USF as well, college dean Edmund J. Smyth, SJ, was personally preparing a generation of undergraduates, most of them the first of their families to attend college, for scholarship admission to the graduate and professional schools of the Ivy League and other leading universities. Dennis Kennedy '62, a plumber's son, went on to hold the Samuel Beckett Professorship of Drama and Theatre Studies at Trinity College, Dublin. Peter Ueberroth graduated from San Jose State in 1959 before going on to success in the travel business, the chairmanship of the 1984 Olympics, and the commissionership of baseball. Over in Moraga, meanwhile, at St. Mary's College, conducted by the Christian Brothers, the San Francisco–born, San Rafael–raised Robert Hass took his undergraduate degree in 1963, then went on for an M.A. and a Ph.D. in English at Stanford, where he studied with poet-critic Yvor Winters. In the decades to come, Hass would emerge as a highly respected poet and, by then a member of the English faculty at UC Berkeley, would serve two terms as poet laureate of the United States.

When it came to the question of entering the establishment, there was always an advantage to Cal Berkeley and Stanford. Throughout the 1950s there seemed a one-way connection between Stanford and the Harvard Law School, such as that taken by Derek Bok, Stanford '51, later professor of law and president of Harvard. Interestingly enough, for someone of such distinguished East Coast Anglo-Dutch lineage, Bok had come of age in the 1940s on the edges of the émigré community of Los Angeles, his charismatic mother being a close friend of Gerald Heard, Christopher Isherwood, the Huxleys, and other members of the Berthold and Salka Viertel circle: boyhood associations, Bok later recalled, that had a formative influence on his intellectual and imaginative development.

Three Stanford graduates of this era made it to the United States Supreme Court. Sandra Day O'Connor '50 was from Arizona. Anthony Kennedy '58, a Sacramento lawyer appointed to the Ninth Circuit of the United States Court of Appeals, had to wait until Robert Bork (for strict construction) and Douglas Ginsburg (for marijuana) failed Senate confirmation before he assumed his seat. Raised in San Francisco, the son of the attorney for the board of education, Stephen Breyer '59 earned an Eagle Scout badge and completed Lowell High School with a near-straight-A record (except for one B) and debated Jerry Brown of St. Ignatius to a draw, no mean achievement. Breyer's Stanford degree led to a Marshall scholarship to Oxford, followed by Harvard Law, followed by a clerkship on the Supreme Court, followed by a professorship at Harvard and an appointment to the Supreme Court.

Dianne Goldman, later Feinstein, Stanford '55, laid down the foundations for a future political career by winning election to the student body vice presidency, the highest political office a woman could legally hold at Stanford, given the 3.3-to-1 ratio of men to women: which suggested certain dangers for an attractive woman running for office, such as Feinstein herself experienced when, in the midst of a campaign speech at a fraternity house, she was rushed into a shower and drenched. Elected student body vice president, Feinstein refused to issue any parking passes for the Big Game weekend to the fraternity until the membership formally apologized to her, reinforcing the tested political adage "Don't get mad, get even." As an undergraduate and a student politician, Feinstein displayed the reconciling, harmonizing traits of a member of the Silent Generation. Jewish on her father's side, Russian Orthodox on her mother's, educated at the Convent of the Sacred Heart High School, Feinstein chose Judaism upon reaching her majority. She remained, however, thoroughly ecumenical in attitude and, to her father's distress, was pinned for a while to a varsity football player en route to becoming a Presbyterian minister. She was, in short, already a consensus builder, with a distinctive ability to form alliances with the male establishment, a trait that would serve her well in later years as mayor of San Francisco and United States senator.

In academic terms, Stanford in these years was in the process of its big breakthrough to prominence. Lagging behind but also in a take-off mode was UCLA. If one were an African American and an athlete—as Bruins Tom Bradley, Jackie Robinson, Woody Strode, and Rafer Johnson would tell you—UCLA had already arrived, bringing to campus a pioneering generation of African American students. Nobel Prize winner Ralph Bunche would also note that one did not have to be an athlete to be a successful African American at UCLA, although it did help. So too would the Jewish community of Los Angeles see in UCLA its own special place, although by the 1950s, the student body had diversified considerably. If progressive left-liberal politics had been characteristic of an earlier UCLA generation, by the 1950s another UCLA trait, a certain love of the good life, redolent of the suburban country club, had asserted itself. UCLA supported a flourishing fraternity and sorority culture, as the brothers at the Phi Gamma Delta (Fiji) House at 611 Gayley might tell you, citing the Friday afternoon kegger parties at the frat house, or the spur-of-the-moment beer busts in one or another of the nearby canyons, or the 1953 football season in which eight Fijis were starting for the Bruins, helping to take coach Red Sanders's team to the Rose Bowl. Throughout the season, for home games at the Coliseum, the Fiji brothers organized a flatbed truck with slat sides, from which the beer flowed freely. Then there were the weekend dances at the Hollywood Palladium or the dance parties aboard steamers heading for Catalina or the spring break gatherings in which fraternities and sororities would rent houses at Balboa and Newport, with some of the senior Fijis keeping a place full-time at Malibu.

When social chronicler Martin Mayer covered UCLA for *Esquire* in November 1961, the message that the new UCLA chancellor Franklin Murphy was preaching—namely, that Los Angeles was making the transition to a serious city and UCLA was the actualizer and reflection of that transition—provided Mayer the organizing principle for his coverage. Mayer, however, did not like Los Angeles and hence approached with skepticism the entire UCLA experience. UCLA was a commuter school, Mayer argued, with seventy-five hundred of its twelve thousand undergraduates living at home and working a job. Just because the students were beautiful did not mean that they were dumb, although, as Mayer believed, Los Angeles was "the home of the one-idea mind, beatnik or Buddhist or Bircher, and once the mind has found its idea it ceases to work."[3] Mayer had missed the point, Oxford graduate and UCLA teaching assistant Richard Gilbert argued a few years later. UCLA embodied the pleasure principle, and the pleasure principle was not inimical to learning. A Londoner and Oxonian, Gilbert discerned a fundamental tension between life and learning at UCLA, especially noticeable in the "herds of colorful nymphets, looking like film extras milling around a stage California campus. . . . The contrast between these creatures, and the drab, black-stockinged undergraduates of Oxford was powerful." Conflict was not absent in the lives of these "luscious girls," these "Lolitas in sprayed-on jeans," a conflict that was emblematic of a larger tension in UCLA itself: between academic work and the joy of life, which in their case involved being sexy and finding a husband. A surprising number of co-eds, Gilbert noted, had to resort to psychiatric counseling to deal with the tension between doing well in class and getting their M.R.S. degrees. This tension could be especially trying on an intellectually ambitious co-ed. UCLA was also the first university Gilbert had ever encountered in which cars and parking spaces played a determining role, to the point that students scheduled classes not in terms of the content of a specific course but whether it was given early enough in the day for anyone taking it to find parking. Then there was a certain disconnect between culture and intelligence, meaning that UCLA students could be as intelligent as any Oxford student, but in their own distinctive way, with a certain detachment and insouciance. Correcting bluebooks for the Western Civilization survey taken by some six hundred students, Gilbert came up with such gems as: "St. Augustine was illuminated by divine power" ("AC or DC?" Gilbert asked); or—this in an essay on *The Song of Roland*—"He charged in against the dragon relying on God to help him, and if he didn't, well that's the way the cookie crumbles." Yet Gilbert confessed to admiring the UCLA undergraduates, drawn from the top 12 percent of high school seniors in the state. Secretly, he admired the zany things they said, their indifference to politics ("politics," one of his students told him, "is strictly for the birds"), and, most of all, their ability to handle with aplomb the underlying pressures of American life, actualized in their case by a pressure to get good grades that was way beyond anything he had experienced at Oxford.[4]

Arriving at Berkeley in the spring of 1953, Joan Didion entered the Cal experience at the early mid-point of a rising tide of well-being, culminating in the Camelot chancellorship of Glenn Seaborg. Didion's presence at Cal had been facilitated, ironically, by the support—or was it indifference?—of her parents to the Stanford rejection. As might be expected, Didion pledged Delta Delta Delta, one of the most selective of sororities on campus, which assuaged the sense of displacement she had experienced when turned down by Stanford. Cal was a much more intellectually challenging place than Stanford she discovered to her satisfaction when she wrote a paper for a friend at Stanford on Conrad's *Nostromo*, and he got an A, and she then submitted it at Berkeley and received a B minus. Berkeley had a challenging faculty, Didion found, together with a flourishing on-campus literary life organized around the *Daily Cal*, the *Occident* literary magazine, the *Blue and the Gold* yearbook, and the *Pelican* humor review. Sorority life at Tri Delt, finally, helped render the behemoth Berkeley campus less anonymous and lonely.

Still, there was another side to all of this. Joan Didion could never be just another sorority girl from the Valley on the lookout for a husband; and she was too much a member of the Silent Generation, she would later write, in her ambivalence to feel-good social action and a false sense of community. "We were silent," she later noted, "because the exhilaration of social action seemed to many of us just one more way of escaping the personal, of masking for a while that dread of the meaningless which was man's fate."[5] Didion is echoing the French existentialism that constituted such force among religiously skeptical Silents harboring intellectual ambitions: a postwar sense—nurtured by Sartre, Malraux, and Camus, but evident as well in such popular writers as Françoise Sagan—that orthodoxies had crumbled in the twentieth century. Even believing Silents bothering to think were nurturing themselves on the existentialism of Søren Kierkegaard, Martin Buber, and Paul Tillich, believers who conditioned their orthodoxy with uncertainty and dread. The classics of existentialism were now available in quality paperbacks, with good translations, to be read late into the evening and discussed over coffee and Gauloise cigarettes in cafés, preferably while wearing (for those truly under the influence of French writers and the foreign films being screened by Pauline Kael at the Berkeley Cinema Guild) a turtleneck sweater and beret.

Four years after her graduation, Didion returned to Berkeley in the fall of 1960 to confront in the course of doing an article for *Mademoiselle* the campus that had meant so much to her and remained, as she would later suggest, California's best idea of itself. From one perspective, it was a most idyllic place, perfect for a *Mademoiselle* article oriented toward an affluent young female readership, young women from Didion's own background, sorority girls. It was also a campus in the final phases of Silent Generation ascendancy. With the exception of the ongoing resistance to compulsory ROTC, Chancellor Seaborg at Berkeley, like Chancellor Murphy at UCLA, governed a student body focused primarily upon personal advancement and upward mobility, eager to please. Photographs show young men in crew or Princeton cuts, loafers, chinos, and short-sleeved shirts when it was warm, sweaters or Pendletons when breezy; the young women in skirts and blouses and sweater sets. Social occasions—dances, receptions at the chancellor's residence, other formal events—show the men in coats and ties, a number of them clenching pipes between their teeth, lit or unlit, the young women wearing the satiny gowns of the era, their hair in ponytails or poodle cuts. The pipe represented some form of statement, Chancellor Seaborg noted in his memoirs. Exactly what was being stated remained obscure. The pipe represented something akin, perhaps, to the enigmatic eye patch worn by the man in the Hathaway shirt advertisements, suggesting a present suavity and Hemingwayesque past. Didion saw and described all this, with an eye for readers of *Mademoiselle* as to what the young women were wearing, including the facts that only transfers from Wellesley wore knee socks and that girls from Central and Southern California used a lot of eye make-up.

Yet Didion also noted a disquieting lack of motivation in many students: a passivity, a reluctance to articulate goals for themselves, their purchase of mimeographed notes for lecture courses, a certain sense of unease in the air. "Call it the weather," she notes, "call it the closing of the frontier, call it the failure of Eden; the fact remains that Californians are cultivating America's lushest growth of passive nihilism right along with their bougainvillea. Enterprises that seemed important in the East, where the world is scaled to human beings, lose their significance beneath California's immense, bland sky; transient passions fade in the face of the limitless Pacific." UC Berkeley was large and complex, unforgiving, Didion said, and could be very lonely and alienating. There was an acute shortage of dormitories, and it was too easy for many undergraduates to become isolated and lost in their apartments or boarding houses. "The campus offers none of the cohesive spirit that a college like Smith or even a university like Stanford does," Didion noted; "only alumni say 'We' and only then through clouds of nostalgia and the pages of the alumni magazine." That is what gave such a value, for the girls who qualified, to sorority memberships, which Tri Delt Didion dutifully chronicled, telling the story of a young woman who spent her first two years at Berkeley alone in her private boarding house and made no real friends but joined a sorority in her junior year and was now going to parties on Fraternity Row and in private apartments, was being invited to fraternity/sorority dances at the Fairmont and Mark Hopkins hotels in San Francisco, and was getting good grades.

Yet for all that a sorority or fraternity offered, Didion cautioned, it could also imprison. On campus and beyond Sather Gate was a great big world filled with artistic and ambitious guys, unaffiliated, living in dorms or rented rooms, catching foreign flicks on Telegraph, questioning the establishment, whom even a Tri Delt might like to date. "I used to go out with boys I wouldn't dream of marrying," a transfer sorority girl told Didion. "Sometimes now I miss that." Berkeley, a faculty member told Didion, was increasingly becoming a place for people preparing for the learned professions. Berkeley was "big, rich, and, like its students, peculiarly undefined, oddly amoral," Didion concluded of her alma mater. "Someone has yet to say: 'This is what we mean.' Until someone does, Berkeley will continue to be a brilliant faculty, a beautiful plant, and an extravagantly good research facility, [but] will continue to just miss being a great university in the sense that only Harvard has been in this country. In the meantime, lost souls will not find themselves in those eucalyptus groves of academe. For Berkeley is a great place only for students capable of self-definition. It is a place of great riches, but it gives them up readily only to people of great expectations."[6]

A failure to define goals, Didion had noted, a reluctance to talk about oneself. Yet certainly an entire generation, even of Silents, could not remain totally silent when it came to connecting to their time of life. Music offered an outlet. Over the Labor

Day weekend of 1961, four Silents—brothers Brian and Carl Wilson, their cousin Mike Love, and a friend, Al Jardine—using rented instruments, recorded a demonstration tape in the Wilson home at 3701 West 119th Street in the suburban community of Hawthorne in southern Los Angeles County, while their parents were visiting Mexico City. The name of the song, written primarily by Brian Wilson, was "Surfin'." Thereby was launched, however tentatively, one of the most important mythic brandings of Southern California since the creation of the orange crate label: a branding that would put youth, Silent and Boomer alike, and a youth-oriented culture of surfing, beach life, cruising, parties, school, and romance, at the forefront of the California identity via the records and albums and live performances of the Beach Boys, as they would soon be known.

The Beach Boys were at once typical of the generation coming of age in 1950s Southern California and naturally talented as musical performers. This combination of generational experience with musical genius and performance virtuosity—energized by dream-wish and fantasy—conferred on the Beach Boys an iconic power that rendered their songs compelling distillations of imaginative experience. Before it was over—before, that is, the creativity of the Beach Boys peaked and they were turned into a non-stop nostalgia machine—their songs proved capable of distilling on a subliminal level that dream of youth, that sense of being young on the Coast of Dreams, emanating from high school yearbooks.

The Beach Boys were suburban, raised in a white middle-class suburb near the ocean. They attended the local high schools and junior college, worshipped at the local Presbyterian church, learned to sing there and at school, to play their instruments (initially) on a most rudimentary basis, and, in Brian Wilson's case, to become mesmerized by harmonic singing, whether from J. S. Bach or, his favorites, the Hi-Lo's and the Four Freshmen. Dennis Wilson surfed, the only Wilson brother to do so, and Brian played baseball for Hawthorne High, where he had a girlfriend, Judy Bowles, and where the brothers performed on special school occasions, as documented, among other places, in the 1960 Hawthorne High yearbook *El Camino*. All this suggested an idealized, or at the least normal, suburban experience from this period, were it not for the fact that the boys' father, Kansas-born Murry Gage Wilson, a semi-failed middle manager (Southern California Gas, Goodyear Tire & Rubber, where he lost an eye in an industrial accident) was a sadist who verbally, psychologically, and physically abused his offspring (Brian later claimed that a blow from his father left him deaf in one ear) in the midst of their *Leave It to Beaver* life in a way that would in a later era bring down the wrath of the district attorney's office, should it ever be reported. For the Wilson brothers, their cousin Mike Love, and their friend Al Jardine, the very deficiencies of life in Hawthorne—centered for the Wilson boys on their abusive father—intensified through reverse compensation the musical narrative they were developing as, initially, the Pendletones (named after the shirt) in high school and junior college, their actualized daydream of young Californians singing in harmony of life in a world that resembled their own, only better.

It was Dennis Wilson, the only true surfer in the group, who first suggested to Brian, "Hey, surfing's getting really big. You guys ought to write a song about it," which prompted Brian and his cousin Mike Love to write "Surfin'."[7] Behind that simple suggestion was not only the genesis of the Beach Boys' first record to make the Los Angeles charts (number 33 as of 29 December 1961) but a connection to a place and an activity poised for take-off. When Candix Records folded shortly after the release of "Surfin'," the Beach Boys and their father, who acted as their agent, never wanting to relinquish any control over the boys, opened negotiations with Capitol Records. The boys' first 45 from Capitol had "Surfin' Safari" on one side and on the other "409," a hot rod song co-authored by Brian Wilson, and here was achieved a connection to another teenage obsession: hot rods, cruising, dragging the main. Based in common experience, the preoccupations of these and later songs— surfing ("Surfin' Safari," "Surfin' USA," "Surfer Girl,"), cars ("Little Deuce Coupe," "409," "I Get Around," "Don't Worry, Baby"), school ("Be True to Your School,"), teenage romance ("Wendy," "Help Me, Rhonda")—upgraded such themes into near mythological status as Beach Boys songs became the anthems and icons of Southern California life among the young, broadcast nationally to the teenagers of America, drawing them into life on the Day-Glo shores of the sundown sea.

Growing up in such an environment, seeking themes for their songs, the Beach Boys could not help but mythologize a landscape and way of life that was already so surreal, so proto-mythic, in its setting. Cars and the beach, surfing, the California Girl, all this fused in the alembic of youth: Here was a way of life, an iconography, already half-released into the chords and multiple tracks of a new sound. The songs of the Beach Boys upgraded an overnight place into national identity by connecting its myth to young America and inviting young America to buy into the dream, to find its own Southern California, if only within itself, wherever radios were playing and whatever cars were cruising down whatever streets. Cars, after all, had been liberating young Americans since the 1920s, and at no time was this more true than among the Silent Generation in the postwar era when hot rods, customized cars, and sports cars became increasingly available. Hot rods came first and least expensively, for the hot rod was a prewar automobile—Model T's, the Fords and Chevys of the early 1930s (especially the Fords, which had introduced the V8 engine in 1932)—available in the postwar period for transformation into a racing machine capable of speeds of more than a hundred miles per hour. With its existing used car stock, its paved open spaces for racing, its dry lake beds in remote areas, Southern California soon emerged as the epicenter of hot rod culture. The first Hot Rod Exhibition, held in January 1948 at the National Guard Armory in Los Angeles, attracted some ten thousand attendees and helped to launch Hot Rod magazine, which reached a circulation of three hundred thousand by 1950.

Hot rods were by definition customized, but the customized car as a separate genre came into its own in the 1950s. Customizing began with a more expensive and later model automobile—a Ford, a Chevrolet, a Mercury, a Buick from the 1940s—which was then modified not so much for racing purposes but as a style statement: channeled (lowered) to sit more closely to the pavement, its rear wheels skirted with metal shields, its windows top-chopped to half their normal size, to create an atmosphere of mystery, the front or rear end of the car raked downward in pure attitude, exhaust pipes extended, painted pin-striping and decorative motifs, such as flames, running along the surface, suggestive of explosive power beneath the hood. As in the case of all artistic genres, customizing could be traced to a founding school of artists and the prototypes they created, most notably the Barris brothers, Sam and George, of Compton, where Sam in 1949 began to stylize his two-door 1949 Mercury and, two years later, created for his friend Bob Hirohata a customized 1951 Mercury that, shown at the 1952 Motorama, created a sensation, as well as establishing a signature car, the Hirohata '51 Merc, that, like all classic prototypes, guided a generation of customizers. Meanwhile, in an ascending order of affluence, came the next development: the sports car, whether foreign (the two-door MG especially) or such domestic efforts as the 1952 Nash Healey, the 1953 Chevrolet Corvette, the 1953 Studebaker Starliner, the 1954 Kaiser Darrin, the 1955 Ford Thunderbird, and the Ford Mustang, debuting in 1964. The Detroit sports car expressed the affluence of the 1950s and like certain films of the period—Alfred Hitchcock's *To Catch a Thief* (1955), for example—brought the look and ambience of Europe, initially pioneered by the MG, to affluent American car buyers.

High school and college yearbooks of the era, especially those from Southern California, testify to the increasing presence of automobiles on high school and college campuses and the availability of nearby bowling allies, creameries, drive-in restaurants, and other automobile-related hang-outs. Much of the teenage slang of the period (*burn rubber, a gas, cherry, drag, crash, haul ass, jacked up*) was derived from this Southern California world of driving and cars. For the students of Fairfax, Hollywood, Beverly Hills, North Hollywood, Woodrow Wilson, David Starr Jordan, and Orange Union high schools in the Southland, as well as for the high school students of the Bay Area and the San Joaquin and Sacramento valleys, cruising constituted a ritualized salute to the time just before adulthood that such performers as the Ventures, Dick Dale, Jan and Dean, and the Beach Boys were celebrating and that George Lucas would immortalize in *American Graffiti* (1973).

Like cars, the beach was not an exclusively Southern California place or artistic theme. Far from it: Since ancient times the beach—as site, occasion, and metaphor—had represented across various permutations a place outside of place, and a time outside of time, offering a suspension of the ordinary and an opportunity to glory in the human body and the physical world and thereby, paradoxically, to experience spiritual renewal. In Southern California, with its three hundred miles of coast between Santa Barbara and San Diego, the beach emerged in the twentieth century as the central resort, the shared public space, a compelling opportunity for pleasure and renewal. "The sun of Los Angeles," novelist and political scientist Eugene Burdick observed in *Holiday* for October 1957, "is the center of an elaborate and complex myth. The citizens believe that their sun is tamed, gentle, caressing, and, above all else, healthful. And, the myth runs, this sun glows down on a sensuous luxuriant paradise where everything from children to oranges grows better and bigger. This is not the almost tropical sun of Hawaii or the alternately thin and blistering sun of Arkansas or the moderate bourgeois sun of France. This is a kind sun, a boon of nature, a sun designed for Utopia." Beach culture, Burdick argued, was in so many ways a fundamental premise of Southern California. It appeared to have made the teenagers of the region taller and more athletic, certainly more tan and blond, than elsewhere in the nation. And it seemed to be bringing into the coastal lifestyle, so Burdick speculated, a certain psychological passivity, or at the least a more relaxed way of relating to daily life. It was not necessary to be active in the sun, Burdick speculated. "Merely to be in the sun is itself socially desirable, perfectly understood and pleasant. On every decent day, and many that are not, the beaches will be lined with young people stretched out and taking the sun. To an extent that is startling to newcomers, all activities are moved outdoors—sports, classes, barbecues, dances, concerts, banquets, graduation exercises. And if one has nothing to do, he can just sit in the sun. There is no society I know of where just the simple possession of a tanned skin is so highly valued."[8]

Jack London first publicized surfing to an American audience following a 1907 visit to Hawaii. George Freeth, a champion surfer of Irish-Hawaiian descent based out of Redondo Beach, introduced the sport to Southern California shortly there-after. Before and after World War I, Freeth and the famed Hawaiian surfer Duke Kahanamoku further popularized the sport through surfing exhibitions up and down the south coast. By the late 1930s, surfing had emerged as the sport of choice among a small elite of Hollywood stars (Jackie Coogan, Buster Crabbe, Joel McCrea, Paul Gregory, Gary Cooper, and David O. Selznick among them) and upper-middle-class businessmen and professionals who favored the beaches of Malibu, Palos Verdes, Huntington, and San Onofre. Starting in the 1940s, surfing made a transition from a limited upper-register pursuit to the signature activity of a more bohemian lifestyle and was further popularized by the evolution of early surfboards, built of redwood, many of them weighing a hundred pounds or more, to the lighter and more maneu-verable fiberglass-covered balsa-wood prototype designed and built in 1949 by a young bohemian surfer (and dropout aeronautical engineer) Robert Wilson Simmons in a garage off Malibu, using materials and designs evolved during the war.

In the 1950s, entering its third phase, surfing became a way of dropping out of Cold War California for young men—Tom Wert (nom de surf Opai), Terry Tracey (nom de surf Tubesteak), Miki Dora (nom de surf Da Cat), Mickey Munoz, Kemp Aaberg, and the others—who did not want to fit in, did not want to be drafted or to finish college and wear gray flannel suits to an office, but merely wanted to surf. While avoiding the overt ideologies of the Beats, surfing nevertheless embodied a lifestyle statement rejecting the conventional expectations for young people in the Eisenhower era. Living in rented rooms or homemade beach shacks in canyons, avoiding work and the draft (the calcium deposits formed on feet and kneecaps from prolonged surfing helped in this regard), Tubesteak and Da Cat emerged as iconic figures of surfing culture as an alternative approach to life.

As in the case of the Beats, surfing culture had its underside. Miki Dora—a raffish and charismatic Hungarian-born charmer whose good looks, wiles, and social graces masked an underlying sociopathy—supported himself as a sneak thief, specializing in live-action, real-time entries into upscale parties (like Cary Grant in *To Catch a Thief*, Dora was known to don a tuxedo for certain occasions), followed by a quick extraction of cash from guests' purses left in bedrooms and the scooping up of available jewelry (Dora once nabbed an Oscar), followed by a quick exit. Surfing could attract the troubled, the marginal, especially those fleeing dysfunctional family situations and looking for a supportive community. As in the case of the Beats and the jazz scene, drugs would make serious inroads into surfing in the 1960s, taking out the vulnerable with an almost generational sweep. But all this—the drugs, the side effects and after-effects of promiscuity on groupie beach girls running headlong into the sexual revolution, the crises of middle age when forty arrived so unexpectedly—belonged, in the main, to Boomers and the post-1963 era.

During the 1950s surfing had not yet lost its innocence or become a multi-billion dollar business. Thanks to Tracey a.k.a. Tubesteak, a young Southern Californian experienced an encounter that would result in a novel, followed by a movie, *Gidget* (1959), that would set the stage for the media-driven surfer craze propelled by the Beach Boys. Émigré Frederick Kohner had arrived in Los Angeles during the war not speaking a word of English. By the summer of 1956 Kohner was hearing stories from his teenaged daughter Kathy of how on the beach she had traded her sack lunch for a surfing lesson from a guy called Tubesteak and how Tubesteak and his friends were calling the diminutive Kathy a *gidget*, a nickname combining *girl* and *midget*, and how Gidget, now her nom de surf, had been accepted into the surfer group as a sort of mascot. A professional screenwriter with an Academy Award nomination, Kohner grasped the implications of his daughter's story and produced a novel, *Gidget: The Little Girl with Big Ideas* (1957), written in the first person and filled with teenage argot and surfer talk, which he sold to Columbia for $50,000. Released in 1959 and starring Sandra Dee, *Gidget* provided audiences with a conventional ending. Thanks to the influence of Gidget, a level-headed girl despite her surfing, the two surfer dropouts who befriend her, Kahuna and Moondoggie, return to the workforce and college respectively, reconciled to adult roles and conventional society. Trained as an Air Force pilot before dropping out, Kahuna will now fly for an airline. Moondoggie gives Gidget his promise pin. The two of them look forward to life together after Moondoggie finishes law school. Thanks to Gidget, Freddy Kohner, Hollywood, and Sandra Dee, surfing made its peace with the Eisenhower era.

During the Second World War, anxieties regarding young people—teenaged V-girls, for example, running away from home and to follow their boyfriends to military bases—led to a kind of Red Scare regarding juvenile delinquency lasting into the postwar period. The Zoot Suit Riots of June 1943 were, essentially, a confrontation of one set of teenagers against another, a rumble between rival gangs, teenaged

Mexican Americans and teenaged military. The Los Angeles Youth Project established in the aftermath of the riots documented gang life and turf in South Central Los Angeles and established programs of outreach and counseling. Fear that the country, not just California, was facing an epidemic of juvenile delinquency persisted into the postwar era. In 1948 Governor Earl Warren established a Commission on Social and Economic Causes of Crime and Delinquency, chaired by USC social work professor Arlien Johnson, to investigate the problem further. Released in June 1949, the commission's report cited a wide range of causes, with extensive attention paid to the children of the some 150,000 seasonal migrant workers in the state, for whom poverty and a sense of dislocation seemed to be tempting to misbehavior. In 1950 the San Francisco Police Department established a task force to deal with, as usage then put it, the gangs of teenage punks who were roaming the streets of the city, armed with blackjacks, brass knuckles, knives, and long chains (one gang was alleged to have a secret cache of eight pistols, a Tommy gun, and 4,500 rounds of ammunition), picking fights, beating up people on streetcars, invading theaters looking for trouble. In one month alone, January 1950, seventeen juveniles under the age of eighteen were arrested in such instances. A spate of California-based novels—Karl Brown's *Incorrigible* (1947), Ray Morrison's *Angels Camp* (1949), Lange Lewis's *The Passionate Victims* (1952), and John B. Sanford's *The Land That Touches Mine* (1953)—dealt with one or another aspect of the juvenile problem.

The signature manifestation of this postwar anxiety was Nicholas Ray's film *Rebel Without a Cause* (1955), set in Los Angeles and starring James Dean, Natalie Wood, and Sal Mineo as troubled teenagers. On the one hand, the film seems to be yet another documentation of the juvenile delinquency crisis, so common to the era. It was, in fact, inspired by an earlier (1944) psychological study of troubled urban youth. Yet *Rebel Without a Cause* represented a shift of attitude. In it, the parents are to blame, having, among other faults, placed too much faith in suburban Southern California as a matrix for their offsprings' development and not connecting with them on a deeper level.

As *Rebel Without a Cause* suggested, adults were backing off an unwarranted suspicion of their children and looking to their own obligations to their offspring. The significance of this shift, historian Kirse Granat May argues, is that it set the stage for a dramatic reversal of attitude by the World War II generation toward its Silent and Boomer progeny, a reversal that, intensified over the next half decade and more, would result in the appropriation of California's youth as the emblem par excellence of Eisenhower- and Kennedy-era well-being. During World War II, the argument goes, the older generation was asking the younger generation to fight and die and was hence anxious regarding its relationship to its offspring, projecting such fears as a juvenile delinquency epidemic. The outbreak of the Cold War exacerbated matters by creating yet another gulf between generations, in this case, the fear that young people might be subverted. By the mid-1950s, however, an equilibrium had been achieved, and the World War II generation began to see in its youth not those who might reject the system but those who affirmed and embodied it. Hence,

May points out, the almost mantra-like attribution of conventional ambitions—education, work, home, and family—attributed to the media stars of the period, most notably Annette Funicello, who made the transition from Mouseketeer to the star of a spate of post-*Gidget* beach movies set in Southern California. The entire myth and mise-en-scène of beach life, in short, whether the surf sounds of the Beach Boys and Jan and Dean, the film *Gidget,* or the other Southern California beach movies that followed—*Beach Party* (1963), *Bikini Beach* (1964), *Muscle Beach Party* (1964), *How to Stuff a Wild Bikini* (1965)—were not about rebellion but its exact opposite: the ultimate acceptance of conventional values by an entire generation. While Burt Lancaster and Deborah Kerr, embodying the World War II generation, might make adulterous love on the beach in *From Here to Eternity* (1953), ten years later Annette Funicello, Frankie Avalon, and the others had less rebellious pursuits in mind.

This tenuous détente was challenged, however, by the simultaneous rise of rock 'n' roll, starting in the mid-1950s. With its cross over origins in sexually sly African American race music, as white DJs called it, rock 'n' roll—as music and as lyrics—threatened to destabilize the message of innocence and social compatibility being assembled, in part, out of Southern California materials. Rock 'n' roll was black and poor Southern white, restless and subversive, and the older generation knew it and feared rock 'n' roll as a result. Clean-cut teenaged singers such as Pat Boone, Frankie Avalon, Ricky Nelson, and Fabian were promoted as acceptable alternatives, with Pat Boone making his film debut in the upbeat teenage comedy *Bernardine* (1957), older generation music provided by Johnny Mercer. Even rock 'n' roll's wildest wild man, Elvis Presley, was toned down and, significantly enough, brought to the beach in such seaside epics as *Blue Hawaii* (1961), *Fun in Acapulco* (1963), *Girl Happy* (1965), and *Paradise Hawaiian Style* (1966).

If there was one figure from young California in this era that most intrigued the media, it was the California Girl, in all her manifestations. Innumerable photographs in mass circulation magazines celebrated the California Girl as the embodiment of all that the state promised. First and most obviously, she appears on the beach in a bikini, fetching, athletic, bodacious. She personifies the bounteous physicality of the California myth, as in the case of Jocie Kilbrough, a recent graduate of Hollywood High and the heroine of Ira Wallach's comic novel *Muscle Beach* (1959), whom her admirer Carlo Cofield, a spindly egghead from the East, describes as having the most beautiful body in the world. "Southern California has the prettiest girls in the United States," photographer Russ Meyer, producer-director of *The Immoral Mr. Teas* (1959) and other nudie films, told *Esquire* in May 1963, "and I have to be where the source is."[9] Yet many of the sumptuous California Girls depicted in magazine layouts were college students, preparing for such conventional futures as teaching and marriage. "Education is the main reason for college," UCLA senior Carolyn Tindall told *Look* in September 1959. "But if you find someone you want to marry, it's even better." (Tindall planned to marry that June.) Stanford, Claudia Andreason told *Look* in the same article, represented "a steppingstone to anything you want to do, including marriage." Andreason wanted to teach music, marry, and have three or four children.[10]

This tendency to put marriage and child-raising at the center of the impending life cycle helps explain, in part, the lavish attention paid in yearbooks to junior and senior proms, with high schoolers dressed up in such an adult manner, as if they could barely await their future, together with the frequent inclusion of the baby pictures of graduates, suggesting their own generation and the generation that they in turn would soon be bringing into the world. How else to explain the almost ritualized protocols of going steady, the Couples category in so many yearbooks, celebrating the teenage Silents who had found each other at a young age and were recognized as such by the high school community, all this prefiguring the early marriages of an entire generation? Here was a generation nurtured on the myths and expectations of their suburbanizing parents, dreamily reinforced by the teenaged-boy-meets-teenaged-girl themes of 1950s and early 1960s music, which for all the assertive sexuality of the rock 'n' roll rebellion remained dominated by stories of teenagers falling in love and living happily ever after.

Behind the serene and joyous surfaces of the high school and college yearbooks of these years can be glimpsed, simultaneously, the ordinariness of everything, its celebration of orthodoxy and convention, as well as surfacing suggestions of impending conflicts. 1950s California, high school and college, seemed so overwhelmingly white, as if the world itself were only white, which throws into relief the young men and women of color one encounters in these yearbooks, especially in urban areas. African American and Asian students sport the same styles and emblems of convention as their white counterparts: the same clothes, the same hair styles for the girls, the same membership in teams and clubs, the same block sweaters and cheerleading regalia, the same posing in tuxedos and long dresses for junior and senior proms. Here was a generation, the Silent and minority, doing its best to fit into the dominant culture. The Japanese American students posing for their yearbook pictures had, one and all, spent part of their childhood behind barbed wire. African Americans and Mexican Americans, meanwhile, were beleaguered by a whole range of restrictions and discriminations, overt and covert, that would soon flare forth into open conflict.

Among whites there were also significant tensions. The key issue at the UCLA *Daily Bruin* by the mid-1950s, for example, was the battle between a self-perpetuating board of editors, anchored in the leftist muckraking era epitomized by the editorship of Clancy Sigal—in which a card-carrying Communist or two were on the staff—and student government, which by the mid-1950s was dominated by suburban types out of sympathy with the leftism of the *Daily Bruin* staff and had organized a take-over. Tension had been building for a number of years, pitting one kind of UCLA student—commuters to Westwood from the inner city, left-leaning Red Diaper babies, significantly Jewish—against a non-Jewish suburbanized Republican ascendancy. As early as 1948 a group of such students was openly calling the *Daily Bruin* the "People's Bruin" and were protesting its left-leaning editorials. Two years later, more than fifteen hundred UCLA students signed a petition to end the self-perpetuating editorial board of the campus newspaper. During the Korean War, the *Daily Bruin* further enraged the campus majority when it argued for the withdrawal of American troops and defended convicted spies Ethel and Julius Rosenberg. By 1956 the Student Council of the Associated Students of UCLA had gained control of the newspaper. Even so, undergraduates in this era—Fay Abrahams Stender and Mario Savio, a decade apart at UC Berkeley yet both Silents—would soon be playing crucial roles in conflicts to come.

14

Brubeck!

Jazz Goes to College

BY 1946 jazz was changing. Tensions that had remained suppressed during the war now surfaced in two developments, bebop and progressivism, which ended the emotional certainties of the big band era, the sheer sense of being part of something communal and big. Originating in Harlem in the late 1930s, bebop was a discordant, counter-establishment style whose wild flurries of dissonant notes expressed the musical worldview of African American musicians and a few white fellow travelers who for various reasons—civilian status, their sense of themselves as outsiders, their cultivation of rebellion in a variety of forms—had missed being part of the great big surge of unifying emotion that had helped sustain the American home front, even the war front. No one attended a bebop performance in order to dance. First and most obvious, bebop was not danceable. Bebop was abrupt music from a sax, aggressive, even angry. Bebop was melody turned inside out, dissected almost, its harmonics over-charged, its line and pattern fragmented. Second, bebop had a solitary, existential edge. Realized most powerfully in its solos, bebop was about being alone, very alone, and against the world. As brilliant as Dizzy Gillespie's band might be in musical terms, and as much as it might mean to a postwar generation of rebellious young people who dug Dizzy to the point of rolling their hat brims back like Dizzy did or wearing a version of Dizzy's black horn-rimmed glasses, African American or white, you could not dance to the discordant runs and inverted harmonies of bebop, no matter how encouraging the music might be to the libido. Bebop belonged to nightclubs, small and smoky, not to cavernous dance halls.

Black crossover music, meanwhile, which might have then inspired a new form of dancing as it would in the 1950s, was nipped in the bud, as Lionel Hampton found out in January 1946 when Decca refused to release his new album, tentatively entitled *Rock and Roll Rhythm*, on the basis that the music was too cacophonous, meaning, as Hampton himself would later remark, too black. From the Decca experience, Hampton learned that the time for crossover had not come. The armed forces, after all, had not yet been desegregated. And when the crossovering would begin, it would be whites crossing over into black music, not vice versa. "I stayed in the black groove," noted Hampton of 1946, 1947, and 1948. "You'd know my band was black just from listening to it."[1]

Progressive music, moreover, together with the music of what would soon be called Third Stream, blending American jazz and European classical, was equally non-danceable. Confronted with progressive bands, couples, black and white alike, tended to turn toward the musicians and listen rather than dance, and this tendency would soon help bring the big band era to conclusion. Progressivism was a form of rebellion, in this case rebellion on the part of a white avant-garde against the perceived banality of so much big band music and the firewall that seemed to exist between the popular and the highbrow. Progressivism and later developments in the Third Stream wanted jazz to move in the direction of the atonal and abstract and thus make available to the American big band the rebellious energies of concert music in the twentieth century.

Significantly enough, the years that would see the advent of progressivism in the big band, from 1946 onward, would also be a period of productive creativity on the part of French émigré composer Darius Milhaud, then teaching at Mills College in Oakland. Milhaud had devoted himself to bringing the sounds and idioms of jazz to the full orchestra and concert auditorium. Before his return to France in the fall of 1947, Milhaud composed and had performed a variety of compositions—symphonies; concertos for cellos, violin, and piano; a concerto for marimba; chamber music; orchestral suites; songs; a grand opera based on the life of Simón Bolívar—all fully expressive of Milhaud's belief that jazz was a high art form totally compatible with serious music. No one, however, attended a Darius Milhaud concert to dance, however jazzy his rhythms and syncopations. Whether classical music was appropriating jazz, or jazz was appropriating classical music, the end result was an increasingly unbusy dance floor.

This empty dance floor was creating problems in 1946 for two brilliant California-based big band leaders, Artie Shaw and Stan Kenton. Based by 1946 in Los Angeles (Kenton) and Beverly Hills (Shaw) when not on the road (which seemed almost always), each of these Southern Californians was a genius in his field. While Shaw and Kenton might have their differences—Shaw the brilliant clarinetist, Kenton the competent pianist; Kenton agonizing over the breakup of his first marriage in 1946, Shaw breezing through the first four of his seven marriages by 1947 (Elizabeth Kern, daughter of Jerome Kern, followed by actress Lana Turner, followed by actress Ava Gardner, followed by novelist Kathleen Winsor)—these differences could not conceal their common interest in pushing the envelope of the American popular music they each had mastered.

Even before the war, both Shaw and Kenton had been toying with the idea of bringing an intensified element of musical intellectualism to the big band sound. In 1937 Kenton took a full year off from touring and Hollywood studio jobs to study musical theory. Shaw, for his part, was so ambivalent about the big band scene that he spent the entire year of 1935 in Bucks County, Pennsylvania, trying to write a novel. By 1936 Shaw had already disbanded one band and formed another as an expression of his dissatisfaction. In 1939 Shaw entered the belly of the beast, at least as far as big band music and dancing were concerned, with his famous denunciation of jitterbug. When Shaw reassembled his band, it was as a twenty-three-piece orchestra that—astonishing for a dance band in this era—included violins, violas, and cellos. One of his offerings, "Concerto for Clarinet," featured in the Paramount film *Second Chorus* (1940), clearly pointed in the direction of a Third Stream amalgam of popular and classical music. Kenton, whose all-time personal hero was George Gershwin, was making his band so big, so blaring, so intricate that it bombed completely at the Roseland Ballroom in New York in early 1942. Far from being intimidated, the very next year, Kenton recorded for Columbia Records what almost instantly became his signature piece, "Artistry in Rhythm," based on a theme from Ravel's *Daphnis et Chloé.*

During the war Shaw and Kenton each had prominent and socially representative battlefield and home front gigs. Enlisting in the Navy in 1942, Shaw spent two years in the South Pacific as leader of the Rangers, a Navy band that played for Marines under fire in such forward battle zones as Guadalcanal, where Shaw and his men came under Japanese attack. By October 1943 Shaw, by then a decorated chief petty officer, was diagnosed, along with a number of his musicians, as suffering from combat fatigue after nearly a year and a half on the front lines.

Stan Kenton, meanwhile, was holding down an equally representative gig as the featured orchestra on *The Bob Hope Show,* broadcast nationally and heard overseas on the Armed Forces Radio Network, a platform that allowed Kenton and his orchestra to be heard by millions of listeners. Hope thought that the Stan Kenton band played too loudly, too intricately, and negotiated a solution whereby Kenton could play it Kenton's way during the audience warm-up but Hope's way—which is to say, more smoothly, more danceably—during the actual broadcast. The Kenton Orchestra also accompanied Hope, comedian Jerry Colonna, and singer Frances Langford on domestic tours and did stints at the Hollywood Canteen in Los Angeles, where soldiers, sailors, and Marines were entertained.

The end of the war left both Shaw and Kenton depressed and under psychiatric care. Kenton was talking about quitting music altogether, going to medical school, and training as a psychiatrist. By then, having played through the second half of 1945 at the Paramount Theater in New York from increasingly intricate charts, he had brought his Artistry in Rhythm Orchestra to Carnegie Hall itself, a decidedly non-dance venue. Despite the critical success of this Carnegie Hall concert, Kenton and his musicians had to make a living, and so the year 1946 found the Stan Kenton Artistry in Rhythm Orchestra back on the road, playing forty-eight of the forty-eight states, most of them in one- or two-night stands, almost exclusively in dance halls or similar venues. Yet despite these dance-oriented gigs, so dependent upon an easily accessible melody and beat, Kenton continued to employ the increasingly intricate arrangements of Pete Rugolo and went so far as to cart around a set of oversized symphonic kettledrums for the use of Shelly Manne in an effort to intensify concert effects. On that tour, the Kenton Orchestra gave concerts at the San Francisco Opera House and the Hollywood Bowl, where some 17,500 people roared their approval of Kenton's "Concerto to End All Concertos" — but did not dance. Two years later, Kenton reorganized his musicians into a forty-piece minia-ture symphony orchestra featuring a sixteen-piece string section. With the help of such talented musicians as Bud Shank on flute and saxophone, Art Pepper on alto sax, and trumpeters Shorty Rogers, Chico Alvarez, Buddy Childers, and Maynard Ferguson, Kenton took his militantly dissonant sound on a full-scale frontal attack, playing such works as composer Bob Graettinger's ultra-modern *City of Glass* suite, in four nerve-racking parts.

Like Kenton, Artie Shaw was doing his best to remain simultaneously employed and progressive. Reestablishing his band in late October 1944 after his release from the Navy, Shaw went back on tour, playing standards on a circuit that included Minneapolis, Chicago, Akron, Columbus, Cleveland, and, finally, New York City. By April 1945 Shaw was in California, playing the Golden Gate Theater in San Francisco, followed by engagements in Oakland and the Dorsey Brothers' Casino Gardens Ballroom on the Santa Monica Pier. With both his full band and the Gra-mercy Five combo, meanwhile, Shaw was recording standards for Victor. In one sense, it was like old times. And yet Shaw himself later confessed to feeling a sense of malaise during this period, of trying to put himself back together again, of look-ing for new ways to do music. On 18 November 1945, after just a year back in the big band business, Shaw once again disbanded his group. RCA took revenge by not releasing many of the cuts Shaw had recorded until well into the LP era.

Throughout 1946 Shaw struggled to regain the old magic with yet another group, this time a pickup combo of studio musicians. In a series of recordings for Musicraft Records in Hollywood, Shaw sought to blend jazz and pop with four-part arrange-ments of brass, reeds, strings, and the voices of, among others, Kitty Kallen, and Mel Tormé and the Mel-Tones. From this period came the classic four-disc 78 rpm album *Artie Shaw Plays Cole Porter*, issued by Musicraft in the summer of 1946 and featured in the sound track of the 1946 Cole Porter biopic *Night and Day*. The 1946 Musicraft recordings turned out to be for Shaw a farewell to music itself on the part of a restless musician who had peaked in one musical idiom but was uncertain of another. True, Shaw returned to big band music in 1949 with an eighteen-piece group, telling *Down Beat* on 23 September 1949 that this time he would play only the music the dancers wanted during his forthcoming tour. When Shaw began his tour in Boston, however, he began it almost defiantly with a performance of Ravel's *Pièce en Forme de Habanera* (1907–8). *Time* reported on 26 September 1949 that while "a few horn-rimmed jazz intellectuals" appreciated the Ravel, the rest of the crowd was hostile, including one thwarted dancer who yelled, "Artie, you stink!"

By 1954 the big band era was over, and only the older generation seemed to care. Teenagers were on the verge of discovering a new kind of danceable music, rock 'n' roll and its variations; and the older crowd—college kids, young professionals, a developing intelligentsia—were discovering the pleasures of a plenteously emergent form, modern jazz, that had rapidly become 1950s mainstream. With his black horn-rimmed glasses, hip haircut, dark shirt, and madras tie, the Bay Area–based jazzman Dave Brubeck epitomized the postwar GI Bill generation, the essence of 1950s cool. People listened to the music of the Dave Brubeck Quartet. No one danced. And they theorized, the intelligentsia especially. And in so doing, they felt connected to something big, deep, and important: something reverberating with the achievement and promise of the postwar era. They were making the scene, defining themselves through jazz.

How did this happen? How did dancers become listeners? And how did the listeners, the jazz aficionados, liberate themselves from a restrictive venue of smoky gin joints and become a mass audience? Part of the answer was technical: the high-fidelity phonograph, for one thing, and the vinyl 33 rpm long-play record, the LP, each being introduced to American consumers by the early 1950s. Some two dozen record companies, *Time* reported, were making money as of late 1954 off jazz recordings, and not just jazz specialists such as the Berkeley-based Fantasy, with its brightly colored LPs, but such mainstream, even highbrow, labels as Victor, Westminster, Vanguard, and Columbia, for whom Brubeck was now recording. The first release of the Dave Brubeck Quartet for Columbia, *Jazz Goes to College* (1954), topped the charts. Hi-fi and LP technology, however, were common to the record industry as a whole and were helping to create a mass audience for classical, pop, folk, Broadway, even stand-up comedy. Hi-fi LPs were primarily the medium and only part of the message: the part that reinforced the notion of the home as an entertainment center and privacy as an increasingly appreciated value. What message were the Dave Brubeck Quartet and all the other notable jazz groups communicating in their various orientations and styles? Where had they come from and how had they been formed, these messages regarding tradition and modernism, heat and coolness, art and life, the conduct of life, black and white, East and West, New York and California?

Jazz, first of all, arose on the West Coast, most powerfully out of Los Angeles; and it was black, very black, even before the in-migration of thousands of African American defense workers during the war. Centered along Central Avenue between Vernon and Forty-second Street north to south from the downtown and coming to maturity in the late 1930s and early 1940s, the jazz culture of Los Angeles had its gurus (jazz instructor Sam Browne, for example, who taught a generation of musicians passing through Jefferson High School), its impresarios and taste-makers (Big John Dolphin, from whose record store on Central disc jockeys would broadcast behind the front window), its jazz-friendly radio stations, especially KHJ, even its own record label (Dial, in Hollywood). Into and through this culture, a generation of jazz greats, either L.A. born and bred or coming of age in the city—Eric Dolphy, Charlie Mingus, Hampton Hawes, Art Farmer, Dexter Gordon, Wardell Gray,

Buddy Collette, Chico Hamilton, to name a few—acquired their chops, played their first gigs, jump-started their careers in the jazz-soaked streets of South Central. Although Dexter Gordon and Wardell Gray played out their recently recorded tenor sax duel "The Hunt" and "The Chase" at the local Elks Club on 6 July 1947, most gigs had the benefit of one or another of the jazz joints—bars mainly, but a restaurant or two, and a number of after-hour breakfast clubs—centered on Central. The Downbeat, the Memo, Lovejoy's, the Last Word, the Turban Lounge, the Ritz, the Haig on Wilshire, just down from the Brown Derby (where in the spring of 1952 the Gerry Mulligan Quartet would record its classic version of "My Funny Valentine," with Chet Baker on trumpet), the Surf, the Jungle Room, the Capri on La Cienega, Trouville on Beverly at Fairfax, the Swing and Cotton clubs in Hollywood: only the most exacting local historian is capable of chronicling the appearances and disappearances of these venues. Among the better known were the Chicken Shack at Vernon and Central and the Bird in the Basket at 1356 North Vine in Hollywood, where late-night revelers could enjoy Southern fried chicken as well as jazz, and the Club Alabam—a majestic room, saxophonist Art Pepper later remembered, with a sweeping bandstand and fancy curtains and waitresses in abbreviated costumes— next to the equally ambitious Dunbar Hotel, catering to the local black elite and such visiting celebrities as Lionel Hampton and Duke Ellington.

It was a black scene, but not exclusively so, jazz being one of the few ways in these discriminatory and segregated decades through which blacks and whites could make meaningful contact with each other. The most important impresario of the mid-1940s, Billy Berg, was Jewish and insisted that his venue remain integrated, which meant that such celebrities as Lana Turner, Ava Gardner, John Barrymore, Orson Welles, and John Steinbeck felt comfortable dropping in. Jazz, in fact, was offering to those who cared about such things a momentary reconciliation between black and white and would continue to do so through the 1950s, although it would be a mistake in Jim Crow Los Angeles to push the extent of this reconciliation too far. At the same time, however, Nat King Cole met with fierce resistance when he tried to buy a home in Hancock Park. Eric Dolphy resigned his scholarship at USC because he felt discriminated against. The LAPD continued to stop cars containing interracial couples, and Billy Eckstine was pulled over when the police noticed that he was driving a shiny new Cadillac with New York license plates.

Still, jazz did continue to nurture an inter-racial dialogue, however tenuous. Semanticist S. I. Hayakawa—then at the University of Chicago, soon to be on the faculty at San Francisco State, and himself an accomplished jazz pianist—worked up a series of academic lectures, broadcast on, among other venues, the pioneering Chicago FM station WFMT in the spring of 1954, tracing the beginnings of jazz in the slavery era in the borderlands, as Hayakawa put it, between the field and the plantation house. Had black people remained only in the fields, Hayakawa argued, their music would have remained folkloric. Had they assimilated fully to the mansion, however, which is to say, to white culture, they might have lost their musical heritage in a generation or two. As it was, jazz developed from an interaction, a tension, between African memory and a mastery of white music. Memoirs by black musicians frequently contain vignettes in which white colleagues helped black artists get gigs, such as drummer Shelly Manne's helping pianist Hampton Hawes, recently released from the Army, get a recording contract with Contemporary Records, including a $300 payment for back union dues. In 1960 Dave Brubeck threatened to cancel some $60,000 worth of college circuit contracts when officials at two Southern institutions objected to the onstage presence of his black bassist, Eugene Wright. Brubeck stared, and the college officials, including at least one Southern governor, blinked, and the tour went on as scheduled.

Still, there was tension; and it often went the other way, from black to white. Wright himself came under fire from some black musicians for joining the otherwise all-white Brubeck Quartet; and the oft-repeated observation, first made by Miles Davis, that the Brubeck Quartet could not swing encoded a race-related argument. From the beginning, which is to say, as early as New Orleans in the pre–World War I era, black musicians were fearing that white America would rip off their music. By the 1930s, *Village Voice* jazz critic Nat Hentoff reports, that fear had become a reality as the big bands of Benny Goodman, Tommy and Jimmy Dorsey, and Artie Shaw outgrossed the technically more proficient bands of Duke Ellington, Count Basie, Jimmie Lunceford, and Cab Calloway. Even worse, whites were wont to heckle these black bands when on tour and deny them hotel and restaurant accommodations. Even ordering take-out sandwiches from a deli could prove a hassle, as the Duke Ellington band discovered to its dismay during a 1944 appearance in St. Louis. White theater owners and booking agents expressed fears that unless the lights were perfectly adjusted the light-skinned Billie Holiday might be taken for white when she played the Fox Theater in Detroit with Count Basie. On the other hand, traveling with the white Artie Shaw band (the first black singer to do so), Holiday was banned from the stage when Shaw broadcast live coast-to-coast from the Lincoln Hotel in New York.

In December 1945 Billy Berg booked Dizzy Gillespie and Charlie (Yardbird) Parker into his one-story stucco club on North Vine, an event that jazz historian Ted Gioia has described as the "D-day landing of bebop on the Pacific seaboard."[2] Unlike D-day, however, Parker's Southern California landing—with the exception of the brilliant eight-week stint at Berg's and three successful recording sessions for Dial—was a disaster subsequently interpreted by East Coast jazz critics and historians, with some exaggeration, as proof positive of the chasm existing between authentic jazz, meaning New York bebop, and the less than informed preferences of California. Defenders of the coast, on the other hand, are wont to argue that Parker was appreciated in Southern California, even revered; but his life was already a train wreck, and Southern California cannot be blamed for what the demons of genius, the wounds of race, and assorted pathologies, expressed and fueled by gargantuan ingestions of heroin, morphine, whiskey, and (in truly terrible times) California port wine at a dollar a gallon, were doing to the Bird's ability to stay alive, much less show up to his gigs and display his genius. Bird Parker's California sojourn functions as an overture in reverse to the emergence of West Coast jazz as epitomized in the Dave Brubeck Quartet. In every way possible, no two people could be more unlike than Parker and Brubeck, nor could any other two iconic figures better exemplify the genius, limitations, and vulnerabilities of bebop on one coast, cool jazz on the other, and listening America in between.

Even before Bird, age twenty-five, arrived in Los Angeles, there were signs of trouble. Roused from a drug-induced sleep, he left his train during a stop in Arizona and wandered out into the desert, valise and instrument case in hand, looking for a fix. Pulled back to the train by a fellow musician, Parker spent the rest of the trip strapped into his bunk. Once in L.A., Parker scored a semi-fix (a prescription for a three-day supply of morphine) from a general practitioner in the Wilshire district whom Bird lied to regarding painful kidney stones while dropping a twenty on the desk. On opening night at Berg's, Parker was two sets late, as, high on morphine, he downed two complete Mexican dinners (Conquistadors, Berg called this specialty of the house) in a back room. No matter: Once ready, Parker passed through the crowd en route to the stage, improvising on "Cherokee"; and the people there that night, hearing Bird's intricate chord progressions, later compared themselves to those lucky enough in 1913 to be in the audience at the premiere of Stravinsky's *Rite of Spring*; for these sounds—these chords, these progressions, this interplay of Parker and Gillespie—represented a whole new way of making American music: broadcast live that night on Armed Forces Radio, as if to announce to a war-weary generation that new times, better times, were coming.

Bird played Berg's, and it would have been enough; and the Armed Forces Radio show was taking Gillespie's and Bird's music to a brand-new (and significantly white) audience. L.A. impresario Norman Granz, meanwhile, was arranging for two sell-out concerts at the Philharmonic Auditorium in January 1945: two nights of twenty-eight hundred seats filled with ticket-buying Los Angelenos willing to hear the latest in jazz musicianship from Parker, Gillespie, trumpeter Al Killian, Willie Smith on the alto sax, and Charlie Ventura and the great Lester Young on tenor. On night two, in one of those serial duels favored by bebop musicians, Lester Young took down Charlie Ventura, then Bird took down Young with a solo on "Lady Be Good" that left no doubt who was the champ.

Had Charlie Parker boarded the United airliner for New York that February with the rest of the Parker/Gillespie All-Stars, he would have left behind, all things considered, a happy story. But Parker had found a dealer by the name of Emry Byrd, better known as Moose the Mooche, a onetime Jefferson High track star and honor student, felled by poliomyelitis, surviving on crutches as the proprietor of a shoeshine stand on Central Avenue from which he dealt heroin and cannabis. Booze slackened and coarsened Bird's playing, but heroin seemed, at least for the moment, to sharpen his senses, or at least to mask his high, although Bird would soon develop an odd set of mannerisms—a sudden flinging of his arms into space, among other gestures—that signaled his condition. In any event, Bird Parker became a full-fledged heroin addict: which was why he sold his United Airlines ticket for one hundred dollars, skipped the flight back to New York, and stayed on in L.A. Even with this, it might have worked out, or at the least redounded to the credit of L.A. in the jazz world. Parker got a gig at the Finale, at 115 South San Pedro Street in Little Tokyo, whose original owners and inhabitants were still in the interment camps.

The Finale was a membership club. You brought your own booze in a brown paper bag, paid a membership fee of $2 at the door, and were provided with glasses, ice, mixers, and, as it turned out, some of the best jazz (Stan Getz, Zoot Sims, Miles Davis, Gerry Mulligan, Hampton Hawes, Shorty Rogers, Charlie Ventura, among others) in the country in the spring of 1946 outside of New York. Even better, Los Angeles attorney Marvin Freeman and Hollywood music store owner Ross Russell (the Tempo Music Shop at on Hollywood Boulevard) joined up to form Dial Records and with a cash advance of $100 from the Tempo Shop cash register signed Bird to a handwritten contract, subsequently formalized, although Freeman and Russell were astonished to learn that Bird had already assigned half of his royalties to his dope dealer Emry Byrd, then serving time in San Quentin. In the last week of March 1946, on a gray, wet Thursday afternoon, Charlie Parker, alto sax, Miles Davis, trumpet, Lucky Thompson, tenor sax, Dodo Marmarosa, piano, Arv Garrison, guitar, Vic McMillan, bass, and Roy Porter, drums, assembled at the Radio Recorders studio on Santa Monica Boulevard in Hollywood (after one brief rehearsal the previous evening) and across the next seven hours of takes and retakes, with an all-business Parker pacing the proceedings, recorded a series of master cuts—Parker's "Moose the Mooche," a tribute to his dealer, the "Yardbird Suite," "Ornithology," and "A Night in Tunisia"—that have remained standards for more than sixty years.

Unfortunately, Parker never managed to return to Dial his signed lead sheets for copyright, and so neither he nor Dial could capitalize on their success beyond the first records sold. By that time, despite the positive outcome of the session, Parker was descending further into addiction, vagrancy, and malnutrition. With his dealer out of circulation, Parker returned to gallon jugs of port wine and, after a period of disappearance, was found living in a garage in South Central. Rescued by friends, Bird tried to recover but was in such bad shape he flubbed a second Dial session, despite the restorative assistance of six tablets of phenobarbital.

Matters soon came to a head at the Civic Hotel near the Finale Club where Charlie was staying. One terrible night he appeared twice in the lobby stark naked, asking the manager for change to use the pay phone. Later that night, returned forcibly to his room, he set his mattress afire when he fell asleep smoking. The fire department came, followed by the cops, and when Bird offered the cops attitude they blackjacked him unconscious, wrapped him in a blanket, and hustled him off to the psychopathic ward of the county jail, which was where, ten days later, Dial co-owner Ross Russell and another friend, Howard McGhee, who had previously rescued Bird from the McKinley Avenue garage, found the most talented jazz musician of his or any other era, lying on an iron cot in a small cell, wearing prison pajamas and a straightjacket. It took all of Dial co-owner Marvin Freeman's legal skills and behind-the-scenes juice to have criminal charges (indecent exposure, resisting arrest, suspected arson) dropped, and his case referred to the chambers of Superior court judge Stanley Mosk, a liberal known for his broader sympathies, who diverted Parker to the Camarillo State Hospital for a minimum of six months.

A cluster of Mission Revival buildings north of Los Angeles, Camarillo was considered the country club of such facilities, and Parker, off drugs and booze, soon seemed a new man, working in the hospital's vegetable garden, laying bricks (even talking about leaving music for masonry), playing a C-melody saxophone in the hospital band. A girlfriend, Doris Sydnor, moved to California from New York, got a room and a waitress job nearby, gathered Bird's scattered personal effects together, and, when she could, made visits. Released after six months to the custody of Russell, Parker had two final recording sessions at Dial: one great ("Bird's Nest," "Cool Blues"); one starting bad, with Howard McGhee finding Charlie asleep, fully clothed, in a bathtub that morning and bringing him to the studio badly hung-over, but the Bird pulled himself together to record with McGhee on trumpet, Wardell Gray on tenor, Dodo Marmarosa on piano, Barney Kessel on guitar, Red Callender on bass, and Don Lamond on drums his own "Relaxin' at Camarillo" and three originals by McGhee ("Cheers," "Stupendous," and "Carvin' the Bird") that over the decades have kept their high place in the Parker canon. A few days later, Charlie (Yardbird) Parker and Doris Sydnor caught—just barely, with two or three minutes to spare—that United airliner to New York Parker had deliberately missed seventeen months earlier.

Because Parker had crashed so severely in Los Angeles—drugs, booze, a nervous breakdown, six months of incarceration—California got blamed. Over time, the appreciative audiences that had greeted Parker at Berg's and the Finale were minimized, as was the faith shown in him by Dial Records and the talented local musicians willing to jam or to record. As late as 1988, Clint Eastwood's film *Bird* was advancing this argument: that Southern California just could not dig the Bird. He was too big, too hot, too good, too bebop—dare one say too black?—for the superficial certainties of the Coast. So went the argument, and it held.

Like many such stereotypes, this scenario held some truth. The Los Angeles of the 1940s was a Jim Crow town, and Parker recognized this through whatever haze of drugs or booze hung between him and reality. He and the music he played were black, having arisen out of Harlem, where black America enjoyed a community, however embattled, and a sense of common culture. In the phraseology of W.E.B. Du Bois, bebop came from the depths, from the souls, of the Black Folks, and while white intellectuals such as Norman Mailer might understand, might dig it, might even daydream—as Mailer put it in his seminal essay "The White Negro," published in *Dissent* in the spring of 1957—of transitioning themselves to the hipness, the alienation, the existential panache, of black culture, such was not the expectation, over time, of white mid-America, however much it might appreciate jazz. Bird Parker's music encoded too much pain, too much defiance, for full white consumption; or, from a slightly different perspective, only the most alienated of self-styled white elites—the intellectuals of Greenwich Village, the Beats of North Beach San

Francisco—would dare think of trying to cross over, body and soul, to a black republic called bebop.

Look at the Bird himself. Was he merely a drunk and a druggie who happened to
be a genius, or were the drugs, the booze, the descents into squalor, the price Bird
had to pay for his blackness as well as for his talent? Was the disorderly and short (he
died in 1955 at age thirty-four) life of the Bird prophetic evidence—like the contemporary career of dramatist Jean Genet in France—that the agonies and hypocrisies
of modern times were too much to bear for artists of a certain sort, who must per-
force go underground into drugs, booze, and sociopathies of many sorts (to include,
in Genet's case, the life of a career criminal) and thereby become heroes not only
to their peer group but to bourgeois intellectuals ambivalent to their culture, hence
enjoying vicariously the bolder defiances of the underground?

Which brings up the issue of drugs. An entire generation of jazz greats was marching alongside Parker—even following him—into addiction. "To play like Bird, you
have to do like Bird!" became for their rallying cry.[3] The question itself might be
asked: Was jazz itself an especially vulnerable occupation in terms of addiction
since jazz had arisen in significant measure out of repression and discrimination? If
so, were these dynamics even more operative in the wartime and postwar 1940s, with
the psychological scarring of segregation continuing through the suburbanizing era
and an even more powerful drug, heroin, becoming increasingly available by the
1940s and better able to be managed on the bandstand than booze or marijuana?

By 1950 *Down Beat*, the *Variety* of jazz, was expressing alarm at the inroads drugs
were making, a theme explored by the film *The Man with the Golden Arm* (1955).
Village Voice jazz critic Nat Hentoff—against the advice of many, who said that it
would damage the cause—was by 1957 arranging a public symposium at the Newport
Jazz Festival to address the problem. Past, present, and future, there was much to talk
about, as so many jazz musicians were experiencing a drug culture that would soon
be spreading to a wider constituency. On the Coast, such brilliant black musicians
as Dexter Gordon, Frank Morgan, Wardell Gray, Hampton Hawes, and Miles Davis
had already become addicted to heroin, Morgan at the age of seventeen. Heroin
had ended Gray's career by 1954, and in May 1955, at age twenty-five, he died in Las
Vegas, most likely from an overdose. Davis got busted in L.A. in 1950, won acquittal
in January 1951, but remained a user for the rest of his career. Dexter Gordon was not
so lucky. Busted for heroin in late 1952, Gordon spent two years in the state prison
at Chino. He would later do time in federal prison in Texas and Kentucky, followed
back home in California by a stint at Folsom. Howard McGhee, who rescued Bird
Parker, most likely saving his life, from the unheated garage on McKinley Avenue,
developed a $500 a week habit, which eventually landed him behind bars at Rikers
Island. Hampton Hawes started using heroin some time in late 1948 or early 1949
and by the spring of 1950 had a serious habit. Busted for dealing in November 1958,
Hawes was sentenced to ten years in the penitentiary at Fort Worth, Texas, where
he served half his sentence before being granted clemency by President Kennedy
in August 1963. These and so many other brilliant black musicians had more than

their fair share of white counterparts. Even Paul Desmond of the Dave Brubeck Quartet, the ultimate Mr. Cool, developed a Benzedrine habit when he was playing at the San Francisco Presidio during the war that almost cost him his teeth. Some white musician users—Gerry Mulligan, for example, who spent six months in the Los Angeles sheriff's honor farm in 1953—managed to recover. In the case of two West Coast jazzmen, however, Chet Baker and Art Pepper, heroin—more than their talent—became the determining force in their lives.

Born in Oklahoma, brought to California in 1940 as a boy, and raised in Glendale and Hermosa Beach, Baker started out as the Jimmy Dean of West Coast jazz: a handsome and talented trumpeter and singer who, like Dean, conveyed a certain mystique—hip, explosive yet contained—just by being there. Heroin, however, and an addict's life—an $800 to $1,000 a week habit, arrest after arrest in Europe and the United States, expulsions from West Germany and Italy, a beating outside the Trident Club in Sausalito in 1968, most likely connected to a drug deal gone bad, in which his assailants deliberately tried to knock out his teeth to impair his playing— soon cost Baker the career he might have had; and in May 1988, his once handsome face reduced to a Kabuki mask of dissipation, Baker fell mysteriously to his death in Amsterdam, a victim of either murder or suicide. The Jean Genet of West Coast jazz, at once a genius and a career criminal, Art Pepper followed heroin into a lifetime of sociopathic behavior and dealings in the drug underworld leading to four imprisonments, the last of which—a sentence of two to twenty years handed down in October 1960—could have kept him in San Quentin into old age, had not drummer Shelly Manne vouched for Pepper's parole in 1964 with a gig at the Manne Hole nightclub he had recently opened in L.A. In the joint or out, however, Pepper sustained the stance and attitudes of a con—withdrawn, narcissistic, sociopathic— for most of his adult life. Pepper's autobiography *Straight Life* (1979) constitutes a no-holds-barred odyssey through the jazz, junk, and underworld life, unembarrassed and unapologetic, hence possessed of a disquieting integrity and power.

Heroin and all the damage it could cause was very much on Nat Hentoff's mind through the 1950s, and in a chapter entitled "Junk" in *The Jazz Life* (1961), he surveyed the growing body of medical and scientific literature on the subject. From these sources, Hentoff distilled an argument. Drugs and booze, went his scenario, had always been part of the jazz life, due to the very nature of jazz itself. Jazz had arisen in the bars and clubs of New Orleans, driven by the sale of booze. As jazz moved north and went partly white, booze gave way to marijuana, which is where it settled until the postwar era, when a more intricate jazz demanded a more intricate drug, heroin. Hentoff, however, had serious issues with this scenario, which made booze and drugs a fixed necessity for the rigors of jazz improvisation. Such a scenario made drugs a co-equal in jazz performance, which, Hentoff argued, was clearly not the case.

When it came to the social aspects of such an argument as opposed to the musical, Hentoff was more accepting. Jazz was by definition on the margins, went this scenario, and jazz musicians knew it. Hence they were tempted to see themselves, simultaneously, as rejected by the mainstream but above it as well. Drug usage, heroin especially, reverberated with the false but seductive siren call of easing the pain of marginalization by transforming it into the avant-garde. Drug usage defied the squares. The fact that jazz attracted—perhaps even required—so many musicians who were adolescent, even infantile, in personality structure compounded the problem. Such personalities were by definition fragmented, dependent, hence liable to addiction. One could play well yet remain a child or adolescent into adult life, hence disposed toward a security blanket called H, heroin, horse. According to a survey made in the late 1940s, Hentoff pointed out, fifty-three percent of the 357 musicians surveyed admitted to trying heroin at least once. Sixteen percent of them had become regular users.

Dave Brubeck did not do drugs, nor was he a boozer. He was, rather, a religiously oriented family man who would eventually convert to Roman Catholicism and devote himself late in life to the composition of sacred music. Raised on cattle ranches in Contra Costa and Amador counties, Brubeck was taught to play the piano at the age of four by his mother, a pianist who had studied in England under Dame Myra Hess before giving up thoughts of the concert stage. Brubeck's two older brothers, Howard and Henry, became composers and music educators. In September 1942 Brubeck married writer and radio actress Iola Whitlock, whom he had met as an undergraduate at the College of the Pacific (COP) in Stockton, where Brubeck had initially enrolled as a pre-veterinary student before switching to music. The couple would stay together across a lifetime, with Iola raising their six children, keeping the books, and generally managing things for the Dave Brubeck Quartet.

Graduating from COP in 1942, Brubeck spent four years in the Army, two years stateside and two years in Europe. Originally assigned to band duty, Brubeck was shipped to Europe in the summer of 1944 as a rifleman (a copy of Paul Henry Lang's *Music in Western Civilization* and one of Oswald Spengler's *Decline of the West* were part of his five-pound allotment), headed for the Battle of the Bulge until the commanding officer of the replacement center at Metz, a music-loving West Point regular, had him pulled for duty—a PFC in a warrant officer's slot—as leader of a hastily organized (and unauthorized) twenty-eight-piece band called the Wolf Pack, comprised in part of soldiers wounded in action and, Brubeck later believed, the first racially integrated unit in the Army. Touring the front, Brubeck and his men came close to the Battle of the Bulge and were twice lost behind enemy lines, but the Wolf Pack survived the war, in one instance because a friendly officer sent them to the rear, out of harm's way, on the eve of a major German attack. Offered a bandleader's warrant, Brubeck chose to remain a PFC so as to rotate as soon as possible back to the States when the war was over.

Fall 1946 found Brubeck at Mills College in Oakland, studying theory and composition with Darius Milhaud, the modernist French Jewish émigré composer who had long since been incorporating jazz motifs into his work. Brubeck had studied briefly with Milhaud before going into the Army and while on active duty in

Southern California had two lessons from Arnold Schoenberg, then teaching at UCLA. However brief, these sessions indicated Brubeck's desire to connect with High Modernism in theory and practice, despite the fact that Brubeck had the effrontery to argue back when Schoenberg demanded that he be able to account for every note—every note!—in a composition, something near impossible to such an inveterate improviser and noodler on the keyboard. The second session ended with Schoenberg shouting and Brubeck, by mutual agreement, ending his studies with the modernist master.

Such a connection with modernism—as a matter, primarily, of intuition and ear but with some grasp as well of theory and the canon—pursued by Brubeck and others in the postwar period helped jazz cool down from the heat of the bebop era as represented by Bird Parker in New York and Howard McGhee in L.A. By the early 1950s, bebop was beginning to dry up along Central Avenue, having peaked, perhaps, on 12 June 1947 in the MacGregor Studio on Western Avenue in Holly-wood in the recorded bebop duel between tenor saxophonists Dexter Gordon and Wardell Gray, challenging each other in increasingly shorter solos (32-bar, 16-bar, 8-bar, 4-bar), a session released by Dial Records as *The Hunt* and *The Chase* in several 78 rpm discs. Beat novelist John Clellon Holmes considered these record-ings the national anthem of the Beat movement. Jack Kerouac agreed, placing this heated music at the center of *On the Road* (1957). Brubeck and his generation—Gerry Mulligan, Ornette Coleman, Eric Dolphy, Jimmy Giuffre, Charlie Mingus, and the others on the Coast or in the East—wanted to absorb the best of bebop and go on to the future. As was the case with so many other developments in the 1950s, modernism had a monopoly on cultural traffic in that direction.

As Dave Brubeck would always believe, Stan Kenton had led the way. As a nine-teen-year-old college student with his own band, Brubeck had closely followed the radio broadcasts of the Kenton Orchestra from the Rendezvous Ballroom in Balboa. Passing through Los Angeles in 1943, Private Brubeck made a cold call on Kenton at his home, asking him to look over "Prayer of the Conquered," a jazz arrangement inspired by the war. Reviewing the manuscript that night in his studio dressing room after the Bob Hope show, Kenton was encouraging but non-committal. Back in civilian life after the war, Brubeck called on Kenton once again, this time to inquire about a piano slot in Kenton's orchestra, but Kenton already had a pianist, Pete Rugolo, another Bay Area musician, born in Italy, raised in Santa Rosa, also a former student of Milhaud at Mills.

Following his release from the service, Dave Brubeck returned to Mills on the GI Bill to resume his studies with Milhaud. It would be an exaggeration, however, to present Brubeck as a theorist or to suggest that what he learned from Milhaud was primarily theoretical. Brubeck appreciated history and theory and would in 1949 teach a highly successful jazz history and theory course at the UC Extension in San Francisco, preparing lectures that were later published in *Down Beat*. Brubeck's approach to music and to Milhaud was that of a working musician. What, in short, could be played? How did history and theory translate into improvised music? This is not to deny that Brubeck was, as the 1950s put it, an egghead when it came to music; indeed, his prominent signature black horn-rimmed glasses alone declared an iconic eggheadedness to college audiences. College, in fact, was a favored Brubeck venue and métier, not just in terms of the college audience he would cultivate but the college-educated musicians he recruited. From his mother and from his studies at COP, Brubeck had absorbed a respect for, and some knowledge of, the classical canon. Yet the heavy lenses of his glasses also told another story. Born with a severely crossed eye that required infant glasses to correct, Brubeck suffered from dyslexia, although the term was not in use at the time and, indeed, was never referred to by Brubeck in later years as anything more than "my problem."[4] Yet this problem severely curtailed Brubeck's ability to read music and almost cost him his degree from COP. It also underscores the significance of Brubeck's debate with Arnold Schoenberg during the war when Schoenberg insisted that a composer must keep track of every note and know what it was doing in every bar. By talent and by disability, Brubeck was an improviser, a spontaneous composer, not a tracker of notes.

And yet jazz, Brubeck knew from the beginning (and would later theorize concerning), was not a matter of pure improvisation. Jazz—or at least the jazz he cared to practice—proceeded on three levels. First, there was "the subconscious, almost effortless flow of new material from the creator," which is to say, the performing musician. "The performer at this level," Brubeck believed, "has neither desire nor need for a preconceived pattern because he knows that the music comes from a source of infinite imagination and limitless variety." At a second and lower level was the encounter of the performing musician with the canon, with other music, either his own or someone else's: "quotes," Brubeck describes them, employing a common term, "which intrude like the human ego into the flow of creative ideas." Third, "at a still lower creative level is the performance based on a backlog repertoire, in which runs and patterns, cadences and progressions are worked out to meet each situation."[5]

Jazz, in short, represented for Brubeck a blend of improvisation, quotes, patterns, and harmonic progressions. Each dimension, moreover, even improvisation, was governed by law, however deceptively. Brubeck's beloved teacher Darius Milhaud (after whom Brubeck named his firstborn son) was himself a composer in rebellion against an overly rigid or academic notion of compositional theory or practice, yet Milhaud was not a musical anarchist. Far from it: Milhaud was a composer who knew which rules he could break and which he could not; and he communicated to Brubeck this sense of law within a pattern of improvisation ("You cannot be free until you have mastered the rules," he told his pupil) in a way that the dyslexically challenged young musician could assimilate.

From Milhaud as well Brubeck absorbed a wealth of musical "quotes"—from Stravinsky, from Schoenberg, from the classical masters—that would lend to his playing an aura of assimilated scholarship, a connection to the wider world of serious music that supplemented and upgraded his spotty formation. Brubeck would soon be announcing his intention to devote part of his year to composition and would eventually become himself a recognized composer of choral music: this California country boy, with the possibility of Indian blood in his veins from his father's side of the family, pulling together the worlds of jazz and classical music so intuitively on his own terms, with difficulty, not as an autodidact, but as a college man, a veteran studying on the GI Bill under the supervision of an acknowledged European master.

While back at Mills following the war, Brubeck in 1946 formed an experimental octet that was soon putting classical-modernist notions into jazz practice: Third Stream such music was called, paralleling what Stan Kenton was doing at the time. Jazz impresario Jimmy Lyons, who had first introduced Kenton's music to a national audience, secured for the octet a weekly broadcast slot on KNBC radio, with Lyons providing the narration. Such interpretation was sorely needed. The Brubeck Octet—four Milhaud protégés from Mills, three San Francisco State students (Paul Desmond on alto sax, Ron Crotty on bass, Cal Tjader on drums) and non-academic amateur Robert Collins on trombone—was playing some far out stuff, hardly recognizable as jazz at all. Still, when the octet addressed such familiar standards as "The Way You Look Tonight," "Love Walked In," "What Is This Thing Called Love?," "September in the Rain," "Let's Fall in Love," "You Go to My Head"), one can sense the pangs of a new music struggling to be born, at once avant-garde yet melodically recognizable.

By 1949 the newly formed Dave Brubeck Trio (Brubeck on piano, Cal Tjader on drums, Ron Crotty on bass) was playing a much more toned down style of music at the Burma Lounge in Oakland and Ciro's in San Francisco, where the trio shared billing with Sarah Vaughan. The trio also cut four sides for Coronet Records and inherited the octet's Monday night slot with Jimmy Lyons on radio station KNBC. Across the 1950s jazz on the Coast was in the process of cooling down, differentiating itself from the ascendancy of bebop prevalent in the East. To alto saxophonist Paul Desmond's way of thinking, bebop, the Charlie Parker effect, constituted a form of McCarthyism in music. "It was equally analogous to a totalitarian state, in some ways," Desmond later remembered of touring the East Coast in 1952. "You either played the Holy Writ, or the party line, or you were outlawed."[6] The problem: There was, or ever could be, only one Charlie Parker. The Parker effect, the party line, could only produce Parker imitators and wannabes, and Desmond was looking for his own style, which he would soon be finding as a member of the Dave Brubeck Quartet.

Hyper-modernism was also a professional dead end. Tenor saxophonist Ornette Coleman, for example, was so avant-garde he could rarely get any L.A. gigs and was forced to support himself as an elevator operator at Bullock's Wilshire. Not until March 1958 would Coleman get a chance to record. The resulting album, *Something Else!*, while a succès d'estime in avant-garde circles, did not take Coleman off Poverty Row. Listening to Ornette Coleman, Paul Desmond observed, "was like being locked in a red room with your eyelids pinned open."[7]

Brubeck was only part of the cooling-down process, and not even its leading edge. That role belonged to the Los Angeles–area musicians loosely centered on two men — trumpeter, composer and arranger Milton (Shorty) Rogers and trumpeter-arranger Miles Davis — and one place, the Lighthouse Café at 30 Pier Avenue, Hermosa Beach. Born (1924) Milton Michael Rajonsky in Lee, Massachusetts, and raised in New York City, Shorty Rogers landed in Hollywood in 1946 after stateside service as an Army musician as a member of the trumpet section of Woody Herman's First Herd and later joined Stan Kenton as trumpeter and arranger. Rogers went on to compose and score sound tracks for the movies, including *The Wild One* (1953).

Articulate and outgoing, Rogers was a formally trained composer as well as a talented performer, and he knew his classical music — Hindemith and Schoenberg were favorites — to the point of relaxing by following classical music on his phonograph from a score opened across his lap. As a theorist Rogers envisioned jazz as moving, like chamber music, into purer realms, which meant, for one thing, freeing itself from the tyranny of repetitive and monotonous rhythm (two-beat Dixieland, four-beat swing, eight-beat boogie-woogie) in favor of an improvisation emphasizing not noise or beat but intelligent (and cooled-down) musicianship. Rogers further refined these notions through studies with Los Angeles musical theorist Wesley La Violette and a conducting apprenticeship with André Previn. A saxophonist and jazz composer, La Violette was also a student of Far Eastern religion and philosophy, Zen Buddhism especially, and so he very much wanted things to quiet down, including jazz.

In addition to everything else he was doing, Shorty Rogers had a band, the Giants, steadily playing at Zardi's in L.A., which functioned as a moveable feast for the up-and-coming jazz musicians of the Southland: musicians such as saxmeisters Zoot Sims, Art Pepper, and Jimmy Giuffre, bassist Don Bagley, and drummer Shelly Manne, many of them Stan Kenton veterans. An LP cut by an expanded Rogers group on 8 October 1951 — it included Hampton Hawes on piano, John Graas on French horn, and Gene Englund on tuba — was issued by Capitol as *Modern Sounds* and remains a signature moment in the development of an intricate and cooled-down West Coast sound.

The Miles Davis Nine, meanwhile, was adding momentum to the movement with a series of records for CM Blue Note explicitly and vividly entitled *The Birth of the Cool* (1949). "Miles Davis had come to town and began playing at the Oasis and other clubs," Hampton Hawes remembered. "He was a dentist's son out of East St. Louis and had gone to the Juilliard School in New York. That was some heavy shit; not many cats were going to music schools in those days. But good music doesn't necessarily come out of that kind of knowledge so he went into the streets. Since he couldn't play high like Dizzy he compensated by picking all the pretty notes — got strong out of his weakness — and later blazed his own trail."[8]

In May 1949 bassist Howard Rumsey, another Kenton veteran, was lobbying John Levine, owner of the waterfront Lighthouse Café at Hermosa Beach. During the war, Rumsey pointed out, Hermosa Beach was a jumping place, packed with defense workers and military on leave. Now it was deadsville. Why not start a Sunday afternoon jazz session to liven up the place? Levine bought into the proposal; and from the very first Sunday afternoon session, 29 May 1949 (Don Dennis on trumpet, Dick Swink on tenor sax, Arnold Kopitch on piano, Bobby White on drums, Howard Rumsey on bass) the Lighthouse Café was a success.

Initially, from 1949 to 1951, the Lighthouse programs were based on a pickup culture common to jazz, as musicians such as Hampton Hawes, Wardell Gray, Teddy Edwards, Bud Shank, Art Pepper, Chet Baker, and Sonny Criss dropped by on any given weeknight or Sunday afternoon to jam with Rumsey and assorted regulars. In 1951, however, Rumsey formed a permanent group, the Lighthouse All-Stars (Shorty Rogers on trumpet, Jimmy Giuffre on reeds, Frank Patchen on piano, Shelly Manne on drums, and Rumsey on bass). The rest was history. Across the decade, the Lighthouse—staffed by the All-Stars in their Hawaiian shirts, playing to an audience frequently attired in swimwear, the surf rolling in nearby, the sun overhead—emerged as the epicenter of cool jazz on the Coast, noted, among other things, for Sunday afternoon jam sessions running continuously from 2:00 P.M. to 2:00 A.M. When Miles Davis joined the All-Stars for a recording session on Sunday, 13 September 1953 (five cuts, "Infinity Promenade," " 'Round Midnight," "Night in Tunisia," "Drum Conversation," "At Last"), two major streams of West Coast cool converged. Nothing could have been cooler as far as the cooling down of West Coast jazz was concerned.

Gerry Mulligan, meanwhile, working on the Coast since 1952, was cooling down as well. Already, while in the East, playing baritone sax in Claude Thornhill's Society Orchestra, Mulligan had come to believe that less could be more. "There were times," Mulligan later reminisced of his stint with Thornhill, "when I would be sitting in the middle of the sax section and the whole bank would be playing around me so softly that I just could not hear myself blow. You see, at that low dynamic level, the blend of sound was so perfect that all the different notes coming out of the different horns sounded like one solid chord. It taught me an unforgettable lesson about the power of restraint, the beauty of delicate shading, and the impact, not of loud blowing—which was characteristic of swing and bop—but of softness."[9]

The restrained style of Miles Davis was another early influence on Mulligan, so much so that Mulligan left Thornhill in September 1948 to join Davis's group playing at the Royal Roost in New York and later had Davis record some of his early music for Capitol on the now classic 1949 album *Move*. Forming his own quartet after moving to the Coast (Mulligan on baritone sax, Chet Baker on trumpet, Chico Hamilton or Larry Bunker on drums, Carson Smith on bass), Mulligan eliminated the piano entirely in an effort to achieve a purer, more relaxed sound. The string bass, Mulligan argued, was sufficient to establish background for contrapuntal interplay. J. S. Bach proved that a long time ago. (Like Brubeck, Mulligan knew his music, Bach, Stravinsky, Ravel, and Prokofiev being special favorites.) "When a piano is used in a group," Mulligan noted, "it necessarily plays the dominant role; the horns and bass must tune to it as it cannot tune to them, making it the dominant

tonality. The piano's accepted function of constantly stating the chords of the progression makes the solo horn a slave to the whims of the piano player. The soloist
is forced to adapt his line to the changes and alterations made by the pianist in the
chords of the progression."[10] Fans of Hampton Hawes might disagree, pointing to
the vibrant yet restrained piano solos played by Hawes on Artur Rubinstein's practice
Steinway in an all-night recording session for Contemporary Records held in the
gymnasium of the Los Angeles Police Academy near Chavez Ravine on the night of
12 November 1956.

Up in the Bay Area, vibraphonist Cal Tjader—who had played in Brubeck's octet—
was quieting Latin jazz down, a seemingly impossible task. Tjader's pianist, Vince
Guaraldi, was on his own time developing a playing style so cooled down, so minimalist, that it sometimes threatened to disappear altogether. Tjader's guitarist, Eddie
Duran, was doing something similar. By 1955 the Fantasy LP *Modern Music from San
Francisco* was offering testimony to the muted minimalism of the West Coast jazz
movement. Even drummers were quieting down, with the Chico Hamilton Quintet
becoming the epitome of the West Coast cooled-down style. Drummer Shelly Manne
had never liked the Kenton sound. Playing it, he remarked, was like chopping wood.
Like so many other West Coast jazzmen, moreover, Manne experimented best when
he experimented on standards, as testified to in August 1957 when Shelly Manne
and His Men recorded the songs from *My Fair Lady* in an album that stylishly and
symptomatically fused Broadway, Hollywood, jazz, and ultra-cool.

Dave Brubeck needed coolness—needed melody, line, smoothness, occasional
sweetness even—if his own style of chordic, experimental, sometimes aggressive
playing were to attain its best effect. Brubeck found that partner, that alter ego, in
alto saxophonist Paul Desmond, and the two of them formed an association unique
to jazz history. They had met briefly during the war, early in the summer of 1944,
when Brubeck, scheduled to be shipped out, auditioned in San Francisco for a place
in the Presidio band and failed, his auditors unimpressed by Brubeck's pile-driving,
polytonal treatment of "Rosetta" and a blues number. In contrast to Brubeck—
shipped overseas to Patton's Third Army when one last effort to stay stateside, an
agricultural exemption order sought by his father for the family ranch, only came
through when Brubeck was already on the troop ship—Desmond remained safely
in San Francisco for the duration, playing alto sax with the 253rd AGF Band and
catching an occasional off-duty gig in and around the city.

Born in San Francisco in 1924 of Moravian-Czech descent, with some Jewish
ancestry on his father's side, Desmond grew up in the city as Paul Emil Breitenfeld,
the son of a silent movie organist, composer, arranger, and music teacher, spending
a few years with relatives in New Rochelle, New York, when his mother's deteriorating mental health demanded his father's full attention. At Polytechnic High Breitenfeld distinguished himself as a writer for the campus newspaper and a clarinetist
and saxophonist with the school band, having acquired his skills from his father,
the music teachers of the San Francisco Unified School District, and assiduous

attendance, when possible, at big band appearances at local hotels and other live music events throughout the city. Following high school, Desmond got a job in San Diego with the Jack Buckingham Society Orchestra playing at Top's Café on the Pacific Highway near Lindbergh Field, then returned to the Bay Area as a clarinetist with the Eddie Duran band before, racing ahead of the draft, he enlisted as an Army musician. By then he had changed his last name to Desmond in honor of Johnny Desmond, then a singer with Gene Krupa.

Following the war, Desmond pursued an English degree at San Francisco State, seriously thinking—along with hundreds of thousands of equally literary veterans on the GI Bill across the nation—of making it as a writer for *Esquire*, the *New Yorker*, or a similar New York venue. The lengthy typewritten diary Desmond kept during these years, together with the few short stories he managed to complete, suggests that he was not delusional in his literary ambitions. Desmond could write and write well, and perhaps might have had a creditable career at his typewriter, becoming, say, a local reporter or a regional man of letters or perhaps even a New York–based critic or writer of comic sketches. The problem was, while Desmond was a competent writer (and an ambitious reader, who might comfortably have gone on for a Ph.D.), he was already en route, whether he knew it or not, to becoming a jazz saxophonist of genius.

In 1947 Brubeck recruited Desmond for his ultra-progressive octet. Desmond also began playing with Brubeck at the Cellar in the basement of the Geary Theater in San Francisco and at the Band Box near Stanford in Palo Alto, in a trio—Norman Bates on bass, Frances Lynne, vocalist—led by Desmond, who held the contract. It was in Palo Alto, Desmond later recalled, that he and Brubeck began to evolve the beginnings of an extraordinary artistic rapport—a confluence of performance talent resulting in a fusion of music greater than the sum total of its parts—that would soon propel them into national reputation.

But not before Desmond—graduated from SF State and newly divorced—took a job upstate at the Feather River Inn without signing over the Band Box contract to Brubeck, who was supplementing his meager musical earnings selling sandwiches over the lunch hour in downtown San Francisco office buildings. Brubeck and Desmond remained estranged from each other for the better part of two years, until the winter of 1949–50, with Desmond spending most of that time in New York, playing with the Jack Fina Band at the Waldorf-Astoria and doing his best to improve his skills at local venues without being overwhelmed by bebop.

The Dave Brubeck Trio, meanwhile, was recording 78 rpms ("Laura," "Indiana," "Blue Moon," "Undecided," "Tea for Two") for Coronet, a struggling local label. Brubeck was also further developing his polytonal block chord style of playing, from which he would break out into single-note lines or light-fingered improvisation. When Coronet folded, the Brubeck Trio was acquired by a new label, Fantasy, a Berkeley subsidiary of an East Bay chemical company owned by jazz aficionados Max and Sol Weiss. When LPs began to replace 78s, Fantasy pressed its records in assertive shades of red, green, and purple and marketed them in innovative covers annotated with ultra-hip liner notes. Thanks to Fantasy, such Bay Area jazz talents as Brubeck, Cal Tjader, and Vince Guaraldi, together with far-out comics Mort Sahl and Lenny Bruce, first reached a wider audience.

Tracking Brubeck's rise via radio broadcasts and the jazz press and contrasting it with his own routine duties in an hotel orchestra in New York, Desmond resolved to apologize to Brubeck for the cavalier way he had denied him the Band Box contract and reconnect with him and Bay Area jazz. Proceeding systematically, Desmond began to study the Brubeck Trio arrangements he could hear via records and radio and to explore how he could once again fit in. Returning to San Francisco, Desmond called on Dave and Iola Brubeck in November 1949 at their apartment on Eighteenth Street in the Castro district and began the process of making amends. Paul Desmond was a man of great personal charm—a vulnerable bachelor type, with wit and a gift for friendship, at whom it was hard for Dave and Iola Brubeck to stay mad—and as 1950 progressed Desmond was increasingly sitting in with the trio when he could, to include a session at the Burma Lounge in the spring that was informally recorded by Desmond for purposes of further analysis. When a good contract came in from Ciro's on Geary Street in San Francisco shortly thereafter, Brubeck added Desmond and another octet veteran, trumpeter Dick Collins, to the group; and the Dave Brubeck Trio became a quintet.

The quintet was reduced to a quartet in 1951 and stayed that way. Yet despite early and frequent shifts in the bassist and drummer slots, together with Desmond's later recording with his own quartet and with Gerry Mulligan, the Brubeck-Desmond connection remained active until Paul's death in 1977 from lung cancer. Desmond was an incessant smoker, a martini aficionado, a ladies' man forever falling in and out of love. He also maintained an ongoing, if manageable, relationship to the drug scene, not heroin most likely, but certainly a lingering taste for Benzedrine and, in the 1950s, a now-and-then experimentation with LSD. Philosophically, Desmond was a well-read existentialist, an artist, a sophisticated urbanite, and liking it that way. Brubeck, by contrast, was a ranch kid who had grown into a devoted family man. A virtual non-drinker, Brubeck developed an allergy to cigarette smoke. Yet to see the two of them on the stage together in the 1950s, in their professorial coats and ties and black horn-rimmed glasses, was to encounter iconic personalities: jazzmen, no longer on the margins of society, but cool and dapper eggheads developing an art form—jazz to be listened to, jazz as an emergent genre of modern music.

But first, the Dave Brubeck Quartet, with Paul Desmond, as it would soon become known, had to build up its skills and reputation locally, and then broaden its reach: from San Francisco to the Bay Area to Southern California to the rest of the nation and, as it turned out, to an international audience. San Francisco provided a supportive place to start from. The city enjoyed distinct but overlapping jazz traditions and venues. New Orleans–style Dixieland had come to San Francisco just before World War I and never left. By the 1950s Dixieland—as represented in such figures as Jelly Roll Morton, Bob Scoby, Earl (Fatha) Hines, Turk Murphy, Muggsy Spanier, and George Lewis—was centered largely in such joints as the Hangover, the Tin Angel, the New Orleans Swing House, and a number of hotel bars keyed to the tourist trade.

For all its pretenses to sophistication, San Francisco maintained a color line. Visiting performers such as Oscar Peterson and Sammy Davis Jr. were forced to lodge west of Van Ness at such "colored" hotels as Manor Plaza and the Booker T. Washington. African American venues (Elsie's Breakfast Club, Jackson's Nook, The Plantation, Club Alabam, the New Orleans Swing House, The Booker T. Washington Hotel Lounge, Shelton's, Blue Mirror, Wally's, Soulville, Jimbo's Bop City) were clustered in the Western Addition and the Fillmore. Of these, Jimbo's Bop City at Post and Buchanan, serving chicken, setups, and jazz, was the most notable, both for its featured musicians (Bird Parker, Dexter Gordon, John Coltrane, and Frank Foster, with Gordon and Foster still in Army uniform, engaging one night in an epic bebop duel till dawn based on "Perdido"), its vocalists (Ella Fitzgerald, Billy Eckstine, Sammy Davis Jr., an aspiring San Francisco State student named Johnny Mathis), and its visiting celebrities (Lionel Hampton, Louis Armstrong, Billie Holiday): all of this coalescing to energize Bop City during the 1950s as an African American jazz venue of national importance.

Of the white (but not exclusively so) jazz venues of the city (the Jazz Showcase on lower Market near the Ferry Building, the Jazz Workshop on Broadway, the Down-beat, Ciro's, Say When, Jumptown, the Macamba, the Black Hawk at Turk and Hyde), the Black Hawk was most notable as both a venue for visiting talent across a crowded decade (Charlie Parker, Miles Davis, a regular through the 1950s, the Gerry Mulligan Quartet, the Modern Jazz Quartet, Erroll Garner, George Shear-ing, Dorothy Dandridge, Anita O'Day, Dinah Washington, Shorty Rogers, Al Hib-ber, Art Pepper, Hampton Hawes, Chet Baker, Ed Norvo, Charles Mingus, Shelly Manne, Oscar Peterson, Stan Getz, and Art Tatum making one or another or even multiple appearances) and such talented younger local players coming out of Mills and SF State as Brubeck, Desmond, Tjader, and saxophonist John Handy. Run as an unpretentious, no-nonsense place by its bartender owners, John Noga and Guido Cacianti, who left the musical bookings to bassist Vernon Alley, the Black Hawk charged fifty cents at the door and sixty-five cents for a drink and kept a screened-off space for underage listeners. Fantasy Records had a relationship to the Black Hawk, with Fantasy co-owners Max and Sol Weiss eventually buying into the place, which was part of the reason the Dave Brubeck Quartet, now under contract to Fantasy, got its initial contract and played there, when not on the road, for the first half of the 1950s before concentrating on concert engagements. Taking to the road in Brubeck's 1949 Kaiser Vagabond, sleeping on air mattresses when necessary, the quartet would tour the country in the fall and spring, then return to the Black Hawk for a summer engagement.

The Bay Area was providing the quartet a good home base and springboard, once things got started in the right direction, including supportive critics such as Ralph Gleason of the *Chronicle*, willing to promote local talent, and poets such as Ken-neth Rexroth, who saw in jazz, as it was developing, the perfect accompaniment to contemporary poetry as spoken word with an existentialist edge. By this time, moreover, the Brubeck-Desmond artistic partnership had entered its major phase. In April 1951, unable to pay Desmond to join him, Brubeck accepted a gig at the Zebra Lounge in Honolulu. On the afternoon of 1 May, Brubeck was giving swimming lessons to his sons Darius and Michael at Waikiki Beach. Diving headlong into a wave, Brubeck hit a submerged sandbar, severely damaging his hands and neck. The ambulance driver taking Brubeck to the hospital thought the injuries were mortal, given the angle of Brubeck's bent neck. Brubeck spent a month in traction. It took longer for his fingers to heal, and for the rest of his life he would frequently experience pain in his fingers when he played.

Brubeck's playing style could not but help but be affected, although to what degree would remain a matter of controversy. His polytonal block chord of playing, it can be argued, became more dense, more pronounced, more Bartók than Bach—hence more dramatically matched, by way of contrast, to the smooth and precisely controlled melodic line of Desmond's alto. The partnership, some critics have speculated, kept Desmond from connecting with his music at the deepest possible levels in terms of emotion and inventiveness. Not true, other critics argued; Desmond needed Brubeck's block-chordic wall of sound to achieve his own dexterity, the way a tennis player needs a net. There was a fundamental lightness to Desmond requiring Brubeck's density. And besides: Brubeck could play as subtly as anyone when he chose to. Desmond, furthermore, was temperamentally incapable of running his own show. Iola Brubeck did the bookings and tracked the proceeds. Desmond was guaranteed a steady salary together with featured billing and a generous share of the profits from a quartet that would soon be grossing more than a quarter million dollars a year.

In any event, the partners at first worked out their relationship against the background of a shifting rhythm section. In the fall of 1956, drummer Joe Dodge, worn down from the quartet's demanding travel schedule, stepped down and was replaced by Joe Morello, a Stan Kenton veteran then playing with the Marian McPartland Trio at the Hickory House in New York. In early 1958 bassist Norman Bates left the quartet for similar reasons and was replaced by Eugene Wright, a veteran of the Cal Tjader Quintet, whom Brubeck and Desmond knew and admired from their joint appearances with Tjader at the Black Hawk. Morello, who was white, and Wright, an African American, soon achieved a rapport akin to that achieved by Brubeck and Desmond. Morello, moreover, liked to solo, Buddy Rich style, and was good at it—too good, some critics suggested, too long and too loud, edging into set pieces on the edge of banality. Brubeck disagreed. He liked Morello's drumming. It played well on the concert stage. It suggested to neophytes what jazz was all about; and needless to say, Brubeck's pounding piano could stand up to anything. Desmond, however, had his difficulties, now that a twosome had become a two-by-twosome, with a drummer and a bassist eager to show their stuff. Desmond adjusted, but only after some conflict, and critics noted that as the late 1950s turned into the early 1960s Desmond tended to stand at the edge of the group when onstage, as if he were watching a performance in which he would intermittently participate.

On the morning of 8 November 1954, Dave Brubeck found himself on the cover of *Time*, vividly illustrated by Boris Artzybasheff. Already, on 10 November 1952, *Time* had briefly profiled the quartet when it was playing the Band Box in Manhattan and coming to national recognition. The November 1954 profile, however, focused in on the Brubeck Quartet as a case study of how a new kind of jazz—intricate, improvised, intellectualized, quintessentially modern—was sweeping the country in and through such figures as Oscar Peterson, Art Tatum, Gerry Mulligan, Erroll Garner, and Chet Baker (each featured in prominent photographs), with the Dave Brubeck Quartet serving as paradigm and icon of the entire movement. From the formation of the quartet in 1951 and its appearances at the Black Hawk in San Francisco and the Haig in Los Angeles, such recognition had been building. As early as 1951, *Playboy*, a new magazine based out of Chicago, conducted what it claimed to be the most extensive jazz poll ever. The Brubeck Quartet won first place in the category of instrumental combo, Brubeck took first place in piano, and Desmond placed first in alto sax. *Metronome* gave the quartet its first-place Editors' Choice in 1952, and *Down Beat* accorded the quartet similar honors in 1953, together with an appreciative essay by Nat Hentoff.

Taking jazz to college audiences played the major role in propelling the Dave Brubeck Quartet to national prominence. Middle-class Americans were attending college in great numbers, and listening to jazz became an emblem of this expanded identity. Brubeck cultivated the college crowd assiduously at innumerable college concerts and such resulting LP albums as *Jazz at the College of the Pacific*, *Jazz at Oberlin College*, and Brubeck's first release with Columbia, *Jazz Goes to College*, which in four months, *Time* pointed out, outsold Liberace. Listening to the quartet at one of the numerous college venues it was playing each year by the mid-1950s, students could see themselves flatteringly refracted in the music: hip, assured in their taste, heading for big things. The popularity of the quartet with the editors of *Playboy*—indeed, *Playboy*'s rapport with the college jazz market in general—had its ironies, given Brubeck's conservative Christian values; yet for an undergraduate of the 1950s *Playboy*—as yet restrained by the limitations of the era, its young ladies not that divergent from the Vargas Girls of *Esquire*—was tapping into the fantasy life of the postwar consumerist culture being experienced by an entire college generation.

Brubeck took jazz national, starting from California and broadening out to college audiences and to places like Storyville in Boston, where college was the local industry. (Desmond's playing on the album *Dave Brubeck at Storyville*, Brubeck claimed, was the best, the absolute best, Paul had done so far for the quartet.) By mid-decade *High Fidelity*, *Hi-Fi Music at Home*, and *Hi-Fi and Movie Review* were each giving quality space to jazz coverage. By the end of the decade the *New Yorker* had established a jazz department, the *Saturday Review* was carrying jazz features and reviews twice a month, and *Esquire* was back in the jazz reviewing game after a decade's absence. *Playboy*, meanwhile, had long since been advocating an appreciation of jazz as a signature characteristic of a sophisticated bachelor's lifestyle. At the other end of the spectrum, Paulist priest Norman O'Connor, Catholic chaplain at Boston University and a friend of Brubeck's, pictured with him in the *Time* profile, was DJing a weekly jazz program on radio station WBUR-FM and hosting a weekly television show, *Father O'Connor's Jazz*, on educational channel WGBH. Established in 1954 by Gregory Wein with the financial backing of cigarette heiress Elaine Lorillard (who would date Desmond briefly after her divorce), the annual Newport Jazz Festival became a national institution.

At the opening of the decade, a jazz LP was lucky to sell five thousand to ten thousand copies. Fantasy, however, knew it had a good thing as of the early 1950s when LPs by the Dave Brubeck Quartet began to be ordered in quantities of forty thousand to fifty thousand a quarter. Brubeck, Ellington, and Garner were by the late 1950s averaging a hundred thousand an album in sales, a figure also reached by the Shelly Manne–André Previn LP of songs from *My Fair Lady*. The Modern Jazz Quartet was commanding $1,000 a night; Brubeck and Garner, $4,000 to $5,000 a week. In 1955 Brubeck himself—selling sandwiches a mere five years earlier to make ends meet—passed the $100,000 mark in annual income.

The overseas market was growing exponentially, which led to commercial and State Department–sponsored tours. It was the Cold War, and the United States needed friends, and so in 1956–57 the State Department dispatched the Dizzy Gillespie's orchestra to the Near East, the Benny Goodman orchestra to the Far East (after a command performance at the royal palace at Bangkok, King Bhumipol Adulyadej jammed briefly on the saxophone with Goodman and his rhythm section), and the Wilbur de Paris combo to Africa. In 1958 the Woody Herman and Louis Armstrong orchestra toured South America under State Department auspices, and the Dave Brubeck Quartet was sponsored on a three-month, seventy-concert tour of Europe, the Middle East, and the Indian sub-continent. By the mid-1950s letters to Brubeck (many of them meticulously answered, one suspects, by Iola) were increasingly coming from abroad, as modern jazz and Brubeck himself went international. Preserved today in the Brubeck Archives of the University of the Pacific, such letters testify to the personal significance of jazz to correspondents in postwar England, France, and Italy and, with special intensity, to young people from behind the Iron Curtain (Poland in particular, where the quartet played fourteen concerts in seven cities), who revered American jazz as an art form embodying values of freedom and personal expression severely repressed in their collective societies.

Worldwide fame and high income, however, did not always translate to critical acceptance. For a number of reasons—his piano technique, the question of whether the Brubeck Quartet could swing, its sheer success in reaching a popular audience—the group came in for more than its fair share of criticism. Even such an ostensible fan as *Chronicle* critic Ralph Gleason, the dominant voice in West Coast jazz criticism, could never fully give himself to Brubeck's style of playing and the overall sound of the quartet, although Gleason kept his reservations to himself, given the phenomenal success of the quartet and what it was accomplishing for West Coast jazz. Brubeck's orientation toward an aggressive polychordal attack irked more than a few critics, who tended to exaggerate Brubeck's reliance on this technique and to ignore his skill in other styles.

The swing question was at once musical and racial in its implications. In its early years, the quartet's rhythm section, ever shifting in personnel, played a secondary role to Brubeck's and Desmond's improvisations, which frequently became intricate, even erudite, in pattern and reference. Brubeck's interest in classical music was also cited in this regard. The quartet was not playing jazz at all, some critics charged, but a hybrid of jazz, classical, standard, and other elements, a kind of chamber music for cognoscenti as opposed to jazz for the hip. Hence the alleged lack of swing, which was also a code word for an alleged and financially successful hijacking of authentic jazz, which was black, by an all-white group (until early 1958 when bassist Eugene Wright was added) playing to an all-white audience on all-white college campuses. No one ever accused Brubeck of personal prejudice. In his many writings on jazz, for one thing, Brubeck went out of his way to attribute the origins and early vitality of jazz to its African American creators and performers. As a composer, he would later turn to the writings of Martin Luther King Jr. for text and inspiration. Brubeck refused to play segregated colleges in the South. In the Jim Crow 1950s, however, it is easy to see in retrospect how black musicians might resent the over-the-top success of the quartet in white venues still redolent of exclusion. Black jazzmen, for example, were virtually non-existent in the Hollywood studios where so many white jazzmen found work.

Even white hipsters, of the Norman Mailer variety—who had found in jazz the cutting edge of the marginal, the existential, the subversive—can be sympathized with as they beheld their signature art form going mainstream, with atmospheric joints in marginal neighborhoods being replaced by college campuses. Writing in the *Philadelphia Jazz Digest* for March 1956, baritone saxophonist Billy Root, who said he learned to play in funky little clubs around Philadelphia, pooh-poohed every aspect of the quartet's performance, especially Dave's playing. The whole notion of taking jazz to college, Root opined, was ridiculous, as was the intellectualization of jazz by the college crowd. The Dave Brubeck Quartet did not represent musicians throwing themselves into it, body and soul, Root charged, in the way that Bird, Bud Powell, Lester Young, Art Tatum, and Dizzy Gillespie threw themselves into it. The quartet provided, rather, a performance, an act, for the pretentious and uninformed. As far as Dave Brubeck was concerned, Root fumed, Dave Brubeck was the Liberace of jazz!

Ouch! Yet Brubeck developed a thick skin and managed to laugh all the way to the bank. But Root's assessment, however erroneous and ungenerous, testified to the cleavage that had developed between jazz as anti-establishment and jazz as a mainstream and intellectualized art form. This cleavage, moreover, had reverberations in matters of race, class, coasts, and attitudes toward life. Billy Root was white, but the musicians he revered were black, and that blackness said something important to Root: something about jazz being not only an alternative way of music but an alternative way of life. The college crowd were not exactly the people Root hung out with in those funky little places around Philadelphia. The Brubeck Quartet, moreover, came from the other coast, where jazz had cooled down and gone mainstream, and where white jazz musicians worked steadily in Hollywood studios and earned a decent living. In addition to recording Leith Stevens's sound track for *The Wild One*, Shorty Rogers also recorded Elmer Bernstein's score for *The Man with the Golden Arm* and had a bit part in the movie. Up north, Vince Guaraldi, whose *Cast Your Fate to the Wind* LP was a crossover hit, wrote soundtracks for Christmas television specials based on the *Peanuts* comic strip and gave concerts in Grace Cathedral.

It all went back to Bird, to Charlie Parker. As far as jazz was concerned, and other things as well, the East Coast was where it was authentically happening. The West Coast was show business. Yet even as this critique was being advanced, it was on the verge of being out of date. By going national, as the Dave Brubeck Quartet had helped it do, jazz had de-regionalized itself. From this perspective, West Coast jazz, California jazz—as was the case with so many things going on in California in this era: architecture, planning, freeways, higher education, leisure, personal self-actualization, environmental awareness—had helped work out a larger American solution. Indeed, it could be argued, jazz from the South, jazz from the East, had to pass through the alembic of postwar California as part of a necessary process of nationalization. Mainstreaming such as this had its risks, and the Dave Brubeck Quartet received more than its fair share of bad-mouthing as it took to the road day after day, night after night, year after year. Tough-guy purists such as Billy Root might scoff at the repetitive nature of such gigs on long road trips and the later college concert tours, claiming that it turned jazz into a performance, an act devoid of authenticity. But the same objections could be made against Nashville for a similar projection of country music. The quartet, whether its members were fully aware of it or not, were in the vanguard of the democratization of jazz. The 1950s were about such extensions because millions now wanted connection to a broader range of cultural opportunities.

Which explains, in part, why in 1960 the Brubecks rented their home in the hills of Oakland and moved to Wilton, Connecticut. Designed by F. D. Thorne in the early 1950s, with the minute involvement of the Brubecks, the ultra-modern cantilevered structure of concrete, brick, redwood beams, and glass soared out from its steep incline on three levels. *Chez* Brubeck represented an architectural equivalent of modernist jazz, a Fantasy recording turned into a home, a celebration of the modernist postwar Bay Area identity. He was spending too much time getting back to California from the road, Brubeck explained, not to mention that road expenses were depleting his income and that, like so many people experiencing surges of income, he was developing a tax problem ($10,000 in back taxes, his accountant told him) and was technically, albeit temporarily, broke.

Brubeck might also have added that since jazz had gone national and international, the East Coast offered a more convenient place from which to tour. Other West Coast musicians who had already made or would soon be making the same decision to relocate to the East Coast included Gerry Mulligan, Eric Dolphy, Charles Mingus, Howard McGhee, Dexter Gordon, and Paul Desmond, who at the same time that the Brubecks were moving sublet his flat on Telegraph Hill in San Francisco and moved to a penthouse apartment at Fifty-fifth Street and Sixth Avenue in Manhattan. Desmond lived there for the rest of his life, the consummate New York bachelor and man-about-town, an habitué of Elaine's on the Upper East Side, a frequent diner at his favorite restaurant, the French Shack, near his apartment, seen there in the company of one or another of the high-fashion models he squired around town or merely dining alone on an off evening, keeping company with himself over martinis, wine, and dinner with a book.

When jazz became national, its epicenter shifted to New York, where it had been when Bird Parker first set out for Los Angeles in late 1945. Important talents remained on the West Coast, but they had each made peace with not being at the center of the action. Others were in jail or otherwise out of commission from substance abuse. (By the early 1970s, Chet Baker was making his living pumping gas.) Jazz itself, moreover, would soon be going into eclipse as the 1960s unfolded and the Baby Boomer generation turned wholeheartedly to a new kind of music.

The rise and fall of the Monterey Jazz Festival tells the story. The festival was the brainchild of California's leading jazz fan and promoter, Jimmy Lyons, although Lyons gave equal credit for the idea to Ralph Gleason of the *Chronicle*. Born in Peking, where his parents were Presbyterian missionaries, and raised in Cleveland Heights, Lyons began his radio career in 1939 as an announcer on station KVOE, Santa Ana, broadcasting live from Balboa Beach, where he first heard Stan Kenton and became enraptured with the new music. During the war, Sergeant Lyons produced the jazz-oriented *Jubilee Show* for the Armed Forces Radio Service, showcasing such talents as Dizzy Gillespie and Charlie Parker and a young Miles Davis. Lyons's father had been expert in producing church pageants, and son Jimmy was a natural showman. In the world of jazz, he seemed to know everyone. He met Miles Davis when Davis was sixteen, buying him his first drink at a party for Duke Ellington in Beverly Hills. He met Mel Tormé in Los Angeles in the late 1930s when Tormé, then a drummer, had just dropped out of the Chico Marx Band and begun his career as a singer. After spending 1947 as an advance man for Woody Herman, Lyons moved to San Francisco, where he secured a radio gig on KNBC thanks to program director Paul Speegle. Lyons later had a show, *Discapades*, on San Francisco radio station KFRC, late-night clear channel, heard by millions, and a television program on KRON-TV, channel 4.

As a disc jockey, Lyons modeled himself on Dave Garroway of Chicago, presenting himself to his audience as the essence of knowledgeable cool. Lyons loved to showcase new talent: Oscar Peterson, Gerry Mulligan, Chet Baker, the Dave Brubeck Octet and, later, the Dave Brubeck Trio, and still later, the Dave Brubeck Quartet with Paul Desmond, with whom Lyons remained lifelong friends and with whom he shared a common interest in martinis. (It was Lyons who scattered Desmond's ashes from a plane flying over Big Sur, tossing a pitcher of martinis to the wind for good measure.) Briefly tiring of the city scene, Lyons moved to Big Sur in 1953, opening a country store with a sign on the counter reading BEBOP SPOKEN HERE. When *Time* omitted to cite Lyons's early sponsorship of the Brubeck groups, Brubeck came forward in the Herb Caen column to say that he owed his start in great part to Jimmy Lyons, as did so many other West Coast jazz musicians. Later, Brubeck and Mulligan would compose two jazz standards for Lyons, "The Lyons Busy" and "Line for Lyons."

To promote the Monterey Jazz Festival locally, Lyons and Gleason gave a no-host luncheon on the wharf in Monterey for 120 leading citizens, persuading them to form the Monterey Jazz Festival, Inc., a non-profit educational corporation. Lyons raised $6700 in long-term no-interest loans at the lunch. The festival opened on 3 October 1958, with jazz composer and musician John Lewis serving as musical director, and closed with a $1,000 profit. Lyons had paid off his $6,700 debt by the end of 1959. By 1961 the festival was netting $12,500 and had proven a critical success. Emceed by comedian Mort Sahl, the first festival featured Harry James and His Orchestra, the Dizzy Gillespie Quintet (Lyons tried to arrange for Dizzy to make his appearance on an elephant), Billie Holiday (six months before her death, formally attired in a sheath dress and mink stole, in precarious health, helped to the stage by Buddy DeFranco and Gerry Mulligan), the Gerry Mulligan Quartet with Art Farmer, the Modern Jazz Quartet, and the Dave Brubeck Quartet with Paul Desmond. Delayed until 1:00 A.M. when it was supposed to go on at 10:00 the previous evening, the Cal Tjader Sextet wowed the audience with a Latin rhythm jam session. The 1958 session also included a Saturday afternoon symposium, moderated by Ralph Gleason, with Louis Armstrong, Gillespie, Lewis, and others, entitled "Jazz: An International Language."

The second festival, held in October 1959, which Ralph Gleason believed to have been the high point of the series, featured an equally impressive national Who's Who of jazz talent: Zoot Sims, Ben Webster, Coleman Hawkins, Woody Herman, Earl Hines, Vernon Alley, Ben Webster, Ornette Coleman, the Count Basie Orchestra, the Oscar Peterson Trio, and Sarah Vaughan, together with a reappearance of the Cal Tjader Quartet and a mini musical review, "Evolution of the Blues," by the San Francisco group Lambert, Hendricks & Ross.

Photographs of the festival show earnest, attentive, and largely white middle-class audiences, listening studiously to the performances. Celebrity regulars at early festivals (Kim Novak, Steve McQueen, Clint Eastwood) tended to be white, as did jazz critics from the East Coast and Europe. Jazz was a black and white affair, and John Lewis balanced his programs accordingly, although the signature talent, much of it regular—Louis Armstrong, Duke Ellington (commissioned to write a special piece for the festival, "Suite Thursday," based on the Monterey novel *Sweet Thursday* of John Steinbeck), Count Basie, Thelonious Monk, Dizzy Gillespie, Miles Davis (flying his Ferarri out from New York), Roberta Flack, Charlie Mingus, John Handy—tended to be African American. At the same time, regulars Gerry Mulligan, Woody Herman, Buddy Rich, and others gave racial balance to the program. Most of the groups, in any event, were integrated, and race remained a dealt-with issue. At the 1963 festival, singer Jon Hendricks made an impassioned plea for the integration of black schoolchildren in Birmingham.

Jazz, however, had become primarily a concert venue, with an emphasis upon intelligent appreciation and audience decorum. As the sixties commenced, Lyons, ever the showman, began to field a more diverse program. It included purist Third Stream jazz, beginning in 1961 with a brass ensemble led by Gunther Schuller; and Dixieland—a special bane to most modern jazz aficionados—introduced in 1963 with appearances by the Teagardens and the Earthquake McGoon Jazz Band, featuring Turk Murphy. In the mid-1960s the festival began to feature, increasingly, blues and rock. The 1967 festival also included performances by Jimi Hendrix, Big Brother and the Holding Company featuring Janis Joplin, Jefferson Airplane, Otis Redding, the Who, Sly and the Family Stone, and the Mamas and the Papas. For *Chronicle* rock critic Joel Selvin, the 1967 Monterey Jazz Festival—with its electrifying performances by Janis Joplin and Jimi Hendrix—constituted a pivotal moment in the evolution of rock.

It also signaled the rejection by young people of a previous generation's appreciation of modern jazz culture. The festival arena itself held seven thousand. Some fifty thousand rock fans showed up, the majority of them attired in the hirsute hippie styles of the movement or semi-nude in the sunshine. For three days, crowds milled about the Monterey Fairgrounds as amplified music and the scent of marijuana filled the air. Joplin used the F-word from the stage, amplified loud and clear. Sly refused to sing until his favorite stool was brought onstage, causing a twenty-five-minute delay—all this in contrast to the cool professionalism of the jazz performers and the well-behaved clean-cut audiences who had so recently come to hear them.

For some time now, problems had been developing, most conspicuously disorderly drinking. At the conclusion of the 1962 festival, an empty vodka bottle sitting atop a broken bongo drum suggested to Ralph Gleason ominous things to come. Loud conga drumming by predominately black drummers before and after (and sometimes during) performances became commonplace, upsetting the white Monterey establishment that had initially welcomed and financed the festival. Hookers flocked into town. A trashed fairground proved another problem as oversized crowds camped out on the premises, bereft of proper water or sanitation facilities. Then there was the dancing. By 1967 the crowds dancing in the aisles during performances had become thicker and thicker and more Dionysian. This was not cool jazz. This was a new music and a new era. You did not dance to modern jazz. You listened.

V

DISSENTING OPINIONS

15

Largest State in the Nation

A Rebellion Against Growth and
the Destruction of Environment

IN January 1962, anticipating the surpassing by California of New York as the most populous state in the nation, Governor Edmund G. (Pat) Brown began to formulate plans for a statewide celebration for the final three days of December. With characteristic exuberance, Brown envisioned the celebration as equal in scope and intensity to the celebration of the centennial of statehood in 1949 and appointed a blue ribbon committee to organize the festivities. Brown called for "the biggest party the state has ever seen" to celebrate the triumphant growth of California. "On that day," exulted the governor, "the balance of the most powerful nation of the world will shift from the Atlantic to the Pacific....The implications are vast," Brown declared in a statewide television broadcast. "Our voice in Washington will carry new authority. Our responsibilities will increase many fold."[1]

Almost on cue, the editors of *Look* and *Life* began to prepare full-book considerations of California for the fall. Throughout the 1950s, coverage of California in national magazines had been growing steadily in volume and enthusiasm in such publications as *Life, Look, Holiday, Time, Newsweek, U.S. News & World Report, Fortune, Business Week, Changing Times*, and the *New York Times Magazine*. Even such unexpected publications as *Cosmopolitan, McCall's, Mademoiselle, Better Homes and Gardens, Reader's Digest*, and *America*, chimed in with California stories. California guidebooks, meanwhile, showed a comparable progression: one in 1953, one in 1959, three in 1961, and three in 1962. Each magazine examined California from its own perspective. *Holiday* returned to California on three occasions with lavish coverage of California as vacationland. *Fortune* and *Business Week* covered economic growth. *Changing Times* covered the cost of living; *Better Homes and Gardens*, interior design and lifestyle. Edited by the Jesuits, *America* expressed concerns for the ability of the Roman Catholic Church to keep pace, institutionally, with all the growth. *Time* ran cover stories on Dave Brubeck, Goodwin Knight, and

Joan Baez that saw California as point of origin for national trends. The *New York Times Magazine* published five lengthy essays on California culture and politics, including an ambitious cross-comparison between New York and California by veteran observer Bruce Bliven, who had previously written about the topic for *Harper's*. The year 1962 constituted an annus mirabilis of coverage: the full-book treatments by *Newsweek* on 10 September, *Look* on 25 September, and *Life* on 19 October, as well as solid ongoing coverage in other news magazines.

All this commentary, taken cumulatively, suggests a national fixation on California as a newly emergent way of life, recognizably American, as writer Wallace Stegner would put it, only more so. In text and photographs, article after article in this cavalcade of commentary took a more or less approving look at California as economic engine, growth machine, lifestyle experiment, and national bellwether of the American future. "So leap with joy," wrote California poet and Pomona College professor Richard Armour in the special issue of *Look*:

> Be blithe and gay,
> Or weep, my friends, with sorrow.
> What California is today,
> The rest will be tomorrow.[2]

The high point of such discourse was Remi Nadeau's *California: The New Society* (1963), which painstakingly examined every aspect of life in the Golden State as, simultaneously, both an affirmation of and a departure from the norm, with implications for the American future. Only *Esquire* took a somewhat jaundiced and satirical look at life in the Golden State in a May 1963 symposium entitled "California: Too Much, Too Soon."

Ironically, even *Esquire*'s skeptical response to the emergence of California as the largest state in the nation met with the approval of many Californians. First of all, Governor Brown's three-day extravaganza more or less fizzled. Crowds were small and celebrations lackluster. In San Francisco, the three-day observance met with outright hostility, with the *Chronicle* editorializing over "the blight and the miseries that planless growth has brought to this golden state."[3] A number of dissenting demographers argued that it would not be until 1964, even 1965, that California would surpass New York in population. The general media myth of California, in short—the belief that it was a great big beautiful and growing place, where the California Dream had become the American Dream writ large—was provoking serious dissent among many Californians, who agreed with *Esquire* that California had experienced too much, too soon. Its culture was edging into banality, and its environment was being ruined by growth.

Resistance to growth had already surfaced in November 1960 in the debates surrounding Proposition 1, calling for the ratification of the Burns-Porter Act authorizing the State Water Project. Despite Brown's ardent campaigning on its behalf, Proposition 1 barely passed. Once again, the *San Francisco Chronicle* had been an outspoken opponent of a measure that it believed would promote runaway growth in Southern California by bringing to this region the water resources of the North. The sectional partisanship of the *Chronicle,* moreover, contained within itself the theme and dynamic of a larger argument. Runaway growth—especially in Southern California, but not exclusively there—was destroying not only the environment but the culture and quality of life of California. So why exacerbate the problem with a State Water Project that would finalize the destruction? Just as San Francisco had halted its destruction by freeways, the *Chronicle* editorialized, it was now time for San Francisco to lead the crusade against the big-growth promoters whom the San Francisco environmental writer T. H. Watkins dubbed the Water Hustlers.

As far as Watkins was concerned, the State Water Project was a white elephant in the making. The project, Watkins warned, was over-planned, under-financed, environmentally catastrophic to the wild rivers on the North Coast and to the San Francisco Bay–Sacramento River delta region, an instance, in short, of hydrological overkill correctly depicted by the *Chronicle* as the new Octopus threatening to strangle California as the railroad was alleged to have done in the past. It was also, in part, the fantasy child, Watkins argued, of state and Army Corps of Engineers technocrats eager to prove themselves builders superior to their colleagues at the federal Bureau of Reclamation. The State Water Project was, finally, a self-fulfilling prophecy as far as growth was concerned: justified, that is, by the very growth that it would engender—growth that would not occur, were the State Water Project to be left unbuilt.

As far as environmental writing and publishing was concerned, the 1960s witnessed the emergence of a two-pronged attack on apocalyptic and Green fronts, each of them activist-oriented. Nowhere was this more evident than in the Exhibit Format books issued by Sierra Club Books, many of them edited by Sierra Club executive director David Brower. By Exhibit Format, the Sierra Club meant that each book in this series—folio-sized, skillfully designed, dramatically illustrated with artistic photographs—constituted a book version of a museum or gallery exhibit in its three-dimensional interplay of image, text, and spatial arrangements, intended at once to delight and persuade. As such, the Sierra Club Exhibit Format books possessed a connection, symbolic and actual, to Edward Weston's edgy photographic essay *California and the West* (1940), sixty-four photographs of western landscapes, many of them showing signs of human or environmental deterioration, or combinations thereof—including the body of a migrant who had died alone, trying to cross the Mojave Desert—in keeping with that sense of erosion of people and land so characteristic of the photography in the late years of the Great Depression.

Editor of the *Sierra Club Bulletin* from 1946 to 1953, while serving simultaneously as an editor at the University of California Press for environmentally oriented titles, David Brower became executive director of the Sierra Club in 1952. No one, it can be safely argued, was better suited for the positon, whether in terms of mountaineering experience, organizational abilities, or skills as an activist and communicator, and he had an ego to match his good looks and leading-man demeanor. Before the war, Brower had made some two hundred ascents of Sierra Nevada peaks, in many cases opening entirely new routes. A skilled downhill skier, Brower also pioneered the art of ski mountaineering in winter ascents of such impressive peaks as Mounts Lyell, Clark, Starr King, and North Palisade. Brower's *Manual of Ski Mountaineering* (1942) went through several editions. During the war Brower served in the elite Tenth Mountain Division in Italy, winning the Combat Infantryman's Badge, a Bronze Star, and three battle stars, and reaching the rank of captain. Following V-E Day, Brower commanded the Tenth Mountain's climbing school and spent weekends mountaineering or skiing in the Alps and Dolomites. Outdoorsman, environmental writer, skilled editor, Brower was, in short, sent from Central Casting as far as the Sierra Club and its publishing program were concerned.

Across the 1960s, under Brower's direction, the books issued by the Sierra Club set new standards for environmental publishing in the United States, in terms of both design distinction and propaganda value. In 1962, for example, even as Governor Pat Brown was urging Californians to celebrate becoming the largest state in the nation, Sierra Club Books issued *In Wilderness Is the Preservation of the World*, with text from Henry David Thoreau and photographs by Eliot Porter. The noted environmental writer Joseph Wood Krutch wrote the introduction. The very next year, Sierra Club Books issued *The Last Redwoods* (1963), with photographs by Philip Hyde, text by François Leydet, and foreword by Secretary of the Interior Stewart Udall. Nineteen sixty-three saw as well the publication of *The Place No One Knew: Glen Canyon on the Colorado*, with photographs by Eliot Porter. Almost immediately came *Gentle Wilderness: The Sierra Nevada* (1964) with photographs by Richard Kauffman and text from John Muir's *My First Summer in the Sierra* (1911). The next year, there appeared *Not Man Apart* (1965), dealing with Big Sur, with poetry by Robinson Jeffers and photographs by Ansel Adams, Philip Hyde, Eliot Porter, Edward Weston, and others. That same year, the Sierra Club also published historian Holway Jones's magisterial *John Muir and the Sierra Club: The Battle for Yosemite* (1965), elegantly designed and lavishly illustrated.

Thus within four years, David Brower and the publications committee of Sierra Club Books—operating out of San Francisco, a city that was highly suspicious of California's headlong rush to become the largest state in the nation—envisioned, edited, and raised private funds to publish outstanding books and such subsidiary publications as calendars and posters promoting awareness of just how much of the environment was being lost, and would continue to be lost, by runaway growth, if left unchecked. Here in the Exhibit Format series were Green visions of California, poetic and reassuring, that were also conservationist manifestos, calling for action on behalf of redwoods, the Sierra Nevada, Big Sur, and other endangered California places.

Running parallel to the Sierra Club publications was a growing list of titles from Sunset Books devoted to the regions, cities, state parks, and back trails of California. The most comprehensive of these volumes, assembled under the direction of Sunset editor Paul Johnson, was *Beautiful California* (1963). The Sunset volumes—aimed at a middle-class audience, the very people who had been busy transforming

California since the war—were fundamentally optimistic regarding the ability of California to remain an attractive place while taking in millions of new residents. Indeed, on a visit to the Vatican Governor Brown presented the Pope with a copy of *Beautiful California* as the governor's way of assuring the Pontiff that all was well with the Golden State.

Even as Green visions were being advanced by the Sierra Club, a sequence of dystopian jeremiads, increasingly apocalyptic in tone, was chronicling the destruction of California by runaway growth. Writing mid-decade in the *Saturday Review, Chronicle* environmental writer Harold Gilliam, former assistant to Secretary of the Interior Stewart Udall, summarized the social psychology motivating these dystopian laments. "The roots of the resentment," noted Gilliam, "are deep. Everyone who has lived in California more than a few months remembers a pleasant orchard that has been uprooted for a factory or shopping center, a favorite picnic spot that has been graded for tract houses, an unspoiled beach that has been paved for parking, a living stream that has been entombed in a culvert, a rustic country lane that has been converted into a roaring highway. Thousands of residents have been displaced by freeways, and tens of thousands live in neighborhoods now dominated by their stench and racket."[4]

What Gilliam was setting forth in the simplest of personal terms, urbanist and cultural historian Lewis Mumford addressed on a more philosophical basis in an address before the Institute on Planning for the North Central Valley at UC Davis on 12 January 1962, remarks later published in the *Sierra Club Bulletin*. Entitled "California and the Human Prospect," Mumford's remarks, given to planners and assorted public officials, were keyed to the impending emergence of California as the largest state in the nation. Not surprisingly, Mumford was outspokenly hostile to postwar growth in California. His critique, however, while keyed to California, was part of his larger critique of an American society that had become, Mumford argued, mechanical, repetitive, soulless, anti-biological, anti-environmental, anti-human, bowed down in slavish adoration of the Machine. When thinking about "the population explosion, the freeway explosion, the recreation explosion, the suburban explosion (or should one say 'the slurban explosion' ?)...all working toward the same blank goal—that of creating more and more featureless landscapes, populated by more and more featureless people," Mumford could not help but remember the impact of his first visit to the ancient Italian town of Pompeii, buried under the ashes of Vesuvius in A.D. 79. The landscape around this provincial Roman town resembled that of California: the same vineyards, olive groves, and wheat fields, the same mountains and sunshine. Yet the quality of life enjoyed by the estimated twenty-five thousand citizens of this provincial Roman community stood in dramatic contrast to the quality of life currently being endured by so many Californians.

The architecture and planning of Pompeii exceeded that of any California suburb, Mumford argued. Homes were built of lasting materials and were decorated with murals and mosaics. The citizens of Pompeii enjoyed a wide range of public amenities, including games and theatrical performances in a well-built amphi-theater, to which they could stroll on foot. Pompeians even enjoyed better bread, baked from whole wheat flour ground on the premises, in contrast to the "devital-ized foam-rubber loaf, laden with additives and substitutes, mechanically sliced for built-in staleness" available to Californians in the local supermarket. Above all else, Pompeians enjoyed community, enjoyed living together in their city, knowing one another, sharing a society that had its deep deficiencies—slavery, most conspicu-ously—as well as its achievements. Pompeii, in short, without even setting itself up to be a model city, served human nature and community and enhanced the human prospect.

Contemporary California, by contrast, Mumford continued, was dominated—as was the rest of the nation—by the automobile, the ultimate machine, treated as a god "to be flattered with prayers and propitiated by human sacrifices—some forty thousand dead by motor accidents every year—a million injured, many of them maimed for life." Many Californians were spending up to three hours a day on free-ways. Steam shovels and bulldozers, meanwhile, were leveling the environment, as Californians hovered over their backyard barbecues in the belief that they were re-experiencing the simplicities of pioneer life. "If you ask me how California can be improved, without altering our prevailing view of life, without changing our rou-tines, without attaching ourselves to more public purposes and higher human ends than those we now respect," Mumford concluded, "I must answer with a sad smile that no serious improvements are possible on those old terms."[5]

Thus the stage was set for a growing documentation of what runaway growth was doing to California. Taken cumulatively, these laments expressed a resentment—a fear even—and, more hopeful, a call for planning that would lead to a half cen-tury of environmental activism extending into the twenty-first century, with mixed and uncertain results. In *Death of a Valley* (1960) photographer Dorothea Lange and environmental writer Pirkle Jones documented how Berryessa Valley in Napa County had been cleared of all human habitation to create the twenty-mile Lake Berryessa reservoir impounded by Monticello Dam, built by the United States Bureau of Reclamation on Putah Creek at the junction of Napa, Yolo, and Solano counties. Lange had gained her first fame documenting the human erosion of the Great Depression, followed by her coverage of population growth in wartime Cali-fornia. Now she was covering the removal—building by building, farm by farm, tree by tree, fence post by fence post—of an entire rural culture so as to serve through water storage and distribution the growing population of the region. One way of life, one California, was yielding to another as the eleven-mile-long Berryessa Valley was depopulated through eviction and scraped clean by bulldozers.

The Yosemite Valley, meanwhile, so *Look* magazine was reporting on 25 September 1962, was becoming, each summer, a camping slum. Would-be campers were forced to wait long hours just to get into the park. When they arrived, they were required to park their campers or pitch their tents side by side in over-crowded campsites, which *Look* documented with photos of campers cheek by jowl. California Tomorrow, a

Sacramento-based advocacy group, issued the first jeremiad of the decade, *California Going, Going...* (1962) by California Tomorrow executive director Samuel E. Wood and president Alfred E. Heller, publisher of the *Nevada County Nugget*. Appearing almost simultaneously with Governor Pat Brown's call for a statewide celebration of California's becoming the largest state in the nation, *California Going, Going...* documented in a relatively sober manner—policy-wonkish, a later generation might describe it—of how weak planning, non-planning even, was allowing the air, land, water, natural resources, and beauty of California to be squandered in a headlong and heedless embrace of growth. The following year, California Tomorrow supplemented this manifesto with the even more policy-wonkish *The Phantom Cities of California* (1963), documenting the near-impossibility of proper planning controls in the multi-jurisdictional political environment of California that allowed local tax requirements and preferences to aggregate with other equally tax-hungry cities and towns to form regional power blocs, phantom cities, capable of authorizing, collectively, runaway growth. As long as growth was managed only on the local level, Wood and Heller argued, it would remain runaway, resulting in "unsightly intrusions of subdivisions, cars, roads, parking spaces, sewage, exhaust, strip development, *slurbs*—sloppy, sleazy, slovenly, slipshod, semi-cities."[6]

The next three installments in this developing genre of population and land-use apocalypse became increasingly more personalized and embattled in tone. They bore the imprint of New York–based publishing houses of national reputation, suggesting New York's awareness of California as a fast-forwarded mirror image of itself and the paradigm of runaway growth California was offering the entire nation. In 1965 Macmillan issued *The Destruction of California* by Raymond F. Dasmann, chairman of the division of natural resources at Humboldt State. A zoologist and biologist, trained at UC Berkeley in forestry, range management, and plant ecology, Dasmann was motivated, in part, to document what growth was doing to the California environment when, driving across the San Francisco–Oakland Bay Bridge early in 1963, he saw the electronic sign the Division of Highways had installed, with Governor Brown's encouragement, documenting the population growth of California as it raced to overcome New York. His question was: Was California becoming a better place? Was the San Francisco Bay Area becoming better than the region and the city he remembered from his student days in Berkeley in the late 1930s?

Flying south to Los Angeles shortly thereafter, Dasmann asked himself the same question as he beheld the smog-ridden suburban sprawl of the Southland. "It is disturbing to a man to find himself out of step with the parade of his times," Dasmann wrote in his preface, "even if he suspects that others also hear the beat of that different drum. I often wish I could join in the elation of the real estate developer, building the suburbs for tomorrow's masses, confident that the masses will come and his products will be in demand. Or the secure and comfortable feeling that must envelop the engineer, who with full public support and approval channels yet one more river toward the ever-thirsty southland, or builds one more power station on some previously unvanquished headland. To be in the organized army, even under

an idiot commander, brings feelings of comradeship and security lacking to the gue-
rilla sniping from the rocks. But if the army is marching to the wrong place, to fight
the wrong battle, for the wrong cause, what can you do?"[7] What Dasmann decided
to do, most obviously, was scientifically document the destruction of natural California by this runaway growth, which he proceeded to do in the measured tones of
an environmental scientist.

Richard G. Lillard, by contrast, ramped up the amperage of anxiety and anger in
his *Eden in Jeopardy: Man's Prodigal Meddling with his Environment—The Southern California Experience* (1966), published by Alfred A. Knopf. A native Southern
Californian, a Stanford graduate with a Ph.D. in American civilization from the
University of Iowa, Lillard surveyed the Southland from his Spanish Revival home
in Bel Air. The problem was, however—and this being the equivalent of Dasmann's
passing the population sign on the Bay Bridge—bulldozers operating in the canyon
above Lillard's home in 1952 pushed tons of mud on houses below, including his,
and nine years later, insult added to injury, Lillard lost his home in the great Bel Air
fire, which tended to further concentrate Lillard's mind on the problem of runaway
growth. The resulting *Eden in Jeopardy* constitutes the most powerful Southern California jeremiad of the decade, surpassed only later by Mike Davis's *City of Quartz*
(1990) and *The Ecology of Fear* (1998) as an edgy investigation of and lament over
what runaway growth has wrought in Southern California.

To Lillard's way of thinking, Southern California was being destroyed by a self-
fulfilling set of paradoxical assumptions operating across seventy-five years, escalating with new intensity in the postwar era. For the settlement of Southern California
to be successful required a theory of settlement, together with an emotional response.
That theory, Lillard documented, was the garden-variety American theory of progress. The psychological and emotional response to progress was boosterism, a sense
of well-being in the present and confidence in an endlessly unfolding future. The
problem was, progress, as Southern California defined it, could only feed on more
progress, lest it fail to believe in itself; and boosterism, as a result, could only fuel
itself with even more boosterism, lest it suddenly disbelieve the story it was telling
itself. Hence there was in American Southern California, almost from the beginning, an omnivorous need for progress to corroborate itself with more progress and
for boosterism to boost itself with more boosterism. Southern Californians not only
got used to change, they were soon seeing in change corroboration of the very narrative they were telling themselves. The vast majority of Southern Californians,
Lillard argued, even those who had come to the region in relatively recent times,
were eager to share narratives with each other—in a ritual authenticating membership in the Southern California community—of how things used to be one way and
were now another, how this shopping center had once been a lima bean field, how
that suburb had once been farmland.

The primary icons of current development, Lillard argued—at once serving practical necessity, progress, and boosterism—were the automobile, the freeway, and the
bulldozer. All this conferred upon Southern California an unresolved irony. "The

booster," Lillard wrote, "with his progress, presumably his capital solace, lives forever dissatisfied with the present and cannot leave things alone. He and the majority who believe in progress cannot be happy, contented, contemplative, aesthetic, or religious. Since use is all, nothing is to be treasured or left alone and looked at, or only meditated on, talked about, and enjoyed. Nothing is for a lifetime. Nothing is taboo." Arrayed in battle against the booster, Lillard continued—leaving no doubt in which camp he belonged—"are a minority made up of conservationists, of utopists, of thoughtful historians, of perennial individuals, or artists in living, of appointees to relatively powerless public commissions, and idealists (whom the other side calls sentimentalists)."[8]

The forces of righteousness were not doing that well, unfortunately, if one is to judge from William Bronson's *How to Kill a Golden State: A Graphic Report on the Crisis of Ugly California*, published in 1968 by Doubleday—and the most apocalyptic presentation of the decade, given the fact that Bronson had been roaming California since the fall of 1963, camera in hand, documenting the Golden State as a ruined paradise. What set Bronson off, he tells us, was the *Beautiful California* volume from Sunset. Bronson respected the volume as book-making art, but its claim that it was presenting the complete picture of California did not, he believed, jive with the facts. "We live in Ugly California," Bronson argued. "And despite the valiant struggling by those who know and care about what is happening, the ugliness grows at a rate that outraces all our present efforts to control it. The dimensions of ugliness are varied and often overlap: freeways/autos/smog/urban sprawl/strip development/ *ad nauseam*—pollution—destruction of wildlife—dreariness of landscape and small towns—ugly social sores—filthy streets—cheap-jack architecture, and more."

The very disjointedness of Bronson's syntax, its near-hysterical tone, underscores the anxiety of a third-generation Californian, born in 1926, when there were slightly less than five million people in the state, and the California of October 1967, approaching the twenty million mark. California, Bronson argued, was the victim of its own success. It led the world in mass affluence and had become "standing testimony to man's infinite capacity to befoul and destroy in the quest for an ever-higher standard of living."[9] Having established his argument, Bronson proceeded to present his readers with a visual and textual refutation of *Beautiful California* across three hundred images of smog-ridden skies, belching smokestacks, polluted debris-strewn rivers and creeks, carelessly sited industrial dumps and other trash sites, billboard-ridden city streets, freeways carving up cities and rustic landscapes, telephone poles and electrical transmission lines as far as the eye can see, sprawling suburbs with their ticky-tacky architecture (with a full-page presentation, words and music, of Malvina Reynolds's "Little Boxes"), bulldozers at work everywhere, violated coast and wetlands, redwood forests being brutally logged.

All these indictments, taken cumulatively—from Wood and Heller in 1962, Dasmann in 1965, Lillard in 1966, and Bronson in 1968, each of them so aware of the damage being done by runaway growth—might have led to a kind of collective despair. Each of these indictments, however, was linked to a call for corrective action, which is to say, to a program of statewide planning based on a balanced philosophy of environmentalism and managed growth. Even Bronson, despite the edgy negativity of his indictment, remained hopeful. A distinction must be made, Bronson argued, "between pollution, which is reversible, and destruction, which is not.... Nothing is impossible; if we can go to the moon, we can re-create a decent environment."[10]

Each of these indictments, then, must also be read as a call for corrective environmentalism through planning, public advocacy, journalistic coverage of abuses, and political action. California Tomorrow was advocating the consolidation for planning purposes of metropolitan regions—regional cities, they were called—with power over regional growth and at the state level a central planning board, backed by a legislatively approved statewide program of planning and growth management. To promote its cause, California Tomorrow in 1965 founded a journal, *Cry California*, which William Bronson edited. *Cry California* ran articles by the leading environmental writers of the state: Bronson himself, as editor, and, among others, landscape architect Garrett Eckbo, environmental writer T. H. Watkins, Allan Temko and Richard Reinhardt from the *Chronicle*, journalist and television personality Mel Wax, newspaper publisher Alfred Heller, and Samuel Wood, formerly attached to the Departments of Agriculture and the Interior in Washington. The advisory board of *Cry California* included such well-known figures as architect Nathaniel Owings, investor William Matson Roth, attorney Clarence Heller, and Caspar Weinberger, each of San Francisco; Stanford professor Wallace Stegner and physician-activist Russell Lee of Palo Alto; assorted notables from Sacramento, Berkeley, Atherton, Menlo Park, Monterey, and Santa Barbara; and columnist Neil Morgan in San Diego. The lack of Los Angeles area representation was notable, as was the strong influence of Alfred Heller of Grass Valley and Harold Berliner of Nevada City in the Gold Country. In terms of its writers and its advisory board, then, which overlapped, *Cry California* represented a recapitulation of the prewar Progressive détente, dominated by Northern Californians, that had founded the environmental movement in the state earlier in the century. The *Cry California* community included Republicans and Democrats, the very wealthy and working journalists, Christians and Jews, bound together by education, professional status, and an environmentalism motivated by a conviction of responsible stewardship for a California under threat from runaway growth.

The recruitment of Professor Wallace Stegner of Stanford to the *Cry California* cause spoke for itself. As novelist and historian, Stegner was arguably the most respected writer on and spokesman for the Far West, where he had been raised and which he knew intimately and chronicled in fiction and non-fiction. Stegner also embodied the cultural prestige of Stanford University, a role he shared with Mel and Bill Lane, publishers of *Sunset*. In the mid-1950s Stegner was recruited by David Brower to the Sierra Club, where he sat on the publications committee, and to the campaign to resist plans by the Bureau of Reclamation to a series of dams in the Grand Canyon. At Brower's urging, Stegner agreed to edit for Alfred A. Knopf a collection of essays, *This Is Dinosaur: Echo Park Country and Its Magic Rivers* (1955), opposing the dams. Had he listened to Stegner more closely, Brower later admitted, he would have refused to have been party to the agreement to trade off the dams endangering Dinosaur National Monument, which Reclamation relinquished, in favor of allowing the Glen Canyon Dam to be built on the Colorado, creating Lake Powell. Stegner was himself a suburbanite, living on a mountaintop in Los Altos Hills in an Eichler-inspired home with sweeping views, furnished in Scandinavian modern. He eschewed a defensive regionalism and sojourned each summer in Greensboro, Vermont, that most Eastern of places, where he would set one of his best novels, *Crossing to Safety* (1987). During the Kennedy administration, he served as a special assistant to Interior Secretary Stewart Udall. As writer and activist, in short, Wallace Stegner epitomized the establishment orientation of the California Tomorrow/*Cry California* enterprise, which lamented the destruction of California by runaway growth but nevertheless envisioned, through planning and politics, a balanced program of environmentalism and human use.

By the late 1960s, by contrast, David Brower—brooding over the damming and flooding of Glen Canyon, which he now considered the greatest mistake of his career—was moving in a more radical direction, more Green, more intransigent, so that not even the Sierra Club could offer him a militant enough venue. If *Cry California* stood for planning and negotiation, even the occasional compromise, Brower increasingly believed that an environmental Armageddon was taking shape, a battle between the forces of darkness and light. Initially, Brower tried to bring the Sierra Club to this way of thinking, but it resisted. In 1969, ousted from the directorship of the Sierra Club for extremism, he formed his own more militant group, Friends of the Earth. The onetime outdoorsman, so recognizable in a California context, the skilled and sensitive editor believing in the efficacy of beautiful books, had become the arch-druid, armed for battle, taking no prisoners.

Helping to radicalize Brower and the many other environmentalists who would follow him down this intransigent path were the arguments set forth by Stanford biologist Paul R. Ehrlich in his best-selling *The Population Bomb* (1968), predicting the starvation of hundreds of millions of people around the planet in the 1970s and 1980s due to global over-population. The fact that such wholesale starvation did not occur—a fact that critics of Ehrlich frequently point out—in no way diminishes the power of *The Population Bomb* at the time of its publication. The book struck a chord in the kinds of Californians who were most concerned about over-population and runaway growth in the state. Now they had at their disposal a global argument. What was happening in California was happening around the world, they could now claim, or at the least they could now conjoin the two arguments as they fought runaway growth locally.

The Population Bomb, however, went deeper in its values and arguments than any complaint that growth in California was being mismanaged. Ehrlich—speaking, like

Stegner, from the bully pulpit of Stanford and all that Stanford suggested to a sector of the California elite—was making an argument against people, period. There were just too many of them, and they were increasing too quickly for either nature or the various economies of the globe, or combinations thereof, to provide them with the necessities of life. In the debate provoked by his book and continuing thereafter, Ehrlich—by now the head of the Center for Conservation Biology at Stanford and the founder of the Zero Population Growth movement—became progressively more bleak, more apocalyptic, more outspokenly Malthusian in his outlook; and this struck his supporters as the proper response. In years to come, the more militant wing of environmentalists in California—not only David Brower but a host of other environmental spokespersons, including by then a more militant Wallace Stegner and the Sierra Club that had initially resisted Brower's militancy—embraced the Zero Population Growth point of view, which included a growing Malthusian edge when it came to balancing the needs of people and the needs of the environment. In short, they went Green, very Green: which is to say, they edged into an Inhumanism, a preference for place over people, that Robinson Jeffers would have understood perfectly: a preference for nature—increasingly perceived as Planet Earth, an integrated Pangaeaic entity, alive in the totality of its processes—over the people who were doing so much damage to this sacred place.

The growing Greenness—a fusion of an almost theologized concern for exploited nature and a disregard (if only through leaving it unstated) of the human element in the man-nature equation, all this catalyzed and propelled forward by a growing sense of environmentalism as a radical and savvy political movement, playing nonnegotiable hardball if and when necessary—was implicit in the newly issued *Ecotactics: The Sierra Club Handbook for Environmental Activists* (1970) and *Action for Wilderness* (1972), the proceedings of the twelfth annual Wilderness Conference in Washington, D.C., edited by Elizabeth Gillette as part of the Sierra Club Battle Book series. In 1972 University of Southern California legal scholar Christopher Stone, writing in the *Southern California Law Review*, advanced on behalf of the Sierra Club, which was opposing in the courts efforts by the Disney Corporation to develop a ski resort in Mineral King Valley in the Sequoia National Park in Tulare County, an argument that trees, as living entities, had standing before the law. Stone's essay, "Should Trees Have Standing? Toward Legal Rights for Natural Objects"—extending, as it did, legal rights to inanimate but living entities—represented a pivotal development in the Green argument and also a powerful tool in its political and legal arsenal; for if animals had standing before the law, as had already been established, and trees had standing, as was now being argued, then the way was open for rivers, streams, lakes, wetlands, stones even, whole ecologies, to be seen as possessed of comparable standing as well. All nature had standing, went the Green argument; and Californians had better start absorbing that lesson and responding to those rights.

The writing of California history, meanwhile, was growing more environmentally oriented, especially in terms of the water resources of the state. Thanks to the Rivers of America series inaugurated by the publishing house of Farrar & Rinehart and continued by Holt, Rinehart and Winston, studies such as *The Sacramento: River of Gold* (1939) by Julian Dana and *The Salinas: Upside-Down River* (1945) by Anne Fisher had placed a great California river at the center of the environmental and social history of its region. In 1959 UC Santa Barbara historian Robert Kelley, a Stanford Ph.D. with a taste for the outdoors, broke new ground with *Gold vs. Grain: The Hydraulic Mining Controversy in California's Sacramento Valley—A Chapter in the Decline of the Concept of Laissez Faire*, issued by Arthur H. Clark. Kelley chronicled how hydraulic mining filled the Sacramento River with sludge and silt, which oozed up and over the banks of the river and destroyed vast sections of agricultural land until federal judge Lorenzo Sawyer put an end to hydraulic mining in 1884 through court order. Judge Sawyer's decision, Kelley argued, represented the first foray of the federal courts into the technology and environmental impact of water use in California. Up to that time, California had been a laissez-faire state, heedless of environmental outcome. From then on, environmentalists had a new tool, the court order, in their arsenal.

While the State Water Project did not result, as many had feared, in the wholesale loss of the wild rivers of the North, numerous smaller waterways—smaller rivers, creeks, brooks, rills, many of them feeding into small lakes and ponds—were sacrificed; and the downstream flow of rivers below dams was severely curtailed, to the growing distress of Water Resources engineer William Berry, a devoted angler who had played an important role in planning the project. Like canaries brought deep into mines to detect poisonous fumes, anglers, by definition environmentalists, were among the first to detect a drop-off in fish due to the diversions and dams of the State Water Project. Not that Berry became a radical environmentalist, but the very fact that a state engineer was beginning to sense the fundamental paradox of the project spoke for itself. The State Water Project was designed to impound water that would otherwise flow into the sea and to make that water serve growth. Not only did the impounding of water curtail fishing, environmentalists argued, it was the largest self-fulfilling prophecy of all. The project would not only serve the present needs of California, it would stimulate further growth, and this growth, in turn, would demand further expansions of the project, which would make even further growth possible, and so forth, in an open-ended progression, leading to the loss of even further streams, hence fewer places to fish.

By the early 1960s, 86 percent of the population of California was living in cities and suburbs. The more sprawl became a fact of life, the more did the small towns of California emerge as focal points of lifestyle choice and anti-growth resistance. In the 1950s and early 1960s, an entire genre of San Franciscan—Irish American Catholics with a multi-generational connection to San Francisco, especially its police and fire departments—was removing itself to the small towns of Novato in northern Marin County and Petaluma, Sebastopol, and Santa Rosa in Sonoma County. Responding to this migration, the Vatican separated this region from the Archdiocese of San Francisco in February 1962 and established the Diocese of Santa Rosa, with its own bishop. This migration of San Franciscans to Sonoma County cannot be interpreted as a self-consciously anti-growth statement. In Sonoma County, these Catholic San Franciscans were in one sense re-creating San Francisco in more sunny and suburban circumstances. Yet growth had helped push them out of the city, increasing the cost and competitiveness of life, and changing things beyond recognition to a disquieting degree.

While the small towns of California lacked the impressive numbers of the Santa Rosa migration, they were playing out an even more powerful imaginative and psychological drama of one California being chosen over the other. Most growth in the postwar era occurred within the footprint of Spanish and Mexican California, which is to say, from San Diego north to Marin, up to seventy miles inland from the coast. Two coastal communities, Santa Barbara and Carmel-by-the-Sea—each of them privileged enclaves—were conspicuously anti-growth, as were their hinterlands in the counties of Santa Barbara and Monterey. Santa Barbara County pioneered the establishment of greenbelt preserves and practiced a pro-ranch, pro-agriculture zoning. The entire Monterey Peninsula, meanwhile, kept itself off the growth grid by limiting freeway access to the region. South of Monterey, the even more inaccessible Big Sur, served only by the Pacific Coast Highway—and that intermittently, given the frequency of rock slides—supported fewer inhabitants than had lived there in the nineteenth century. While sustaining high levels of growth in the San Francisco Bay Area and in San Diego, Orange, and Los Angeles counties, Spanish and Mexican California had in its mid-zone, from Santa Barbara to Santa Cruz, an undeveloped center increasingly characterized by anti-growth sentiment.

Historian and contemporary chronicler Remi Nadeau characterized the regions outside the Spanish and Mexican footprint as rimland California and asserted, "The rimland—from the wave-assaulted cliffs of the coast to the glaciated Sierra crags—is the aesthetic soul of California."[11] Nadeau and others were witnessing by the early 1960s an out-migration to rimland small towns by Californians, whether long-term residents or recent arrivals, looking for more accessible communities and an environmentally oriented way of life. That meant Arcata, Eureka, and Fort Bragg on the North Coast, and Mendocino and Bolinas for a more bohemian and artistically inclined clientele. South of San Francisco, small towns gaining attention included Half Moon Bay and La Honda on the southern San Mateo County coast and Santa Cruz further south, where the University of California was developing a rustic Oxbridge campus. According to writer-resident Charles Jones, La Honda offered a way of life that was rapidly becoming impossible in the suburbs of fast-growing California: an environmentally friendly way of life, intimately associated with the satisfactions of living within a sustained and sustaining ecology, blessed by daily human contact and community. Cherishing these values, the three thousand citizens of La Honda, a town fifty miles south of San Francisco, fought off a dam and reservoir the state wished to build so as to serve a projected population of 160,000 by the year 2080.

City planner David Yeadon, meanwhile, tiring of life in Los Angeles, was embarking upon a full-scale inventory of the small towns of California—north, central, and south, including those of the Central Valley and southern desert—from the point of view of environment, culture, and livability. The results of Yeadon's survey— *Exploring Small Towns* (1973), published in two volumes, one for Southern and one for Northern California—constitute a prophetic inventory of communities that would in the remaining twenty-five years of the twentieth century either balloon with runaway growth or, be colonized by environmentalists and become models of a deliberately fashioned California lifestyle based on environmental, aesthetic, and anti-growth values. Towns such as Carlsbad, Cucamonga, Temecula, Warner Ranch, and Hanford were destined to be transformed by growth in the years to come. San Juan Capistrano, Monterey, Gilroy, Tiburon, Benicia, Glen Ellen, Sonoma, Colusa, Marysville, and Red Bluff would experience growth but not lose their character. Cambria, San Simeon, Bodega, and Mendocino would become enclaves of alternative values, successfully (for the time being) resisting change. The small towns of the Gold Country would experience an even more distinctive transformation, combining commercial success—vineyards, wineries, hotels, restaurants, heritage sites—with alternative values and a lifestyle based upon Sierra foothill living in Gold Rush towns surprisingly resilient in their environment, architecture, and street plans. The towns of the Gold Country, whether in the Mother Lode or such other places as Weaverville in Trinity County, Grass Valley and Nevada City in Nevada County, or Truckee near Donner Lake in the High Sierra, would make their peace with tourism, finding in it an economy that could be sustained alongside environmental, aesthetic, and heritage-related value.

Rural California, small-town California, state park California, coastal California, the California of desert and mountain—so guidebooks argued overtly or by implication—were to be visited and enjoyed as ends in themselves, but also as California places that could very well be lost to runaway growth. Even the downsides of California as natural environment—earthquakes and wildfires, most notably— must be learned to be lived with in a spirit of acceptance and respect. The interpretive effort to live with the downsides of the California environment began with such publications as Robert Iacopi's *Earthquake Country* (1964) from Sunset Books. Earthquakes, Iacopi argued, were facts of nature that should be lived with consciously and with respect as part of the California lifestyle. Californians need not be obsessed with these dangers, but neither should they ignore them. Each demanded a creative response, whether in terms of architecture, engineering, building materials, or urban and regional planning. To ignore such precautions—especially, to ignore them in the midst of runaway growth—was to ignore a central requirement of an environmentally responsible California way of life.

So too would it be irresponsible to ignore the coast of California, all eleven hundred miles of it, with its larger and smaller bays, its landings and estuaries, its coves and wetlands. Fortunately, the coast was not ignored by environmentally conscious Californians as the state approached the most populous status so welcomed by Governor Brown. In Northern California, in and around the San Francisco Bay, environmentalists achieved their most conspicuous success. In 1957 *Chronicle* environmental writer Harold Gilliam produced *San Francisco Bay*, a classic of environmental writing, in which he poetically set forth the topography and tides, fish, fauna, and flora, and shifting patterns of sunshine, wind, and fog of the great bay and its tributaries around which more than half the population of California had settled by the first decade of the twentieth century. That very settlement, continuing in the inter-war era and booming in the postwar period, had brought with it serious environmental consequences. Sure enough, a mere two years later, in December 1959, the Army Corps of Engineers issued a report on behalf of the Department of Commerce entitled *Future Development of the San Francisco Bay Area, 1960–2020*. The Corps of Engineers report embraced wholesale, without reservation, the notion that growth across the next sixty years would inevitably fill in the San Francisco Bay, reducing it to a mere channel. No apologies, no laments were offered. These were the facts, reported the Corps. Already, as of 1959, 42 percent of Bay lands that could be "reclaimed" (meaning "filled in" in engineer terminology) had been reclaimed, and another 325 square miles of Bay lands "susceptible of reclamation" were in the process of being converted, at the minimal rate of 3.6 square miles a year that had been established between 1940 and 1957. A bay that had astonished the European world when it was first discovered; that had been cited by Daniel Webster in 1850 as a reason, almost in and of itself, that California should be admitted to the Union; a bay around which there had emerged one of the most beautiful cities of the world, and two of the world's most impressive bridges, and nine counties of suburban and agricultural settlement; a bay central to the trade and strategic defense of the nation—this bay was with bureaucratic detachment being cited as part of the environment that must inevitably be lost to growth.

In Berkeley, Kay Kerr, wife of the newly appointed president of the University of California, learned of the Corps of Engineers report and was appalled. As a resident of the Berkeley Hills, Kay Kerr lived in daily enjoyment of the Bay. She especially relished sharing this view when officially entertaining as first lady of the university. And now the Corps of Engineers was predicting the inevitable evolution of paved and developed flatlands for her guests to enjoy, with only a channel surviving to bring the waters of the delta through the Golden Gate. Even more disturbing to Kerr's way of thinking, because they were more immediate, were the plans of the city of Berkeley to fill in and develop two thousand acres of tidelands on its Bay front.

Determined to act, Kay Kerr turned to two of her close friends for help, Sylvia McLaughlin, wife of UC regent Donald McLaughlin, and Esther Gulick, wife of economics professor Charles Gulick. The trio began to hold teatime meetings with other interested Berkeleyites in the Gulick home on Grizzly Peak Road. The group soon organized itself as the Save San Francisco Bay Association, with Jan Koneckny, a professor of chemistry, as president. The association had an overlapping membership with the San Francisco Bay Committee of the Sierra Club. Two prominent members of the Sierra Club succeeded Koneckny—a Czech émigré committed to a European-style philosophy of respectful and aesthetic waterfront development—as president. It was the first time in the seventy-six year history of the Sierra Club that the Club was involving itself in an urban-centered conservation fight.

Most important, the Save San Francisco Bay Association turned to the Institute of Governmental Studies at UC Berkeley and the noted planner Mel Scott to investigate the entire problem of runaway Bay fill. In the course of his distinguished career, Scott had produced, among his many publications, a crucial prewar plan for Los Angeles, a comprehensive survey of the San Francisco Bay Area, and the first draft of the plan for the Bay Area Rapid Transit. The report written by Scott and issued by the Institute in October 1963, *The Future of San Francisco Bay*, ranks as perhaps the most influential planning document in California history. Bayside properties, Scott documented, were in either public or private hands. Those properties in private hands tended to be under the control of a narrow span of owners. Regardless of ownership, a disturbing amount of development was under way or being planned for these sites. A significant percentage of the 276 miles of San Francisco Bay shoreline was either developed, being developed, or scheduled for development by such public entities as the Division of Highways; the San Francisco International Airport and the Port of Oakland, which operated the Oakland Airport, for runway development; and the cities of Emeryville, Sausalito, San Rafael, Corte Madera, and other polities. In the private sector, even more dramatically, the Westbay Community Associates — a joint venture by Lazard Frères, Crocker Land, and the Rockefellers—were planning development along twenty-seven miles of San Mateo County shoreline, 10,179 acres in all, for apartment buildings, hotels, office parks, a convention center, light industry, and port facilities, using bulldozed soil from the nearby San Bruno Mountains for 3,274 acres of fill. Further south, the Leslie Salt Company had already filled in 4,200 acres of salt ponds to create land for the Redwood Shores development and had plans for even further expansion. Across the Bay, the Atchison, Topeka, and Santa Fe Railway had plans for 3,400 acres of Bayside development, 1,000 of it in fill, along the shores of Emeryville, Berkeley, El Cerrito, Albany, and Richmond. (The city of Richmond itself had plans to fill in its tidelands for industrial development.) To the south, in the city of Alameda, Utah Construction and Mining had plans for the development (commercial zones and nearly six thousand housing units) on 890 acres of Bay Farm Island, which involved the filling in of considerable wetlands. By 1963, in short, the process of Bay fill so vividly predicted by the Corps of Engineers was boldly under way—and was being opposed, in the main, only by the Sierra Club and the Save the Bay Association. The question became: Could such people, however influential in their own spheres, bring to a halt, or at the least put under some form of regulation, what now seemed to be yet another inevitable result of population growth in California, the tragic loss of a majestic bay of incalculable environmental importance?

Only a political solution seemed to offer any hope. In Washington, the Kennedy administration—spoken for in these matters by Secretary of the Interior Stewart Udall—was projecting a sympathetic attitude regarding conservation. The Sierra Club had persuaded Udall to write the foreword to Harold Gilliam's *Island in Time:*

The Point Reyes Peninsula (1962), yet another Sierra Club Exhibition Format book keyed to preservationist legislation, in this case the establishment of a federal preserve on the Point Reyes peninsula north of San Francisco, where the Douglas fir forest on Inverness Ridge was being logged into oblivion. The effort was successful, and on 13 September 1962 President Kennedy signed legislation authorizing the acquisition by the federal government of this property. California congressman Clem Miller, author of the bill, stood to the President's left with a copy of *Island in Time* under his arm. Two years later, the signing by President Lyndon Johnson of the Wilderness Act on 3 September 1964, creating the National Wilderness Preservation System, positioned the federal government even more powerfully to play a conservation role by formally defining wilderness, strengthening the hold of the federal government on 9.1 million acres of national forest wilderness areas, and setting up mechanisms for further acquisitions and conservationist efforts.

San Francisco Bay, unlike Point Reyes, was not a wilderness area that could be brought under the jurisdiction of the federal government. It was, rather, an environmental entity and ecosystem under the jurisdiction of multiple authorities connected to the federal government, the state of California, and the nine counties and thirty-two cities lining the Bay. Hence the formation of the Association of Bay Area Governments in 1961, designed to create a coordinating forum for these entities; and it was ABAG that encouraged the Save the San Francisco Bay Association, the Sierra Club, and other interested groups to seek a statewide political solution to the Bay fill problem. These Berkeley-based forces turned to local assemblyman Nicholas Petris for help. A scholarly attorney, an avid Hellenophile, and a book collector, Petris epitomized the humanistic liberalism of his Berkeley-Oakland constituency and accepted the Save-the-Bay mandate with enthusiasm. Blocked by powerful lobbyists, however, Petris's legislation remained stalled in committee.

Petris needed help, Kay Kerr decided, needed political muscle, and Kerr knew where to find it: across the Bay in San Francisco, in the person of State Senator J. Eugene McAteer. Kerr met McAteer for lunch at Castagnola's, a restaurant on Fisherman's Wharf in which McAteer was an investor and maintained a small office for private business, in an effort to recruit the powerful state senator to the cause. In one sense, the two were opposites: the elegant and by definition privileged wife of the president of the University of California, and the hard-charging war hero, lawyer, politician, and successful entrepreneur, an orphan, up from nowhere, living in the exclusive St. Francis Wood, president of the Olympic Club, where he played handball, a ferociously demanding sport that fully reflected McAteer's hard-charging attitude toward life. Essential to McAteer's upward mobility, however, had been his undergraduate years at UC Berkeley when he had been a standout varsity football player. Kerr knew McAteer from UC Berkeley alumni circles, and this was, initially, her strongest link to him; for it would take time to recruit McAteer fully to the cause.

The San Francisco McAteer represented, after all, while Democratic, was also business-oriented and had not, all things considered, accrued much of a track record in conservation matters. Witness the Embarcadero Freeway. McAteer, in fact, had only recently been associated with a proposal to build a North Bay Bridge anchored on Alcatraz and Angel Island. Yet McAteer wanted to run for mayor; hence he knew that he had to broaden his base to include liberal environmentalists. As his conversations with Kerr continued, McAteer began to see the saving of the San Francisco Bay as a parade he could get out in front of en route to City Hall. Soon, at Kerr's urging, the San Francisco Planning and Urban Renewal Association (SPUR) was encouraging McAteer to lead the crusade, thus connecting McAteer to the liberal wing of the local Democratic establishment.

And so, in relatively short order, McAteer joined Assemblyman Petris in the conservation fight. In February 1964 the two of them secured $75,000 in state funds to create a study group to investigate the entire question of Bay fill and report back to the legislature. Governor Brown made McAteer the chairman of the study group, and McAteer, in turn, recruited former *San Francisco Examiner* reporter Joseph Bodovitz, now with SPUR, to direct the commission and write its report. After twelve weeks of public hearings around the Bay Area, followed by a month for writing, Bodovitz and his SPUR team produced yet another remarkable document, building upon Mel Scott's earlier tour de force. In sixty-four well-written pages, Bodovitz recapitulated the facts and added to the sense of emergency that had emerged from the hearings. He also updated all relevant data on the thirty-four proposed Bay fill projects currently under way, which Bodovitz characterized as a "frenzy of development." Legislators were taken aback to find the Bodovitz report back on their desks in such short order and—even more unexpectedly—only $45,000 of the $75,000 appropriated having been spent. The population of the Bay Area, argued the report, was approaching the four million mark. By 2020 some fourteen million people could be expected to be living in the region. Yet there was no single governmental mechanism available to evaluate and regulate, project by project, not only the thirty-four developments under way but whatever projects the future might hold. The San Francisco Bay Conservation and Development study group, the Bodovitz report argued, should be elevated into a four-year commission charged with drawing up a comprehensive plan, with enforceable regulatory procedures, for the conservation and proper development of San Francisco Bay.

To get the McAteer-Petris Act of 1965 passed through the legislature and signed by Governor Brown, McAteer enlisted the support of KSFO disc jockey Don Sherwood, who hammered away at the topic on his wildly popular early morning program aimed at commuters. A pioneer in the shock-jock genre, Sherwood had no trouble gaining the attention of his extensive Northern California audience, whom he urged to write or telegram the governor and legislators in support of the bill. Sherwood rallied his listeners to enclose a small packet of dirt with their letters, with the appended caution: "You'll wonder where the water went / If you fill the Bay with sediment," paraphrasing a currently popular ad for Pepsodent toothpaste. At one point in the campaign, Sherwood phoned Governor Brown early one morning, got him out of bed in the governor's mansion, and interviewed him on the progress of the McAteer-Petris bill: which was a good move, as it turned out, for Governor Brown, alarmed by the ferocious lobbying of the private sector against the bill, was rumored to be wavering in his support. The McAteer-Petris Act passed the legislature and was signed by Brown in May 1965, and the twenty-seven member San Francisco Bay Conservation and Development Commission (BCDC) went into operation. In 1969, after another heated battle, the commission became permanent.

On 28 January 1969, as plans were under way to make BCDC permanent, the blowout of Oil Well A-21 beneath Drilling Platform A of the Union Oil Company, five and a half miles offshore in the Santa Barbara Channel, provoked a crisis that offered the most dramatic possible corroboration of the conservationists' contention that the environment was in serious danger. Even such an avid environmentalist as Interior Secretary Udall had assured concerned Santa Barbarans that there would be nothing to worry about when the federal government authorized the construction of twelve offshore oil drilling platforms across fifty miles, eight of them in state waters, within three miles of the shore, and four of them in federal waters, between the three- and twelve-mile limit. Santa Barbarans—seventy-five thousand of them in the city proper, another seventy-five thousand in the region—were understandably skittish regarding the federal decision. In 1925, after all, an offshore earthquake had leveled their city, sending a massive wave up State Street and killing twenty Santa Barbarans. Most of the drilling platforms would be anchored onto earthquake-prone sites. Platform A stood directly over an angular fault and was a mere four miles from the epicenter of a recent earthquake. The seabed 188 feet beneath the twenty-story-high Platform A structure was a network of minor fault lines and fissures. Nevertheless, the leases were signed for Federal Lease Tract 402, and a consortium of oil companies that included Gulf, Mobil, and Texaco under the leadership of the Union Oil Company of California began drilling.

By 28 January 1969, after fourteen days of drilling, Well A-21 under Platform A had been drilled to a maximum depth of 3,500 feet, and the drill pipe was being removed in ninety-foot increments. Seven of them already rested in racks on the side of the platform. At 10:45 A.M., with a loud noise, a torrent of dark gray mud mixed with gas shot into the air ninety feet above the deck, saturating it with a dark and oily ooze. Amidst a storm of falling mud, the crew on Platform A went into action. The 2,759 feet of drill pipe remaining in Well A-21 was detached from the rig and dropped to the bottom of the drill shaft. The next step: to close the wellhead itself by sealing it off by jamming shut a four-ton steel valve by two electrically powered rams, then pumping heavy mud into the well via a small-diameter Kelly pipe inserted beneath the sealed surface. No sooner was the drill pipe dropped, however, and the rams applied to the valve, and the pipeline of heavy mud inserted—all this taking between ten and fifteen minutes—than bubbles created by escaping gas began to appear around the platform, followed by large boils of heaving water eight hundred feet east of the platform. The bubbles indicated gas and oil escaping through multiple fissures in the seabed, and the more formidable boils were lining up above an even larger geological fault.

The following months—indeed, all things considered, the following two years—witnessed the playing out of a complex drama involving efforts to seal Well A-21, the growing oil slick created by the leakage, and political efforts to deal with the catastrophe. On the coping front, Red Adair blowout control experts from Houston arrived on the scene within days and did their best to contain the situation, complicated by a stuck valve. By midnight on 7 February 1967, Well A-21, injected with heavy mud and cement, was technically under control. Four days later, however, leakage resumed and remained a problem—in the well itself and throughout the surrounding network of faults and fissures—for months to come, as experts continued to try to deal with the situation. Fifty days into the crisis, the 1,500-foot east-west fault line under Platform A was still spilling oil. One hundred days into the crisis, an estimated 3.2 million gallons of oil had entered the channel.

The oil slick created by this leakage had spread out over 150 square miles by 30 January, a mere two days into the crisis. By Friday, 31 January—fed at the rate of some 210,000 gallons a day—the slick had reached 200 square miles in extent. Initially, winds and tidal action kept the slick offshore. But by 4 February the oil slick had breached the fence of plastic pontoons laid out on the water and flowed into the Santa Barbara harbor and adjacent beaches. Floating fences of linked telephone poles were next put in place and proved somewhat more effective. Other cleanup techniques included the spraying of the slick from airplanes with chemical emulsions intended to break down oil density and the dumping of straw at the rate, eventually, of some 2,500 bales a day, capable of absorbing five to six times its weight in oil. In certain instances, suction pumps were used to remove oil from the surface of the channel, or compressed air was released from a pipe on the seabed of the harbor to push the slick upward via the bubble that was created and thereby reduce its density and holding power. Eventually, more than a thousand workers, many of them local residents, were retained by the Union Oil Company to work on beach cleanup, which initially consisted of raking up contaminated straw from the beaches and later involved steam-blasting, sand-blasting, and other industrial techniques.

An oil slick of such monumental proportions, lasting so long, moving down the coast to Ventura County and to the islands of Anacapa, Santa Cruz, Santa Rosa, and San Miguel, extending for sixty miles offshore, parallel to the mainland, took a terrible toll of marine birds, mammals, fish, and undersea vegetation. The great kelp forests beneath the surface of the channel proved the most resistant to oil contamination. Not so with other forms of undersea vegetation. Damage to fish stocks was uncertain, with experts debating its extent. A number of migrating whales, later washed ashore in Northern California, might have suffered damage from the oil slick through which they swam on their accustomed routes to the North; and there was damage done, including death—not a massacre, fortunately—to the elephant seals, sea lions, and seals on their island rookeries. When it came to sea birds, however—especially diving birds such as grebes, loons, murres, and cormorants plunging directly into the slick, but seagulls also, proving the most hardy and resistant, and a smaller number of brown pelicans—the damage was visible and devastating. The California Department of Fish and Game estimated that 3,686 seabirds had been lost in the first four months to smothering, starvation, loss of body heat, or chemical poisoning. Photographs of the mass treatment of damaged birds by volunteers washing them carefully in metal tubs, or photographs of oil-blackened birds dying onshore, or already dead—their oil-drenched wings spread out grotesquely on the sand of the beaches—provided iconic images for television crews and press photographers covering the catastrophe.

The Santa Barbara Oil Spill, as it came to be known, up to that time the greatest oil spill in American history, would in the long run offer the environmental movement a catalyzing and defining event. Almost immediately, a Get Oil Out (GOO) movement surfaced in Santa Barbara, city and county. Secretary of the Interior Walter Hickel and President Richard Nixon flew out to inspect the damage. The Senate held hearings in Washington. A presidential panel was appointed. California congressman John V. Tunney, accompanied by a Jacques Cousteau aquanaut, dove to a depth of two hundred feet to inspect the oil leaks. The Sierra Club was on hand from the beginning, fanning outrage on a statewide and national basis, monitoring every move the Union Oil Company made, disputing its statistics, criticizing its well-capping and cleanup performances. Surprisingly enough, given the drama of the oil spill and the worldwide publicity it engendered, there was no defining response from either the Reagan administration in Sacramento or the Nixon administration in Washington. Government, after all, needed the royalties and tax revenues, and the nation needed the gasoline. Yet the Santa Barbara Oil Spill did convince Californians to manage the coast on a comprehensive, statewide basis. In November 1972 voters approved Proposition 20, the Coastal Initiative, declaring it state policy "to preserve, protect, and where possible to restore the resources of the coastal zone for the enjoyment of the current and succeeding generations." Three years later, the California Coastal Zone Conservation Commission established by Proposition 20 issued a 433-page *Coastal Plan* (1975) containing 162 policy statements on threats and challenges facing the California coast, together with policy and administrative responses.

As Governor Brown was anticipating the emergence of California as the largest state in the union, Berkeley writer Theodora Kroeber was seeing her book *Ishi in Two Worlds* (1961) through the University of California Press. Kroeber's father, UC Berkeley anthropologist Alfred Kroeber, had traveled north to Oroville, Butte County, in August 1911 to encounter Ishi after this last survivor of the Yahi people had emerged from the forest, following the destruction of his cache of tools and supplies by marauding whites and the death of his mother and sister in the aftermath of that raid. A photograph of Ishi, taken at the time, reveals nothing less than the later image of a death camp survivor: ragged, emaciated, a haunted look of bewilderment and unspeakable pain etched into his face. Kroeber secured for Ishi home and employment at the Museum of Anthropology connected to the University of California campus in San Francisco, where Ishi lived out his days until his death from tuberculosis in 1916. Ishi's legacy, as Theodora Kroeber developed it forty-six years later, was not only the anthropological drama of Ishi making the transition from the Stone Age to modernity in a matter of weeks but the fundamental intelligence, moral character, and resilient personality of a man required by fate to make a leap across ten thousand years of human culture. Ishi the Californian of his time and Ishi the Stone Age survivor were harmonized in a continuity that bespoke the fundamental unity and endurance of human nature, at its best when in connection with the natural environment and an appropriate and caring society. In vignette after vignette, Kroeber—inspired by her father's deep friendship with Ishi, love for him even, and the message of human nature and human culture Ishi had taught this sophisticated anthropologist—presented in *Ishi in Two Worlds* moments that revealed the elusive mystery of this unique man. Ishi calmly took the train with Professor Kroeber from Oroville to Oakland shortly after his emergence from the forest, despite the fact that when he first saw the train he thought it was a demon. Almost insouciantly, a few months later Ishi was taking the streetcar and ferry boat over to Berkeley from the medical campus in San Francisco to visit his friend Mrs. Saxton Pope, wife of a UC anthropologist who had debriefed him in Oroville, sitting quietly with her in the parlor of her Berkeley home as she poured tea. Ishi learned to respect and to use skillfully the white man's tools, with a special appreciation for the white man's matches. Watching aviator Lincoln Beechy fly over San Francisco Bay, Ishi noted that while Beechy flew well, a hawk flew better. Walking the wards of the UC hospital, Ishi offered his healing company to patients, as required. He saved the money he earned as a janitor at the museum in gold coins, which he delighted to arrange in even stacks of four according to the Yahi method of counting. Dying, Ishi said simply to Kroeber in his last illness: "You stay. I go."[12] Ishi, then, taken as a symbol of California, taken as a natural saint of Green, incorporated within himself multiple dimensions of meaning: the Ishi of Yahi people whom American California had destroyed; the Ishi of Alfred Kroeber, challenging Kroeber and an entire generation of anthropologists to encounter, understand, and learn to respect the depth of aboriginal culture in its California variations; and finally, the Ishi of Theodora Kroeber's 1961 book, an Ishi rescued from history as a warning against destructive patterns in society and as a bridge to a better California. In two very different worlds, he had harmonized nature and technology. Enduring change beyond measure, he had blended one California with another. In forest and civilization alike, Ishi had lived with equilibrium and prudence. Theodora Kroeber encouraged Californians of another generation to do likewise.

16

People of Color

The Beginning of the End for
Jim Crow California

F ROM the beginning, American California was a multi-racial, multi-ethnic
society, although it frequently did its best to reject that identity. Through
statute, social suppression, and recurrent slight, people of color were kept in
their place. Yet across the decades, enduring all manner of injustice and exploita-
tion, non-white Californians prevailed, with the glaring and genocidal exception
of Native American Californians, who came close to being driven into extinction.
California entered the twentieth century a de facto Jim Crow state, segregated by
custom and real estate covenant, if not outright legislation, although in the case of
its miscegenation laws segregation was explicitly enforced. By mid-century, signs
were emerging that Jim Crow California was on the verge of not change exactly, but
at least the beginnings of change. In various racial groups, the Second World War
had accelerated the process. While centered on the war and postwar years, however,
the story of the beginning of the end for Jim Crow California extends back in time
to the nineteenth century and must be told as such. Certain other developments
unfolded almost a century later, in the 1960s. As in the case of the nation itself, the
process continued into the twenty-first century. In this vital matter, as in so much
else, American society remained a work in progress.

The story begins with the Japanese. Between 1942 and 1945, they most conspicuously experienced the effects of prejudice. In the nineteenth century, Americans
in California persecuted the Chinese and in the 1880s successfully lobbied for federal legislation banning them from further immigration to the United States. At
the time, the anti-Chinese movement of the nineteenth century constituted the
most conspicuous attack on the Pacific Coast against Asians. In the twentieth century, with the Chinese population of California reduced to negligible numbers, the
attention of the anti-Asian lobby turned to the Japanese; and for forty years a campaign of hostility against Japanese immigrants to California raged, so severe and

so well-orchestrated Carey McWilliams in 1945 described it as an out-and out-war between California and Japan. The culmination of this war was the ethnic cleansing from the Pacific Coast in 1942 of 110,000 Japanese through Executive Order 9066 and their forced removal into ten relocation centers (renamed concentration camps in the mid-1960s), administered by the War Relocation Authority. With surprising rapidity, this internment, made in the name of wartime security, began to generate open protest by 1944, well before the war was over. The decision of the federal government, announced in January 1943, to allow interned Japanese Americans to volunteer for two elite Army combat units to fight in the European theater represented an implicit acknowledgment of the very contradiction inherent in interning American citizens wholesale, as a group, sheerly on the basis of race. The brilliant performance and heroic casualties sustained by the all-Japanese-American 100th Infantry Battalion and 442nd Regimental Combat Team in some of the fiercest fighting in northern Italy, together with the outstanding record of other *Nisei* attached to Army and Marine units in the South Pacific as intelligence evaluators, interrogators, and translators further underscored what over the next forty years would be seen as the terrible injustice, born of racial antagonism, leveled against the Japan-born *Issei*, forbidden by law to become citizens, and their American-born *Nisei* offspring.

As early as 17 December 1944, the War Department announced that, one year hence, the exclusion orders against the Japanese on the West Coast would be rescinded. A day later, Dillon Myer, the thoroughly decent federal official in charge of the War Relocation Authority, announced that all Relocation Centers would be closed by the end of 1945 and that the WRA would cease operation by June 1946. For whatever it was worth, internees had time to get ready, to make preparations, psychological and physical, for return. Would they go home, as many decided to do, or would they head into the midwestern and eastern states where evacuation had not been in effect, hence regions of the country not as soaked in ambiguity and sorrow as California, from which more than half of the internees had come and to which most of the returnees were now heading? Some internees delayed their release for a few months so that their children might finish the semester, even graduate from high school, testimony to the culture, family loyalty, and general concern with self-improvement characteristic of Japanese families. Many aged internees delayed their release because they came from prejudiced areas and were fearful of returning there or heard reports of returnees being mistreated. Some five thousand internees scheduled for repatriation to Japan—many of them *Kibei*, Japanese born in the United States but educated in Japan and strongly Japanese in culture—were returning to the Japanese homeland and not to their homes of origin in the United States, motivated by admixtures of anger, bitterness, disillusionment, or sheer fatigue. Over time, many would reclaim their citizenship—which the courts judged to have been renounced under forced circumstances, hence revocable—and returned to the United States to resume their American lives. Since the ten camps were each, without exception, in remote regions of Arkansas, Colorado, Wyoming, Idaho, Utah, California, and Arizona, the trip home under late wartime or early postwar conditions was arduous, especially for Californians returning from out of state. Memoirs are replete with stories of return by train, Greyhound bus, or private automobiles, used and battered, purchased with scrupulously accumulated camp earnings.

The camp years ended with the dropping of atomic bombs on Hiroshima and Nagasaki. However these atomic attacks might be justified in terms of avoiding an invasion of the Japanese homeland and the saving of millions of lives, they nevertheless represented an ultimate act of violence against not soldiers, not sailors, not Marines, but civilians, men, women, and children in their physical selves, flesh and bone. Many American internees lost family in these attacks. However loyal they were in their American identity—and who could have proven their loyalty more than these interned citizens, sending their sons to fight for the Republic on foreign soil—they felt a shudder of fear. This new technology of death had not been used to end the war in Europe but to end the war against Japan, which under the conduct of war by the Allies, as far as Germany and Japan were concerned, meant an air war directly against the German and Japanese people, a war of civilian extermination now apocalyptically completed by the hellfire of atomic attack. The atomic obliteration of Hiroshima and Nagasaki offered a kind of catharsis among all but the most extreme of anti-Japanese racists on the Pacific Coast. What more could one people do to another, even if such a people felt morally justified, than to incinerate them into oblivion or condemn them to die terrible deaths over time? Surely, the Japanese were paying for the crimes of the fascist era.

Historians can document only some thirty violent attacks against *Issei* and *Nisei* returnees. The atomic victory against Japan seems momentarily to have quelled on-site violence or at least sated all but the most irreconcilable of racists. Most telling, the worst episode occurred eight months before the bombs were dropped, in January 1945 in Placer County, where two Army privates, absent without leave, the eighteen-year-old brother of one of them, and a local bartender, on two separate occasions night-raided, shot up, fire-bombed, and attempted to dynamite barns on the repossessed ranch of the Doi family, recently released from the Amache Relocation Center in Colorado. Brought to trial in April 1945, the four men faced overwhelming evidence but were acquitted—in spite of a warning by the presiding judge that the jurors must ignore issues of race, color, or creed in their deliberations—after their defense attorney described in detail the Death March on Bataan and evoked the specter of a fifth column of Japanese he claimed had been sent earlier to the United States: a repeat, in short, of a charge widely circulating in the immediate aftermath of Pearl Harbor. Minor incidents continued in Placer County and Solano County to the south in the two years that followed: refusals of service in restaurants, the breaking of a window in a store opened by a *Nisei* decorated for heroism, the refusal of a San Francisco barber to cut the hair of Army Captain Daniel Inouye, in uniform, a Combat Infantryman's badge and a row of ribbons on his tunic, one sleeve empty from the arm he had lost in Italy.

Incidents such as this, together with anti-Japanese statements from various organizations reported in the press, drove the Sixth Army commander, four-star General

Joseph (Vinegar Joe) Stilwell, a veteran of Asian service in peace and war, to outspoken distraction, which was not difficult to do in General Stilwell's case. "The *Nisei*
bought an awful big hunk of America with their blood," Vinegar Joe announced
from Sixth Army Headquarters, Presidio, San Francisco. "You're damn right those
Nisei boys have a place in the American heart, now and forever. And I say we soldiers
ought to form a pickaxe club to protect Japanese Americans who fought the war
with us. Anytime we see a barfly commando picking on those kids or discriminating
against them, we ought to bang him over the head with a pickaxe. I'm willing to be a
charter member. We cannot allow a single injustice to be done to the *Nisei* without
defeating the purposes for which we fought."[1]

Mary Masuda, a *Nisei*, knew what General Stilwell was talking about. Released
early from the Gila Relocation Center in Arizona, Mary Masuda returned to her
home in Talbert, Orange County. Shortly after her arrival, on the night of 4 May
1944, a posse of men called at her home, threatening physical injury if she tried to
remain. Mary Masuda's brother, Staff Sergeant Kazuo Masuda, had recently lost
his life in Italy, using his mortar to turn back two German attacks. When Sergeant
Masuda was posthumously awarded the Distinguished Service Cross, the WRA, the
War Department, and General Stilwell cooperated to make the award a pointed
attack against barfly commandos and their ilk. In ceremonies held on the porch of
the Masuda home, General Stillwell read the citation describing how Staff Sergeant
Kazuo Masuda, leading a night patrol into heavily mined territory, had held off a
German attack with an improvised mortar position, losing his life but allowing his
men to escape. "I've seen a good deal of the *Nisei* in service," Stilwell said to Mary
Masuda, "and never yet have I found one of them who did not do his duty right up to
the handle." Since Sergeant Masuda's mother was still, technically, an enemy alien,
Stillwell could not present the Distinguished Service Cross directly to her because
of Army regulations. He presented it instead to Mary Masuda, who then gave the
medal to her mother. "In accepting this distinction for my brother," Mary Masuda
told General Stilwell, "I know that he would want me to say that he was only doing
his duty as a soldier of our beloved country."[2]

Not so approving as General Stilwell or as forgiving as Mary Masuda, however,
were the courts of California when it came to adjudicating cases involving *Issei*
and *Nisei* property. Personal belongings and other property in the custody of the
WRA were, in the main, meticulously inventoried, tagged, stored, and returned
upon release. Some property was lost or stolen, as might be expected in an operation
of this magnitude, but there was next to no systemic pilferage. Local arrangements,
however, were more mixed in outcome. Some *Issei* and *Nisei* returned to find that,
while they were incarcerated, their local Caucasian friends or business partners had
taken good care of their property. In so many other instances, however, documented
during the claims process following the war, thousands of other families returned to
find their properties alienated in one way or another to new ownership or trashed
to the point that many businesses could not be revived. The Japantowns of San
Francisco and Los Angeles had been re-colonized, largely by African Americans,

although some families were able to reestablish themselves. Other families discovered that a trusted lawyer or business partner had become a devious double-dealer while they were in the camps. Many returnees did not have the funds to fight such thievery in court and simply walked away from what they had owned from investment and sweat equity before the war.

Even worse were the land grabs orchestrated with governmental assistance. No sooner were the Japanese interned in early 1942 than sharks began to circle around the nearly $66 million in landholdings left behind. The Alien Land Laws of 1913, 1920, 1923, and 1927 prohibited ownership of property in California by those ineligible for citizenship. That meant the *Issei*. To circumvent this law, *Issei* frequently bought land in the name of their American-born *Nisei* offspring, who were citizens and held it for them in trust. With the internment, such end runs around the Alien Land Laws began to show their legal vulnerability, especially as local interests and the state of California itself began to work in tandem. Between 1944 and 1948, Attorney General Robert Kenny of California launched fourteen escheat (state confiscations) actions against *Issei*-purchased properties transferred to *Nisei* offspring—this in contrast to the mere fourteen escheat actions that had been initiated over the previous thirty years. In June 1945 the legislature appropriated some $200,000 to finance such confiscations.

Hence the crucial importance of the resistance of the Oyama family to the seizure of their six acres outside Chula Vista, San Diego County, previously purchased in the name of their six-year-old American-born son, Fred. Argued by ACLU attorney Abraham Lincoln Wirin, a Russian-born Jewish American with degrees from Harvard and Boston University, *Oyama v. State of California*, filed in August 1944, met with a resounding defeat at the trial court level one year later, but was taken by Wirin to the state supreme court, where, most unexpectedly, it prevailed, thanks to questioning from the bench and an outspoken opinion by Chief Justice Phil Gibson. So, too, did the Oyamas prevail before the United States Supreme Court in January 1948, their case anchored in a Fourteenth Amendment equal protection argument stating that since *Issei* were not allowed to become citizens, they were being denied equal protection under the law when it came to bestowing property on their offspring. Thanks to the Oyama decision, momentum was lost to escheat suits concurrently under way in California and the Alien Land Laws themselves. In January 1948 California attorney general Fred Howser stopped all escheat proceedings. Over the next few years, without being formally repealed, the Alien Land Laws of California, rejected by the US Supreme Court, went into eclipse.

The civil rights movement had its most intense expression and resolution in the American South and the halls of Congress. Also of importance—indeed, of prophetic importance, given the involvement of Thurgood Marshall on behalf of the NAACP—was the lawsuit brought in February 1945 by Gonzalo and Felicitas Mendez, a naturalized Mexican American asparagus farmer and his Puerto Rico–born wife, against the Westminster School District of Orange County. In September

1944, UC Berkeley historian Mark Brilliant tells us in *Color Lines: Civil Rights Struggles on America's "Racial Frontier," 1945–1975* (forthcoming from Oxford University Press), the Mendezes sought to enroll their three children, together with two of the children of Gonzalo's sister Soledad Vidaurri, in the Seventeenth Street School in Westminster, a small town in agricultural Orange County. Faced with the prospect of enrolling five Mexican American children at the "American" (the code name for all-white) Seventeenth Street School, administrators ruled on the very morning that the children showed up that only the two lighter-skinned Vidaurri children could attend the school. The darker-skinned Mendez children would have to attend the Hoover School, a rundown operation reserved for Mexican American children. Sixty years later, one of the children, Sylvia Mendez, remembered the shock when, as an eight-year-old wearing a freshly ironed dress, her hair neatly braided, she was refused admission to the school that her lighter-skinned cousins were allowed to attend.

Retaining the services of lawyer David Marcus, a Spanish-speaking Jewish American married to a Mexican American immigrant, the Mendezes launched a class action suit against the Orange County School District on behalf of an estimated five thousand Mexican American families in the county. As was the case in most other Southern California counties, the children of the majority of these Mexican Americans and undocumented Mexican residents had long since been forced to attend segregated schools, most of them substandard in facilities and programs. The spurious legal basis for such Jaime Crow segregation, as it might be called, were long-standing interpretations that Mexicans, being of whole or partial Indian descent, came under the constitutionally reinforced segregation of Native American and Asian children (*Mongolian* was the particularly offensive term employed) into separate schools, a practice based allegedly on linguistic and cultural differences. This was the argument lawyers for the Westminster School District made as *Mendez v. Westminster School District of Orange County* was filed in the United States District Court in the Southern District of California in February 1945. The children of Mexican descent, ran the school district argument, were being segregated not on the basis of skin color but on the basis of linguistic and cultural differences demanding a separate educational track.

In arguing his case, David Marcus took a twofold approach, one straightforward, the other more nuanced. Segregated schools, Marcus argued, were under-funded and second-rate, hence intrinsically unequal as far as American citizens were concerned, hence unconstitutional. Federal judge Paul McCormick had difficulties with Marcus's first argument, given evidence provided by school district administrators of how they were trying, successfully to an extent, to upgrade schools serving a Mexican clientele. Surprisingly, however, Judge McCormick bought Marcus's second argument. "A paramount requisite in the American system of public education," McCormick ruled on 18 February 1946, "is social equality. It must be open to all children by unified school association regardless of lineage." The school district appealed McCormick's decision to the Ninth Circuit in San Francisco. Marcus was thus forced into the more theoretical waters of his second argument: Segregated schools, even those that were equal in programs and facilities, or were the recipients of good-faith efforts to bring them to such a condition, were nevertheless discriminatory and unconstitutional. Separate could never be equal—period.

At this point, the Legal Defense and Educational Fund of the NAACP, as represented by its attorney Thurgood Marshall, sensing the breakthrough nature of the Mendez case, filed an amicus brief in support of Marcus as *Mendez v. Westminster* came under the scrutiny of the Ninth Circuit. The Ninth Circuit decision issued on 14 April 1947, however, sidestepped the sweeping implications of Marcus's argument, which would await the resolution of *Brown v. Board of Education* before the United States Supreme Court in 1954. The Ninth Circuit did decide, however, that while state law did allow for the segregation of Native Americans and Asians, it did not allow for the segregation of children of Mexican descent, who were, legally, not Indians, whatever their mixed ancestry, or Asians, but white people; and under California law white people could not be segregated.

From one point of view, the decision of the Ninth Circuit represented a partial defeat. The federal Court of Appeals did not accept Marcus's and Marshall's more sweeping and inclusive argument that separate could never be equal. It did, however, nominally end the segregation of children of Mexican descent. This, in turn, represented a victory strong enough to dissuade the Westminster School District from appealing to the Supreme Court.

Mendez v. Westminster, moreover, reinforced a certain fatigue factor in the effort to sustain, officially, segregationist practices in the public schools of California. And no one was more fatigued than Governor Earl Warren. As a citizen of the Bay Area, Warren had come of age as a politician in a part of the state that did not practice the rigid segregation of children of Mexican descent, no doubt, in part, because there were so few of them in the region. Personally, moreover, Warren had an abiding appreciation of the Spanish and Mexican origins of California. As a boy growing up in Bakersfield, Warren had had Mexican American friends. One of his closest friends in later life—and Earl Warren did not make friends easily!—was actor Leo Carrillo, the descendant of a pioneer Californio family. Each year, the Warrens would attend the Old Spanish Days festivities in Santa Barbara, where Carrillo was a presiding celebrity. It did California no good, Warren had long argued, to segregate people of the same descent and culture as the citizens of its neighboring commonwealth, Mexico. And even more hemispherically, Warren argued, how could the United States deal effectively with the nations of Latin America if one of its most important states, California, discriminated against Hispanic peoples?

Two years before *Mendez v. Westminster* was ruled on by the Ninth Circuit, Warren had tried, unsuccessfully, to get a school desegregation bill through the legislature. *Mendez v. Westminster* encouraged him to renew the effort, and within two months of the decision Warren signed into law a bill rescinding the right of school districts to segregate children of Native American and Asian descent. There was no need to cite Mexican American children in this new law, since they, being white people by law, had not been named in the original statute. A powerful shot had been fired across the segregationist bow. *Mendez v. Westminster* revealed, simultaneously, the power of the courts, especially the federal courts in civil rights cases, and the postwar reentry of Mexican Americans into public life in California.

That same year, health educator and social worker Edward Roybal was running for the Los Angeles City Council, seeking to become the first Mexican American on that board since 1881. By birth, Roybal was a New Mexican, the descendant of seventeenth-century Spanish pioneers, hence an aristocrat, an Hispanic Knicker-bocker, belonging to a group that had always distinguished itself from descendants of later migrations. Nevertheless, once Roybal arrived in Los Angeles in 1922 as a boy of six, he became a Boyle Heights Los Angeleno, a Mexican American, expe-riencing discrimination as he wended his way through public grammar school, Roosevelt High School, and a stint in the Civilian Conservation Corps, followed by UCLA and legal studies at Southwestern. Running in a district that was only 34 percent Hispanic, Roybal lost his first bid for the council. By the time of his second run, however, in 1949, Roybal had considerably widened his community support—essential in a district that was 45 percent white, 15 percent African American, and 6 percent other—thanks in significant measure to the tutelage of community orga-nizer Fred Ross.

No history of dissent and community organizing in California in the prewar and postwar period—indeed through the 1980s—can be considered without reference to Fred Ross. Lean, ascetic, living throughout his life on minimal levels of support, Ross absorbed his all-encompassing radicalism as one would become converted to religious faith. Born in 1910 in San Francisco into a solidly Republican family, raised in Los Angeles, Ross graduated from the University of Southern California in 1936, whereupon he tried and failed to secure employment as a schoolteacher. As an alter-native, Ross went to work as a manager at the Arvin Migratory Labor Camp of the Farm Security Administration, where he counseled residents in community orga-nizing and self-government. During the war, Ross worked with interned Japanese Americans, first as a staffer with the War Relocation Authority, then as a member of the American Friends Service Committee, counseling internees regarding their rights, arranging for housing and employment in non-restricted areas so that intern-ees might win parole from the camps. Following the war, Ross sharpened his skills in Chicago under Saul Alinsky, who sent Ross back to Los Angeles in August 1947 to help organize the Community Service Organization within the Mexican American community. In short order, the CSO registered fifty thousand new voters, a plurality of them Hispanic, helped Edward Roybal win election to the city council in 1949, and won a number of cases involving police brutality. In the process, Ross recruited and appointed to a staff position a promising young Navy veteran by the name of César Chávez. "He discovered me, he inspired me," Chávez would later remark. "He thought I had what it took to be an organizer. He gave me a chance, and that led to a lot of things."[3]

Roybal's election to the city council constituted a dramatic victory for a segregated community treated as a criminal class by the Los Angeles police. By 1954 Roybal was running for lieutenant governor: unsuccessfully but historically as no Mexican American candidate had openly aspired to that position for seventy-five years. In 1958 Roybal lost once again, this time in a race for county supervisor, amidst credible suspicions of voter fraud. In 1962, after thirteen years on the Los Angeles City Council, Roybal won election to the House of Representatives, representing East Los Angeles, Downtown, and parts of Hollywood—the first Hispanic congressman from California since the election of Romualdo Pacheco in 1879—and remained in the House until his retirement in 1993. *Mendez v. Westminster* and the election of Edward Roybal to the Los Angeles City Council in 1949 can be considered the actual and symbolic beginning of a liberation struggle that would last for the rest of the century.

At the center of this struggle, initially, remained the non-Mexican-American Fred Ross and the Community Service Organization movement. By the late 1950s, however, Mexican American leaders trained by Ross were in the forefront of the struggle: figures such as Roybal himself on the urban front, joined there by nearly one hundred elected Mexican American officials by 1960, and in the harvest fields by such labor organizers as Ernesto Galarza, César Chávez, and Dolores Huerta. In cities, on the local level, better community-police relations remained on the forefront of the developing Mexican American political agenda, followed by the effort to secure state pensions in lieu of social security for aged Mexican Americans and others, Chinese especially, who, while longtime residents, had through no fault of their own never managed to regularize their citizenship.

On the agricultural front, the challenge was profoundly Mexican and Mexican American—or more precisely, Mexican national versus Mexican American—for since 1942, in the *bracero* program, Mexican national labor had been being used to supplant Mexican American or legal resident Mexican labor in the agricultural fields of the state. Initially, President Roosevelt had deep reservations regarding proposals, in the aftermath of Pearl Harbor, to authorize a regulated guest worker program between Mexico and the United States, since the nation was still in the throes of a job shortage. So why export American jobs, however marginal, to foreign nationals, however nearby? And second—although this argument never fully surfaced—there were an estimated 1.5 million Mexican immigrants, legal and illegal, in the United States as of Census 1940. A significant portion of this population was involved in migratory labor. So why undercut the employment of these tax-paying citizens of the United States, even if one did not have much sympathy with their illegal colleagues? Even more subtle, especially for Democrats, was the notion that the United States had always imported its labor through immigration leading to citizenship. A new model was now being proposed—the importation of temporary foreign labor detached from a pathway to citizenship, an affront to immigrant working America, who tended to vote Democratic.

By 1942, however, the draft had begun to take its toll as far as available agricultural labor was concerned. Mexican Americans were enlisting at impressive rates as well as being drafted. And so Roosevelt authorized the guest worker *bracero* program, organized on a relatively informal basis between individual states and Mexico under the general supervision, initially, of the Farm Security Administration, followed in June 1943 by the War Manpower Commission, followed in January 1948 by the Bureau of Employment Security of the United States Department of Labor and renewed successively into the postwar period, most recently in July 1949. All in all, more than 430,000 *braceros* worked in the United States between 1942 and 1950. At the height of the war, *braceros* were also employed in maintaining rail lines, with some forty thousand Mexican nationals by April 1944 working on twenty-four railroad lines, half the total force of railroad maintenance workers in a nation at war.

From the point of view of most growers, the *bracero* program was a great success, bringing as it did strong, capable, eager, and compliant field labor to the harvest, at reasonable rates, under governmental supervision. Arriving by railroad at small-town stations, *bracero* contingents were frequently fêted by welcoming bands and speeches, followed by a barbecue. Many growers, familiarizing themselves with Mexican culture, sponsored special holiday celebrations on Mexican national days. These *braceros*, after all, were keeping alive an agricultural Industry that would otherwise be in serious trouble, and they were doing it, all things considered, with minimal difficulties. *Braceros*, in turn, were being paid what they considered generous wages. (Eighty cents to a dollar an hour as of 1959, as opposed to eighty cents a day in Mexico.) After a year or more in the United States, many could save up to a thousand dollars and return to their home villages affluent and respected men. No wonder, then, defenders of the *bracero* program pointed out, at each center of recruitment on the Mexico–United States border vastly more candidates for *bracero* status were showing up than were needed.

Hence the wetback problem, an almost inevitable result of the *bracero* program, critics charged, with increasing numbers of Mexican nationals, eager to experience the rewards of working in El Norte, crossing the border illegally—swimming across the Rio Grande, as folklore had it, hence getting their backs wet—in increasing numbers as the *bracero* program continued. Once an illegal had established himself in the American labor market, he could make the transition to legal status by being vouched for for a work permit. The larger the farm operation, the greater the tendency to hire wetbacks, such as at the DiGiorgio farms at Arvin near Bakersfield, where immigration officials arrested 315 illegals in 1949. Formally supervised *braceros*, migrants with work permits, and illegals, then, constituted a formidable component of organized agricultural labor in Arkansas, Texas, New Mexico, Arizona, and California by the outbreak of the Korean War in 1950. As might be expected, the Korean War encouraged growers to argue on behalf of even further strengthening and regularization of the *bracero* program through passage of a proposed Public Law 78, reauthorizing and expanding it. Congress passed Public Law 78 in July 1951, and despite warnings from the Department of Labor, fearful of union resistance and other complications, President Truman signed the bill. Between 1950 and 1960, more than 3.3 million Mexican nationals crossed the border in organized and supervised contingents for harvest work in the United States.

From the point of view of growers in the states affected, the *bracero* program was a boon. From the point of view of Mexican American migrant workers, as well as legally resident migrant workers of Mexican or other ancestry, however, the wholesale importation of Mexican nationals constituted a tax-supported, union-busting, scabbing operation of heroic magnitude, analogous to the use of convict labor on public works or mercenaries in the military. How could wages and living conditions in the American migrant workforce ever be improved, they asked, when the competition, reinforced by government, consisted of Mexican nationals coming from a totally different economy and hence willing to work under totally different conditions? Would American auto, aircraft, or steel workers, American railroad workers or stevedores, American plumbers, carpenters, or electricians ever tolerate such legally sanctioned displacement? But these were urban-based industries, organized by union labor, protected by federal and state statutes. The agricultural industry, by contrast, remained rural and off the grid, seen, if at all, by city dwellers in the form of bent-backed workers, glimpsed from a passing automobile, tending the soil in a distant field with short-handled hoes. In California, as elsewhere, there was much mechanization under way in agriculture, and even more talk of mechanization to come; yet the industry still depended, most basically, through a cycle of planting, tending, and harvest, on bodies bent to the ground in repetitive tasks under a searing sun.

In California, the counter-attack against the *bracero* ascendancy came, initially, from the Community Service Organization movement spearheaded by Fred Ross. The CSO movement, however, was urban-oriented, aimed at community organization, voter turnout, the regularization of citizenship, and, eventually, the posting of a full-time lobbyist in Sacramento to advocate the pension proposal and other Mexican American initiatives. As such, the CSO model depended upon urban density, which was why Ross in June 1952 took the movement to East San Jose, the second-largest Mexican American community in the state.

Ernesto Galarza, meanwhile, was advancing the cause among migrant farm workers, Hispanic in the main but not exclusively so. Born in Mexico in 1905, raised in Sacramento, Galarza held a doctorate in economics from Columbia and in 1947 joined the National Farm Labor Union as director of research and education, before being sent by his superiors to Arvin, south of Bakersfield in the southern San Joaquin Valley, with a next-to-impossible assignment: to unionize the migrant workers at DiGiorgio Farms, one of the largest agribusiness operations in the state and one of the biggest contractors for *bracero* labor—and an employer willing to look the other way when it came to the hiring of illegals, provided that the illegals not rock the boat as far as wages and working conditions were concerned. Galarza tried his best to organize Local 218 of the National Farm Labor Union and met with some success, signing up more than thirteen hundred farm workers; but he soon found out that he had merely provoked a colony of wasps. Local 218 went out on strike in October 1947, and DiGiorgio Farms went into Red Alert, quite literally, smearing the walkout as Communist-inspired and appealing to State Senator John Tenney, chair of the state senate Committee on Un-American Affairs, which held hearings. Even more devastating, DiGiorgio Farms brought in phalanxes of *braceros* and illegals to break the strike, which soon happened; and within short order, two years at the most, not one person associated with Local 218 remained on the workforce of DiGiorgio Farms. It was one thing, Galarza recognized, to talk about the rights of workers to organize, as guaranteed by Section 7 of the National Labor Relations Act of 1935. It was another thing entirely to oppose a corporate entity with an inspired but hastily organized ragtag union of migrant workers for whom the organizing efforts of the 1930s were but a distant memory, facing the full power of strikebreaking Mexican national labor, whether legitimatized through the *bracero* program or otherwise.

Like *Mendez v. Westminster*, the unsuccessful strike at DiGiorgio Farms by Local 218 of the National Farm Labor Union nevertheless anticipated and to a certain extent set the stage for the emergence, in time, of yet another expression of Mexican Americans' refusal to accept their restriction to third-class status, in this instance, in the fields by foreign labor, whether *braceros* or wetbacks. And as far as wetbacks were concerned, even the federal administrators running the *bracero* program knew that they had a problem in the flooding of the agricultural migratory workforce with illegals, beyond federal control, breaking the law and subverting the values of American citizenship, taking away jobs from American citizens, especially returning veterans from World War II and the Korean War. By mid-1954, three years after the passage of Public Law 78 had stabilized and expanded the *bracero* program for more than a decade, the Eisenhower administration was putting in motion Operation Wetback, a massive roundup by Immigration and Naturalization Service Border Patrol agents and local police and sheriff's deputies of illegals throughout California and the Southwest. Within a year, more than a million illegals, the so-called wetbacks, had either been rounded up and deported to Mexico or, fearing arrest, had returned to Mexico voluntarily.

The United States did not seem to be willing or able to make up its mind regarding its need for Mexican national labor, in the fields or elsewhere, but seemed, rather, to lurch from one extreme to the other, either porous borders and the creation of a welcoming de facto market for Mexican national labor, or roundups and deportations. The Eisenhower administration was justifying Operation Wetback on grounds that illegals were taking away jobs from veterans. But was there really such a massive market for backbreaking stoop labor in the fields of California and the Southwest among American veterans, Mexican American or otherwise, removed from the barrios and integrated through military experience and able through the GI Bill to acquire training for better-paying jobs in the service industries and trades? The quality and dignity of Mexican American citizenship was coming under assault. The Farm Workers Union movement was, however unintentionally, pitting Mexican Americans against their counterparts from south of the border, whether *bracero* or illegal. While the rounding up of illegals helped Mexican Americans choosing to do migrant labor, there remained a disturbing element of racial prejudice, ethnic cleansing even, in the rounding up and deportation of people of color on such a massive scale, hard-working Mexican people in search of a better life. A prejudicial side effect was being set in motion by Operation Wetback, an equating, whether intended or unintended, voiced or not voiced, of wetbacks and Mexican Americans.

Thus the challenging complexity faced by the first generation of union organizers, Ernesto Galarza, first of all, with his higher degrees, and César Chávez, raised in migrant circumstances in Arizona and California. As a Navy enlisted man during the Second World War, however, Chávez was young, restive, and outspoken when it came to the discrimination that kept him and other Mexican American sailors busy chipping paint, day in and day out, excluded from more prestigious and challenging assignments. While still in uniform, in the town of Delano, Chávez was arrested when he refused to sit in the upper balcony section reserved for Mexicans at the local movie theater. At the police station, Chávez later remembered, a baffled desk sergeant, confronted by what he recognized to be an illegal arrest for violating a law that was not legally on the books, sent Chávez off with a warning. The incident reveals the steel in Chávez's soul that existed alongside the goodness and piety that was also there and would, in time, transform him into a charismatic Catholic union leader. Fred Ross and the Community Service Organization movement galvanized Chávez's talents as an organizer. Chávez joined in 1952 and traveled throughout California for a number of years as a CSO activist and organizer. By birth and upbringing, however, Chávez was not urban-oriented. He knew and feared, as so many Mexican Americans of his generation did, the servitude of the harvest fields, but he sensed there as well an inescapable destiny. As important as the CSO victories might be, whether in voter registration, victories at the polls, or the struggle for old-age pensions, the cause of Mexican Americans, Chávez recognized, could never be detached from agriculture and the land; and that meant the well-being of agricultural workers, so many of them of Mexican descent, under-organized, hence under-housed and under-paid as they performed the repetitive tasks essential to the very survival of society. The manifest absurdities of Operation Wetback—especially the devaluation of Mexican American identity connected inevitably to the roundup of Mexican nationals—further oriented Chávez in the direction of agricultural organizing.

In August 1958, Chávez moved to Oxnard, Ventura County, an epicenter of *bracero* employment, with the intention of organizing a CSO chapter. In the months that followed, Chávez focused his CSO organizational efforts on agricultural issues and agriculture-related strategies. So effective were his organizing efforts— pickets, the strengthening of the local Farm Placement Bureau; a campaign of personalized lobbying, grower to grower, in favor of Mexican Americans and legal Mexican nationals on a job-by-job basis—the CSO became, within a year, the de facto hiring hall for the region. These achievements were not everything, not the defeat of an agribusiness giant, only small victories, resulting from a painstaking identification on a job-by-job basis of jobs held by *braceros* and a job-by-job replacing of these *braceros* with Mexican American or legal Mexican national workers. But it was, all things considered, a breakthrough, not the least in the mind of César Chávez, now promoted to the national director of the CSO movement, replacing Fred Ross.

And so too was it significant in 1961 when Dolores Huerta of the CSO became a full-time lobbyist in Sacramento. Across the next thirty years, Huerta, like Chávez, would emerge as a union and civil rights activist of national stature. She was born in New Mexico, like Edward Roybal, but raised in Stockton since childhood, along with two brothers and two sisters, by her partially disabled grandfather and divorced mother, a ferociously hard-working woman who supported her family as a cook during the Depression, then made the transition to hotelkeeper when she purchased two down-market hotels from a Japanese family being sent to a relocation camp. The family lived in one hotel, and Dolores and her siblings served as maintenance and cleaning staff for both. Dolores Huerta grew up in mid-range, mid-American circumstances: not rich but not poor either, a Girl Scout, enrolled by her mother in piano, violin, and dance lessons, a majorette in local parades. Graduating from Stockton High School in 1947, she attended Delta College, affiliated with College of the Pacific, and went into teaching. Huerta, however, knew the prejudices of a rough-and-tumble Central Valley town: the rebuffs and denials at school, the final grade of C in senior high school English after a succession of A's during the course (she could not have possibly written her own work, her teacher declared, explaining the final grade), the time on V-J Day when her brother, celebrating American victory in his brand-new zoot suit, was beaten on the street.

Huerta left teaching for a career in grassroots CSO organizing, personally recruited by Ross, and was sent by Ross to Sacramento: a twenty-five-year-old, educated, Mexican American woman with a college degree, married and busy with her growing family, yet a most effective lobbyist as well, if one were to judge from the passage in the summer of 1961 of Assembly Bill 5, sponsored by San Francisco assemblyman Phillip Burton and signed into law by Governor Pat Brown in July 1961, granting pension rights to longtime residents, the majority of them Mexican, previously denied eligibility because of defective documentation of citizenship. This latest victory by the CSO further defined its civic focus; and at its annual convention in March 1962, the CSO put itself formally on record that it was a civic organization and not a labor union. And so César Chávez and Dolores Huerta resigned from the CSO in favor of pro-union activism. In the Delano area the two of them organized an effort leading to the founding in September 1962 in Fresno of the Farm Workers Association. Thus began a union—renamed the United Farm Workers Organizing Committee in 1966 and the United Farm Workers in 1972—that, in conjunction with Filipino American farm workers led by Larry Itliong, in September 1965 launched a grape strike, *huelga*, that would become a crusade of national importance to the civil rights movement.

The importance of Filipino American farm workers to the Delano grape strike signified a bridge being built between two minority groups. In very small numbers,
Filipino men had been in California since the mid-nineteenth century, classified as
Manila men or Luzon Indians. With the entry of the United States into the Philippines as a result of the Spanish-American War, a trickle of *pensionados* began to
arrive, young men from good families sent to the United States by the American
colonial government for education and training that would fit them for colonial
administration and other professional pursuits in the new American protectorate.
Between 1910 and 1938, another fourteen thousand or so Filipino students not on
government scholarship were also studying in the United States. Coming from the
more affluent and educated classes in the Philippines, poised and well-mannered,
the so-called fountain pen boys were prized as domestic help, full- or part-time, in
upper-register California households. Many of them, however, unable to find such
comfortable positions, were forced into the fields as migrant workers, which is where
the next great wave of Filipino migration was headed: workers from the less-educated
classes, imported initially into Hawaii by the Hawaiian Sugar Planters Association,
then brought, increasingly, into California in the mid-1920s at the rate of approximately four thousand per year for the rest of the decade after federal legislation had
severely curtailed Chinese and Japanese migration. Little Manila enclaves grew up
in Los Angeles, Watsonville, San Jose, San Francisco, and Stockton, the largest such
settlement. Filipinos held American passports but were not citizens, nor were they
eligible for citizenship. They were, however, officially under the protection of the
United States, which governed the Philippines, and herein they took on distinctive
characteristics. First of all, they had been inculcated in the Philippines, through
the American-sponsored educational system and through the general point of view
of a colonial society strongly under American influence, in the belief that all men
were created equal, in fact and under the law, and that included them. Second, they
spoke English, excellently in many cases, thanks once again to the American sponsored educational system in the Philippines. Filipino migrant workers did not see
themselves as aliens. They existed, rather, in a midway zone between Filipino and
American identity and hence adjusted rapidly to American circumstances.

Coming from a highly socialized culture in the Philippines, Filipino men, the
majority of them young or early middle-aged, enjoyed social life and were possessed
of developed social skills. They were good conversationalists and good dancers and
made every effort to dress well in their off hours, which enabled them, among other
things, to attract the attention of younger white women in cities and small towns
alike. In response to the Filipino market, a new business, taxi-dancing, developed,
gaining momentum throughout the 1930s. For ten cents a dance, each dance lasting
a minute, Filipino men could enjoying dancing with young women, predominately
white or light-skinned Hispanics. Los Angeles alone had half a dozen such places,
frequented by Filipino men in MacIntosh suits, double-breasted and English cut,
like William Powell wore in the movies and representing a considerable investment
on the part of an individual migrant worker. Here on the dance floor, Filipino men

ceased for the moment to be migrant workers at the bottom of the social ladder and experienced themselves—their small strong bodies moving across the dance floor, the feel of a young woman in their arms—as men, proper men, respected men, electric in their attraction to the opposite sex.

When taxi-dance establishments were opened in the late 1920s in smaller towns or when young Filipino men tried to date local white girls in rural areas, a perfect storm for violence coalesced. In October 1929 in Exeter, a small farming community in the San Joaquin Valley, Filipino farm laborers, defending themselves against an attack, stabbed two white men. A mob of three hundred white men formed, marched to a nearby Filipino labor camp, ordered the residents out, and burned the camp to the ground. Three months later, in January 1930, an even worse five-day riot broke out in the Pajaro Valley near Watsonville, protesting, among other things, the opening of a Filipino dance hall in the nearby town of Palm Beach. This time, the mobs that formed and re-formed over the five-day period ranged from two hundred to five hundred and were bent on a pogrom, a racial cleansing, most horribly expressed in the execution of Fermin Tobera, a young Filipino lettuce picker, by a group of young white men from privileged backgrounds, allegedly using a tommy gun so as to create a clear-cut message to Filipino workers in the area to clear out. Locally, the Filipino community rallied, although it avoided talk of armed resistance. In Washington the Philippine Commissioners to the United States requested a formal investigation of the Tobera murder, and in the Philippines itself a day of national observance was organized. San Jose congressman Arthur Free rose in the House to blame the riots upon Filipino migrant workers "luring young white girls into degradation."[4] Headlines and speeches in the Salinas Valley and beyond were equally lurid, compounded by the mistaken belief, first reported on 30 January 1930, that a sixteen-year-old girl was being held captive at a labor camp by Filipino farm workers. Speeches and newspaper reports hammered away as well at the notion that these disturbances were somehow Communist-inspired. Anti-Filipino attacks, meanwhile, spilled over to San Jose and Los Angeles.

The Watsonville Riots, as these disturbances came to be known, did not result in any indictments. The riots did result, however, in an intensification of anti-Filipino agitation, together with sporadic outbreaks of anti-Filipino demonstrations stopping short of full-scale riots. Efforts coalesced to banish Filipinos from the fields and canneries of Central California, indeed, to banish them from entering the United States at all and to repatriate Filipinos already in the country. The banning of Filipino entry into the United States, however, was unconstitutional, since the Philippines were an American protectorate. So, ironically, anti-Filipino agitation helped pass the Tydings-McDuffie Act of 1934, otherwise known as the Philippine Independence Act, granting independence to the Philippines as of 1946; but also, now that independence had been granted, reducing to an annual quota of fifty—only fifty!—the number of Filipino migrants who could legally enter the United States each year. The following year, on 11 July 1935, Roosevelt signed the Filipino Repatriation Act, which said that the United States would bear the expenses of any Filipino wishing to return to the homeland. The Department of Labor went so far as to charter a special train leaving New York for San Francisco, stopping along the way at Cleveland, Chicago, and St. Louis, to deliver a trainload of Filipinos to the passenger ship *President Coolidge* for transportation to Manila. Intended to lure some 45,000 Filipinos back to the Islands, the Repatriation Act succeeded in removing only 2,190.

However difficult things were in the United States, the majority of Filipinos in the United States were determined to stay—and to continue efforts at organization, beginning with the Filipino-dominated Agricultural Workers League formed in 1930 and the Filipino Labor Union formed in Salinas in October 1933, intended to unite an estimated thirty thousand farm workers, vegetable workers and shippers, labor contractors, and allied businessmen into a statewide union, Filipino and non-Filipino alike, to push for a minimum wage of thirty-five cents per hour, an eight-hour day, recognition of the union as a bargaining agent and hiring hall, and, most important, the total banishment of discrimination in employment on the basis of race. Going out against lettuce growers in Salinas in August and September 1935, the Filipino Labor Union, to everyone's surprise, achieved an almost total victory, piquing the interest of big labor, which for the first time glimpsed an opportunity for recruitment in the harvest fields and canneries of California. Within a few years, the California Federation of Labor, the American Federation of Labor, and the Congress of Industrial Organizations were active in a number of farm workers, vegetable workers and shippers, and cannery workers unions throughout Central California. One of these unions, the Filipino Agricultural Workers Association, enrolled more than six thousand Filipino farm laborers and contractors in the fields surrounding Stockton, Sacramento, and a number of other Central Valley cities. By 1940 the Filipino Agricultural Laborers Association, now renamed the Federated Agricultural Laborers Association, had more than thirty thousand members throughout California and had organized or was in the process of organizing numerous successful labor actions. Filipino solidarity, together with Filipino social and organizational skills, in short, had put the Filipino agricultural unions in the vanguard of the farm labor movement.

The Second World War offered even further opportunities. By late 1943 the United States Army had established three Filipino units: the 1st Filipino Infantry Regiment, the 1st Battalion of the 2nd Filipino Infantry Regiment, and the 1st Reconnaissance Battalion (Special). These units saw extensive service in the Pacific, culminating in the liberation of the Philippines. In February 1943, moreover, just before the 1st and the 2nd embarked for overseas, hundreds of Filipino infantrymen were sworn in as citizens at ceremonies at Camp Beale. Following the war, hundreds of Filipino American soldiers, as they now were, serving in the Philippines, brought home Filipina war brides, bringing to the United States for the first time a significant number of Filipina women and thus allowing for family formation on a hitherto unprecedented scale. Opportunities for citizenship were extended even further with the passage of the Filipino Naturalization Act, authorizing citizenship to any Filipino living in the United States prior to March 1943. The Immigration and Nationality

Act of 1952, also known as the McCarran-Walter Act, finally, had strong provisions for quotas reuniting relatives of citizens and permanent residents.

Thus by the late 1950s, the Filipino community of California, while still strongly represented in migrant labor, had been expanded to include Filipino American families with American-born children, urbanized, with a strong representation in Stockton, the Bay Area, and Los Angeles, and high levels of home ownership, given the eligibility of so many Filipino men for veteran loans and other forms of veteran financing. In the mysterious alchemy of history, their citizenship, prosperity, and civil rights remained linked to the memory of those who had gone before them: Fountain pen boys in the early 1900s, struggling to stay awake over their books after a day of hard work and night classes; migrant farm laborers, bent under the searing sun, crowded into spartan dormitories, organizing, organizing, living as they aged in single occupancy hotel rooms, such as those of the International Hotel in San Francisco, their possessions and memories crowded into a few square feet—and yet remembering as well the long-ago days in which they had come together and formed a union and those sweet nights they had glided across the dance floor.

During the Second World War—with the exception of one voluntary all-Chinese-American unit requested by General Claire Chennault of Flying Tiger fame to create further solidarity with Chinese allies—Chinese Americans were not segregated in the military. A new confidence characterized Chinese American life in the years following the war analogous to the transformations of American soldiers in World War I expressed by the song "How 'Ya Gonna Keep 'Em Down on the Farm After They've Seen Paree?" No Asian group played a more important role in the establishment of the state in the nineteenth century than the Chinese. The Chinese were more than immigrants. They were founders. The trans-Sierra railroad they built reflected the Great Wall of China itself in its magnitude and importance. The levees the Chinese constructed in the Sacramento Valley remained serviceable, crucial in fact, into the twentieth century. Among other enterprises—laundries, restaurants, grocery stores, brick kilns—the Chinese pioneered the fishing industry in California and constituted the first wave of agricultural workers following Americanization. Entering the domestic service of the affluent, they became trusted household retainers to the oligarchy—cooking their food, caring for their children, helping to establish domestic culture—and, in doing this, became shadow members of influential families. Survey photographs of California in the post–Civil War era, and you find the Chinese everywhere: in their own urban settlements, hence in groups almost exclusively male, but also as farm workers in planting and harvest, fishermen drying their nets on the shores of San Francisco and Monterey bays, cooks and housemen on ranches north and south, housemen on the great estates, attired in silken coats with mandarin collars. They are almost always men, for the migration of Chinese women to California was banned by law.

While other concentrations of Chinese existed throughout the state, Chinatown San Francisco was the largest and most strategically located colonial enclave projecting China onto the North American continent. In the nineteenth century and well into the twentieth, this paradigmatic projection challenged white California to come to terms with the people and culture of this commanding portion of the human race. The China Trade between New England and China had, beginning in the 1790s, first brought California to American attention and nurtured that awareness in the golden age of Bryant and Sturgis, whose ships kept New England, California, and China linked in a network of exchange. In the early American period, Bay Area figures such as journalist Benjamin Parke Avery and lawyer-politician Anson Burlingame understood the need for this connection and, each of them in turn, served terms as United States minister to China. For such patrician figures— including Charles Crocker, construction chief for the trans-Sierra railroad—hiring the Chinese in great numbers, bringing them individually into their households as trusted domestics, the Chinese connection was positive, if not exactly egalitarian. The lower down the white California pecking order one found oneself by the 1870s, a decade of depression and unemployment, however, the more the Chinese became, in UCLA historian Alexander Saxton's term, the Indispensable Enemy in whom could be found a convenient cause and scapegoat for every sort of misery.

The story of this persecution—summarized in San Francisco demagogue Denis Kearney's cry, "The Chinese must go!"—culminated, if not in an ethnic cleansing of Chinese from California, then at least in their banishment by federal statute in the 1880s from any further immigration. Yet even with this victory in hand, it would be almost surreal, if it were not so painful, to chronicle the continuing persecution by ordinance leveled by white San Francisco against its Chinese citizens. Efforts were made to bar Chinese from fishing, a measure declared unconstitutional by federal judge Lorenzo Sawyer. Another ordinance, Order Number 1569, dated 26 May 1880, attempted to bar the Chinese from running a laundry without the specific permission of the San Francisco Board of Supervisors. No permission would be given, moreover, unless the laundry was in a building constructed from either brick or stone, this at a time when of the 320 laundries operating in San Francisco, 310 were in wood buildings, 240 of them run by Chinese. Another ordinance, passed in May 1882 and intended to run concurrently, made it illegal to run a laundry east of Larkin Street, without explicit permission from the board of supervisors upon the recommendation of twelve citizens and taxpayers in the block where the laundry was to operate. The penalty: a fine up to $1,000 and up to six months in prison.

When laundry operator Quong Woo defied the law, he was arrested, convicted, and sentenced—and appealed to the federal court. On 1 July 1885, more than two hundred Chinese were refused laundry licenses under the new ordinance. Laundry operator Yick Wo fought the case up to the Supreme Court of California and lost, then won in federal court with a Fourteenth Amendment argument, calling for equal protection under the law. Justice Stephen Field, meanwhile, voided the conviction of Quong Woo on the basis that the supervisors had no right to delegate their licensing authority to twelve citizens on any given block. Only for reasons of health and/or good morals, Field opined, could a laundry be shut down. Field's decision provided the route on which the board of supervisors now re-launched its attack, passing an ordinance on 18 June 1883 requiring all laundries to be inspected by health officials and fire wardens. Once again, there was an arrest, in this case of laundryman Soon Hing, and an appeal. This time, however, Justice Field, having made the initial ruling regarding health, morals, and safety, upheld the city. From that time forward, Chinese laundries were kept under control—but not eliminated entirely—via health and safety requirements.

On the one hand, this harassment can be seen as a minor chapter in the story of anti-Chinese persecution, unless one happened to be laundry operators Yick Wo, Quong Woo, Soon Hing, or the hundreds of other Chinese operators being affected, or, in the case of the fishing ban, fisherman Ah Chong, who also sued and won a favorable decision from Judge Sawyer. Attempts at imaginative literature at the time, however—specifically a series of apocalyptic short stories and novels dealing with a Chinese invasion of the United States—reveal the deeper fear behind this warfare by harassing ordinance. No category of Chinese-related fiction was stronger, Taiwanese scholar Li-min Chu notes, especially in the 1880s, than essays, short stories, and novels—such as *Last Days of the Republic* (1880) by P. W. Dooner and *A Short and Truthful History of the Taking of California and Oregon by the Chinese in the Year* A.D. *1899* (1882) by Robert Woltor—together with a number of overland novellas, either predicting or describing in an early instance of Yellow Peril ideology a Chinese invasion and takeover of the United States for which the Chinese of California, centered on Chinatown San Francisco, served as a reconnaissance in force and fifth column.

Other fictive themes isolated and analyzed by Li-min Chu include tales of opium dens, tong wars, deceit, and vengeance (the Fu Manchu stereotype, it might be called) and more positive stories of loyalty from servants and comic Chinese shtick of various sorts that can be traced back to Bret Harte. When it came to sexual matters, Li-min Chu finds one continuing preoccupation among white writers, miscegenation, meaning sexual attraction between Chinese and white and the usually tragic results—from the nineteenth- and early twentieth-century point of view—of a mixed-race heritage. Hardly any of this fiction involves sexually aggressive Chinese males, although there are a number of stories of erotically charged emotional attachments by Chinese male servants to their white female employers. The celibacy enforced on the Chinese men of California through immigration restriction was forced on them in fiction as well. Chinese females, by contrast, are depicted as objects of honorable, if disquieting, romantic love from white males, although the outcome of these unions is almost always tragic.

Along with the laundry ordinances that so bedeviled Chinatown San Francisco were an equal number of measures based on the assumption that the Chinese were a disease-ridden people. Between 1875 and 1885, the board of supervisors deported forty-eight Chinese immigrants for leprosy and elephantiasis, a disease frequently confused with leprosy in that era. Ironically, when bubonic plague was detected in Chinatown in March 1900, at a time when it had erupted in Hong Kong and spread to India, both the leaders of the Chinese community and the white establishment initially went into denial, although with federal help a full-scale battle of disinfectant efforts and rat-proofing of buildings against the disease was launched in Chinatown. When bubonic plague reappeared in San Francisco between 1907 and 1909, all seventy-seven people who died from the disease were white. Pre-Earthquake Chinatown did possess more than its fair share of haphazardly constructed, badly ventilated, rat-ridden, over-crowded living spaces devoid of plumbing and related amenities, as might be expected in a restricted ghetto peopled almost entirely by working men. Then there was the question of vice, whether brothels or opium dens or combinations thereof. At this point, a racist point of view might have been gratified by the mere noting of these places, but they did exist, as, once again, might be expected in an all-male society; indeed, printed maps from the final decades of the nineteenth century are in the collection of the Society of California Pioneers color-coding the brothels of Chinatown. The color-coding of brothel clients, however, remains an unanswered question. Certain it was, however, that whites frequented the basement gambling and opium dens of the district. Connected to prostitution, gambling, and opium was another fixed image of San Francisco Chinatown as a violent arena of hatchet men engaged in gang (tong) warfare in the back alleys and underground tunnels of the Chinese quarter. The San Francisco newspapers of the era delighted in covering prostitution, gambling, tong wars, and related topics for their white readership. Once again, there was evidence to justify this perception, although racial stereotyping and urban folklore had a way of escalating this particular scenario. The novella *Edith: A Story of Chinatown* (1895) by Harry M. Johnson represents an early anti-prostitution tract at a time when American writers were beginning to address this topic. In the short story "The Third Circle," published in the *Wave* in the 1890s, Frank Norris tells an horrific tale of a young white woman kidnapped into sexual slavery while visiting Chinatown.

As far as the reflections and refractions of nineteenth-century fiction were concerned, the Chinese remained entrapped in stereotype: either demonized as invaders, damned as menaces to public health, painted as addicts of violence and vice, or begrudgingly accepted as quaint and colorful retainers. At this point, Edith Maude Eaton took Chinese-related fiction in a new direction. English on her father's side, Chinese on her mother's, Eaton wrote under her girlhood name, Sui Sin Far, and is today considered the foundress of Asian American literature. As a newspaper-woman in San Francisco and Seattle at the turn of the century, Eaton mastered the setting and themes of Chinese life on the Pacific Coast; hence her stories succeed as regional realism at a time when a generation of women writers—Mary Wilkins Freeman and Sarah Orne Jewett of New England, Edith Wharton of New York, ex-Nebraskan Willa Cather, Ellen Glasgow of Virginia, Kate Chopin of New Orleans, Margaret Collier Graham of Southern California—were placing their female characters in highly localized settings. Having wrestled with the implications of her dual ethnicity across a lifetime, Sui Sin Far brought a whole new level of depth to the fictional depiction of Chinese people and the classic themes of Chinese-related fiction, including attractions across the color line. The refined perceptions of Sui Sin Far exercised their influence. In the first three decades of the twentieth century, in the nationally published fiction of such Bay Area writers as Charles Caldwell Dobie, Hugh Wiley, and Idwal Jones, the image of the Chinese of California, although remaining ensconced in stereotypes, nevertheless tended to shed negative assessments in favor of presentations that, while adhering to the exotic, endowed Chinese protagonists with an enlarged humanity. Even the Charlie Chan mystery stories of Earl Derr Biggers, published between 1925 and 1932 and spinning off film versions through the 1940s, represent—for all their stereotyping, for which they are today roundly criticized—an enhancement of Chinese humanity via the intelligence, wisdom, good humor, courage, and loving fatherhood of the celebrated Chinese American detective.

On the national level, this opening to Chinese humanity was paced by novelist Pearl Buck, who had lived long in China as the daughter of Protestant missionaries and later the wife of a missionary. Buck's novel *The Good Earth* (1931) won the Pulitzer Prize and, together with successor novels in the same setting and spirit, set the stage for her 1938 Nobel Prize in literature. Californian Alice Tisdale Hobart, another China veteran like Buck, sustained the literary momentum created by Buck with *Oil for the Lamps of China* (1934), a novel centered on an idealistic American businessman trying to bring material and social progress to China. In 1934 Stanford sociologist Richard LaPiere was awarded a Rockefeller grant to study Chinatown San Francisco. In addition to scholarly writing, LaPiere turned to fiction as well to express his affection and high regard for the Chinese of the city. Set in nineteenth-century China, LaPiere's first novel, *Son of Han* (1937), tells the story of how a young man of modest background is barred from his goal of becoming a respected scholar through family and other forms of social obligation. In his second novel, *When the Living Strive* (1941), LaPiere tells the exactly opposite story: how Lew Gan migrates to California from China, settles in Chinatown San Francisco, first finds work as a houseboy, then becomes a successful importer and civic leader, negotiates the reconstruction of Chinatown in the aftermath of the Earthquake and Fire of April 1906, and spends his senior years as a respected elder.

Two years after the publication of LaPiere's *When the Living Strive*, a twenty-six-year-old immigrant by the name of Chin Y. Lee—born in Hunan, China, and having lived as well in Burma, India, and Indochina—arrived in Los Angeles. Learning of an opening on the San Francisco newspaper *Chinese World*, Lee moved to Chinatown San Francisco, which he covered for three years as a columnist and editor while writing programs for Radio Free Asia. Following the war, Lee spent two years at the Yale Drama School acquiring an M.F.A. degree and for the rest of his life worked as a novelist, short story writer, freelance arts critic, and, at one point, a scriptwriter for Twentieth Century–Fox. His greatest success as a novelist was *The Flower Drum Song* (1957), brought to Broadway in December 1958 as a musical by Rodgers and Hammerstein and released as a film in 1961. C. Y. Lee, as he signed his novel, had enjoyed a thorough education in Chinese classics, including classic prose fiction, and *The Flower Drum Song* is possessed of that distinctive blend of fairy tale and social realism characteristic of the classic Chinese novel: a sense of enchantment, that is, fused with the details of everyday life. Hence the sociology and social realism of *The Flower Drum Song* are surprisingly vital, despite its fairy-tale quality.

The Chinatown San Francisco covered by C. Y. Lee as a newspaper columnist was a complex and integrated society, responding to city, state, and national law but also self-governed by twenty-eight family associations: Dere, Yee, Lee, Chan, and Wong, among others, together with five associations representing fusions of families, such as the Lung Kong Tin Yee Association, representing the Low, Quan, Jang, Chew, and other families. Not only did these families govern themselves through associations, they also apportioned out among themselves various businesses. The Dere family, for example, ran fruit and candy stores. The Yees and the Lees owned and ran the better restaurants and supplied most of the professional cooks.

Next upward in the hierarchy came some district associations, keyed to the districts in China from which residents came. By the 1940s there were eleven such district associations operative in Chinatown. The Chinese Six Companies stood at the apex of self-governing organizations. The elders of the Six Companies constituted a *gran signori* for Chinatown, presiding over and serving the community at the highest level, accruing and investing capital, organizing charities, conducting the largest Chinese-language school in Chinatown, raising relief for the homeland in time of need, playing a determining role in the annual Chinese New Year's Parade. Also operative were various trade guilds representing cooks, laundry workers, cigar makers, garment makers, and merchant seamen, which also functioned as social organizations for their respective populations. And then, of course, there were the tongs, shadowy associations of single men, many of them, such as the Chee Kung Tong, bonded together by secret oaths and rituals. In earlier days, the tongs ran protection rackets throughout Chinatown, and they still, as of the 1940s, had a hand in gambling and other illicit activities, although the slave-trade prostitution culture of Chinatown was by a now a thing of the past, thanks in part to the vigilance of the Chinatown Squad of the San Francisco Police Department but even more to the still-inadequate but growing presence of Chinese women in the community, immigrant and American-born, and the development of family life.

This was the Chinatown San Francisco Jade Snow Wong grew up in and where by the 1950s she was living as an established writer and ceramic artist whose girlhood memoir *Fifth Chinese Daughter* (1950) sold 250,000 copies. Born in 1922, Wong grew up in Chinatown in a Christian family making the transition from Chinese to Chinese American. In the Chinese American side of her development, Wong graduated from Mills College, apprenticed herself as a ceramicist, and opened her own successful pottery business. During the Second World War, she was asked to dedicate a Liberty ship. Margaret Chung, meanwhile, the first American-born Chinese female physician in the United States, had also established herself in Chinatown and by the Second World War had become a celebrity to American pilots flying in the Far East, for whom a visit to Dr. Chung was a rite of good luck en route to or returning from the Pacific. A bohemian on the sly as well as an established figure, the attractive Dr. Chung had a number of lesbian relationships with local and Hollywood celebrities. By the 1950s Chinatown San Francisco had become an Americanized place, with its own chamber of commerce, branch library, public school, Optimists Club, Sportsmen's Club, Asian American Bar Association, Chinese American Citizens Alliance lodge, Miss Chinatown Beauty Pageant, medical clinics, daycare centers, clubs for the elderly, clubs for the young, Catholic and Protestant churches, a YMCA and a YWCA, ballroom dancing classes, newspapers in Chinese and English, a Chinese-language movie theater, funeral parlors, antique stores, a drum and bugle corps, a sports car club, nightclubs, and celebrities such as Charlie Low, the polo-playing owner of Forbidden City, actor-antique specialist Ching Wah Lee, and, by then, Jade Snow Wong and C. Y. Lee. On 17 October 1957, Herbert P. Lee, twenty-four, was sworn in as San Francisco's first Chinese American policeman. Previously, the department had denied admittance to Chinese candidates, so it said, because they could not meet the five-foot nine-inch height requirement. Officer Lee stood at five feet nine and a half inches.

In *The Flower Drum Song*, C. Y. Lee presents Chinatown as an urban enclave that in the aftermath of the Second World War, the subsequent establishment of the People's Republic, the Korean Conflict, and the Cold War was receiving into American life four distinct generations: refugee elders (Wang Chi-yang, age sixty-three, the Old Master from Hunan, a widower, comfortably ensconced in a two-story home three blocks from Grant Avenue, thoroughly Chinese in organization and routine, and Madam Tang, the widowed sister of his late wife); the refugee middle-aged and young (Chang Ling-yu, age forty, a Berkeley Ph.D. in political science; Linda Tung, a divorced adventuress intent on a singing career); the American-born who remained strongly Chinese in culture (Wang Ta, age twenty-eight, Wang Chi-yang's eldest son, a medical student); and the younger American-born (Wang San, a teenager, preferring baseball to Confucius). Each of these characters is in one or another stage of development regarding Americanization. Wang Chi-yang, the Old Master, has brought China with him. Madam Tang, his sister-in-law, loves the citizenship lessons she is taking, looks forward to citizenship, and is already more than half American. So too Chang Ling-yu, the UC Berkeley Ph.D., is glad to be out of Communist China, wants to get rich, and has left academia for the grocery business. Wang Ta, also a UC graduate, is studying medicine and is caught between two worlds, especially when it comes to his love life. His younger brother Wang San barely understands Chinese and prefers hot dogs to any number of the exquisite Chinese dishes C. Y. Lee has his characters enjoying in the course of the novel. By the conclusion of *The Flower Drum Song*, the central characters have either begun, continued, or completed a complex journey to Americanization. Wang Ta becomes engaged to May Li, a young immigrant from the old country, who sings the traditional Flower Drum Song but looks forward to an American future. Chang Ling-yu is planning the first supermarket in Chinatown. Even Wang

Chi-yang, the Old Master, has agreed to seek Western medical help for his persistent cough.

To suggest the primacy of the African American struggle for civil rights in the late 1950s and 1960s is not in any way to devalue the importance of other peoples of color to the emerging civil rights movement in California. From the beginning, American California had been a Jim Crow society; indeed, the Constitutional Convention meeting in Monterey in the summer of 1849 briefly considered the possibility of banishing all African American migration to California, thereby creating an early version of an apartheid state. While this extreme measure was not adopted, African Americans were given next to no civil rights in the nascent state, were prohibited from testifying in court, and in general were relegated to fourth-rate status. Less documented has been the equally recoverable record of African American success as miners, farmers, artisans, business investors, activists in the California Underground Railroad, clergy, and journalists. Which is why, perhaps, amidst all the problems facing African American Los Angeles in the early 1950s—police brutality, restrictive real estate covenants, segregation in schools and employment, underserved ghetto residential districts—the black community took up the issue of just exactly who founded Los Angeles in the first place. Each September since the turn of the century, the city of Los Angeles sponsored a festival reenactment on the Plaza, followed by a civic dinner, of the founding of the city in 1781. By the mid-twentieth century, this pageant had long since become a city-sponsored event. The language attached to the festival was pure RamonaLand, which is to say, it depicted Los Angeles as an outpost of European Spanish civilization. Not so, historian John Weatherwax editorialized in the *Negro History Bulletin* for October 1954. Twenty-six of the original founders of Los Angeles, Weatherwax claimed, were Negroes, sixteen were Indians, and only two were European whites. Only a majority of Hispanics of African descent, Weatherwax argued, inured to the rigors of frontier existence, were willing to volunteer for the hardships of founding a pueblo so far from the settled portions of New Spain.

The founders' controversy continued for the next decade amidst so many much more important events as far as black liberation was concerned; yet the African American community of Los Angeles, in getting behind this campaign to clarify the record, was not indulging in a form of antiquarianism. It made a difference—a true difference, a difference of relevance to the civil rights struggle—to note the large number of Afro-Hispanics, however this figure might be adjusted, present at the founding. Matters reached a crisis in 1961 when black cultural groups threatened to picket the Plaza commemoration and dinner if the Afro-Hispanic contribution to the founding of the city continued to be ignored. Elected with the strong support of the African American community, Mayor Sam Yorty agreed. It was time to acknowledge, Yorty announced, just exactly who had founded the city. Otherwise, he would cancel any public support for the festival. Organizers responded by canceling the pageant in favor of a simple announcement by a mounted horseman in costume depicting Felipe de Neve, the governor of Alta California in 1781, announcing that, yes indeed, the City of Angels had been founded.

Los Angeles County itself, meanwhile, was leveling off from a wartime and post-war increase of its black population from 97,000 as of 1940 to 440,000 as of 1962. During the war, the defense industry had spiked this growth, increasing the African American population of all California from 124,306 in 1940 to 462,172 by 1950, centered in Los Angeles, the Bay Area, and San Diego. The very nature and texture of African American life in California was being changed. In the early 1900s, the African American middle class, along with the white middle-class, had discovered Los Angeles and Southern California and for very much the same reasons had moved there accordingly. By the 1920s, black Los Angeles tended to be middle class and Republican, or, if Democratic, peopled by such established members of the community as members of the Brotherhood of Sleeping Car Porters or related organizations. This Los Angeles produced architect Paul Williams, Nobel Prize winner Ralph Bunche, Mayor Tom Bradley, the Liberty Savings and Loan Company, the Golden State Mutual Life Insurance Company, a network of impressive metropolitan churches, a newspaper—the *California Eagle*, edited since 1912 by Charlotta Bass—and the allied resort community at Lake Elsinore. This African American Los Angeles also produced, cumulatively, a generation of jazz greats first developing their talents in the prewar period. While San Francisco could not match Los Angeles in the scale, scope, or affluence of its black community, it nevertheless also supported a solidly established African American society, characterized by sustained and sustaining employment rates. Following the influx of black migrants to Los Angeles in the mid- to late 1930s and the accelerating pace of this migration during and following the Second World War, Los Angeles had emerged by the late 1950s as an epicenter of African American society in the United States. In Northern California, Oakland was en route to becoming a black majority city. Given these numbers, it is not surprising that Jim Crow California should come under renewed attack.

The first assault against Jim Crow California was the most fundamental, because it involved a racist assessment of human worth and a restriction by the state of a fundamental human right. Section 69 of the California Civil Code forbade the marriage of a white person "with a Negro, mulatto, Mongolian or member of the Malay race." Not even the Alien Land Acts leveled against the Japanese represented a more negative judgment based on race or a more egregious intrusion by the state into personal freedom. How best to attack Section 69, however, became the question. Similar restrictions were on the books of many states, and as of the 1940s the question of interracial marriage, even in the minds of those who would not favor legal restrictions, remained a delicate topic edging into taboo. The legal and theoretical basis for resistance would come from the most unexpected of quarters, the First Amendment, protecting freedom of religion. This, at least, is the way that Los Angeles attorney Daniel Marshall, president of the Catholic Interracial Council of Los Angeles, saw the matter when in 1947 his family's former high school babysitter, Andrea Dena Perez, a Mexican American, sought his help. She had fallen in love with an African American, Perez informed Marshall and his wife. His name was Sylvester Scott Davis Jr. and the two of them wished to be married in the Catholic Church. Strongly influenced by the writings of the Jesuit moralist John LaFarge, the Harvard-educated convert son of the noted American artist and a lifelong proponent of equal rights for minorities, Marshall saw an opening, if Perez and Davis were willing to challenge the system. They agreed. On 1 August 1947 Perez and Davis filed for a marriage license in Los Angeles County and were refused. Seven days later Marshall filed *Perez v. Sharp*, naming the head of the Los Angeles County Marriage License Bureau as correspondent. Sylvester Scott Davis, Jr., and Andrea Dena Perez, Marshall argued, were being denied the right to practice their religion in the form of a sacramental marriage according to the rites of the Roman Catholic Church. The Archdiocese of Los Angeles, however, fearing the negative reaction of the general public, refused to assist Marshall in any way whatsoever, although Father LaFarge himself did provide a strong letter of support.

When *Perez v. Sharp* reached the California Supreme Court in 1948, it met the active and previously unexpected support of Justice Roger Traynor, a former UC Berkeley law professor. Sensing the legal ambiguities surrounding Marshall's First Amendment argument, Traynor shifted discussion to Marshall's Fourteenth Amendment argument involving equal protection before the law. Traynor's questioning—revolving around the issue of whether the state could abrogate a fundamental human right for an entire group of citizens, strictly on the basis of either racist attitudes or shaky anthropology or a combination thereof—constituted a tour de force of legal inquiry. Six months later, the California Supreme Court issued its decision, declaring, in a one-vote majority, that California's anti-miscegenation law was illegal. Each of the concurring judges seemed to have a differing opinion as to exactly why this was the case. In December 1948 Andrea Perez and Sylvester Davis received a marriage license from Los Angeles County, and the following May they were married in a nuptial mass in St. Patrick's Church in East Los Angeles.

Where, however, were the newly married couple to live? And could public accommodations of any sort be denied them because of race or color? The answer was, unfortunately, they could be denied public accommodation in scores of places, and they would be able to buy or rent only in areas designated by real estate covenant as available to people of color. The successful assault against discrimination in public accommodations, implemented by the Unruh Civil Rights Act of 1959, had a most improbable genesis, as improbable as its sponsor himself, Jesse Marvin Unruh, assemblyman from the Sixty-fifth District, centered on USC, Exposition Park, and South Central Los Angeles.

Already, the influence of white judges on crucial civil-rights-related cases had asserted itself. What would have been the outcome in *Oyama v. State of California*, for example, without the brilliant and thoroughly unexpected line of questioning advanced by Chief Justice Phil Gibson? And what would have happened to *Perez v. Sharp* without the intervention of Justice Robert Traynor? The influence of an individual judge, whether on the trial or appellate level, was in a class by itself. It would be naïve, moreover, to detach this influence from an individual judge's life experience, social and cultural heritage, personal psychology, and, to be sure, philosophy and approach to the law. The 1930s, for example, could not have witnessed such a wholesale repression of the labor movement as occurred in California without the backing of ultra-right judges from agricultural areas. Hence the importance of liberal judges, or even open-minded moderate judges, slowly but steadily assuming positions on the bench in the postwar era. Judge Stanley Mosk is perhaps the most dramatic case in point. A liberal, serving as clemency secretary and, later, executive secretary to Governor Culbert Olson, Mosk was appointed by Olson to the superior court in Los Angeles, thereby becoming the youngest superior court judge in California. Mosk took a leave of absence during the war to serve as a private first class in the Army Transportation Corps, returned to the bench, then ran successfully for attorney general of California in 1958, serving two terms before going on the California Supreme Court, where he would write a grand total of 1,486 opinions. Mosk epitomized a new kind of presence on the bench and before the bar: liberal, Jewish, learned, openly committed to the reform of society in the matter of racial discrimination.

Jesse Unruh, however, was another matter. He was a legislator, not a judge, a hardscrabble Kansas-born, Texas-raised evangelical Protestant, one of the Folks drifting into Southern California during the Depression via Route 66, then making a go of it, of sorts, in the promised land. Following service as an enlisted man in the United States Navy during World War II, rejected by the Army Air Corps for pilot training because of his flat feet, Unruh attended USC on the GI Bill, graduating in 1948. Given his background—the deprivation, the sense of coming from third-class status, resentment of the big shots who seemed to be running the world—Unruh could have easily gone right, cracker right, blaming people of color for his circumstances. Unruh went left, however, although he never detached himself from the gritty realities of day-to-day power politics—to include a restructuring of his district so that it stayed white—despite an almost ferocious commitment to redressing wrongs leveled against people of color.

Starting in late 1958, Unruh pulled off a legislative end run that fast-forwarded the civil rights movement not only in California but across the nation. In the late fall of 1958, Unruh's legislative assistant Marvin Holen, a UCLA-trained lawyer, read an item in the *Los Angeles Herald* noting that the state supreme court had upheld a refusal by the Hollywood Professional School, a private institution, to exclude a young black woman, strictly because of her race. Holen passed the item on to Unruh, who was outraged. Early in the 1959 session, with Unruh serving as chairman of the Ways and Means Committee, the most powerful committee in the assembly, Unruh commissioned Holen to draft a law, Assembly Bill 2702, prohibiting discrimination on the basis of race in a wide variety of accommodations serving the public throughout the state: hotels, cemeteries, fraternal organizations, train and bus stations, airports, "in all business establishments of every kind whatsoever," in a key phrase crafted by Holen. Even more dramatically, another Unruh associate, Nathaniel Colley—an African American graduate of Tuskegee and Yale Law School who had risen from private to captain during World War II — added a monumental preamble: "All persons within the jurisdiction of this state are free and equal." It was that simple. Jesse Unruh, as he would pungently phrase it, had gotten ticked off about what had been done to one individual black girl and had decided to do something about it, and, being chairman of the Ways and Means Committee, as it turned out, he could do plenty.

Assembly Bill 2702 went to the senate, which was controlled by the rural counties, and there it languished, as the conservative rural senators intended, in a graveyard for bills known as the Governmental Efficiency Committee. After two or three months of such neglect, Unruh countered with a bold and brilliant move. No senate bill, none whatsoever, he declared, would be heard by the assembly Ways and Means Committee until his civil rights bill was heard by the senate. Aghast, the conservative senators consulted their options and discovered that they had none. Unruh had the legal authority and the political muscle to carry out his threat. Assembly Bill 2702 — soon to be known as the Unruh Civil Rights Act — was heard, and it passed, and Governor Pat Brown signed it forthwith.

The next great advance in civil rights legislation in California, the Rumford Act of 1963, banning discrimination in housing, had a more tumultuous history, suggestive, in part, of the backlash to come. Ever since Giants star Willie Mays had been denied the home of his choice in San Francisco in the fall of 1957, sentiment against housing segregation, whether enforced by covenant, gentlemen's agreements in the real estate industry, neighborhood pressure, or a combination thereof, had emerged in the minds of liberal California as the next big segregationist policy to be tackled. Coming out of nowhere, the Unruh Civil Rights Act of 1959 only accelerated the determination of liberal Californians to end Jim Crow practices in statewide real estate, sales and rentals alike. Initially, efforts were made to extend the Unruh Act to the housing sector, but with little success. It soon became obvious that a separately framed fair housing act was required. No one was more convinced of this than Governor Brown, and by early 1953 Brown and Berkeley assemblyman Byron Rumford, an African American pharmacist with a master's in public administration, had joined forces to get such a law through the legislature. Sensitive to the developing civil rights movement in the South, Brown, Rumford, and their allies were confident that the time was right to end housing discrimination in California. Brown worked tirelessly on behalf of Assembly Bill 1240, spending as much energy — even more, he later declared — as he had expended in pushing through the State Water Project three years earlier. Passed by the assembly on 25 April 1963, the Rumford Fair Housing Act, as it came to be called, languished in the state senate, as had the Unruh Civil Rights Act before it. By this time, however, Jesse Unruh had become speaker of the assembly; and after an epic of maneuvering, with Unruh once again using assembly leverage against the senate, an amended Assembly Bill 1240 passed the senate on the last hour of the last night of the 1963 legislative session, was rushed back to the assembly, and, with the clock approaching midnight, passed the assembly sixty-three to nine and was immediately signed by Governor Brown into law.

Unlike the Unruh Civil Rights Act, the Rumford Fair Housing Act went right to the core of private value, housing, and met with fierce resistance from the California Real Estate Association. Within three months, the association had secured some 767,000 signatures to put Proposition 14 on the November 1964 ballot, recalling the recently passed Rumford Act. Initially, supporters of fair housing thought that the momentum of the Lyndon Johnson versus Barry Goldwater presidential campaign would work in their favor. As it turned out, however, Californians split the difference, voting for both Lyndon Johnson and Proposition 14. Two years later, the schizophrenia in the matter of fair housing continued. On the one hand, Ronald Reagan now sat in the governor's chair. On the other hand, the California Supreme Court in May 1966 overturned Proposition 14, a decision the United States Supreme Court reaffirmed a year later, and the matter of fair housing was thrown back into the legislature at a time of growing political division between left and right. Still, a beachhead had been established for people of color in California, although, all things considered, it remained a narrow beachhead in constant danger of being pushed back into the sea, whether by legislative act or voter initiative or combinations thereof. Without these landings, however, there could be no continuing campaign. The postwar era witnessed the beginning of the end for Jim Crow California.

17

Cool, Not Cool

Headlines and Transitions

I N October 2007 the Orange County Museum of Art opened an exhibition entitled Birth of the Cool: California Art, Design, and Culture at Midcentury. Edited by exhibition curator Elizabeth Armstrong, a specialist in modernism, the illustrated catalog included seven provocative essays defining California Cool in the 1950s. While centered on Southern California, the exhibition and the essays were of relevance to the San Francisco Bay Area as well, especially in discussions of Eichler homes, Dave Brubeck, and the influence of Zen. Emerging from the images and text of the exhibition and the catalog was nothing less than a revelatory probe into the aesthetics of the California that had been achieved in the postwar era. The Birth of the Cool exhibition explored architecture, furniture and appliance design, abstract art, West Coast jazz, experimental cinema, and graphics (including architectural signage, posters, LP albums, and book covers), together with such iconic personalities as Peggy Lee, June Christy, Dave Brubeck, Frank Sinatra, Chet Baker, and architectural photographer Julius Shulman. Both the exhibits and the essays asked the question: Why this stylized restraint, this coolness, this distance and reserve, in the 1950s California style?

As in the case of most everything else Californian, a larger American process was at work. The 1950s in general showed an appreciation of coolness, gaining force over the decade and culminating in the cool, ironic, detached style of Jack and Jackie Kennedy. In California, however, coolness was not merely the prerogative of an avant-garde elite, as tended to be the case elsewhere in the nation. Coolness — which is to say, modernism, California style — tended, rather, to project itself into the mass culture being created in postwar California. The Case Study House program, for example, developed prototypes that were not merely works of art in themselves but models for mass housing, at least in its more upscale sectors. Cool jazz, West Coast jazz, became a music of choice for an entire college generation. LP albums, meanwhile, vividly dramatized to a mass audience the power of photography as a cool art form, just as *Vogue* and *Life* had done for the prewar era. Abstract expressionism—also known as abstract classicism or hard-edged expressionism—reconfigured the world as geometry and color, with the messiness of the human condition left far behind. The furniture of Charles and Ray Eames actualized a world in which new materials—plastic, shaped plywood, aluminum—were sculpted into forms that were at once minimalist and biomorphic, allowing Californians (and others) to sit, as it were, on space itself, or at the least to make of sitting a form of stabilized flight. California Cool performers, meanwhile—Gerry Mulligan, Miles Davis, Chet Baker, Julie Christie, Peggy Lee, Shelly Manne, the Dave Brubeck Quartet, the Lighthouse All-Stars—took American standards and cooled them down to stylized detachment. California Cool architects reduced homes to basics, creating pavilions of roofs over glass, rising from concrete, possessed of the serenity of classic Japan.

What were the causes for all this? Was there a specifically Californian dimension to it all? The essayists of the Birth of the Cool catalog put forward a number of suggestions, which can be augmented and amplified. First of all, there was the European connection, as in Danish Modern furniture, for example, also popular in this era, together with other aspects of Scandinavian design that sought to pare down architecture, furniture, appliances, whatever, to as minimalist a presentation as possible. This postwar tendency, in turn, can in its European dimension be traced to the prewar Bauhaus or even earlier movements. From this perspective, California, Southern California especially, rising so rapidly in its material dimension, with so much to be designed rapidly and efficiently, required for purposes of quality control a quick fix of aesthetic modernism, which Europe, Scandinavia especially, provided. This infusion of European design repeated the way in which Austrian Secessionism, thanks to photographs in architectural magazines, pointed Irving Gill in the early 1900s in the direction of an entirely new kind of architecture for Southern California.

Then there is the issue of corporate-driven affluence. As a number of essays in the Birth of the Cool catalog suggest, California, Southern California especially, was created in the postwar era, in significant measure, by a super-infusion of corporate investment and defense spending. There was, to put the matter simply, a lot of money flowing through the society, hence a lot of jobs and careers open to talent, hence the filling in of domestic space with iconic manifestations of the new consumer lifestyle—stereophonic sound systems, electric appliances, modernist furniture, abstract art and sculpture, Space Age silver and flatware, fabrics in unprecedented colors, designer jewelry and eyewear. The world, in short, was filling up with stylized consumer items enlivened by design. Hence the effort to keep this consumption under control by banishing clutter from interiors, appliance design, and related items. Once again, a discernible California trait was repeating itself: the movement toward the Simple Home, stripped of Victorian clutter, that swept California in the early 1900s and found expression in the bungalow domestic Craftsman architecture of that era. Coolness, from this perspective, constituted a kind of asceticism, an insistence upon choice and restraint, in a world filling up with consumer goods.

And as far as defense spending was concerned, there was the question of the Cold War itself. California Cool represented a certain existential stance, a defiance even, of a world that had Strategic Air Command bombers in the sky, armed with atomic weapons, on a 24/7 basis; that was testing atomic weapons in the Nevada desert; and that in general was preparing itself for the scenario so brilliantly advanced by Stanley Kubrick in *Dr. Strangelove* (1964), namely, the ending of the world by atomic holocaust. To be cool, from this perspective, was, subconsciously at least, to conduct oneself with insouciance and panache before an openly acknowledged prospect of nuclear annihilation.

Undeveloped by the Birth of the Cool essayists, however, or at least only peripherally touched upon, was the question of California itself, which had experienced accelerated growth and an influx of people from elsewhere. Coolness, from this perspective, reflects the culture of a society based, in part, upon a rejection of Elsewhere, a choice of California, and the tensions resulting therefrom. Thus the architecture of postwar California did not materialize postwar domesticity with the wealth of reference and historical narrative characteristic of subdivision development in California in the prewar period. Mediterranean Revival itself, after all, so dominant in the 1920s, was a form of storytelling, of bringing tales from elsewhere to the Pacific Coast, subdivision by subdivision. And even in the 1930s—for all the distinctiveness of the International Style, for all the trendiness of Art Deco and Streamline Moderne—architects continued to design and developers continued to build more than California's fair share of Cape Cod, Dutch Colonial, Georgian Revival, and Edwardian classicism. But with so many Americans coming in so rapidly from so many other places, postwar California faced a challenge not only in design but also in the evolution of its sensibility. A common aesthetic, as de-regionalized as possible, had to be developed, one emphasizing, as far as possible, a non-hierarchical, non-historical point of view. Emptying the world out as far as design was concerned, downplaying volatilities of emotional response, establishing an easy-to-understand lingua franca, cool, California Cool, became the answer.

And yet no sooner was this coolness established than California began to show signs of heating up: signs of protest, dissent, social change. The Birth of the Cool catalog concludes with a month-by-month calendar of coolness in 1959. Things heated up in 1960. The execution of Caryl Chessman that May at San Quentin, followed shortly by major disturbances in City Hall San Francisco when a subcommittee of the House Un-American Activities Committee came there to hold hearings, suggested a new direction for the new decade, one oriented toward dissent and social protest, hot, not cool, engaged, passionate, messy, and ambiguous.

Resistance had been building since the 1940s among people of color. Equally early had been the resistance of the Hollywood Ten in 1949 to the HUAC hearings in Washington, which received national attention, especially when a number of well-known screenwriters refused to testify and were sentenced to a year in jail for contempt of Congress. McCarthyism, moreover, had a tendency to subjugate, even scrub away, white dissent in the early 1950s. Yet the founding of the Mattachine Society in Los Angeles between 1948 and 1950, while it faced its own McCarthyism-related crisis in 1953, which led to founder Harry Hay's resignation, signaled the advent of a new level of organized dissent among homosexuals that over the next half century and more would profoundly transform American society.

Raised briefly in Chile, then living with his family in Los Angeles after 1919, the English-born Harry Hay was a Marxist, a member of the Communist Party in the 1930s and 1940s. Graduating from Los Angeles High School in 1929, Hay spent two years at Stanford before returning to Los Angeles, where he pursued, intermittently, a career as understudy for assorted motion picture and Hollywood Playhouse Repertoire Theatre actors. An experienced horseman from his high school years working on a ranch in Smith Valley, Nevada, Hay also worked as a stunt rider in B westerns. Hay's homosexual life, by definition an underground activity, began following graduation from high school, where he served as ROTC captain and commencement speaker. While at Stanford, Hay made contact with the gay subculture of San Francisco.

Hay's background might have led to a somewhat inconclusive life as a bit player in the flourishing gay subculture of the motion picture industry. Yet Hay was a political activist, not only in Los Angeles, where he participated in the Milk Strike demonstrations of 1934, but also in San Francisco, to which he traveled that summer to participate in the General Strike. His activities in the 1930s veered back and forth between at-risk political agitation, theatrical involvements (with actor Will Geer, his lover, Hay was present at the founding of the Hollywood Theatre Guild to produce in 1935 *Waiting for Lefty* and *Till the Day I Die* by Clifford Odets), the Hollywood Film and Photo League, and the Lester Horton Dance Theater, where he played percussion. By the mid-1930s, Hay was in the process of earning a respectable walk-on role in Hollywood history. He had, after all, appeared with Anthony Quinn at the Hollytown Playhouse, and had collaborated on a short film, *Heavenly Music*, which won an Oscar in 1943. He was maintaining, meanwhile, his activist involvement in such organizations as Upton Sinclair's 1936 End Poverty in California campaign for governor, the Hollywood Anti-Nazi League, and similar groups.

Harry Hay was also an avid and largely self-instructed intellectual, with a growing interest in, and knowledge of, anthropology, Jungian analysis, and ethno-musicology, which is to say, folk music as an expression of culture, especially among the repressed. In 1937 Hay helped an aspiring folksinger by the name of Woodie Guthrie get a job singing on radio station KEVD, Los Angeles. Hay's interest in anthropology had its origins, in part, in his contact with Native Americans during ranching experiences in Nevada. His interest in Jungian psychology came in part from his efforts to live the straight life. Under the influence of his Jungian therapist, Hay, then employed by the Works Progress Administration, in September 1938 married Anita Platky, a fellow Party member.

The 1940s saw Harry Hay pursue the kind of eclectic life that was possible in Southern California during the war and immediate postwar years: a blend of defense work, union organizing, continuing studies in anthropology and Marxist theory, which he taught at the Southern California Labor School, activism in the growing folksinging movement, Communist Party activities, and, in 1948, activism on behalf of the Henry Wallace campaign for President. At this point, 1948, forces began to coalesce. Interviewed by Alfred Kinsey, Hay was profoundly impressed by the arguments in Kinsey's *Sexual Behavior in the Human Male* (1948) that 10 percent of American males were homosexual.

Initially, Hay, now separated from his wife, proposed the formation of a group calling itself Bachelors for Wallace. The organization lasted a nanosecond, but it was nevertheless a gay organization, however in the closet. Discussions of the Kinsey Report continued with Hay and his circle, which now included Hay's lover, designer Rudi Gernreich, Hay having left behind once and for all any effort to lead the straight life. Hay's divorce would become final in September 1951. In November 1950, Hay prepared a working paper, "Preliminary Concepts," for a homosexual study and activist group, which held its first meeting in Los Angeles that December. The group called itself the Mattachine Society, in honor of the Mattachines of the French Renaissance, an organization of unmarried young men, many of them clerics, encouraged by society to satirize at stated intervals the establishment, including the Church, and in general disclose the machinations and underside of conventional life.

The esoteric origins of the designation Mattachine for this trailblazing gay rights organization came, in significant measure, from the fusion of Marxist theory, history, and anthropology at the core of Harry Hay's early efforts, in a series of manifestos and working papers, to set forth the aims of the new group. Simply but powerfully, Hay postulated that homosexuals in the United States as of the early 1950s were a repressed minority. From the perspective of the early twenty-first century, Hay's formulation might at first glance seem to be stressing the obvious. From the perspective of the early 1950s, however, a powerful concept—at once simple, comoplex, and compelling—was being advanced. Although genetic evidence was not available at the time—and Hay at this point had an open mind on the nature-versus-nurture issue as far as homosexuality was concerned—the Kinsey Report had postulated a shared sexual identity, however covert and fragmented, for 10 percent of the American male population, who nevertheless remained on the books as criminals. Hay's anthropological studies, beginning with the role of the *berdache* in Native American culture—men living as women, or even women living as men, thought to possess two spirits, and accorded a stable and respected place in Native American life—projected the claims of the Kinsey Report back into the past. In the majority of societies Hay studied, homosexuals, and to a lesser extent lesbians, were accorded a stable, even respected, status—or, at the least, were not persecuted and were allowed, at intervals, as in the case of the French Mattachines, to express their own take on a society dominated by heterosexuals. Marxist theory encouraged Hay to put these anthropological, historical, and Kinsey Report researches into the context of a liberation movement aimed at establishing full civil rights for gay people.

All this was very tenuous as of the early 1950s, a Los Angeles–based study group, with only vague goals regarding social activism, but it contained within itself, thanks to Harry Hay, a revolutionary concept. Homosexuality was not merely a personal condition. It was the basis of an entire class, and this class was a repressed minority in the classic sense of that term. Republicans, Democrats, college-educated professionals, the blue-collar working class, Catholics, Protestants, Jews, whites, blacks, Asians: homosexuality, Hay and his colleagues were arguing, made them a class, a minority, however diverse and cross-cultural in composition. This assertion, moreover—namely, that homosexuals held equal status in this class identity, however different and unequal in other aspects of their personal and social existence—had a revolutionary implication, especially as it was arising at the height of McCarthyism and fierce resistance to anything even remotely suggesting the civil rights movement that would surface in the late 1950s. In 1955, in San Francisco, a new group, the Daughters of Bilitis, was privately and discreetly entertaining similar concepts. Initially formed as a social group, the Daughters of Bilitis—named in honor of a lesbian song cycle by the French poet Pierre Louÿs—became more political after it formed a connection with the Mattachine Society and its magazine *ONE* and in 1956 founded its own publication, the *Ladder*.

From this perspective, the sense of class identity and solidarity surfacing in the Mattachine Society and the Daughters of Bilitis paralleled the prior and continuing efforts of people of color in California, Mexicans and Filipinos especially, to define themselves as a repressed minority group and to struggle against that repression through community organizing and union activism. Gay liberation, however, perhaps because it was such a revolutionary concept, would take more time to develop itself; indeed, Hay himself and some of the other founders resigned from the Mattachine Society in mid-1953 because they wanted it to maintain its activist bent and not evolve as a mere study group. In the American South, the African American–oriented civil rights movement would soon be occupying center stage in the late 1950s and early 1960s as far as liberation movements were concerned. Black activism, including organized resistance, fueled the gay activism evident in the Stonewall Riots of June 1969 in New York, which took gay liberation mainstream as a resistance movement. In years to come, Queer Theory, as it was later developed, postulated alternatives to Hay's theory of a repressed minority, especially among the followers of French philosopher Michel Foucault, who argued that merely to define Queerness as a permanent condition was to allow the larger society to call the shots. All things considered, mainstream gay activism remained centered for more than a half century on the simple argument of Harry Hay that homosexuality was part of the human condition, previous societies had recognized this fact, and it was time for Americans to do the same.

In the case of Caryl Chessman, an equally radical notion was being put forth, namely, that condemned prisoners were an oppressed class as well, repressed by the death penalty, and required liberation. In May 1948 in the Superior Court of Los Angeles County, Caryl Chessman, a twenty-seven-year-old career criminal, was convicted under Section 209 of the California Penal Code, a Little Lindbergh law, for the kidnapping of and sexual attacks against two women in a remote Lovers' Lane section of the county, a capital offense, and the following month was sentenced to death. By July 1948 Chessman was confined to Cell 2455 on Death Row, San Quentin, where he would remain for more than eleven years, successfully fighting his case. Why the Chessman case dragged on for so long following Chessman's first sentencing, through eight stays of execution, involved a number of issues.

First of all, there was the case itself: Chessman the Red Light Bandit, approaching lovers parked in their cars by night, red cellophane covering a spotlight mounted on the hood of his car so as to simulate a police vehicle, followed by armed robbery and, in two cases, sexual assault. In that *Front Page* era, with five newspapers vying for readers' attention, the saga of the Red Light Bandit provided excellent copy for crime reporters, made even more dramatic when Chessman was assigned to the court of Judge Charles W. Fricke for trial, a judge noted for sending people to the gallows or gas chamber. As hostile as he was in the first place to Chessman, a career criminal charged with kidnapping in the course of armed robbery, Judge Fricke became even more unsympathetic when Chessman, rejecting the public defender assigned to him, insisted upon defending himself in court, and Judge Fricke was forced to allow him to do this, although he did assign to Chessman a public defender to be on hand as counsel.

Chessman's insistence on defending himself immersed his trial almost immediately in a morass of legal error that would keep it under judicial review for the next twelve years. First, there was the obvious issue of Chessman's competence to defend himself in a capital case, although time would reveal him as a complex and brilliant man. Second, Judge Fricke refused to provide Chessman with daily transcripts of the trial, as might be expected, on the grounds that the prosecuting deputy district attorney, J. Miller Leavy, did not make the same request. Third, the long-term trial transcripts that were prepared by an aging court reporter, Ernest Perry, who passed away shortly after the trial, were riddled with errors and gaps and, even when transcribed, were recorded in a sketchy system long out of date or merely supplemented with a bridge narrative composed by Perry. When the court hired an outside stenographer to complete the transcript, finally, he turned out to be not only the uncle by marriage of the prosecuting attorney, compensated at almost three times the going rate for such work, but an alcoholic as well, with questionable work habits, given to a frequently arbitrary rendition, so it was later alleged, of the original highly compromised transcript. For more than a decade of appeal and re-appeal in state and federal courts, this problematic transcript and its alleged violations of due process in a capital case, kept Caryl Chessman alive on Death Row through repeated appeals in state and federal courts. His death sentence was upheld in each instance, and a new date was set for execution by the Superior Court of Los Angeles County. In at least one instance, Chessman came within hours of going to the gas chamber. Still, he prevailed, researching and preparing his case with the help, initially, of Rosalie Asher, a lawyer and legal librarian who devoted herself to the case.

In 1954 Chessman made an end run around the process by selling his autobiography *Cell 2455, Death Row* to Prentice-Hall, which soon had on its hands a bestseller. While the text of *Cell 2455, Death Row* was obviously edited for publication, it was substantially Chessman's work, an apologia that would become a classic of prison literature. Chessman knew that he had an image problem. A career criminal, in and out of reformatories and prisons on various charges since his teenage years—car theft and joyriding, initially, escalating into burglary and armed robbery, together with assorted parole violations—Chessman had been convicted and sentenced to death on the technical charges of kidnapping in the course of robbery, which is to say, he moved his female victims at gunpoint from the front seat of the car to the back seat; but his real offense as far as his image was concerned, although this was not a capital crime, was the sexual assaults, in one instance rape (without penetration due to Chessman's impotence, but a form of sexual assault nevertheless) and in the second instance forced oral copulation. The victim of this second crime, moreover, seventeen years old at the time, was within a few years confined to the state hospital at Camarillo. At least one psychiatrist had diagnosed her schizophrenia as being rooted not necessarily in her sexual assault by the Red Light Bandit but in a separate cluster of causes; nevertheless, a scenario had been established: a young woman, sexually assaulted by Chessman, now hopelessly debilitated. Had Chessman merely committed these sexual assaults, not in the course of armed robbery, he would not have been liable for the death penalty under California law; yet the heinous nature of the sexual assaults was stressed throughout his trial, and they created for Chessman a reputation that, in the court of public opinion as well as with the jury itself, edged his technical moving of two victims a few feet in the course of armed robbery into a capital offense.

Historian Theodore Hamm argues that Chessman became, in significant measure, a loathed poster boy for the rash of sexual assaults reaching near-epidemic proportions in greater Los Angeles in the immediate postwar years, including the infamous Black Dahlia murder. Chessman embodied in the public mind at the time, Hamm notes, a dangerous fusion of sexual deviance and sociopathy linked—however subliminally—to fears that Chessman, as outlaw and sexual predator, embodied a more pervasive fear within postwar society that things might just be coming apart. Chessman, after all, was in one side of his life story a member of the Folks gone bad: a Michigan-born hardscrabble Anglo-American Protestant, raised in poverty in Glendale during the Depression, his mother a housebound invalid, the family barely surviving on Chessman's father's scant wages as a venetian blind repairman. Southern Californians had always been fascinated by Folks gone bad, but in times past the spectacular crimes of such Folks usually involved murder born of sexual jealousy or the prospect of an insurance payment. In Chessman's case, however, there was at the core of his persona a powerful and pervasive sociopathy, linked to sexual deviance—and subliminally, Theodore Hamm suggests, to fears of homosexuality, Chessman having spent most of his life in all-male reformatory and prison environments—that transformed him in the course of the trial into an embodiment of deep social fears among public and jury alike, a jury who thus recommended a death sentence in a case that would otherwise have just sent him away for many years, but not to Death Row. If indeed things might be in danger of falling apart, as Southern California, making the transition from the Second World War to the Cold War feared, then Chessman embodied the kind of figure who, in Southern California's worst nightmare, might rise up out of the confusion as something more than the Red Light Bandit. Chessman himself did not help his case in the course of the trial. However unschooled he might be, he was a brilliant man, and his brilliance was connected to an all-pervasive arrogance, verbally and physically expressed in the courtroom. To his dying day (literally), Chessman denied being the Red Light Bandit. He never apologized nor threw himself on the mercy of the court.

The very process of legal appeal demanded not only technical arguments relating to the transcript and other trial errors but the creation of a counter-persona to the sexually deviant sociopath of 1948. In *Cell 2455, Death Row* Chessman advanced a counter image: the unjustly convicted convict as existential hero. Four years of legal research on his own behalf had formed and sharpened Chessman's already formidable intelligence. Like the narrator of Albert Camus's *The Stranger* (1942), Chessman projects himself in *Cell 2455, Death Row* as, first of all, falsely condemned and, second, seeing in the process that had brought him to Death Row an acting out by society, on the cruelest possible level, of its fear of those who refused to conform. By being thus excluded from the system, Chessman suggested, he had become a philosophical protagonist, an outsider, unjustly condemned to a punishment that was in and of itself futile and barbarous. *Cell 2455, Death Row* touched a nerve, made a connection, with a stream of dissent continuing through the 1950s. Thanks to *Cell 2455, Death Row*, the Chessman case struck a deep chord in Europe and Latin America as well as the United States, especially as the case dragged on from year to year, court to court, in what by the late 1950s had emerged as a cause célèbre probing not only the validity of the death penalty, which Europe was in the process of rejecting, but the very nature of modern society itself. By this time, Chessman— thanks to royalties from his autobiography and two ensuing books, the last smuggled out of San Quentin, and the growing notoriety of the case—had attracted a team of top defense lawyers, most notably the famed criminal defense attorney George T. Davis of San Francisco, who had secured Tom Mooney's pardon in 1939 in a California case that had also attained international dimensions.

On the other edge of the equation, as the Chessman cased moved, inevitably, toward its conclusion, was the figure of Edmund G. (Pat) Brown, governor of California since 1958, hence possessed of awesome powers of clemency in capital cases. Although Pat Brown's pathway to the governorship had been as a prosecutor, he was not, by definition, hostile to the notion of clemency. Indeed, after leaving the governorship, Brown wrote a book chronicling the clemency granted to twenty-three of the fifty-nine death penalty cases he had reviewed as governor, far more than any previous governor of California. Brown was convinced of Chessman's guilt from the time he first reviewed the case as attorney general. He therefore found himself on the horns of a dilemma. By continuing to deny his guilt, Chessman was, in effect, not asking for clemency when his appeal for clemency reached Governor Brown in mid-October 1959, since clemency was an act of executive mercy contingent upon an admission of guilt. Brown was being asked, in effect, to grant clemency as a form of reprieve, based, in part, upon Chessman's faulty trial but based as well, to a disquieting degree, on some acknowledgment of Chessman's innocence, which Brown rejected. To this as well were added two more arguments from Chessman supporters throughout the United States and abroad. Were not nearly twelve years on Death Row a form of cruel and unusual punishment, it was argued? And were not Chessman's books in and of themselves proof that he had been rehabilitated? And besides, ran a concurrent third argument, was not the death penalty itself a barbarous embarrassment? What good would the execution of Caryl Chessman bring about?

By late 1959 matters were coming to a head. For those supporting execution, Chessman had long since made a mockery of the legal system. "I do not see how we can offer life as a prize for one who can stall the legal process for a given number of years," noted Judge Richard Chambers of the Ninth Circuit Court of Appeals in an unusually harsh statement. "We are told of his agonies on Death Row. True, it would be hell for most people. But here is no ordinary man. I think he has heckled his keeper long enough."[1] For a growing number of Californians, however, together with an equally growing national and international cadre of those opposing Chessman's execution, the very fact that Chessman had been on Death Row so long was not only in and of itself a form of cruel and unusual punishment but an indication of both a flawed trial and Chessman's probable innocence. By the time Chessman's eighth date with Death Row approached, petitions and demonstrations throughout Europe, Brazil, and the United States were demanding a reprieve. On the evening of 18 February 1960, having again reviewed the case and finding no cause for a reprieve, Pat Brown returned to the governor's mansion following a deliberative dinner with his clemency advisers and, with reluctance and foreboding, awaited Chessman's execution on the morrow.

At 9:00 P.M. Brown received a call from his son Edmund G. Brown Jr., universally known as Jerry, who had recently left the Jesuit order after nearly four years of study for the priesthood and was completing a bachelor's degree in classics at UC Berkeley. In an unprecedented father-son conversation, Jerry Brown argued with his father for clemency, basing his arguments not so much on the guilt or innocence of Chessman, although this was involved, but on the ambiguity involved in the death penalty itself as a deterrent and the continuing risk of executing the innocent or the unfairly tried. In this conversation, not only were two generations, father and son, confronting each other, two differing points of view came into dialogue:

the pragmatic liberalism of Pat Brown, a Republican-turned-Democrat, deeply Progressive in his instincts, proud of the California he was helping to create as governor, and his son Jerry: a rebel of sorts from the beginning, whose decision to join the Jesuits had caused his parents such grief, and who was now a student at UC Berkeley, where dissent had been a way of life since the 1930s. Jerry Brown's arguments to his father were philosophical, sharpened by eight years of Jesuit education in high school and college, but were animated as well by a certain zeitgeist in the air at Berkeley and other places as well, critical of cool California, corporate California, modernist California, the largest state in the nation.

In Pat Brown's recollection of the conversation, his son provided the governor with a way out. "Dad," Jerry asked, "can't you give him a sixty-day stay and go to the legislature to ask for a moratorium on the death penalty?" There was not a chance in a thousand, Brown replied, that the legislature would vote for a moratorium. "They've turned down the last eight in a row." Jerry countered: "But Dad, if you were a doctor and there was one chance in a thousand of saving a patient's life, wouldn't you take it?"[2] Brown agreed. He would grant Chessman a sixty-day reprieve and call the legislature into special session to consider the entire question of the death penalty. Picking up the telephone, Brown instructed his thoroughly surprised clemency secretary Cecil Poole to inform the warden of San Quentin that Chessman's execution would be postponed for sixty days.

The review of the death penalty Brown was proposing went nowhere. It was not even reported out of the senate Judiciary Committee, where it failed on an eight-to-seven vote, despite an eloquent brief by Brown against the death penalty, in which were echoed many of his son's arguments. For the ninth time in ten years, the state of California confirmed the death penalty. Shortly thereafter, the superior court in Los Angeles, for the ninth time, assigned Caryl Chessman a date for execution, Monday, 3 May 1960, at 10:00 A.M. Some 200 letters and telegrams were pouring into Brown's office, demanding clemency. Chessman's legal team, meanwhile, continued to work on appeals to the federal district court and the United States Supreme Court.

On the night of 2 May 1960, Caryl Chessman was moved into the holding cell adjacent to the gas chamber. To the end, he asserted his innocence and maintained the persona he had created for himself. "Now my long struggle is over," Chessman wrote his attorney George T. Davis shortly before his execution. (Even then Davis was trying for a last-last-minute intervention by the federal district court or the Supreme Court.) "Yours isn't. This barbarous, senseless practice, capital punishment, will continue. In our society other men will go on taking that last walk to death until...when? Until the citizens of this State and this land are made aware of its futility. Until they realize that retributive justice is not justice at all. I die with the burning hope that my case and my death will contribute to this awareness, this realization. I know that you will personally do all in your power, as citizen and lawyer, to convince your fellows that justice is not served, but confounded, by vengeance and executioners. Good luck."[3]

Approaches to San Quentin were cordoned off as an unusual number of demonstrators, many of them high school and college students, gathered for an all-night vigil. Marlon Brando, Shirley MacLaine, Phyllis Kirk, and Steve Allen traveled to Sacramento by chartered airplane to join the protest. Norman Mailer, Aldous Huxley, Christopher Isherwood, and Dorothy Parker signed a petition. Albert Schweitzer and Brigitte Bardot sent telegrams. Even as Chessman was strapped in the chair, efforts at reprieve were under way and might have been successful, had time allowed. Federal district court judge Louis Goodman had just authorized from San Francisco a thirty-minute stay so as to read a writ only then presented to him by Rosalie Asher and George T. Davis, but the pellets had already been dropped by the time Goodman's telephone call went through. The pellets fell at 10:05 A.M., and by 10:12 A.M. Caryl Chessman was dead.

Demonstrations broke out in California, other parts of the United States, Latin America, and Europe. United States embassies were attacked in Lisbon, Stockholm, Montevideo, and dozens of other cities. Twenty-eight years later, Brown was still pondering the case that in so many ways put his own political career in jeopardy. "The shadow of the gas chamber, and of Caryl Chessman, hung over my last years," Brown later wrote. "And when Ronald Reagan defeated me by almost a million votes in 1966, the same issue and its surrounding aura of weakness and vacillation had a lot to do with it." Chessman, Brown admitted, "was a nasty, arrogant, unrepentant man, almost certainly guilty of the crimes he was convicted of, but I didn't think those crimes deserved the death penalty then, and I certainly don't think so now. And his trial was so badly tainted by that faulty transcript that his sentence should have been commuted by *someone* to life without possibility of parole. By the time I became the someone with that power, other people—myself included as attorney general—had successfully stoked the fires of public indignation so high against him for 'heckling his keeper' that such action was virtually impossible, especially for an elected official with a responsibility to his constituency and the programs he hoped to implement for the common good. I firmly believe all of that. I also believe that I should have found a way to spare Chessman's life."[4]

Ten days following Chessman's execution, demonstrations broke out at City Hall, San Francisco, on Friday 13 May 1960, protesting hearings being held there by a HUAC subcommittee and reinforcing the atmosphere of protest created by the execution. The demonstrators—a significant number of them Berkeley-based activists and college students, the same sort of people who had demonstrated for Chessman— were peaceful and well-mannered as they picketed. HUAC staff, however, seeking to pack the board of supervisors chambers with a favorable audience, had assigned the bulk of seats in the chamber to patriotic groups, including the Daughters of the American Revolution. During the morning session, those hostile to the committee who managed to get into the chambers were vociferous in their shouts and groans of disapproval, thereby raising tensions. Before the afternoon session, a crowd of between three hundred and four hundred, young people in the main, hostile to the

HUAC hearings, sensing that they were on the verge of being excluded, began to grow visibly restive as people waited in line in the second-floor corridor. The crowd began to mill about, shout, and sing protest songs. A group of subpoenaed witnesses, demanding that their family and friends be admitted to the afternoon proceedings, were especially outspoken. The crowd outside City Hall, meanwhile, had grown to some four thousand people but was conducting itself in an orderly manner, thanks, no doubt, to the fact that a total of one hundred police officers, fifteen of them on horseback, were keeping order.

By 1:15 P.M., matters were growing more and more tense. Some fifty-five police officers were in the building, attempting to keep order and growing more agitated along with the crowd. That morning, presiding superior court judge Clarence Morris had complained to Police Chief Thomas Cahill that demonstrations outside City Hall and on the second floor outside the board of supervisors chambers were disturbing court sessions elsewhere in the building. The noise was greater than it had been that morning. "Sieg Heil!" some jeered, along with other choice epithets the police found especially offensive. At this point, Inspector Michael Maguire of police intelligence ordered the fire hoses along the wall of the second floor unrolled. "You want this?" Maguire demanded of the crowd. "Go ahead!" came the cry from a protestor. Almost simultaneously, the hoses were turned on the crowd as demonstrators surged toward the chambers where the hearings were about to be held. Chaos ensued. The high-pressure hoses dispersed most of the crowd. A number of demonstrators were washed down the grand staircase, which soon became a cascade of water flowing over dangerously slippery marble, flooding the rotunda floor below. Women demonstrators were especially vulnerable to the high-pressure hoses, which in a number of cases reduced their clothing to transparency. Other demonstrators, including a number of women, were dragged down the staircase by police, their heads and inert bodies painfully banging against each stair, and loaded into paddy wagons outside City Hall. Among the fifty-five police in the building, billy clubs were much in evidence.

The HUAC held its hearings within the locked chamber until 5:10 P.M. Sixty-four demonstrators, meanwhile, had been arrested and carted off in paddy wagons to the Hall of Justice, where they would spend the night behind bars. The four newspapers of the city covered the disturbances with banner headlines, and San Francisco found itself, as might be expected, galvanized into opposing camps: the vast majority, backed by newspaper editorials over the following days, opposing the demonstrations, hardly anyone voicing support, with the dramatic exception of *San Francisco Chronicle* columnist Herb Caen. "The accomplishments of the Un-American Activities Committee are debatable," Caen wrote in the *Chronicle* for 16 May 1960. "McCarthyism seems to have been its only lasting contribution. Some of the students were demonstrably out of line. Shall we blame it on their youth and inexperience? The predictable reaction of the police was ill-advised. A criminologist who refuses to be identified said: 'One of the marks of a mature police department is its ability to keep demonstrations from turning into riots.' And the bureaucratic mind at work was best or worst shown by a high City Hall official (not Christopher) who couldn't understand any show of concern: 'What're you getting excited about? Hell, they're just a bunch of Beatniks.'"[5] Mayor George Christopher, however, continued to describe Friday, 13 May 1960 as a black day for San Francisco. Not since the General Strike of 1934 had there been such demonstrations in the city.

At the same time, however, official San Francisco realized that it had a problem on its hands. Herb Caen was right. The police had mismanaged the demonstrations. Turning the fire hoses on the crowd had been a provocation, not proper crowd management, and had escalated the demonstrations to a whole new level of violence. The San Francisco Fire Fighters Union, Local 798, issued a statement noting that no firemen were involved in turning the hoses against the crowd and that the only firemen involved in the entire event were the members of the Salvage Corps sent in to handle the water damage at City Hall. When the demonstrators came to trial, en masse, half of them represented by San Francisco attorney Jack Berman, they opted, on Berman's advice, to be heard not by a jury but by municipal judge Albert Axelrod, who following hearings, dismissed all charges. Only one student demonstrator, Robert Meisenbach, twenty-two, of UC Berkeley, was granted a continuance on felony charges of assaulting a police officer. Tried in April 1961 in a superior court jury trial, Meisenbach was acquitted.

However anti-climactic in outcome, the events of 13 May 1960 provoked, not only in San Francisco but in California and throughout the nation, a lively discussion in the press, zeroing in on the alienation and political activism of the students who had come to City Hall that morning to demonstrate. Something new was happening, which some writers linked, as a matter of genesis and development, to the anti-ROTC demonstrations at Berkeley earlier in the decade. The Silent Generation was no longer silent, or at the least it was capable of helping to mass thousands of demonstrators outside of City Hall to protest the HUAC.

In the cool/not cool, equation, the demonstrations surrounding the execution of Caryl Chessman and the San Francisco City Hall HUAC hearings were definitely in the not cool category, as for that matter were the community organizing concurrently under way in the Mexican American community, the union movement among Mexican American and Filipino American migrant workers, the efforts in Sacramento to end racial discrimination in housing and public accommodations, and the still obscure yet revolutionary demands for equal rights for homosexuals and lesbians being advanced by the Mattachine Society and the Daughters of Bilitis. For all their referencing of "Cool!" as a mark of approval, the Beats of San Francisco were spending the bulk of their time pursuing more kinetic connections to experience. Down at Big Sur, Henry Miller and his friends were not cool. They were, rather, passionately engaged in an almost old-fashioned rejection of the structures, reservations, and distances of corporate modernism, California style. The Zen Buddhism of Alan Watts and his Marin County friends was cool, in one sense, connected as it was to an ultra-detached Zen aesthetic; but Zen was an alternative vision as well, running parallel to the Vedantism of the Southern California circle and representing a form of resistance, active and passive, to California as mass society. The Sierra Club and the *Cry California* crowd, meanwhile, and all the other environmentalists protesting the headlong development of the state, were not being cool, either, but were, rather, engaged in what they considered to be a take-no-prisoners struggle against the forces of darkness. From this perspective the year 1960, with its dramatic disturbances, possesses in retrospect prophetic suggestions of things to come.

Notes

Chapter 1
San Fernando

1 "The Tract Way of Life," *Look* (25 September 1962), 36.

Chapter 2
Designs for the Good Life

1. *Landscape for Living* (1950), 61, 64.
2. "The Accepted Architectural Look of the Mid-20th Century," *House Beautiful* (9 January 1957), 36.

Chapter 3
Urban Expectations

1. *It Must Be the Climate* (1941), 55, 59.
2. Raymond Chandler to George Harmon Coxe, 9 April 1939, *Selected Letters of Raymond Chandler*, edited by Frank MacShane (1981), 7.
3. Deborah Day, "Biography," *A Guide to the Roger Randall Dougan Revelle Papers, 1928–1979*, Archives of the Scripps Institution, 24.
4. Nancy Scott Anderson, *An Improbable Venture: A History of the University of California, San Diego* (1993), 79.
5. Memo of Clark Kerr to Roger Revelle, 7 June 1960; Memo of Roger Revelle to Clark Kerr, 17 February 1961, Revelle Papers, Box 16, file 29.
6. Anderson, *An Improbable Venture*, 89.
7. Bert Boudin, *Fortress on a Hill: Founding the University of San Diego and the San Diego College for Women, 1942–1963* (2001), 140.

Chapter 4
Baghdad by the Bay

1. *Baghdad by the Bay* (1949), 211.

Chapter 5
The Cardinal, the Chief, Walter O'Malley, and Buff Chandler

1. Francis J. Weber, Hermine Lees, and Joanne Wittenburg, A *History of the Archdiocese of Los Angeles* (2007), 33.
2. Michael Parrish, *For the People: Inside the Los Angeles County District Attorney's Office, 1850–2000* (2001), 40.
3. Joe Domanick, *To Protect and to Serve: The LAPD's Century of War in the City of Dreams* (1994), 111–12.
4. "The Untold Story of Chavez Ravine," *Los Angeles* (April 1962), 16.
5. Ibid.
6. Thomas S. Hines, "Housing, Baseball, and Creeping Socialism: The Battle of Chavez Ravine, Los Angeles, 1949–1959," *Journal of Urban History* (February 1982), 130.
7. John Thomas Kean, *Fritz B. Burns and the Development of Los Angeles* (2001), 176.
8. Francis Marien, SJ, "Los Angeles and the Idea of a City," *America* (30 November 1957), 261.
9. Joe Scott, "The Deb Deluge," *Los Angeles* (December 1967), 82.
10. Maurice Zolotow, "Land of Nod," *Theatre Arts* (April 1956), 86.
11. Cecil Smith, "The Greatest Gift of All," *Music Center: A Living Memorial to Peace*, a Special Supplement of the *Los Angeles Times* (6 December 1964), 30.

Chapter 6
Downsides and Dividends

1. Arthur Millier, "Will and Ariel Durant—Down the Home Stretch," *Los Angeles* (May 1965), 43.
2. David Halberstam, *The Powers That Be* (1979), 287.
3. Bernard Wolfe, "Manners and Morals on the Sunset Strip," *Esquire* (August 1961), 50.
4. Richard Austin Smith, "Los Angeles, Prototype of Supercity," *Fortune* (March 1965), 99.
5. Ray Duncan, "The Painful Rejuvenation of Downtown," *Los Angeles* (November 1963), 31.
6. Francis J. Weber, *His Eminence of Los Angeles* (2 vols., 1997), II, 442.
7. "A Police Chief Talks of 'Police Brutality.'" *U.S. News & World Report* (10 August 1964), 33–34.
8. Joe Domanick, *To Protect and to Serve: The LAPD's Century of War in the City of Dreams* (1994), 179–80.
9. Ibid., 184.
10. Ibid., 185.

Chapter 7
Warren, Nixon, Knight, Knowland

1. "The Gentleman from California," *Theodore H. White at Large: The Best of His Magazine Writing, 1939–1986* (1992), 356.
2. Ibid., 357.

3. Checkers Speech of 23 September 1952, *American Speeches: Political Oratory from Abraham Lincoln to Bill Clinton*, edited by Ted Widmer (Library of America, 2006), 511.
4. Richard B. Harvey, "Governor Earl Warren of California," *California Historical Society Quarterly* (March 1967), 47–48.
5. "Don Juan in Heaven," *Time* (30 May 1955), 16.
6. Ethan Rarick, *California Rising: The Life and Times of Pat Brown* (2005), photograph caption following page 184.
7. Earl Behrens, "California, the New Men," *States in Crisis: Politics in Ten American States, 1950–1962*, edited by James Reichley (1964), 182.
8. Ibid., 183.

Chapter 8
Cold War Campus

1. Verne A. Stadtman, *The University of California, 1868–1968* (1970), 397–98.
2. www.rand.or/about/history, accessed 29 June 2008.
3. James L. Clayton, "Defense Spending: Key to California's Growth," *Western Political Quarterly* (June 1962), 26.
4. *The Centennial Record of the University of California, 1868–1968*, edited by Verne Stadtman (1967), 35.
5. David Gardner, "Driving Mr. Kerr," *California Monthly* (February 2004), 25.
6. Clark Kerr, *The Uses of the University* (1963), 41.
7. Ibid., 124–26.
8. Clark Kerr, *The Gold and the Blue: A Personal Memoir of the University of California, 1949–1967*, vol. 1, *Academic Triumphs* (2001), 286.
9. Ibid., 286–87.

Chapter 10
Mare Nostrum

1. Paul S. Taylor, "Central Valley Project: Water and Land," *Western Political Quarterly* [June 1949), 232.

Chapter 11
Provincials, Baghdaders, and Beats

1. Ron Fimrite, "Lucius Beebe," *San Francisco Chronicle* (5 February 1966), 8.
2. "Birth of the Cool," *San Francisco Chronicle* (8 June 2003), D1.

Chapter 12
Big Sur

1. Van Wyck Brooks, *Scenes and Portraits: Memories of Childhood and Youth* (1954), 191–92.
2. Rosalind Sharpe Wall, *A Wild Coast and Lonely: Big Sur Pioneers* (1989), 185–88.
3. Jonathan Fryer, *Isherwood* (1978), 188.
4. Brian Finney, *Christopher Isherwood: A Critical Biography* (1979), 174.
5. Fryer, *Isherwood*, 196.
6. *In My Own Way* (1972), 299.

Chapter 13
Silent Generation

1. Carolyn See, "Autobiographical Statement," *Contemporary Authors Autobiography Series* 22 (1955), 212.
2. Joan Didion, "On Being Unchosen by the College of One's Choice," *Saturday Evening Post* (6 April 1968), 18.
3. Martin Mayer, "University in the Sun," *Esquire* (November 1961), 113.
4. Richard Gilbert, "A Good Time at UCLA: An English View," *Harper's* (April 1965), passim.
5. Joan Didion, "On the Morning After the Sixties," *The White Album* (1979), 206–7.
6. Joan Didion, "Berkeley's Giant," *Mademoiselle* (January 1960), 90, 106, 107.
7. David Leaf, *The Beach Boys* (1985), 27.
8. Eugene Burdick, "The Sun and Its Worshippers," *Holiday* (October 1957), 64.
9. "Why Do You Like Living in California?" *Esquire* (May 1963), 78–79.
10. "Beauties from Two Top Campuses," *Look* (29 September 1959), 69.

Chapter 14
Brubeck!

1. Lionel Hampton, *Hamp: An Autobiography* (1999), 91.
2. Ted Gioia, *West Coast Jazz: Modern Jazz in California, 1945–1960* (1992), 16.
3. Ross Russell, *Bird Lives! The High Life and Hard Times of Charlie (Yardbird) Parker* (1973), 260.
4. John Salmon, "What Brubeck Got from Milhaud," *American Music Teacher* (February/March 1992), 260.
5. "Brubeck Plays Brubeck," *Philips Music Herald* (Winter 1956), 13.
6. Gene Lees, *Meet Me at Jim & Andy's: Jazz Musicians and Their World* (1988), 256.
7. Ibid., 264.
8. Hampton Hawes and Don Asher, *Raise Up Off Me: A Portrait of Hampton Hawes* (1979), 37.
9. Arnold Shaw, "West Coast Jazz," *Esquire* (September 1955), 128.
10. Nat Shapiro and Nat Hentoff, "A Quiet Beat in California," *High Fidelity* (April 1955), 430.

Chapter 15
Largest State in the Nation

1. "Governor Plans Big Party for Day California Is Tops," *San Francisco Chronicle* (7 January 1962), 2; Ethan Rarick, *California Rising: The Life and Times of Pat Brown* (2005), 255–56.
2. Richard Armour, "I Loved You, California," quoted in Rarick, *California Rising*, 256.
3. Rarick, *California Rising*, 256.
4. Harold Gilliam, "Beating Back the Bulldozers," *Saturday Review* (23 September 1967), 67.
5. Lewis Mumford, "California and the Human Prospect," *Sierra Club Bulletin* (December 1962), 42–59.
6. Samuel E. Wood and Alfred E. Heller, *The Phantom Cities of California* (1962), 5.
7. Raymond F. Dasmann, *The Destruction of California* (1965), 5–6.
8. Richard G. Lillard, *Eden in Jeopardy* (1966), 20.
9. William Bronson, *How to Kill a Golden State* (1968), 9–10.

10. Ibid., 10.
11. Remi Nadeau, *California: The New Society* (1963), 88.
12. Theodora Kroeber, *Ishi in Two Worlds* (1961), 238.

Chapter 16
People of Color

1. Allan Bosworth, *America's Concentration Camps* (1967), 214.
2. Ibid., 213–14.
3. Fred Ross obituary, *New York Times* (2 October 1992), A22.
4. Howard A. DeWitt, *Anti-Filipino Movements in California*, 55, quoting the *San Francisco Chronicle* for 26 January 1930.

Chapter 17
Cool/Not Cool

1. Edmund G. (Pat) Brown with Dick Adler, *Public Justice, Private Mercy: A Governor's Education on Death Row* (1989), 38.
2. Ibid., 39–40.
3. Brad Williams, *Due Process: The Story of Criminal Lawer George T. Davis and His Thirty-Year Battle Against Capital Punishment* (1961), 330.
4. Brown, *Public Justice, Private Mercy*, 52.
5. *A Focus on Rebellion*, selected and edited by Albert T. Anderson and Bernice Prince Biggs (1962), 32–33.

Bibliographical Essay

Chapter 1
San Fernando

David Halberstam's *The Fifties* (1993) is a valuable general survey of the era. See also "The Fifties," *Esquire* (June 1983). General studies of growth in California during this period include Carey McWilliams, *Southern California: An Island on the Land* (1946) and "Look What's Happened to California," *Harper's* (October 1949); Clifford Zierer, editor, *California and the Southwest* (1956); Richard Bernard and Bradley Rice, editors, *Sunbelt Cities: Politics and Growth Since World War II* (1983); and Gerald Nash, *The American West Transformed: The Impact of the Second World War* (1985). See also John Anson Ford, *Thirty Explosive Years in Los Angeles County* (1961). Guides and promotional literature from this era include John Crow, *California as a Place to Live* (1953); Irving Stone, "California, a Land to Dream On," *Holiday* (December 1954); Philip Ault, *How to Live in California* (1961); and Maidee Thomas Nelson, *California, Land of Promise* (1962). A critical look at the origins of American suburbia is Robert M. Fogelson, *Bourgeois Nightmares: Suburbia, 1870–1930* (2005). See also Mark Baldassare, *Trouble in Paradise: The Suburban Transformation in America* (1986). Also of value, throughout, is Remi Nadeau, *California: The New Society* (1963).

Two historians, W. W. Robinson and Kevin Roderick, have most effectively chronicled the rise of the San Fernando Valley. Among other publications, see Robinson's *San Fernando Valley, A Calendar of Events* (1938); "San Fernando Tells California Story," *Westways* (October 1950); *The Story of San Fernando Valley* (1961); and *Fabulous San Fernando Valley* (1962). Roderick's *The San Fernando Valley: America's Suburb* is the best overall survey of the subject. For the geographer's perspective, see Clifford Zierer, "San Fernando—A Type of Southern California Town," *Annals of the Association of American Geographers* (March 1934); Louis Guzman, "San Fernando: Two Hundred Years in Transition," *California Geographer* (1962); and Richard Preston, "The Changing Landscape of the San Fernando Valley Between 1930 and 1964," *California Geographer* (1965). See also this bound pamphlet: John Baur, *William Paul Whitsett: A Biographical Sketch* (1987). Regarding the lifestyle of the San Fernando Valley in this period, see Noel Busch, "The San Fernando Valley," *Holiday* (December 1951); Art Seidenbaum, "A New Look at San Fernando Valley," *Southern California Prompter*

(September 1960); and Patricia McBroom, "The Ducal Life in Northridge," *Los Angeles* (September 1963).

Regarding the actual move to California, see Vivien Robinette, *We Moved to California* (1951); D. Berrigan, "They Escaped from Civilization," *Saturday Evening Post* (14 August 1954); "Booming California: Want to Move There?" *Changing Times* (February 1957); "That California Way of Life," *Changing Times* (January 1960); Neil Kuehnl, "What It's Really Like to Move to California," *Better Homes and Gardens* (August 1961); and Doyce Nunis, "California, Why We Come: Myth or Reality," *California Historical Society Quarterly* (June 1965). The 19 October 1962 issue of *Life* is devoted entirely to California. See especially "If You're Thinking of Going There, What to Know About and Look For."

The population growth resulting from such migration can be traced through Margaret Gordon, *Employment Expansion and Population Growth: The California Experience, 1900–1950* (1954); Warren Thompson, *Growth and Changes in California's Population* (1955); William Thomas Jr., editor, "Man, Time, and Space in Southern California: A Symposium," *Annals of the Association of American Geographers* (September 1959); "California's New Boom Era," *Business Week* (2 April 1960); Ernest Engelbert, editor, *Metropolitan California* (1961); Arthur Karinen and David Lantis, "The Population of California, 1950–1961," *Annals of the Association of American Geographers* (December 1961); Howard Gregor, "Spatial Disharmonies in California Population Growth," *Geographical Review* (January 1963); Winston Crouch and Beatrice Dinerman, *Southern California Metropolis: A Study in Development of Government for a Metropolitan Area* (1964); and the University of California College of Environmental Design, *The Metropolitan Future* (1965). See also Richard Erickson, "Will There Be Room Enough for Coming Thousands?" *California Monthly* (October 1962).

An overview of sub/urban life in the San Francisco Bay Area can be found in William Chapin, Alvin Hyman, and Jonathan Carroll, photographs by Michael Bry, *The Suburbs of San Francisco* (1969). The texture of town and suburban life south of San Francisco can be gleaned from Frank Stanger, *South from San Francisco: San Mateo County, California—Its History and Heritage* (1963). See also Samuel Chandler, *"Gateway to the Peninsula": A History of the City of Daly City* (1973) and Ken Gillespie and Bunny Gillespie, "The History of Daly City," www.ci.daly-city.ca.us/about/history.htm. See also Linda Wickert Garvey, *San Carlos Stories: An Oral History for the City of Good Living* (2000). Regarding the East Bay, see Edward Staniford, *El Cerrito: Historical Evolution* (1976); Arthur Young, *The Improvers of Lafayette* (1981); Beth Bagwell, *Oakland: The Story of a City* (1982); Edna May Andrews, *History of Concord: Its Progress and Promise* (1986); and Sandy Kimball and Dennis Goodman, *Moraga's Pride* (1987). See also R. Coke Wood and Leonard Covello, *Stockton Memories* (1977); and Gaye LeBaron and Joann Mitchell, *Santa Rosa: A Twentieth-Century Town* (1993). Regarding Fresno in this period, see "Fresno: 'Where the Goodness of Life Abounds,'" *Fortnight* (11 June 1951).

Guides to the sub/urban life of Southern California include Scott O'Dell, *Country of the Sun* (1957); Andrew Hepburn, *Southern California* (1959); editors of Sunset, *Southern California* (1959); and Bill Murphy, *The Dolphin Guide to Los Angeles and Southern California* (1962). Regarding Orange County, see Richard Dale Batman, "Orange County, California: A Comprehensive History," *Journal of the West* (January, April, July, and October 1965). See also Pamela Hallan-Gibson, *The Golden Promise: An Illustrated History of Orange County* (1986). Other county histories of relevance to this chapter include W. W. Robinson, *The Story of Riverside County* (1957); and Walter Schuiling, *San Bernardino County: Land of Contrasts* (1984). Regarding the rise of the cities and towns of Southern California, see W. W. Robinson, *Ranchos Become Cities* (1939). My composite history of Southern Californian townships has been derived from a reading of numerous city histories. Of these, Donald Pflueger, *Covina: Sunflowers, Citrus, Subdivisions* (1964) and Michele Zack, *Altadena, Between Wilderness and*

City (2004) can be taken as representative—and outstanding—examples. Regarding Palm Springs in this period, see "Palm Springs, the Pains of Becoming a Metropolis," *Los Angeles, Magazine of the Good Life in Southern California* (November 1962). Regarding Lakewood, see Arthur Will, "The Lakewood Story," *Western City* (March 1954); John Todd, *A History of Lakewood, 1949–1954* (1984); "Lakewood, Community History," www.colapublib.org/history/lakewood; and "The Lakewood Story," www.lakewoodcity.org/about_lakewood/community/lakewoodhistory, accessed on 29 June 2008.

Regarding the rise of suburbia in this era, see Kenneth Jackson, *Crabgrass Frontier: The Suburbanization of the United States* (1985). To interpret the meaning of these suburbs, I was guided by Constance Perin, *Everything in Its Place: Social Order and Land Use in America* (1977); Rob Kling, Spencer Olin, and Mark Poster, editors, *Postsuburban California: The Transformation of Orange County Since World War II* (1991); and John Findlay, *Magic Lands: Western Cityscapes and American Culture After 1940* (1992). A contemporary assessment of importance is "Suburbia-Exurbia-Urbia: The New Breed," *Newsweek* (1 April 1957). Regarding Disneyland, see *Disneyland: The First Quarter Century* (1979). Affirmations of suburbia include Phyllis McGinley, "Suburbia: Of Thee I Sing," *Harper's* (December 1949); John Cheever, "Moving Out," *Esquire* (June 1983); and D. J. Waldie, *Holy Land: A Suburban Memoir* (1996). Skeptical assessments include John Keats, *The Crack in the Picture Window* (1957); R. E. Deegan, "Unclosed Frontier: Southern California," *America* (8 February 1958); "Tract Way of Life" and "The Ivy Crime," *Look* (25 September 1962); and the novels *The Man in the Gray Flannel Suit* (1955) by Sloan Wilson and *No Down Payment* (1957) by John McPartland. See also "Newport: The Ordeal of Status," *Los Angeles* (May 1964). The lyrics and music for Malvina Reynolds's "Little Boxes" can be found in her *Little Boxes and Other Handmade Songs* (1964).

Regarding the sexual tensions so evident in McPartland's novel, see Howard Kitching, M.D., *Sex Problems of the Returned Veteran* (1946). Alfred Kinsey, Wardell Pomeroy, and Clyde Martin issued *Sexual Behavior in the Human Male* in 1948. The critical response to the Kinsey Report can be accessed through Donald Porter Geddes, *An Analysis of the Kinsey Reports on Sexual Behavior in the Human Male and Female* (1954), which contains Lionel Trilling's classic essay. See also Jerome Himelhoch and Sylvia Fleis Fava, *Sexual Behavior in American Society: An Appraisal of the First Two Kinsey Reports* (1955). Regarding Kinsey himself, see Marjorie Dent Candee, "Alfred Charles Kinsey," *Current Biography* (1954); and Cornelia Christenson, *Kinsey: A Biography* (1971). The topic of postwar consumerism is brilliantly treated by Lizabeth Cohen in *A Consumer's Republic: The Politics of Mass Consumption in Postwar America* (2003). The saga of the Swanson TV dinner can be traced in Linda Keene, "Fame for the Inventor of the TV Dinner Is Frozen in Time," *Seattle Times* (24 September 1999); "TV Dinner," www.fiftiesweb.com/pop/tv-dinner.htm accessed on 6/29/08; and "The History of TV Dinners," www.inventors.about.com/od/inventionsalphabet/a/tv_dinner.htm. Regarding the rise of McDonald's, see Ray Kroc with Robert Anderson, *Grinding It Out, The Making of McDonald's* (1977); John Love, *McDonald's, Behind the Arches* (1986); and "History of the Historic Site of the Original McDonald's in San Bernardino," www.route-66.com/mcdonalds/history.htm.

Regarding religion and suburbia, see Joseph How Jr., "The Church Alive and Changing," *Christian Century* (5 January 1972). Regarding the classic film *Rebel Without a Cause* (1955), see the relevant analysis by Tom Dirks at www.filmsite.org/rebel.html. Regarding the juvenile delinquency scare, see Duane Robinson, *Chance to Belong: Story of the Los Angeles Youth Project, 1943–1949* (1949); Howard Whitman, "Teen-Age Punks: San Francisco Tries to Tame Them," *Collier's* (29 April 1950); and the novels *Incorrigible* (1947) by Karl Brown, *Angels Camp* (1949) by Ray Morrison, *The Passionate Victims* (1952) by Lange Lewis, and *The Very First Time* (1959) by Richard Fisher. On a happier note, see *Ozzie* (1973) by Ozzie Nelson;

John Leonard, "Sneer Not at 'Ozzie and Harriet,'" *U.S. News & World Report* (14 September 1992); and Daniel Polsby, "Ozzie and Harriet Had It Right," *Harvard Journal of Law and Public Policy* (Spring 1995). See also "The Adventures of Ozzie and Harriet" in Horace Newcomb, editor, *Museum of Broadcast Communications Encyclopedia of Television* (1997).

Chapter 2
Designs for the Good Life

The relationship between the California lifestyle and domestic architecture can be explored through "The California Way of Life," *Life* (22 October 1945) and "California—What a Way to Live," *McCall's* (July 1963). See also "Apartments Designed for Single People," *Architectural Record* (June 1951). In 1998 the Stanford University Libraries issued *Sunset Magazine, a Century of Western Living, 1898–1998: Historical Portraits and a Chronological Bibliography of Selected Topics*, with essays by Michael Keller, L. W. (Bill) Lane Jr., Kevin Starr, and Tomas Jaehn. The outdoor lifestyle can be traced through *Bill Magee's Western Barbecue Cookbook* (1949); the *Sunset Patio Book* (1952); and *Sunset's Ideas for Building Barbecues* (1951). See also Frans Evenhuis and Robert Landau, *Hollywood Poolside: Classic Images of Legendary Stars.* Regarding Koret sportswear, see www.koretfoundation.org/about/history.html.

For a glimpse into the rich tradition of California landscape painting, see Ruth Lilly Westphal, *Plein Air Painters of California: The Southland* and *Plein Air Painters of California: The North* (1986). See also Steven Nash, *Facing Eden: 100 Years of Landscape Art in the Bay Area* (1995). Regarding the public gardens of California, see Helaine Kaplan Prentice, with photographs by Melba Levick, *The Gardens of Southern California* (1990); and Eric Sigg, *California Public Gardens: A Visitor's Guide* (1991). Of special value is *Tangible Memories: Californians and Their Gardens, 1800–1950* (2003) by Judith Taylor, M.D., and Harry Butterfield. See also "Garden Homes in the Golden Land," *Holiday* (September 1951); and "A Grand Tour of San Marino Gardens," *Los Angeles* (April 1962). Regarding the garden orientation of Wallace Stegner's suburban California novels, see the University Microfilms International Dissertation Information Service reprint (1990) of the 1987 Bowling Green State University Ph.D. thesis by James Russell Burrows, "The Pastoral Convention in the California Novels of Wallace Stegner." See also Forrest Robinson and Margaret Robinson, *Wallace Stegner* (1977); and *The Geography of Hope: A Tribute to Wallace Stegner* (1996), edited by Page Stegner and Mary Stegner.

The third edition of Thomas Church's *Gardens Are for People* (1995) includes illuminating essays by Grace Hall and Michael Laurie. See also Thomas Church, *Private World: A Study of Intimate Gardens* (1969). Also informative is the Web site http://gardenvisit.com. Garrett Eckbo was a prodigious writer. Of relevance to this chapter are *Landscape for Living* (1950), *The Art of Home Landscaping* (1956, revised and enlarged in 1978 as *Home Landscape: The Art of Home Landscaping*), *Urban Landscape Design* (1964), and *The Landscape We See* (1969). See also Marc Treib and Dorothée Imbert, *Garrett Eckbo: Modern Landscapes for Living* (1997). Lawrence Halprin's thought can be traced through *Cities* (1963), *Freeways* (1966), and *Notebooks 1959–1971* (1972). See also Jacques Leslie's 1996 "A Profile of Lawrence Halprin," at www.well.com/user/jacques/lawrencehalprin.html; and Paul Bennett, "Lost in Translation," *Preservation* (May/June 2004).

Gwendolyn Wright's *Building the Dream: A Social History of Housing in America* (1981) commands the subject. For the California dimension of the story, see Charles Nordhoff, *California for Health, Wealth, and Residence* (1872); and Frank Taylor, *Land of Homes* (1929). Regarding a wartime effort to achieve density in civilian housing, see "Park La Brea Apartments," *Architect and Engineer* (February 1944). Details regarding the design and furnishings of the homes of Levittown can be found in Georgia Dullea, "The Tract House as Landmark," *New York Times* (17 October 1991). The government documents section of the California State Library has a collection of pamphlet guides for the Cal-Vet loan program.

The best overall consideration of developers and the development process is Edward Eichler and Marshall Kaplan, *The Community Builders* (1967). Regarding Fritz Burns as a developer, see James Thomas Keane, *Fritz B. Burns and the Development of Los Angeles* (2001). Regarding the partnership of Burns and Henry J. Kaiser and the Garden City goals of Panorama City, see Greg Hise, *Magnetic Los Angeles* (1997). Also consulted was an unpublished essay/lecture by Hise from the mid-1990s entitled "The Garden Metropolis: Community Builders and Post–World War II Urban Expansion in the United States." Regarding James Francis Cardinal McIntyre, see Francis Weber, *His Eminence of Los Angeles* (2 vols., 1997). Regarding the Gellert brothers of San Francisco, see Ken Zinns, "The Sunset Developers," at www.outsidelands.org/sunset-developers.html and "Sunstream Homes," at www.sunstreamhomes.com/history/html. Regarding the development of Stonestown by the Stoneson brothers, see "Stonestown," at www.outsidelands.org/stonestown.html. Henry Doelger's obituary is in the *San Francisco Chronicle* for 26 July 1978. David Bohannon's obituary is the *San Jose Mercury News* for 17 March 1995. See also the obituary by Gary Marsh in the *Business Journal* for 27 March 1995. Regarding the career of Hillsdale Garden Apartments architect Edwin Wadsworth, see the obituary in the *San Francisco Chronicle* for 31 July 1999. Regarding Bohannon's San Lorenzo Village, see the history of this project at www.slvha.com/docs/hstryass.html.

LA's Early Moderns: Art, Architecture, Photography (2003) by Victoria Dailey, Natalie Shivers, and Michael Dawson, with an introduction by William Deverell, is a comprehensive and commanding introduction to this subject. Owen Gingerich interviewed Charles Eames for the *American Scholar* (Summer 1977). See also Lisa Sanders, "In the Footsteps of Bauhaus," *Forbes* (31 July 1995). Thomas Hines's *Richard Neutra and the Search for Modern Architecture* (1982) and *Irving Gill and the Architecture of Reform* (2000) are classics of architectural history. See also David Gebhard, *Schindler* (1980). For general impressions of domestic architecture in this era, see Douglas Honnold, *Southern California Architecture, 1769–1956* (1956); Reinhold Publishing, *A Guide to the Architecture of Southern California* (1956); and the editors of *Sunset*, *New Homes for Western Living* (1956). Regarding J. R. Davidson, Harwell Hamilton Harris, Gregory Ain, and Raphael Soriano, see Esther McCoy, *The Second Generation* (1984), introduction by Cesar Pelli. Regarding Gregory Ain, see David Gebhard, Harriette Von Breton, and Lauren Weiss, *The Architecture of Gregory Ain: The Play Between the Rational and High Art* (1980); and Susan Freudenheim, "A Living Legacy Endures," *Los Angeles Times* (16 October 2002). See also Patrick Pascal, David Gebhard, and Julius Shulman, *Kesling Modern Structures: Popularizing Modern Living in Southern California, 1934–1962* (2002). The Case Study project can be studied through Esther McCoy, *Modern California Houses: Case Study Houses, 1945–1962* (1962); and Elizabeth A. T. Smith, editor, *Blueprints for Modern Living: History and Legacy of the Case Study Houses* (1989), with essays by Esther McCoy, Thomas Hines, Helen Searing, Kevin Starr, Elizabeth A. T. Smith, Thomas Hine, Reyner Banham, and Dolores Hayden. Two studies of crucial importance to Case Study House #22 are James Steele and David Jenkins, *Pierre Koenig* (1998) and Joseph Rosa, *A Constructed View: The Architectural Photography of Julius Shulman* (1994). See also the entry "Julius Shulman" at www.usc.edu/dept/architecture/shulman/biography/index.html. Regarding Eichler homes, see Jerry Ditto, Lanning Stern, and Sally Woodbridge, *Eichler Homes: Design for Living* (1995), photography by Marvin Wax; and Paul Adamson and Marty Arbunich, *Eichler: Modernism Rebuilds the American Dream* (2002), photographs by Ernie Braun. See also Kathleen Sullivan's obituary for Eichler marketing director James San Jule in the *San Francisco Chronicle* (13 March 2003). Regarding Eichler architects A. Quincy Jones and Frederick Emmons, see Esther McCoy's portrait in *Arts & Architecture* (May 1966). See also Cory Buckner, "The Other Quincy Jones," *Interior Design* (March 2002). Regarding the career of William Wurster and the soft modernism of the San Francisco Bay Area, see Marc Treib, editor, *An Everyday Modernism: The Houses of William Wurster* (1995), with essays by David Gebhard, Daniel Gregory, Greg Hise, Dorothée Imbert, Alan Michelson, Richard Peters, Caitlin Lempres, Marc Treib, and Gwendolyn Wright. Regarding architecture in Northern California and the Bay Area in this period, see Pierluigi Serraino, *NorCalMod: Icons of Northern California Modernism* (2006); Dave Weinstein, with photography by Linda Svendsen, *Signature Architects of the San Francisco Bay Area* (2006); and Rob Keil, *Little Boxes: The Architecture of a Classic Midcentury Suburb* (2006).

Regarding the Tiki craze, see Sven Kirsten, *The Book of Tiki: The Cult of Polynesian Pop in Fifties America* (2000). Richard von Busack wrote "Tiki It to the Limit: From Mugs to Music, the Tiki Fever of the 1950s Has Returned as a Suburban Cult" for *Metro, Silicon Valley's Weekly Newspaper* (4 January 1996). The article can be found at www.metroactive.com/papers/metro/01.04.96/tiki-9601.html. Dennis McLellan's obituary of Hawaiian haberdasher Waltah Clarke appeared in the *Los Angeles Times* (11 May 2002). See also Charles Perry, "Foods of the Tiki Gods," *Los Angeles Times* (17 January 2001); and Steven Kurutz, "Cracking the Code of the Zombie," *New York Times* (28 November 2007).

Of great value is Mary A. van Balgooy, "Designer of the Dream: Cliff May and the California Ranch House," *Southern California Quarterly* (Summer 2004). *Sunset Western Ranch Houses* by the editorial staff of *Sunset* in collaboration with Cliff May appeared in 1946. In 1958 the book was reissued by *Sunset* as Cliff May, *Western Ranch Houses*, and it was republished in 1997. In January 1957 *House Beautiful* extolled the ranch house in "Accepted Architectural Look of the Mid-Twentieth Century."

Chapter 3
Urban Expectations

The Zimmerman Report was issued in a boxed edition of eleven mimeographed volumes on 31 March 1945. Regarding the rise of San Diego in the postwar period, see Anthony Corso, "San Diego: The Anti-City," in *Sunbelt Cities: Politics and Growth Since World War II* (1983), edited by Richard Bernard and Bradley Rice. A valuable introduction to San Diego history is Robert Mayer, editor, *San Diego: A Chronological and Documentary History, 1535–1976* (1978). In 1960 Richard Pourade, editor emeritus of the *San Diego Union*, issued *The Explorers*, the first installment of his seven-volume history of the city. The other volumes are *Time of the Bells* (1961), *The Silver Dons* (1963), *The Glory Years* (1964), *Gold in the Sun* (1965), *The Rising Tide* (1967), and *City of the Dream* (1977). See also Iris Engstrand, *San Diego: California's Cornerstone* (1980); Raymond Starr, *San Diego: A Pictorial History* (1986); and Roger Showley, *San Diego: Perfecting Paradise* (1999). Interpretive portraits include Shelley Higgins, *This Fantastic City, San Diego* (1956); Syd Love and the editors of *San Diego* magazine, *San Diego: Portrait of a Spectacular City* (1969); Dan Berger, Peter Jensen, and Margaret Berg, *San Diego, Where Tomorrow Begins* (1987); and Theodore Fuller, *San Diego Originals* (1987). Also of interest is the pamphlet *San Diego Firsts* by Lucinda Eddy and Richard Crawford (1995), issued by First Interstate Bank and the San Diego Historical Society. Edmund Wilson's essay "The Jumping-Off Place" appears in *The American Jitters: A Year of the Slump* (1932).

Regarding San Diego during World War II, see Roger Lotchin, *The Bad City in the Good War: San Francisco, Los Angeles, Oakland, and San Diego* (2003). See also Lotchin's invaluable *Fortress California, 1910–1961: From Warfare to Welfare* (1992). The distinctive relationship between San Diego and the Navy is fully discussed in Bruce Linder, *San Diego's Navy: An Illustrated History* (2001). See also Abraham Shragge, "'I Like the Cut of Your Jib': Cultures of Accommodation Between the U.S. Navy and Citizens of San Diego, California, 1900–1951," *Journal of San Diego History* (Summer 2002). See also Edward J. P. Davis, *The United States Navy and U.S. Marine Corps at San Diego* (1955); and Robert Witty, *Marines of the Margarita: The Story of Camp Pendleton* (1970). Also of interest are "Jennies to Jets," *San Diego* (April 1950); and Lucius Johnson, "Snug Harbor: Where Do Old Sea-Dogs and Leathernecks Drop Anchor?" *San Diego* (December 1951).

Under the Perfect Sun: The San Diego Tourists Never See (2003) by Mike Davis, Kelly Mayhew, and Jim Miller is a comprehensive and unique investigation into oligarchic ownership and power in San Diego across the twentieth century. It is also the first installment and founding text of the investigative history of San Diego that is only now being written. For a 1950s point of view, see Mary Harrington Hall, "Who Runs San Diego?" *San Diego* (July 1961); and Joe Howard, *History of San Diego Rotary Club 33* (1981). See also Sally Bullard Thornton, "'An Atmosphere of Friendliness': The Cuyamaca Club," *Journal of San Diego History* (Fall 1983). The obituary of Clinton McKinnon can be found in the *Los Angeles Times* for 1 January 2002. Regarding Bishop Charles Buddy and the creation of the University of San Diego in this period, see Iris Engstrand and Clare White, *The First Forty Years: A History of the University of San Diego, 1949–1989* (1989); and Burt Boudoin, *Fortress on a the Hill: Founding the University of San Diego and the San Diego College for Women, 1942–1963* (2001). See also "Catholic Growth," *San Diego* (May 1959).

The library of the San Diego Historical Society in Balboa Park maintains an extensive file of clippings on the life and times of C. Arnholt Smith. For Smith's version of his rise and fall, see the interviews he gave Neal Matthews and Linda Nevin, published as "Mr. San Diego: Born with the Century" and "Mr. San Diego: The Decline of a Western Tycoon" in *San Diego's Weekly Reader* (19 and 26 March 1992). See also "C. Arnholt Smith Chosen Mr. San Diego 1961," *San Diego Union-Tribune* (29 November 1960). Regarding the early years of the tuna industry of San Diego, see Edward Soltesz, "Pole Fishing for Tuna, 1937–1941," *Journal of San Diego History* (September 1991). Also of interest is Arnold Fernandes, "The Rise and Fall of the Tuna Industry in San Diego," at http://home.flash.net/afernand/. For the background to sailing on San Diego Bay, see Iris Engstrand and Cynthia Davalos, *The San Diego Yacht Club: A History, 1886–2000* (2000). Regarding Ted Williams and the San Diego Padres, see Leigh Montville, *Ted Williams: The Biography of an American Hero* (2004); and Peter Rowe, "Going to Bat for Ritchey," *San Diego Union-Tribune* (30 March 2004). See also William Swank and James D. Smith III, "This Was Paradise: Voices of the Pacific Coast League Padres, 1936–1958," *Journal of San Diego History* (Winter 1995).

Roger Revelle's papers are on deposit at the Library of the Scripps Institution of Oceanography in La Jolla, with a detailed biographical sketch by archivist Deborah Day, "A Guide to the Roger Randall Dougan Revelle Papers, 1928–1979." See also the brief and splendid illustrated biography *Roger* (1996) by Judith Morgan and Neil Morgan, issued by the Scripps Institution. Histories of La Jolla include Howard Randolph, *La Jolla Year by Year* (1955); Patricia Schaelchlin, *La Jolla: The Story of a Community, 1887–1987* (1988); and Patricia Daly-Lipe and Barbara Dawson, compilers, *La Jolla: A Celebration of Its Past*, edited by Steele Lipe (2002). The "La Jollans Are Talking About" department ran in *San Diego* magazine throughout the 1950s. See also these *San Diego* articles (July 1950): Doris Christman, "The Green Dragon Colony"; "La Jolla: The Town with the Funny Name"; and "La Jolla's Favorite Spot Is Its New Marine Room." See also Neil Morgan, "Jewel City: Baubles, Bagels, and Beads," *San Diego: The Unconventional City* (1972). In *The Films of Gregory Peck* (1984), John Griggs gives a brief sketch of Peck's boyhood in La Jolla. Regarding Florence Chadwick, see the entries in *Current Biography 1950* (1951) and "Chadwick, Florence, swimming," www.hickoksports.com/biograph/chadwicf.shtml. Regarding Maureen Connolly, see the entry "Connolly, Maureen C. (Mrs. Brinker), tennis," www.hickoksports.com/biograph/connolym.shtml.

Growth in San Diego in this period can be traced in Philip Pryde, editor, *San Diego: An Introduction to the Region* (1984). See also Donald Appleyard and Kevin Lynch, *Temporary Paradise? A Look at the Special Landscape of the San Diego Region* (1974). Regarding Linda Vista, see Mary Taschner, "Boomerang Boom: San Diego, 1941–1942," *Journal of San Diego History* (Winter 1982); Christine Killory, "Temporary Suburbs: The Lost Opportunity of San Diego's National Defense Housing Projects," *Journal of San Diego History* (Winter–Spring 1993); and Norma H. Handy, *Linda Vista, 1940–1954* (1993). Contemporary assessments include Joe Knefler, "The Migration Keeps Rolling: San Diego Real Estate, 1954," *San Diego* (December 1954); and James Britton, "Art of the City, 1968," *San Diego* (November 1958). Regarding the shifting self-image of San Diego in this period, see Lucinda Eddy, "Visions of Paradise: The Selling of San Diego," *Journal of San Diego History* (Summer 1995); and Nathan Glazer, "Notes on Southern California," *Commentary* (August 1959). San Diego's conception of itself is suggested by J. P. Smith Jacobs, "Ode to Us," *San Diego* (July/August 1954). Regarding the Mexican American community of the city, see Robert Alvarez, "The Lemon Grove Incident: The Nation's First Successful Desegregation Court Case," *Journal of San Diego History* (Spring 1986); and Alberto López Pulido, "Nuestra Señora de Guadalupe: The Mexican Catholic experience in San Diego," *Journal of San Diego History* (Fall 1991).

Regarding Donal Hord, see Alice Craig Greene, "San Diego's Donal Hord," *San Diego* (July 1950). Regarding Archie Moore, see Greene's "Archie" in *San Diego* (January 1956). Regarding *San Diego* magazine itself, see the eight-page typescript memoir by founder and executive editor Edwin Self, "The San Diego Magazine Story," dated 23 September 1962, in the library of the San Diego Historical Society. For a listing of San Diego–based films, see Gregory Williams, "Filming San Diego: Hollywood's Back Lot, 1898–2002," *Journal of San Diego History* (Spring 2002). Regarding Oakley Hall and San Diego, see "Oakley Hall's San Diego," *San Diego* (October 1956). See also James Mills's review of *Warlock* in *San Diego* (September 1958). For the background of *Confetti for Gino* by Lorenzo Madalena, see "Italian Colony Portrait," photographs by Ted Lau, *San Diego* (October 1959). Regarding H. H. Lynde, see Gertrude Gilpin, "Novelist Has Two Names," *San Diego Evening Tribune* (3 December 1958). Judith and Neil Morgan wrote *Dr. Seuss & Mr. Geisel: A Biography* (1995). Regarding Max Miller, see Neil Morgan, "Max Miller's Waterfront Is Heart of Our City," *San Diego Union-Tribune* (19 July 1992). Regarding Erle Stanley Gardner on his ranch in Temecula, see the portrait "About Books" in *Southern California Rancher* (May 1960). Regarding Raymond Chandler, see Frank MacShane, *The Life of Raymond Chandler* (1976); and Tom Hiney, *Raymond Chandler: A Biography* (1997). In *The Long Embrace: Raymond Chandler and the Woman He Loved* (2008), Judith Freeman delineates the unusual and complex relationship between Raymond and Cissy Chandler. See also *Selected Letters of Raymond Chandler* (1981), edited by Frank MacShane. Neil Morgan's extraordinary productivity as a columnist in this period can be glimpsed in the anthologies *My San Diego* (1950), *Crosstown* (1955), *My San Diego, 1960* (1960), *Neil Morgan's San Diego* (1964), and *San Diego: The Unconventional City* (1972). Morgan's astuteness as a social commentator on a broader canvas is evident in *Westward Tilt* (1963), *The Pacific States* (1967), and *The California Syndrome* (1969).

Regarding Convair and the B-36, see "A Giant of a Plane," *American History* (February 2003). See also Ralph Friedman, "San Diego: Here We Go Again," *San Diego* (April 1951). For speculation regarding San Diego's role in the forthcoming age of jet passenger travel, see Frank Wigham, "What's Going to Happen Next?" *San Diego* (October 1957). Regarding the 880, see "880! Convair Tools Up for Its Jet-Age Gamble," *San Diego* (October 1957).

For the history of the Scripps Institution, see Elizabeth Noble Shor, *Scripps Institution of Oceanography: Probing the Oceans, 1936–1976* (1978). Regarding the founding of UCSD, see Nancy Scott Anderson, *An Improbable Venture: A History of the University of California, San Diego* (1993). See also John Walsh, "San Diego: New General Campus for University of California Plots an Unconventional Course," *Science* (8 May 1964). See also Abraham Shragge, "Growing Up Together: The University of California's 100-Year Partnership with the San Diego Region," *Journal of San Diego History* (Fall 2001). Also of value is Kenneth Lamott, "La Jolla's New University: Olympus on a Mesa," *Harper's* (August 1966). Regarding San Diego State, see Alexander Bevil, "From Grecian Columns to Spanish Towers: The Development of San Diego State College, 1922–1953," *Journal of San Diego History* (Winter 1995). See also Barbara Greaves, "San Diego State: The Awkward Years," *San Diego* (January– February 1950). Regarding California Western University, see James Britton, "The California Western Situation," *San Diego* (August 1959). Regarding San Diego's first Nobel Prize winner in residence, see Mary Harrington Hall, "All Sides of Harold Urey," *San Diego* (November 1960). Regarding the need for San Diego to change its ways once it had a UC campus, see Kramer Rohfleisch, "Climate for a University: Is San Diego Ready?" *San Diego* (November 1960). Roger Revelle's correspondence with Clark Kerr can be found in Box 16, File 29 of the Revelle Papers in the library of the Scripps Institutions of Oceanography. Regarding the rich tradition of art in San Diego, see Bram Dijkstra, *Masterpieces of San Diego Painting: Fifty Works from Fifty Years, 1900–1950* (2008).

Chapter 4
Baghdad by the Bay

Of the writing of books on San Francisco, there is no end. Recent histories of relevance to this chapter include Oscar Lewis, *San Francisco: Mission to Metropolis* (1966); Robert Mayer, *San Francisco: A Chronological and Documentary History* (1974); Doris Muscatine, *Old San Francisco: The Biography of a City from Early Days to the Earthquake* (1975); John Bernard McGloin, SJ, *San Francisco: The Story of a City* (1978); Robert W. Cherny and William Issel, *San Francisco: Presidio, Port, and Pacific Metropolis* (1981); Charles Fracchia, *City by the Bay: A History of Modern San Francisco, 1945–Present* (1997); and Gray Brechin, *Imperial San Francisco: Urban Power, Earthly Ruin* (1999). The Works Progress Administration published the guidebook *San Francisco: The Bay and Its Cities* (1940), which city archivist Gladys Hansen revised and updated in 1970. See also Randolph Delehanty's *San Francisco: The Ultimate Guide* (1989); and *San Francisco, A Sunset Pictorial* (1969). The April 1961 issue of *Holiday* was devoted to San Francisco and is of special relevance to this chapter. For the overall look of San Francisco in this period, see Gene Wright, *San Francisco Love Affair: A Photographic Romance, 1949–2000* (2006).

The Daniel E. Koshland San Francisco History Center of the San Francisco Public Library possesses the invaluable *San Francisco Clippings: California Biographies* files (six volumes in three series). This collection contains a wealth of obituaries and biographical profiles, upon which I have drawn freely. The Koshland History Center also contains innumerable other information files dealing with every aspect of San Francisco. Scores of them are of relevance to the 1950s. Regarding the personalities of the era, the following *San Francisco Chronicle* obituaries are of relevance: Dean Maddox (25 September 1955); Charles Blyth (26 August 1959); Charles Harney (8 December 1962); Hector Escobosa (23 November 1963); Arthur Caylor (9 June 1965); Howard Gossage (10 July 1969); James Albert Pike (8 September 1969); Robert Watt Miller (20 February 1970); Adrien Falk (15 April 1971); Justin Herman (31 August 1971); Ira Blue (9 January 1974); Dan London (25 May 1974); Imogen Cunningham (25 June

1976); Robert Patterson/Freddie Francisco (10 November 1976); Benjamin Swig (1 November 1980); Paul Speegle (7 June 1982); Elmer Robinson (9 June 1982); Charles McCabe (2 May 1983); Thomas Mellon (25 May 1983); Antonio Sotomayor (12 February 1985); Prescott Sullivan (24 May 1985); George R. Reilly (7 August 1985); Turk Murphy (1 June 1987); Richard Egan (22 July 1987); Stanton Delaplane (19 April 1988); Joseph Mazzola (18 August 1989); C. Julian Bartlett (28 January 1992); Abe Mellinkoff (16 June 1992); Scott Newhall (27 October 1992); Marc Spinelli/Count Marco (29 October 1996); Frederick Walter Kuh (12 November 1997); Hal Lipset (9 December 1997); William Winter (9 November 1999); Art Hoppe (3 February 2000); Vernon Alley (5 October 2004); John Monaghan (2 June 2005); Allan Temko (26 January 2006). See also the obituary for Willis Egan, SJ, in the *Los Angeles Times* (9 February 1981).

Harold Gilliam commands the field of environmental writing. The following are of special value: Gilliam, *San Francisco Bay* (1957); Gilliam and Michael Bry, *The Natural World of San Francisco* (1967); Gilliam, *For Better or For Worse: The Ecology of an Urban Area* (1972); and Gilliam, *Weather of the San Francisco Bay Region* (second edition, 2002). See also Mike Sullivan, *The Trees of San Francisco* (2004). The architecture of the city can be traced through Roger Olmsted and T. H. Watkins, *Here Today: San Francisco's Architectural Heritage*, photographs by Morley Baer and others, (1968); David Gebhard, Roger Montgomery, Robert Winter, John Woodbridge, and Sally Woodbridge, *A Guide to Architecture in San Francisco and Northern California* (1973); Leslie Mandelson Freudenheim and Elisabeth Sacks Sussman, *Building with Nature: Roots of the San Francisco Bay Region Tradition* (1974); Sewall Bogart, *Lauriston: An Architectural Biography of Herbert Edward Law* (1976); Charles Hall Page and Associates, *Splendid Survivors: San Francisco's Downtown Architectural Heritage* (1979); and Richard Longstreth, *On the Edge of the World: Four Architects in San Francisco at the Turn of the Century* (1983). See also Lewis Mumford, "Sky Line," *New Yorker* (7 December 1963).

For the look of San Francisco as defined by colored postcards in the 1900–1940 era, see Glenn D. Koch, *San Francisco's Golden Age Postcards and Memorabilia, 1900–1940* (2001), based on the author's collection of five thousand San Francisco postcards. Regarding the stained-glass heritage of the city, see Edith Hopps Powell, *San Francisco's Heritage in Art Glass*, photography by Brian Moran (1976).

Regarding Herb Caen, see Barnaby Conrad, editor, *The World of Herb Caen: San Francisco, 1938–1997*, commentary and captions by Carol Vernier (1997). See also G. Manning, "Young Mr. San Francisco," *Collier's* (24 June 1950); and Grover Sales, "Herb Caen: His Power Is Awesome," *Holiday* (March 1970). See also April Lynch and Edward Epstein, "Herb Caen Wins Pulitzer Prize. Columnist Cited as 'Voice and Conscience of SF for 58 Years,'" *San Francisco Chronicle* (10 April 1996). Caen described his own method of operation in "Confessions of a Columnist" in *Don't Call It Frisco* (1953). In addition to the books discussed in the text, Caen also produced in this period a *Guide to San Francisco* (1957), a *New Guide to San Francisco and the Bay Area* (1958), and *Only in San Francisco* (1960). See also Caen's "San Francisco's Most Glamorous Women," *Collier's* (31 January 1953); and "San Francisco," *Look* (12 January 1954). Of special value is Steve Wiegand, "Herb Caen, S.F. Legend, Dies at Age 80," *Sacramento Bee* (2 February 1997).

Business histories of relevance to this chapter include Frank Morton Todd, *A Romance of Insurance, Being a History of the Fireman's Fund Insurance Company of San Francisco* (1929); Roos Brothers, Inc., *The Story of Roos Brothers, Outfitters Since 1865* (1945); Ruth Teiser, *An Account of Domingo Ghirardelli and the Early Years of the D. Ghirardelli Company* (1945); Charles Flammer, *The Philosophy of Quality: A Way of Life; Fifty Years in the Service of A. Schilling and Company* (1947); David Warren Ryder, *The Story of Sherman Clay and Company* (1947); Edward Hungerford, *Wells Fargo, Advancing the American Frontier* (1949); Robert Ingram, *A Builder and His Family, 1898–1948: Being the Historical Account of the Contracting, Engineering, and Construction Career of W. A. Bechtel* (1949); W. & J. Sloane, *The Story of Sloane's* (1950); Charles Coleman, *PG&E of California: The Centennial Story of Pacific Gas and Electric Company, 1852–1952* (1952); Neill Compton Wilson, *Southern Pacific: The Roaring Story of a Fighting Railroad* (1952); Marquis James, *Biography of a Bank: The Story of Bank of America* (1954); Daniel Volkmann, *Sixty-Five Years of A. Schilling and Company* (1959); Ruth Waldo Newhall, *The Folger Way: Coffee Pioneering Since 1850* (1960); Reed Hunt, *Pulp, Paper and Pioneers: The Story of Crown Zellerbach Corporation* (1961); William Bronson, *Still Flying and Nailed to the Mast: The First Hundred Years of the Fireman's Fund Insurance Company* (1963); Carol Green Wilson, *Gump's Treasure Trade, A Story of San Francisco* (1965); Robert Ingram, *The Bechtel Story: Seventy Years of Accomplishment in Engineering and Construction* (1968); George Koster and Elizabeth Summers, *The Transamerica Story* (1978); David Siefkin, *Meet Me at the St. Francis: The First Seventy-five Years of a Great San Francisco Hotel* (1979); MJB, *1881–1981: 100 Years of History* (1981); Philip Fradkin, *Stagecoach: Wells Fargo and the American West* (2002). See also Jade Snow Wong, "San Francisco: The Bazaar," *Holiday* (April 1961); Nora Leishman, "The City of Paris," *Argonaut: Journal of the San Francisco Museum and Historical Society* (Summer 2003). See also "Gump's Goes Modern," *Time* (30 May 1949); "Tourism Is Getting Bigger," *American City* (June 1963). Regarding residence clubs, see "Room, Board and Maybe Romance (36 Clubs)," *California Living/San Francisco Sunday Examiner and Chronicle* (11 June 1967).

Biographies and memoirs of business personalities include Eric Hoffer, *Working and Thinking on the Waterfront: A Journal, June 1958–May 1959* (1969); *Ralph K. Davies: As We Knew Him* (1976); Ruth Bransten McDougall, *Coffee, Martinis, and San Francisco* (1978); Frances Bransten Rothman, *The Haas Sisters of Franklin Street* (1979); Cyril Magnin and Cynthia Robins, *Call Me Cyril* (1981); Frances Bransten Rothman, *My Father, Edward Bransten: His Life and Letters* (1982); and John A. Sutro Sr., *A Life in the Law* (bound typescript of an oral history interview conducted by Sarah Sharp for the Bancroft Library, 1986). See also G. S. Perry, "Debonair Dan, the Magnificent Innkeeper, St. Francis Hotel," *Saturday Evening Post* (10 January 1953); David Dalin and John Rothmann, "Henry U. Brandenstein of San Francisco," *Argonaut* (Summer 2004). Regarding Howard Gossage, see Warren Hinckle, "Remembering Howard Gossage," *California Living/San Francisco Sunday Examiner and Chronicle* (1 December 1974). See also Howard Gossage, *Is There Any Hope for Advertising?* edited by Kim Rotzoll (1987), and *The Book of Gossage* (1995). Regarding Charles E. Williams, see Executive Biographies, www.williams-sonomainc.com/com/com_bio.cfm. Regarding Walter Landor, see Ken Kelley and Rick Clogher, "The Ultimate Image Maker," *San Francisco Focus* (August 1992).

Edmund Wilson's slightly ambivalent portrayal of James Martin MacInnis can be found in *The Forties: From Notebooks and Diaries of the Period*, edited with an introduction by Leon Edel (1983). See also John Wesley and Bernie Averbuch, *Never Plead Guilty: The Story of Jake Ehrlich* (1955); Brad Williams, *Due Process: The Story of Criminal Lawyer George T. Davis and His Thirty-Year Battle Against Capital Punishment* (1961); Melvin Belli with Robert Blair Kaiser, *Melvin Belli: My Life on Trial, an Autobiography* (1976); James P. Walsh, *San Francisco's Hallinan: Toughest Lawyer in Town* (1982). See also Dean Dickensheet, *Great Crimes of San Francisco* (1974); and Thomas Garden Barnes, *Hastings College of the Law, The First Century* (1978). The partial papers of Joseph L. Alioto are on deposit at the San Francisco History Center.

Regarding the restaurants of San Francisco, see Ruth Thompson and Louis Hanges, *Eating Around San Francisco* (1937); Matty Simmons and Don Simmons, *On the House* (1955); and Frances de Talavera Berger and John Parke Custis, *Sumptuous Dining in Gaslight San Francisco, 1875–1915* (1985). See also John Briscoe, *Tadich Grill: The Story of San Francisco's Oldest Restaurant* (2002). Regarding the restaurants of Fisherman's Wharf, see Warren Chase

Merritt, *Fisherman's Wharf, San Francisco* (1958). See also Herb Caen, "*Holiday* Handbook of San Francisco Restaurants," *Holiday* (April 1961); and Calvin Kentfield, "San Francisco: The Water Front," *Holiday* (April 1961). Also of relevance to this chapter is and Jane Chamberlin, Hank Armstrong, and Dustin F. Leer, *Saloons of San Francisco: The Great and Notorious* (1982).

Regarding the jazz culture of San Francisco, see Jesse Hamlin, "Jazz Helped Break the Color Barrier. Blacks and Whites Mixed Freely in San Francisco Clubs," *San Francisco Chronicle* (8 February 1998). Regarding the Old Spaghetti Factory, see "Old Spaghetti Factory's Treasures Sold," *San Francisco Chronicle* (19 March 1984). Regarding the hungry i, see John Weaver, "San Francisco: hungry i," *Holiday* (April 1961); and Don Asher, "The hungry i," *Image, Sunday San Francisco Examiner and Chronicle* (31 May 1992). Regarding the Purple Onion, see Jane Ganahl, "Laughter Peels Anew at Purple Onion," *San Francisco Chronicle* (15 March 2004). See also these memoirs: Lenny Bruce, *How to Talk Dirty and Influence People, An Autobiography* (1965); and Phyllis Diller with Richard Buskin, *Like a Lampshade in a Whorehouse: My Life in Comedy* (2005). See also Ronald Collins and David Skover, *The Trials of Lenny Bruce: The Rise and Fall of an American Icon* (2002). For a highly skeptical view of the entire scene, see Alice McIntyre, "Depressed in California," *Esquire* (May 1963).

Regarding Don Sherwood, see Laurie Harper, *Don Sherwood: The Life and Times of "The World's Greatest Disc Jockey"* (1989). Regarding the 49ers, see Dan McGuire, *San Francisco 49ers: All About the Thirteen Wild and Woolly* (1960). See also John McGilvray, *The Shriners' Finest Hour* (1955). For the background to the championship University of San Francisco football and basketball teams, see John Bernard McGloin, SJ, *Jesuits by the Golden Gate: The Society of Jesus in San Francisco, 1849–1969* (1972). Regarding the 1951 USF championship football team, see Aram Goudsouzian, "The House That Russell Built," *California History* (Fall 2007). See also Ryan Callan, "The Indomitable 1951 Football Dons," http://usfdons.collegesports.com/trads/football_trad.html. Regarding the Giants, see Joe King, *San Francisco Giants*, introduction by George Christopher (1958); Russ Hodges, *My Giants* (1963); and Art Rosenbaum, *The Giants of San Francisco* (1963). See also Benjamin Rader, *Baseball: A History of America's Game* (1992); and Kevin Nelson, *The Golden Game: The Story of California Baseball* (2004). Regarding Seals Stadium and Candlestick Park, see Daniel Bacon, "Sandlots to Stadiums: The Baseball Parks of San Francisco," *Argonaut* (Fall 2001).

For an inventory of the attractions of Golden Gate Park, see Katherine Wilson, *Golden Gate: The Park of a Thousand Vistas* (1947). For Golden Gate Park in the 1950s, see "For a Sunday Afternoon in May," *Sunset* (May 1954); and Frank Cameron, "Don't Keep Off the Grass," *Saturday Evening Post* (25 September 1954). For the history of the park, see Raymond Clary, *The Making of Golden Gate Park: The Early Years, 1865–1906* (1980); and Christopher Pollock, "Bygone Golden Gate Park," *Argonaut* (Summer 2004). Also of value is Margot Patterson Doss, *Golden Gate Park at Your Feet* (1970).

For the modernism/anti-modernism backgrounds to art in San Francisco, see Society for Sanity in Art, Inc., *Exhibition of Paintings and Sculpture, California Palace of the Legion of Honor, San Francisco, August 10 to October 6, 1940* (1940); and Beatrice Judd Ryan, "Rise of Modern Art in the Bay Area," *California Historical Society Quarterly* (March 1959). Regarding Haig Patigian, see Peter Garland, "The Greatest Bohemian of Them All," *Argonaut* (Fall 1998). Regarding other artists under discussion, see Randolph Falk, *Bufano* (1975); Thomas Albright, *Art in the San Francisco Bay Area 1945–1980: An Illustrated History* (1985); and Susan Landauer, *The San Francisco School of Abstract Expressionism*, introduction by Dore Ashton (1996). Regarding Dong Kingman, see www.dongkingman.org/about2.html. See also the retrospective catalog *Modernism—Twenty-five Years* (2 vols., 2005), issued by the Modernism gallery of San Francisco.

Regarding the general history of theater in San Francisco, see Edmond McAdoo Gagey, *The San Francisco Stage: A History* (1950). Regarding the achievement of Actors' Workshop, see "Rise of Repertory Theater," *Time* (14 February 1964); and Robert Brustein, "Health in an Ailing Profession," *New Republic* (30 January 1965). Regarding its decline, see F. H. Gardner, "Actors' Workshop is Dead," *Nation* (19 September 1966). Regarding its successor company, see John R. Wilk, *The Creation of an Ensemble: The First Years of the American Conservatory Theater* (1986). Regarding ballet in the city, see Cobbett Steinberg, *San Francisco Ballet: The First Fifty Years* (1983). Regarding the symphony, see Leonora Wood Armsby's *We Shall Have Music* (1960) and her earlier "The San Francisco Symphony Orchestra: First Decade," *California Historical Society Quarterly* (September 1946). Regarding Pierre Monteux as a beloved public figure, see Herb Caen's portrait in *Don't Call It Frisco*, 120–25. Regarding the San Francisco Opera, see Arthur Bloomfield, *50 Years of San Francisco Opera* (1972). Regarding Adler, see Kevin Starr, "Kurt Herbert Adler: Notes Towards a Biography," *San Francisco Opera* (19 November 1978). For an overall view of the arts during this era, see Allan Temko, "The Flowering of San Francisco," *Horizon* (January 1959).

William H. Chambliss castigated fin-de-siècle society in *Chambliss' Diary; or, Society as It Really Is* (1895). Julia Cooley Altrocchi lauded it in *The Spectacular San Franciscans* (1949). For an assessment of the period under discussion, see Stephen Birmingham, "San Francisco: The Grand Manner," *Holiday* (April 1961). *Life* covered the opening night and the annual Opera Ball and Fol-De-Rol on 16 November 1953, 1 October 1956, and 19 November 1962. An idea of club life in San Francisco in this period can be gleaned from: Theodore Bonnet, editor, *Annals of the Olympic Club, San Francisco* (1914); Olympic Club of San Francisco, *One Hundred Years, 1860–1960* (1960); John van der Zee, *The Greatest Men's Party on Earth* (1974), Arthur Hargrave, *The Family Story* (1978); the eight volumes of the *Annals of the Bohemian Club*, published between 1900 and 1997; and Kimball Livingston, *San Francisco Yacht Club, Founded 1927* (2002). Society bandleader Ray Hackett was profiled by Albert Morch in the *San Francisco Examiner* for 17 June 1973.

Church histories from the period include Trinity Episcopal Church, *One Hundred Years a Parish* (1949); Louis Alfred Peterson, *History of 100 Years in San Francisco, 1849–1949, First Presbyterian Church* (1950); First Baptist Church, *1849–1949: A History of the First Baptist Church, San Francisco* (1950); First Unitarian Church, *One Hundred Years, 1850–1950* (1950); and Othmar Tobisch, *The First One Hundred Years of the New Jerusalem Society of San Francisco, 1852–1952* (1952). See also Howard Thurman, *Footprints of a Dream: The Story of the Church for the Fellowship of all Peoples* (1959). See also Sherwood Eliot Wirt, *Crusade at the Golden Gate* (1959); and "Minister for the Beatniks," *Newsweek* (16 March 1959). Regarding the Diocese of California, see Edward Lambe Parsons, *The Diocese of California, a Quarter Century, 1915–1940* (1958). See also the bound pamphlet by C. Julian Bartlett, *A Great Cathedral Rises in the West* (1960). Bishop James Pike's books include *Beyond Anxiety* (1953), *The Church, Politics and Society* (1955), *The Next Day* (1957), *A Time for Christian Candor* 1963, and *The Other Side* (1967). See also W. Stringfellow and A. Towne, *The Bishop Pike Affair* (1967).

For the facts and figures of Catholic San Francisco, see the yearly *Official Catholic Directory* for the years under discussion. See also *Catholic San Francisco: Sesquicentennial Essays*, edited by Jeffrey Burns (2005). For the texture of daily life in Catholic San Francisco during this period, see Kevin Starr, "I Grew Up Catholic in San Francisco," *City of San Francisco* (21 October 1975). Regarding the Irish of the city, see James P. Walsh, editor, *The San Francisco Irish, 1850–1976* (1978). See also Paul B. Fay Jr., *The Pleasure of His Company* (1966); and *Memoirs of Charles Kendrick*, edited and annotated with an introduction by David Warren Ryder (1972). Of special value is Bernice Scharlach, *Big Alma: San Francisco's Alma Spreckels* (1990). Regarding the University of San Francisco, see John Bernard McGloin,

SJ, *Jesuits by the Golden Gate: The Society of Jesus in San Francisco, 1849–1969* (1972); Eric Abrahamson, *The University of San Francisco School of Law: A History, 1912–1987* (1987); and Alan Ziajka, *Legacy of Promise: 150 Years of Jesuit Education at the University of San Francisco* (2005). Regarding the Paulists, see Thomas Denis McSweeney, *Cathedral on California Street: The Story of St. Mary's Cathedral, San Francisco, 1854–1891, and of Old St. Mary's, A Paulist Church, 1894–1951* (1952). See also the bound brochure *One Hundredth Anniversary, 1873–1973, St. Dominic's Church, San Francisco* (1973).

Regarding the Jewish community of San Francisco in the era under discussion, see Michael Moses Zarchin, *Glimpses of Jewish Life in San Francisco* (1952). See also Jacob Voorsanger, *The Chronicles of Emanu-El* (1900); Edgar Myron Kahn, *Early San Francisco Jewry* (1955); Irena Narell, *Our City: The Jews of San Francisco* (1981); and Bernice Scharlach, *Dealing from the Heart: A Biography of Benjamin Swig* (2000). See also Fred Rosenbaum, *Architects of Reform: Congregational and Community Leadership, Emanu-El of San Francisco, 1849–1980* (1980); and Louis Blumenthal, *Three Generations of Service to the Community, 1877–1954: The Story of the San Francisco Jewish Community Center and the YM-YWHA* (1954). For local color in the Jewish community, see Jerry Flamm, *Hometown San Francisco: Sunny Jim, Phat Willie, and Dave* (1994). For the arrival of psychiatry and psychoanalysis, see Jurgen Ruesch, M.D., *Langley Porter Institute and Psychiatry in Northern California, 1943–1975* (1978). See also the Centennial Edition of the *Red and White* yearbook issued by the Lowell High School Student Association, text by Archibald Jeter Cloud (1956).

Regarding the neighborhoods of San Francisco, see the series "Cities Within the City" by Anita Day Hubbard in the *San Francisco Bulletin* (August–November 1924). Regarding the demographics of the city, see San Francisco Department of City Planning, *The Population of San Francisco: A Half-Century of Change* (1954). See also Leonard Austin, *Around the World in San Francisco* (1940). Regarding the government of San Francisco, see Douglas McPhee, *San Francisco's Six Years of Achievement Under the New Charter: The Story of a City Whose People Decided to Have a Better Government* (1938). See also John Constantinus Bollens, *The Problem of Government in the San Francisco Bay Region* (1948). For further background, see James P. Walsh, "Abe Ruef Was No Boss: Machine Politics, Reform, and San Francisco," *California Historical Society Quarterly* (Spring 1972); and Philip J. Ethington, *The Public City: The Political Construction of Urban Life in San Francisco, 1850–1900* (1994).

Regarding the mayors under discussion, see David Wooster Taylor, *The Life of James Rolph, Jr.* (1934); *In Memoriam, Angelo J. Rossi, 1878–1948*, issued by the Stanford Parlor #76, Native Sons of the Golden West (1949); Helen Abbot Lapham, *Roving with Roger* (1971); and George Dorsey, *Christopher of San Francisco* (1962). Other politicians and soon-to-be politicians can be explored through John Jacobs, *A Rage for Justice: The Passion and Politics of Phillip Burton* (1995); James Richardson, *Willie Brown: A Biography* (1996); and Ethan Rarick, *California Rising: The Life and Times of Pat Brown* (2005). See also Kevin Starr, "Jerry Brown: The Governor as Zen Jesuit," in Walsh, editor, *The San Francisco Irish*, 127–40. Regarding unions, see Steven Schwartz, *Brotherhood of the Sea: A History of the Sailors' Union of the Pacific, 1885–1985* (1986). For the politics of the Jewish community, see David Gil Dalin, "Public Affairs and the Jewish Community: The Changing Political World of San Francisco Jews" (Ph.D. dissertation, Political Science, Brandeis University, 1977). Regarding St. Anthony's Dining Room, see Madeline Hartmann, *The Man Behind the Miracle* (2000).

Regarding population growth in the region, see Marybeth Branaman, *Growth of the San Francisco Bay Area Urban Core* (1956); and Kingsley Davis and Eleanor Langlois, *Future Demographic Growth of the San Francisco Bay Area* (1959). The single most important consideration of the spatial development of the City of San Francisco can be found in the extended essay by UC Berkeley geography professor James E. Vance Jr. entitled "Geography and Urban Evolution in the San Francisco Bay Area," in the second volume of the magisterial anthology issued by the Institute of Governmental Studies at UC Berkeley, *The San Francisco Bay Area: Its Problems and Future*, edited by Stanley Scott (3 vols., 1966–1972), containing key essays on all aspects of planning and development in the Bay Area by such noted experts as Vance, Catherine Bauer Wurster, T. J. Kent Jr., Mel Scott, and others. Regarding the overall development of the Bay Area, see Lawrence Kinnaird, *History of the Greater San Francisco Bay Region* (3 vols., 1966).

Regarding planning in an earlier era, see Judd Kahn, *Imperial San Francisco: Politics and Planning in an American City, 1897–1906* (1979). See also Thomas J. Kent Jr., *City and Regional Planning for the Metropolitan San Francisco Bay Area* (1963). Planning in San Francisco in the war and postwar period can be traced through San Francisco Planning Commission, *Postwar Improvements: A Handbook for Making a Sound Program for San Francisco* (July 1944); San Francisco Planning Commission, *The Master Plan...A Brief Summary of the Master Plan as Adopted by the City Planning Commission on December 20, 1945 with an Outline of the Task Ahead* (1946); San Francisco District Attorney, *Survey of Housing Conditions in San Francisco as of May 1, 1947*, prepared by Edmund G. Brown (1947), *Second Report* (1947), *Third and Final Report* (May 1948); and Steven Warshaw, *The City of Gold: The Story of City Planning in San Francisco* (1960). Mel Scott's thought can be traced through his *New City: San Francisco Redeveloped, Replanned, and Rebuilt Under the Community Development Act of 1945* (1947) and *San Francisco Bay Area: A Metropolis in Perspective* (1959). See also Scott's "What's Stopping Urban Redevelopment?" *American City* (April 1948). See also Allan Temko, "San Francisco Rebuilds Again," *Harper's* (April 1950); and Welton Beckett and Associates, *The Development of the Golden Gateway, Prepared for the Redevelopment Agency of San Francisco* (1960). For the significance of downtowns in this era, see M. Fogelson, *Downtown: Its Rise and Fall, 1880–1950* (2001); and Michael Johns, *Moment of Grace: The American City in the 1950s* (2003).

For an overall view of transportation, see Richard M. Zettel, "Urban Transportation in the San Francisco Bay Area," *The San Francisco Bay Area: Its Problems and Future* (vol. 2, 1966). *Life* covered the cable car controversy on 24 February 1947. See also George H. Harlan, *Of Walking Beams and Paddle Wheels: A Chronicle of San Francisco Bay Ferry-Boats* (1951); "Last Bay Auto Ferries," *Sunset* (December 1955); and Nancy Olmsted, *The Ferry Building: Witness to a Century of Change, 1898–1998* (1998). Regarding the San Francisco skyline in this era, see Roger Olmsted and T. H. Watkins, *Here Today: San Francisco's Architectural Heritage* (1968). Regarding the Crown Zellerbach and John Hancock buildings, see San Francisco Museum of Art, *Two Buildings: San Francisco 1959* (1959). Regarding the restoration of the Palace of Fine Arts, see Ruth Newhall, *San Francisco's Enchanted Palace* (1967). Regarding the restoration of Victorians, see Judith Waldhorn, *A Gift to the Street*, photographs by Carol Olwell (1976).

For the overall history of San Francisco journalism, see John Roberts Bruce, *Gaudy Century: The Story of San Francisco's Hundred Years of Robust Journalism* (1948). The *San Francisco Examiner* published its Golden Jubilee edition on 4 March 1937. The *News* published its Golden Jubilee edition in 1953. The *Call-Bulletin* published its Call-Bulletin Centennial on 10 October 1955. For examples of the *Chronicle*'s reportage and columns from this era, see *The San Francisco Chronicle Reader*, edited by William Hogan and William German (1962). For the colorful background of the era, see Warren Hinckle, *If You Have a Lemon, Make Lemonade* (1973). Regarding Scott Newhall, see the oral history issued by the Bancroft Library in 1990, "Scott Newhall: A Newspaper Editor's Voyage Across San Francisco Bay: San Francisco *Chronicle*, 1935–1971, and Other Adventures," with an introduction by Karl Kortum (interviews conducted by Suzanne B. Riess, 1988–1989). See especially, Appendix N, "Herb Caen's Return to the *Chronicle*," 555C–G. Also of value is John Luce, "My Search for Scott Newhall," *San Francisco Magazine* (July/August 1968). For the writings of Charles McCabe, see the collections *The Fearless Spectator* (1970), *Tall Girls Are Grateful* (1973), and *The Good Man's Weakness* (1974). See also *The Charles McCabe Reader,* foreword by Gordon Pates and James P. Degnan (1984). Regarding the Herb Caen–Art Cohn rivalry following Herb Caen's return to the *Chronicle,* see "Caen vs. Cohn," *Newsweek* (27 January 1958). Regarding Caen's success as a columnist, see William Rivers, and David Rubin, *A Region's Press: Anatomy of Newspapers in the San Francisco Bay Area* (1971), 96–101. For Margot Patterson Doss's columns, see her *San Francisco at Your Feet* (1974). See also "N.Y. Times Ending Western Edition," *San Francisco Chronicle* (17 January 1964).

Chapter 5
The Cardinal, the Chief, Walter O'Malley, and Buff Chandler

As interpretations of Los Angeles, Mike Davis's *City of Quartz: Excavating the Future in Los Angeles* (1990) and *Ecology of Fear: Los Angeles and the Imagination of Disaster* (1998) are in a class by themselves. General histories of Los Angeles include Remi Nadeau, *Los Angeles: From Mission to Modern City* (1960); John Chapman, *Incredible Los Angeles* (1967); W. W. Robinson, *Los Angeles, A Profile* (1968); Lynn Bowman, *Los Angeles: Epic of a City* (1974); John Weaver, *Los Angeles: The Enormous Village, 1781–1981* (1980); Bruce Henstell, *Sunshine and Wealth: Los Angeles in the Twenties and Thirties* (1984); and Andrew Rolle, *Los Angeles: From Pueblo to City of the Future* (revised and expanded second edition, 1995). See also the high school geography textbook, Mel Scott, *Metropolitan Los Angeles: One Community* (1949). Regarding ordinary life in this era, see Carolyn Kozo Cole and Kathy Kobayashi, *Shades of LA: Pictures from Ethnic Family Albums* (1996). For portraits of colorful personalities from this period, see Cecilia Rasmussen, *LA Unconventional: The Men and Women Who Did LA Their Way,* foreword by Kevin Starr (1998). For a satirical view of things, see Cynthia Lindsay, *The Natives Are Restless* (1960).

Regarding the founding of Los Angeles see *The Founding Documents of Los Angeles: A Bilingual Edition,* edited by Doyce Nunis Jr. (2004). See also Maurice and Marco Newmark, *Census of the City and County of Los Angeles California for the Year 1850 Together with an Analysis and an Appendix* (1929). Regarding the transition of Los Angeles to an American city, see William Deverell, *The Whitewashed Adobe: The Rise of Los Angeles and the Remaking of Its Mexican Past* (2004). See also Janet Abu-Lughod, "Los Angeles Becomes 'Anglo,'" *New York, Chicago, Los Angeles: America's Global Cities* (1999).

The environmental history of Los Angeles, past and present, is chronicled in Blake Gumprecht, *The Los Angeles River: Its Life, Death and Possible Rebirth* (1999). See also Jared Orsi, *Hazardous Metropolis: Flooding and Urban Ecology in Los Angeles* (2004); and William Deverell and Greg Hise, *Land of Sunshine: An Environmental History of Metropolitan Los Angeles* (2005).

The planning and development of Los Angeles can be traced through Robert Fogelson, *The Fragmented Metropolis: Los Angeles 1850–1930* (1967); William Fulton, *The Reluctant Metropolis: The Politics of Urban Growth in Los Angeles* (1997); Greg Hise, *Magnetic Los Angeles: Planning the Twentieth-Century Metropolis* (1997); Greg Hise and William Deverell, *Eden by Design: The 1930 Olmsted-Bartholomew Plan for the Los Angeles Region* (2000); Catherine Mulholland, *William Mulholland and the Rise of Los Angeles* (2000); John Thomas Keane, *Fritz B. Burns and the Development of Los Angeles* (2001); and Tom Sitton and William Deverell, editors, *Metropolis in the Making: Los Angeles in the 1920s* (2001);

Guidebooks of use to this chapter include Lee Shippey, *The Los Angeles Book,* photographs by Max Yavno (1950); Robert Huston, *This Is Los Angeles: A Complete Guide Book* (1950); J. P. Bernard, *Non-Tourist Los Angeles* (1959); Bill Murphy, *The Dolphin Guide to Los Angeles and*

Southern California (1962); and Robert Cameron and Jack Smith, *Above Los Angeles* (1990). Regarding the automobile and aircraft industries of Los Angeles in this era, see Clifford Zierer, *California and the Southwest* (1956). Regarding the waterfront, see Lawrence Allison, "Our Warring Waterfronts," *Los Angeles* (March 1964); and Digby Diehl, "The Surprising Harbor," *Los Angeles* (August 1966). Roger Butterfield predicted the postwar rise of the city in "Los Angeles," *Life* (22 November 1943). That growth was documented by *Life* in "A New Mayor, a New Councilwoman...And 400 New Angels Every Day" (13 July 1953). See also "From Los Angeles of 1952 to Los Angeles of 2052," *American City* (May 1952).

Regarding the Roman Catholic culture of Los Angeles, see Msgr. Francis J. Weber, Hermine Lees, and Sister Joanne Wittenburg, SND, *A History of the Archdiocese of Los Angeles* (2007). Regarding the life and career of James Francis Cardinal McIntyre, see Weber's comprehensive *His Eminence of Los Angeles* (2 vols., 1997). See also Weber's *Magnificat: The Life and Times of Timothy Cardinal Manning* (1999), *Encyclopedia of California's Catholic Heritage* (2001), and *Cathedral of Our Lady of the Angels* (2004). For a portrait of McIntyre at the height of his authority, see Jack Alexander, "Private Life of a Catholic Cardinal," *Saturday Evening Post* (12 September 1953). Regarding McIntyre's contemporaries in the Los Angeles religious establishment, see Geoff Miller, "Our Churches and Their Leaders," *Los Angeles* (October 1961). See also Robert Berger, photographer, text by Alfred Willis, *Sacred Spaces: Historic Houses of Worship in the City of Angels*, introduction by Kevin Starr (2003). Of special importance is Max Vorspan and Lloyd Gartner, *History of the Jews of Los Angeles* (1970).

Regarding resistance to McIntyre, see John Leo, "Catholicism in Los Angeles—The DuBay Case," *Commonweal* (10 July 1964); Robert Blair Kaiser, "The McIntyre Controversy," *Los Angeles* (August 1964); Gail Cottman, "The Nuns' Rebellion," *Los Angeles* (March 1968); "Fighting Nuns," *Newsweek* (1 April 1968); and Kenneth Lamott, "A Quiet Revolt," *Horizon* (Winter 1970). For the rebellious nuns' side of the story, see Anita Caspary, *Witness to Integrity* (2003). For a rebuttal, see the reviews by Charles A. Coulombe in *The Los Angeles Lay Catholic Mission* (November 2003). See also "My Immaculate Heart" by Jeanne Cordova, in *Lesbian Nuns: Breaking Silence*, edited by Rosemary Curb and Nancy Manahan (1985), surprisingly critical of certain aspects of the IHM breakaway movement.

For a scholarly assessment of the Los Angeles Police Department, see Gerald Woods, *The Police in Los Angeles: Reform and Professionalization* (1993). For a reporter's inside look, see Joe Domanick, *To Protect and to Serve: The LAPD's Century of War in the City of Dreams* (1994). Daryl F. Gates, with Diane Shah, *Chief: My Life in the LAPD* is filled with colorful detail of the LAPD during Parker's administration. See also the two notices in *American City*: "One Building Houses All Los Angeles Police Activities" (November 1949) and "Los Angeles Photographs All Persons Arrested" (August 1953). For a general survey of crime in this period, see Michael Parrish, *For the People: Inside the Los Angeles County District Attorney's Office, 1850–2000*, foreword by Kevin Starr (2001). See also the equally colorful, if untrustworthy, Mickey Cohen, *In My Words* (1975). Regarding the Black Dahlia case, see the startling revelations in Steve Hodel, *Black Dahlia Avenger: The True Story* (2003). Regarding the 1950 Los Angeles crime wave, see Howard Whitman, "Don't Go Out Alone at Night in LA," *Collier's* (28 October 1950). See also "'Best' Police Force vs. Worst Crime Wave," *Newsweek* (22 February 1954). For a selection of speeches by Chief William Henry Parker, see *Parker on Police*, edited by O. W. Wilson (1957). For articles covering Parker and the LAPD during Parker's tenure as chief, see Dean Jennings, "Portrait of a Police Chief," *Saturday Evening Post* (7 May 1960); Wesley Marx, "Parker, the Cop as Crusader," *Los Angeles* (August 1962); Bill Davidson, "The Mafia Can't Crack Los Angeles," *Saturday Evening Post* (31 July 1965). Parker outlined his response to the national rioting in the summer of 1964 in, "Crisis in Race Relations: A Police Chief Talks of 'Police Brutality,'" *US News & World Report* (10 August 1964). In *To Protect and to Serve*, Joe Domanick gives a crisp and detailed account of the Watts riots. See also the narrative and documents presented in www.usc.edu/libraries/archives/cityinstress/mccone/part3.htm.

Regarding the recreational culture of Los Angeles during this era, see Mike Ebert, *Griffith Park, A Centennial History* (1996). For beach culture during this era, see Eugene Burdick, "The Sun and Its Worshippers," *Holiday* (October 1957); Buck Lowry, "Malibu, How You've Changed," *Los Angeles* (January 1963); and Gil Thomas, "The Young Side of Town: South Bay," *Los Angeles* (May 1965). See also Arthur Verge, *Los Angeles County Lifeguards* (2005). For the sports culture of Los Angeles during this period, see Robert Oates, *The Los Angeles Rams* (1955); Tim Cohane, "Has Pro Football Killed the College Game?" *Look* (29 September 1959); and "The Most Interesting 9," *Los Angeles* (May 1962). For the hotel and restaurant culture of the era, see Cynthia Lindsay, "A Harvest of Restaurants," *Holiday* (October 1957); Bill Ballantine, "Los Angeles," *Holiday* (November 1958); Eugene Burdick, "Food for the Angels—Perino's," *Holiday* (December 1958); and Mike Fessier Jr., "Westside's Ingenious Innkeepers," *Los Angeles* (January 1966). See also George Christy, *The Los Angeles Underground Gourmet* (1970); and the pamphlet *Confrérie des Chevaliers du Tastevin Sous-Commanderie de Los Angeles, 1955–2005: A History* (2005). For Barney's Beanery, www.qs-pasadena.com/barneysbeanery/default.asp. For a general view of good times in this era, see the reminiscences collected in "O Happy Days!" *Los Angeles Times Magazine* (4 February 1990).

Regarding the history of public housing in Los Angeles in this era and the Chavez Ravine controversy, Don Parson, *Making a Better World: Public Housing, the Red Scare, and the Direction of Modern Los Angeles*, foreword by Kevin Starr (2005) commands the subject. See also Thomas S. Hines, "Housing, Baseball, and Creeping Socialism: The Battle of Chavez Ravine, Los Angeles, 1949–1959," *Journal of Urban History* (February 1982). For contemporary assessments, see Charles Abrams, "Rats Among the Palm Trees," *Nation* (25 February 1950); and Jo Hindman, "Homes Into Kindling: Urban Renewal, Our Latest Demolition Team," *American Mercury* (December 1959).

Neil Sullivan, *The Dodgers Move West* (1987) commands the topic. For further background on the Dodgers, see Paul Zimmerman, *The Los Angeles Dodgers* (1960); and Stanley Cohen, *Dodgers! The First 100 Years* (1990). For baseball culture in California before it went big league, see Kevin Nelson, *The Golden Game: The Story of California Baseball*, foreword by Hank Greenwald (2004). Mayor Norris Poulson told it from his perspective in "The Untold Story of Chavez Ravine," *Los Angeles* (April 1962). For a point-by-point refutation of Poulson's arguments, see the *Chavez Ravine Fact Book* (9 April 1962) at http://content.cdlib.org/ark:/13030.hb2c6005wk. See also John Lardner, "The War for Chavez," *Newsweek* (16 December 1957); and Tim Cohane, "The West Coast Produces Baseball's Strangest Story," *Look* (19 August 1958). For Poulson's background, see W. W. Robinson, *Mayors of Los Angeles* (1965). For Poulson's sense of the challenges facing Los Angeles, see "Problems of Fastest-Growing City in the US: Interview with Norris Poulson, Mayor of Los Angeles," *U.S. News & World Report* (16 September 1965).

Regarding Walter O'Malley, the official Web site www.walteromalley.com is highly informative. Regarding the effect of Dodger Stadium and other modernist developments on the spatial arrangements and prior minority cultures of Los Angeles, see Eric Avila, *Popular Culture in the Age of White Flight: Fear and Fantasy in Suburban Los Angeles* (2004); and the essays gathered in, Charles Salas and Michael Roth, editors, *Looking for Los Angeles: Architecture, Film, Photography, and the Urban Landscape* (2001). Regarding the coming of the Giants to San Francisco, see Joe King, *San Francisco Giants*, preface by Ford Frick, introduction by George Christopher (1958). Regarding the arrival of the Dodgers, see Kevin Nelson, "Los Angeles Dodgers vs. San Francisco Giants, April 1958," *California History* (Fall 2005). See also the two-part retrospective by Steve Springer in the *Los Angeles Times* (7, 8 October 2007).

Chapter 6
Dividends and Downsides

Regarding the history of the Los Angeles oligarchy, see Michael Regan, *Mansions of Los Angeles* (1965); Margaret Leslie Davis, *Dark Side of Fortune: Triumph and Scandal in the Life of Oil Tycoon Edward L. Doheny* (1998); Clark Davis, *Company Men: White-Collar Life and Corporate Cultures in Los Angeles, 1892–1941* (2000). See also Jane Wilson, *Gibson, Dunn & Crutcher, Lawyers: An Early History* (1990); and the essays gathered in Tom Sitton and William Deverell, editors, *Metropolis in the Making* (2001). Regarding the oligarchic elite of this era, see Frank Riley, "The Power Structure: Who Runs Los Angeles?" *Los Angeles* (December 1966); and "Ahmanson, an Interview" *Los Angeles* (January 1967). Regarding the debutante culture, see Joan Winchell, "Partyline," *Los Angeles* (January 1964); and Josh Scott III, "The Deb Deluge," *Los Angeles* (December 1967). See also Jean Halliburton Stevens, "Society Among the Angels," *Los Angeles* (July 1961); and "Stage-Struck Society: The Leaguers Leap," *Los Angeles* (March 1962). For the social scene in satellite communities, see "The Satellites" in the Los Angeles special edition of *Holiday* (October 1957); and Ray Duncan, "Pasadena: The Old Order Changeth," *Los Angeles* (December 1963). Regarding the premier charity of the social elite, see Margaret Leslie Davis, *Children's Hospital and the Leaders of Los Angeles* (2002).

The Jesuit debate regarding the soul of Los Angeles can be traced in Francis Marien SJ, "Los Angeles and the Idea of a City," *America* (30 November 1957), followed by the response of Eugene Schallert, SJ, in *America* (18 January 1958). The Los Angeles vs. San Francisco debate can be followed in R. L. Duffus, "The Two States of California," *New York Times Magazine* (18 December 1955); and Herb Caen and Jack Smith, "A Tale of Two Cities: A Sibling Rivalry," *Saturday Evening Post* (3 November 1962). See also Nathan Glazer, "Notes on Southern California," *Commentary* (August 1959). Maurice Zolotow blasted the theatrical culture of Los Angeles in "Land of Nod," *Theatre Arts* (April 1956). Regarding art collecting among the elite, see Winifred Haines Higgins, "Art Collecting in the Los Angeles Area, 1910–1960" (Ph.D. dissertation, Art History, UCLA, June 1963); and the magisterial Suzanne Muchnic, *Odd Man In: Norton Simon and the Pursuit of Culture* (1998). See also Patricia Carr Bowie, "A Cultural History of Los Angeles, 1850–1967," (Ph.D. dissertation, History, USC, June 1980). Regarding the musical history of the region, see Richard Drake Saunders, editor, *Music and Dance in California and the West* (1948); Howard Swan, *Music in the Southwest, 1825–1950* (1952); John Northcutt, *Symphony: The Story of the Los Angeles Philharmonic Orchestra* (1963); and Kenneth Marcus, *Musical Metropolis: Los Angeles and the Creation of a Music Culture, 1880–1940* (2004). See also the articles Charles Davenport, "County Full of Music," *Los Angeles* (February 1962); and Henry Sutherland, "Requiem for the Los Angeles Philharmonic Auditorium," *Southern California Quarterly* (September 1965).

Regarding the Chandler family, David Halberstam, *The Powers That Be* (1979) commands the subject. See also the authorized Robert Gottlieb and Irene Wolt, *Thinking Big: The Story of the Los Angeles Times, Its Publishers, and Their Influence on Southern California* (1977). See also these contemporary accounts: "Those Tireless Chandlers," *Newsweek* (30 April 1956); "L.A.'s Mighty Chandlers," *Look* (25 September 1962); and John Corry, "The Los Angeles Times," *Harper's* (December 1969). Regarding Dorothy Chandler, see these obituary-related articles: Charles Champlin, "Her Vision Gave City Its Heart," *Los Angeles Times* (8 July 1997); Rick Lyman, "Dorothy Buffum Chandler," *New York Times* (8 July 1997); and Joan Didion, "Willpower," *Los Angeles Times* (13 July 1997). See also Gloria Ricci Lothrop, "Strength Made Stronger: The Role of Women in Southern California Philanthropy," *Southern California Quarterly* (Summer/Fall 1989). Regarding Otis Chandler, see Charles Moritz, editor, *Current Biography Yearbook, 1968.* See also Mary McNamara, "Mom Is Watching,"

Los Angeles Times (19 October 2003); and these obituaries: David Shaw and Mitchell Landsberg, "A Lion of Journalism," *Los Angeles Times* (28 February 2006); and Mitchell Landsberg, "Mourners Recall an Original," *Los Angeles Times* (7 March 2006).

The opening of the Music Center was the cover story for *Time* (18 December 1964). The *Los Angeles Times* issued a 119-page supplement, *Music Center: A Living Memorial to Peace* (6 December 1964), containing twenty-eight articles on every phase of the facility. See also Charles Davenport, "The Music Center and Mrs. C," *Los Angeles* (May 1962); and Ray Duncan, "A Connoisseur's Key to the Music Center," *Los Angeles* (December 1964), with a number of informative inserts.

The literary culture of Los Angeles has inspired a number of incisive studies. Of use to this chapter have been Sam Bluefarb, *Set in LA: Scenes of the City in Fiction* (1986); Norman Klein, *The History of Forgetting: Los Angeles and the Erasure of Memory* (1997); Paul Vangelisti with Evan Calbi, *L.A. Exile: A Guide to Los Angeles Writing, 1932–1998*, photographs by Jen Calbi (1999); David Fine, *Imagining Los Angeles: A City in Fiction* (2000); William Alexander McClung, *Landscapes of Desire: Anglo Mythologies of Los Angeles* (2000); and Ehrhard Bahr, *Weimar on the Pacific: German Exile Culture in Los Angeles and the Crisis of Modernism* (2007). A valuable bibliographical guide is W. W. Robinson, "Books About Los Angeles," in *Los Angeles, A Profile*. See also Althea Warren, "Writers of California," *Library Journal* (15 June 1953); and Lawrence Clark Powell, "Some Angelic Reading Matter," *Westways* (June 1965). See also Powell's *California Classics: The Creative Literature of the Golden State* (1971). Of critical value to this chapter is David Ulin, *Writing Los Angeles: A Literary Anthology* (2002). See also Elizabeth Ward and Alain Silver, editors, *Raymond Chandler's Los Angeles* (1987); David Reid, editor, *Sex, Death, and God in L.A.* (1992); and Scott Timberg and Dana Gioia, *The Misread City: New Literary Los Angeles* (2003). Regarding survivors from the prewar era, see Charles Champlin, "A Warm Climate for Cultural Life," *Life* (20 June 1960); J. M. Edelstein, *Jake Zeitlin: A Garland on the Occasion of His 65th Birthday* (1967); Arthur Millier, "[Merle Armitage] The Master of Manzanita," *Los Angeles* (March 1962); Wesley Marx, "Upton Sinclair: The Rebel in Retirement," *Los Angeles* (June 1962); and Robert Bobrow, "Jake the Bookie," *Los Angeles* (May 1964). See also Peter Richardson, *American Prophet: The Life and Work of Carey McWilliams* (2005). Regarding the extraordinary career of Franklin Murphy, see Margaret Leslie Davis, *The Culture Broker: Franklin D. Murphy and the Transformation of Los Angeles* (2007). See also Andrew Hamilton and John Jackson, *UCLA on the Move During Fifty Golden Years, 1919–1969* (1969). For the reforms and upgrading of USC by President Norman Topping, see Manuel Servin and Iris Higbie Wilson, *Southern California and Its University: A History of USC, 1880–1964* (1969).

For a list of visiting scholars at the Huntington in this period, see John Pomfret, *The Henry E. Huntington Library and Art Gallery from Its Beginnings to 1969* (1969),147–80. Regarding the ongoing English involvement with L.A., see "Two out of England," *Los Angeles* (April 1962). For a general survey of early modern prewar Los Angeles, see the essays in, Victoria Dailey, Natalie Shivers, and Michael Dawson, *LA's Early Moderns*, introduction by William Deverell (2003). Regarding the Durants, see Arthur Millier, "Will and Ariel Durant: History in the Home Stretch," *Los Angeles* (May 1965). Regarding Ray Bradbury, see the authoritative William Nowlan, *The Ray Bradbury Companion* (1975). See also Charles Davenport, "The Magic World of Ray Bradbury," *Los Angeles* (March 1962); and Marilyn Fletcher and James Thorson, *Reader's Guide to Twentieth-Century Science Fiction* (1989). Regarding Irving Wallace, see Dave Sheehan and Charles Davenport, "The Boccaccio of Brentwood," *Los Angeles* (August 1962); and John Riley, "Seven Minutes in LA," *Los Angeles* (August 1969). Regarding Alison Lurie, see http://people.cornell.edu/pages/a128/html/bio.html.

Regarding the new bohemia of Sunset Strip, see Bernard Wolfe, "Manners and Morals on the Sunset Strip," *Esquire* (August 1961); D. M. Whitworth, "Sunset Strip," *Westways*

(December 1964); and Mike Fesier Jr., "Sunset Boulevard's New Bohemia," *Los Angeles* (December 1965). Regarding Sunset Boulevard itself, see Amy Dawes, *Sunset Boulevard: Cruising the Heart of Los Angeles* (2002). Regarding the Garden of Allah in this period, see Charles Champlin, "The Glorious Garden," *Southern California Prompter* (Stember 1960). Regarding Wilshire Boulevard, see Ralph Hancock, *Fabulous Boulevard* (1949); Esther McCoy, photographs by Marvin Rand, "Face of the City: Wilshire Boulevard," *Western Architect and Engineer* (September 1961); and Kevin Roderick, with research by J. Eric Lynxwiler, *Wilshire Boulevard: Grand Concourse of Los Angeles* (2005). Spencer Crump, *Ride the Big Red Cars: How Trolleys Helped Build Southern California* (fifth edition revised, 1970) is essential to the understanding of space, travel, and time in L.A.

The contemporary response to the emergence of metropolitan/regional Los Angeles in this era can be traced through "A City—200 Miles Long?" *U.S. News & World Report* (16 September 1955); "Los Angeles in a New Image," *Life* (20 June 1960); American Geographical Society, *Los Angeles Focus* (May 1962); Robert de Roos, photographs by Thomas Nebbia, "Los Angeles," *National Geographic* (October 1962); Richard Austin Smith, "Los Angeles, Prototype of Supercity," *Fortune* (March 1965); and "Anatomy of a Super City," *Los Angeles* (October 1967). Christopher Rand's *New Yorker* series was published as *Los Angeles: The Ultimate City* (1967). See also the lavishly illustrated Paul C. Johnson and the editors of *Sunset*, *Los Angeles: Portrait of an Extraordinary City* (1968).

The political and administrative response to metropolitanization in this era is evident in the exhaustive sixteen-volume report from the John Randolph Haynes and Dora Haynes Foundation, *Metropolitan Los Angeles: A Study in Integration* (16 vols., 1952–55), especially the first volume of the series, Edwin Cottrell and Helen Jones, *Characteristics of the Metropolis* (1952). See also Winston Crouch and Beatrice Dinerman, *Southern California Metropolis: A Study in Development of Government for a Metropolitan Area* (1964); and the remarkable essays in Allen Scott and Edward Soja, editors, *The City: Los Angeles and Urban Theory at the End of the Twentieth Century* (1996). Reyner Banham compared London to Los Angeles in "LA Is...Exactly Like London," *Los Angeles* (November 1968). Reyner Banham's *Los Angeles: The Architecture of Four Ecologies* (1971) was perceptively reviewed by John Margolies in *Architectural Form* (November 1971). See also "Pop-up City," *Newsweek* (23 August 1971). For another Englishman's view, see Richard Gilbert, *City of the Angels* (1964). Regarding the effort to revive downtown Los Angeles, see Ray Duncan, "The Painful Rejuvenation of Downtown," *Los Angeles* (November 1963); Walt Anderson, "Downtown: The Doomcriers Foiled Again," *Los Angeles* (August 1967); Gilbert Thomas, "Civic Center's Rebirth: Uptown at the Downtown," *Los Angeles* (March 1966); and Cynthia Joyce, "Bunker's Comeback: Return of the Hill," *Los Angeles* (May 1968). Regarding the emergence of Westside development, see "20th Century City," *Time* (13 January 1958); Wes Marx and Gil Thomas, "The Westside Story," *Los Angeles* (February 1962); J. Lee Anderson, "Hollywood: The Myth Becomes a City," *Los Angeles* (February 1964); and Robert Carson, "Upper Los Angeles," *Los Angeles* (January 1966). Regarding the influence of UCLA on the Westside through its extension program, see Frank Riley, "The Hidden Campus," (April 1965). Regarding the overnight popularity of LACMA, see Arthur Millier, "The Museum Gets Its Second Wind," *Los Angeles* (February 1967). Regarding the planning and architectural aspects of Westside development, see Charles Davenport, "The Look of the City: Is Beauty Within Reach?" *Los Angeles* (April 1962); Gil Thomas, "The Face Changers," *Los Angeles* (September 1964); Frederick Carleton, "A Champagne Wedding for Art & Architecture," *Los Angeles* (April 1965); and "A Formless City Takes Form," *Los Angeles* (January 1966).

Francis Carney, "The Decentralized Politics of Los Angeles," *The Annals of the American Academy of Political and Social Science* (1964) is a seminal statement. Ed Ainsworth, *Maverick Mayor: A Biography of Sam Yorty of Los Angeles* (1966) is an early and sympathetic biography. See also "At Home with the Yortys," *Los Angeles* (June 1962). Yorty reflected on the Watts riots and related topics in "What to Do About Slums, Riots, City Ills: Interview with Sam Yorty, Mayor of Los Angeles," *U.S. News & World Report* (21 August 1967).

Chapter 7
Warren, Nixon, Knight, Knowland

Theodore H. White's "The Gentlemen from California: Nixon, Knowland, Knight, Warren" first appeared in *Collier's* (3 February 1956) and was reprinted in *Theodore H. White at Large: The Best of His Magazine Writing, 1939–1986* (1992). Regarding President Eisenhower's medical history at the time, see C. W. Hughes and others, "A Review of the Late General Eisenhower's Operations," *Annals of Surgery* (1971); and Clarence Lasby, *Eisenhower's Heart Attack: How Ike Beat Heart Disease and Held on to the Presidency* (1997).

For the general history of politics of California in this era, see Dean Cresap, *Party Politics in the Golden State* (1954); Leonard Rowe and William Buchanan, "Campaign Funds in California: What the Records Reveal," *California Historical Society Quarterly* (September 1962); Earl Behrens, "California," in James Reichley, editor, *States in Crisis: Politics in Ten American States, 1950–1962* (1964); Henry Turner and John Vieg, *The Government and Politics of California* (second edition, 1964); Eugene Dvorin and Arthur Misner, editors, *California Politics and Policies: Original Essays*, (1966); Gladwin Hill, *Dancing Bear: An Inside Look at California Politics* (1968); Royce Delmatier and others, *The Rumble of California Politics* (1970); and Michael Paul Rogin and John Shover, *Political Change in California: Critical Elections and Social Movements, 1890–1966* (1970). See also Carey McWilliams, "Look What's Happened to California," *Harper's* (October 1949). Of great usefulness to this chapter is Brett Melendy and Benjamin Gilbert, *The Governors of California: From Peter H. Burnett to Edmund G. Brown* (1965).

Regarding cross-filing, see Dean McHenry, "Cross Filing of Political Candidates in California," *Annals of the American Academy of Political and Social Science* (1946); Robert Pitchell, "The Electoral System and Voting Behavior: The Case of California's Cross-Filing," *Western Political Science Quarterly* (June 1959); Gladwyn Hill, "California: State of Confusion," *New York Times Magazine* (12 November 1961); and H. Brett Melendy, "California's Cross-Filing Nightmare: The 1918 Gubernatorial Election," *Pacific Historical Review* (August 1964).

General studies of California politics of relevance to this chapter include Winston Crouch, *California Government and Politics* (1956); Philip Schlessinger and Richard Wright, *Elements of Government in California* (1962); Bernard Hyink, Seyom Brown, and Ernest Thacker, *Politics and Government in California* (1963); Eugene Lee, *California Votes* (1963); Leroy Hardy, *California Government* (1964); Gerald Nash, *State Government and Economic Developments: A History of Administrative Policies in California* (1964); Joseph Harris, *California Politics* (1965); and Ruth Ross, *California's Political Process* (1973).

For contemporary assessments of Whitaker and Baxter, see Carey McWilliams, "Government by Whitaker and Baxter," *Nation* (5 May 1951); "The Partners," *Time* (26 December 1955); William Worden, "Tales of the Kingmakers," *Saturday Evening Post* (23 May 1959); and Irwin Ross, "The Supersalesmen of California Politics: Whitaker and Baxter," *Harper's* (July 1959). See also Stanley Kelley, *Professional Public Relations and Political Power* (1956); and Robert Pitchell, "The Influence of Professional Campaign Management Firms in Partisan Elections in California," *Western Political Quarterly* (June 1958). See also Gabrielle Morris's *Oral History Interview* with Clement Sherman Whitaker Jr., on deposit at the California State Archives in Sacramento.

The most comprehensive history of the rise of conservatism in Southern California is Lisa McGirr, *Suburban Warriors: The Origins of the New American Right* (2001). See also

Matthew Dallek, *The Right Moment: Ronald Reagan's First Victory and the Decisive Turning Point in American Politics* (2000). For contrasting versions of the Pasadena school controversy, see David Hulburd, *This Happened in Pasadena* (1951); and Mary Louise Allen, *Education or Indoctrination* (1956). Regarding the UNESCO debate, see Glen Adams, "The UNESCO Controversy in Los Angeles, 1951–1953: A Case Study of the Influences of Right-Wing Groups on Urban Affairs" (Ph.D. dissertation, History, University of Southern California, 1970). See also Paul Jacobs, "Assault on UNESCO," *Commonweal* (27 May 1955). Regarding fluoridation, see John Mueller, "The Politics of Fluoridation in Seven California Cities," *Western Political Quarterly* (March 1966). Other items of use to this chapter regarding the rise of the Right include Norman Cousins, "How Communism Is Gaining in California," *Saturday Review* (11 April 1953); Henry Ehrlich, "Setback for the Far Right," *Look* (29 September 1962); and Jim Wood, "California Republicans: Are the Birchers Taking Over?" *Reporter* (7 May 1964). See also Eugene Burdick's novel *The Ninth Wave* (1956). For the influence of William Randolph Hearst in this period, see David Nasaw, *The Chief: The Life of William Randolph Hearst* (2000). My sense of the McCarthyite Los Angeles city councilman Edward J. Davenport is based upon an unpublished essay by Don Parson, "The Darling of the Town's Neofascists: The Bombastic Political Career of Edward J. Davenport," (45 pages typewritten, 1998), generously provided me by the author. Also of importance is Markell Baer, *Story of the California Republican Assembly* (1948, revised 1955).

Biographies of Richard Nixon of use to this chapter include the skeptical Earl Mazo, *Richard Nixon: A Political and Personal Portrait* (1959); the hostile William Costello, *The Facts About Nixon: An Unauthorized Biography* (1960); the comprehensive Roger Morris, *Richard Milhous Nixon: The Rise of an American Politician* (1990); and the exhaustively researched and insightful Irwin F. Gellman, *The Contender: Richard Nixon, the Congress Years, 1946–1952* (1999). *Life* ran Donald Jackson's "The Young Nixon" on 6 November 1970. Also of use were Ernest Brashear, "Who Is Richard Nixon?" *New Republic* (1 September 1952); Mark Blackburn, "Nixon in California," *New Republic* (27 October 1952); and William Roger, "The Man Who Might Be President: Richard Nixon's Success Story from the Inside," *Frontier* (September 1955). Nixon's Checkers Speech of 23 September 1952 is reprinted in the Library of America volume *American Speeches: Political Oratory from Abraham Lincoln to Bill Clinton*, edited by Ted Widmer (2006). Nixon gave his side of the story in *Six Crises* (1962). See also Garry Wills, "The Checkers Speech," *Esquire* (June 1983). Regarding the support of Nixon by the *Los Angeles Times*, see David Halberstam, *The Powers That Be* (1979), 256–66. Congressman Jerry Voorhis told his side of the story in *Confessions of a Congressman* (1947). Evidence of the hostility generated by Nixon among liberals can be seen in Mark Harris's comic noir novel *Mark the Glove Boy; or, The Last Days of Richard Nixon* (1964), concerning a psychological stalking of Nixon during the 1962 gubernatorial campaign.

The most comprehensive biographies of Earl Warren are Ed Cray, *Chief Justice: A Biography of Earl Warren* (1997); and Jim Newton, *Justice for All: Earl Warren and the Nation He Made* (2006). See also the Warren portrait in *The Governors of California. The Public Papers of Chief Justice Earl Warren*, edited by Henry Christman, appeared in 1959. See also *The Memoirs of Earl Warren* (1977). Carey McWilliams depicted Earl Warren as a man of the Right in "Warren of California," *New Republic* (18 October 1943). See also McWilliams's "Machines, Political and Slot," *New Republic* (28 May 1949). Novelist and fellow Old Blue Irving Stone provided the opposite point of view in *Earl Warren: A Great American Story* (1948). See also the largely admiring, Leo Katcher, *Earl Warren: A Political Biography* (1967). The best investigation of Warren's political style is Richard Harvey, "Governor Earl Warren: A Study in 'Non-Partisan' Republican Politics," *California Historical Society Quarterly* (March 1967).

Two biographies are of critical importance to my understanding of the details and significance of the gubernatorial election of 1958: Gayle Montgomery and James Johnson, *One Step from the White House: The Rise and Fall of Senator William F. Knowland* (1998); and Ethan Rarick, *California Rising: The Life and Times of Pat Brown* (2005). See also the chapter on Brown in *The Governors of California*. There is no critical biography of Goodwin J. Knight. See however, the catalog *The Golden Heritage of Goodwin Knight: The 31st Governor of the 31st State: Published on the Occasion of an Exhibit of His Papers* (Stanford University Libraries, October 1975), with a warm introduction by fellow former governor Edmund G. Brown and an informative essay by Virginia Knight. See also the portrait in *The Governors of California* and the cover story on Knight and his presidential prospects, "Don Juan in Heaven," *Time* (30 May 1955). Regarding Knight's Horatio Alger boyhood and authorship, see Gene Kramer and Alan Cline, "Hidden Talent of Governor Knight Comes to Light," *The Sacramento Bee* (5 January 1954). Also consulted was a file of Knight's speeches, campaign brochures, and other ephemera on file at the California State Library.

Regarding the resurgence of the Democratic Party in California in the 1950s, see Frances Carney, *The Rise of the Democratic Clubs in California* (1958); and James Q. Wilson, *The Amateur Democrat: Club Politics in Three Cities* (1962). See also Earl Behrens and Dan Fowler, "New Faces, New Power," *Look* (29 September 1959). Regarding the difficulties of political organizing in suburban Southern California, see Winston Crouch and Beatrice Dinerman, *Southern California Metropolis: A Study in Development of Government for a Metropolitan Area* (1963), 261–91.

William L. Roper chronicled the drying up of funds for Knight in 1957 in "Knight into Pawn," *Nation* (23 November 1957). For George Christopher's resistance to Knight's senate campaign, see "The Californians," *Time* (24 March 1958). *Life* (30 September 1957) captured the campaign at its height in "California, Here It Comes for Big Stakes." Richard Rovere analyzed the 1958 Republican primary for the *New Yorker* (14 June 1958). Regarding the growing partisanship in California politics evident in the 1958 and 1962 gubernatorial campaigns, see Totton Anderson, "Extremism in California Politics: The Brown-Knowland and Brown-Nixon Campaigns Compared," *Western Political Quarterly* (June 1963). Regarding the 1962 campaign, see Totton Anderson and Eugene Lee, "The 1962 Election in California," *Western Political Quarterly* (June 1963). Pat Brown and his department heads set forth their goals in *California: The Dynamic State* (1966). For assessments of Pat Brown as governor, see "The California of the Pat Brown Years: Creative Building for the Golden State's Future," edited by Martin Schiesl, a special issue of *California Politics and Policy*, published by the Edmund G. (Pat) Brown Institute of Public Affairs, California State University, Los Angeles (1997). See also Francis Carney, "Remembering Pat Brown: California's Last Progressive Governor," *The Riverside Press-Enterprise* (25 February 1996).

Chapter 8
Cold War Campus

Critical to an understanding of the industrial history of California is Forest G. Hill, "The Shaping of California's Industrial Pattern," *Proceedings of the Thirteenth Annual Conference of the Western Economic Association* (1956). Also of importance are Robert Glass Cleland and Osgood Hardy, *March of Empire* (1929); Ewald T. Grether, *The Steel and Steel-Using Industries of California* (1946); Frank Kidner, *California Business Cycles* (1946); Philip Neff, "Industrialization in Southern California," *California Looks Ahead: Papers Presented Before the Pacific Southwest Academy* (June 1946); Nedra Belloc, *Wages in California: War and*

Postwar Changes (1948); James J. Parsons, "California Manufacturing," *Geographical Review* (April 1949); Robert K. Arnold, *The California Economy, 1947–1980* (Stanford Research Institute, 1961); Victor Fuchs, *Changes in the Location of Manufacturing in the United States Since 1929* (1962); John W. Reith, "The Supply of Fuel and Power for Los Angeles," *Festschrift: Clarence F. Jones*, edited by Merle C. Prunty Jr. (*Northwestern University Studies in Geography* no. 6 (May 1962); and W. H. Hutchinson, *Oil, Land, and Politics* (1966). Regarding the defense aspects of this history, see Wytze Gorter and George H. Hildebrand, *The Pacific Coast Maritime Shipping Industry, 1930–1948* (2 vols., 1952–54); Clifford M. Zierer, editor, *California and the Southwest* (1956); Sterling Brubaker, *The Impact of Federal Government Activities on California Economic Growth, 1930–1956* (a 1959 UC Berkeley Ph.D. dissertation issued as a report by the Economics Department of the Bank of America in 1958); James L. Clayton, "Defense Spending: Key to California's Growth," *Western Political Quarterly* (June 1962); Roger W. Lotchin, *Fortress California, 1910–1961: From Warfare to Welfare* (1992). The continuing boom documented in a number of instances, including "California's New Boom Area," *Business Week* (2 April 1960), came under serious challenge by Ceyom Brown in "Southern California's Precarious One-Crop Economy," *Reporter* (7 January 1960).

Regarding the aerospace industry in general, see H. O. Stekler, *The Structure and Peformance of the Aerospace Industry* (1965). The special importance of aviation and aerospace to the defense economy of Southern California can be traced in Frank J. Taylor and Lawton Wright, *Democracy's Air Arsenal* (1947); William G. Cunningham, *The Aircraft Industry: A Study in Industrial Location* (1951); Andrew Hamilton, "Rocketdyne: Roar of the Future," *Westways* (October 1961); Wesley Marx, "Vandenberg: Home on the Missile Range," *Los Angeles* (May 1962); Andrew Hamilton, "Aerospace: Umpire for the Air Force," *Westways* (July 1962), "Northrop: Where Technologies are Mastered," *Westways* (March 1963), and "Douglas: The Lengthened Shadow," *Westways* (February 1964); Seymour L. Chapin, "Garrett and Pressurized Flight: A Business Built on Thin Air," *Pacific Historical Review* (August 1966); Charles D. Bright, *The Jet Makers: The Aerospace Industry from 1945 to 1972* (1978); and Glyn Jones, *The Jet Pioneers: The Birth of Jet-Powered Flight* (1989). See also Electronics Committee, Los Angeles Chamber of Commerce, *Report on the Electronics Industry, Los Angeles Metropolitan Area* (1955). Regarding the breaking of the sound barrier, see Tom Wolfe, *The Right Stuff* (1979). See also Patrick Mott, "An American Ace," *Los Angeles Times* (8 October 1997); and Jose Cardenas, "Edwards Remembers Its Conquerors of the Sky," *Los Angeles Times* (12 October) 1997.

Mike Gruntman's *Blazing the Trail: The Early History of Spacecraft and Rocketry* (2004) commands the subject. The transition of aerospace from missiles to space exploration can also be traced through Max Wesley, "The Quick Change from Rocketry to Diversity," *Los Angeles* (October 1961); Art Seidenbaum, "From Here to the Moon," *Los Angeles* (January 1962); and Andrew Hamilton, "Aerojet: From the Depths of the Sea to Outer Space," *Westways* (January 1963) and "Lockheed—Seaplane to Space," *Westways* (December 1963). Hughes Aircraft as think tank was profiled by Andrew Hamilton in "Shangri-La for Deep Thinkers," *Westways* (February 1962). The rise of RAND is chronicled by Virginia Campbell in "How RAND Invented the Postwar World," *Invention and Technology* (Summer 2004). See also Alex Abella, *Soldiers of Reason: The RAND Corporation and the Rise of the American Empire* (2008); and the Web site www.rand.org/about/history. Cecilia Rasmussen chronicled the bizarre career of John Parsons in the *Los Angeles Times* (19 March 2000). The effort to reapply aerospace know-how to civilian programs can be traced through Wesley Marx, "Our Aerospace Industry: Will It Run Away Too?" *Los Angeles* (February 1963); Ray Duncan, "The Aerospace Economy: Go or No Go?" *Los Angeles* (February 1964); "Aerospace 1965: The Cold Statistics," *Los Angeles* (February 1965); "Aerospace: A New Life for a Billion-Dollar Industry? With an Interview with Edmund G. Brown," *U.S. News & World Report* (24 May 1965); and W. J. Coughlin,

"Next Step: Aerospace Programs to Apply Space-Age Know-How to the Nation's Social and Economic Problems," *Missiles and Rocketry* (15 November 1965).

Regarding the rise of Caltech, see Judith R. Goodstein, *Millikan's School: A History of the California Institute of Technology* (1991). See also William M. Cramer with Margaret Leslie Davis, *A Lone Traveler: Einstein in California* (2004). Regarding the rise of Stanford, see Rebecca S. Lowen, *Creating the Cold War University: The Transformation of Stanford* (1997); C. Stewart Gillmor, *Fred Terman at Stanford* (2004); and Leslie Berlin, *The Man Behind the Microchip: Robert Noyce and the Invention of Silicon Valley* (2005). See also David Packard, *The HP Way: How Bill Hewlett and I Built Our Company*, edited by David Kirby with Karen Lewis (1995). I interviewed Arthur Rock extensively in August 1994. See also Arthur Rock and Morris Kronfeld, "Some Considerations of the Infinite," *Financial Analysts Journal* (November 1958); and Arthur Rock, "Strategy vs. Tactics from a Venture Capitalist," *Harvard Business Review* (November–December 1987).

Verne A. Stadtman, *The University of California, 1868–1968* (1970) presents the overall history of the university. Stadtman also edited *The Centennial Record of the University of California, 1868–1968* (1967). Also of relevance are William Carey Jones, *Illustrated History of the University of California* (1901); *The Semicentenary of the Celebration of the Founding of the University of California* (1919); William Warren Ferrier, *Origin and Development of the University of California* (1930); Robert Sibley, editor, *The Golden Book of California* (1937); *Endowed Chairs of Learning* (1947); Russell H. Fitzgibbon, *The Academic Senate of the University of California* (1968); Albert G. Pickerell and Mary Dornin, *The University of California: A Pictorial History* (1968); and Patricia A. Pelfrey, *A Brief History of the University of California* (second edition, 2004). For the texture and detail of life at Cal across the decades, see *There Was Light, Alumni Essays: A Collection of Essays by Alumni of the University of California, Berkeley* (1996), edited by Jean Stone and Irving Stone (1996).

Regarding the presidency of UC, see Monroe E. Deutsch, editor, *The Abundant Life: Benjamin Ide Wheeler* (1926); and William Warren Ferrier, *Henry Durant: First President, University of California* (1942). Regarding certain outstanding faculty from the turn-of-the-century period, see Cornelia Stratton Parker, *An American Idyll: The Life of Carelton H. Parker* (1919); Benjamin Putnam Kurtz, *Charles Mills Gayley* (1953); and James E. Watson, "Bernard Moses' Contribution to Scholarship," *California Historical Society Quarterly* (June 1963). See also "Memorial to Professor H. Morse Stephens," *School and Society* (17 May 1919); and Charles B. Faulhaber, "Henry Morse Stephens," *Newsletter of the Friends of the Bancroft Library* (Spring 2006). Regarding the UC Berkeley campus itself, see Verne Stadtman, *California Campus: The University of California at Berkeley* (1961); Ansel Adams and Nancy Newhall, *Fiat Lux* (1967); Benjamin B. Ehrich, *Photographic Guide to the University of California, Berkeley* (1969); and Loren W. Partridge, *John Galen Howard and the Berkeley Campus: Beaux-Arts Architecture in the "Athens of the West"* (1978).

Regarding science at UC Berkeley, see Ira Michael Heyman, *The Nobel Tradition at Berkeley* (1984); see also J. L. Heilbron, *Lawrence and His Laboratory: A History of the Lawrence Berkeley Laboratory* (1989). For early views of the cyclotron, see "4,900-ton Atom Smasher Financed by Rockefeller," *Science* (19 April 1940); and "Super-K.O. for Atom," *Newsweek* (14 October 1940).

Clark Kerr documented his remarkable career in his highly readable two-volume memoir, *The Gold and the Blue: A Personal Memoir of the University of California, 1949–1967*, volume 1, *Academic Triumphs*, foreword by Neil J. Smelser (2001); volume 2, *Political Turmoil*, with the assistance of Marian L. Gade and Maureen Kawaoka, foreword by Neil J. Smelser (2003). Kerr's 1963 Godkin Lectures at Harvard appeared as *The Uses of the University* (1963). Regarding Kerr himself, see David Pierpont Gardner, "Driving Mr. Kerr," *California Monthly* (February 2004); and the extensive obituary by Stuart Silverstein and Rebecca Trounson,

"Renowned UC Leader Dies," *Los Angeles Times* (2 December 2003). See also Ira Michael Heyman's review of *The Gold and the Blue* in the *Book Review of the Los Angeles Times* (21 October 2001).

Regarding the history of education in California, see William W. Ferrier, *Ninety Years of Education in California* (1937); and Roy W. Cloud, *Education in California* (1952). The California State Assembly issued *A Master Plan for Higher Education in California, 1960–1975* in February 1960. Assemblywoman Dorothy M. Donahoe was profiled in *California Schools* (March 1959). The background to the Master Plan for Higher Education is exhaustively and elegantly set forth by John Aubrey Douglass in *The California Idea and American Higher Education: 1850 to the 1960 Master Plan* (2000). See also Arthur G. Coons, *Crises in California Higher Education* (1968). Regarding the development of the State College system, see Glenn S. Dumke, "Higher Education in California," *California Historical Society Quarterly* (June 1963). See also Louis H. Heilbron, "Higher Education for the Millions," in, Edmund G. Brown and others, *California: The Dynamic State* (1966). Heilbron, the first chairman of the newly constituted state college system, was profiled in *California Schools* (August 1959). See also the history of the California State College and University system by Donald R. Gerth, James O. Haehn, and associates, *An Invisible Giant* (1971).

The multi-campus UC system was first profiled by *Time* as "the big, big C" on 28 July 1958. Clark Kerr and the multi-campus system was the *Time* cover story for 17 October 1960. See also Eugene Burdick, "Colossal U. by the Pacific," *New York Times Magazine* (6 May 1962); "Will There Be Enough Room for the Coming Thousands?" *California Monthly* (July–August 1962); "Fever of a Mass Thrust for Knowledge," *Life* (19 October 1962); "California: As Enrollment Bulge Hits Higher Education System, State Banks on Its Master Plan," *Science* (3 April 1964); William Trombley, "Expanding University of California," *Saturday Evening Post* (16 May 1964); Neil Morgan, "The State as a Campus," *Holiday* (October 1965); and "After Berkeley: California Looks Ahead," *Newsweek* (4 October 1965). For surveys of the architecture of the new UC campuses, see the *Architectural Record* for November 1964. For the integrated library system, see M. J. Voigt and J. H. Treyz, "New Campuses Program: San Diego (UCSD), Irvine (UCI), and Santa Cruz (UCSC)," *Library Journal* (15 May 1965); Robert M. Hayes, "Institute of Library Research," *Library Journal* (1 October 1966); and Jerome Cushman, "Instant College Libraries," *Library Journal* (1 February 1967).

For the UC Berkeley campus during this period, see Glenn T. Seaborg with Ray Colvig, *Chancellor at Berkeley* (1994). See also Irving Stone, "University of California," *Holiday* (8 December 1950); and Stone's anthology *There Was Light: Autobiography of a University, Berkeley 1868–1968* (1970). For the storm clouds on the Berkeley horizon, see W. J. Rorabaugh, *Berkeley at War: The 1960s* (1989). Regarding the rise of UCLA, see Andrew Hamilton and John B. Jackson, *UCLA on the Move During Fifty Golden Years, 1919–1969* (1969). See also Ernest Carroll Moore, *I Helped Make a University* (1952); Edward A. Dickson, *University of California at Los Angeles: Its Origin and Formative Years* (1955); Lawrence Clark Powell, "Beanfields, Builders, and Books: The First Quarter Century of the Los Angeles Campus of the University of California," *Historical Society of Southern California Quarterly* (December 1964); *UCLA: A Pictorial Treasury*, photography by Phil Schermeister (1989). *Time* profiled Chancellor Franklin Murphy on 21 October 1966. Regarding the library program at UCLA, see the *Library Journal* for 1 September 1962 and the profile "A Graduate Research Library Designed to Expand" in the *Architectural Record* for September 1966. Regarding UC Davis, see Ann F. Scheuring, *Abundant Harvest: The History of the University of California, Davis* (2001). Regarding UC Santa Barbara, see Robert Kelley, *Transformations: UC Santa Barbara, 1909–1979* (1981). *Time* profiled the proposed UC Santa Cruz campus as "Oxford on the Pacific" on 21 December 1962. Russell Kirk praised the program in his "Academic Order and the Humane Scale," *National Review* (23 March 1965). *Architectural Record* profiled the developing campus in its issues of April 1967 and May 1969. See also James L. Jarrett, "Santa Cruz After One Year," *Saturday Review* (21 January 1967).

Chapter 9
Freeways to the Future

Herbert Marshall Goodwin submitted "California's Growing Freeway System" as his doctoral dissertation at UCLA in 1969. Issued that year in two volumes by University Microfilms, Goodwin's exhaustive study commands the subject and is the source for innumerable details in this chapter, as are the volumes from this period of *California Highways and Public Works*, the official publication of the Division of Highways, Department of Public Works, State of California. Also of importance are the relevant volumes of the *California Highway Patrolman*, the official publication of the California Association of Highway Patrolmen. Also of relevance is the portfolio by photographer James B. Jennings, *Richmond–San Rafael Bridge: A Photographic Story* (1955).

My interpretation of freeways has been shaped by two classic studies: *Freeways* (1966) by Lawrence Halprin and *L. A. Freeway: An Appreciative Essay* (1981) by David Brodsly. I am especially grateful to Brodsly's study, which is brilliantly interpreted and comprehensively researched. A useful history of highways is Felix Riesenberg Jr., *The Golden Road* (1962). As far as the earlier history of highway construction is concerned, see Ben Blow, *California Highways: A Descriptive Record of Road Development* (1920). Regarding convict labor, see Elford Eddy, "Hope for the Convict: How the State of California Is Turning Prisoners into Road Workers and Saving Money," *Sunset* (June 1924). Regarding the first phases of motor tourism, see Edward Fletcher, *An Auto Trip Through San Diego's Back Country* (1906); and Don DeNevi and Thomas Moulin, *Motor Touring in Old California* (1979). Two crucial articles are Frederic I. Paxson, "The Highway Movement, 1916–1935," *American Historical Review* (January 1946); and John C. Burnham, "The Gasoline Tax and the Automobile Revolution," *Mississippi Valley Historical Review* (December 1961). See also Daniel J. B. Mitchell, "Earl Warren's Fight for California's Freeways," *Southern California Quarterly* (Summer 2006).

Regarding the general history of motoring in Southern California, see Phil Townsend Hanna, *The Wheel and the Bell: The Story of the First Fifty Years of the Automobile Club of Southern California* (1950); J. Allen Davis, *The Friend to All Motorists: The Story of the Automobile Club of Southern California Through 65 Years, 1900–1965* (1967); and Richard R. Mathison, *Three Cars in Every Garage: A Motorist's History of the Automobile and the Automobile Club in Southern California* (1968). See also Ashleigh E. Brilliant, "Some Aspects of Mass Motorization in Southern California, 1919–1929," *Southern California Quarterly* (June 1965). See also Brilliant's *The Great Car Craze: How Southern California Collided with the Automobile in the 1920s* (1989).

Reyner Banham's *Los Angeles: The Architecture of Four Ecologies* (1971) is a classic study. Architectural historian Richard Longstreth analyzes the early impact of the automobile on Los Angeles in "Don't Get Out: The Automobile's Impact on Five Building Types in Los Angeles, 1921–1941," *ARRIS: Journal of the Southeast Chapter of the Society of Architectural Historians* (1996); "Innovation Without Paradigm: The Many Creators of the Drive-in Market," in *Images of an American Land: Vernacular Architecture in the Western United States* (1997), edited by Thomas Carter; "The Forgotten Arterial Landscape: Photographic Documentation of Commercial Development Along Los Angeles Boulevards During the Interwar Years," *Journal of Urban History* (May 1997); and "The Diffusion of the Community Shopping Center Concept During the Interwar Decades," *Journal of the Society of Architectural Historians* (September 1997). For the 1950s perspective, see Wilfred Owen, *Cities in the*

Motor Age (1959). Regarding the spatial and planning impact of the automobile in Southern California, see William Leroy Thomas, "Man, Time, and Space in Southern California: A Symposium," *Annals of the Association of American Geographers* (1959). For the politics of freeways and smog, see the relevant chapters by county supervisor John Anson Ford in *Thirty Explosive Years in Los Angeles County* (1961).

For an overall assessment of the Arroyo Seco Parkway, see H. Marshall Goodwin Jr., "The Arroyo Seco: From Dry Gulch to Freeway," *Southern California Quarterly* (March 1965). See also A. D. Griffin, "Arroyo Seco: Pasadena Freeway, First in West, Has 20th Birthday," *California Highways and Public Works* (January/February 1961). Contemporary accounts of the construction and dedication of the Arroyo Seco Parkway can be found in the following articles in *California Highways and Public Works*: A. D. Griffin, "Arroyo Seco" (January 1940) and "Proposed Arroyo Seco Parkway to Los Angeles Business Center Through Elysian Park" (October 1940); and Amerigo Bozzani, "Governor Olson Dedicates and Opens Arroyo Seco Freeway" (January 1941). See also the commemorative brochure *The Arroyo Seco Parkway. Dedication Ceremonies, Monday, Dec. 30, 1940* in the California State Library. Freeway congestion is suggested by "California Patrolman: He Safeguards the Freeway," *Look* (29 September 1959); Henry Ehrlich, "The Great Freeway Fight," *Look* (25 September 1962); and "A Fight Against the Frightful Freeway," *Fortune* (September 1966).

The developing smog crisis is chronicled in Chip Jacobs and William Kelly, *Smogtown: The Lung-Burning History of Pollution in Los Angeles* (2008). See also the following *Los Angeles Times* articles: "City Hunting for Source of 'Gas Attack'" and "Haze Causes Eyes to Burn" (27 July 1943); "City 'Smog' Laid to Dozen Causes" (18 September 1944); "Blanket Over Downtown Area Lifts" (24 September 1944); "Man-Made 'Smog'" (25 September 1944); "County Moves for Fumes Czar" (27 September 1944); "'Smog' Blankets City Again" (26 October 1944); "Citizens Drafted to Aid in Fight Against Fumes" (10 November 1944); "Federal Health Study of Fumes Nuisance Asked" (21 November 1944); "Expert Says Smog Can Be Eliminated" (28 November 1944); and "Fumes Again in Evidence" (9 December 1944). The continuing smog crisis can be chronicled through "Los Angeles: Forgotten Sun," *Newsweek* (23 December 1946); Charles L. Senn, "General Atmospheric Pollution: Los Angeles 'Smog,'" *American Journal of Public Health* (July 1948); "Airborne Dump," *Time* (25 April 1949); "LA Kills Smog With Kindness," *Business Week* (24 February 1951); A. M. Zarem and W. E. Rand, "Smog," *Scientific American* (May 1952); "Smog and Health," *Newsweek* (4 May 1953); "Uproar over Smog," *Business Week* (14 November 1953); Jack Jones, "Smog Crisis in Los Angeles," *Frontier* (November 1953); "Smoggy California," *Newsweek* (16 November 1953); "Blight on the Land of Sunshine," *Life* (1 November 1954); "Smoggy Nightmare," *Time* (1 November 1954); "To Grips with Smog?" *Newsweek* (13 December 1954); Richard P. Eckles, "Los Angeles Pioneers in the Fight Against Smog," *The Reporter* (30 December 1954); "Los Angeles in Torment: The Valley of Smog," *Fortune* (April 1955); "Auto Exhaust Accused for LA Smog," *American City* (July 1956); Ray Duncan, "Pollution in Paradise," *Holiday* (October 1957); "Los Angeles Pinpoints Auto Exhaust as Uncontrolled Air Pollution Source," *American City* (May 1958); Arnold Nicholson, "Los Angeles Battles the Murk," *Saturday Evening Post* (19 December 1959); R. B. Niese, "Blowing the Lid off Los Angeles's Smog Pot," *American Mercury* (January 1960); R. Boardman, "California Closes In on Smog," *Science Digest* (April 1960); "Auto-Intoxication in Los Angeles," *Time* (3 July 1964); George H. Fisher, "Twenty Years of Smog in Los Angeles," *Frontier* (June 1965); and "When a Smog Blanket Smothers a City," *U.S. News & World Report* (15 November 1965). Regarding A. J. Haagen-Smit, see William S. Barton, "Puzzle of Smog Production Solved by Caltech Scientist," *Los Angeles Times* (20 November 1950); A.J. Haagen-Smit, "The Control of Air Pollution," *Scientific American* (January 1964); Al Martinez, "Haagen-Smit, Pioneer in Study of Smog, Dies at 76," *Los Angeles Times* (19 March 1977). The following Web sites were also consulted:

www.arb.ca.gov/ba/omb/50thfinal/tsldoo6.htm; www.arb.ca.gov/brochure/history.htm; www.pbs. org/now/science/smog.htmls; and www.autolife.umd.umich.edu/Environment/E_Overview.

Regarding Los Angeles's continuing struggle with traffic, see "Los Angeles Works to Solve Traffic Problem," *American City* (April 1947); "Los Angeles: The Art of Living Bumper to Bumper," *Look* (18 September 1956); and "Modern Transit Proposed for Los Angeles," *American City* (January 1961). Regarding Los Angeles's continuing infatuation with monorail, see "Los Angeles's Transit Problem: The Way Out Is Up," *Business Week* (17 May 1952); "Monorail Is Latest Relief Proposed for Los Angeles Traffic," *American City* (March 1953); "Subways in the Sky," *Popular Science* (October 1953); Glenn L. Black, "Monorail for Los Angeles," *Railroad Magazine* (December 1953); and Robert Buhrman, "What Time's the Next Air Cushion to the Airport?" *Los Angeles* (August 1970). Ray Bradbury reminisced regarding his advocacy of monorail in "L.A.'s Future Is up in the Air," *Los Angeles Times* (5 February 2006).

Regarding BART, the following reports were of value: San Francisco Department of City Planning, *A Subway and Rapid Transit System for San Francisco* (1950); Parsons, Brinckerhoff, Quade & Douglas, *Regional Rapid Transit: A Report to the San Francisco Bay Area Rapid Transit Commission, 1953–1955* (1956); Stanford Research Institute, *Report on Organizational and Financial Aspects of a Proposed Rapid Transit System for the San Francisco Bay Area Rapid Transit Commission* (1956); and San Francisco Bay Area Rapid Transit Commission, *Report to the Legislature of the State of California, December 1957* (1957). See also "Good-By to Traffic Jams," *Newsweek* (19 July 1965); Richard M. Zettel, "SF Bay Area Transportation Study," *California Highways and Public Works* (July–August 1965) and "BART," *California Highways and Public Works* (July–August 1966). Regarding the scenic highway movement, see California Interdepartmental Coordinating Committee on Scenic Highways, *Report on the Preliminary Plan for Scenic Highways* (1962). Regarding the reportage of Paul Pierce, see Paul Pierce, *Take an Alternate Route*, introduction by Gene Autry (1968).

Chapter 10
Mare Nostrum

Three studies—Robert Kelley, *Battling the Inland Sea: American Political Culture, Public Policy, and the Sacramento Valley, 1850–1986* (1989); Norris Hundley, Jr., *The Great Thirst: Californians and Water, a History* (revised edition, 2001); and Ethan Rarick, *California Rising: The Life and Times of Pat Brown* (2005)—are crucial to this chapter. Also of importance are the following Department of Water Resources (DWR) histories on file in Government Publications at the California State Library: DWR, "Decade of Action" (1969); "After Forty Years, Milestones for DWR," *DWR News* (Fall 1996); DWR, *California's Water History* (1999); "California State Water Project: Past, Present, Future," *DWR News* (Special Edition, 2001). See also the DWR Web sites www.publicaffairs.water.ca.gov/swp/history.cfm and wwwswpao. water.ca.gov/publication/bulletin/96/text for relevant documents. The Government Publications section of the California State Library in Sacramento maintains an extensive collection of official reports relevant to the water history of California. All such documents in this bibliography, unless otherwise cited, can be found in the CSL collection, indicated as GP/CSL.

Also of value to this chapter is J. D. Strauss and George H. Murphy, "California Water Law in Perspective," *68 West's Annotated California Codes 1–49* (1956). See also Wallace Smith, *Garden of the Sun* (1939); and Stephanie S. Pincetl, *Transforming California: A Political History of Land Use and Development* (1999); and David Carle, *Drowning the Dream: California's Water Choices at the Millennium* (2000). Always indispensable as a source of reference is William L. Kahrl, *The California Water Atlas* (1979). Also of value regarding early planning is the collaboratively produced *A Modern History of Tulare County* (1974).

The California State Library BioLetter File has been consulted for Elwood Mead, Edward Hyatt, A. D. Edmonston, and Carley V. Porter. Regarding Mead, see also E. Green and S. Wilsey, "The Practical Scholar—A Life of Elwood Mead," *The Elwood Mead Professorship of Engineering at Colorado State University* (n.d.). For a sense of the excitement felt by Los Angeles as the Colorado River Aqueduct was being built, see Lynn D. Smith, "392 Miles for a Drink to Make Southland Blossom Like the Rose. Thousands of Workmen Push Construction Across the Desert and Through Mountains of World's Greatest Aqueduct," *Los Angeles Saturday Night* (13 February 1937). Ellwood Mead joined W. W. Schlecht and C. E. Grunsky to produce the *Report of the All-American Canal Board* (1920). See also Imperial Irrigation District, *Facts: The Boulder Dam All-American Canal Project* (1924); and the Imperial Irrigation District Web site www.iid.com/water.

The most commanding history and analysis of the Central Valley Project was made by UC Berkeley economist Paul S. Taylor in "Central Valley Project: Water and Land," *Western Political Quarterly* (June 1949). Regarding the construction of Shasta Dam, see Pacific Constructors, Inc., *Shasta Dam and Its Builders* (April 1945); and Al M. Rocca, *The Shasta Dam Boomtowns: Community Building in the New Deal Era* (1993). For the visual documentation of the project, see *Once upon a Dam Site: Howard Colby's Shasta Dam Photographs, 1938–1950*, edited by Peter Palmquist (1987). See also "Shasta Dam," *Time* (13 September 1938).

Regarding the Feather River project, see Alan Jones, "Oroville Dam at Twenty-Five," *DWR News* (Spring 1993). The *Oroville Mercury* covered the Feather River project ground-breaking in a special edition (31 May 1957). The dedication program is available at the California State Library. See also "Governor Knight Launches Feather River Project Job," *California Highways and Public Works* (March–April 1957). Also of value are the DWR reports "Information on Feather River Project," (November 1954) and "Economic Impact of the Construction of the Oroville Dam and Power Plant," (October 1956), in GP/CSL. *The Sacramento Bee* covered A. D. Edmonston's retirement and career on 24 August 1955. Regarding the work of William L. Berry on the water plan, his son William L. Berry Jr. has written an unpublished reminiscence, based in part on Berry's diaries, which he has generously provided me.

The full text of the California Water Resources Development Bond Act of 1959 (Burns-Porter) is in GP/CSL. For an analysis of the Burns-Porter Act, see the bound brochure in GP/CSL: Harvey O. Banks and Jean O. Williams, consultants, "The Burns-Porter Act: A California High Water Mark" (April 1984). For biographies of Burns and Porter, see the entries in *Members of the California Legislature and Other State Officials* (1961). GP/CSL holds an important collection of documents relevant to the State Water Project. They include the following DWR publications: "Summary of Data and Information Concerning State Water Facilities as Provided in the Burns-Porter Act" (August 1960); William E. Warne, director, "Water for the Millions" (December 1964); "State Water Project Inspection by Governor Edmund G. Brown and City and County Officials" (22 April 1966); and "Water: California's Challenge and Opportunity" (September 1967). In November 1974 the DWR issued *Bulletin No. 200*, a comprehensive history in six volumes of the California State Water Project, which is a model of its kind. For a sense of the arguments waged on behalf of Burns-Porter, see Sydney Kossen, "California's $2 Billion Thirst," *Harper's* (March 1961); and Hugo Fisher, "Water—Life Blood of the West," in Edmond G. Brown and others, *California: The Dynamic State* (1966). The long history of area-of-origin updates can be traced in www.norcalwater.org/area_of_origin.html. The continuing legal and statutory history of the California Water Plan can be traced through http://rubicon.water.ca.gov/v1cwp/apA.html. Regarding Southern California's continuing thirst, see the authoritative Steven P. Erie, *Beyond Chinatown: The Metropolitan Water District, Growth, and the Environment in Southern California* (2006). For the life and career of Harvey Banks, see the obituaries in the *Austin American-Statesman* (25 September 1996) and the *Sacramento Bee* (27 September 1996).

Chapter 11
Provincials, Baghdaders, and Beats

The three standard literary histories of San Francisco are Franklin Walker, *San Francisco's Literary Frontier* (1939); Oscar Lewis, *Bay Window Bohemia* (1956); and Lawrence Ferlinghetti and Nancy J. Peters, *Literary San Francisco: A Pictorial History from the Beginnings to the Present Day* (1980). See also *The Western Gate: A San Francisco Reader*, edited by Joseph Henry Jackson (1952). Also of value is George Rathmell, *Realms of Gold: The Colorful Writers of San Francisco, 1850–1950* (1998). For Frank Norris's explorations of the literary possibilities of San Francisco, see the essays in *The Literary Criticism of Frank Norris*, edited by Donald Pizer (1964). Regarding Frank Norris himself, see Franklin Walker, *Frank Norris, A Biography* (1932); and Joseph McElrath Jr. and Jesse Crisler, *Frank Norris, A Life* (2006). Charles Caldwell Dobie's pioneering article "Frank Norris; or, Up from Culture," appeared in the *American Mercury* for April 1928. See also the introductions by Kevin Starr to the Penguin Books editions of *McTeague* and *The Octopus*. Regarding Gertrude Atherton, see Emily Wortis Leider, *California's Daughter: Gertrude Atherton and Her Times* (1991). See also Atherton's *Adventures of a Novelist* (1932) and *My San Francisco, A Wayward Biography* (1946). Regarding Kathleen Norris, see Deanna Paoli Gumina, *A Woman of Certain Importance: A Biography of Kathleen Norris* (2004). See also Norris's *My San Francisco* (1932) and *Family Gathering* (1959). Regarding Miriam deFord, see Mitchell Thomas, "The City's 'Most Remarkable' Writer," *San Francisco Chronicle* (5 January 1973). Regarding Oscar Lewis, see the Book Club of California anthology *A Widely Cast Net*, edited by Wayne Bonnett (1996). See also the obituary by Harre Demoro in the *San Francisco Chronicle* (14 July 1992). Regarding Idwal Jones, see the obituary in the *San Francisco Chronicle* (18 November 1964). See also Jones's novel *Vermillion* (1947) and the memoir *Chef's Holiday* (1952). Regarding Jack Boyle, author of the Boston Blackie stories, see the introduction by Edward D. Hoch to Jack Boyle, *Boston Blackie* (1979). My interpretation of Dashiell Hammett's *The Maltese Falcon* (1929) is based upon the Arion Press annotated edition of 1983.

Biographical information regarding the many San Francisco writers mentioned in this chapter was gleaned from the extraordinary scrapbook volumes *San Francisco Clippings* in the Daniel E. Koshland History Center of the San Francisco Public Library. The following *San Francisco Chronicle* obituaries were also of use: Samuel B. Dickson (2 March 1974); George L. Harding (2 September 1976); James deTarr Abajian (14 March 1986); and C. Albert Shumate (2 October 1998). Ron Fimrite prepared and extensive obituary for Lucius Beebe (5 February 1966). Beebe also pre-prepared his own obituary for the *Chronicle* (6 February 1966). See also Scott Newhall, "Lucius Beebe of the *Chronicle*" (7 February 1966); and Herb Caen, "Beebe on Beebe," *San Francisco Chronicle* (13 February 1966). See also Walter P. Gray III, "The Last Edwardian Gentleman," *Trains* (January 2000). Also of interest are "Beebe Heir Is Pal Clegg. Dog Inherits, Too," *San Francisco Sunday Examiner Chronicle* (10 April 1966). Regarding Edmund Wilson's experiences of San Francisco, *The Forties* (1983), 193–201.

Regarding the fine printing tradition of San Francisco, see James D. Hart, *Fine Printing: The San Francisco Tradition* (1985). See also Robert D. Harlan, *John Henry Nash: The Biography of a Career* (1970); and Joseph Torchia, "Half a Century of Beauty," *San Francisco Chronicle* (15 February 1977). Regarding the bookstores of San Francisco, see Richard Dillon, *The Bay Area Bookmen* (1961); and James D. Hart, *Rare Book Stores in San Francisco Fifty Years Ago* (1984). See also Jerry Carroll, "Gentile World of the Rare Book Dealer," *San Francisco Chronicle* (25 January 1983). Regarding Paul Elder, see Maitland Zane, "A Bookman Bows Out," *San Francisco Chronicle* (4 October 1968); Carl Nolte, "Old SF Bookstore Closing," *San Francisco Chronicle* (10 February 1960); and the *Chronicle* obituary (9 April 1997). David Magee wrote the memoir *Infinite Riches: The Adventures of a Rare Book Dealer* (1973).

Regarding Warren Howell, see the superb "Reminiscences of Warren R. Howell" by Jeremy Norman, *AB Bookman's Weekly* (11 February 1985). See also the obituary in the *San Francisco Examiner* (12 January 1984). Regarding the Book Club of California, see David Magee, *The Hundredth Book: A Bibliography of the Publications of the Book Club of California and A History of the Club* 1958); and *Second Reading: Selections from the Quarterly News-Letter, 1933–1963* (1965). Regarding the Roxburghe Club, see *Roxburghe Club of San Francisco: Chronology of Twenty-five Years, 1928–1953* (1954).

Regarding Baghdad writers, the following *San Francisco Chronicle* obituaries were useful: Eugene Burdick (27 July 1965); Kenneth Lamott (21 August 1979); Charles McCabe (2 May 1983); Rollo May (19 November 1987); Stan Delaplane (19 April 1988); and Alice Adams (28 May 1999). See also the essays by Gordon Pates and James P. Degnan in *The Charles McCabe Reader* (1985). See also the obituary for Albert Joseph Guerard in the *Stanford Report* (13 November 2000). Numerous Web sites were consulted for Niven Busch, Erskine Caldwell, Ernest K. Gann, C. S. Forester, Evan S. Connell Jr., Ernest J. Gaines, Tillie Olsen, Kay Boyle, Mark Schorer, Oakley Hall, and Erik Erikson. Regarding the decidedly non-Baghdadian Eric Hoffer, see Calvin Tomkins, *Eric Hoffer: An American Odyssey* (1968); James D. Koermer, *Hoffer's America* (1973), James T. Baker, *Eric Hoffer* (1982); and Tom Bethell, "The Longshoreman Philosopher," *Hoover Digest* (2003).

Regarding the post-Earthquake Bohemia, see Warren Unna, *The Coppa Murals: A Pageant of Bohemian Life in San Francisco at the Turn of the Century* (1952); Henry Herman Evans, *Bohemian San Francisco* (1955); and Joanne Lafler, "The King of Telegraph Hill," *Argonaut* (Summer 2004). Miriam deFord profiled George Sterling in *They Were San Franciscans* (1941). Sterling himself was one of the editors of *Continent's End: An Anthology of Contemporary California Poets* (1925), and some of his best poetry can be found in this volume. Regarding Telegraph Hill, see David F. Myrick, *San Francisco's Telegraph Hill* (1972). See also Clarence David Greenhood, *PG: The Green Knight, 1871–1951, In Memory of Porter Garnett* (1951).

Ann Charters's *The Portable Beat Reader* (1992) is a masterpiece of the anthologist's art. Regarding the San Francisco Literary Renaissance and the Beats, see Thomas Parkinson, *A Casebook on the Beat* (1961); Bruce Cook, *The Beat Generation* (1971); David Meltzer, *The San Francisco Poets* (1971); and Michael Davidson, *The San Francisco Renaissance: Poetics and Community at Mid-Century* (1989). Regarding the Beats' use of San Francisco as a physical place, see Bill Morgan, *The Beat Generation in San Francisco: A Literary Guidebook* (2003). See also Raymond S. Dondero, *The Italian Settlement of San Francisco* (1974); Stewart E. Perry, *San Francisco Scavengers: Dirty Work and the Pride of Ownership* (1978); Alessandro Baccari, Vincenza Scarpaci, and Gabriel Zavattaro, *Sts. Peter and Paul Church: The Chronicles of the Italian Cathedral of the West, 1884–1984* (1985); Richard Dillon, *North Beach, the Italian Heart of San Francisco: Photographs by J. B. Monaco, 1856–1938*, photo editor Lynn L. Davis (1985). See also Richard Ben Cramer, *Joe DiMaggio: The Hero's Life* (2000).

In June 2003 the *San Francisco Chronicle* ran a four-part series of reminiscences regarding the Beat era. It included "The Birth of the Cool: 1953–1960" (8 June); "City Lights and the Counterculture: 1961–1974" (9 June); "City Lights Enters the Modern Age: 1975–2003" (10 June); and "Lawrence Ferlinghetti: A Portrait in Words" (11 June). Regarding the Beats of Southern California, see Lawrence Lipton, *The Holy Barbarians* (1959); and John Arthur Maynard, *Venice West: The Beat Generation in Southern California* (1991). Kenneth Rexroth's *An Autobiographical Novel* (1966) is in reality a detailed memoir. See also Rexroth's *American Poetry in the Twentieth Century* (1971). Rexroth profiled the movement in "San Francisco's Mature Bohemians," *Nation* (23 February 1957). Biographies relevant to this chapter include Neeli Cherkovski, *Ferlinghetti: A Biography* (1979); Barry Silesky, *Ferlinghetti: The Artist in*

His Times (1990); Barry Miles, *Ginsberg: A Biography* (1989); Michael Schumacher, *Dharma Lion: A Critical Biography of Allen Ginsberg* (1992); Ann Charters, *Kerouac: A Biography* (1973); Warren French, *Jack Kerouac: Novelist of the Beat Generation* (1986); Gerard Nicosia, *Memory Babe: A Critical Biography of Jack Kerouac* (1985); and Lee Bartlett, *William Everson: The Life of Brother Antoninus* (1988). See also Ann Charters, editor, *The Portable Jack Kerouac* (1995); and Albert Gelpi, *Dark God of Eros: A William Everson Reader* (2003). Also of interest is Carolyn Cassady, *Off the Road: My Years with Cassady, Kerouac, and Ginsberg* (1990).

Regarding the influence of City Lights, see Jack Foley, "City Lights Books," *Argonaut* (Fall 2001). Regarding Thomas Merton as a Beat, see Paul Elie, *The Life You Save May Be Your Own: An American Pilgrimage* (2003). Regarding the Catholicism of Philip Lamantia, see the two articles by Stephen Schwartz in *San Francisco Faith, the Bay Area's Lay Catholic Newspaper*: "The Road Less Traveled: San Francisco Beat Poet Turns Traditional Catholic," (November 1998) and "A Mystic and Tormented Believer" (June 2005). See also John Clellon Holmes, "The Philosophy of the Beats," *Esquire* (June 1983).

For a skeptical look at the Beat lifestyle, see Francis Joseph Rigney and Douglas Smith, *The Real Bohemia: A Sociological and Psychological Study of the Beats* (1961). See also "Squaresville USA Versus Beatsville," *Life* (21 September 1959); and George B. Leonard Jr., photographed by Cal Bernstein, "The Bored, the Bearded, and the Beat," *Look* (19 August 1958). Of relevance as well is Nan Alamilla Boyd, *Wide Open Town: A History of Queer San Francisco to 1965* (2003). Regarding café society during this same era, see Kenneth Tynan, "San Francisco: The Rebels," *Holiday* (April 1961); and Barnaby Conrad, *Name Dropping: Tales from My Barbary Coast Saloon*, foreword by Herb Caen (1994). For Herb Gold's perspective, see his *Travels in San Francisco* (1990), "When San Francisco Was Cool," *Image/San Francisco Examiner* (2 June 1991), and *Bohemia, Where Art, Angst, Love, and Strong Coffee Meet* (1993).

Howl is republished in *Allen Ginsberg: Collected Poems, 1947–1980* (1984). See also Allen Ginsberg, *Howl: Original Draft Facsimile, Transcript and Variant Versions*, edited by Barry Miles (1986). Regarding the composition of *Howl*, see Jonah Raskin, *American Screen: Allen Ginsberg's "Howl" and the Making of the Beat Generation* (2004). See also Raskin's "'Six at the Six' at 50—Return of SF's Poetic Beat," *San Francisco Chronicle* (30 September 2005). Regarding the *Howl* controversy, see "Big Day for Bards at Bay: Trial over Howl and Other Poems," *Life* (9 September 1957); John G. Fuller, "Ginsberg Trial," *Saturday Review* (5 October 1957); and David Perlman, "How Captain Hanrahan Made 'Howl' a Best-Seller," *The Reporter* (12 December 1957). See also *The Poem That Changed America*, edited by Jason Shinder (2006).

Regarding the New York origins of the Beats, see Leslie Berlowitz and Rick Beard, *Greenwich Village: Culture and Counterculture* (1991). Regarding the *Paris Review* crowd, see Gay Talese, "Looking for Hemingway," *Esquire* (June 1983). Regarding the non-Beat poets of the Bay Area, see Cynthia Haven, "The Un-Beats," *San Francisco* (July 2002). Regarding Josephine Miles, see the obituary in the *San Francisco Chronicle* (14 May 1985). See also the two volumes of the American Poets Project of the Library of America: *Yvor Winters, Selected Poems*, edited by Thom Gunn (2003); *Muriel Rukeyser, Selected Poems*, edited by Adrienne Rich (2004). For the enigmatic Weldon Kees, see James Reidel, *Vanished Act: The Life and Art of Weldon Kees* (2003). See also Anthony Lane, "The Disappearing Poet," *New Yorker* (4 July 2005); and the entry by Dana Gioia in *The Oxford Encyclopedia of American Literature* (2004). See also Gioia's preface to Kees's one-act play "The Waiting Room," published by the Press at Colorado College in a limited edition (Winter 1999). See also Daniel Gillane and Robert Niemi, *The Bibliography of Weldon Kees*, foreword by Donald Justice, introduction by Dana Gioia (1997). *San Francisco State Magazine*, issued by San Francisco State University, profiled Walter Van Tilburg Clark (Spring 2007) and Ruth Witt-Diamant (Spring/Summer 2008).

Chapter 12
Big Sur

Of importance to this chapter are Denis Hale and Jonathan Eisen, *The California Dream* (1968); and Richard Cándida Smith, *Utopia and Dissent: Art, Poetry and Politics in California* (1995). See also Erik Davis, *The Visionary State: A Journey Through California's Spiritual Landscape*, photographs by Michael Rauner (2006). Regarding the Big Sur region, see Tomi Kay Lussier, *Big Sur: A Complete History and Guide* (1979); John Woolfenden, *Big Sur: A Battle for the Wilderness, 1869–1985* (1985); and the anecdote-filled memoir by Rosalind Sharpe Wall, *A Wild Coast and Lonely: Big Sur Pioneers* (1989). See also John Walton, "The Land of Big Sur: Conservation on the California Coast," *California History* (Winter 2007). Of great use as well are: Paul Henson and Donald J. Usner, *The Natural History of Big Sur* (1993); and Gary S. Breschini and Trudy Haversat, *The Esselen Indians of the Big Sur Country* (2004). The Big Sur novel can be experienced in Ruth Comfort Mitchell, *Corduroy Road* (1923); Dan Totheroh, *Deep Valley* (1942); and Elizabeth Smart, *By Grand Central Station I Sat Down and Wept* (1945).

For the photographic record, see also Jeff Norman, *Big Sur* (2004) in the Images of America series from Arcadia Publishing. Regarding the larger Monterey identity, see John Walton, *Storied Land: Community and Memory in Monterey* (2001). Regarding the founding of Carmel-by-the-Sea and its bohemian art colony, see Franklin Walker, *The Seacoast of Bohemia* (1973). For a definitive contemporary account, see Van Wyck Brooks, *Scenes and Portraits: Memories of Childhood and Youth* (1954), chapter 10, "California," 189–209. For bohemian life in San Francisco prior to the Earthquake, see Warren Una, *The Coppa Murals: A Pageant of Bohemian Life in San Francisco at the Turn of the Century* (1952). See also the Carmel portions of Jack London's novel *The Valley of the Moon* (1913), reprinted by the University of California Press with a foreword by Kevin Starr in 1999. J. Smeaton Chase writes of the San Carpóforo Cañon in *California Coast Trails: A Horseback Ride from Mexico to Oregon* (1913). Regarding the creation of Hearst Castle, see the relevant portions in David Nasaw, *The Chief: The Life of William Randolph Hearst* (2000).

Tim Hunt edited *The Collected Poetry of Robinson Jeffers* (4 vols., 1988) for the Stanford University Press. For biographical background regarding Jeffers, see Melba Berry Bennett, *The Stone Mason of Tor House: The Life and Work of Robinson Jeffers* (1966). Although no scholarly biography of Jeffers has yet appeared, the critical response to Jeffers's poetry—much of it from California, where Jeffers remains a major figure—has been voluminous. Of special value to this chapter is Lawrence Clark Powell's pioneering *An Introduction to Robinson Jeffers* (1932), a printed and bound edition of Powell's doctoral dissertation to the Faculty of Letters at the University of Dijon, updated as *Robinson Jeffers: The Man and His Work* (1940). I also enjoyed a number of conversations with the late Lawrence Clark Powell regarding Jeffers and Henry Miller, which are reflected in this chapter. Of great importance to me in understanding the overall arc of Jeffers's career is the review essay by Dana Gioia, "Strong Counsel," *Nation* (19 March 1988), reprinted in Robert Brophy, editor, *The Robinson Jeffers Newsletter: A Jubilee Gathering, 1962–1988* (1988). I also acknowledge as a matter of detail and interpretation my indebtedness to Radcliffe Squires, *The Loyalties of Robinson Jeffers* (1956); Frederic Carpenter, *Robinson Jeffers* (1962) in the Twayne series; Robert Brophy, *Robinson Jeffers: Myth, Ritual, and Symbol in his Narrative Poems* (1973); and James Karman, *Robinson Jeffers, Poet of California* (1995). Also of value are the essays anthologized by Robert Brophy in *Robinson Jeffers: Dimensions of a Poet* (1995). See also Mark Griffith, "Robinson Jeffers and Greek Tragedy," *Jeffers Studies* (Spring 2003). Regarding Una Jeffers, see the memoir by Edith Greenan, *Of Una Jeffers*, edited with an introduction by James Karman (1998).

Ella Young wrote her memoirs as *Flowering Dusk: Things Remembered Accurately and Inaccurately* (1945). Regarding the Native Americans of Big Sur, see Alfred Kroeber, *Handbook of Indians of California* (2 vols., 1925), II, 544–49. Wendy Leeds-Hurwitz, *Rolling in Ditches with Shamans: Jaime de Angulo and the Professionalization of American Anthropology* (2004) is the best introduction to this fascinating figure. See also the brief biography by Gui de Angulo as the afterword to: Jaime de Angulo, *Indian Tales* foreword by Darryl Babe Wilson (2003); and Robert Brightman, "Jaime de Angulo and Alfred Kroeber: Bohemians and Bourgeois in Berkeley Anthropology," in *Significant Others: Interpersonal and Professional Commitments in Anthropology*, edited by Richard Handler (2004), 158–95. *Don Bartolomeo* and *The Lariat* were separately published by the Turtle Island Foundation as volumes 3 and 5 respectively of the *Jaime de Angulo Library* (5 vols., 1974). In 1979 Bob Callahan assembled *A Jaime de Angulo Reader* for the Turtle Island Foundation. The anthology included *Don Bartolomeo* and *The Lariat*, together with de Angulo's posthumously published account of his field research in Modoc County, *Indians in Overalls* (1950).

Regarding Henry Miller, see the two biographies Mary V. Dearborn, *The Happiest Man Alive* (1991); and Robert Ferguson, *Henry Miller, A Life* (1991). The official biography of Jiddu Krishnamurti is Pupul Jayakar, *Krishnamurti: A Biography* (1986). See also the three-volume biography by Mary Lutyens: *Krishnamurti, the Years of Awakening* (1975), *Krishnamurti, the Years of Fulfillment* (1983), and *The Open Door* (1988). There is also the composite biography by Lutyens, *The Life and Death of Krishnamurti* (1990). See also the perceptive essay-review "Prophet Motive" by Joan Ococella in the *New Yorker* (7 January 2008).

Regarding Aldous Huxley, see Sybille Bedford, *Aldous Huxley: A Biography* (2 vols., 1973). See also Anita Loos, *Kiss Hollywood Goodbye* (1947), 148–57, for details of Aldous and Maria Huxley's life in Hollywood. For Huxley's essays and correspondence regarding his experimentation with drugs, see Huxley, *Moksha: Writings on Psychedelics and the Visionary Experience (1931–1963)*, edited by Michael Horowitz and Cynthia Palmer (1977).

There is no critical biography of Gerald Heard, but his California career can be assembled from Huxley and Isherwood titles. See also the Gerald Heard official Web site, including biography and bibliography, at www.geraldheard.com. Regarding Christopher Isherwood, see Alan Wilde, *Christopher Isherwood* (1971); Jonathan Fryer, *Isherwood* (1978); Brian Finney, *Christopher Isherwood: A Critical Biography* (1979); and Peter Parker, *Isherwood: A Life Revealed* (2004). Of special value to this chapter is *Christopher Isherwood, Diaries*, vol. 1, 1939–1960, edited and introduced by Katherine Bucknell (1996). See also Isherwood's *My Guru and His Disciple* (1980). For general background, see Carl Jackson, *Vedanta for the West: The Ramakrishna Movement in the United States* (1994).

For environmental comparisons of Northern and Southern California, see the two Sunset books *Northern California* (1959) and *Southern California* (1962). Regarding the September 1892 Buddha Jinks of the Bohemian Club of San Francisco, see *The Annals of the Bohemian Club*, vol. 3, 1887–1895, edited by Robert H. Fletcher (1909), 187–94. Regarding Sadakichi Hartmann, see the anthology *Sadakichi Hartmann: Critical Modernist*, edited by Jane Calhoun Weaver (1991). Regarding the long dialogue between San Francisco and the Asia-Pacific, see Kevin Starr, "Beyond Gump's: The Unfolding Asian Identity of San Francisco," *Pacific Rim Report* (June 2006).

Regarding Alan Watts, see his autobiography *In My Own Way* (1972); and Monica Furlong, *Zen Effects: The Life of Alan Watts* (1986). See also the Web site www.alanwatts.com for Watts's lengthy bibliography. Regarding Watts's friends Henry and Sumi Jacobs, see the photo-essay "California's Offbeat Intellectuals," *Look* (29 September 1959). Regarding Watts's father-in-law Gavin Arthur, see Ferlinghetti and Peters, *Literary San Francisco*, and the Web site www.solsticepoint.com/astrologersmemorial/arthur.html. See also the Web site www.astroqueer.tripod.com/charts/gavinarthur.html.

For biographical information, text, and cogent analysis, Ann Charters's *The Portable Beat Reader* (1992) is crucial to any understanding of the poets of the San Francisco Literary Renaissance. *The Collected Poems of Philip Whalen* (2007) were edited by Michael Rothenberg, foreword by Gary Snyder, with an introduction by Leslie Scalapino. See also the extensive interview of Whalen by David Meltzer in *Poetry Flash* (August/September 1999) at www.poetryflash.org/archive.282.wahlen.html and the obituary by Tony Perry in the *Los Angeles Times* (29 June 2002). For the poetry of Lew Welch, see *Ring of Bone: Collected Poems, 1950–1970* (1979). Regarding Welch himself, see Aram Saroyan, *Genesis Angels: The Saga of Lew Welch and the Beat Generation* (1979). Regarding Joanne Kyger, see the biography by Bill Berkson in volume sixteen of the *Dictionary of Literary Biography* (1983). See also Linda Russo, " 'To Be Jack Spicer in a Dream': Joanne Kyger and the San Francisco Renaissance, 1957–65," *Jacket* #7 (1999) at www.jacketmagazine.com/07/spicer-russo.html. Regarding the pilgrimage of Ginsberg, Orlovsky, Snyder, and Kyger to India, see Deborah Baker, *A Blue Hand: The Beats in India* (2008).

The best insight into Gary Snyder's development during the 1950s and early 1960s can be had in Gary Snyder, *The Real Work: Interviews and Talks, 1964–1979*, edited with an introduction by William Scott McLean (1980). Although there is no definitive biography of Snyder, biographical references are abundant in critical commentary dealing with the poets of the San Francisco Literary Renaissance and the criticism Snyder's own work has inspired. In this regard, Bob Steuding's pioneering *Gary Snyder* (1976) for the Twayne series, David Kherdian's *A Biographical Sketch and Descriptive Checklist of Gary Snyder* (1965), and *The Gary Snyder Reader: Prose, Poetry, and Translations 1952–1998* (1999) offer valuable chronologies, especially *The Gary Snyder Reader*, upon which this chapter is heavily dependent for the reprint of Snyder's early poetry and a very revealing interview with the *Paris Review*. See also the transcript of Snyder's appearance before the Commonwealth Club of California—*The Commonwealth* (15 December 2002) and the Gary Snyder entry at the UC Davis Department of English Web site, www.english.ucdavis.edu/people/faculty-web-pages?gary-snyder. Also of value to this chapter are Charles Molesworth, *Gary Snyder's Vision: Poetry and Real Work* (1983); and James W. Kraus, "Gary Snyder's Biopoetics: A Study of the Poet as Ecologist" (Ph.D. dissertation, American Studies, University of Hawaii, May 1986). See also Dana Goodyear, "Zen Master," *New Yorker* (20 October 2008).

Regarding the rock climbers of Camp 4, see Steve Roper, *Camp 4: Recollections of a Yosemite Rockclimber* (1994); and Glen Denny, *Yosemite in the Sixties* (2007). See also *The Vertical World of Yosemite: A Collection of Writings and Photographs on Rock Climbing in Yosemite*, edited by Galen A. Rowell (1984). For further examples of Rowell's work, see *Mountains of the Middle Kingdom: Exploring the High Peaks of China and Tibet* (1983); and *Galen Rowell: A Retrospective*, compiled by the editors of Sierra Club Books (2007).

Regarding the San Francisco Zen Center, see David Chadwick, *Crooked Cucumber: The Life and Zen Teachings of Shunryu Suzuki* (1999). Regarding Esalen, see Walter Truett Anderson, *The Upstart Spring: Esalen and the Human Potential Movement: The First Twenty Years* (1983); and Jeffrey J. Kripal, *Esalen: America and the Religion of No Religion* (2007). Also of value regarding the early years are David Drury, "Questing at Big Sur," *Los Angeles* (July 1966); and Leo Litwak, "The Esalen Foundation: 'Joy is the Prize,' " *New York Times Magazine* (31 December 1967). See also Michael Murphy, *Golf in the Kingdom* (1972). For a contemporary assessment, see "Where 'California' Bubbled Up," *Economist* (double issue 22 December 2007—4 January 2008). Ann Charters chronicles Jack Kerouac's Big Sur breakdown in chapter 30 of *Kerouac: A Biography* (1973). See also Dennis McNally, *Desolate Angel, a Biography: Jack Kerouac, the Beat Generation, and America* (1979).

Chapter 13
Silent Generation

Regarding the sequence and meaning of American generations, see William Strauss and Neil Howe, *Generations: The History of America's Future, 1584–2069* (1991). Otto Butz first described the Silent Generation in "Defense of the Class of '58," *New York Times Magazine* (25 May 1958). As a chronicle in local context of wartime service, to include deaths while on active duty, see the memorial edition of the Santa Cruz High School yearbook, *World War II Service Cardinal* (1948) in the California Collection of the California State Library (CSL). The CSL maintains an extensive collection of numerous yearbooks from the postwar to 1963 era. Many local public libraries throughout the state also maintain locally relevant yearbook collections, and over the years I have consulted numerous titles. Of special interest are such centennial and semi-centennial editions as Lowell High School, San Francisco, *Red and White, Centennial Edition* (1956); and Orange Union High School, *The Orange and White: The Golden Anniversary Story of Orange High, 1903–1953* (1953). Also of use was *Berkeley High School Yellow Jackets Fiftieth Reunion, 1949–1999* (1999). Whenever appropriate, these yearbooks are cited by school and title in the text. See also Marshall Stimson, "History of Los Angeles High School," *Historical Society of Southern California Quarterly* (1942).

Regarding childhood in this era, see Gary Soto, editor, *California Childhood: Recollections and Stories of the Golden State* (1988). Regarding the high school scene in this era in Los Angeles, see Bonnie J. Morris, *The High School Scene in the Fifties: Voices from West L.A.* (1997). See also Robert A. Jones, "Coming Home to the Faraway '50s," *Los Angeles Times* (12 October 1997). James Q. Wilson portrayed David Starr Jordan High School, Long Beach, in "The Young People of North Long Beach," *Harper's* (December 1969). Susan Sontag chronicled her high school years in "Pilgrimage," *New Yorker* (21 December 1987). See also the entry in Charles Moritz, editor, *Current Biography, 1969* (1969). See also the extensive obituary of Sontag by Margalit Fox in the *New York Times* for 29 December 2004. Regarding the Evenings on the Roof concerts at the home of Frances Mullen and Peter Yates attended by Sontag, see Howard Swann, *Music in the Southwest* (1952), 275–76. Sontag returned to Southern California themes in her novel *In America* (2000), based on the life of the Polish-born actress Helena Modjeska. Richard Rodriguez described his early Sacramento years in *Hunger of Memory* (1982). Other memoirs of value to this chapter include Ted Pejovich, *The State of California: Growing Up Foreign in the Backyards of Eden* (1989); and Tony Cohan, *Native State: A Memoir* (2003). Regarding Joan Brown, see the catalogs UC Berkeley, University Art Museum and Pacific Film Archive, *On Painting: The Work of Elmer Bischoff and Joan Brown*, essays by Christopher Brown and David Simpson (1992); and College of Notre Dame, Belmont, the Wiegand Gallery, *Working Together: Joan Brown and Manuel Neri, 1958–1964*, essay by Whitney Chadwick (1995). Regarding Richard Serra, see the Web sites www.pbs.org/art21/artists/serra/index.html and www.guggenheimcollection.org/site/artist_bio_144A.html. Regarding Claude Jarman Jr., see Monique Benoit, "Movie Star Who Left Hollywood," *San Francisco Chronicle* (30 May 1966); Norman K. Dorn, "'The Yearling' Just Got Tired of Tearing His Soul Out for a Camera," *Datebook/San Francisco Sunday Examiner and Chronicle* (14 February 1971); and Ezekiel Green, "The Man Behind the Film Festival," *California Living/San Franciso Sunday Examiner and Chronicle* (15 September 1977). Regarding Margaret O'Brien, see the entries in David Thomson, *A Biographical Dictionary of Film* (1976) and James Vinson, editor, *Actors and Actresses*, volume 3 of *The International Dictionary of Films and Filmmakers* (1984). Regarding Natalie Wood, see Suzanne Finstad, *Natasha: The Biography of Natalie Wood* (2004). Joan Baez's autobiography is *And a Voice to Sing With: A Memoir* (1987). See also Hedda Garza, *Joan Baez* (1991). John McPhee profiled Joan Baez in the *Time* cover story for 23 November 1962. Regarding the music of Rick Nelson, see the Web site www.classicbands.com/nelson.html.

The development of the junior college movement in California can be traced through: A. A. Gray, "The Junior College in California," *School Review* (September 1915); J. Sachs, "Junior Colleges in California," *Educational Review* (January–May 1918); Merton E. Hill, editor, *The Functioning of the California Public Junior College* (1938) and *The Junior College Movement in California, 1907–1948* (1949); and Sidney W. Brossman and Myron Roberts, *The California Community Colleges* (1973). See also the doctoral dissertation on deposit at the California State Library: Diana Northrop Lockard, "Watershed Years: Transformations in the Community Colleges of California, 1945–1960" (Education, the Claremont Graduate School, 1986). See also the typescript reports on deposit at the California State Library: Carl G. Winter, "History of the Junior College Movement in California" (21 December 1964); and Albert S. Rodda, "Commentary on the History of California Community Colleges" (1 April 1986). For an early portrait of Los Angeles City College, see "Junior College: Los Angeles Two-Year School is Biggest in the U.S.," *Life* (13 May 1946). See also *Parallels: A History of the Los Angeles Community College District* (1976). Regarding Foothill College, see "Jet Age Junior College," *Look* (25 September 1962). Regarding vocational education, see Wesley P. Smith, *A History of Vocational Education in California, 1900–1975* (1979). John Kautz was profiled in the *Lodi News-Sentinel* on 16 April 2004. Carolyn See chronicles her youth and education in the memoir *Dreaming: Hard Luck and Good Times in America* (1995). See also See's candid autobiographical statement in *Contemporary Authors Autobiography Series* (volume 22, 1995). See also the Web site www.carolynsee.com. Joan Didion's early writings have been listed in Fred Rue Jacobs, *Joan Didion—Bibliography* (1977). See also the pioneering Twayne study: Mark Royden Winchell, *Joan Didion* (1980). Of particular relevance to this chapter are Didion's essays "On Going Home" in *Slouching Towards Bethlehem* (1968) and "In Bed" in *The White Album* (1979).

An early glimpse into student life at UCLA is afforded in the two profiles "Bertrand Russell Rides Out Collegiate Cyclone" and "Early Spring in California Takes UCLA Boys and Girls to Beach," *Life* (1 April 1940). Also of interest are "Art Rides High at a Great University," *Life* (20 May 1957); and Martin Mayer, "University in the Sun," *Esquire* (November 1961). See also the portraits in "Fever of a Mass Thrust," *Life* (19 October 1962); and William Trombley, "The Exploding University of California," *Saturday Evening Post* (16 May 1964). Regarding Judy Chicago's experiences at UCLA, see her memoir *Through the Flower: My Struggle as a Woman Artist* (1977). See also Susan Stocking, "Through the Feminist Looking Glass with Judy Chicago," *Los Angeles Times* (9 July 1972), an early profile. Regarding the ups and downs of the UCLA *Daily Bruin*, see George L. Garrigues, "Loud Bark and Curious Eyes: A History of the UCLA *Daily Bruin*, 1919–1955" (1997), a bound typescript history on deposit at the California State Library.

Irving Stone reminisced on his days at UC Berkeley in *There Was Light: A Collection of Essays by Alumni of the University of California, Berkeley, 1868–1996* (1996), edited by Irving Stone, updated by Jean Stone. Joan Didion profiled UC Berkeley in "Berkeley's Giant: The University of California," *Mademoiselle* (January 1960). Regarding the golden age of UC Berkeley, see Glenn T. Seaborg's memoir *Chancellor at Berkeley* (1994). See also Irving Stone, "University of California," *Holiday* (December 1950); Robert Sibley, *University of California Pilgrimage: A Treasury of Tradition, Lore, and Laughter* (1952); "Big, Big C," *Time* (28 July 1958); and Donald Gutierrez, "Bohemia Berkeley," *California Monthly* (April 2002). A rare UC Berkeley faculty autobiography is John D. Hicks, *My Life with History: An Autobiography* (1968).

Regarding the California State College/University system, see Donald R. Gerth and James O. Haehn, *An Invisible Giant: The California State Colleges* (1971). See also Benjamin Franklin Gilbert, *Pioneers for One Hundred Years: San Jose State College, 1857–1957* (1957);

and Myron Roberts, "Life at an Off-Ramp U," *Los Angeles* (September 1968). Anne Burke interviewed Anne Rice regarding her years at San Francisco State in the *San Francisco State Magazine* (Spring 2006). Regarding Willie Brown and John Burton at San Francisco State, see James Richardson, *Willie Brown: A Biography* (1996).

Regarding life at Stanford, see Edith Mirrielees, *Stanford: The Story of a University* (1959); Mirrielees, editor, *Stanford Mosaic: Reminiscences of the First Seventy Years at Stanford University* (1962); and Margo Baumgartner Davis, *The Stanford Album: A Photographic History, 1885–1945* (1989). Regarding Dianne Feinstein at Stanford, see Jerry Roberts, *Dianne Feinstein: Never Let Them See You Cry* (1994). Regarding Michael Murphy, see Jackie Krentzman, "In Murphy's Kingdom," *Stanford* (January/February, 1998). Regarding Justices Anthony Kennedy and Stephen G. Breyer, see the biographies at www.oyez.org.

Histories of private institutions in this era include George Hedley, *Aurelia Henry Reinhardt: Portrait of a Whole Woman* (1961); Andrew F. Rolle, *Occidental College: The First Seventy-five Years, 1887–1962* (1962); Charles W. Cooper, *Whittier: Independent College in California Founded by Quakers, 1887*, preface by Jessamyn West (1967); Manuel P. Servin and Iris Higbie Wilson, *Southern California and Its University: A History of USC, 1880–1964* (1969); Kara Pratt Brewer, *Pioneer or Perish: A History of the University of the Pacific During the Administration of Dr. Robert E. Burns, 1946–1971* (1977); E. Wilson Lyon, *The History of Pomona College, 1887–1969* (1977); Gerald McKevitt, SJ, *The University of Santa Clara: A History, 1851–1977* (1979); Kevin Starr, *Commerce and Civilization: Claremont McKenna College, the First Fifty Years, 1946–1996* (1998); Burt J. Boudoin, *Fortress on the Hill: Founding the University of San Diego and the San Diego College for Women, 1942–1963* (2001); and Alan Ziajka, *Legacy and Promise: 150 Years of Jesuit Education at the University of San Francisco* (2005). See also Warren Hinckle, *If You Have a Lemon, Make Lemonade* (1974).

My discussion of the media response to young people in California during this era is strongly guided by and dependent upon Kirse Granat May, *Golden State, Golden Youth: The California Image in Popular Culture, 1955–1956* (2002). Regarding the importance of automobiles to young people, see Christopher Buckley, *Cruising State: Growing Up in Southern California* (1994). Regarding hotrods, see the Web site www.gregburch.net/cars/hotrod. html. See also "Gangway!" *Time* (26 September 1949). Regarding customizing, see the Web site http://rodandcustommagazine.com/techarticles/86378. Regarding car-related slang in the era, see the Web sites http://cougartown.com/slang.html and www.fiftiesweb.com/fashion/slang.htm. See also Harold Wentworth and Stuart Berg Flexner, *Dictionary of American Slang* (1967); and Howard Junker, "As We Used to Say in the '50s: A Short Course in Tribal Linguistics," *Esquire* (June 1983).

Mauricio Mazón analyzed the Zoot Suit Riots in *The Zoot Suit Riots: The Psychology of Symbolic Annihilation* (1985). Regarding the aftermath of these riots, see Duane M. Robinson, *Chance to Belong: Story of the Los Angeles Youth Project, 1943–1949* (1949). Regarding the Warren Commission on Juvenile Delinquency, see Anne Roller Issler, "California and Its Migrants," *Survey* (October 1949). For later disturbances, see Howard Whitman, "Teen-aged Punks: San Francisco Tries to Tame Them," *Collier's* (29 April 1950); and Michela Robbins, "The Inside Story of a Girls' Reformatory," *Collier's* (8 October 1953). Statistics and attitudes of the California Youth Authority in this era can be garnered from its *Biennial Reports*. See also State of California, Department of Youth Authority, *A Statistical Report of Youth Authority Activities for the Years 1953–1963* (1964) and *Characteristics of California Youth Authority Wards* (1964). Regarding grooming in high schools during the era, see Gene David Six, "Dress and Grooming Standards in California Secondary Schools," (Ed.D. dissertation, School of Education, University of Southern California, January 1969).

Rebelliousness in the music of the era is documented in Glenn C. Altschuler, *All Shook Up: How Rock 'n' Roll Changed America* (2003). See also Thomas B. Morgan, "The Adoration of Frankie, Ricky, and Kookie," *Esquire* (June 1983); and David Rensin, *All for a Few Perfect Waves: The Audacious Life and Legend of Rebel Surfer Miki Dora* (2008).

Regarding athletics in California life, see Kevin Starr, "The Sporting Life," *California Historical Society Quarterly* (Winter 1984). Regarding the pleasure principle in California life, see "Happy Hedonism," *Newsweek* (10 September 1962). Regarding the long history of the beach, see Lena Lencek and Gideon Bosker, *The Beach: The History of Paradise on Earth* (1999). Regarding California beach life in this era, see Eugene Burdick, "Sun and Its Worshippers," *Holiday* (October 1957); "Beach Club Living: Cabanas, Cocktails, and the Unlisted Self," *Los Angeles* (August 1961); and "California's Rugged Buggies" and "North California Beaches: Some Like It Cold," *Look* (25 September 1962). See also Bob Thompson, *Sunset Beachcombers' Guide to the Pacific Coast* (1968); and Arthur C. Verge, *Los Angeles County Lifeguards* (2005). Regarding the literature of the beach, see W. W. Robinson, "Books of the California Seacoast," *Westways* (June 1963); and the "On the Malibu Coast" section of, Lawrence Clark Powell, *The Little Package* (1964).

California as surf country is described in Bank Wright, *Surfing California: A Complete Guide to the California Coast* (1973). Regarding surfing culture in the 1930s, see Robert Sides, "Surf Slaloms," *Saturday Night* (12 February 1938). Regarding Robert Wilson Simmons, see Tom Wolfe, *The Pump House Gang* (1968); and Dennis Romero, "A Shadow on the Waves," *Los Angeles Times* (26 September 1994). Regarding the surf scene in the late 1950s and early 1960s, see Sheila Weller, "Malibu's Lost Boys," *Vanity Fair* (August 2006).

Mass circulation magazines of the period frequently chronicled the Southern California lifestyle. See, for example, "Paradise by the Month," "The Lush Palm Springs Look," and "Wine and Food: Big Business" in *Look* (29 September 1959); and "California: The Search for Sensation" and "The Way-Out Way of Life" in *Look* (25 September 1962). Charles Phoenix collected the photographs of Southern Californians documenting themselves in *Southern California in the '50s: Sun, Fun, Fantasy* (2001) and *Southern California Land: Mid-Century Culture in Kodachrome* (2004). The key interpretation of Southern California in this era was by fifth-generation Southern Californian Remi Nadeau, *California: The New Society* (1963). *Newsweek* devoted an issue to California on 10 September 1962. Intellectually ambitious think pieces include R. D. Miller, "Southern California Riddle," *American Mercury* (May 1956); Nathan Glazer, "Notes on Southern California," *Commentary* (7 August 1959); C. Page Smith, "Picnic Coast: A Study of Southern California," *Current History* (6 May 1961); and Bruce Bliven, "How Did Southern California Get That Way?" *Reporter* (18 January 1962). The spate of Southern California histories and guidebooks includes Carey McWilliams, *Southern California: An Island on the Land* (1946); Scott O'Dell, *Country of the Sun* (1957); the editorial staff of *Sunset*, *Southern California* (1959); Andrew Hepburn, *Southern California* (1959); Philip H. Ault, *How to Live in California* (1961); Bill Murphy, *The Dolphin Guide to Los Angeles and Southern California* (1962); and Keith Monroe, *California* (1963). See also the more skeptical, Cynthia Lindsay, *The Natives Are Restless* (1960).

Regarding the Beach Boys, the following treatments are of relevance to this chapter: David Leaf, *The Beach Boys* (1985); Timothy White, *The Nearest Faraway Place: Brian Wilson, the Beach Boys, and the Southern California Experience* (1994); and Peter Ames Carlin, *Catch a Wave* (2006). See also Brian Wilson, *Wouldn't It Be Nice? My Own Story*, with Todd Gold (1991). See also the obituary for Jan Berry in the *New York Times* (28 March 2004). An early poem titled "The California Girl" appeared in *Sunset* (November 1915). For a more intellectualized approach to this phenomenon, see Neill York, "California Girls and the American Eden," *Journal of American Culture* (April 1984). See also "Beauties From Two Top Campuses," *Look* (29 September 1959); and "California Lassie Universally Classy," *Life* (19 October 1962). Later variations include J. Shepherd, "California Classic: The Berkeley Girl," *Look* (28 January 1966); "How to Be a California Girl," *Look* (26 December 1967); and "Special

Season of the Young: Some Beautiful Girls," *Life* (10 July 1970). See also Chapter 8, "The Ascent of Women" in Nadeau's *California: The New Society*.

Chapter 14
Brubeck!

Ted Gioia's *West Coast Jazz: Modern Jazz in California, 1945–1960* (1992) commands the subject and is the point of departure and constant source of reference for this chapter. See also Gioia's *Jazz, the Imperfect Art: Reflections on Jazz and Modern Culture* (1988), especially his treatment of Dave Brubeck. See also Robert Gordon, *Jazz West Coast: The Los Angeles Jazz Scene of the 1950s* (1986); and *Central Avenue Sounds: Jazz in Los Angeles*, edited by the Central Avenue Sounds Editorial Committee (1998).

Regarding bebop, see Ira Gitler, *Jazz Masters of the Forties* (1966) and *Swing to Bop: An Oral History of the Transition to Jazz in the 1940s* (1985); A. B. Spellman, *Four Lives in the Bebop Business* (1966); and Guthrie P. Ramsey Jr., *Race Music: Black Cultures from Bebop to Hip-Hop* (2003). Of crucial relevance is Ross Russell, *Bird Lives! The High Life and Hard Times of Charlie (Yardbird) Parker* (1973). Regarding Brubeck's own anti-segregationist stance, see Ralph J. Gleason, "Racial Issue 'Kills' Brubeck Jazz Tour of the South," *San Francisco Chronicle* (12 January 1960). See also Brubeck's impassioned essay "Face the Problem!" *Music Journal 1964 Annual Anthology* (1964).

A systematic examination was made of the following subdivisions of Series I of the Dave Brubeck Collection in the Special Collections department of the University Library of the University of the Pacific in Stockton, California: C. Personal Correspondence and Fan Mail; D. Biographies, Interviews, Itineraries, Notes, Discographies; E. Clippings, including periodical articles. It would be impossible to cite such abundant material by title. Individual articles from the collection that are of special importance, however, will be cited in this bibliographical essay in standard format as separate entries.

Also in the Special Collections of the University of the Pacific Library are the Paul Desmond Papers, especially the typewritten diary Desmond kept between 22 January 1947 and 12 January 1955. In his comprehensive biography *Take Five: The Public and Private Lives of Paul Desmond* (2005), Doug Ramsey makes extensive and skillful use of this material. *Take Five* is crucial to this chapter as a source of information, interpretation, and reference.

There is no definitive biography of Dave Brubeck, although, given the closeness of Desmond and Brubeck, *Take Five* contains an abundance of Brubeck-related material. See also Barry Ulanov, "Dave Brubeck," *Metronome* (March 1952); "The Man on Cloud Number 7," *Time* (8 November 1954); "Dave Brubeck," *Current Biography* (1956); Robert Rice, "The Cleanup Man," *New Yorker* (3 June 1961); and Arnold J. Smith, " The Dave Brubeck Quartet: A Quarter of a Century Young," *Down Beat* (25 March 1976). Belgian jazz critic Juul Anthonissen wrote a biographical study of Brubeck for the boxed CDs *Dave Brubeck, Time Signatures: A Career Retrospective* from Columbia/Legacy (1992). See also the important article by University of North Carolina music professor John Salmon, "What Brubeck Got from Milhaud," *American Music Teacher* (February/March 1992). Brubeck himself outlined his theory of jazz on a number of occasions. See, for example, the two-part essay based on his UC Extension lectures "Jazz' Evolvement as Art Form," *Down Beat* (27 January 1950 and 10 February 1959); "Brubeck Plays Brubeck," *Philips Music Herald* (Winter 1956); and "Jazz Perspective," *Scholastic* (5 April 1957). Brubeck meditated on his own education in music in short articles for *Guideposts*, "Fragile Moments...When God Speaks in Whispers" (January 1958), "Words That Changed My Life" (April 1958), and "Short Cut to Real Freedom" (July

1965). See also Nat Hentoff, "Jazz Fills Role of Classical Composition, Brubeck Learns," *Down Beat* (2 June 1954). To trace further Brubeck's growing attraction to classical music in this period, see "Dave Brubeck...Boogie-Woogie Meets Bartok," *International Musician* (1956); and Miles Kastendieck, "In Carnegie Hall Brubeck Jazz Makes History," *New York Journal-American* (12 December 1959).

For an obituary of Elizabeth Ivy Brubeck, Dave's mother, see the *San Francisco Chronicle* for 15 October 1964. For the background and early life of Iola Brubeck, see David Levinson, "Shasta High's Top Student Married a Celebrity," *Redding* [California] *Record-Searchlight* (2 May 1956).

General considerations of the jazz world by critics that proved of value include André Hodeir, *Jazz: Its Evolution and Essence*, translated by David Noakes (1956); *Jazz: New Perspectives on the History of Jazz by Twelve of the World's Foremost Jazz Critics and Scholars*, edited by Nat Hentoff and Albert J. McCarthy (1959); Nat Hentoff, *The Jazz Life* (1961) and *Jazz Is* (1976); Leonard Feather, *The Passion for Jazz* (1980); Gary Giddins, *Riding on a Blue Note: Jazz and American Pop* (1981); and Marian McPartland, *All in Good Time* (1987). Relevant autobiographies include Hampton Hawes and Don Asher, *Rise Up Off Me: A Portrait of Hampton Hawes* (1979); Red Callender and Elaine Cohen, *Unfinished Dream: The Musical World of Red Callender* (1985); *Miles: The Autobiography of Miles Davis*, with Quincy Troupe (1989); Paul Horn with Lee Underwood, *Inside Paul Horn: The Spiritual Odyssey of a Universal Traveler* (1990); and Art Pepper and Laurie Pepper, *Straight Life: The Story of Art Pepper* (updated edition, 1994). Studies of individual musicians of value to this chapter include Vladimir Simosko and Barry Tepperman, *Eric Dolphy: A Musical Biography and Discography* (1979); Brian Priestley, *Mingus, A Critical Biography* (1984); Steve Voce, *Woody Herman* (1986); and John Chilton, *The Song of the Hawk: The Life and Recordings of Coleman Hawkins* (1990). Regarding the overall importance of Stan Kenton, see Carol Easton, *Straight Ahead: The Story of Stan Kenton* (1973); and William F. Lee, *Stan Kenton: Artistry in Rhythm*, foreword by Mort Sahl (1980). Regarding the Kenton-Brubeck connection, see the recorded remarks of Brubeck at the Newman Club of Boston University published as "The Jazz Scene Today," *Down Beat* (3 June 1953); and Harry Frost, "Alike yet Unalike: Dave Brubeck and Stan Kenton," *Down Beat* (21 November 1963).

Profiles of jazz musicians of value to this chapter include Raymond Horricks, editor, *These Jazzmen of our Time* (1959) and *Profiles in Jazz: From Sidney Bechet to John Coltrane* (1991); Valerie Wilmer, *Jazz People* (1970); Joe Goldberg, *Jazz Masters of the Fifties* (1973); Michael Ullman, *Jazz Lives: Portraits in Words and Pictures* (1980); Linda Dahl, *Stormy Weather: The Music and Lives of a Century of Jazz Women* (1984); and Gene Lees, *Meet Me at Jim & Andy's: Jazz Musicians and Their World* (1988). For an informative tribute to John Handy, see Andrew Gilbert, "Handy's Work," *San Francisco State Magazine* (Fall/Winter 2007).

Regarding the cooling down of West Coast jazz, see the following contemporary assessments: Barry Ulanov, "Cool Jazz," *Vogue* (18 March 1952); Nat Shapiro and Nat Hentoff, "A Quiet Beat in California," *High Fidelity Magazine* (April 1955); Arnold Shaw, "West Coast Jazz," *Esquire* (September 1955); and George Marek, "How Jazz Got Cool," *Good Housekeeping* (March 1955). Regarding the Lighthouse All-Stars, see the liner notes for the 1985 Contemporary CD *At Last! Miles Davis and the Lighthouse All-Stars*.

Regarding the San Francisco milieu as it relates to the rise of the Dave Brubeck Quartet, see R. Gehman and E. Condon, "San Francisco Jazz," *Saturday Review* (15 March 1958); E. Salzman, "Real Bay City Jazz," *Saturday Review* (12 July 1958); C. H. Garrigues, "A Decade of Jazz at the Black Hawk," *San Francisco Examiner* (15 March 1959); William Moore, "Note of Nostalgia for a Jazz Great," *San Francisco Chronicle* (13 June 1973); Kent Williams, "Remembering the Hawk (And All That Jazz)," *California Living/San Francisco Sunday Examiner and Chronicle* (19 February 1984); and John Ross, "When Jazz Was the

Thing," *Datebook/San Francisco Sunday Examiner and Chronicle* (23 May 1993). Regarding the Oakland home of the Brubecks as an icon of Bay Area modernism, see Grace House, "Jazz and Rocks in a Hilltop House," *San Francisco Examiner* (5 December 1954). Regarding Brubeck's development of a college audience, see "Jazz Does Campus Comeback," *Oakland Tribune* (24 March 1947)); Rod Nordell, "Jazz at Oberlin College," *Christian Science Monitor* (19 January 1954); Raymond Lowery, "Brubeck Finds College Receptive to his New Style of Music," [Raleigh, North Carolina] *News and Observer* (17 March 1955); Dave Brubeck, "The New Jazz Audience," *Playboy* (August 1955); Jack Cahalan, "Jazz Comes to Notre Dame," *Scholastic* (23 January 1959); and "Applause for Brubeck Rocks LC Chapel," [Lawrence College] *Laurentian* (6 February 1959). Regarding the jazz seminars of S. I. Hayakawa at the Blue Note in Chicago, see Robert Lewis Shayon, "Syncopated Semantics," *Saturday Review* (5 June 1954).

Regarding the rise in the polls of the Dave Brubeck Quartet, see "Dave Brubeck, Success of the Year," *Metronome Jazz Yearbook* (1955); and Robert Santelli, "Dave Brubeck Hall of Fame," *Down Beat* (December 1994). Regarding the quartet on the international scene, see "Dave Brubeck, the Beat Heard 'Round the World," *New York Times Magazine* (15 June 1958); and Meredith Hindley, "Dave Brubeck: Ambassador of Cool," *Humanities* (November/December 2006). See also Leonard Feather, *The New Year Book of Jazz* (1958), 17–21.

Regarding Brubeck and the critics, see "Brubeck vs. the Critics," *Jazz World* (July 1957); and Gene Lees, "About This Man Brubeck," *Down Beat* (22 June 1961). See also George Laine, "Brubeck vs. Critics: Who Swings?" *Independent* (3 August 1957). Favorable assessments of Brubeck include Barry Ulanov, "Dave Brubeck," *Metronome* (March 1952); "Subconscious Pianist," *Time* (10 November 1952); Murray Kempton, "The Cool One," *New York Post* (5 October 1954); Nat Hentoff, "Inside Dave Brubeck," *Record Whirl* (May 1955); Milton R. Bass, "The Lively Arts," [Massachusetts] *Berkshire Eagle* (13 January 1959); and Arthur J. Sasso, "Sounds of Brubeck," *Caper* (May 1959). Outright hostility can be found in Billy Root, "Cool? Dave Brubeck Is Cold!" *Philadelphia Jazz Digest* (March 1956); Mike Hawker, "Brubeck?—He's Childish," *Melody Maker* (11 May 1957); Paul Wright, "Brubeck: A Personal Opinion," *Coda* (January 1961); Tony Brown, "Jazz—Or Party Tricks?" *Melody Maker* (25 November 1961); and Raymond Horricks, "Dave Brubeck, a Formula and a Dilemma," *These Jazzmen of Our Time*, 161–68. For the growing appreciation of Paul Desmond's playing, see Nat Hentoff, "Altoist Paul Desmond Is Vital Factor in Success of Dave Brubeck Quartet," *Down Beat* (18 April 1952); "Coronation Ceremonies Nearing for Brubeck," *Down Beat* (11 February 1953); Russ Wilson, "Desmond Hits No. 1 on Alto Jazz Note," *Oakland Tribune* (10 December 1955); and John S. Wilson, "Music: Jazz Is Tested at Stadium," *New York Times* (16 July 1956).

Regarding the life and times of Jimmy Lyons, see the obituaries in the *Los Angeles Times* (11 April 1994) and *Down Beat* (August 1994). Regarding the founding of the Monterey Jazz Festival, see Jimmy Lyons with Iran Kamin, *Dizzy, Duke, the Count, and Me: The Story of the Monterey Jazz Festival* (1958); and William Minor and Bill Wishner, *Monterey Jazz Festival: Forty Legendary Years*, foreword by Clint Eastwood (1997). For favorable responses to the festival, see "Big Blast of Jazz," *Life* (19 October 1962); and Ralph J. Gleason, "Jazz Scene: Monterey," *Sunday Bonanza/San Francisco Chronicle* (15 September 1963). The decline of the festival as far as jazz is concerned can be traced through Don DeMicheal, "Falling Angel? Monterey Jazz Festival Report," *Down Beat* (8 November 1962); Richard Hadlock, "The Festival Must Grow Up," *San Francisco Examiner* (4 October 1964); and Philip Elwood, "Playing It Too Safe?" *San Francisco Examiner* (27 August 1967). Regarding the momentous 1967 festival, see Joel Selvin, "Three Days That Shook the Music World," *This World/Sunday San Francisco Examiner and Chronicle* (14 June 1992).

Chapter 15
Largest State in the Nation

Guidebooks to California propelled by its population growth and rivalry to New York include Andrew Hepburn, *Southern California* (1959); Phillip H. Ault, *How to Live in California* (1961); Robert K. Arnold, *The California Economy* (1961); *California and the West: A Mobil Travel Guide* (1962); Bill Murphy, *The Dolphin Guide to Los Angeles and Southern California* (1962); Keith Monroe, *California: How to Live, Work and Have Fun in the Golden State* (1963); and Thomas B. Lesure, *All About California—The State That Has Everything* (1964). *Newsweek* devoted an entire issue to California on 10 September 1962, as did *Look* on 25 September 1962 and *Life* on 19 October 1962. *Business Week* ran a cover article on the Northern California economy on 2 April 1960. *U.S. News & World Report* compared and contrasted New York and California in "Two 'Empire States'—How They Compare" (24 December 1962). For coverage of California in the *New York Times Magazine* for this period, see Bruce Bliven, "East Coast or West, Which?" (12 March 1961); Gladwin Hill, "California: State of Confusion" (12 November 1961); and Eugene Burdick, "From Gold Rush to Sun Rush" (14 April 1963). See also Bruce Bliven's "The California Culture," *Harper's* (January 1955) and "How Did Southern California Get That Way?" *Reporter* (18 January 1962). *Esquire* took a skeptical view of the whole phenomena in its issue for May 1963. For Governor Brown's plans to celebrate California's emergence as the largest state in the nation, see "Governor Plans Big Party for Day California is Tops," *San Francisco Chronicle* (7 January 1962), 2. For further details regarding Brown's plans for a statewide celebration, see Ethan Rarick, *California Rising: The Life and Times of Pat Brown* (2005), 255–56. For Governor Brown's point of view on growth and related matters, see his *California: The Dynamic State* (1966).

T. H. Watkins set forth his arguments against the State Water Project in the "California, the New Romans" section, Part II, *The Water Hustlers* (1971). Watkins reveals his lyrical green side in *On the Shore of the Sundown Sea* (1973), poetic meditations on life on the California coast, from Southern California to Mendocino.

David Brower's earlier edited publications include *A Climber's Guide to the High Sierra* (1949), *The Meaning of Wilderness to Science* (1960), *The Sierra Club: A Handbook* (1957); and *Wilderness: America's Living Heritage* (1962). See also Brower's *The Sierra Club Wilderness Handbook* (1967). Regarding Brower himself, see the biography in, R. Peattie, *The Sierra Nevada*, 7–9. John McPhee chronicles Brower in *Encounters with the Archdruid* (1968). See also Brower's memoirs *For Earth's Sake* (1990) and *Work in Progress* (1991). Other works inspired by the Exhibit Format series include *This California*, photographs by Michael Bry, text by George Stewart (1965); and Paul Webster and the editors of the *American West*, *The Mighty Sierra: Portrait of a Mountain World*, foreword by Francis Farquhar (1972).

Lewis Mumford speculated on "California and the Human Prospect" in the *Sierra Club Bulletin* (December 1962). *Look* (25 September 1962) covered "California's Crowded Wilderness." Wallace Stegner assessed the challenges facing California in Edmund G. Brown and others, *California: The Dynamic State* (1966), 210–24. Regarding Stegner, see Jackson Benson, *Wallace Stegner: His Life and Work* (1996); and Philip Fradkin, *Wallace Stegner and the American West* (2008), especially 184–98. See also James Hepworth, "The Revolutionary," *Outside* (September 1993). For a comprehensive view of land use and development in California, Stephanie Pincetl's *Transforming California: A Political History of Land Use and Development* (1999) commands the field. Aside from documents discussed in the text, other planning manifestos with origins in the 1960s include, Robert Durrenberger, compiler, *California: Its People, Its Problems, Its Prospects* (1971); Robert Fellmeth, and others, *Power and Land in California* (1971); and California Land-Use Task Force, *The California*

Land: Planning for People (1975). Publisher Walter Kaufmann of Los Altos reissued in book format Christopher Stone's *Should Trees Have Standing? Toward Legal Rights for Natural Objects*, foreword by Garrett Hardin (1974).

Regarding the campaign to save San Francisco Bay, see Harold Gilliam, *Between the Devil and the Deep Blue Bay: The Struggle to Save San Francisco Bay* (1969); and Rice Odell, *The Saving of San Francisco Bay: A Report on Citizen Action and Regional Planning* (1972), from the Conservation Foundation in Washington, D.C., especially 10–27. For an even more ambitious treatment of conservation efforts in the Bay Area and the establishment of the Golden Gate National Recreation Area, see Amy Meyer with Randolph Delehanty, *New Guardians for the Golden Gate: How America Got a Great National Park*, foreword by I. Michael Heyman (2006). Regarding the ecology of San Francisco Bay, see Joel Walker Hedgpeth, *Introduction to Seashore Life of the San Francisco Bay Region and the Coast of Northern California* (1962).

For an evocation of the California coast, see *Discovering the California Coast* (1975) from Sunset Books. In addition to Robert Easton's *Black Tide: The Santa Barbara Oil Spill and Its Consequences* (1972), which is central to my discussion, see also Wesley Marx, *Oil Spill* (1971), part of the Battlebook series of Sierra Club Books. Regarding oil and the undersea environment off Southern California, see Kenneth Orris Emery, *The Sea Off Southern California: A Modern Habitat of Petroleum* (1960). See also Rimmon Fay and others, *Southern California's Deteriorating Marine Environment* (1972).

Chapter 16
People of Color

Carey McWilliams's *Prejudice, Japanese-Americans: Symbol of Racial Intolerance* (1945) is of commanding importance to this chapter. See also Jacobus tenBroek, Edward Barnhart, and Floyd Matson, *Prejudice, War, and the Constitution* (1954); and Roger Daniels, *The Politics of Prejudice: The Anti-Japanese Movement in California and the Struggle for Japanese Exclusion* (1962). Regarding the evacuation and internment of the Japanese, the following—among other titles already cited in *Embattled Dreams: California in War and Peace, 1940–1950* (2002)—proved, once again, useful: Dorothy Swaine Thomas, with the assistance of Charles Kikuchi and James Sakoda, *The Salvage: Japanese-American Evacuation and Resettlement* (1952); Allan Bosworth, *America's Concentration Camps*, introduction by Roger Baldwin (1967); Audrie Girdner and Anne Loftis, *The Great Betrayal: The Evacuation of the Japanese-Americans During World War II* (1969); Edward Spicer and others, *Impounded People: Japanese-Americans in the Relocation Centers* (1969); and John Armor and Peter Wright, *Manzanar*, commentary by John Hersey, photographs by Ansel Adams (1988). Of special importance is the narrative by Dillon S. Myer, head of the War Relocation Authority, *Uprooted Americans: The Japanese-Americans and the War Relocation Authority During World War II* (1971). Photographic documentations of camp life include Ansel Adams, *Born Free and Equal: Photographs of the Loyal Japanese-Americans at Manzanar Relocation Center Inyo County, California* (1944); Maisie and Richard Conrat, *Executive Order 9066: The Internment of 110,000 Japanese-Americans* (1972); and Mamoru Inouye, with an essay by Grace Schaub, *The Heart Mountain Story: Photographs of Hansel Mieth and Otto Hagel of the World War II Internment of Japanese-Americans* (1997). Other visual titles of value are Allen Eaton, *Beauty Behind Barbed Wire: The Arts of the Japanese in Our War Relocation Camps*, foreword by Eleanor Roosevelt (1952); and *Chiura Obata's Topaz Moon: Art of the Internment*, edited with text by Kimi Kodani Hill (2000). For Jack Matsuoka's coverage of Poston Camp through cartoons, see his *Poston Camp 2, Block 211* (2003).

Memoirs of camp life consulted for this chapter include Jeanne Wakatsuki Houston and James D. Huston, *Farewell to Manzanar* (1973); *Remembering Heart Mountain: Essays on Japanese-American Internment in Wyoming*, edited and contributions by Mike Mackey (1998); Toshio Mori, *Unfinished Message*, introduction by Lawson Fusao Inada (2000); Noboru Shirai, *Tule Lake: An Issei Memoir*, translated from the Japanese by Ray Hosoda (2001); Hiroshi Kashiwagi, *Swimming in the American: A Memoir and Selected Writings* (2005); and Kiyo Sato, *Dandelion Through the Crack: The Sato Family Quest for the American Dream* (2007). Of special value is the anthology of reminiscences *Only What We Could Carry: The Japanese-American Internment Experience*, edited with an introduction by Lawson Fusao Inada (2000). Of particular relevance to this discussion is *Greenmakers: Japanese-American Gardeners in Southern California*, edited by Naomi Hirahara (2000).

While supplemented with other sources and highlighted by my own interpretations, my discussions of *Oyama v. State of California* and *Mendez v. Westminster, Perez v. Sharp*, Fred Ross and the Community Service Organization, the Rumford Fair Housing Act, and Proposition 14 are dependent upon Mark Brilliant, *Color Lines: Civil Rights Struggles on America's "Racial Frontier," 1945–1975* (2009). Based upon his 2002 doctoral dissertation at Stanford, directed by Professor David Kennedy, *Color Lines* is a comprehensive and authoritative narrative, anchored in an exhaustive use of primary sources, such as the Fred Ross papers at Stanford, of the struggle for civil rights by minorities in California during these years. See also the Web site www.mendezvwestminster.com and the sixty-year retrospective Tyche Hendricks, "An Early Blow for Equality," *San Francisco Chronicle* (9 May 2007).

Regarding Fred Ross, see the relevant portions of Sanford Horwitt, *Let Them Call Me Rebel: Saul Alinsky—His Life and Legacy* (1989). See also Burt A. Folkart, "Fred Ross: Worked Quietly…" *Los Angeles Times* (1 October 1992); and Mark Arax, "UFW Memorial Honors Lifelong Activist Fred Ross," *Los Angeles Times* (19 October 1992). For an obituary of Ross, see Jerry Roberts, "Fred Ross—Helped Unionize Farm Workers," *San Francisco Chronicle* (1 October 1992). See also Sanford D. Horwitt, *Let Them Call Me Rebel: Saul Alinsky, His Life and Legacy* (1989).

Regarding the early history of farm labor in California, see the magisterial Richard Steven Street, *Beasts of the Field: A Narrative History of California Farmworkers, 1769–1913* (2004). Regarding the later history of Mexican labor in the fields of California, see the two classic studies: Paul S. Taylor, *Mexican Labor in the United States: Imperial Valley, California* (1928); and Carey McWilliams, *North from Mexico: The Spanish-Speaking People of the United States* (1949). Regarding repatriation in the 1930s, see Francisco E. Balderrama and Raymond Rodríguez, *Decade of Betrayal: Mexican Repatriation in the 1930s* (1995). For Mexican American life in Los Angeles in the prewar and postwar era, see the classic Beatrice Griffith, *American Me* (1948). Regarding the fear of Mexican American juvenile delinquency, see Carey McWilliams, "Nervous Los Angeles. The 'Wolf-Crusade'" *Nation* (10 June 1950). For a case study in the rise of agribusiness in the same era, together with a comprehensive bibliography of the subject, see Mark Arax and Rick Wartzman, *The King of California: J. G. Boswell and the Making of a Secret American Empire* (2003). Regarding the *bracero* program, see Ernesto Galarza, *Merchants of Labor: The Mexican Bracero Story* (1964); and Henry P. Anderson, *The Bracero Program in California* (1976). See also James F. Rooney, "The Effects of Imported Mexican Farm Labor in a California County," *American Journal of Economics and Sociology* (October 1961). See also "A New Deal for the Mexican Worker," *Look* (29 September 1959). Regarding Operation Wetback, see Juan Ramon García, *Operation Wetback: The Mass Deportation of Mexican Undocumented Workers in 1954* (1980). Regarding Leo Carrillo, see his *The California I Love* (1961).

César Chávez chronicled his early life and career in, Jacques E. Levy and César Chávez, *César Chávez: Autobiography of La Causa* (1975). Fred Ross chronicled his early relationship with Chavez in *Conquering Goliath: César Chávez at the Beginning* (1989), published by the United Farm Workers. See also Frederick John Dalton, *The Moral Vision of César Chávez* (2003).

Howard DeWitt, *Anti-Filipino Movements in California: A History, Bibliography, and Study Guide* (1976) commands the subject and is of crucial importance to this chapter, as is Lorraine Jacobs Crouchett, *Filipinos in California: From the Days of the Galleons to the Present* (1982). See also Irene Norell, *Literature of the Filipino-American in the United States: A Selective and Annotated Bibliography* (1976). Two USC master's theses were of special value: Valentin Aquino, "The Filipino Community in Los Angeles" (1952); and Mario Paguia Ave, "Characteristics of Filipino Social Organizations in Los Angeles" (1956). Of late there have been a number of important doctoral dissertations in the field of Filipino American studies, which have also been of importance to this chapter. Issued by UMI Dissertation Services, these doctoral dissertations include Linda Nueva España Maram, "Negotiating Identity: Youth, Gender, and Popular Culture in Los Angeles's Little Manila, 1920s–1940s" (History, UCLA, 1996); Arleen Garcia deVera, "Constituting Community: A Study of Nationalism, Colonialism, Gender, and Identity Among Filipinos in California, 1919–1946" (History, UCLA, 2002); Estella Habal, "'We Won't Move': The International Hotel Anti-Eviction Movement, 1968–1979, and the Filipino-American Community" (History, UC Davis, 2003); and Dawn Bohulano Mabalon, "Life in Little Manila: Filipinas/os in Stockton, California, 1917–1972" (History, Stanford, 2003). See also Herminia Quimpo Meñez, *Folklore Communication Among Filipinos in California* (1980).

As stated in the text, the documentation and scholarship of the Chinese in the United States are formidable. Of relevance to this chapter are Gunther Barth, *Bitter Strength: A History of the Chinese in the United States: 1850–1870* (1964); Alexander Saxton, *The Indispensable Enemy: Labor and the Anti-Chinese Movement in California* (1971); Jack Chen, *The Chinese of America* (1980); Elmer Clarence Sandmeyer, *The Anti-Chinese Movement in California* (1991); and Jean Pfaelzer, *Driven Out: The Forgotten War Against Chinese Americans* (2007). Regarding the persecution of the Chinese in San Francisco, William J. Courtney, "San Francisco's Anti-Chinese Ordinances: 1850–1900" (M.A. thesis, History, University of San Francisco, 1956), republished in 1974 by R and E Research Associates of San Francisco, was especially helpful. See also John T. C. Fang, *Chinatown Handy Guide* (1959). Regarding crime in Chinatown, see Kevin J. Mullen, *Chinatown Squad: Policing the Dragon from the Gold Rush to the 21st Century* (2008).

Crucial to any understanding of the engagement of white writers in California with the Chinese is the Ph.D. dissertation by Li-min Chu, "The Images of China and the Chinese in the *Overland Monthly*, 1868–1875, 1883–1935" (English, Duke, 1965), republished in 1974 by R and E Research Associates of San Francisco. Regarding Sui Sin Far (Edith Maude Eaton), see Annette White-Parks, *Sui Sin Far/Edith Maude Eaton: A Literary Biography*, foreword by Roger Daniels (1995). The stories of Sui Sin Far can be found in *Mrs. Spring Fragrance and Other Writings*, edited by Amy Ling and Annette White-Parks (1995). See also Annette White-Parks, "A Reversal of American Concepts of 'Other-ness' in the Fiction of Sui Sin Far," *MELUS* (Spring 1995). Hugh Wiley's Chinatown San Francisco fiction can be found in *Jade and Other Stories* (1922), *Manchu Blood* (1927), and *The Copper Mask and Other Stories* (1932). Regarding C. Y. Lee, see the interview by Lia Chang at http://asianconnections.com/entertainment/columns/lia.chang/003.php. For background on San Francisco's Chinatown, see Charles Caldwell Dobie, *San Francisco's Chinatown*, illustrations by E. Y. Suydam (1936); Vincent McHugh, "San Francisco: Little Chinatown," *Holiday* (April 1961); Helen V. Cather, *The History of San Francisco's Chinatown* (1974); Thomas W. Chinn, *Bridging the Pacific: San Francisco Chinatown and Its People* (1989); and Yong Chen, *Chinese San Francisco, 1850–1943: A Trans-Pacific Community* (2000). See also Jade Snow Wong, *No Chinese*

Stranger (1975); and Judy Tzu-Chun Wu, *Doctor Mom Chung of the Fair-Haired Bastards: The Life of a Wartime Celebrity* (2005). Of special value is Victor Nee and Brett de Bary Nee, *Longtime Californ': A Documentary Study of an American Chinatown* (1972). Regarding Victor Nee, see his Web site at www.soc.cornell.edu/faculty/nee.html.

The bibliography of Afro-Americans in California is extensive. Of general relevance to this chapter are: Rudolph M. Lapp, *Afro-Americans in California* (1987); Gordon Wheeler, *Black California: The History of African-Americans in the Golden State* (1993); and Lawrence B. de Graaf, Kevin Mulroy, and Quintard Taylor, *Seeking El Dorado: African Americans in California* (2001). Regarding the East Bay, see Lawrence P. Crouchett, Lonnie G. Bunch III, and Martha Kendall Winnacker, *Visions Toward Tomorrow: The History of the East Bay Afro-American Community, 1852–1977* (1989). Regarding Los Angeles, see Josh Sides, *L.A. City Limits: African-American Los Angeles from the Great Depression to the Present* (2003). Three Ph.D. dissertations available through University Microfilms and/or UMI Dissertation Services are also of relevance: James Adolphus Fisher, "A History of the Political and Social Development of the Black Community in California, 1850–1950" (History, State University of New York at Stony Brook, 1971); Alonzo Nelson Smith, "Black Employment in the Los Angeles Area, 1938–1948" (History, UCLA, 1978); and Delores Nason McBroome, "Parallel Communities: African-Americans in California's East Bay, 1850–1963" (History, University of Oregon, 1991). Articles of relevance to this chapter include Rudolph M. Lapp, "Negro Rights Activities in Gold Rush California," *California Historical Society Quarterly* (March 1966); Lawrence B. de Graaf, "The City of Black Angels: Emergence of the Los Angeles Ghetto, 1890–1930," *Pacific Historical Review* (August 1970); and James A. Fisher, "The Political Development of the Black Community in California, 1850–1950," *California Historical Society Quarterly* (September 1971). See also John M. Weatherwax, "Los Angeles, 1781," *The Negro History Bulletin* (October 1954); and Wesley Marx, "The Negro Community: A Better Chance," *Los Angeles* (March, 1962). Regarding Charlotta Bass, see her *Forty Years: Memoirs from the Pages of a Newspaper* (1960). See also Horace Cayton, "America's Ten Best Cities for Negroes," *Negro Digest* (October 1947) for a positive assessment of Los Angeles.

For a complete discussion of the Unruh Civil Rights Act of 1959, see the relevant sections of Bill Boyarsky, *Big Daddy: Jesse Unruh and the Art of Power Politics* (2008). See also Lawrence P. Crouchett, *William Byron Rumford: The Life and Public Services of a California Legislator—A Biography* (1984). For a brief review of the career of Justice Stanley Mosk, see the California State Supreme Court printed transcript *Celebration Session Honoring the Record Service of Justice Stanley Mosk* (7 January 2000) on deposit at the California State Library. Of great importance is the California State Archives State Government Oral History Program's *Oral History Interview with Honorable Stanley Mosk*, interview by Germaine LaBerge (Regional Oral History Office, UC Berkeley, 1998), on deposit at the California State Library.

Chapter 17
Cool, Not Cool

Birth of the Cool: California Art, Design, and Culture at Midcentury (2007) was edited by Elizabeth Armstrong for the Orange County Museum of Art, with essays by Michael Boyd, Frances Colpitt, Dave Hickey, Thomas Hine, Bruce Jenkins, Elizabeth A. T. Smith, and Lorraine Wild, with contributions by Anna Brouwer and Mary Trent. My discussion of Harry Hay and the founding of the Mattachine Society is dependent upon the superbly annotated anthology *Radically Gay: Gay Liberation in the Words of Its Founder Harry Hay*, edited by Will Roscoe (1996). I am especially indebted to Roscoe's chronology for clarifying certain disputed points. See also Stuart Timmons, *The Trouble with Harry Hay: Founder of the Modern*

Gay Movement (1990). For the Los Angeles background of the Mattachine Society, see Daniel Hurewitz, *Bohemian Los Angeles and the Making of Modern Politics* (2007).

Regarding the Chessman case, see Theodore Hamm, *Rebel and a Cause: Caryl Chessman and the Politics of the Death Penalty in Postwar California, 1948–1974* (2001). Governor Edmund G. (Pat) Brown tells his side of the story in *Public Justice, Private Mercy: A Governor's Education on Death Row*, with Dick Adler (1989). See also the relevant portions of Brad Williams, *Due Process: The Story of Criminal Lawyer George T. Davis and His Thirty-Year Battle Against Capital Punishment* (1961). Regarding the demonstrations at San Francisco City Hall on 13 May 1960, see the first-rate anthology of newspaper reports and magazine commentary, *A Focus on Rebellion*, selected and edited by Albert T. Anderson and Bernice Prince Biggs (1962).

Acknowledgments

Golden Dreams was researched over a five-year period at the California State Library in Sacramento, the Dave Brubeck Archives at the University of the Pacific in Stockton, the Bancroft Library in Berkeley, the department of special collections at the Green Library of Stanford University in Palo Alto, the Gleeson Library of the University of San Francisco, the Daniel E. Koshland San Francisco History Center of the San Francisco Public Library, the Los Angeles Public Library, the Doheny Memorial Library at the University of Southern California in Los Angeles, the Archives of the Scripps Institution of Oceanography in La Jolla, and the San Diego Historical Society. At each of these institutions, I was assisted by archivists, librarians, and support staff.

At the California History Room of the California State Library, I was helped by its director Gary Kurutz, curator of special collections, and librarians John Gonzales, Kathy Correia, Catherine Hanson, Karen Paige, Michael Dolguskin, and Marianne Leach. At the Dave Brubeck Archives at the University of the Pacific, Shan Sutton, head of special collections, Michael Wurtz, archivist, and Trish Richards, special collections assistant, came to my aid. At the Bancroft Library in Berkeley, I wish to thank its director Professor Charles Faulhaber, its collections manager Lorna Kirwan, and Susan Snyder, head of public service. At the department of special collections of the Green Library at Stanford University, Mattie Taormina, head of public services, was most helpful. At the Daniel E. Koshland San Francisco History Center, city archivist Susan Goldstein and librarians Christina Moretta, Tami Suzuki, Tom Carey, and Tim Wilson, together with photo collection assistant Jeff Thomas, proved most helpful, as did reference librarian Joe Garity at the Gleeson Library. At the Los Angeles Public Library, I enjoyed the able assistance of Carolyn Cole and Bettie Webb of the photograph collection. At the Doheny Memorial Library, I wish to thank Dace Taube, director of the regional history collection, Shahla Bahavar, director of public service, and Sue Tyson, instruction and reference librarian, for their special assistance. At the San Diego Historical Society, Chris Travers, director of the Booth Historical Photograph Archives, was most helpful, as were Carol Myers and Kevin McManus.

At Oxford University Press, I began *Golden Dreams*, the seventh volume of the Americans and the California Dream series, under the direction of my longtime editor, the legendary Sheldon Meyer. With Sheldon's lamented passing, executive editor Susan Ferber assumed the task with exacting precision and panache. I am especially grateful to her for help in paring down a lengthy manuscript. Through production, I had the good fortune to be once again in the hands of India Cooper and Joellyn Ausanka. I am especially grateful to India Cooper for her exhaustive, line-by-line fact-checking. Naturally, I assume personal responsibility for any errors that managed to survive this exacting process. Marie Nuchols and Peter Brigaitis of Denton, Texas, prepared the index. I continue to be represented by the finest literary agent on the Coast, Sandra Dijkstra, who over the years, along with her husband Bram, has become a cherished friend.

Fifty years ago, at the epicenter of the era dealt with in this book, I met Sheila Gordon in San Francisco. Today, my wife Sheila and I are blessed with seven beloved grandchildren. In researching and writing this book, I enjoyed the opportunity to travel back in time and memory to our first years together—in Army service in Germany and at Harvard—when, in the delightful company of our daughters, Marian and Jessica, we looked to the future and beheld the promise of American life.

Index